Encyclopedia of World Cultures

Volume V

EAST AND SOUTHEAST ASIA

ENCYCLOPEDIA OF WORLD CULTURES

David Levinson
Editor in Chief

North America
Oceania
South Asia
Europe (Central, Western, and Southeastern Europe)
East and Southeast Asia
Russia and Eurasia / China
South America
Middle America and the Caribbean
Africa and the Middle East
Bibliography

The Encyclopedia of World Cultures was prepared under the auspices and with the support of the Human Relations Area Files at Yale University. HRAF, the foremost international research organization in the field of cultural anthropology, is a not-for-profit consortium of twenty-three sponsoring members and 300 participating member institutions in twenty-five countries. The HRAF archive, established in 1949, contains nearly one million pages of information on the cultures of the world.

Encyclopedia of World Cultures
Volume V
EAST AND SOUTHEAST ASIA

Paul Hockings
Volume Editor

G.K. Hall & Co.
Boston, Massachusetts

MEASUREMENT CONVERSIONS

When You Know	Multiply By	To Find
LENGTH		
inches	2.54	centimeters
feet	30	centimeters
yards	0.9	meters
miles	1.6	kilometers
millimeters	0.04	inches
centimeters	0.4	inches
meters	3.3	feet
meters	1.1	yards
kilometers	0.6	miles
AREA		
square feet	0.09	square meters
square yards	0.8	square meters
square miles	2.6	square kilometers
acres	0.4	hectares
hectares	2.5	acres
square meters	1.2	square yards
square kilometers	0.4	square miles

TEMPERATURE

$°C = (°F - 32) ÷ 1.8$

$°F = (°C × 1.8) + 32$

First published 1993
by G.K. Hall & Co., an imprint of Macmillan Inc.
866 Third Avenue
New York, NY 10022

10   9   8   7   6   5   4   3   2   1

Macmillan, Inc., is part of the Maxwell Communication Group of Companies.

Library of Congress Cataloging-in-Publication Data
(Revised for volume 5)

Encyclopedia of world cultures.

 Includes bibliographical references, filmographies, and indexes.
 Contents: v. 1. North America / Timothy J. O'Leary, David Levinson, volume editors —v. 3. South Asia / Paul Hockings, volume editor —v. 5. East and Southeast Asia / Paul Hockings, volume editor.
 1. Ethnology—Encyclopedias. I. Levinson, David, 1947–
GN307.E53 1991 306'.097 90–49123
ISBN 0–8168–8840–X (set : alk. paper)
ISBN 0–8161–1808–6 (v. 1 : alk. paper)
ISBN 0–8161–1812–4 (v. 3 : alk. paper)

Contents

Contributors

Greg Accaioli
Department of Anthropology
University of Western Australia
Nedlands, W.A.
Australia

Bugis

Kathleen M. Adams
Department of Anthropology
Beloit College
Beloit, Wisconsin
United States

Alorese; Toraja

R. H. Barnes
Institute of Social and Cultural Anthropology
Oxford University
Oxford
England

Kédang; Lamaholot

Dieter Bartels
Center for the Study of Social Conflicts
State University of Leiden
Leiden
The Netherlands

Ambonese; Moluccans—North; Moluccans—Southeast

Andrew Beatty
Wolfson College
Oxford University
Oxford
England

Nias

Sawa Kurotani Becker
Department of Anthropology
University of Colorado
Boulder, Colorado
United States

Burakumin

Geoffrey Benjamin
Department of Sociology
National University of Singapore
Singapore

Temiar

John R. Bowen
Department of Anthropology
Washington University
St. Louis, Missouri
United States

Gayo; Ogan-Besemah

Harald Beyer Broch
Ethnographic Museum
University of Oslo
Oslo
Norway

Bonerate

Kacha-ananda Chob
Tribal Research Institute
Chiang Mai University
Chiang Mai
Thailand

Yao of Thailand

Clark E. Cunningham
Department of Anthropology
University of Illinois—Urbana-Champaign
Urbana, Illinois
United States

Atoni

Jean DeBernardi
Department of Anthropology
University of Alberta
Edmonton, Alberta
Canada

Chinese in Southeast Asia

Robert K. Dentan
Department of Anthropology
State University of New York—Buffalo
Amherst, New York
United States

Senoi

Alain Y. Dessaint
American Psychological Association
Washington, D.C.
United States

Lisu; T'in

May Ebihara
The Graduate School and University Center
City University of New York
New York, New York
United States

Khmer

Ronald K. Edgerton
Department of History
University of Northern Colorado
Greeley, Colorado
United States

Bukidnon

Kirk Endicott
Department of Anthropology
Dartmouth College
Hanover, New Hampshire
United States

Semang

Enya P. Flores-Meiser
Department of Anthropology
Ball State University
Muncie, Indiana
United States

Samal Moro

James J. Fox
Research School of Pacific Studies
Australian National University
Canberra, Australian Capital Territory
Australia

Ata Sikka; Rotinese

Charles O. Frake
Department of Anthropology
Stanford University
Stanford, California
United States

Subanun

Antonio J. Guerreiro
Ethnologie Comparative de l'Asie du Sud-Est
Centre National de la Recherche Scientifique
Paris
France

Modang

Thomas N. Headland
Department of Anthropology
Summer Institute of Linguistics
Dallas, Texas
United States

Agta; Philippine Negritos; Tasaday

Paul Hockings
Department of Anthropology
University of Illinois—Chicago
Chicago, Illinois
United States

*Buddhist; Indonesian; Singaporean; Taiwanese;
Visayan*

Ying-Kuei Huang
Institute of Ethnology
Academia Sinica
Nankang, Taipei
Taiwan

Bunun

Carol Ireson
Department of Sociology and Anthropology
Willamette University
Salem, Oregon
United States

Lao

W. Randall Ireson
Department of Sociology and Anthropology
Willamette University
Salem, Oregon
United States

Lao

Neil Jamieson
Callao, Virginia
United States

Vietnamese

Cornelia Ann Kammerer
Department of Anthropology
Brandeis University
Waltham, Massachusetts
United States

Akha

Charles Kaut   *Tagalog*
Department of Anthropology
University of Virginia
Charlottesville, Virginia
United States

Choong Soon Kim   *Korean*
Department of Sociology and Anthropology
University of Tennessee—Martin
Martin, Tennessee
United States

Ruth M. Krulfeld   *Sasak*
Department of Anthropology
George Washington University
Washington, D.C.
United States

Robert Lawless   *Kalingas*
Department of Anthropology
University of Florida
Gainesville, Florida
United States

F. K. Lehman   *Kachin*
Department of Anthropology
University of Illinois—Urbana-Champaign
Urbana, Illinois
United States

E. Douglas Lewis   *Ata Sikka; Ata Tana 'Ai*
Department of Asian Languages and Anthropology
University of Melbourne
Parkville, Melbourne, Victoria
Australia

Margaret Lock   *Japanese*
Department of Humanities and Social Studies in Medicine
McGill University
Montreal, Quebec
Canada

Joel M. Maring   *Palaung*
Department of Anthropology
Southern Illinois University
Carbondale, Illinois
United States

M. Marlene Martin   *Central Thai; Javanese*
Human Relations Area Files
New Haven, Connecticut
United States

Ann P. McCauley   *Balinese*
School of Continuing Education
Johns Hopkins University
Baltimore, Maryland
United States

H. S. Morris   **Melanau**
Withypool, near Minehead
Somerset
England

Satoshi Nakagawa   **Endenese**
Center for Southeast Asian Studies
Osaka International University
Osaka
Japan

Manning Nash   **Burmese; Malay**
Department of Anthropology
University of Chicago
Chicago, Illinois
United States

David J. Nemeth   **Kolisuch'ŏk**
Department of Geography and Planning
University of Toledo
Toledo, Ohio
United States

Emiko Ohnuki-Tierney   **Ainu**
Department of Anthropology
University of Wisconsin
Madison, Wisconsin
United States

Barbara S. Nowak   **Selung/Moken**
Department of Anthropology
Grinnell College
Grinnell, Iowa
United States

Hugh R. Page, Jr.   **Cham**
Department of Religion
California State University—Sacramento
Sacramento, California
United States

Jaganath Pathy   **Muong**
Department of Sociology
South Gujarat University
Surat, Gujarat
India

Nancy Pollock Khin   **Karen**
Department of Anthropology
University of Washington
Seattle, Washington
United States

Frank Proschan   **Kmhmu**
Alexandria, Virginia
United States

Ronald Provencher   **Minangkabau**
Department of Anthropology
Northern Illinois University
DeKalb, Illinois
United States

Susan Rodgers   *Batak*
Department of Sociology and Anthropology
Ohio University
Athens, Ohio
United States

Martin Rössler   *Makassar*
Institut und Sammlung für Völkerkunde
Universität Göttingen
Göttingen
Germany

Clifford Sather   *Bajau; Samal; Tausug*
Research School of Pacific Studies
Australian National University
Canberra, Australian Capital Territory
Australia

Pim (J. W.) Schoorl   *Butonese*
Huizen
The Netherlands

E. Richard Sorenson   *Sea Nomads of the Andaman*
Madras, Tamil Nadu
India

James C. Stewart   *Maguindanao*
Department of Environmental Studies and Planning
Sonoma State University
Rohnert Park, California
United States

Vinson H. Sutlive, Jr.   *Iban*
Department of Anthropology
College of William and Mary
Williamsburg, Virginia
United States

Nicola Tannenbaum   *Shan*
Department of Social Relations
Leigh University
Bethlehem, Pennsylvania
United States

Nicholas Tapp   *Hmong*
Department of Anthropology
Chinese University of Hong Kong
Hong Kong

John Van Esterik   *Lao Isan*
Department of Anthropology
York University
Toronto, Ontario
Canada

Penny Van Esterik   *Lao Isan*
Department of Anthropology
York University
Toronto, Ontario
Canada

Ch. F. van Fraasen   **Ternatan/Tidorese**
Goes
The Netherlands

Michael P. Vischer   **Palu'e**
Research School of Pacific Studies
Australian National University
Canberra, Australian Capital Territory
Australia

Anthony R. Walker   **Lahu**
Department of Anthropology
Ohio State University
Columbus, Ohio
United States

Gehan Wijeyewardene   **Tai Lue**
Research School of Pacific Studies
Australian National University
Canberra, Australian Capital Territory
Australia

Thomas Rhys Williams   **Dusun**
Department of Sociology and Anthropology
George Mason University
Fairfax, Virginia
United States

Inger Wulff   **Yakan**
Department of Ethnography
National Museum of Denmark
Copenhagen
Denmark

Preface

This project began in 1987 with the goal of assembling a basic reference source that provides accurate, clear, and concise descriptions of the cultures of the world. We wanted to be as comprehensive and authoritative as possible: comprehensive, by providing descriptions of all the cultures of each region of the world or by describing a representative sample of cultures for regions where full coverage is impossible, and authoritative by providing accurate descriptions of the cultures for both the past and the present.

The publication of the *Encyclopedia of World Cultures* in the last decade of the twentieth century is especially timely. The political, economic, and social changes of the past fifty years have produced a world more complex and fluid than at any time in human history. Three sweeping transformations of the worldwide cultural landscape are especially significant.

First is what some social scientists are calling the "New Diaspora"—the dispersal of cultural groups to new locations across the world. This dispersal affects all nations and takes a wide variety of forms: in East African nations, the formation of new towns inhabited by people from dozens of different ethnic groups; in Micronesia and Polynesia, the movement of islanders to cities in New Zealand and the United States; in North America, the replacement by Asians and Latin Americans of Europeans as the most numerous immigrants; in Europe, the increased reliance on workers from the Middle East and North Africa; and so on.

Second, and related to this dispersal, is the internal division of what were once single, unified cultural groups into two or more relatively distinct groups. This pattern of internal division is most dramatic among indigenous or third or fourth world cultures whose traditional ways of life have been altered by contact with the outside world. Underlying this division are both the population dispersion mentioned above and sustained contact with the economically developed world. The result is that groups who at one time saw themselves and were seen by others as single cultural groups have been transformed into two or more distinct groups. Thus, in many cultural groups, we find deep and probably permanent divisions between those who live in the country and those who live in cities, those who follow the traditional religion and those who have converted to Christianity, those who live inland and those who live on the seacoast, and those who live by means of a subsistence economy and those now enmeshed in a cash economy.

The third important transformation of the worldwide cultural landscape is the revival of ethnic nationalism, with many peoples claiming and fighting for political freedom and territorial integrity on the basis of ethnic solidarity and ethnic-based claims to their traditional homeland. Although most attention has focused recently on ethnic nationalism in Eastern Europe and the former Soviet Union, the trend is nonetheless a worldwide phenomenon involving, for example, American Indian cultures in North and South America, the Basques in Spain and France, the Tamil and Sinhalese in Sri Lanka, and the Tutsi and Hutu in Burundi, among others.

To be informed citizens of our rapidly changing multicultural world we must understand the ways of life of people from cultures different from our own. "We" is used here in the broadest sense, to include not just scholars who study the cultures of the world and businesspeople and government officials who work in the world community but also the average citizen who reads or hears about multicultural events in the news every day and young people who are growing up in this complex cultural world. For all of these people—which means all of us—there is a pressing need for information on the cultures of the world. This encyclopedia provides this information in two ways. First, its descriptions of the traditional ways of life of the world's cultures can serve as a baseline against which cultural change can be measured and understood. Second, it acquaints the reader with the contemporary ways of life throughout the world.

We are able to provide this information largely through the efforts of the volume editors and the nearly one thousand contributors who wrote the cultural summaries that are the heart of the book. The contributors are social scientists (anthropologists, sociologists, historians, and geographers) as well as educators, government officials, and missionaries who usually have firsthand research-based knowledge of the cultures they write about. In many cases they are the major expert or one of the leading experts on the culture, and some are themselves members of the cultures. As experts, they are able to provide accurate, up-to-date information. This is crucial for many parts of the world where indigenous cultures may be overlooked by official information seekers such as government census takers. These experts have often lived among the people they write about, conducting participant-observations with them and speaking their language. Thus they are able to provide integrated, holistic descriptions of the cultures, not just a list of facts. Their portraits of the cultures leave the reader with a real sense of what it means to be a "Taos" or a "Rom" or a "Sicilian."

Those summaries not written by an expert on the culture have usually been written by a researcher at the Human Relations Area Files, Inc., working from primary source materials. The Human Relations Area Files, an international educational and research institute, is recognized by professionals in the social and behavioral sciences, humanities, and medical sciences as a major source of information on the cultures of the world.

Uses of the Encyclopedia

This encyclopedia is meant to be used by a variety of people for a variety of purposes. It can be used both to gain a general understanding of a culture and to find a specific piece of information by looking it up under the relevant subheading in a summary. It can also be used to learn about a particular region or subregion of the world and the social, economic, and political forces that have shaped the cultures in that region. The encyclopedia is also a resource guide that leads readers who want a deeper understanding of particular cultures to additional sources of information. Resource guides in the encyclopedia include ethnonyms listed in each summary, which can be used as entry points into the social science literature where the culture may sometimes be identified by a different name; a bibliography at the end of each summary, which lists books and articles about the culture; and a filmography at the end of each volume, which lists films and videos on many of the cultures.

Beyond being a basic reference resource, the encyclopedia also serves readers with more focused needs. For researchers interested in comparing cultures, the encyclopedia serves as the most complete and up-to-date sampling frame from which to select cultures for further study. For those interested in international studies, the encyclopedia leads one quickly into the relevant social science literature as well as providing a state-of-the-art assessment of our knowledge of the cultures of a particular region. For curriculum developers and teachers seeking to internationalize their curriculum, the encyclopedia is itself a basic reference and educational resource as well as a directory to other materials. For government officials, it is a repository of information not likely to be available in any other single publication or, in some cases, not available at all. For students, from high school through graduate school, it provides background and bibliographic information for term papers and class projects. And for travelers, it provides an introduction into the ways of life of the indigenous peoples in the area of the world they will be visiting.

Format of the Encyclopedia

The encyclopedia comprises ten volumes, ordered by geographical regions of the world. The order of publication is not meant to represent any sort of priority. Volumes 1 through 9 contain a total of about fifteen hundred summaries along with maps, glossaries, and indexes of alternate names for the cultural groups. The tenth and final volume contains cumulative lists of the cultures of the world, their alternate names, and a bibliography of selected publications pertaining to those groups.

North America covers the cultures of Canada, Greenland, and the United States of America.

Oceania covers the cultures of Australia, New Zealand, Melanesia, Micronesia, and Polynesia.

South Asia covers the cultures of Bangladesh, India, Pakistan, Sri Lanka and other South Asian islands and the Himalayan states.

Europe covers the cultures of Europe.

East and Southeast Asia covers the cultures of Japan, Korea, mainland and insular Southeast Asia, and Taiwan.

Russia and Eurasia / China covers the cultures of Mongolia, the People's Republic of China, and the former Union of Soviet Socialist Republics.

South America covers the cultures of South America.

Middle America and the Caribbean covers the cultures of Central America, Mexico, and the Caribbean islands.

Africa and the Middle East covers the cultures of Madagascar and sub-Saharan Africa, North Africa, the Middle East, and south-central Asia.

Format of the Volumes

Each volume contains this preface, an introductory essay by the volume editor, the cultural summaries ranging from a few lines to several pages each, maps pinpointing the location of the cultures, a filmography, an ethnonym index of alternate names for the cultures, and a glossary of scientific and technical terms. All entries are listed in alphabetical order and are extensively cross-referenced.

Cultures Covered

A central issue in selecting cultures for coverage in the encyclopedia has been how to define what we mean by a cultural group. The questions of what a culture is and what criteria can be used to classify a particular social group (such as a religious group, ethnic group, nationality, or territorial group) as a cultural group have long perplexed social scientists and have yet to be answered to everyone's satisfaction. Two realities account for why the questions cannot be answered definitively. First, a wide variety of different types of cultures exist around the world. Among common types are national cultures, regional cultures, ethnic groups, indigenous societies, religious groups, and unassimilated immigrant groups. No single criterion or marker of cultural uniqueness can consistently distinguish among the hundreds of cultures that fit into these general types. Second, as noted above, single cultures or what were at one time identified as single cultures can and do vary internally over time and place. Thus a marker that may identify a specific group as a culture in one location or at one time may not work for that culture in another place or at another time. For example, use of the Yiddish language would have been a marker of Jewish cultural identity in Eastern Europe in the nineteenth century, but it would not serve as a marker for Jews in the twentieth-century United States, where most speak English. Similarly, residence on one of the Cook Islands in Polynesia would have been a marker of Cook Islander identity in the eighteenth century, but not in the twentieth century when two-thirds of Cook Islanders live in New Zealand and elsewhere.

Given these considerations, no attempt has been made to develop and use a single definition of a cultural unit or to develop and use a fixed list of criteria for identifying cultural units. Instead, the task of selecting cultures was left to the volume editors, and the criteria and procedures they used are discussed in their introductory essays. In general, however, six criteria were used, sometimes alone and sometimes in combination to classify social groups as cultural groups: (1) geographical localization, (2) identification in the social science literature as a distinct group, (3) distinct language, (4) shared traditions, religion, folklore, or values, (5) maintenance of group identity in the face of strong assimilative pressures, and (6) previous listing in an inventory of the world's cultures such as _Ethnographic Atlas_ (Murdock 1967) or the _Outline of World Cultures_ (Murdock 1983).

In general, we have been "lumpers" rather than "splitters" in writing the summaries. That is, if there is some question about whether a particular group is really one culture or two related cultures, we have more often than not treated it as a single culture, with internal differences noted in the summary. Similarly, we have sometimes chosen to describe a number of very similar cultures in a single summary rather than in a series of summaries that would be mostly redundant. There is, however, some variation from one region to another in this approach, and the rationale for each region is discussed in the volume editor's essay.

Two categories of cultures are usually not covered in the encyclopedia. First, extinct cultures, especially those that have not existed as distinct cultural units for some time, are usually not described. Cultural extinction is often, though certainly not always, indicated by the disappearance of the culture's language. So, for example, the Aztec are not covered, although living descendants of the Aztec, the Nahuatl-speakers of central Mexico, are described.

Second, the ways of life of immigrant groups are usually not described in much detail, unless there is a long history of resistance to assimilation and the group has maintained its distinct identity, as have the Amish in North America. These cultures are, however, described in the location where they traditionally lived and, for the most part, continue to live, and migration patterns are noted. For example, the Hmong in Laos are described in the Southeast Asia volume, but the refugee communities in the United States and Canada are covered only in the general summaries on Southeast Asians in those two countries in the North America volume. Although it would be ideal to provide descriptions of all the immigrant cultures or communities of the world, that is an undertaking well beyond the scope of this encyclopedia, for there are probably more than five thousand such communities in the world.

Finally, it should be noted that not all nationalities are covered, only those that are also distinct cultures as well as political entities. For example, the Vietnamese and Burmese are included but Indians (citizens of the Republic of India) are not, because the latter is a political entity made up of a great mix of cultural groups. In the case of nations whose populations include a number of different, relatively unassimilated groups or cultural regions, each of the groups is described separately. For example, there is no summary for Italians as such in the Europe volume, but there are summaries for the regional cultures of Italy, such as the Tuscans, Sicilians, and Tirolians, and other cultures such as the Sinti Piemontese.

Cultural Summaries

The heart of this encyclopedia is the descriptive summaries of the cultures, which range from a few lines to five or six pages in length. They provide a mix of demographic, historical, social, economic, political, and religious information on the cultures. Their emphasis or flavor is cultural; that is, they focus on the ways of life of the people—both past and present—and the factors that have caused the culture to change over time and place.

A key issue has been how to decide which cultures should be described by longer summaries and which by shorter ones. This decision was made by the volume editors, who had to balance a number of intellectual and practical considerations. Again, the rationale for these decisions is discussed in their essays. But among the factors that were considered by all the editors were the total number of cultures in their region, the availability of experts to write summaries, the availability of information on the cultures, the degree of similarity between cultures, and the importance of a culture in a scientific or political sense.

The summary authors followed a standardized outline so that each summary provides information on a core list of topics. The authors, however, had some leeway in deciding how much attention was to be given each topic and whether additional information should be included. Summaries usually provide information on the following topics:

CULTURE NAME: The name used most often in the social science literature to refer to the culture or the name the group uses for itself.

ETHNONYMS: Alternate names for the culture including names used by outsiders, the self-name, and alternate spellings, within reasonable limits.

ORIENTATION
Identification. Location of the culture and the derivation of its name and ethnonyms.
Location. Where the culture is located and a description of the physical environment.
Demography. Population history and the most recent reliable population figures or estimates.
Linguistic Affiliation. The name of the language spoken and/or written by the culture, its place in an international language classification system, and internal variation in language use.

HISTORY AND CULTURAL RELATIONS: A tracing of the origins and history of the culture and the past and current nature of relationships with other groups.

SETTLEMENTS: The location of settlements, types of settlements, types of structures, housing design and materials.

ECONOMY
Subsistence and Commercial Activities. The primary methods of obtaining, consuming, and distributing money, food, and other necessities.
Industrial Arts. Implements and objects produced by the culture either for its own use or for sale or trade.
Trade. Products traded and patterns of trade with other groups.
Division of Labor. How basic economic tasks are assigned by age, sex, ability, occupational specialization, or status.
Land Tenure. Rules and practices concerning the allocation of land and land-use rights to members of the culture and to outsiders.

KINSHIP
Kin Groups and Descent. Rules and practices concerning kin-based features of social organization such as lineages and clans and alliances between these groups.
Kinship Terminology. Classification of the kinship terminological system on the basis of either cousin terms or genera-

tion, and information about any unique aspects of kinship terminology.

MARRIAGE AND FAMILY

Marriage. Rules and practices concerning reasons for marriage, types of marriage, economic aspects of marriage, postmarital residence, divorce, and remarriage.

Domestic Unit. Description of the basic household unit including type, size, and composition.

Inheritance. Rules and practices concerning the inheritance of property.

Socialization. Rules and practices concerning child rearing including caretakers, values inculcated, child-rearing methods, initiation rites, and education.

SOCIOPOLITICAL ORGANIZATION

Social Organization. Rules and practices concerning the internal organization of the culture, including social status, primary and secondary groups, and social stratification.

Political Organization. Rules and practices concerning leadership, politics, governmental organizations, and decision making.

Social Control. The sources of conflict within the culture and informal and formal social control mechanisms.

Conflict. The sources of conflict with other groups and informal and formal means of resolving conflicts.

RELIGION AND EXPRESSIVE CULTURE

Religious Beliefs. The nature of religious beliefs including beliefs in supernatural entities, traditional beliefs, and the effects of major religions.

Religious Practitioners. The types, sources of power, and activities of religious specialists such as shamans and priests.

Ceremonies. The nature, type, and frequency of religious and other ceremonies and rites.

Arts. The nature, types, and characteristics of artistic activities including literature, music, dance, carving, and so on.

Medicine. The nature of traditional medical beliefs and practices and the influence of scientific medicine.

Death and Afterlife. The nature of beliefs and practices concerning death, the deceased, funerals, and the afterlife.

BIBLIOGRAPHY: A selected list of publications about the culture. The list usually includes publications that describe both the traditional and the contemporary culture.

AUTHOR'S NAME: The name of the summary author.

Maps

Each regional volume contains maps pinpointing the current location of the cultures described in that volume. The first map in each volume is usually an overview, showing the countries in that region. The other maps provide more detail by marking the locations of the cultures in four or five subregions.

Filmography

Each volume contains a list of films and videos about cultures covered in that volume. This list is provided as a service and in no way indicates an endorsement by the editor, the volume editor, or the summary authors. Addresses of distributors are provided so that information about availability and prices can be readily obtained.

Ethnonym Index

Each volume contains an ethnonym index for the cultures covered in that volume. As mentioned above, ethnonyms are alternative names for the culture—that is, names different from those used here as the summary headings. Ethnonyms may be alternative spellings of the culture name, a totally different name used by outsiders, a name used in the past but no longer used, or the name in another language. It is not unusual that some ethnonyms are considered degrading and insulting by the people to whom they refer. These names may nevertheless be included here because they do identify the group and may help some users locate the summary or additional information on the culture in other sources. Ethnonyms are cross-referenced to the culture name in the index.

Glossary

Each volume contains a glossary of technical and scientific terms found in the summaries. Both general social science terms and region-specific terms are included.

Special Considerations

In a project of this magnitude, decisions had to be made about the handling of some information that cannot easily be standardized for all areas of the world. The two most troublesome matters concerned population figures and units of measure.

Population Figures

We have tried to be as up-to-date and as accurate as possible in reporting population figures. This is no easy task, as some groups are not counted in official government censuses, some groups are very likely undercounted, and in some cases the definition of a cultural group used by the census takers differs from the definition we have used. In general, we have relied on population figures supplied by the summary authors. When other population data sources have been used in a volume, they are so noted by the volume editor. If the reported figure is from an earlier date—say, the 1970s—it is usually because it is the most accurate figure that could be found.

Units of Measure

In an international encyclopedia, editors encounter the problem of how to report distances, units of space, and temperature. In much of the world, the metric system is used, but scientists prefer the International System of Units (similar to the metric system), and in Great Britain and North America the English system is usually used. We decided to use English measures in the North America volume and metric measures in the other volumes. Each volume contains a conversion table.

Acknowledgments

In a project of this size, there are many people to acknowledge and thank for their contributions. In its planning stages, members of the research staff of the Human Relations Area Files provided many useful ideas. These included Timothy J. O'Leary, Marlene Martin, John Beierle, Gerald Reid, Delores Walters, Richard Wagner, and Christopher Latham. The advisory editors, of course, also played a major role in planning the project, and not just for their own volumes but also for the project as a whole. Timothy O'Leary, Terence Hays, and Paul Hockings deserve special thanks for their comments on this preface and the glossary, as does Melvin Ember, president of the Human Relations Area Files. Members of the office and technical staff also must be thanked for so quickly and carefully attending to the many tasks a project of this size inevitably generates. They are Erlinda Maramba, Abraham Maramba, Victoria Crocco, Nancy Gratton, and Douglas Black. At Macmillan and G. K. Hall, the encyclopedia has benefited from the wise and careful editorial management of Elly Dickason, Elizabeth Kubik, and Elizabeth Holthaus, and the editorial and production management of Ara Salibian.

Finally, I would like to thank Melvin Ember and the board of directors of the Human Relations Area Files for their administrative and intellectual support for this project.

DAVID LEVINSON

References

Murdock, George Peter (1967). _Ethnographic Atlas_. Pittsburgh: University of Pittsburgh Press.

Murdock, George Peter (1983). _Outline of World Cultures_. 6th rev. ed. New Haven: Human Relations Area Files.

Introduction

The national motto of the Indonesian republic, "Bhineka tunggal ika" (Unity amid Diversity), could well stand as the theme of this introductory essay. The diversity, not just of Indonesia but of the whole realm of tropical and subtropical Asia, is quite apparent as one reads through the many dozens of descriptive accounts published here and in the volume on South Asia. Some groups are tiny, while others number in the millions; some are maritime, while others live high in the mountain ranges; some have long flourished in the mainstream of major Eastern civilizations, while others are so remote that they have been effectively cut off from any civilizational influence until the present century, by geography if not by preference.

Geography and Agriculture

If there is a single factor uniting geography and culture throughout this area, it is that in general the lowland areas of Southeast Asia are devoted to the intensive cultivation of one staple crop, rice (*Oryza sativa*); the farming of rice is equally widespread in Japan, Taiwan, and Korea. Evidently the plant was indigenous to southern China, Vietnam, and nearby areas, but it spread south and west from there during the Neolithic period, until in ancient times it occupied most of the land suited to its cultivation in the tropical Asian areas, which up to that point had been densely forested. Although large tracts of that tropical forest still remain in some parts that are unsuited to rice (in Borneo, for example), hundreds of thousands of square kilometers have been devoted to small irrigated paddy fields, which are often terraced to make use of the slopes. Japanese industry, today the world's largest consumer of tropical lumber, is causing extremely rapid deforestation in Borneo (as it has already done in Thailand and the Philippines), with all the usual ensuing environmental damage. Rice is ideally suited to these tropical forest lands: unlike any other cereal crop, rice requires a hot growing season and inundation of the field during part of the growth period, and hence abundant rainfall to feed the rivers. Where irrigated paddy is grown, as in Java or Bangladesh, one can find the densest rural populations in the world. Cultivation of the rice crop is labor-intensive, requiring human labor even more than it does that of water buffalo; this fact tends to keep a large part of the population on the land today.

Ideal though these geographic conditions might be for rice cultivation, they are not found universally in the South-

east Asian area. The floodplains of the larger rivers—the Irrawaddy, Salween, Chao Phraya, Mekong, Red River, and others—with their alluvial soil and plentiful water, were actually terraced and canalized in ancient times, and in some areas (Banaue, in northern Luzon, for example) even the steepest hillsides were terraced for paddy fields. But much of the land is mountainous and not climatically suited to the cultivation of even those varieties of rice that need no irrigation. To the extent that any agriculture can be practiced on the mountains, it consists of the farming of several species of millet that were indigenous to those regions. In general millets (*Panicum* and *Sorghum* spp.) require less sun and less rainfall: some cultivation of them in swiddens is still fairly widespread in the Southeast Asian mountain areas and island interiors. In the equatorial regions—namely, Malaysia, Indonesia, and the southern Philippines—cassava is another widely grown staple. Pepper, cloves, and other spices have been prominent in local cuisine and international trade for several millennia.

During the nineteenth century colonial commercial interests introduced some valuable new plantation crops, largely through private initiative: primarily rubber, but also sugarcane, both of which revolutionized the economy of parts of Southeast Asia, changing the social and geographical landscape—and especially the natural rain forest—in the process. Spices became of even greater economic importance: indeed, it was the great need for spices that first attracted the Dutch to Indonesia four centuries ago.

The area this volume deals with stretches some 5,300 kilometers from east to west and 6,000 kilometers from north to south. While we might well expect such a vast area of the world to show considerable climatic variation, much of the land experiences only two closely related climatic types, mainland and insular (Aw and Af in the Köppen system). Translated into figures, this means that almost everywhere in Southeast Asia except on the high mountains, the temperature in the coldest month of the year is at least 18° C and the rainfall in the driest month is at least 60 centimeters. The insular climate (Af) is a constantly rainy one, and some coastal areas of mainland Southeast Asia also experience this. In the interior of Myanmar (Burma), Thailand, and Cambodia one encounters the mainland climate (Aw), in which the temperature is still above 18° C in the coldest month but there is a dry season in wintertime. The higher mountains of the Southeast Asian mainland, however, are of the Cwa climatic type, which is characterized by temperatures in the coldest month somewhere between 18° and −3° C and in the warmest month higher than 10° C. Coastal areas of Myanmar and Vietnam, as well as Luzon, are somewhat different in climate from these types and are classified as Am, which means that while the temperature of the coldest month still remains above 18° C, there is a monsoon like that which strikes western India: a short dry season in winter is made up for by heavy rains during much of the rest of the year. The South China Sea is notorious for its typhoons (as described in Joseph Conrad's novels *Lord Jim* and *Typhoon*). Mean annual rainfall in the insular sectors of Southeast Asia ranges from 300 to 400 centimeters. On the west coasts of Myanmar and Sumatra, however, it generally goes above 400 centimeters. Throughout the area the natural vegetation is rain forest and the predominant cultivated plant is rice. (New Guinea, the Congo, Central America, and the Amazon Basin are the only other parts of the world that experience such a climate.) In Southeast Asia, the only exception in regard to natural vegetation is Cambodia, which generally has savanna rather than rain forest.

Japan and Korea, however, lie very much farther north than the other countries dealt with in this volume. With the small exception of Okinawa and the Ryukyu Islands which—like neighboring Taiwan—are subtropical, Japan and the peninsula of Korea have a mild climate with well-defined seasons, much like that of Britain. Their climate is classified in the Köppen system as Caf in the south, and as Daw in the more northerly parts of the two countries (Dbw in Hokkaidō). This means that in the south there is a rainy climate with mild winters, the coolest month of the year averaging between 0° and 18° C, whereas in the north of both countries the winters are more severe, and the coldest month averages below 0° C—in other words, snowfall and frost are normal.

The Nations of East and Southeast Asia

Fourteen nation-states now make up the region covered in this volume (population totals were estimated at the beginning of 1992):

Brunei, a small sultanate on the northwest coast of the island of Borneo, surrounded by Malaysian territory. Its capital is Bandar Seri Begawan and its population in 1992 numbered only about 411,000. This wealthy state covers 5,765 square kilometers and is officially Muslim. The population is in fact 66 percent Muslim, 12 percent Buddhist, and 9 percent Christian. Tribal animists account for the remainder of the population.

Cambodia (until recently known as Kampuchea) is a people's republic currently under United Nations supervision in some areas. Its capital is Phnom Penh, and its population in 1992 was estimated at 543,000. The country has an area of 181,035 square kilometers and is bordered by Vietnam and Thailand. Buddhism is the state religion, and most people are Theravada Buddhists. Many others are Marxists and belong to the Khmer Rouge. (For further details, see the article "Khmer.")

Indonesia, the largest and most widespread country in Southeast Asia, is a republic, with Jakarta as its capital. The population was estimated at 195,300,000 in 1992, and the land area is 1,919,443 square kilometers. The dimensions of the country are impressive, for it stretches over 5,100 kilometers from east to west and 2,000 kilometers from north to south. The land area consists of an archipelago of 13,677 large and small islands, of which about 6,000 are inhabited. The population is 87 percent Muslim and 9 percent Christian, but there are also some 1.6 million Buddhists and 3.5 million Hindus. It must be pointed out that the Republic of Indonesia includes Irian Jaya, the western half of the huge island of New Guinea. In this particular volume of the *Encyclopedia of World Cultures,* however, we have excluded coverage of the cultures of Irian Jaya, since they were more appropriately dealt with in volume 2, *Oceania;* those particular cultures are all Melanesian and non-Muslim, whereas the rest of Indonesia is generally Muslim and linguistically Malay. The province of Irian Jaya covers 421,981 square kilometers and had an estimated population of 1.56 million in 1989. (For further details on this, see the article "Irianese.")

Japan (Nippon, Nihon) is a constitutional monarchy with a democratically elected parliament, the Diet. It consists of four major and many small islands and is located in the Pacific Ocean just to the east of Korea and immediately south of the Russian island of Sakhalin. The total land area is 377,708 square kilometers, an area about one-and-a-half times that of Great Britain. (This area will expand very slightly if Russia eventually cedes to Japan some of the Kurile Islands, which the USSR seized at the end of World War II.) The population was estimated in 1992 at 124,270,000, a figure that includes (1989 figures) 681,838 Koreans (most of them long resident in Japan), 137,499 Chinese, 38,925 Filipinos, 6,316 Vietnamese refugees, 5,542 Thais, and (1988 figure) 3,542 Malays, as well as about 60,000 people from other parts of the world. The capital city, Tokyo, once known as Edo, now numbers just over 8 million inhabitants. The vast majority of the Japanese population follows Mahayana Buddhist death rites but also adheres to the native Shintō religion. Christians are a small minority. (For further details, see the article "Japanese.")

Korea, a peninsula of the Asian mainland, lies between Japan and the northeast corner of China. Since 1948 it has been divided into two very different nation-states: North Korea (Inmin Konghwa-guk, Democratic People's Republic of Korea) and South Korea (Han Kook, Republic of Korea). The dividing line between the two Koreas, near the 38th parallel, was established at the end of the Korean War (1950–1953); it is a demilitarized zone of 1,262 square kilometers separating the two nations. North Korea contains the great majority of the peninsula's mineral and forest resources; yet today it is the economy of South Korea that is flourishing, whereas that of North Korea is stagnant and the country has become a military dictatorship under Kim Il-Sung and his son. The capital of North Korea is Pyongyang, and that country has a population of about 22,250,000 and an area of 121,248 square kilometers. In 1986 there were said to be about 200,000 Christians, 400,000 Buddhists, and 3 million Chondogyists (syncretists) in North Korea. South Korea has a population of about 43,305,000, and an area of 99,591 square kilometers; its capital is Seoul. Christians there number about 8.5 million, and the rest of the South Korean population follows a mixture of Buddhist, Confucian, and shamanic practices. (For further details, see the article "Korean.")

Laos is a small inland democratic republic lying to the west of Vietnam. Its capital is Vientiane. The area of the country is 231,399 square kilometers, and its population numbered some 4,158,000 in 1992. The population is mainly Hindu or Buddhist, but about 34 percent of the people follow tribal, animistic religions. (For further details, see the article "Lao.")

Malaysia is a country made up of fifteen federated states. The area is 329,758 square kilometers, and this includes 198,160 square kilometers on the island of Borneo, also called Sarawak and Sabah, which form the eastern part of Malaysia; the remaining part of the country is a peninsula projecting southward from Thailand towards Sumatra. The national population was estimated at 18,200,000 in 1992, including some 350,000 Filipino and 150,000 Indonesian immigrants in Sabah (1990 estimates), most of them illegal settlers. The federal capital is Kuala Lumpur. Islam is the official religion, but there are also numerous Buddhists, Christians, and tribal animists in the country. (For further details, see the article "Malay.")

Myanmar (formerly Burma) has for many years been a military dictatorship. Its capital is Yangon (formerly Rangoon). Although there has not been a reliable census in a long time, the population was estimated at 42,615,000 in 1992. About 68 percent of the people are Theravada Buddhists. The land area is 676,577 square kilometers. (For further details, see the article "Burmese.")

The *Philippine Republic* is another archipelago, made up of about 7,100 islands covering 299,681 square kilometers. Of these Luzon, the largest island, covers a third of the land surface, 104,684 square kilometers; Mindanao in the south covers 94,627 square kilometers. The capital is Manila. In 1992 the population was about 62,380,000. This is the only country in the region that is predominantly Roman Catholic, although there are sizable Muslim populations in the southern islands near the Sulu Sea, and tribal, animistic religions are to be found in most parts of the country. In 1970 a census yielded the following numbers of religious adherents: 31,169,488 Roman Catholics, 1,584,963 Muslims, 1,433,688 Aglipayan, 1,122,999 other Protestants, 475,407 Iglesia ni Kristo, 33,639 Buddhists (mainly Chinese), 863,302 tribal animists and others. Communist sympathizers are also numerous. (For further details, see the article "Filipino.")

Singapore is scarcely more than one city, but it is also one of the wealthiest states in the region and a republic in which Chinese dominate. The state consists of one island and 58 islets, covering only 626 square kilometers. The population in 1992 was approximately 3,062,000. Of these 41.7 percent were Buddhist and Taoist (i.e., the Chinese), with another 18.7 percent Christian, 16 percent Muslim, and 4.9 percent Hindu. (For further details, see the article "Singaporean.")

Taiwan (the Republic of China, or Nationalist China) since 1949 has been a breakaway province of China under a democratic government. It covers 36,179 square kilometers, and its capital is T'ai-pei. The population in 1992 stood at 20,785,000, which included 337,342 aboriginal people (1990 figure). The great majority of the population is of Chinese origin, some 16 million of them speaking Hokkien. The traditional Chinese mix of Buddhism and Taoism with Confucianism is the dominant religion. (For further details, see the articles "Taiwanese" and "Taiwan Aboriginal Peoples.")

Thailand, a democratic kingdom, is a large country centrally located on the Southeast Asian mainland. Its capital is the flourishing city of Bangkok. The area is 513,115 square kilometers, and the population was about 57,200,000 in 1992. In a census of 1983 the population included 47,049,223 Theravada Buddhists, 1,869,427 Muslims, 267,381 Christians, as well as 64,469 Hindus, Sikhs, and adherents of other religions. (For further details, see the article "Central Thai.")

Vietnam is a long, thin, and mainly coastal country forming much of the western margin of the South China Sea. It is a socialist republic, covering 329,566 square kilometers. In 1992 the population was estimated at 68,310,000, but there were an additional 1.5 million Vietnamese living as refugees in Hong Kong, elsewhere in Southeast Asia, or the United States. Because the area has been under strong Chinese influence for 2,100 years Taoism is the traditional religion, but Mahayana Buddhism is also widespread. The country has about 2 million followers of Hoa Hao, a Buddhist sect, and about 2 million more following Caodaism, a religion founded in 1926 that synthesizes Buddhism, Christianity, and Confucianism. In the southern part of the country there are probably some 6 million Roman Catholics, but their religion has been suppressed by the socialist government since the end of the Vietnam War. (See the later section on the war.) Communist sympathizers are very numerous. (For further details, see the article "Vietnamese.")

The Flux of Southeast Asian Civilizations

If one were to draw on a map a continuous line that circumscribed all the territory of Southeast Asia, one would find that the majority of the area so enclosed was in fact sea. The sea has been a determinant of economic and social life in the area since time immemorial. For what we may call insular Southeast Asia (Indonesia, Taiwan, and the Philippines) maritime transportation would seem to have been an essential aspect of civilization. Until the end of the Paleolithic era most of these islands and indeed most of the South China Sea were simply the southeastern continuation of the great Asiatic landmass; but with the rising of sea levels at the end of the Ice Age these islands became cut off from the rest of Asia, around 16,000–12,000 years ago. Some were already populated. Prehistoric cultures developed locally in these islands as they did on the mainland. The land was rich, in many places of volcanic origin, and by 6000–4000 B.C. northern Thailand (at the sites of Spirit Cave and Non Nok Tha) possibly had rice cultivation. Over later centuries this kind of farming became dominant over huge tracts of Southeast Asia. Even the hillsides were terraced for rice cultivation in ancient times—most dramatically, for example, at Banaue in northern Luzon. Neolithic cultures slowly evolved into Bronze Age cultures as the techniques of metallurgy spread. By about 500 B.C. iron, too, had been mastered in central Thailand, as it had in China, and oceanic shipping was no doubt bringing Chinese trade into this area.

Yet major change was slow to follow the introduction of iron. The distinctive rice-eating cultures of the area as yet had no writing systems, no major cities, no universalistic religions. All this was to change very slowly as first China and then India began to extend their influence into the Southeast Asian region. Tropical geography has no doubt been a crucial and limiting factor, determining which staple crop can be grown in each region; but almost as influential has been the long and insidious thrust of civilization emanating from empires and kingdoms alike. For Southeast Asia has been the home and fertile seeding ground to not one but five major civilizations, each being the historical and cultural elaboration of a world religion of great antiquity and wide popular appeal.

None of these civilizational influences was indigenous to the area, but all of them had vast impact.

First we may identify the Hindu sphere. Arising from the earlier Brahmanism of Vedic and post-Vedic India, Nepal, and Sri Lanka, Hinduism took a recognizable form around the seventh century A.D. Soon after that Indian mariners spread eastward on their only phase of foreign ventures, bringing their influence to touch, if not actually establish, the medieval kingdoms of Burma, Thailand, Malaya, Cambodia, southern Vietnam, southern Borneo, Sumatra, Java, Bali, and Lombok. Despite the early trade connections, towns and cities did not appear in any number until A.D. 700, and then they were much more numerous on the mainland than in the islands. At their height in the eleventh and twelfth centuries, Angkor (in Cambodia) covered more than 20,000 hectares, and Pagan (in Burma) covered 10,000 hectares, two of the largest and grandest cities on earth. Yet until about the time of the Muslim arrival in Indonesia (in the fourteenth to fifteenth centuries A.D.) true cities were virtually nonexistent in the archipelago. The celebrated temple complexes at Borobudur and Prambanam in Java were just that, not city complexes; but they did indicate a strong Hindu influence there in the eighth and ninth centuries.

The vast bulk of the Southeast Asian mainland, including Thailand and Cambodia, had already been changed some centuries earlier by the advent of another Indian philosophical and religious system, Theravada Buddhism, which paradoxically had all but disappeared from its homeland by about the sixth century A.D. Buddhism was to provide a permanent philosophical framework for most of the mainland cultures that stretched between Tibet in the west and Vietnam in the east; indeed, from the first century A.D. it became one of the main religious and philosophical strands in the civilizations of China, Korea, and Japan.

Chinese civilization has been a third major influence on Southeast Asia as well as on neighboring Korea and Japan. It was the source of the principles of Taoist thinking, Confucian ethics, and—even more important to millions of people—Chinese mercantilism. Thus the Chinese influence was by no means only associated with the ancient spread of Buddhism, which indeed filtered eastward to Japan and southward through southern China only as far as Vietnam. (The Buddhism of Sri Lanka, Myanmar, and Thailand owes little to China because it was carried to those lands by monks coming from India, and its texts were in the Pali language, written in a script derived from that used for Sanskrit.) The huge Chinese populations to be found today throughout much of Thailand, Singapore, Vietnam, Indonesia, and elsewhere are a forceful reminder of the long and vigorous trade associations that linked the Chinese Empire with these more southerly lands.

For the past few centuries a fourth great civilizing force, also coming from the west, has been the spread of Islam. It reached across India and Southeast Asia not only by the sword but also with the trading vessels that linked much of the Indian Ocean with the western Pacific. Yet it was as late as the fifteenth century before Malaysia and Indonesia were converted; and by then the Portuguese were already at the door—in fact, they attracted Arab traders to Malacca. Today the most populous Islamic lands in the world are to be found in South and Southeast Asia, namely Pakistan, India, Bangladesh, Malaysia, and Indonesia. Islam reached as far as the southern parts of the Philippines but did not travel farther north to Taiwan, Japan, or Korea. Other religions that left their mark on Indian civilization—Jainism, Sikhism, and Zoroastrianism—were of no importance farther east.

The fifth and final influence to be noted has been the more recent European one: it effectively began with Vasco da Gama's voyage to South India from Portugal in A.D. 1498. One hesitates to identify this as a Christian influence, even though that was the religion of these colonial conquerors, because the impact of Christian evangelists in most areas has not been very great. In fact it is only in the Philippines and some pockets of Indonesia, Korea, and Vietnam that one can find Christian communities running to some millions of people; and of these countries only the Philippines can be regarded as predominantly Christian. The real impact of European civilization has been administrative, educational, and commercial, for the recently ended colonial period saw nearly every country of Southeast Asia under fairly direct colonial administration. (Indeed, Taiwan and Korea were for a while under Japanese imperial rule.) This state of affairs was ending everywhere by about 1950; but the modern infrastructure of highways, railways, ports, government buildings, air and postal services, schools, universities, and political and commercial institutions was firmly in place by that time and has altered the face of these Asian lands forever.

This picture of Southeast Asia as an area under the influence of so many historically distinct civilizations must be recognized as a partial one: it is not the whole story. The fact is that on much of the mainland, as in most of the many thousands of inhabited islands, in ancient and recent times, people have commonly subsisted through simple farming or food-collecting strategies, with no reliance whatever on long-distance maritime trade, with no familiarity with any of the great world religions, and with no participation in any city-centered polity. Indeed, civilization in general came rather late to the Southeast Asian area, although it had been recognizable on the Indian subcontinent 5,000 years ago and in China 4,000 years ago. But when one looks elsewhere in the region, one finds few city-states anywhere until well after the sixth century A.D., and nearly all of these reflect a Hindu influence. Islam and the Europeans were yet to arrive, and Chinese traders seldom left much of a mark on indigenous cultures in those early times. (Korea and Japan, being much closer to China, were a rather different story.) To the south there were maritime connections with China, and Java was even attacked by Mongols coming from there in 1293; yet India was the main influence on medieval Malay and Indonesian kingdoms.

The spread of Hinduism was marked by the diffusion of monumental architecture, of writing scripts, and of Brahman priests and scholars, particularly to the royal courts of Southeast Asia. Even today people identifiable as Brahmans may still be found at the royal court in Bangkok, and they exist also in Bali. There is a remarkable correlation between the medieval incidence of Hinduism and irrigated rice cultivation in Southeast Asia: the two were distributed through the same regions. One should not argue that the irrigation was introduced to this area by Brahmans or other Indians, but its surpluses did favor the erection of great Hindu and Buddhist monuments. This was probably because the lax period after the rice harvest, when food was most plentiful, allowed peasant people the time to donate their labor (or be coerced into doing so by soldiers and officials) to build the grand monuments of civilization. Angkor, for example, a cluster of medieval towns, hydraulic engineering projects, and Hindu-Buddhist temples, covered, as we have seen, something like 200 square kilometers.

Korea and Japan

A mountainous spine runs throughout the length of Japan, and another runs more or less parallel to it through eastern Korea. Between these two countries lies the Sea of Japan, the major source of fish in the diet of both. The other staple in that diet is rice, grown in irrigated paddies throughout lowland Japan and Korea. Two other important Japanese crops are tea and mulberries, the latter providing the food for silkworms.

As might be expected from its position at the northeast extremity of China, the Korean Peninsula has been under very strong Chinese influence since the Bronze Age. In 108 B.C. the Han army invaded Korea and conquered the kingdom of Old Chosŏn. Chinese rule lasted from then until A.D. 313, but the influence of the Chinese has never ceased. In the first century B.C. three kingdoms came into existence in Korea as Chinese tributaries (Silla, Koguryŏ and Paekche), a division that lasted till A.D. 668. In A.D. 372 Buddhism first entered Koguryŏ from China, and it soon became the dominant faith, although it has never fully supplanted a local form of shamanism. Confucianism too, as well as Chinese art, architecture, literature, and styles of governance, continued to exert a strong influence on Korea over the centuries. Great Silla became the preeminent power in 668, and ruled a unified Korea until 936. The rest of Korean history down to the present century encompasses the rule of only two dynasties, the Koryŏ (936–1392) and the Yi (1392–1910). During the twentieth century Korea has suffered vastly from the machinations of foreign powers. First, the country found itself caught, late in the nineteenth century, in a power struggle between its three neighbors, China, Japan, and Russia. Then, following a Japanese invasion, it became part of the Japanese Empire from 1910 to 1945. Hundreds of thousands of Koreans ended up as slave labor in Japan, where they or their descendants remain. By 1948 the country had split into two: North Korea, backed by the Soviet Union, and South Korea, backed by the United States and other United Nations forces. The Korean War ended in 1953, but today, forty years later, the land is still divided along the 38th parallel into two hostile states. (For further details, see the article "Korean.")

In the past Japan, Korea, and Taiwan looked to the Buddhism and Confucianism and the arts and letters of China for cultural inspiration. Many of the cultural features of ancient Japan, including the use of *kanji* script, can be traced back through Korea to a Chinese origin. In modern times, however, the orientation of these countries is to the world economy. Japan, South Korea, and Taiwan are nowadays all highly industrialized lands. Early in this century, at the commencement of their industrialization, both Korea and Taiwan were parts of the Japanese Empire, and the Japanese then introduced their management style to the fledgling manufacturing industries of the other two countries. Today Korea and Taiwan find themselves in much the same situation as their mentor, exporting vast quantities of advanced technological products worldwide but importing huge amounts of oil (they produce virtually none). While Australia and New Zealand can adequately supply the meat and fruits needed by Japan, the almost insatiable needs of the Japanese for fish, petroleum, and tropical timbers constitute a long-term threat to the ecology of the western Pacific and raise serious questions about the future stability of the Japanese economy.

Salient features of Japanese and Korean history are outlined in the articles "Japanese" and "Korean." Taiwan will be discussed further in the volume dealing with China (but see also the article "Taiwanese" in this volume).

Historical Geography

A prominent geographical difference between China or India on the one hand and Southeast Asia on the other is that while the former two countries have the absolute minimum length of coastline for such large territories, Southeast Asia has an extremely long coastline. South Asia has very few natural harbors, and the best-known ports are to a large extent artificial. Southeast Asia's mainland, in contrast, has a much indented coastline; and the huge archipelagoes of the Philippines and Indonesia, as well as Japan, add tens of thousands of kilometers to the total coastline of the region. The Philippines as we have seen contains 7,100 islands, including 11 very large ones; Japan includes 4 larger and more than 1,000 smaller islands; and Indonesia has 13,677, including the second-, third- and fifth-largest islands on Earth—it is the largest group of islands anywhere. From the earliest times sea connections must have been of crucial importance in this area, and it was inevitable that the Hindu, the Chinese, and then the Muslim and European influences came with seafaring traders and adventurers in Southeast Asia. In premodern times Malaysia, Indonesia, and other coastal areas were divided among what have been called "harbor principalities," small coastal territories with sultans or chiefs controlling their economies. Although much reduced in their power today, some of these people are still to be found living in ramshackle palaces and bearing the title of sultan. And everywhere that the maritime traders went their alter egos, the pirates, were also to be found. Some of these too have survived to the present day. (See the articles "Bajau," "Samal," and "Sea Nomads of the Andaman.")

In the age of exploration it was the diverse attractions of trade, especially for cloves, nutmeg, mace, pepper, camphor, and Chinese silks, that brought the first European adventurers into the area. The Philippines, seized by Spain in 1571, became the only Spanish colony in Asia, and Spain held it for more than three centuries in close connection with her Mexican territories. The Dutch held Indonesia for a similar length of time, having founded Batavia at the site of Jakarta in 1619. The British acquired Malaya from the Dutch in 1824 and conquered Burma beginning in the same year; between 1859 and 1893 the French added Cambodia, Laos, and Vietnam to their widespread empire as French Indochina. Only Siam (now Thailand) managed to remain beyond formal annexation, although it too was subject to strong British and French commercial exploitation. The Portuguese, so powerful elsewhere, were hardly a force to be reckoned with in Southeast Asia. It is true that d'Albuquerque conquered the great trading port of Malacca, near Singapore, in 1511, thus making the Portuguese the first European traders to venture into Indonesian waters. Yet after their loss of Malacca to the Dutch in 1641, the remote Indonesian island of Timor along with Macao, on the south China coast near Hong Kong, became Portugal's only two East Asian colonies. Portugal was more involved in exploiting the coasts of Brazil and parts of Africa. One other latecomer to the colonial feast was the United States, which as a result of the Spanish-American War of 1898 found itself the guardian of the Philippines, Cuba, and some other Caribbean islands. Virtually all of the colonial holdings survived until the mid-twentieth century, when the Japanese invasion of Southeast Asia in World War II and sundry guerrilla wars finally drove the Europeans and Americans out.

The impact of these colonial powers—or rather of their trading companies—was enormous and, as in India and elsewhere, they developed the infrastructure of the present ten states found in the Southeast Asian region. The two most prominent trading ports, Singapore and Jakarta, were European foundations. In Indochina and Malaysia the valuable plantation crop of rubber was introduced from South America. Tea, originally from China, was another plantation crop that was introduced to Java. In the Philippines the Spanish introduced Roman Catholicism and a Western outlook fostered by the educational system. Elsewhere indigenous customs and faiths were generally left alone by the Europeans, especially by the Dutch. Except for Myanmar, Thailand, and Cambodia, it is true to say that all of the major cities of East and Southeast Asia in modern times are located on the coasts of the region and these are where Western influence was most concentrated. East and Southeast Asia contains some of the world's largest islands, and so it is not surprising that the effects of European colonization and modernization did not always reach far inland. Borneo in particular is so vast that its interior is not well known and is only thinly populated and quite underdeveloped. That island is now divided among three nations: Indonesia, Malaysia, and Brunei.

The Vietnam War

The recent history of Vietnam effectively begins with its declaration of independence in 1945. Then, following the siege of Dien Bien Phu by local guerrilla forces and after that the Geneva Conference, the French, who had administered this region as Tongking, Annam, and Cochin China since 1859, finally withdrew in 1956. Even before this very significant defeat of a major European imperial power, the ongoing civil war in Vietnam had attracted the military attention of a single-minded United States government intent on "beating communism." In 1956 a cease-fire between warring factions had created a demilitarized zone ("DMZ" in military parlance) across the central part of the country. This zone was to separate Communists to the north from Buddhists and Christians to the south; but the United States, siding with the southerners, began to treat the DMZ as a national boundary, which it was never intended to be. By 1965 the United States had documented the return of seventeen ex-soldiers from the north into the southern zone—something completely within their rights—and to counter this "invasion" began a massive buildup of U.S. military forces, with 50,000 from South Korea and some token support from Australia and elsewhere. What ensued was the Vietnam War (1965–1975), in which the United States sent over 2.5 million men and women into the field, only to see over 59,000 of them killed by well-trained guerrilla fighters. In April 1975 the last of the U.S. forces left Saigon, leaving behind a reunited Vietnam under a Communist government, impoverished almost beyond repair. In 1993 Vietnam is still one of the most backward countries of the region, despite its great agricultural potential. The infrastructure the French colonial administration left behind nearly forty years ago is no longer effective, and consequently refugees, mainly "boat people," are still fleeing from Vietnam's poverty and repression in considerable numbers.

Religions

But what of the unity amid this cultural and geographical diversity—or perhaps more accurately, the separate unities? Although the hilly interiors both of islands and of the mainland remain the home of numerous localized animistic religions, Southeast Asia as we have seen has been a meeting place of four major world faiths. Thus the region has a Theravada Buddhist northern sector that stretches through Myanmar, Thailand, and Cambodia and a Muslim southern sector that stretches through Malaysia and Indonesia to the southern Philippines. From its center in the Philippines, Christianity reaches westward to parts of Vietnam, Indonesia, and Malaysia. The northern part of Vietnam, which had been under strong Chinese influence since about 110 B.C., has the Chinese mix of Mahayana Buddhism with Taoism and Confucian philosophy, as do Singapore and Taiwan; and now there is a Communist (officially atheistic) segment in the northeast that reaches down from North Korea and China through Laos and the long finger of Vietnam. No doubt this geographic sketch is a gross oversimplification, but it serves to point out how people in great blocks of territory have been stimulated by contact with greatly different philosophies. Beginning in the second or third century A.D. Hindu influence became widespread in Java, southern Vietnam, southern Sumatra, and Cambodia; but later Islam displaced the power of medieval Hinduism in most of these areas, and so the latter faith is now scarcely noticeable in the region outside of Bali and Lombok. The cultural impact of Hinduism was widespread and of great importance in kingship, the arts, mythology, and the diffusion of writing. Buddhism in Southeast Asian countries of course has roots that go back nearly 2,000 years. Communism has been important here only since the middle third of this century, and Christianity since the arrival of the first European missionaries in the Philippines in the sixteenth century. Sikhism and Hinduism are now to be found among the sizable immigrant populations of Malaysia and Singapore.

All of these influences persist throughout this vast region to this day and are reflected in the latest estimates for religious adherence. For the entirety of Southeast Asia, it is believed that in 1990 there were roughly 178 million Muslims, 65 million Christians, 53 million Buddhists, and 5 million Hindus.

These figures are mere estimates, and they by no means cover the entire Southeast Asian population of 435 million, which also included (in 1990) perhaps 9 million Confucians, Taoists, Sikhs, atheists and nonworshiping Marxists, and at least 125 million tribal animists. What these figures do reflect, then, is the persisting impact in that part of the world of the five diverse civilizations listed earlier.

These figures cannot really be enlarged to include the four countries of East Asia with which this volume deals. The reason is a straightforward one. In Taiwan the Chinese people are commonly simultaneously Buddhists, Taoists, and Confucianists: in the words of a popular dictum, "The three faiths are one." A similar mélange is also encountered in both North and South Korea, where an added element—or a local variant of Taoism—is the widely prevalent shamanism. In Japan it has often been said that one lives as a Shintoist and dies a Buddhist: there these two religions coexist in the lives of many. It was in the ninth century A.D. that Shintō (a Chinese term) and Buddhism became welded together into a single Japanese faith that was called Ryōbu-Shintō or "dual Shintō." The old Shintō deities thus became avatars of the Buddhist deities. In the nationalistic fervor that followed the Meiji restoration in 1867, Shintō rituals were given a new prominence while Buddhism experienced some disfavor. Yet today Buddhist moral teachings, funerals, and concepts of eschatology complement the Shintō pilgrimages, local festivals, and marriage ceremonies in the religious life of most Japanese. In summary, most worshipers in these countries of East Asia tend not to be distinctly of one historic faith or another, as they are in Southeast Asia.

Contemplation of the huge numbers of people living in East and Southeast Asia, a land area of about 4,706,700 square kilometers, prompts me to add that this volume deals with nearly 13 percent of the world's population (just over 5 billion in 1993). The rough geographic limits encompassing this mass are the Chindwin River in the west; the Philippine, Japanese, and Indonesian archipelagoes in the east; the Indian Ocean to the south; and to the north, the Red River (Song Koi) in Vietnam and the Russian territories of Sakhalin and Kamchatka.

Categorization of Cultures

In all of Southeast Asia traditional premodern societies were of three types only. First, there were the tribal societies, dozens of which have been described in the present volume. Their cultures showed great variation, particularly between one region and another. Social fragmentation was a common feature of their former histories. But they did have two distinct kinds of economy. There were the foragers, some of whom traded forest produce with the coastal towns. (See the later discussion.) Some indeed have flourished in the present century through the production of opium, which, though illegal, now commands a huge world market. There were also the swidden farmers, who used slash-and-burn techniques to produce small fields of millet and other foodstuffs on the hillsides; they too often grew opium, in the swiddens of the notorious Golden Triangle. Tribal societies have been quite varied in their cultures, partly for environmental reasons and partly because until recently most have been little affected by the great world religions on account of the geographic remoteness of their territories. Spirit cults, slaving and headhunting have been features of these tribal cultures right down to the twentieth century.

A second type of society was the inland state—though some examples of this should perhaps be described in other terms, as they may have stretched down to the coasts. These states were a stark contrast to the small self-contained tribal societies: they were always based on irrigated rice cultivation, supported large populations, and usually had a hierarchical social organization centered on towns. A rural peasantry labored to produce the staple foods while an extensive bureaucracy and priesthood, mainly in the towns, was subservient to a petty king or raja. The religion of these states throughout the Southeast Asian area was a sometimes uneasy amalgam of Hinduism and Buddhism; the insular areas of Indonesia and the southern Philippines have been Islamized since the fifteenth century, and much of the Philippines has become Christian since the sixteenth century. Premodern Korea and Japan were essentially made up of states of this sort although, as discussed earlier, a Hindu or Islamic component in their region was lacking.

A third kind of society that provided economic integration in premodern times was what van Leur (1955) has called the harbor principality. These were independent trading states, centered on certain seaports and river estuaries, that had a raja, a strong mercantile class, and very often slave labor. Merchants gained products from the inland rice-producing states and even from forest-dwelling tribes, which they then traded to other parts of Southeast Asia, even to southern China and India.

The arrival of European traders some centuries ago did not immediately alter this pattern of societies. Batavia under the Dutch East India Company was simply another harbor principality, as was the later British settlement at Singapore. But eventually the relationship between seaports and inland agricultural regions was to change radically, because the European colonists started developing plantations for coffee, tea, sugar, and in some mainland areas rubber. By the nineteenth century the rajas of Malaysia and Indonesia were subservient respectively to British and Dutch colonial authorities. A prominent feature of the plantation system was its use of indentured labor brought from outside the area—Chinese in Malaysia, Vietnam, and Indonesia, Javanese in Sumatra, and Indians in Malaysia and Sri Lanka. The plantation supervisors were normally European, but middle-level staff on the plantations, as well as on such supporting transportation as the railroads, were commonly half-caste: Anglo-Indians in Malaysia and South India, Burghers in Sri Lanka, mestizos in the Philippines (where sugar was grown), and Dutch or French half-castes in their respective colonial territories.

Whereas many of the plantations survived the Japanese invasion in World War II, European political control did not; and although the British, French, and Dutch did stay on in the area for a while after the war, all of their Southeast Asian colonies had disappeared by about 1960. The fabric of society is now being formed in some countries by the requirements of capitalist development and in other countries by guerrilla warfare and continuing civil strife.

Social Organization

The organization of Southeast Asian societies is in the most general way characterized by kindreds and bilateral descent. This makes a stark contrast with social organization in South Asia, for example, where caste differentiation is a dominant feature, or with the social order in Japan, Korea, and Taiwan, where patrilineages are universal. Even though there was a long Indian cultural influence on much of Southeast Asia, the idea of a caste-organized society did not really diffuse beyond the settlements of Indian invaders. Caste implies a basic rule of patrilineal descent and inheritance, which accounts for the well-known fact that sons in South Asia inherit their father's property and usually follow in his occupational footsteps as well. This is also the case in East Asian countries. In Southeast Asia, by contrast, small families of parents with their children are the universal social unit: the most important corporate unit for landholding, economic activity, and daily social relations is this domestic unit, a family. Beyond this the most common larger social unit is the kindred. Both of them are bilateral rather than lineal. Whereas a caste is a social group with well-defined boundaries and thus a definite, if numerous, set of members, a kindred is not a group but rather a social grouping having no particular boundaries: the kindred of one individual differs from that of another because it is simply definable as the close lineal and collateral kin of an individual, regardless of whether they are related to him or her matrilaterally or patrilaterally. In short, the kindred is a bilateral grouping of one's relatives traced perhaps as far as one's second or third cousins, whereas the Indian caste is a unilineal descent group made up of clans, lineages, and extended families. Chinese and Japanese clans have a structure similar to that of the caste. Put another way, we can visualize the caste as a large group that will continue to exist for centuries, regardless of whether any one particular person is born into it or not. The kindred, in contrast, is Ego-centered and only exists (or can only be defined) in relation to one particular individual (whom anthropologists conventionally call Ego). For this reason the kindred, which is so important in a person's social relations beyond the family level, cannot be a descent group and is not even a corporate group; whereas for Indians the caste, and for Chinese the clan, is the largest descent group. In regard to marriage, we may note that while the domestic unit, the family, is an exogamous unit, the kindred is only rarely definable as exogamous. Indian families are exogamous too, but their castes are always endogamous.

Languages

The Southeast Asian languages belong to three different families. Virtually all languages of insular Southeast Asia are related to Malay and classified as Austronesian (or Malayo-Polynesian); these include the aboriginal languages of Taiwan but do not extend into Irian Jaya. On the mainland, however, another language family, Sino-Tibetan, predominates. It has three main subfamilies: Tibeto-Burman, Tai, and Sinitic, although the last is only represented here among immigrant Chinese populations, including those of Taiwan. Khmer and some tribal pockets of Laos and Thailand can be assigned to a third family, Austroasiatic (also called Munda or Mon-Khmer). The Japanese language cannot be assigned to any family. Korean might be remotely related to it but is probably to be classified as Ural-Altaic.

Despite the large number of languages spoken in each country today, each has an "official" language of wide currency: Burmese in Myanmar, Thai in Thailand, Khmer in Cambodia, Vietnamese in Vietnam, Malay in Malaysia, Chinese and other languages in Singapore, Bahasa Indonesia in Indonesia, Filipino in the Philippines, Laotian in Laos, Mandarin in Taiwan, Korean in Korea, and Japanese in Japan. English is widely used in Malaysia, Singapore, and the Philippines and is common as a second language in big cities of the other countries. French is still spoken by some older Cambo-

dians, Laotians, and Vietnamese, while Japanese is known to older Koreans and Taiwanese. In Indonesia Dutch has been displaced by English as a second (or rather a third) language; for most people there the second language is Bahasa Indonesia, a national language that was made up by a committee in the mid-twentieth century to answer the needs of national integration. It could be loosely characterized as Javanese with a large technical vocabulary borrowed from English and Dutch.

A Note on Placenames

In recent years several important and well-established placenames have been changed by national governments. Thus in 1989 General Ne Win changed the name of Burma to the more literary Myanmar at the behest of his soothsayer. Cambodia was named Kampuchea for a while. In Indonesia (the former Dutch East Indies), most of Borneo is now Kalimantan; Celebes is Sulawesi; Halmahera has long had the alternative name Jailolo Gilolo; Java is Jawa; the Lesser Sundas are Nusa Tenggara; the Moluccas are Maluku; and Sumatra is Sumatera.

Of the various towns that have changed names in recent years, we note that Rangoon, the capital of Myanmar, officially became Yangon in 1989, and that Makassar (in Sulawesi) is now known as Ujung Pandang. Seoul, the capital of South Korea, is also known as Sŏul or Kyŏngsŏng. After the Vietnam War there was extensive renaming of places in the southern part of Vietnam, with Saigon for example becoming Ho Chi Minh City.

A good atlas, such as *The Times Atlas of the World*, usually gives both old and new names in the interest of clarity. Earlier in the century, we might also note, Siam became Thailand, and after independence Dutch New Guinea became Irian Jaya; Malaya (formerly the Straits Settlements and Federated Malay States) joined with Sarawak and Sabah to become Malaysia; and the French provinces of Tongking, Annam, and Cochin China together became Vietnam. North Korea and South Korea were, before 1948, jointly called Corea. Taiwan previously went by its Portuguese name, Formosa.

The Coverage of This Volume

There is no way in which we might have covered, even schematically, all the peoples of East and Southeast Asia in one volume. Even though it may appear that this volume contains many descriptions of minority cultures—those of small tribes or tiny islands, with diminutive populations and a minimal historical impact in the region—we have in fact only been able to offer a small sampling of such cultural descriptions. For example, on the island of Halmahera (area 17,350 square kilometers) on the equator in the eastern part of Indonesia, there are twenty-one cultures, distinguishable in particular by their use of twenty-one distinct languages belonging to two families, but of these we have covered only Tobelorese (but see also "Moluccans—North"and "Ternatan/Tidorese"). Furthermore, for some countries in the region (especially Myanmar, North Korea, Laos, Cambodia, and Vietnam) there has been little or no anthropological research on local cultural groups for over a quarter of a century: this is mainly an effect of socialist government policies prohibiting such research. As a consequence there is a dearth of new information about some of the cultures that are covered in this volume. To the extent possible, we have tried to update previous descriptions of the cultures of those countries (mainly from the volumes edited by LeBar et al., 1964, 1972, 1975) with more recent population and locational data. It is not possible, however, to gauge accurately how the political, economic, and social changes of the last several decades have affected many of the smaller groups, especially in the socialist countries just cited.

The population figures for certain groups are also quite unreliable, although we have tried to be as up-to-date as possible by providing estimates. We did contact the governments of Southeast Asian nations for census data but to little avail, as many of their ethnic groups are not enumerated separately in government censuses. We have also relied on the estimates reported in *Ethnologue,* although these can perhaps be more accurately described as counts of speakers of specific languages rather than counts of the members of ethnic groups. In regard to Vietnam, we want to thank Frank Prochan, who kindly supplied us with a summary of the 1985 census of that country.

At the outset, the editor was faced with the task of selecting from thousands of discrete social units a relatively small number that might represent the cultural, religious, ethnic, social, and economic diversity of the region. As a starting point, forty-six "peoples" included in the World Ethnographic Sample were deemed, by that fact alone, worthy of inclusion here (though in several cases no appropriate living author could be found).

A second procedure was to strive for coverage of peoples who, regardless of how numerous they are, figure prominently in the ethnographic literature.

A third requirement was to ensure that major cultural categories such as the Malays and Tagalog speakers were covered, if only because they often number tens of millions of people. The editor thus saw no difficulty in including articles on groups of different scale and size.

A final factor, a very important one, that helped determine our coverage was which authors might be available. In some cases professional anthropologists volunteered to write about a particular people or tribe with which they were familiar, and of course such offers were never refused. In other cases, however, the obvious person to write about a particular social group—the "authority" on them—was deceased or unavailable. In these instances, where some sort of lacuna in our coverage seemed unavoidable, the project staff came into play. These were people at the Human Relations Area Files (HRAF) office and anthropology students at the University of Illinois, in Chicago, who worked with the editor to produce short articles based on previously published ethnographic literature. Our task was made vastly easier by the existence of two landmark surveys edited by Frank LeBar and others: *Ethnic Groups of Mainland Southeast Asia* (1964) and *Ethnic Groups of Insular Southeast Asia* (1972, 1975). The longer articles have all followed the format established in volume 1 for the entire *Encyclopedia of World Cultures.*

Reference Resources

There are several good, detailed historical and geographical surveys of this region. The standard history of Southeast Asia is by Hall (1981). Cady (1964), le May (1954), and Keyes (1988) can also be recommended. For prehistory and protohistory there are informative, up-to-date articles in Hughes (1985) and in Sherratt (1980). The Indian influence is well covered by Coedès (1968) and le May (1954). Many articles dealing with Southeast Asian history may also be found in Embree (1988). An excellent regional geography is by Fisher (1966), and another standard geography is by Dobby (1973). As far as ethnography is concerned, the surveys edited by LeBar et al. (1964, 1972, 1975), mentioned earlier, have not been superseded unless by the present volume. Three collections of anthropological essays make profitable reading, one edited by Murdock (1960), a second edited by Kunstadter (1967), and a third by Turton and Tanabe (1984). An article by Wertheim (1968) is a masterly survey of Southeast Asian society. Two useful French introductions to the region are by Condominas (1978) and by Cuisinier and de Josselin de Jong (1972). Two other general surveys, both very dated but well illustrated, are Hutchinson (n.d.) and Frey et al. (1937). An introductory account of the mythology of the region is by Luomala (1972), and a more thorough and recent one is by Bonnefoy (1991, 2:913–1141). In fact, Bonnefoy's two volumes are a fine introduction to mythology of the entire world, and their sections roughly correspond to the way volumes of this encyclopedia have been divided. Recent accounts of Buddhism in the area include Buswell (1987), Noriyoshi (1987), and Swearer (1981, 1987). For more on Buddhism, see the bibliography of the article "Buddhist." Van der Kroef (1976) provides an overview of Indonesian religious movements, and Nguyên Trân Huân (1976) does the same for Vietnam. Four excellent histories of the arts have been published for this part of Asia: one dealing with Indonesia (Wagner 1959), one with Indochina (Groslier 1962), one with Japan (Swann 1966), and another dealing with Burma, Korea, and Tibet (Griswold et al. 1964). For the languages of the area one should consult Sebeok et al. (1967), or Huffman (1986). There are many good introductions to Japanese, for example Vaccari and Vaccari (1961). Drews and Hockings (1981) offer a detailed bibliography of bibliographies for the entire region, including Japan, Korea, and Taiwan.

For Japan there exists a multitude of reference works. A basic encyclopedia has been published by Kōdansha (1983). A good brief introduction to the cultural history is Collcutt, Jansen, and Kumakura (1988), and for both Japan and Korea Toynbee (1973) contains some excellent articles. A more detailed account of Japanese cultural history, longer because it consists primarily of translated texts, was prepared by Tsunoda, de Bary, and Keene (1958). An old but fascinating handbook to the traditional culture is by Chamberlain (1971). Useful if brief accounts of the religions of Japan are by Rotermund (1970), Renondeau and Frank (1970), and Renondeau (1976a, b); for recent Japanese sectarian movements, see Rotermund (1976). Ogg (1976) introduces Korean religion. General surveys of Japanese society include Nakane (1970), Norbeck (1976), Passin (1968), Smith and Beardsley (1962), and Yanagita (1970). For further references, see the bibliographies following the articles "Ainu," "Japanese," and "Korean," and a bibliography organized by subject in Collcutt, Jansen, and Kumakura (1988, 225–227).

Most of the countries dealt with in this volume have their own modern novelists, and these are especially numerous in Japan. Many of their works finally have been translated into English and thus have become accessible to Western students. With no pretensions to providing more than a sampling, we offer a short list of novels and a few plays by some of the leading writers of Southeast Asia and Japan (with translation dates; Asian family names are given first).

From Burma/Myanmar: Nu, U, *The People Win Through*; Pe, Hla, *Konmara Pya Zat* (1952). From Indonesia: Echols, John M., ed., *Indonesian Writing in Translation* (1956). From Japan: Akutagawa Ryūnosuke, *Hell Screen* (1948), *Kappa* (1949), *Japanese Short Stories* (1961), *Rashomon and Other Stories* (1952), and *Tales Grotesque and Curious* (1938); Dazai Osamu, *No Longer Human* (1958) and *The Setting Sun* (1950); Edogawa Rampo, *Japanese Tales of Mystery and Imagination* (1957); Hayashi Fumiko, *Floating Cloud* (1957); Hino Ashihei, *Barley and Soldiers* (1939); Kawabata Yasunari, *Snow Country* (1957), *The Sound of the Mountain* (1970), and *A Thousand Cranes* (1959); Kikuchi Kan, *The Madman on the Roof* (c. 1916); Kobayashi Takiji, *The Cannery Boat* (1933); Mishima Yukio, *After the Banquet* (1963), *Confessions of a Mask* (1960), *Death in Midsummer and Other Stories* (1966), and *The Temple of the Golden Pavilion* (1956); Mori Ōgai, *The Wild Geese* (1959); Murasaki Shikibu, *The Tale of Genji* (1935, but written about A.D. 1000); Mushakōji Saneatsu, *Friendship* (1958) and *The Heart Is Alone* (1957); Natsume Sōseki, *Botchan* (1973), *Kokoro* (1967), and *Mon* (1972); Noma Hiroshi, *Zone of Emptiness* (1956); Tanizaki Junichirō, *Diary of a Mad Old Man* (1965), *The Makioka Sisters* (1957), *Seven Japanese Tales* (1964), and *Some Prefer Nettles* (1955); see also the translations by Donald Keene in his three books, *Anthology of Japanese Literature* (1956), *Modern Japanese Literature* (1957), and *Five Modern Noh Plays* (1957); and also Ivan Morris, ed., *Modern Japanese Stories—An Anthology* (1962). From the Philippines: Joaquin, Nick, *The Woman Who Had Two Navels* (1961); Rizal, José, *Noli me tángare* or *The Social Cancer* (1956, 1961) and *The Reign of Greek* (1912). From Thailand: Khu'krit Pramoj, Mọm Ratchawong, *Red Bamboo* (1955).

Several prominent British authors have produced novels that were set in the Southeast Asian area. Of these, the most noteworthy are surely Joseph Conrad's *Almayer's Folly* (1895), *Lord Jim* (1900), *An Outcast of the Islands* (1896), *The Rescue* (1920), *The Shadow-Line* (1917), and *Typhoon* (1902); Graham Greene's *The Quiet American* (1955); W. Somerset Maugham's *The Casuarina Tree* (1926); and George Orwell's *Burmese Days* (1934). Of numerous accounts of European exploration, the most important historically are perhaps Alfred R. Wallace's *The Malay Archipelago* (1869) and the several works of Lafcadio Hearn (later Koizumi Yakumo). The above literary titles have not been included in the following bibliography, as most have come out in numerous editions.

Acknowledgments

The editor thanks Paul Wheatley and Anthony R. Walker for their valuable advice on the coverage of ethnic groups in Southeast Asia and Robert L. Messer for his advice on the Vietnam War. In addition, the help of Joyce Drzal, film librarian at the University of Illinois, provided up-to-date information on the distributors for all films listed in the filmography. Their aid, together with that of several anthropology students at the University of Illinois, is gratefully acknowledged.

Bibliography

Bonnefoy, Yves, ed. (1991). *Mythologies*. English translation edited by Wendy Doniger. Chicago and London: University of Chicago Press.

Buswell, Robert Evans, Jr. (1987). "Buddhism in Korea." In *The Encyclopedia of Religion*, edited by Mircea Eliade. Vol. 2, 421–426. New York: Macmillan; London: Collier Macmillan.

Cady, John Frank (1964). *Southeast Asia: Its Historical Development*. New York: McGraw-Hill.

Chamberlain, Basil Hall (1971). *Japanese Things; Being Notes on Various Subjects Connected with Japan*. Rutland, Vt., and Tokyo: Charles E. Tuttle.

Coedès, Georges (1968). *The Indianized States of Southeast Asia*. Honolulu: University of Hawaii Press.

Collcutt, Martin, Marius Jansen, and Isao Kumakura (1988). *The Cultural Atlas of the World: Japan*. Alexandria, Va.: Stonehenge Press.

Condominas, Georges (1978). "L'Asie du Sud-est." In *Ethnologie régionale*. Vol. 2, 283–375. Encyclopédie de la Pléiade. Paris: Éditions Gallimard.

Cuisinier, Jeanne, and P. E. de Josselin de Jong (1972). "Le Monde malais." In *Ethnologie régionale*. Vol. 1, 1300–1407. Encyclopédie de la Pléiade. Paris: Éditions Gallimard.

Dobby, Ernest Henry George (1973). *Southeast Asia*. 11th ed. London: University of London Press.

Drews, Lucy, and Paul Hockings (1981). "Asia Bibliographies." In *Anthropological Bibliographies: A Selected Guide*, edited by Margo L. Smith and Yvonne M. Damien, 89–141. South Salem, N.Y.: Redgrave Publishing.

Embree, Ainslee T. (1988). *Encyclopedia of Asian History*. 4 vols. Edited by Ainslee T. Embree. New York: Charles Scribner's Sons; London: Collier Macmillan.

Fisher, Charles Alfred (1966). *South-East Asia: A Social, Economic, and Political Geography*. 2nd ed. London: Methuen.

Frey, Ulrich, et al. (1937). *Vorder- und Südasien in Natur, Kultur und Wirtschaft*. Handbuch der geographischen Wissenschaft. Potsdam: Akademische Verlagsgesellschaft Athenaion.

Griswold, Alexander B., Chewon Kim, and Peter H. Pott (1964). *The Art of Burma, Korea, Tibet*. New York: Crown Publishers.

Groslier, Bernard Philippe (1962). *The Art of Indochina, including Thailand, Vietnam, Laos, and Cambodia*. New York: Crown Publishers.

Hall, Daniel George Edward (1981). *A History of South-East Asia*. 4th ed. London: Macmillan.

Huffman, Franklin E. (1986). *Bibliography and Index of Mainland Southeast Asian Languages and Linguistics*. New Haven: Yale University Press.

Hughes, James, ed. (1985). *The World Atlas of Archaeology*. Boston: G. K. Hall.

Hutchinson, Walter (n.d.; c. 1920). *Customs of the World: A Popular Account of the Manners, Rites, and Ceremonies of Men and Women in All Countries*. Vol. 1. London: Hutchinson.

Keyes, Charles F. (1988). *The Golden Peninsula: Culture and Adaptation in Mainland Southeast Asia*. New York: Macmillan; Kōdansha International.

Kōdansha (1983). *Kōdansha Encyclopedia of Japan*. 9 vols. Tokyo and New York: Kōdansha International.

Kunstadter, Peter, ed. (1967). *Southeast Asian Tribes, Minorities, and Nations*. Princeton, N.J.: Princeton University Press.

LeBar, Frank, ed. (1972). *Ethnic Groups of Insular Southeast Asia*. Vol. 1, *Indonesia, Andaman Islands, and Madagascar*. New Haven: HRAF Press.

LeBar, Frank, ed. (1975). *Ethnic Groups of Insular Southeast Asia*. Vol. 2, *Philippines and Formosa*. New Haven: HRAF Press.

LeBar, Frank, Gerald C. Hickey, and John K. Musgrave, eds. (1964). *Ethnic Groups of Mainland Southeast Asia*. New Haven: HRAF Press.

le May, Reginald Stuart (1954). *The Culture of South-East Asia: The Heritage of India*. London: George Allen & Unwin. [Several reprints.]

Leur, Jacob C. van (1955). *Indonesian Trade and Society: Essays in Asian Social and Economic History*. The Hague: Van Hoeve.

Luomala, Katherine (1972). "Indonesian (Malaysian) Mythology." In *Funk & Wagnalls Standard Dictionary of Folklore, Mythology, and Legend*, edited by Maria Leach and Jerome Fried, 518–521. San Francisco: Harper & Row.

Murdock, George Peter, ed. (1960). *Social Structure in Southeast Asia*. Viking Fund Publications in Anthropology, no. 29. Chicago: Quadrangle Books; London: Tavistock Publications.

Nakane, Chie (1970). *Japanese Society*. Berkeley and Los Angeles: University of California Press.

Nguyên Trân Huân (1976). "Les sectes religieuses au Vietnam." In *Histoire des religions*, edited by Henri-Charles Puech. Vol. 3, 449–473. Encyclopédie de la Pléiade. Paris: Éditions Gallimard.

Norbeck, Edward C. (1976). *Changing Japan*. 2nd ed. New York: Holt, Rinehart, & Winston.

Noriyoshi, Tamaru (1987). "Buddhism in Japan." In *The Encyclopedia of Religion*, edited by Mircea Eliade. Vol. 2, 426–435. New York: Macmillan; London: Collier Macmillan.

Ogg, Li (1976). "Les religions de la Corée." In *Histoire des religions*, edited by Henri-Charles Puech. Vol. 3, 474–494. Encyclopédie de la Pléiade. Paris: Éditions Gallimard.

Passin, Herbert (1968). "Japanese Society." In *International Encyclopedia of the Social Sciences*, edited by David L. Sills. Vol. 8, 236–249. New York: Macmillan, Free Press; London: Collier Macmillan.

Renondeau, Gaston (1976a). "Le syncrétisme japonais." In *Histoire des religions*, edited by Henri-Charles Puech. Vol. 3, 495–510. Encyclopédie de la Pléiade. Paris: Éditions Gallimard.

Renondeau, Gaston (1976b). "Le Shintô d'état." In *Histoire des religions*, edited by Henri-Charles Puech. Vol. 3, 511–519. Encyclopédie de la Pléiade. Paris: Éditions Gallimard.

Renondeau, Gaston, and Bernard Frank (1970). "Le bouddhisme japonais." In *Histoire des religions*, edited by Henri-Charles Puech. Vol. 1, 1320–1350. Encyclopédie de la Pléiade. Paris: Éditions Gallimard.

Rotermund, Hartmut O. (1970). "Les croyances du Japon antique." In *Histoire des religions*, edited by Henri-Charles Puech. Vol. 1, 958–991. Encyclopédie de la Pléiade. Paris: Éditions Gallimard.

Rotermund, Harmut O. (1976). "Les nouvelles religions du Japon." In *Histoire des religions*, edited by Henri-Charles Puech. Vol. 3, 520–541. Encyclopédie de la Pléiade. Paris: Éditions Gallimard.

Sebeok, Thomas A., et al., eds. (1967). *Current Trends in Linguistics*. Vol. 2, *Linguistics in East Asia and South East Asia*, edited by Yuen Ren Chao, Richard B. Noss, and Joseph K. Yamagiwa. The Hague: Mouton Publishers.

Sherratt, Andrew (1980). *The Cambridge Encyclopedia of Archaeology*. Edited by Andrew Sherratt. New York: Crown Publishers; Cambridge University Press.

Smith, R. J., and Richard K. Beardsley, eds. (1962). *Japanese Culture: Its Development and Characteristics*. Viking Fund Publications in Anthropology, no. 34. Chicago: Aldine Publishing.

Swann, Peter C. (1966). *The Art of Japan from the Jōmon to the Tokugawa Period*. New York: Crown Publishers.

Swearer, Donald K. (1981). *Buddhism and Society in Southeast Asia*. Chambersburg, Pa.: Anima Publications.

Swearer, Donald K. (1987). "Buddhism in Southeast Asia." In *The Encyclopedia of Religion*, edited by Mircea Eliade. Vol. 2, 385–400. New York: Macmillan; London: Collier Macmillan.

Toynbee, Arnold J., ed. (1973). *Half the World: The History and Culture of China and Japan.* New York: Holt, Rinehart, & Winston; London: Thames & Hudson.

Tsunoda, Ryusaku, William Theodore de Bary, and Donald Keene, eds. (1958). *Sources of Japanese Tradition.* New York and London: Columbia University Press.

Turton, Andrew, and Shigeharu Tanabe, eds. (1984). *History and Peasant Consciousness in South East Asia.* Senri Ethnological Studies, no. 13. Osaka: National Museum of Ethnology.

Vaccari, Oreste, and Enko Elisa Vaccari (1961). *Complete Course of Japanese Conversation-Grammar: A New and Practical Method of Learning the Japanese Language.* Tokyo: Maruzen; Charles E. Tuttle; Kyobunkan.

Van der Kroef, Justus M. (1976). "Mouvements religieux modernes d'acculturation en Indonésie." In *Histoire des religions,* edited by Henri-Charles Puech. Vol. 3, 1110–1141. Encyclopédie de la Pléiade. Paris: Éditions Gallimard.

Wagner, Frits A. (1959). *Indonesia: The Art of an Island Group.* New York: McGraw-Hill.

Wertheim, W. F. (1968). "Asian Society: Southeast Asia." In *International Encyclopedia of the Social Sciences,* edited by David L. Sills, 423–438. New York: Macmillan, Free Press; London: Collier Macmillan.

Yanagita Kunio (1970). *About Our Ancestors—The Japanese Family System.* Tokyo: Japan Society for the Promotion of Science.

PAUL HOCKINGS

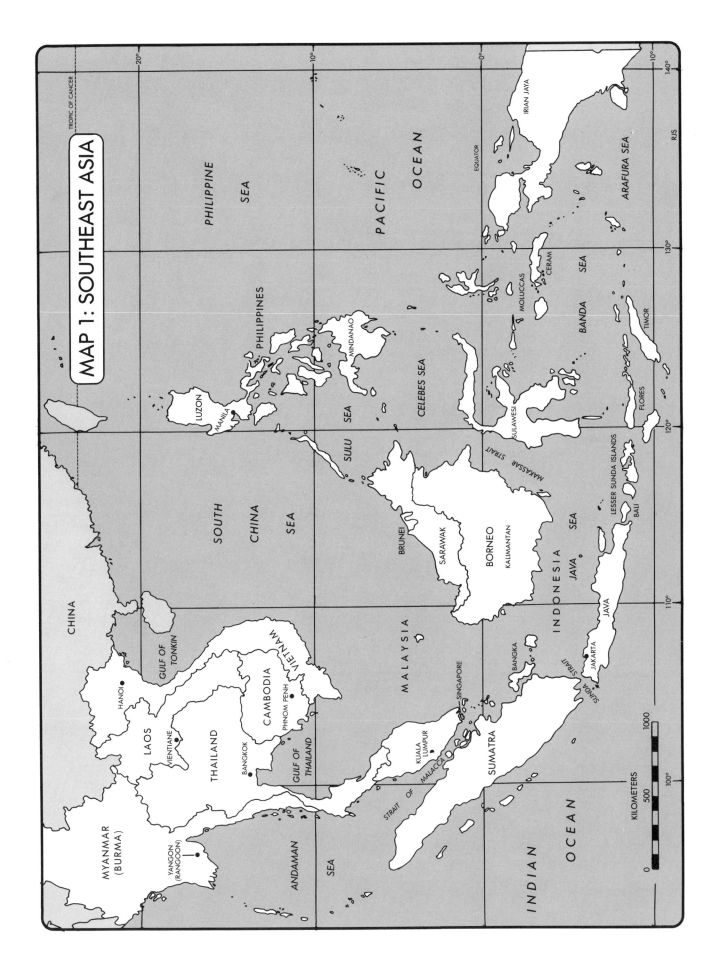

MAP 1: SOUTHEAST ASIA

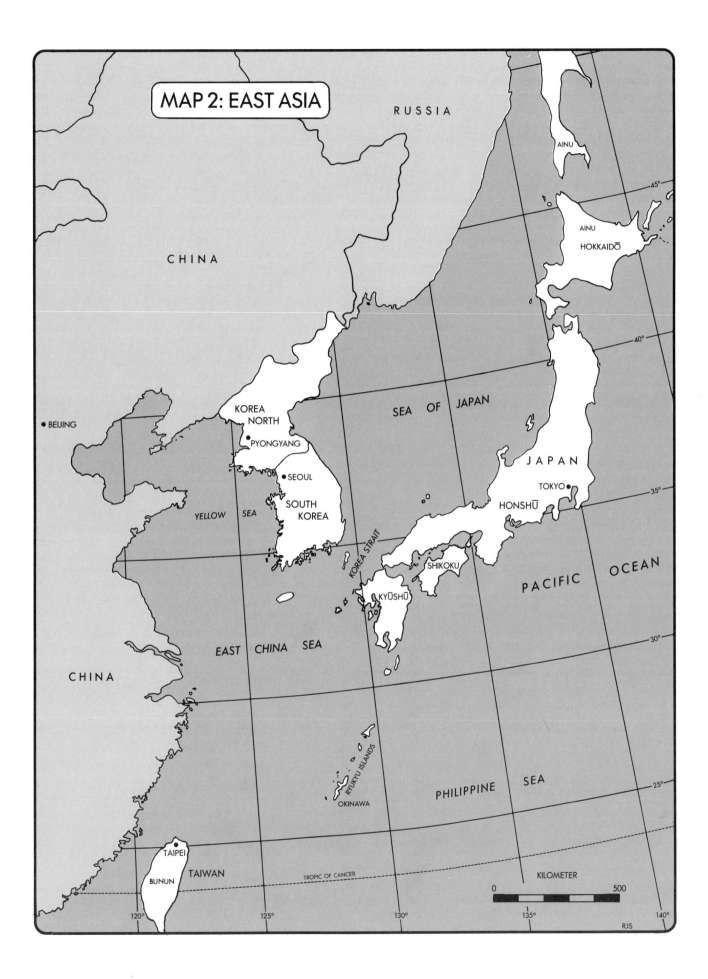

MAP 2: EAST ASIA

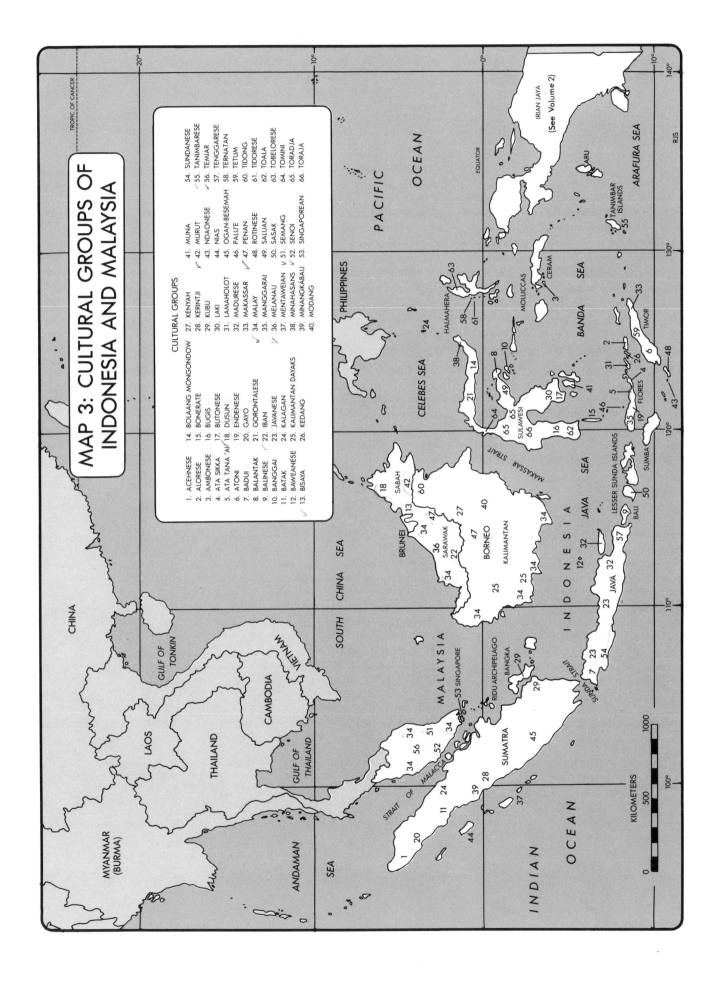

MAP 3: CULTURAL GROUPS OF INDONESIA AND MALAYSIA

CULTURAL GROUPS

1. ACEHNESE
2. ALORESE
3. AMBONESE
4. ATA SIKKA
5. ATA TANA 'AI
6. ATONI
7. BADUI
8. BALANTAK
9. BALINESE
10. BANGGAI
11. BATAK
12. BAWEANESE
13. BISAYA

14. BOLAANG MONGONDOW
15. BONERATE
16. BUGIS
17. BUTONESE
18. DUSUN
19. ENDENESE
20. GAYO
21. GORONTALESE
22. IBAN
23. JAVANESE
24. KALAGAN
25. KALIMANTAN DAYAKS
26. KEDANG

27. KENYAH
28. KERINTJI
29. KUBU
30. LAKI
31. LAMAHOLOT
32. MADURESE
33. MAKASSAR
34. MALAY
35. MANGGARAI
36. MELANAU
37. MENTAWEIAN
38. MINAHASANS
39. MINANGKABAU
40. MODANG

41. MUNA
42. MURUT
43. NDAONESE
44. NIAS
45. OGAN-BESEMAH
46. PALU'E
47. PENAN
48. ROTINESE
49. SALUAN
50. SASAK
51. SEMANG
52. SENOI
53. SINGAPOREAN

54. SUNDANESE
55. TANIMBARESE
56. TEMIAR
57. TENGGARESE
58. TETUM
59. TIDONG
60. TIDORESE
61. TOALA
62. TOBELORESE
63. TOMINI
64. TORADJA
65. TORAJA
66. TORAJA

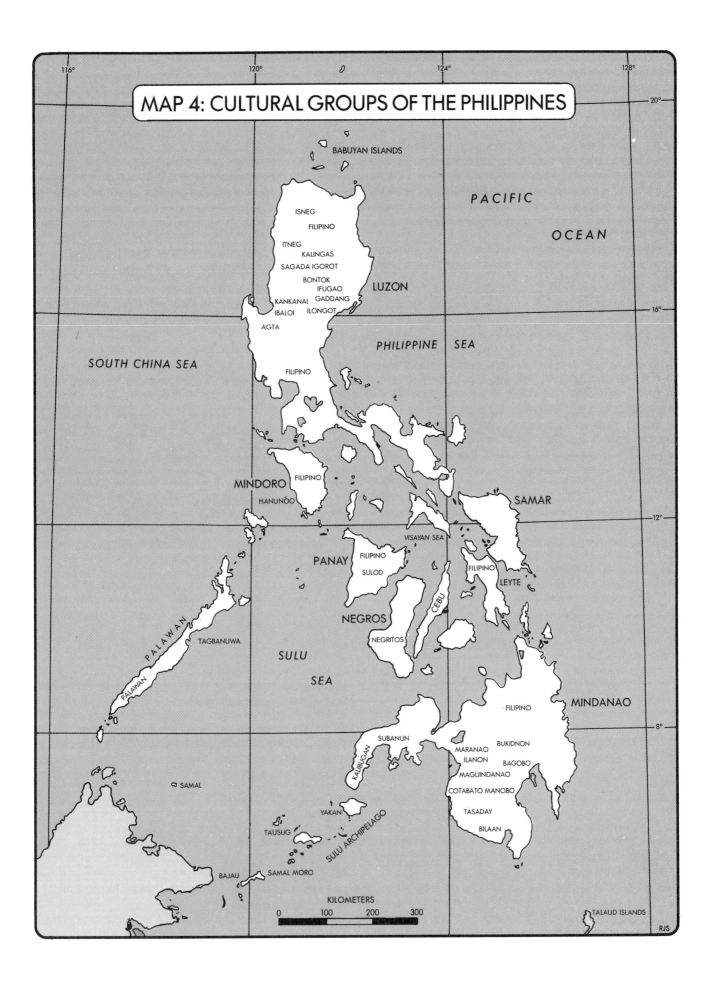

MAP 4: CULTURAL GROUPS OF THE PHILIPPINES

BABUYAN ISLANDS

PACIFIC

OCEAN

ISNEG

FILIPINO

ITNEG
KALINGAS
SAGADA IGOROT
BONTOK
IFUGAO
KANKANAI GADDANG
IBALOI ILONGOT
AGTA

LUZON

PHILIPPINE SEA

SOUTH CHINA SEA

FILIPINO

FILIPINO

MINDORO

HANUNÓO

SAMAR

VISAYAN SEA

PANAY FILIPINO

SULOD

FILIPINO

LEYTE

CEBU

NEGROS

PALAWAN

TAGBANUWA

NEGRITOS

SULU

SEA

MINDANAO

FILIPINO

SUBANUN

BUKIDNON

MARANAO

ILANON BAGOBO

MAGUINDANAO

COTABATO MANOBO

TASADAY

BILAAN

KALIBUGAN

SAMAL

YAKAN

SULU ARCHIPELAGO

TAUSUG

SAMAL MORO

BAJAU

KILOMETERS

0   100   200   300

TALAUD ISLANDS

RJS

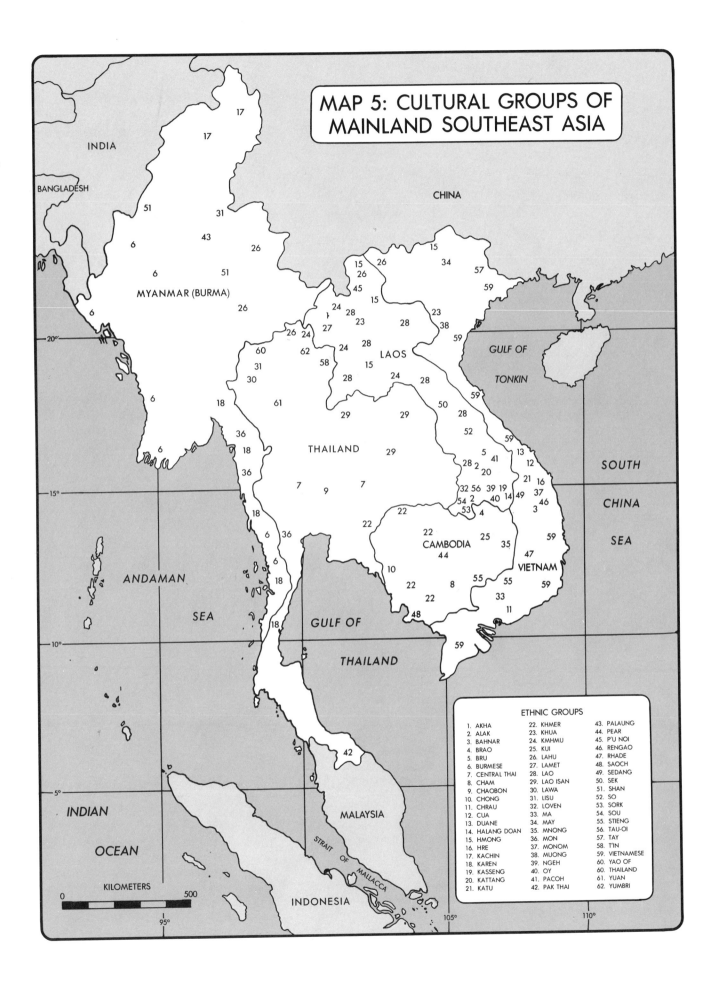

MAP 5: CULTURAL GROUPS OF MAINLAND SOUTHEAST ASIA

ETHNIC GROUPS

1. AKHA	22. KHMER	43. PALAUNG
2. ALAK	23. KHUA	44. PEAR
3. BAHNAR	24. KMHMU	45. P'U NOI
4. BRAO	25. KUI	46. RENGAO
5. BRU	26. LAHU	47. RHADE
6. BURMESE	27. LAMET	48. SAOCH
7. CENTRAL THAI	28. LAO	49. SEDANG
8. CHAM	29. LAO ISAN	50. SEK
9. CHAOBON	30. LAWA	51. SHAN
10. CHONG	31. LISU	52. SO
11. CHRAU	32. LOVEN	53. SORK
12. CUA	33. MA	54. SOU
13. DUANE	34. MAY	55. STIENG
14. HALANG DOAN	35. MNONG	56. TAU-OI
15. HMONG	36. MON	57. TAY
16. HRE	37. MONOM	58. T'IN
17. KACHIN	38. MUONG	59. VIETNAMESE
18. KAREN	39. NGEH	60. YAO OF
19. KASSENG	40. OY	60. THAILAND
20. KATTANG	41. PACOH	61. YUAN
21. KATU	42. PAK THAI	62. YUMBRI

Encyclopedia of World Cultures

Volume V

EAST AND SOUTHEAST ASIA

Acehnese

ETHNONYMS: Achehnese, Achinese, Atchinese, Atjehnese, Ureung Aceh, Ureung Baroh, Ureung Tunong

Orientation

The Acehnese are a group numbering more than 2.6 million who inhabit the northern portion of the island of Sumatra in Indonesia. They are distinguished from their neighbors primarily by their adherence to the Muslim (Sunni) faith. Acehnese may be divided into two subgroups: the hill people (who are physiologically homogeneous proto-Malays) and the lowland coastal people (who are physiologically heterogeneous). The Acehnese language belongs to the Malay Subfamily of the Indonesian Branch of Austronesian and is most closely related to the Cham languages of Indochina; most Acehnese also speak Bahasa Indonesia.

History and Cultural Relations

Early Acehnese history indicates that it was once ruled by Buddhists who were originally from India. The Sunni Islam religion came to the region probably in the twelfth century, and perhaps earlier. The Acehnese had their first sultan, who controlled a harbor, in the sixteenth century, but it was not until the seventeenth century that the entire area was politically united as a sultanate. The Acehnese resisted colonial European power, which appeared in approximately 1509 and which became prevalent under the Dutch by 1601. The Acehnese did not surrender officially to the Dutch until 1903, and even then resistance continued until World War I. Although declared a part of the new state of Indonesia in 1945, the Acehnese effectively ruled themselves until 1961.

Settlements

Most Acehnese live in villages, also known as *meunasah*, or prayer houses, since each village contains one or more of these. Villages are located in the midst of the inhabitants' rice fields.

Economy

Most Acehnese subsist through agriculture, primarily by raising rice; in the lowland areas, wet-rice culture is most common, and in the hills, dry-rice culture. Other important crops include sugarcane, tobacco, rubber, peanuts, coconuts, areca, maize, pepper, and, in some areas, coffee. Approxi-mately one-third of the people raising crops do so as sharecroppers, and there are tens of thousands of agricultural laborers as well. Cattle and water buffalo are frequently raised for meat and as draft animals. In coastal areas, Acehnese fish with casting nets, seines, lines, and traps. The Acehnese are well known as metalworkers who fashion weapons as well as goods of gold and silver. Women weave high-quality cotton and silk textiles. Trade is important as a means of bringing cash to the village, and young men are expected to leave the village to trade or work during the first year of marriage.

Kinship

Acehnese kinship terminology is Hawaiian, but it makes sharp distinctions between older and younger kin of the same generation. The nuclear family forms the basic social unit, but society is organized also on a principle of bilateral descent. Patrilineal descent groups are sibs or *kawom*, of which there are four; they were once a means of security and revenge in times of conflict, but now appear to have lost most or all of their function. Matrilineal descent groups, or *karong*, function as residential groups among the uxorilocal Acehnese.

Marriage and Family

The Acehnese follow Islamic law in marriage prohibition, and they forbid marriage with kin in one's own line of descent or with anyone within three degrees of relatedness. Polygyny still exists among the wealthy. Marriage, which requires the consent of the parents of both bride and groom, takes place after the groom delivers the bride-price to the bride's representatives in the prayer house. Following marriage, the couple lives with the bride's family, and the bride's parents support the bride and her children for a period of time, depending on the size of the bride-price. Inheritance follows Islamic law: for every share given to a female, two are given to a male. Offspring receive inheritance from both parents, with sons receiving agricultural land and daughters dwellings.

Sociopolitical Organization

Although under Indonesian control, the Acehnese also have an elected village chief (*keuchi*) who regulates family law and rice growing, as well as an elected religious authority (*teungku*) who adjudicates matters pertaining to Islamic law. These two officers work together with a village council made up of mature men. Between the village and federal administrative levels is a lower-district level (*mukim*) comprised of those villages that are served by a single mosque; it is administered by a priest (*imeum*). There is also an upper-district level comprised of several villages and mukim; it is governed by an *uleebalang*. Prior to Indonesian control it had a great deal of autonomy, and the uleebalang office was passed down through patrilineal succession.

Acehnese of the nineteenth century were divided into four separate groups based primarily on religious or governmental function, but these have given way to a division based on whether one is an *ulama* (religious scholar) or not.

Religion and Expressive Culture

Acehnese are considered among the most zealous of all Indonesians in their Islamic beliefs. They are especially concerned with the pilgrimage to Mecca, the tithe, and the fast during Ramadan. There also survive traditional beliefs in the supernatural, as well as magic associated with agriculture and female shamanism.

Bibliography

Jayawardena, Chandra (1977). "Women and Kinship in Aceh Besar, Northern Sumatra." *Ethnology* 16:21–38.

Reid, Anthony (1979). *The Blood of the People: Revolution and the End of Traditional Rule in Northern Sumatra*. Kuala Lumpur: Oxford University Press.

Siegel, James T. (1979). *Shadow and Sound: The Historical Thought of a Sumatran People*. Chicago: University of Chicago Press.

DANIEL STROUTHES

Agta

ETHNONYMS: Alta, Arta, Baluga, Dumagat, Negritos, Pugut

Orientation

Identification. The Agta consist of eight ethnolinguistic groups, numbering in total about 7,000 people. They are nomadic hunter-gatherers scattered widely over several thousand square kilometers of dense rain forest in eastern Luzon in the Philippines. They appear phenotypically different from other Filipinos because of their Negroid features: dark skin, kinky hair, and small size. The height and weight averages for men are 153 centimeters (60 inches) and 45 kilograms (99 pounds). Women's averages are 144 centimeters (56 inches) and 38 kilograms (84 pounds). They are generally referred to as "Negritos."

Location. The Agta groups are located all along the eastern side of Luzon Island between 14° and 19° N and 121° and 123° E in the provinces of Cagayan, Isabela, Aurora, Quirino, Quezon, Camarines Norte, and Camarines Sur. In the previous century this whole area was at least 90 percent covered by dipterocarp tropical lowland forest. By the 1980s the area covered by primary forest was about 40 percent, with

another 20 percent covered by secondary forest. The rest of the area was (in the early 1980s) grassland (about 13 percent), brushland (11 percent), or farms (16 percent). The fast-accelerating deforestation in recent years is the result of commercial logging and the high influx of colonist farmers from other areas of Luzon. The area is classed as true rain forest, with an average yearly rainfall of from 361.8 centimeters per year in the deforested flatlands, to 712.5 centimeters per year in the mountainous forests. Mean annual temperature is 26° C. Mean relative humidity is 87 percent. There is no pronounced dry season.

Demography. In the 700-square-kilometer Casiguran area of northern Aurora Province, in 1900, the non-Agta farmers numbered 2,067 and the Casiguran Agta numbered 1,000. By 1984 the Casiguran Agta population had declined to only 609 and the non-Agta peoples numbered 35,000. Thus, the Agta population density in 1984 was one Agta per square kilometer, but the overall population density was 59 persons per square kilometer. The Agta are suffering such a severe population decline not as the result of out-migration or a low birth rate, but solely because of an exceptionally high death rate. (For the rest of this essay, the numerical figures refer to the Casiguran Agta population of northern Aurora; these figures may be accepted as roughly general for most other Agta groups.) The Agta crude death rate (45/1,000 per year) is higher than their crude birth rate (43/1,000 per year). Average Agta life expectancy at birth is only 21.5 years. The infant mortality rate is 342 (per 1,000 live births), and 49 percent of the children die before the age of 15. The total fertility rate is high, with women who live to the age of 45 having an average of 6.3 live births each. What are the causes of the high Agta death rates? The main killer is disease, with 80 percent of the deaths attributed to that cause. The biggest killer disease is tuberculosis (12 percent of the adult deaths), followed by pneumonia and gastrointestinal illnesses. Five percent of the adult deaths are from leprosy. The morbidity of the population is high as well, with Agta suffering chronically from malnutrition, malaria, intestinal parasites, alcoholism, and unsanitary living conditions. Homicide is frequent; 21 percent of the adult males die from that cause. The homicide rate is one of the highest on record for any population (326/100,000 per year). Twelve percent of the female deaths result from complications from childbirth. Suicide is extremely rare, and the Agta do not practice infanticide. Three percent of the deaths are from accidents.

Linguistic Affiliation. The Agta groups speak eight distinct languages that, like those of their non-Negrito neighbors, belong to the Austronesian Language Family. Most of these Agta languages are unintelligible to their agricultural neighbors; thus they are not simply dialects of those neighbors' languages, as has frequently been suggested, but separate languages.

History and Cultural Relations

An important historical fact concerning these nomadic Negrito foragers is that they have not lived isolated from, nor independently of, other peoples, as was assumed and taught until the 1980s. Recent research has established that the Agta peoples have carried on intense symbiotic interaction with farming peoples not only for centuries, but for millennia. The ancestors of today's Agta, and of all Philippine Negritos, are assumed to be the aboriginals of that archipelago, having migrated into those islands 20,000 to 30,000 years ago. Much later, around 3000 B.C., Austronesian-speaking peoples began migrating into the Philippines, probably from Taiwan. Gradually the Negritos switched from their isolated and independent hunting and gathering lifestyle as they increasingly developed symbiotic relationships with Austronesian farmers. For most Agta groups, this switch occurred by around 1000 B.C. From this time on, Agta traded and interacted heavily with farming populations. The more recent twentieth-century history of the Agta is another story. After thousands of years of living a relatively stable and adaptive life in the rain forest, they are today undergoing severe deculturation; their forest is being cut back, immigrants are depleting their game and fish resources, they are being herded onto small reservations by the government, and change is being imposed on them by various development agencies.

Settlements

Agta live in small and widely scattered camp groups throughout the forest. While 60 percent of Agta camps are in the forest (the other 40 percent are found on the coastal beaches of the Pacific Ocean, in open brushland, or in coconut groves), few camps are located directly under the forest canopy. Because of the Agta's fear of falling trees during storms, forest camps are usually situated in small open areas away from trees, such as on dry riverbeds or in small gardens. Camps are small, consisting of from three to seven kin-related nuclear households, with a mean average of six. A family will rarely reside in a camp of non-related kin. Agta move their camps often. In one study they were found to move, on average, every 18 days, and in another study every 29 days.

Housing. Agta may live in simple lean-tos, sleeping directly on the ground, or in small huts on stilts with a bamboo or palm wood floor about one meter above the ground, and with a thatch roof. Usually there are no side walls. Houses are very small, with an average floor size of only 3.9 square meters and a per capita floor space of only 1.2 square meters. Mean household size is 4.3 people. Most households (79 percent) are composed of simple nuclear families (parents and dependent children). Seventeen percent are of augmented nuclear families (e.g., with a cousin or grandparent present), and only 4 percent are composite (i.e., with two related couples sharing the same hearth).

Economy

Subsistence and Commercial Activities. The most salient economic activity of the Casiguran Agta, until the 1960s, was hunting. Men spent a major part of their time hunting large game (wild pigs, deer, monkeys) with bow and arrow or borrowed homemade shotguns. Their economy for many hundreds of years has revolved around an institutionalized exchange relationship with non-Agta farmers. Until recently, the main feature of this exchange was the trade of wild meat for starch foods from farmers. As the game declined during the 1960s, the Agta gave more and more of their economic time to working as unskilled laborers for the growing farming population. In 1984 Agta men gave only 6 percent of their daily activity time to hunting. Agta are no strangers to agriculture. They have helped non-Agta farmers seasonally in their fields since prehistoric times, and they were cultivating small slash-and-burn fields of their own when first observed by Spaniards in the eighteenth century. Each year about 25 percent of Agta families make tiny desultory fields that average one-seventh of a hectare in size. In a good year these fields produce enough rice (their main starch food) to feed the population for only 15 days. Only 6 percent of the daily activity of all adults (both men and women) is given to working in these fields. The biggest single economic activity of the Agta is collecting forest products for trade. The main product was formerly wild meat. In the 1980s it was rattan. In 1984 men spent 25 percent of their daily activity in rattan collecting, and women, 17 percent. They also work frequently on nearby farms for wages (12 percent of the daily time of men, and 6 percent of women).

Division of Labor. There is a very weak division of labor between the sexes. Women participate with their husbands in hunting on about half of the hunting trips (in Cagayan some women even secure game with bow and arrow themselves). Both sexes contribute equal amounts of time to work in their own gardens. Both sexes collect forest products for trade, and both work as casual laborers for farmers. Both men and women collect firewood for their own hearths, and both engage in housebuilding, carrying water, etc. Only women weave baskets and mats, and only women wash clothes. Only men spear fish in deep water on coral reefs, and only men climb high trees to collect wild honey.

Land Tenure. Agta do not own land, nor usually show interest in doing so. Land tenure is a foreign concept to them. Instead, they see land as a free good.

Kinship, Marriage, and Family

Kin Groups and Descent. Kinship is very important to the Agta, and their social organization is based almost exclusively on it. Descent is bilateral. They do not have lineages, clans, or cognatic descent groups. Rather, it is the personal kindred that is important to them.

Kinship Terminology. Kinship terms reflect an Eskimo classification, with lineal relatives distinguished from collaterals in the first ascending and descending generations from Ego, as well as in Ego's own generation. There is no distinction between cross and parallel cousins. Cousin terminology may be Eskimo or Hawaiian, depending on the context and the level of contrast required. The Agta language has a total of fifteen kinship terms of reference, six of which also serve as terms of address, plus seven more kinship terms used for address only.

Marriage. Agta marriages are monogamous. They practice strict kin exogamy, but manifest a preference for group endogamy. Marriages between distantly related consanguines are extremely rare, as are unions between affines. In 1984, 17 percent of the Casiguran Agta adults in northern Aurora were married to partners from other Agta ethnolinguistic groups, and 11 percent (two men and twenty-five women) were married to non-Agta farmers. Residence is bilocal—the couple may live with either the husband's or the wife's parents. In 1978, 48 percent of the households were virilocal, 35 percent were uxorilocal, 8 percent were neolocal, and 8 percent were ambiguous. Divorce is infrequent, with only 18 percent of the adults ever having been divorced. Most cases of divorce occur between couples who are newly married or who are still in a trial period of incipient marriage. It is quite uncommon for a couple with dependent children to divorce.

Sociopolitical Organization

Like other hunter-gatherer societies, Agta political organization is weak. There are no chiefs or formal group leaders of any kind beyond the nuclear household. Organized social life is controlled primarily by the nuclear family heads (i.e., the father and mother). Women participate equally with their husbands in decision making. Secondarily, social organization is based on the personal kindred. Social control is therefore quite weak. Individuals tend to do what they wish. If individuals go against the norms of the camp, or manifest disruptive deviant behavior, they will first be put in their place through oblique criticism, and then by ostracism. If that does not work, families will just move away. There are no laws or fines for keeping people in line, except ostracism. Conflicts are usually resolved by one of the families moving away and, in fact, moving is the primary mechanism for resolving interpersonal problems between families.

Religion and Expressive Culture

Religious Beliefs.   The Agta are animists, although some of their beliefs have been modified by Roman Catholicism and, more recently, by Protestant missionaries. In contrast to most traditional animists, however, the Agta do not take their religion very seriously. There is a lack of systematic beliefs in their religion, and it takes a secondary place in their ideology, exerting less control over their daily lives than is usual among tribal peoples. Agta hold to a strong belief in a spirit world containing many classes of supernatural beings. Depending on the class of spirit, these beings are said to reside in trees, underground, on rocky headlands, or in caves. There are two general classes of these beings: *hayup* (creature) and *belet* or *anito* (ghost). The latter are always malignant. Ghosts are wandering disembodied souls of deceased humans. The ghosts of recently deceased adult relatives are especially feared, as they are prone to return to the abode of their family during the night, causing sickness and death. There are several types of hayup. These nonhumans are bipedal, and may appear in human form. Agta view these as having some influence over processes of nature, health, and the economic success or failure of humans. Most hayup are malignant, others are neutral, and a few can be called upon for help in curing disease.

Religious Practitioners.   In northern Aurora, 8 percent of the Casiguran Agta adults are shamans, of whom one in five is a woman. These religious practitioners do only white magic. A shaman (*bunogen*) is defined by the Agta as an individual who has a familiar spirit "friend" (*bunog*) who aids him or her in diagnosing and treating disease. The primary role of shamans is curing. They do not practice sorcery.

Ceremonies.   Shamans may treat their patients with herbal medicines and simple prayers to their spirit "friends." For difficult cases, they may conduct a séance. In such cases, shamans will enter into a trance state, chanting prayers over the patient until they are possessed by their familiar spirits. These chants are sung in a form of glossolalia, not in the normal Agta language. They do not have a sacrificial system, as do other Philippine animistic societies, but they do sometimes offer small gifts to the hayup spirits if they are taking something from the forest. These gifts may consist of a few grains of rice, a few drops of honey, or a piece of thread from a man's G-string. In some areas, when a new garden is cleared, a shaman may set up a small table with spirit offerings of betel quid and food. Herbal medicinal treatments, séances, and simple sacrifices are the only religious ceremonies.

Arts.   Agta women weave baskets and sleeping mats, and men make many types of fine arrow. Permanent body decorations consist of designed scarring on the back (and sometimes the chest) and teeth filing. Their traditional music consists of singing solos, using a three-tone scale, and the use of three types of simple musical instruments: a simple stringed instrument, a bamboo Jew's harp, and hunting bows, which they sometimes strum. They have no custom of dancing.

Death and Afterlife.   Agta have only a vague and casual interest in the afterlife, the realm of the dead, immortality, or the future; nor do they seek religious experiences. They do have a great fear of death, and it is the fear of sickness and death that activates Agta religious behavior.

See also Philippine Negritos

Bibliography

Griffin, P. Bion, and Agnes Estioko-Griffin (1985). *The Agta of Northeastern Luzon: Recent Studies.* Cebu City: San Carlos Publications.

Headland, Thomas N. (1986). *Why Foragers Do Not Become Farmers: A Historical Study of a Changing Ecosystem and Its Effect on a Negrito Hunter-Gatherer Group in the Philippines.* Ann Arbor, Mich.: University Microfilms International.

Headland, Thomas N. (1987). "Kinship and Social Behavior among Agta Negrito Hunter-Gatherers." *Ethnology* 26: 261–280.

Headland, Thomas N. (1988). "Ecosystemic Change in a Philippine Tropical Rainforest and Its Effect on a Negrito Foraging Society." *Tropical Ecology* 29:121–135.

Headland, Thomas N. (1989). "Population Decline in a Philippine Negrito Hunter–Gatherer Society." *American Journal of Human Biology* 1:59–72.

Peterson, Jean T. (1978). *The Ecology of Social Boundaries: Agta Foragers of the Philippines.* Urbana: University of Illinois Press.

THOMAS N. HEADLAND

Ainu

ETHNONYMS: Aino, Emischi, Ezo, Hokkaidō Ainu, Kurile Ainu, Sakhalin Ainu

Orientation

The Ainu are a group of people in northern Japan whose traditional life was based on a hunting, fishing, and plant-gathering economy; the word _ainu_ means "man." Only about 18,000 Ainu now live on Hokkaidō, the northernmost island of Japan, but the population was much larger in the past and their homeland included at least southern Sakhalin, the Kurile Islands, northern parts of Honshū (the main island of Japan), and adjacent areas.

Not only was their hunting-gathering economy vastly different from that of the neighboring Japanese, Koreans, and Chinese, who had been agriculturalists for several millennia, but they spoke a language of their own, and certain physical characteristics distinguished them from their neighbors.

Far from being monolithic, Ainu culture has been rich in intracultural variation. This article introduces only some of the major differences and similarities among the three major Ainu groups: the Kurile, Sakhalin, and Hokkaidō Ainu. The Hokkaidō Ainu and the Sakhalin Ainu reside on the island of Hokkaidō and the southern half of the island of Sakhalin, respectively. Some use the term "Kurile Ainu" to refer only to the Ainu who occupied the central and northern Kurile Islands, excluding the Ainu on the southern Kuriles, whose way of life was similar to that of the Hokkaidō Ainu. Others use the label "Kurile Ainu" to refer to the Ainu on all the Kurile Islands, which is the practice followed in this article. The island of Sakhalin south of 50° N had always been the homeland of the Sakhalin Ainu, while the territory north of 50° N belonged to the Gilyaks and other peoples.

History and Cultural Relations

The Sakhalin Ainu, with an estimated population between 1,200 and 2,400 in the first half of the twentieth century, most likely migrated from Hokkaidō, possibly as early as the first millennium A.D., but definitely by the thirteenth century. They had extensive contacts with native populations on Sakhalin and along the Amur, including the Gilyaks, Oroks, and Nanais. It is likely that Chinese influence reached the island by the first millennium A.D. and intensified during the thirteenth century when northern Sakhalin submitted to Mongol suzerainty subsequent to the Mongol conquest of China. The period between 1263 and 1320 saw the Mongol colonization and "pacification" of the Gilyaks and the Ainu. The Sakhalin Ainu fought valiantly until 1308, finally submitting to the suzerainty of the Yuan dynasty, the Mongolian dynasty that ruled China and to whom the Ainu were forced to pay tribute. The tribute system, together with trade with other peoples along the way, merged with the Japanese–Hokkaidō Ainu trade during the fifteenth century. As a result, Japanese ironware reached the Manchus while Chinese brocade and cotton made their way to Osaka in western Japan. With the weakening of Manchu control over Sakhalin, the tribute system was abandoned at the beginning of the nineteenth century. By then, the Japanese and Russians were racing to take political control of the island and exploit its rich natural resources.

The impact of the Japanese government on the Sakhalin Ainu intensified under the Meiji government established in 1868. Many Japanese were sent to southern Sakhalin to exploit its resources. The Sakhalin Ainu came under Russian control in 1875 when southern Sakhalin came under Russian control, but Japan regained the area in 1905; the territory north of 50° N remained under Russian control throughout history. Between 1912 and 1914, the Japanese government placed the Sakhalin Ainu, except those on the remote northwest coast, on reservations, drastically altering their way of life. With the conclusion of World War II, southern Sakhalin again was reclaimed by the USSR and most of the Ainu were resettled on Hokkaidō.

The history of contact with outsiders is equally important for the Hokkaidō Ainu, whose territory once extended to northeastern Honshū. As the Japanese central government expanded its control toward the northeast, the Ainu were gradually pushed north from their southernmost territory. Trade between the Ainu and the Japanese was established by the mid-fourteenth century. With the increased power of the Matsumae clan, which claimed the southwestern end of Hokkaidō and adjacent areas, the trade became a means for the Japanese to exploit the Ainu during the sixteenth century. Although there were numerous revolts by the Ainu against Japanese oppression, the revolt in the mid-seventeenth century by a famous Ainu political leader, Shakushain, was the most significant. Shakushain rose to the forefront of the Ainu resistance in the mid-1660s, but his forces were crushed when the Matsumae samurai broke the truce, slaying Shakushain and his retinue. This event marked the last large-scale resistance by the Hokkaidō Ainu.

In 1779, the Matsumae territory on Hokkaidō came under the direct control of the Tokugawa shogunate in order to protect Japanese interests against Russian expansion southward. The administrative hands changed again in 1821 to the Matsumae and then back to the shogunate in 1854. Drastic changes took place shortly after the establishment of the Meiji government in 1868, as the new government abolished residential restrictions for the Ainu and the Japanese, allowing them to live anywhere on Hokkaidō. The Japanese were encouraged to emigrate to Hokkaidō to take advantage of the natural resources. Most significant, the new government issued the Hokkaidō Aboriginal Protection Act. The Ainu on Hokkaidō were forced to attend Japanese schools established by the government and to register in the Japanese census. Beginning in 1883, the Ainu were granted plots of land and encouraged to take up agriculture. They were removed from their settlements and resettled on land more suited to agriculture, causing drastic changes in Ainu society and culture.

The long history of Ainu contact with outsiders, especially the Japanese, has undermined the Ainu way of life. The Ainu have long been a minority population in Japanese society, suffering prejudice, discrimination, and economic impoverishment. In recent years, the Ainu have made positive efforts to improve their social and political position in Japanese society as well as to establish their own cultural identity.

In addition to ecological factors, the history of contact with outsiders is responsible to a large degree for the major differences in the way of life among these groups of Ainu. For example, because of a lack of contact with metal-using populations, the Kurile Ainu continued to use stone and bone implements and to manufacture pottery long after the Hokkaidō and Sakhalin Ainu had started to use metal goods obtained in trade with their neighbors. The Ainu on the central and northern Kuriles had long been in contact with the Aleuts and Kamchadals. From the end of the eighteenth century, Russians and Japanese, who were hunting sea otters in the area for their furs, exploited the Ainu and transmitted diseases, causing a decline in the population. In 1875 the central and northern Kuriles came under the political control of the Japanese government, which made several attempts to "protect" the Ainu, but the last survivor in this area died in 1941.

Settlements

There was considerable variation in the permanency of Ainu settlements. Until the turn of the century, the basic pattern of the Sakhalin Ainu was a seasonal alternation of settlement between a summer settlement on the shore and a winter settlement farther inland. In the winter settlement, they built semisubterranean pit-houses. Ainu settlements were usually located along the shore, with houses in a single line parallel to the shore. The Kurile Ainu migrated even more frequently. In contrast, on Hokkaidō, permanent settlements were located along the rivers, which were rich in fish from mouth to source—an unusual situation for hunter-gatherers.

Most Ainu settlements, regardless of region, were small, usually consisting of fewer than five families. An exception was the Hidaka-Tokachi District on Hokkaidō, which enjoyed the most abundant natural resources and the densest population of all the Ainu lands. Here, especially along the Saru River, a few settlements housed about thirty families, and more than half the settlements in the valley exceeded five families.

Economy

The Ainu were basically a hunting-gathering population but fish from the sea, rivers, and lakes was an important source of food for most Ainu. Ainu men fished and hunted sea and land mammals, while women were responsible for gathering plants and storing food for the cold season. Large animals such as bear, deer (in Hokkaidō), musk deer, and reindeer (in Sakhalin) were usually caught using individual techniques of hunting, although cooperation among individuals sometimes took place, especially among the Hokkaidō Ainu. They used the bow and arrow, the set-trap bow, the spear, and various kinds of traps for hunting land mammals, often combining different methods. The hunting techniques of the Hokkaidō Ainu were on the whole technologically more developed than those of other Ainu. They used trained dogs for hunting, and, in some areas, even for fishing. In addition, they used aconite and stingray poison for hunting, which ensured that wounded animals would fall to the ground within a short distance. Large fish such as trout and salmon were important foods, obtained by means of detachable spearheads. The Ainu also used nets, various traps, weirs, and the line and fishhook.

Animal domestication was most highly developed among the Sakhalin Ainu, who engaged in selective breeding to create strong and intelligent male sled dogs and in castration of the dogs to preserve their strength for pulling the sleds, which were an important means of transportation dur-

ing the harsh winters. The Hokkaidō Ainu alone engaged in small-scale plant domestication prior to the introduction of agriculture by the Japanese government.

Kinship, Marriage, and Family

There are some basic features of sociopolitical organization that are shared by most of the Ainu groups, although their finer workings vary from region to region. Among most Ainu groups, the nuclear family is the basic social unit, although some extended families are present. In most Ainu settlements, males related through a common male ancestor comprise the core members who collectively own a hunting ground or a river with good fish runs. Although some scholars emphasize that among the Ainu along the Saru River in Hokkaidō women related through females comprise a corporate group, the exact nature of the group is unclear. Among these Hokkaidō Ainu, an individual is prohibited from marrying a cousin on his or her mother's side. Among most Ainu groups, a few prominent males in the community practice polygyny.

Sociopolitical Organization

Nowhere among the Ainu does political organization extend beyond the settlement, although occasionally a few extremely small settlements form a larger political unit, or a small settlement belongs politically to an adjacent larger settlement. Ainu political leaders are usually not autocratic; elders in the settlement are usually involved in decision making and executing the rules.

Although the formalized ideology prohibits women from participating in the major religious activities that provide the basis of sociopolitical powers for males, there are a number of culturally constituted ways for women to exercise nonformalized power, as discussed in the section on shamanism.

Religion and Expressive Culture

Separation of religious dimensions of Ainu life from others distorts the way Ainu view their lives, since religion is the perspective that pervades their life. Thus, even the disposal of discarded items such as food remains and broken objects is guided by the spatial classification of the Ainu universe and its directions, which derive from religious and cosmological principles. What we call economic activities are religious activities to the Ainu, who regard land and sea animals as deities and fish and plants as products of deities.

Religious Beliefs.   An important concept in the Ainu belief system is the soul, owned by most beings in the Ainu universe. According to tradition, the soul becomes perceptible when it leaves the owner's body. For example, when one dreams, one's soul frees itself from the sleeping body and travels, even to places where one has never been. Likewise, a deceased person may appear in one's dreams because the soul of the deceased can travel from the world of the dead to that of the living. During a shamanistic performance, the shaman's soul travels to the world of the dead to snatch back the soul of a dead person, thereby reviving the person nearing death.

This belief underlies the Ainu emphasis on proper treatment of the dead body of humans and all other soul owners in the universe, resulting in elaborate funeral customs ranging from the bear ceremony, discussed later, to the careful treatment of fish bones, which represent the dead body of a fish. Without proper treatment of a dead body, its soul cannot rest in peace in the world of the dead and causes illness among the living to remind the Ainu of their misconduct. Shamans must be consulted to obtain diagnosis and treatment for these illnesses.

The soul has the power to punish only when it has been mistreated. Deities (*kamuy*), in contrast, possess the power to punish or reward at will. Some scholars believe that among the Ainu nature is equated with the deities. Others claim that only certain members of the universe are deified. The Ainu consider all animal deities to be exactly like humans in appearance and to live just like humans in their own divine country—an important point in Ainu religion. Animal deities disguise themselves when visiting the Ainu world to bring meat and fur as presents to the Ainu, just as Ainu guests always bring gifts. The bear thus is not itself the supreme deity but rather the mountain deity's disguise for bringing the gift of bear meat and hide.

In most regions, the goddess of the hearth (fire) was almost as important as the bear. Referred to as "Grandmother Hearth," she resides in the hearth, which symbolizes the Ainu universe. Other important deities include foxes, owls (the deity of the settlement), seals, and a number of other sea and land animals and birds. The importance of each varies from region to region. In addition, there are the goddess of the sun and moon (in some regions, the sun and moon represent two phases of one deity), the dragon deity in the sky, the deity of the house, the deity of the *nusa* (the altar with *inaw*, ritual wood shavings), the deity of the woods, the deity of water, and others.

Evil spirits and demons—called variously *oyasi, wen-kamuy* (evil deity), etc.—constitute another group of beings in the universe who are more powerful than humans. They exercise their destructive power by causing misfortunes such as epidemics. The smallpox deity is an example. Some of them are intrinsic or by definition bona fide demons, whereas others become demons. For example, if a soul is mistreated after the death of its owner, it turns into a demon. The Ainu devote a great deal of attention to evil spirits and demons by observing religious rules and performing exorcism rites. Human combat with demons is a major theme in Ainu epic poems, discussed later. Characteristically, the deities never deal directly with the demons; rather, they extend aid to the Ainu if the latter behave as directed.

Religious Practitioners. Shamanism is not an exclusively male role. Sakhalin Ainu shamanism differs considerably from Hokkaidō Ainu shamanism. Among the Sakhalin Ainu, with regard to the symbolic structure, the shamanistic ritual represents the process of cooking, a role assigned to women in Ainu society. Shamanism is highly valued among the Sakhalin Ainu, and highly regarded members of society of both sexes, including heads of settlements, may become shamans. Although shamans sometimes perform rites for divinations of various sorts and for miracles, most rites are performed to diagnose and cure illnesses. When shamans are possessed by spirits, they enter a trance and the spirit speaks through their mouths, providing the client with necessary information such as the diagnosis and cure of an illness or the location of a missing object.

Among the Hokkaidō Ainu, shamanism is not highly re-

garded and shamans are usually women, who collectively have lower social status than men. The Hokkaidō Ainu shaman also enters a possession trance, but she does so only if a male elder induces it in her by offering prayers to the deities. Although she too diagnoses illnesses, male elders take over the healing process. Male elders must consult a shaman before they make important decisions for the community. In other words, the politically powerful male cannot even declare a war without consulting the shaman—an intriguing cultural mechanism to balance formalized and nonformalized power.

Ceremonies. Among the rich and varied Ainu religious beliefs and practices, the bear ceremony is perhaps the most important religious ceremony among both the Sakhalin and Hokkaidō Ainu, for whom the bear represents the supreme deity in disguise. From the Ainu perspective, the bear ceremony is a "funeral ritual" for the bear. Its purpose is to send the soul of the bear back to the mountains through a proper ritual so the soul will be reborn as a bear and revisit the Ainu with gifts of meat and fur.

The process of the bear ceremonial takes at least two years. Among the Sakhalin Ainu another, less elaborate, "after ceremony" follows several months after the major ceremony, thereby further extending the process. A bear cub, captured alive either while still in a den or while walking with its mother upon emerging from the den, is usually raised by the Ainu for about a year and a half. Sometimes women nurse these cubs. Although the time of the ceremony differs according to region, usually it is held at the beginning of the cold season; for the Sakhalin Ainu, it takes place just before they move inland to their winter settlement.

The bear ceremony combines deeply religious elements with the merriment of eating, drinking, singing, and dancing. All participants don their finest clothing and adornments. Prayers are offered to the goddess of the hearth and the deity of the house, but the major focus of the ceremony is on the deity of the mountains, who is believed to have sent the bear as a gift to humans. After the bear is taken out of the "bear house," situated southwest of the house, the bear is killed. The Sakhalin Ainu kill the bear with two pointed arrows, while the Hokkaidō Ainu use blunt arrows before they fatally shoot the bear with pointed arrows, and then strangle the dead or dying bear between two logs. Male elders skin and dress the bear, which is placed in front of the altar hung with treasures. (Ainu treasures consist primarily of goods such as swords and lacquerware obtained in trade with the Japanese. They are considered offerings to the deities and serve as status symbols for the owner.) After preliminary feasting outside at the altar, the Ainu bring the dissected bear into the house through the sacred window and continue the feast.

Among the Hokkaidō Ainu, the ceremony ends when the head of the bear is placed at the altar on a pole decorated with ritual wood shavings (inaw). An elder offers a farewell prayer while shooting an arrow toward the eastern sky—an act signifying the safe departure of the deity. The Sakhalin Ainu bring the bear's skull, stuffed with ritual shavings, bones, eyes, and, if a male bear, the penis, to a sacred place in the mountains. They also sacrifice two carefully chosen dogs, whom they consider to be servant-messengers of the bear deities. Although often taken as a cruel act by outsiders, the bear ceremony expresses the Ainu's utmost respect for the deity.

The bear ceremonial is at once religious, political, and economic. The host of the bear ceremony is usually the political leader of the community. It is the only intersettlement event, to which friends and relatives as well as the politically powerful from nearby and distant settlements may come to participate. Offerings of trade items, such as Japanese lacquerware or swords and Chinese brocades, are a display of wealth, which in turn signifies the political power of the leader and his settlement.

The bear ceremony expresses the formalized cosmology in which men are closer to the deities than are women. The officiants of the ceremony must be male elders and the women must leave the scene when the bear is shot and skinned.

Arts. While Ainu religion is expressed through rituals as well as in daily routines like the disposal of fish bones, nowhere is it better articulated than in their highly developed oral tradition, which is comparable to the Greek tradition. For the Ainu, the oral tradition is both a primary source of knowledge about the deities and a guide for conduct. There are at least twenty-seven native genres of oral tradition, each having a label in Ainu, that may be classified into two types: verses (epic or lyric) to be sung or chanted, and narrative prose. While the prose in some genres is in the third person, first-person narration is used in the rest: a protagonist tells his own story through the mouth of the narrator-singer. The mythic and heroic epics are long and complex; some heroic epics have as many as 15,000 verses. While the mythic epics relate the activities of deities, the heroic epics are about the culture hero who, with the aid of the deities, fought demons to save the Ainu and became the founder of the Ainu people. Among the Hokkaidō Ainu, the culture hero descended from the world of the deities in the sky and taught the Ainu their way of life, including fishing and hunting and the rituals and rules governing human society. Some scholars contend that the battles fought by the culture hero are battles that the Ainu once fought against invading peoples.

Ainu carving, weaving, embroidery, and music are of high aesthetic quality. Traditionally, these activities were a part of their daily lives rather than separate activities. While Hokkaidō Ainu relied most extensively on garments made of plant fibers, the Sakhalin Ainu wore garments made of fish skin and animal hides. The Kurile Ainu, who knew basketry but not weaving, used land- and sea-mammal hides and bird feathers for their clothing.

Bibliography

Ainu Bunka Hozon Taisaku Kyōgikai (Committee on the Protection of Ainu Culture), ed. (1970). *Ainu minzokushi* (The Ainu people). Tokyo: Daiichi Hōki.

Batchelor, John (1927). *Ainu Life and Lore: Echoes of a Departing Race.* Tokyo: Kyobunkwan. Reprint. 1971. New York: Johnson Reprint Corp.

Chiri, Mashio (1973-1976). *Chiri Mashio chosakushū* (Collected works by Chiri Mashio). 5 vols. Tokyo: Heibonsha.

Harrison, John (1953). *Japan's Northern Frontier.* Gainesville: University of Florida Press.

Hattori, Shirō, ed. (1964). *Bunrui Ainugo hōgen jiten* (An Ainu dialect dictionary with Ainu, Japanese, and English indexes). Tokyo: Iwanami Shoten.

Hilger, Mary Inez (1968). "Mysterious 'Sky People': Japan's Dwindling Ainu." In *Vanishing Peoples of the Earth,* edited by Robert L. Breeden, 92-113. Washington, D.C.: National Geographic Society.

Higler, Mary Inez (1971). *Together with the Ainu.* Norman: University of Oklahoma Press.

Kindaichi, Kyōsuke (1925). *Ainu no kenkyū* (Study of the Ainu). Tokyo: Naigai Shōbō. Reprint. 1944. Tokyo: Yashima Shōbō.

Koganei, Yoshikio (1893-1894). "Beiträge zur physischen Anthropologie der Aino." *Mitteilungen der medizinichen Fakultät der Kaiserlichen Universitat zu Tōkyō* 2:1-249, 251-402.

Munro, Neil Gordon (1963). *Ainu Creed and Cult.* New York: Columbia University Press.

Murdock, George Peter (1934). "The Ainus of Northern Japan." In *Our Primitive Contemporaries,* 163-191. New York: Macmillan.

Nihon Minzokugaku Kyōkai, ed. (1952). *Saru Ainu kyōdō chōsa hōkoku* (Report of the joint research on the Saru Ainu). *Minzokugaku Kenkyū* 16(3-4).

Ohnuki-Tierney, Emiko (1974). *The Ainu of the Northwest Coast of Southern Sakhalin.* New York: Holt, Rinehart & Winston. Reprint. 1984. Prospect Heights, Ill.: Waveland Press.

Ohnuki-Tierney, Emiko (1981). *Illness and Healing among the Sakhalin Ainu.* Cambridge and London: Cambridge University Press.

Piłsudski, Bronislov (1912). *Materials for the Study of the Ainu Language and Folklore.* Cracow: Spółka Wydawnicza Polska.

Takakura, Shinichirō (1960). *The Ainu of Northern Japan: A Study in Conquest and Acculturation.* Transactions of the American Philosophical Society, n.s. 50, p. 4. Philadelphia.

Torii, Ryūzo (1919). "Études archéologiques et ethnologiques: Les Ainou des Îles Kouriles." *Journal of the College of Science* (Tokyo Imperial University) 42.

Watanabe, Hitoshi (1973). *The Ainu Ecosystem.* Seattle, Wash.: University of Washington Press.

Yamamoto, Toshio (1970). *Karafuto Ainu jūkyo to mingu* (Houses and artifacts of the Sakahlin Ainu). Tokyo: Sagami Shōbō.

EMIKO OHNUKI-TIERNEY

Akha

ETHNONYMS: Ahka/Aka/Ak'a/Akka, Aini/Hani/Houni/ Woni, Edaw/Ikaw/Ikho/Kaw, Kha Kho/Kha Ko/Kho/Ko

Orientation

Identification. Akha refer to themselves as "A$_v$ka$_v$za$_v$," meaning "Akha people." In Myanmar (Burma) and Thailand, speakers of Tai languages call them "Ekaw" (Ikaw/ Ikho) or simply "Kaw," terms viewed as derogatory by Akha. These terms are akin to "Kho" (Ko) used by Tai speakers in Laos, often prefaced by the word *kha*, which means "slave." In China, Akha are classified by the Chinese either as Aini or, together with related peoples, as "Hani" (an official minority nationality). Documents from the Western colonial period use a variety of these ethnic labels, but modern scholarly writing adopts the self-referential ethnonym.

Location. Akha live in villages interspersed with those of other ethnic groups in the mountains of southwest China, eastern Myanmar, western Laos, northwestern Vietnam, and northern Thailand. This region, a part of monsoon Asia, has a wet season from April through August, followed by a dry season.

Demography. Census data are inadequate and unreliable, but experts estimate a total of more than 430,000: some 150,000 in China, 180,000 in Myanmar, 59,000 in Laos, 10,000 in Vietnam, and 34,541 in Thailand (1988). In all these countries, Akha are an ethnic minority, living near Tai-speaking valley-dwellers (e.g., Lue, Shan, Lao, Thai). During the last few decades, some Akha have moved to lowland urban centers.

Linguistic Affiliation. Called "A$_v$ka$_v$daw$_v$," meaning "Akha language," by native speakers, Akha is a tonal language belonging to the Sino-Tibetan Family. Linguists generally assign it to the Southern Loloish Group within the Lolo-Burmese Branch of this language family. Various dialects exist; the best documented is Jeu$_v$g'oe$_v$, spoken in eastern Myanmar and northern Thailand. The speech of one subgroup, A^{v}kui^v (Akhui/Akö/Akhö/Ak'ë) Akha, is not readily intelligible to other Akha. Loanwords, frequently from Tai languages, are often political or technological terms for such things as village headman and truck. Akha have no indigenous writing system, but foreign Christian missionaries have developed several Roman-based and Thai-based scripts. Literacy in Akha is largely restricted to Christians.

History and Cultural Relations

The indigenous oral tradition recounts their southward migration across numerous rivers. Scholars concur with the Akha view that they originated in China; they disagree, however, about whether the original homeland was the Tibetan borderlands or farther south and east in Yunnan Province, the northernmost residence of present-day Akha. The existence of established relations with the Shan prince of Kengtung indicates that Akha were ensconced in eastern Burma by the 1860s and perhaps earlier. They first entered Thailand from Burma at the turn of this century.

Settlements

Villages ranging in size from over two hundred to less than ten houses have been reported. A decline in village size in Thailand since the 1930s has been noted and attributed to the deteriorating ecological and economic situation in the mountains. A traditional community is characterized by two wooden gateways, one upslope and one downslope, flanked by carved female and male figures. These gates mark the division between the "inside," the domain of human beings and domesticated animals, and the "outside," the domain of spirits and wild animals. Also distinctive is a tall four-posted village swing, used in an annual ancestor offering related to the fertility of rice. Houses are sometimes scattered on a slope, but are often built on either side of a ridge with an open avenue in the middle. Smaller paths connect fenced family compounds, which contain a house and rice granary, and, in the case of an extended family, may also include one or more huts for younger couples. Traditionally constructed of logs, bamboo, and thatch, dwellings are of two types: "low house," built on the ground, and "high house," built on stilts. Akha are known for the internal division of their houses into a female side and a male side, paralleling that between the village and the surrounding forest; this division is not retained in the houses of Christians.

Economy

Subsistence and Commercial Activities. The staple of the Akha diet is rice, cultivated mainly by the slash-and-burn (shifting or swidden) method. Known as dry rice, such rice depends solely on rainfall for moisture. Vegetables, including pumpkins, beans, and greens, are planted in rice fields; maize, chilies, soybeans, and cotton are grown in other fields. Where sufficient water is available, irrigated rice fields are built. Although primarily subsistence rice cultivators, Akha have long been involved in cash cropping and trade. In the last century, cotton and opium poppies were the principal cash crops; more recent cash crops are chilies, soybeans, cabbages, and tomatoes. Texts of the oral tradition mention traveling to the lowlands to buy salt and iron, items still obtained in valley markets along with other consumer goods. Gathering of wild fruits, mushrooms, and other edible plants contributes to the food supply. Guns have superseded crossbows in hunting; traps of numerous kinds are set. Game, such as wild boar, deer, bamboo gopher, and jungle fowl, is not as plentiful as in the past, in part because of deforestation. Fishing is done with traps and nets. Pigs, chickens, ducks, goats, cattle, and water buffalo are raised.

Industrial Arts. Villagers make chopsticks and other utensils out of bamboo. Baskets of many types are woven from bamboo or rattan. Until recently, most clothing was made from home-spun cotton, dyed with indigo. Patterns of embroidery and appliqué adorning men's and women's jackets are distinctive of Akha subgroups, as are the stunning women's hats—embellished with silver ornaments, beads, and monkey fur—for which Akha are famous. Each traditional village must have at least one blacksmith to forge iron knives, hoes, and other tools. Silversmiths are rare. Increasingly, Akha engage in wage labor in the highlands and lowlands.

Trade. One or more families in a village may operate a small shop in their home, stocking such items as cigarettes and kerosene. Itinerant traders, either lowlanders or hill-dwelling Yunnan Chinese, come to buy livestock or cash crops, or to sell blankets and other goods. As more roads are built into the highlands, traders are arriving by truck rather than on foot.

Division of Labor.   Hunting is symbolically and in practice a male endeavor; rice cultivation is done by both sexes, though symbolically it is a female activity. Weaving, dyeing, and sewing are also female activities; in certain ritual contexts this domain contrasts with the male domain of hunting. Preparing rice is women's work, but men often cook, especially meat for feasts. This sexual division of labor is enshrined in the Akha religion.

Land Tenure.   Slash-and-burn fields are held in usufruct, that is, while in use; a family's claim to a plot ceases when it is left fallow to allow the forest to regenerate. Irrigated rice fields, on the other hand, are the property of their preparer and can be sold. As Akha are incorporated into the states in which they reside, national land laws—frequently at odds with customary practice—come into effect.

Kinship

Kin Groups and Descent.   Descent is patrilineal. Each child is given a genealogical name, in which the last syllable of the father's name is typically taken as the first syllable and a second syllable is added. Called the Tibeto-Burman genealogical patronymic linkage system, this pattern is a mnemonic device that both memorializes the father and conjoins father and child. It is said that a man should know his patrilineal genealogy back some sixty generations to the named spirits who preceded the first man. Every Akha belongs to a named patrilineage ($a^v jeu_v$; gu). The exogamous unit is not the named lineage but the unnamed sublineage (pa_v). The minimal lineage or patrilineal family ($peh_v za_v$) consists of all those who participate in ancestor offerings together.

Kinship Terminology.   Fundamental to the terminological system are distinctions between patrikin, wife givers, and wife takers. In everyday usage kin terms are used for address, sometimes followed by the name.

Marriage and Family

Marriage.   Akha traditionally marry in their teens or early twenties. Polygyny is permitted. Marriages may be village endogamous or exogamous. Each non-Christian village has a courting ground, where young people gather in the evening to sing and dance. Nowadays radios playing songs in the national language replace Akha love songs. A teenaged girl progresses through graded changes of clothing and ornamentation, culminating in the donning of the high hat which proclaims her marriageability. In general, young people are free to choose their own spouse, although parental approval should be obtained. The wedding ceremony takes place at the groom's family's house. At marriage a woman leaves her father's patrilineal kinship units to join those of her husband. Initial postmarital residence is patrivirilocal; that is, the wife joins her husband, who lives with his father or elder brother. Since only one married couple is permitted to live in a single house, a newly married couple often live in an adjacent hut, taking meals in the main house. After he has children, a married man may move out of his father's house. This household

becomes an independent patrilineal family only when it installs its own ancestor altar. Either spouse can initiate divorce. Before children are born this is common; afterwards, women are constrained by the fact that children remain with the ex-husband. Marriage involves not simply the couple but also their natal patrilineal kin. Wife giving and wife taking relationships are central to Akha society, with wife givers superior to wife takers. Scholars disagree about whether the system can be classified as one of asymmetric alliance, the prototypical mainland Southeast Asian example of which is the Kachin.

Domestic Unit.   Although many patrilineal families (minimal lineage) live in a single compound, it is not, strictly speaking, a residential unit because not all members need reside together; rather, it is a ritually defined unit. Given the developmental cycle of the patrilineal family, membership can range from a nuclear family to an extended family of four generations living in one or more houses.

Inheritance.   At marriage a daughter is given a yoked carrying basket, a hoe, and a knife. Additional gifts are optional; however, a woman leaves with her high hat, which may be laden with silver coins and ornaments. A married son who builds a house of his own may receive livestock, tools, seeds, cash, and household items. The son (often the youngest) who stays with the parents in their old age inherits their house.

Socialization.   Both parents care for children, who are also tended by their older sisters and brothers as well as other kin. Girls, who fetch water and firewood, take on household responsibilities earlier than boys. The mother's brother, believed to have power over the welfare of his nephews and nieces, can perform various ceremonies to ensure that a child grows up healthy and strong.

Sociopolitical Organization

Social Organization.   Lacking stratified social classes, Akha society is egalitarian. Ties of patrilineal kinship and marriage alliance form the fabric of society, binding Akha within and between communities. Relative age is important in social organization; older persons are accorded respect. The village is a fundamental social unit whose members enact agricultural and other rituals in consort.

Political Organization.   Although the Akha oral tradition speaks of princes and city–states, indigenous supralocal political organization is absent. A settlement cannot be founded without a village leader ($dzoe_v ma$), whose house is the first built. Ascension to this office, which is often hereditary, must be ratified by male elders. During the last century and the early part of this century, Akha communities were sometimes included within the spheres of influence of lowland princes. Village headmen, in charge of a single village or a circle of villages, were appointed by these princes. Whereas the traditional village leader is responsible for internal affairs, the village headman is responsible for external relations. Contemporary village headmen are part of the modern national administrative system.

Social Control.   Social order is established and maintained by a system of behavioral rules (zah^v) crosscutting kinship, religion, and etiquette. Customary fines for transgressions of zah[v] are levied by the village leader in conjunction with male elders. Akha are also subject to the national legal system.

Conflict. The oral tradition mentions warriors and warfare, but nonviolence is the norm of everyday life.

Religion and Expressive Culture

Religious Beliefs. Akha religion (zah[v]) can be characterized as animism with an ancestor cult. "Blessing" (gui[v]lah[v]), evidenced by fertility and health in people, rice, and domesticated animals, is sought from ancestors. The being who began everything, including first the sky and then the earth, also gave Akha their zah[v], the rules they live by. Although crucial to the cosmic order, this supernatural is not directly invoked in ceremonies. Rice rituals are addressed to the Rice Mother. Spirits and people are said to have been born of the same mother and to have lived together until a quarrel led to their separation, when the spirits went to the forest and people remained in the village. Since then, spirits have caused illness and other disruptions of human social life. The Akha year is divided into the people's season (dry) and the spirits' season (wet). During the latter, spirits wander into the village, so they must be driven out as part of a yearly ancestor offering. Game have spirit-owners, honored in hunting rites. People and rice have souls, whose flight causes disease. Both Protestant and Catholic missionaries have been active among Akha and have won converts, who typically live apart from traditionalists in Christian villages.

Practitioners. First among these is the village leader, whose ritual responsibilities include initiating the annual rebuilding of the village gates and the swing. Ranked below him is the blacksmith, who plays a yearly ritual role. And below him in ranking is the ritual specialist (pi[v]ma; boe[v]maw), who apprentices to learn by rote the vast corpus of chants for various ceremonies, the three-day funeral being the most important. Offerings to patrilineal ancestors are made by a male family member unless the senior woman has undergone a special initiation, which makes her responsible for annual rice rituals as well. Shamans are held to have been chosen by the spirits.

Ceremonies. The annual ritual cycle consists of nine or twelve ancestor offerings, rice rituals, and other rites such as the building of the village gates. Family ancestor offerings are made in the women's side of the house, whereas hunting ceremonies are held on the men's side. Life-cycle rites include birth rituals, weddings, and funerals. There are also curing and corrective ceremonies of numerous sorts, such as soul calling.

Arts. Jackets, shoulder bags, and women's hats are works of art. Blacksmithing is the only craft with specialists. Many Akha are accomplished singers; indigenous musical instruments include drums, cymbals, and Jew's harps.

Medicine. Numerous botanical medicines are known, such as effective coagulants for wounds. Illness is also treated ritually by specialists in chants and by shamans. Western medical treatment is eagerly sought, though not to the exclusion of traditional cures.

Death and Afterlife. Funeral ceremonies are different for adults survived by at least one son than for adults without male issue or children. Only the former become ancestors and receive offerings after their deaths. Husband and wife become ancestors together in his patriline. Unlike their Buddhist lowland neighbors, Akha bury rather than cremate their dead.

Bibliography

Alting von Geusau, Leo (1983). "Dialectics of Akhazaŋ: The Interiorizations of a Perennial Minority Group." In _Highlanders of Thailand_, edited by John McKinnon and Wanat Bhruksasri, 241–277. Kuala Lumpur: Oxford University Press.

Kammerer, Cornelia Ann (1988). "Shifting Gender Asymmetries among Akha of Northern Thailand." In _Gender, Power, and the Construction of the Moral Order: Studies from the Thai Periphery_, edited by Nancy Eberhardt, 33–51. Monograph 4. Madison: Center for Southeast Asian Studies, University of Wisconsin.

Lewis, Paul (1968). _Akha-English Dictionary_. Data Paper no. 70. Ithaca, N.Y.: Cornell University, Department of Asian Studies, Southeast Asia Program.

Lewis, Paul (1969–1970). _Ethnographic Notes on the Akhas of Burma_. New Haven: Human Relations Area Files.

Lewis, Paul, and Elaine Lewis (1984). "Akha (Kaw)." In _Peoples of the Golden Triangle: Six Tribes of Thailand_. London: Thames & Hudson.

CORNELIA ANN KAMMERER

Alak

The Alak are a central upland group of southern Laos. In 1981 their population was estimated at about 3,000, representing a near doubling of the population since the early 1960s. The Alak speak Alak (Krlak), a Mon-Khmer, Austroasiatic language. Another small group in southern Laos also speaks a language called Alak and calls itself "Alak," although the two groups and their languages are distinct. They are primarily swidden rice horticulturalists who derive some additional income from wage labor. Their religion continues to be basically animist; animal sacrifices and predictions by village sorcerers are important elements.

Alorese

ETHNONYMS: Aloreezen

Orientation

Identification.   The Alorese live on the Island of Alor, in East Nusa Tenggara Province, Indonesia. Alor Regency includes the islands of Alor, Pantar, and Pura. Alor is noted as an area of tremendous cultural and linguistic diversity, possibly owing to its rugged terrain. Estimates of number of ethnolinguistic groups on the island vary greatly. Brouwer (1935) delineated seven primary physical-linguistic divisions on the island. Local officials distinguish thirteen "tribes" (Enga 1988), and Alorese informants speak of between forty-eight and sixty different languages on the island (Adams 1989). Today the Alorese are predominantly Christian, save for those along the coast who tend to be Muslim. Most of this Muslim coastal population originally immigrated from Timor, Flores, South Sulawesi, Java, Ambon, and other nearby islands. Indigenous Alorese residing in the mountainous interior practice either Christian or traditional religions. These autochthonous Alorese are of Papuan stock.

Location.   The Island of Alor lies approximately 30 kilometers off the coast of Timor, between 8°8' and 8°36' S and 124°49' and 125°8' E. The island is 2,884.54 square kilometers in size and the terrain is extremely mountainous, with limited coastal lowlands. The climate is tropical with a rainy season lasting from October to April.

Demography.   In the mid-1980s the population of Alor Regency was estimated as 136,559. Figures are not available for the number of Alorese who have left the homeland to reside or study in the large cities of Indonesia.

Linguistic Affiliation.   The languages spoken on Alor are classified as Austronesian and appear to resemble those spoken on nearby Timor. Some of these languages are also thought to be related to Papuan and East Solorese languages. Cora DuBois, who conducted the most extensive anthropological research on the island, suggests at least eight major language groups. Others have delineated seven primary language groupings on the island: Abui, Adang, Kamang, Kawel, Kelong, Kolana, and Kui-Kramang. As mentioned above, Alorese estimates of the number of mutually unintelligible languages on their island range from forty-eight to sixty. Today, as citizens of Indonesia, most Alorese speak Bahasa Indonesia in addition to their native dialect. Approximately 40 percent of the population uses the national language (Bahasa Indonesia) as their daily language. Roughly 40 percent can speak Bahasa Indonesia but uses another local language on a daily basis. Twenty percent of the population cannot speak Bahasa Indonesia.

History and Cultural Relations

Early historical records for the island are scarce. Alorese residing in the interior of the island remained relatively isolated up until Indonesian independence. For centuries these indigenous Alorese lived in autonomous and at times mutually hostile mountain villages; political organization probably did not exist beyond the village level. The coastal populations have a longer history of ties with the outside world than groups in the interior of the island. It is believed that Javanese aristocrats from the Madjapahit kingdom settled on the coast and intermarried with the local population. Once a Portuguese holding, Alor was relinquished to the Dutch in 1854. Shortly thereafter, in the late nineteenth century, several new groups began to arrive on the coast. The Dutch invasion of South Sulawesi prompted a number of Buginese and Makassarese to flee to Alor. Chinese merchants also began trading activities on the coast at this time. It was not until the arrival of the first Dutch official circa 1908 that individuals on the coast were designated "rajahs" and given title to the interior of the island. According to DuBois the impact of this new political structure on the people of the interior was minimal. Save for some trade relations with coastal peoples, highland political organization continued to be at the village level. The region was occupied by the Japanese during World War II. Following that war, the region was declared a part of the new nation of Indonesia. Protestant missionaries arrived in the 1940s, followed by Catholic missionaries in subsequent decades.

Settlements

Traditionally, Alorese resided in isolated mountain-top settlements; the Dutch relocated a number of these villages for administrative convenience. Villages rarely have more than 150 residents. DuBois describes a traditional Abui village as a cluster of houses around a central dance place (*masang*). Generally each lineage has its own dance place, so some villages have several dance places. Fields are planted behind and between the houses. The Abui traditionally built three types of houses: large carefully constructed lineage houses where feasts are held (*kadang*), regular family houses (*fala*), and field shelters. Traditional houses are elevated and constructed of wood and bamboo, with thatched conical roofs. Today some villages also have cement-built homes with tin roofs. A number of villages also have a church or elementary school in the general area.

Economy

Subsistence and Commercial Activities.   Over 80 percent of the residents of Alor Regency are agriculturalists, 6.38 percent are government workers, 3.84 percent are fishermen, and the remaining 2.5 percent are contractors, traders, or merchants. Farmers plant and harvest maize by hand in swidden fields. Alorese also grow some rice, beans, millet, and cassava. Domestic animals include pigs, goats, and chickens.

Industrial Arts.   Industrial arts are relatively undeveloped on Alor. Wood carving, basketry, pottery, and *ikat* weaving (tying of warp threads in bundles for dyeing before putting them on a loom) are found on the island. These products do not appear to be particularly refined. There is also some metallurgy done on the eastern end of the island.

Trade.   Bronze drums of Javanese origin (*mokos*), gongs, and pigs play key roles in the Alorese economy. Although today a cash economy also exists, these goods remain closely tied to Alorese concepts of wealth and prestige. Particularly in villages, relationships continue to involve the ritualized exchange of these objects. Even Alorese men residing in the main town of Kalabahi speak of a man's wealth as being tied to the number of mokos he possesses. There are numerous stores in Kalabahi. There are also peddlers and several markets on the island, where goods are either bartered or purchased with cash.

Division of Labor. Women and children work in the fields and prepare the family's food. Men tend to the livestock and control and manipulate finances.

Land Tenure. Fields are individually owned. They are given to children (especially females) between the ages of ten and thirteen, although their produce is consumed by the entire family until adulthood. Boys may inherit land from their fathers.

Kinship

Kin Groups and Descent. According to DuBois, kinship is reckoned bilaterally. Central to the Abui kinship system are patrilineages (_hieta_) and male houses (_neng fala_). Female houses (_mayoa fala_) also exist, but their functions are less clearly delineated than those of the male houses. DuBois writes of six types of male house, consisting of six patrilineal descent lines and carrying an assortment of mutual obligations pertaining to marriage, death, finances, etc.

Kinship Terminology. The kinship terminology is classified as Hawaiian-type by DuBois. In the Abui language individuals are distinguished by generation and sex.

Marriage and Family

Marriage. Today Alorese marriages are monogamous, although in the past polygyny was sometimes practiced. According to DuBois, although parents sometimes play a role in selecting spouses for their children, the Alorese have a clear concept of romantic love and most tend to choose their own mates. Although marriage with first and second cousins is prohibited, DuBois cites occasions where second cousin marriage does occur. Marriages in Alor traditionally involve a series of exchanges between affinal groups. Throughout the island, including urban Kalabahi, men speak of being unable to marry without mokos (bronze drums) to offer the bride's family. DuBois notes that other dowry and bride-price payments include gongs, pigs, rice, and maize. Ideally, residence is patrilocal, although this pattern is not always strictly observed. Today, many younger Kalabahi couples tend to aspire to neolocal residence. According to DuBois, divorce is common; the Alorese villagers she worked with averaged "two divorces apiece."

Domestic Unit. The people who cook and share meals around a hearth are considered the most basic domestic unit. The average size of this household group is five persons. In Atimelang, where DuBois conducted her research, the domestic unit ranged from one to eight persons. As a household member, one is generally expected to share in the tasks of everyday living—cooking, cleaning, farming, or contributing part of one's wages to the family.

Inheritance. Sons inherit their fathers' wealth, although according to DuBois, much of the inheritance may be dissipated in costly death feasts (1945:113).

Socialization. Children are reared by their parents, older siblings, and older adult relatives. DuBois notes that as the women are often away in the fields during the day, children are most frequently in the care of their older siblings or left to fend for themselves. Discipline is minimal: ridicule is most frequently used to discourage misbehavior, although corporal punishment may also be administered. Girls are called upon to work in the fields at an earlier age than boys. Children are not considered full-fledged members of society until they become parents.

Sociopolitical Organization

Social Organization. Alorese society is not organized into formal, hierarchical ranks. Although age, sex, occupation, and kinship contribute to determining one's standing on Alor, wealth is the primary means of achieving prestige. Men become wealthy and prestigious through cleverly negotiating a traditional credit system involving mokos (bronze drums), pigs, and gongs. These forms of wealth (particularly mokos) are required payments for marriages, funerals, and the erection of new lineage houses, and may be loaned out for interest. The more drums, gongs, and pigs a man can amass, the more prestigious he becomes.

Political Organization. Traditionally there was no indigenous system of political organization beyond the village level. Today the head of Alor Regency is called a _bupati_ and is appointed by the Indonesian government. A council of local representatives (DPRD) assist the bupati in decision making. The regency is divided into five smaller administrative districts called _kecamatan_, each overseen by a _camat_. These five kecamatan consist of Northwest Alor, Southwest Alor, South Alor, East Alor, and Pantar. Each kecamatan consists of several villages (_desa_), each with a village head (_lurah_). The Indonesian government provides the usual range of services including schools, police, health posts, tax collection, road maintenance, etc.

Social Control. Ridicule and shame are the primary means of sanction on Alor. Personal disputes were traditionally settled by "fines through challenge," whereby an offended individual could purge his shame by publicly challenging his opponents to pay an inflated price for his pig or mokos. An opponent's refusal to comply would be a shameful admission of financial defeat. According to DuBois, occasionally Alorese opponents also engaged in potlatch-like "wealth feuds" to resolve their differences. Today, when disputes cannot be resolved at the local level, the state apparatus may be called upon (police, military force, etc.).

Conflict. Conflict occurs primarily over debts and exchange transactions. Large-scale warfare was extremely rare on Alor. Head-hunting raids to avenge the death of a kinsman (and to provide him with a "spouse") were suppressed in the early 1920s.

Religion and Expressive Culture

Religious Beliefs. The majority of contemporary Alorese has converted to Christianity (precise statistics are not available), although some Alorese adhere to their traditional beliefs. Residents of coastal communities on Alor, in contrast, are predominantly Muslim. The Atimelangers studied by DuBois believed that each individual had two souls. One soul journeyed to the "village below" if the death was natural, and the other soul went to the "village above" if the death was violent. The second soul was thought to linger and potentially cause trouble; funerals were designed to placate it and send it on its way. DuBois notes that there is no consistent theory as to where this second soul ends up. In addition to one's two souls, each individual inherited a number of supernaturals bilaterally from his or her parents. There were also lineage or village guardian spirits (*ulenai*). These spirits were connected to the village's wealth and crops and were represented by large crocodile-like carvings. In addition, there were "Good Beings," supernaturals who take human form and have the power to revive the dead and to travel through water and air. Malignant spirits (*kari, loku*), in the form of female and male witches, were also thought to exist. These evil spirits gained control over people by seducing them; while one slept, the evil spirit was said to step over and urinate on the victim and then proceed to eat his or her liver. DuBois comments that relationships to supernaturals tended to be casual and expedient. People generally ignored these relationships unless some misfortune occurred or a favor (such as harvest success) was desired. At the time of her work, for instance, the Atimelang village guardian spirit had not received a sacrifice or carving in sixteen years. She also states that, aside from funerals, Atimelangers did not appear to devote a lot of energy to the dead. She saw no permanent shrines; those that were made were temporary and of haphazard construction.

Religious Practitioners. The Atimelangers studied by DuBois and Nicolspeyer did not appear to have a large array of religious practitioners. "Water-Lords" (*je-adua*) oversaw harvest rituals, and seers (*timang*), assisted by spirits, performed curing rites.

Ceremonies. Death feasts, rites assuring crops, and sacrifices for the village guardian spirit were the primary rituals in Atimelang. Other spirits were periodically "fed" as well.

Arts. In the Atimelang area, the village guardian spirit is represented by a crocodile-like wood carving. There are also spirit-familiar carvings and "spirit boat" carvings. DuBois notes that the carvings she saw were "crude," made only for sacrificial purposes. Moreover, she states that other Atimelang arts were also relatively unelaborated; basketry design was of the simplest sort, and the mythology was "confused and unstructured" (DuBois 1944:134–135).

Medicine. In addition to Western-style doctors, seers are consulted for various ailments. DuBois speaks of long-delayed death feasts held by parents who fear their children's illnesses were brought on by annoyed spirits. Atimelangers also had "medicines" designed for a number of female concerns (reducing menstrual flow, inducing barrenness, and delaying conception).

Death and Afterlife. According to DuBois, when someone of standing dies, the Atimelangers devote a great deal of energy to the funeral feasts, which entail elaborate financial obligations. Family members incur considerable debts at this time, in the form of mokos, gongs, and pigs. It is believed that one of the souls of the deceased lingers until the conclusion of the final memorial death feast, which might not be held for several years. Until this final feast, the soul may proceed to some unclear destination. As mentioned earlier, DuBois notes that the Atimelangers do not have a well-defined concept of the afterlife.

Bibliography

Adams, Kathleen M. (1989). "Preliminary Survey of Alor." Report submitted to Hewlett-Mellon Fund, Beloit College, Wisconsin.

Brouwer (1935). *Bijdrage tot de anthropologie der Aloreilanden.* Amsterdam: Uitgeversmaatschappij Holland.

Dubois, Cora (1940). "How They Pay Debts in Alor." *Asia,* September, pp. 483–486.

DuBois, Cora (1944). *The People of Alor: A Social-Psychological Study of an East Indian Island.* Minneapolis: University of Minnesota Press. 2d ed. 1960. Cambridge: Harvard University Press.

DuBois, Cora (1945). "The Alorese." *In Psychological Frontiers of Society,* edited by Abram Kardiner, 101–258. New York: Columbia University Press.

Enga, A. H. (1988). *The Guidebook for Touring in Kabupaten Alor.* Kalabahi: Alor.

Indonesia. Biro Pusat Statistik (1981). *Penduduk Nusa Tenggara Timor* (Results of the 1980 Census). Jakarta.

Nicolspeyer (1940). *De Sociale Structuur van een Aloreesche Beevolkingsgroep.* Ryswick: V. A. Kramers.

KATHLEEN M. ADAMS

Ambonese

ETHNONYMS: Alifuru (interior of Ceram), Amboynese, Central Moluccans, Moluccans, Orang Ambon, South Moluccans (exiles in the Netherlands)

Orientation

Identification. The Ambonese most commonly speak Ambonese Malay, live in the Central Moluccas, and are about evenly divided into adherents of Protestant Christianity and Islam. The Central Moluccas (Maluku Tengah) today constitute a subdivision of the province of Maluku in the Republic of Indonesia. Its inhabitants refer to themselves generally as "Orang Ambon," after the name of the most important island and the provincial capital, but various ethnic and island groups use their own appellations, reserving "Orang Ambon" only for the coastal populations of Ambon-Lease and Ceram.

Location. The Central Moluccas are located just below the equator between 3° and 5° S and 126° and 132° E. They encompass the island of Ambon, the Uliasser or Lease Islands (Haruku, Saparua, Nusalaut), Ceram, Buru, Ambelau, Buano, Kelang, Ceramlaut, Gorong, and the Banda Islands. Sizable immigrant populations reside in Jakarta and other large Indonesian cities, and about 40,000 have lived since 1951 as political exiles in the Netherlands. The total land area is about 21,000 square kilometers.

Demography. In 1980 the population of the Central Moluccas was estimated as 554,000, of which 112,000 reside in the provincial capital of Kota Ambon (Ambon City). The average population growth rate is 2.5 percent per year.

Linguistic Affiliation. Originally, various related Austronesian languages were spoken, and they are still spoken in the interiors of Ceram and Buru. These so-called *bahasa tanah* (languages of the land) are also still widely used in Muslim villages of the coastal regions, but have survived in only a few Christian villages there. The Christians are speakers of Ambonese Malay, a derivative of Sumatran Malay that arrived as a lingua franca at least three centuries before the first Europeans arrived. Most Muslims can speak Ambonese Malay. An increasing number of both groups is also familiar with the national language, Bahasa Indonesia, a form of "standard" Malay and the medium of formal communication.

History and Cultural Relations

The region is both culturally and racially located "on the crossroads" between Indonesia and Melanesia. The most outstanding culture trait adopted from Melanesia is the *kakehan*, a secret men's society on Ceram, the only such society in the entire Indonesian archipelago. The Moluccas or "Spice Islands" were originally the only place where nutmeg and cloves were found. Already known in ancient Rome and probably much earlier in China, these coveted spices attracted traders and immigrants from Java and other Indonesian islands, as well as Indians, Arabs, and Europeans. Through intermarriage, a wide spectrum of physical types emerged, often varying widely from village to village, and Ambonese culture became a mind-dazzling amalgam of earlier, indigenous cultural traits with concepts and beliefs of Hindu-Javanese, Arab, Portuguese, and Dutch origin. The Ambonese culture area can be divided into two subcultures, namely the Alifuru culture of the interior tribes of Ceram, and the Pasisir culture of Ambon-Lease and coastal stretches of western Ceram. The Alifuru are horticulturalists who practiced headhunting until pacification by the Dutch shortly before World War I. Most Ambonese clans in the Pasisir region trace their ancestry to the mountain regions of Ceram, and Alifuru culture forms the basis of Ambonese culture. Much of Alifuru culture has been destroyed by zealous Christian missionaries from the Pasisir region who could not perceive that much of what they attacked as "pagan" in Ceram was sacred to themselves in Ambon-Lease. This resulted in the paradox that the Christian villages on Ambon-Lease, converted some 400 years earlier, have conserved their cultural heritage better than the recently converted mountain villages on Ceram, which nowadays find themselves in a cultural limbo and in a state of economic depression. While in the Pasisir region Protestant Christianity and Islam dominate the worldview of their respective followers, traditional beliefs and practices (*adat*) continue to govern social relationships in both religious communities. The rapid expansion of Islam in this region during the fifteenth century was contained with the arrival of the Portuguese (in 1511), who converted most of the "pagan" population to Roman Catholicism during their century of colonial rule. In 1605 the Dutch replaced them, and remained there until 1950. They turned the Christian population into Calvinist Protestants and instituted a spice monopoly despite the fierce resistance of both Muslims and Christians. In the nineteenth century, after the decline of the spice trade, Ambonese Muslims faded into the background while the fortunes of the Christians became ever more closely tied to the Dutch. As trusted and loyal soldiers, they became the mainstay of the Dutch colonial army (KNIL). Belonging to the best-educated groups in the Netherlands Indies, many were employed in the colonial administration and private enterprises outside their homeland. This pattern of emigration has continued in the postindependence period. Muslims, formerly excluded for the most part from education, are now fast catching up with the Christians and competing with them for jobs. After World War II, most Ambonese soldiers remained loyal to the Dutch and fought with them against the Indonesian nationalists. The Dutch transfer of sovereignty to Indonesia led in 1950 to the declaration of an independent Republic of the South Moluccas (RMS), but this failed. Fearing reprisals from the nationalists, some 4,000 Ambonese soldiers and their families were "temporarily" transferred to the Netherlands in 1951. Because of their steadfast attachment to the RMS ideal, their return became impossible. The resulting frustrations led to a series of terrorist actions, including spectacular train hijackings, in the 1970s. During the entire period of exile, the group has displayed strong separatist tendencies, foiling all attempts of the Dutch to assimilate them. Only recently has there been some willingness toward functional integration.

Settlements

With few exceptions, the monoreligious villages range in population from 200 to 6,000 persons. Originally located for defensive purposes on steep mountain ridges, most were forced by the Dutch to relocate to the coast. The tightly clustered houses are often strung along one or more roads running parallel to the beach on a narrow strip of fairly flat land between the sea and mountains. The most prominent feature is either a large church or a mosque. There are two styles of housing. The first is the traditional wood-frame house with dirt floors, walls made from the stems of sago leaves (*gaba-gaba*), and thatched roofs also made of leaves of the sago palm (*atap*). This style is increasingly being replaced by concrete houses with plaster walls and corrugated iron roofs. The square spaces surrounding each house are usually meticulously free of any growth except for fruit- and nut-bearing trees and palms, some of which spread shade. Mostly along the beach there are rows of coconut palms. The land owned by each village is located beyond, in the mountains.

Economy

Subsistence and Commercial Activities. Horticulture is the basis of subsistence. A variety of tuberous plants (yams, cassavas, taros) are grown in family gardens (*kebon*). Sago, growing unattended in swampy regions, continues to be an important staple. Rice, a prestige staple, is almost exclusively cultivated by Javanese transmigrants on Ceram, but the quantity produced is far from sufficient to cover demand and thus most rice is imported. In tracts of lands with mixed growth of perennials (*dusun*), a number of fruit and nut trees, as well as cloves and nutmegs, are grown. These spices are the major cash crops, followed by copra. The main source of protein is fish, caught individually or communally, supplemented by some domestic animals and small game. Commercial fishing and lumbering (mostly on Ceram) are almost exclusively done by foreign companies, usually Japanese, sometimes in conjunction with local enterprises.

Industrial Arts. Only a few specialists are found in villages. Handicrafts are very scarce. Two villages produce low-grade pottery and one engages in metallurgy. Aside from subsistence activities, manual labor is despised, particularly among Christians. Both men and women prefer white-collar jobs as ministers, teachers, administrators, and clerks. Muslims also engage in trading, but most industrial and commercial activities are in the hands of the Chinese, some Arabs, and Muslim immigrants from other parts of Indonesia. A sizable Butonese minority performs most low-level tasks.

Trade. Some villages own cooperatives and/or small stores. Muslim peddlers also visit Christian villages. Markets are found only in Ambon City and a few smaller regional trading centers. Women bring home-grown products to these markets for sale or to supply established merchants.

Division of Labor. Men are seen as providers and perform the more hazardous occupations of fishing and hunting, as well as the heavier tasks in horticulture and house and boat building. Women are responsible for the household but also participate in garden work and fishing near the beach, and do most of the trading.

Land Tenure. Population growth has led to increasing land pressure on Ambon-Lease. Ill-defined boundaries give rise to continuing intra- and intervillage disputes that frequently result in violent clashes. Village land is divided into uncultivated forest land (ewang) and dusun. The former is for joint use, while the latter is divided among various clans, which have the right of usufruct. The dusun is inalienably owned by the village. It reverts back, to be redivided, in the case of a clan's extinction. Indonesian laws make it possible for more and more land to become individual property that can be bought and sold. Recently much of this land has been bought by nonvillagers, mostly Chinese. Land pressure has led to organized and spontaneous migration from Ambon-Lease to Ceram, where land is still plentiful. The Indonesian government has also appropriated Ceramese village land for transplanted Javanese peasants, which has caused increasing tension.

Kinship

Kin Groups and Descent. Whereas in the interior of West Ceram matrilineality is still found, every village in the Pasisir region is made up of a number of patrilineal clans (mata rumah). Several clans form a soa, originally a distinct ward. Each soa has a headman (kepala soa) who represents its clans in the village council. Clan exogamy is no longer universally practiced owing to the adoption of either Christian or Muslim conventions regarding incest. Clan descent is traced to a common ancestor, commonly the man who was the first to arrive at the present locality in ancient times. The clans consist of a number of households (rumah tangga), the closest economic and emotional support units. A third important kin group is the famili (i.e., one's kindred on both the father's and mother's side, which, like the clan, provides support in crisis situations and helps to defray costs on ritual occasions). In recent times, a shift toward bilaterality can be detected, particularly among Christians; it is most pronounced among the exiles in Holland.

Kinship Terminology. Cousin terms are as in the Hawaiian system. The social emphasis on age is reflected by the relative ages of people indicated by most kinship terms.

Marriage and Family

Marriage. Polygynous marriage has been known in Alifuru society, but today monogamy is practiced not only universally among Christians but also, with very few exceptions, among Muslims. Arranged marriages still occur, but usually the youngsters choose their own partners. There are two basic types of marriage: (1) by formal request of the groom's family (kawin masuk minta), and (2) by elopement (kawin lari). The former is considered more honorable and is more common among the relatively prosperous exiles, while the latter is overwhelmingly practiced in the Moluccas because of disagreements with the parents over the choice of partner and/or to avoid the high expenses of a formal wedding. Kawin manua is a form of marriage in which the groom enters the clan of his wife, either to assure her clan's continuity or because of an inability to pay the bride-wealth. The conjugal ties are extremely strong and usually the newlyweds establish their own household shortly after being married. Residence is commonly patrilocal. Divorce is rare.

Domestic Unit. The nuclear family, averaging about ten persons, is the minimal unit, with aging grandparents, grandchildren, single aunts and uncles, cousins, and foster children added on. Membership in the household requires sharing of the workload.

Inheritance. Property is inherited by the surviving sons. Unmarried daughters continue to "eat off the land" belonging to their natal families.

Socialization. Infants and small children are raised by parents and older siblings, as well as by other household members. Upbringing is strongly authoritarian and physical punishment is common after a child grows beyond the toddler stage. Emphasis is placed on filial piety, family allegiance, and respect for elder people. Collectivism is valued above individualism.

Sociopolitical Organization

The province of Maluku is headed by a governor who is directly appointed by the president of Indonesia and is commonly of non-Moluccan origin, as are those holding other key positions. The other offices on the provincial level and below are occupied by Moluccans, but they, like the provincial parliament, have only limited political power.

Social Organization. Traditional Ambonese society is democratically organized to a degree. Elevated status is only afforded by the clan that has the hereditary right to the office of village chief and to religious officials. Furthermore, academicians are highly respected. In postindependence times, however, the status of all these persons has been declining. Status distinctions made between original clans and those that arrived later in a village are also waning.

Political Organization. Within Ambonese society proper, the villages constitute the largest organizational units, each tying separately and directly into the regional components of the national governmental superstructure. They are self-contained and autonomous, dealing with each other as if they were independent ministates. Villages are governed by a council of hereditary office holders headed by the village headman (*raja*). Orders of the Indonesian government to open the councils to anyone chosen in free elections, including non-Ambonese, have been met with great resistance.

Social Control. Villagers still try to avoid the involvement of the police and other governmental authorities in dealing with internal problems. The fear of punishment by the ancestors, who are the founders and guardians of the social value system (adat), is still the most effective prevention of social transgressions. Gossip, public embarrassment, and threats of ostracism are effective devices of social control.

Conflict. In the past, warfare was extremely common and intervillage fighting is still a quite frequent occurrence, resulting in casualties and burning of property. Violence is also common in intravillage fights.

Religion and Expressive Culture

Religious Beliefs. The Ambonese, who generally consider themselves devout Christians or Muslims, have given their respective faiths a certain ethnic exclusivity over the past centuries, which formerly manifested itself in the nonadmittance of fellow believers from other ethnic groups to their churches or mosques. They further indigenized the two universal creeds by syncretizing them with the prior traditional belief system based on ancestor veneration, creating a system in which God is in charge of the universe and salvation and the ancestors are responsible for the proper working of society. Beyond that, the Ambonese succeeded in syncretizing Christianity and Islam, creating an ethnic religion, Agama Nunusaku, which makes it possible for Christians and Muslims to maintain harmony and a common ethnic identity. However, while the harmonious relationships, reinforced by the *pela* alliances, continue to be maintained on the village level, urban religious and political leaders on both sides are attempting to "purify" their respective faiths, leading to a slowly widening rift between Christians and Muslims. Aside from God, whom both Christians and Muslims perceive as the same, the ancestors play the most important role. They are beseeched for blessings, propitiated after transgressions, and invited to all family and village ceremonies. A variety of indigenous Christian and Islamic devils and evil spirits is believed to cause illness and other harm to humans.

Religious Practitioners. The well-organized Moluccan Protestant Church (GPM) allows both men and women to enter the ministry. No such regional organization unites the Muslims, among whom the religious officials are chosen on the community level; in Muslim villages the various offices are often still hereditary. Most villages still have adat "priests" who deal with matters concerning the traditional belief system. The *orang baruba* (healers) cure ailments that Western-style physicians are unable to affect (i.e., those caused by sorcerers [*swangi*] and evil spirits).

Ceremonies. Both Christians and Muslims follow the religious calendars of their respective creeds but some of the ceremonies have taken on a distinct Ambonese meaning and flavor. This is especially true for the life-cycle rituals. No longer universally performed are such traditional ceremonies as the periodic renewal of the roof of the village council house and the cleansing of the village.

Arts. Music, singing, and dancing are the art forms in which Ambonese excel. Aside from traditional dances (e.g., the *cakalele*, a fierce war dance), a number of European dances have survived since Portuguese times among both religious groups. Singing is an integral part of every social occasion and most developed among Christians, who pride themselves on their church choirs. Many leading pop stars and musical groups in Indonesia are of Christian-Ambonese origin, and in Holland Ambonese soloists and bands gained recognition beyond the boundaries of the exile community.

Medicine. Illness is attributed to natural causes, ancestral punishment, and evil forces. Home remedies are used in less serious cases. Generally, Western-style physicians are consulted first and traditional healers are visited if no cure is forthcoming or at the advice of a physician.

Death and Afterlife. After the funeral, one or more rites are conducted to entice the spirit of the deceased, which hovers around its former home, to leave for the abode of the dead. It is generally believed that the spirit will remain on earth until the Last Judgment Day. Christians and Muslims bury their dead.

Bibliography

Bartels, Dieter (1977). "Guarding the Invisible Mountain: Intervillage Alliances, Religious Syncretism, and Ethnic Identity among Ambonese Christians and Muslims in the Moluccas." Ph.D. dissertation, Cornell University.

Bartels, Dieter (1988). *Moluccans in Exile: A Struggle for Ethnic Survival*. Leiden: Center for the Study of Social Conflict, University of Leiden.

Cooley, Frank L. (1962). *Ambonese Adat: A General Description*. New Haven: Yale University, Southeast Asia Studies.

Jensen, Adolf E. (1948). *Die drei Ströme: Züge aus dem geistigen und religiösen Leben der Wemale, einem Primitiv-Volk in den Molukken*. Leipzig: Otto Harrassowitz.

DIETER BARTELS

Ata Sikka

ETHNONYMS: Ata Bi'ang, Ata Krowé, Sika, Sikka, Sikkanese

Orientation

Identification. The Ata Sikka (*ata*, "people," "man"), or Sikkanese, are the people of east-central Flores, an Indonesian island, and are located between Lio and Larantuka. Specifically, the name "Sikka" refers to Sikka Natar, the "village of Sikka" on the south coast, the seat of a Portuguese-Christian native rule between the early seventeenth century and 1954. More generally, the term "Sikka" has been applied to the domain under the rule of the raja of Sikka; to the territories claimed by the tributary mountain domains of Nita and Kangae (which were amalgamated with the domain of Sikka in 1929); and, most generally, to all the lands claimed by these three domains, an area roughly equivalent to the former Dutch *onderafdeling* of Maumere and the present Indonesian administrative region of Kabupaten (regency of) Sikka. The majority of Ata Sikka are concentrated in the western part of their territory. The dialect and customs of the Ata Tana 'Ai of the eastern mountains of Kabupaten Sikka are sufficiently divergent to merit separate description. The terms "Krowé" and "Ata Krowé" have been used by Ata Sikka and commentators alike to refer (a) to the people in the vicinity of Maumere, the port town and administrative center on the north coast; (b) to pagans as opposed to Christians (*ata serani*); and (c) generally to the once non-Christian mountain peoples (Ata 'Iwang) from Nele to Tana 'Ai, including all of those of the subaltern rajadom of Kangae. It is difficult to ascertain whether the term "Krowé" once referred to a separate ethnic group. The administrative adjustments in this century that made the Sikka territory coincident with the Maumere region provided official Sikkanese control over the western border area of Maumere with a large Lionese population.

Location.   The Ata Sikka occupy both the mountains and the coastal stretches of the region of Sikka, a territory extending from the north to the south coast of east-central Flores and roughly from the village of Talibura on the eastern north coast to the river Nanga Bloh in the west (8°30′ to 8°47′ S; 122°02′ to 122°37′ E). A broken, eroded, and irregular terrain, a sharp contrast between coast and mountain, and erratic monsoons with a long dry season produce considerable climatic variation. Since the soil is porous and rivers are few, crops are dependent on irregular rainfall. A major problem for all of western Sikka is the lack of sufficient, well-located drinking water.

Demography.   The national census of 1980 put the total population of the regency of Sikka at 219,650. This number includes approximately 175,000 people who speak Sara Sikka, the Sikkanese language. The remaining inhabitants are Lionese, who reside mainly in the western part of the district, and Ata Muhang, Lamaholot-speaking people who inhabit the far northeastern region of the district.

Linguistic Affiliation.   Sara (way, language) Sikka is an Austronesian language that Wurm and Hattori (1983) include in the Flores-Lembata (Lomblen) Subgroup, Timor Area Group of the Austronesian languages of the Lesser Sunda Islands and Timor. At least three dialects of Sara Sikka can be identified: (1) that spoken by the people in the region of Sikka Natar, the village of Sikka on the south coast of Flores; (2) Sara Krowé, which is spoken in the central hills of the regency of Sikka; and (3) Sara Tana 'Ai, which is spoken by approximately 6,000 people.

History and Cultural Relations

Native tradition attributes the foundation of the rajadom of Sikka to Don(g) Alésu, an ancestor of the royal house of Sikka Natar, who is said to have journeyed to Malakka where he converted to Christianity. Don Alésu then returned to Flores to found the domain of Sikka and to recognize the rajas of Nita and Kangae as his "left" and "right" hands. Documents from 1613 list Sikka as one of the (Portuguese) Christian states of the area. Under the Dutch, the three native domains and their rulers were separately recognized until 1929, when Nita and Kangae were united with Sikka to form a single domain under the raja of Sikka. The Dutch gave the rajadom of Sikka the status of an autonomous region (*daerah swapraja*) under the administrative supervision of the raja of Sikka, who shifted the seat of his government from Sikka Natar to the town of Maumere. The last raja of Sikka to serve as head of government, Ratu Mo'ang Bako Don Josephus Thomas Ximenes da Silva, died in 1952 and within a few years the territory and peoples of the rajadom became part of the modern Republic of Indonesia.

Settlements

Villages of the central saddle of the district are located along peaks of ridges or on other high points; others stretch along roads or parallel the coast. Houses are arranged in rows, usually along either side of a road or major footpath, with traditional village centers marked by one or more large offering stones (*mahé*). Paul Arndt (1933) reports elaborately carved village houses (*woga*) containing ceremonial objects (gongs, drums, shields), which were reserved exclusively for men and used as the place of male circumcision in most non-Christian villages. Such ceremonial structures are no longer found in central Sikka. Arndt speculates that formerly villages were divided into clan quarters or neighborhoods. Each clan within a village designated one house as its clan house. Houses of traditional construction are rectangular and raised on posts a meter or more above the ground. In western Sikka, houses consist of two parts: a gallery (*tédang*) and an inner room (*uné*), with further subdivisions within each part. Such houses increasingly have been replaced by houses constructed directly on packed earth or concrete foundations. Many houses and their courtyards are encircled by low stone walls. During the agricultural season farmers erect makeshift garden huts in distant fields.

Economy

In the past, Sikkanese agriculturalists were almost wholly dependent on the shifting cultivation of dry fields. The techniques of shifting cultivation are still employed in the eastern and western regions of the district but the cultivation of a variety of species of the leguminous lamtoro (*Leucaena* sp.) has increasingly allowed intensive cultivation of permanent unirrigated fields, which has replaced shifting cultivation in much of densely populated central Sikka. The main subsistence crops are rice, maize, and cassava, supplemented by millet, sorghum, and sweet potato. Only the coastal villages have the opportunity for offshore fishing to supplement subsistence agriculture. Commercial fishing, which is a growing industry, is principally in the hands of Butonese, Makassarese, and Chinese entrepreneurs. The traditional economy of central Sikka was radically transformed by the Dutch-induced planting of the coconut palm and sale of copra in the first half of the twentieth century. Clear-cutting of native forests for coconut cultivation and poor management of the coconut plantations resulted in severe degradation of both soil and water resources. In recent years the government has fostered small-scale herding of cattle in some northern coastal areas. Domestic animals include dogs, cats, pigs, goats, ducks, chickens, and horses. Property rights are vested in land, trees, houses, horses, elephant tusks, gold, silver, cloth, and old armaments. The household is the main landowning unit, with residual rights over unclaimed land traditionally belonging to either the "lord of the earth" (_tana pu'ang_) or the raja.

Kinship

Kin Groups and Descent.   In central Sikka, a child belongs to his or her father's descent group. The mother's descent group maintains certain ritual rights and obligations over the children of their women who have married men of other groups. A child's mother's brother must, however, receive a prestation of ceremonial goods from his sister's husband's people at the birth of each child, a payment that dissolves any claim to the child as a member of the mother's group, a claim that group might otherwise make. Communities are divided into large, nonlocalized, nonexogamous, named descent groups (_ku'at_ or _ku'at wungung_), each recognizing its own founding ancestor, possessing its own "history," and sharing a limited number of ritual prohibitions. In Sikka Natar (the village of Sikka) on the south coast, ku'at wungung are associated with wards within the village.

Kin Terminology.   According to Calon and Arndt, there are two published lists of kin terms for western Sikka. Father and father's brother (_ama_) are distinguished from mother's brother (_pulamé_ or _tiu_); mother and mother's sister (_ina_) are distinguished from father's sister (_'a'a_); cross cousins are distinguished from parallel cousins and according to the sex of the speaker; cross cousins who are potential marriage partners (classificatory as mother's brother's daughter and father's sister's son; however, they address each other as _ipar_ or _ipar tu'ang_). There are minor variations of relationship terminologies and the classification of kin among the peoples of central Sikka.

Marriage and Family

Marriage.   In central Sikka and Sikka Natar, marriage is effected by the payment of bride-wealth, reckoned in goods classified as "male" (horses, elephant tusks, gold and silver coins, and cash). Counterprestations from wife givers to wife takers must be paid in classificatorily "female" goods (cloth, pigs, rice, and household furnishings and utensils). Men representing the wife-giving and wife-taking parties in a marriage formally and ceremonially negotiate bride-wealth. When agreement is reached a pig is provoked until it squeals, thereby announcing the marriage of the couple. A Catholic marriage ceremony follows within a few years, in some cases only after the birth of the first child. Marriage is monogamous. Marriage is forbidden (1) between a parent and child, an uncle and niece, or an aunt and nephew; (2) between siblings; (3) between the children of two brothers or the children of two sisters; and (4) between a boy and his father's sister's daughter. According to Arndt, in the past, the desired marriage was between a boy and his mother's brother's daughter. Since the beginning of this century the marriage of first cousins has been discouraged by the church. The people

of Sikka Natar follow a rule of _empat lapis_ (Indonesian: "four layers")—marriage between persons related no closer than as third cousins.

The relations of alliance groups in central Sikka, and most remarkably in Sikka Natar, are ordered by complex exchanges of ceremonial goods and ritual services. Particular exchange cycles are initiated by bride-wealth and its counterprestations. While ceremonial exchange and affinal alliance are generally asymmetric, instances of symmetrical exchange occur within the asymmetric pattern. The mutual obligations of affinally related groups last during the marriage of two of their members and are especially important on the occasion of the death of a spouse. Reduced obligations to exchange goods and ritual services continue to link alliance groups after the death of both a husband and wife. Goods received either as bride-wealth (_ling wéling_, "the clink of the coins"), classificatorily "male" goods, or as counterprestations (_'utang labu wawi paré_, "cloths, blouses, pigs, and rice"), classificatorily "female" goods, are distributed within the receiving group to persons standing in particular kin or affinal categories to the bride and groom. Of special significance are elephant tusks and ceremonial textiles (_'utang_) made by the women of alliance groups. Elephant tusks are nonconsumable goods whose individual movements through exchange chart the histories of alliances in the community. Textiles of a kind and quality suitable for exchange for bride-wealth must be cut, sewn into sarongs, and worn by the women who receive them. They are thus consumable goods that must be constantly replaced by the labor of women. The ceremonial _'utang_ of Sikka Natar are especially notable in that motifs and the structure of motifs incorporated into the overall design of a cloth encode the maternal and paternal identity of the weaver. Once given in return for bride-wealth and worn by recipient women, these cloths exhibit publicly the identity of the wearer in terms of the alliance system of the community.

Throughout Sikka, marriage is by preference village-endogamous, except that royal and noble houses maneuver to increase their political influence by becoming wife givers to nobles of other villages. Arndt reports that a man may spend a year or more in the house of his wife or alternate residence between his own parents' and wife's parents' house before establishing a residence of his own, a practice still followed in Sikka Natar.

Domestic Unit.   A household may include the elderly parents of either husband or wife and a recently married child with spouse. Ten Dam and Arndt report royal houses with up to fifty persons, although the average in Nita is ten per household.

Inheritance.   Property is divided among male siblings, but, according to ten Dam, an elder brother may act on behalf of his other brothers to retain intact for another generation the household's dry fields. One child, with spouse, continues to reside with his or her parents and eventually inherits the house.

Sociopolitical Organization

Social Organization.   Documentary sources and contemporary social life indicate a class of nobles (_ata mo'ang_) related to the raja of Sikka and the former rajas of Nita and

Kangae; a class of freemen or commoners (*ata riwung*); and, formerly, a class of slaves (*ata maha*) made up of debtors and people captured in wars.

Political Organization.   Under the rule of the raja of Sikka in the early 1950s the Maumere region consisted of sixteen parishes, each headed by an officer with the title of *kapitan*. Each parish was divided into villages, each under a village headman (*kepala kampung*). According to Arndt and ten Dam, the traditional political system included titles such as tana pu'ang (lord of the earth) who had ritual rights over the land and authoritative knowledge in questions of *adat* (traditional) law. The tana pu'ang was regarded as a descendant of the founder of a village area, traditionally at enmity with the raja and his representatives.

Social Control and Conflict.   In the period of the rajadom, justice was dealt with by the raja, his representatives, the village headman, and the village elders, including the tana pu'ang. Oaths and ordeals (*jaji*) were once part of the judicial process. Most western Sikkanese villages waged limited warfare against the Lionese on their border. Arndt reports that enemy heads were generally hung at the village entrance on the return from a raid; a coconut was then substituted for the head in the performance of village rituals. Contemporary Sikkanese dispute Arndt's reports of headhunting and claim it was exclusively a Lionese practice.

Religion and Expressive Culture

Religious Beliefs.   Since the early seventeenth century, Catholicism has been associated with the rule of the rajas of Sikka. As a result, native ceremonial life has been virtually replaced by Catholic ritual. The traditional pantheon consisted of a number of coupled deities of which the classificatorily "female" Nian Tana and "male" Lero Wulang, the surface of the earth and the sun and moon respectively, were preeminent and formed a complementary pair. The Catholic deity is called *amapu*, a term invented by early missionaries meaning "source father" or "father of generations." The monadic and masculinely identified Catholic amapu stands in marked contrast to the dualistically male and female deity of the traditional religion. In contemporary religious practice, rosary organizations, which celebrate the Virgin Mary as the feminine complement of amapu, are especially prominent, and serve in Sikkanese thought to maintain the complementarity of the male and female elements of the traditional deity. Belief in generally beneficent spirits of the dead persists throughout contemporary Sikka culture, but the Sikkanese speak of a variety of female spirits or paired spirits whose female aspects are particularly dangerous to humans.

Ceremonies.   Arndt reports that a major focus of the ancient ceremonial life was a male circumcision and initiation ritual, presided over by the *tanah pu'ang*; boys were thereafter confined to the village men's house. There were two categories of curer: *ata rawing*, who were benign curers of either sex, and *ata busung*, who were predominantly male curers who could diagnose the cause of an illness, extract objects from the body, locate witches, and recall the soul. In contemporary Sikka Natar a few women still serve as ata rawing. Most illnesses were believed caused by contact with objects of sorcery stuff (*uru*), by witch's attack, or by confrontation of the soul by a spirit.

Death and Afterlife.   At death the corpse was traditionally wrapped with cloth or mats and buried in the ground. Coastal dwellers sometimes used coffins in the shape of boats. A bush, coconut, or jar was placed on the grave. According to Arndt, the soul journeyed either to Lero Walung or to a seven-layered underworld, through which it progressed by dying and being reborn again and by undergoing various ordeals. Contemporary burials are in accord with Catholic practice but are the occasion for the settlement of outstanding debts of bride-wealth and counterprestations.

See also Ata Tana 'Ai

Bibliography

Arndt, Paul (1932). *Mythologie, Religion und Magie im Sikagebiet (östl. Mittelflores)*. Ende, Flores: Arnoldus-druckerei.

Arndt, Paul (1933). *Gesellschaftliche Verhältnisse im Sikagebiet (östl. Mittelflores)*. Ende, Flores: Arnoldus-druckerei.

Calon, L. F. (1893). "Eenige opmerkingen over het dialekt van Sikka." *Tijdschrift voor Indische Taal-, Land- en Volkenkunde* 35:129–199.

Dam, H. ten (1950). *Kampung Nita dan Sekitarnja.* . . . Bogor (Java): Balai Perguran Tinggi, Fakuktet Pertanian, Bahagian Ilmu Eknomi.

Fox, James J. (1972). "Sikanese." In *Ethnic Groups of Insular Southeast Asia*, edited by Frank M. LeBar. Vol. 1, *Indonesia, Andaman Islands, and Madagascar*, 88–90. New Haven: HRAF Press.

Wurm, Stefan A., and Shiro Hattori, eds. (1983). *Language Atlas of the Pacific Area*. Part 2. Canberra: Australian Academy of the Humanities.

JAMES J. FOX AND E. DOUGLAS LEWIS

Ata Tana 'Ai

ETHNONYMS: Ata 'Iwang, Ata Kangae, Ata Krowé, Krowé

Orientation

Identification.   The Ata Tana 'Ai are a branch of the Sikkanese peoples of eastern Flores. The ethnonym "Ata Tana 'Ai" means "People of the Forest Land," an appellation used both by the Ata Tana 'Ai themselves and by other people of eastern and east central Flores.

Location.   The Ata Tana 'Ai inhabit a region known as Tana 'Ai in the eastern part of the administrative regency of Kabupaten Sikka on the island of Flores in eastern Indonesia. The eastern wall of the Tana 'Ai valley is a range of mountains that runs north and south across the island and rises to the peak of Ili Wukoh (1,446 meters). To the west, Tana 'Ai is bounded by a series of high, broken, and rugged ridges that rise to Mapi (called "Ili Egon" by the central Sikkanese), an active volcano with an elevation of 1,704 meters. Almost the whole of the Tana 'Ai region lies in the catchment of Napun Geté ("Big River" or "Big Valley"), a river that rises at the southern watershed of the island and flows northward to empty into the Flores Sea. Climax vegetation is principally deciduous, with eucalyptus forests altered through the horticulture of the valley's inhabitants. The climate of Tana 'Ai is mild, with distinct rainy and dry seasons. Rains usually begin in November or December. The heaviest rainfall, often accompanied by storms, occurs in January and February. Rainfall decreases steadily from March to May and is rare between July and the beginning of the first intermittent and light precipitation in mid- or late October. In each year between 1977 and 1989 the valley received in excess of 125 centimeters of rain.

Demography. The national census of 1980 put the total population of the regency of Sikka at 219,650. This number includes approximately 175,000 people who speak Sara Sikka, the Sikkanese language. The population of the Tana 'Ai region is approximately 8,000 people.

Linguistic Affiliation. Sara (way, language) Tana 'Ai is a dialect of Sara Sikka, an Austronesian language that Wurm and Hattori (1983) include in the Flores-Lembata (Lomblen) Subgroup, Timor Area Group of the Austronesian languages of the Lesser Sunda Islands and Timor. At least three dialects of Sara Sikka can be recognized: (1) that spoken by the people in the region of Sikka Natar, the village of Sikka on the south coast of Flores, from which the administrative regency takes its name; (2) Sara Krowé, which is spoken in the central hills of the regency of Sikka; and (3) Sara Tana 'Ai, which is spoken by approximately 6,000 people.

History and Cultural Relations

The mythic histories of the ceremonial domains of Tana 'Ai recount the arrival of ancestors who founded the Tana 'Ai clans (*sukun*) and established Tana 'Ai society by the delegation of rights to land and rituals to later ancestors. Direct contact with Europeans came later to the Ata Tana 'Ai than to other peoples of the regency of Sikka. Dutch records to the year 1905 rarely mention the Tana 'Ai region, and Dutch colonial officers began making irregular patrols in the mountains only in the 1930s. Sovereignty over Tana 'Ai was, until the Dutch confirmed the present boundary in 1904, a point of dispute between the rajas of Larantuka (East Flores) and Sikka. Until the 1970s, the principal medium of contact between the Ata Tana 'Ai and outsiders was the Catholic Church, whose mission was staffed primarily by European priests. Since 1970, the regency government has established roads, markets, and schools in the interior of the region.

The Tana 'Ai region is wholly contained within Kecamatan (district of Talibura). The northern region of the district includes, in addition to those of the Ata Tana 'Ai, communities of speakers of Lamaholot, the language of Larantuka (Kabupaten Flores Timur) to the east of Sikka. The Ata Tana 'Ai and Ata Sikka call the Lamaholot speakers of Kabupaten Sikka "Ata Muhang." Despite differences of language, relations of the Ata Tana 'Ai with the Lamaholot-speaking people of the eastern slopes of the Ili Wukoh Range are generally closer than with Sara Sikka-speaking peoples to the west. Ata Tana 'Ai trade regularly with the people of Watubuku on the south coast of East Flores and occasionally cooperate with communities of western Larantuka in the performance of rituals. Some intermarriage of Ata Tana 'Ai with people of Sikka Natar has occurred since the Ata Sikka began opening coconut plantations on the south coast of the Tana 'Ai region in the 1930s.

Settlements

The Ata Tana 'Ai live in single-family-house compounds (*mobo*) constructed in gardens scattered throughout the forests of the valley and the surrounding mountain slopes. Clans and clan branches construct *lepo*, which are larger and more permanent houses of a distinctive architectural style. Hamlets of lepo, called *kloang*, are traditionally the only permanent multidwelling settlements in Tana 'Ai and are ceremonial centers. Since the 1960s the government has encouraged the construction of villages according to a standard layout, and today most Tana 'Ai families or extended families maintain houses in these villages. The density of settlement is greater in the valley of Napun Geté and less on the upper slopes and escarpments of the mountains.

Economy

Subsistence and Commercial Activities. The Ata Tana 'Ai are subsistence horticulturalists, hunters, and gatherers. The economy of the Ata Tana 'Ai is based on the shifting cultivation of rice, maize, and yams. Domestic animals include pigs, goats, chickens, horses, and dogs. The principally vegetable diet is supplemented by the meat of animals sacrificed on ceremonial occasions and by deer and wild pigs hunted in the forests. The forests of Tana 'Ai provide opportunities for gathering wild fruit, vegetables, and materials for building. The Ata Tana 'Ai carry out shifting cultivation with a tool kit consisting of short steel machetes, small iron knives, and dibble sticks. Men use spears and bows and arrows in hunting. Both men and women manufacture a variety of baskets for domestic purposes. Women weave cloth on backstrap looms from thread spun from cotton grown in local gardens. Household utensils, such as metal pots, plastic containers, and Florenese ceramic pots, as well as clothing and items required by schoolchildren, are obtained in the local markets.

Trade. Men of Tana 'Ai maintain trading relationships with men of East Flores, the north coast, central Sikka, and, in some cases, with people of the islands to the east of Flores. A principal trade good is gin or palm wine made from the lontar (*Borassus* sp.) palm, for which Tana 'Ai men exchange pigs, goats, rice, and bamboo and timber for the construction of houses and fences. In recent years most families have derived some cash income from small-scale and occasional trading of copra, coffee, spices, eggs, and chickens in the weekly market on the north coast.

Division of Labor. Whereas the classifications of Tana 'Ai culture associate women with the domestic spheres of house and garden and men with the wild sphere of the forest, there is considerable equality between men and women in laboring for subsistence. Both men and women participate in all the work required for horticulture, although men are expected to provide the labor for the heavy work of clearing the forest and construction of sturdy fences to protect crops from deer and wild pigs. Men, women, and children share the work of burning newly cleared fields, weeding, planting, and harvesting. Men hunt in the forests, often in groups, whereas women weave textiles. Men construct houses and granaries. Men and women share the routine domestic chores of house maintenance and caring for domestic animals. Women usually cook the meals but no opprobrium is attached to a man cooking. Older children, especially adolescent boys and girls, provide care for infants and young children of the household or hamlet and fetch water from springs and streams for their household.

Land Tenure.   Arable land, whether under cultivation or reserve, is divided into fields, which are distributed among the houses of the community. Houses hold rights to their land corporately and by virtue of belonging to clans whose rights to the land are traced in the mythic histories to the founding of the domains. The founding ancestors of each clan were granted land by the ancestors who founded the domain as a whole.

Kinship

Kin Groups and Descent.   The social world of the Ata Tana 'Ai is constructed of smaller groups subsumed within larger groups. An individual's primary group of reference is the lepo, a word that denotes both a physical edifice and a social unit of a particular kind. The principle governing lepo membership is that each Ata Tana 'Ai belongs to the lepo of his or her mother. The membership of the lepo is thus a matrilineal descent group that consists of consanguineally related women and their brothers. The core of the lepo is a group of consanguineally related women in whom is vested commonly shared rights to garden land and ceremonial wealth, and whose decisions regarding the distribution of these resources within the lepo cannot be gainsaid.

Kinship Terminology.   The Ata Tana 'Ai say that among a person's kin are those with whom he or she is méin ha (one blood), and others who are méin pé-péhan (different blood). All the members of a lepo (a person's mother, mother's sisters, mother's sisters' children, mother's brother, brothers, sisters, sisters' children, and, for a woman, her children) are of the same maternal blood, which defines house membership. Kinship traced through men entails relationships of different blood. Thus a person's father, father's siblings, father's siblings' children and, for a man, his children, are conceived to be of different blood.

The classification of cousins is ambiguous in one respect. Mother's sister's son and father's brother's son, and mother's sister's daughter and father's brother's daughter, are classed as brother and sister, respectively. Father's sister's son and mother's brother's daughter are wué wari, the term used without reference to birth order and otherwise used to denote elder and younger siblings and parallel cousins of the same sex. Wué wari cousins can marry. However, a man's father's sister's daughter and a woman's mother's brother's son are both winé and nara, respectively, and wué wari too. While there is no proscription of the marriage of father's sister's daughter and mother's brother's son, such marriages do not occur.

Marriage and Family

Marriage.   Marriage is monogamous with the exception of the tana pu'an, the "source of the domain," who is permitted more than one wife. Marriage is not marked ritually and, unlike the practices of neighboring peoples, the Ata Tana 'Ai do not exchange bride-wealth and counterprestations on the occasion of a marriage. The lepo are the exogamous alliance contracting groups of Tana 'Ai society. Residence is initially with the woman's mother; after the births of children, a couple normally opens its own garden and thereafter resides independently. There is no formal means of divorce. The dissolution of a liaison is most frequently initiated by the husband, who signals his desire by leaving his wife's house.

Domestic Unit.   The domestic unit is the mobo, which is a lifetime garden house in which most families reside. A mobo consists of a woman, her unmarried and recently married children, her husband, and, occasionally, infirm parents or husband's parents who are not attached to a clan-branch house.

Inheritance.   Land and ceremonial wealth are transmitted from mother and mother's sisters to daughters and sister's daughters within the lepo. Because these resources are held corporately by the lepo, there is no inheritance, in the strict sense of the term, of these resources. Domestic animals, textiles, and personal possessions are inherited by a woman's sisters and daughters. Coconut palms, areca, and fruit trees planted by a man in his lifetime are divided among his children and sisters' children. A man's personal possessions (horses, spears, bows and arrows, and knives) are distributed among his mé pu (children and sisters' children) on the occasion of his second-stage mortuary rite.

Socialization.   Responsibility for child rearing is exercised by women and men within the lepo, with parents sharing primary responsibility. Young children frequently spend time in the households of their mother's sisters and brothers and in the lepo of their clan or clan-branch, where they are cared for by the senior woman of the group. Children are generally treated indulgently and are reprimanded verbally. The practice of strict discipline in both state and Catholic primary schools is, in Tana 'Ai, increasingly at odds with the traditional indulgence with which the community treats its children.

Sociopolitical Organization

Social Organization.   Tana 'Ai is divided into seven socially and politically independent ceremonial domains or tana. Each domain consists of a number of clans (sukun), usually five, of which one is pu'an (source, original). The source clan consists of descendants of the founding ancestors of the domain. Each clan consists of a number of lepo, which are ranked according to the precedence of their founding within the clan. One of the elder men of the pu'an house of the clan serves the community as its tana pu'an, in whom is vested ultimate ritual responsibility for the well-being of the domain. All rights to land, residence, exploitation of resources, and ritual status of clans and houses within the domain derive ultimately from the source of the domain as descendant and heir of the domain's founding ancestors. While the Ata Tana 'Ai express a preference for clan endogamy, the alliance system of a domain functions in such a way that only one-third of marriages are endogamous and two-thirds are between men and women of different houses and different clans. In cases of interclan marriage, upon the death of the man, one of his daughters, who is a member of the house and clan of his wife, is returned to his clan in a transaction known as the "return of _ama 'lo'en_" (father's forelock). The purpose of the return of father's forelock is to return a man's blood to his clan in the person of one of his daughters. A man who has married out of his house and clan is viewed as "lost" to his sisters; his daughter, by returning to her "source," replaces her father in his clan and there founds a lepo in alliance to his sisters' house, a new house that is ranked as the "most recent" in the hierarchy of precedence of houses within the clan. The complex network of alliances, reciprocal obligations, and enduring material exchange relationships between houses of different clans, which is formed over time through father's forelock transactions, is fundamental to the coherence and dynamics of the Tana 'Ai social order. Just as the statuses of the clans of a domain are defined by the precedence of their founding in relation to the "source" clan, so too are the houses within a clan ordered in terms of their precedence with respect to the oldest, or "source," house. This precedence is defined in terms of the temporal order in which the father's forelock transactions that founded them occurred. Within both the domain and clans, rights, wealth, and authority are delegated from older and more "central" groups to more recent and more "peripheral" groups.

Political Organization.   In contrast to many of the societies of eastern Indonesia, Tana 'Ai never had an indigenous raja, nor did the Tana 'Ai domains constitute local secular states. The pattern of a diarchical division of power and authority between a secular ruler and a ritual authority, common to other eastern Indonesian societies, is reflected in a division by which women, as the heads of clans, exercise secular authority over domestic and horticultural matters and men, as the ritual specialists of the domain, exercise sacred authority, principally in the execution of ritual. In the thought of the Ata Tana 'Ai, the feminine and masculine domains of authority are complementary and mutually dependent. Women govern within the lepo and men, exercising the delegated authority of their sisters, are the principal medium of relations between lepo and clans, all of which are conceived primarily as ritual in nature. In other terms, the shared hegemony of men and women in community affairs can be categorized as between the pragmatics of subsistence, which are the realm of women, and the pragmatics of alliance and ritual, which are the realm of men. When dealing with secular matters, men are conceived as acting as the delegates of their sisters and clan or lepo mothers. Authority generally is conceived as being delegated from the feminine categories of the universe to the masculine, and from "sources" or "centers" to "peripheries," where women are paradigmatic of sources and men of peripheries. Thus the source of the domain is the chief ritual authority of a domain whereas the senior woman of his lepo represents the authority by which he delegates authority to others. In the political life of the Ata Tana 'Ai, which is principally acted out in rituals, there are those who possess the "right to speak" and those who possess the "right to sit." The former (such as clan ritual specialists and young men) are apparently more active in community affairs, but the latter (such as the source of the domain and senior women) possess greater authority. In Tana 'Ai, women rule within

autonomous social units and men, in whom is vested authority for the conduct of the external affairs of the group, are the "glue" that binds the confederation of diverse clans and houses into the larger domain.

Social Control.   The mythic histories of Tana 'Ai recount rebellions against the sources of the domains, but the recent history of Tana 'Ai has been pacific. Conflicts between individuals most frequently arise from quarrels over rights to plots of land, the boundaries between gardens, the killing of domestic animals found in the forests, and the taking without permission of fruits from cultivated trees and palms. A conflict between members of a lepo is referred to the headwoman and principal male ritualist of that lepo for adjudication. The elder ritualists of a clan settle disputes between people of different lepo within the clan. Men who are expert in the rituals of the domain convene to adjudicate disputes between people of different clans.

Religion and Expressive Culture

Religious Beliefs.   In Sara Tana 'Ai, the phrase _Nian Tana Lero Wulan_ (Land, Earth, Sun, Moon) is a synecdoche for the whole of the world and denotes as well the deity of the Ata Tana 'Ai. The universe consists of a division between two major realms: the earth, which is classified symbolically as female, and the firmament, which is classified as male. The terrestrial realm consists of seven levels or layers, whereas the firmament encompasses eight, an idea expressed in ritual language as _Nian tana pi pitu // Lero wulan tédang walu_ (Land and earth of seven levels // Sun and moon of eight layers). In the myth of creation, the earth and firmament were originally connected by a golden umbilicus. In those days there were neither births nor deaths. Because the sun was near the earth, crops could not grow and the ancestors had nothing to eat. An ancestor cut the umbilicus of the earth and sky and the sun then drifted upward and the earth sank downward, cooling the land sufficiently for crops to yield fruit. With the separation, humans began to die and the sexual congress of men and women became necessary to produce new people. The separation is one element of a complex myth that charts the origins of a thorough system of dual symbolic classification by which the Ata Tana 'Ai represent relations of the cosmos and human beings and the constituent groups of society.

   In addition to ancestral spirits, the forests are home to antipathetically malicious and dangerous spirits known as _nitu noang_. Nitu noang are the aboriginal inhabitants of Tana 'Ai who were banished to the forest, diminished by the ancestors who began cutting trees to make gardens. Only powerful ritual specialists know the names of the nitu noang, by which knowledge they can be controlled.

Religious Practitioners.   In addition to a source of the domain, each domain includes ritual specialists responsible for the conduct of a number of different ceremonial cycles. Ritual specialists are men who are gifted in ritual language and who possess the recondite knowledge of the proper performance of ritual. They are able to summon ancestral spirits and to negotiate with them for assistance for the living.

Ceremonies.   Individuals carry out small rites of sacrifice before entering forests for hunting or gathering. Individual mobo and lepo conduct the "cooling" of new dwellings. Lepo are responsible for burials. Clan branches conduct second-stage mortuary rites. Clans conduct 'lo'é 'unur, the third-stage mortuary rites, and gareng 'lamen, the male initiatory rite of circumcision. Annually ritual specialists of the lepo conduct the rituals of the horticultural cycle in each of the lepo's gardens. At least once a generation, the entire population of a domain gathers under the leadership of the source of the domain and the senior ritualists of the clans to conduct gren mahé, the culminal rituals of the ceremonial system and the only occasion on which the deity is invoked directly by human beings.

Arts. The Ata Tana 'Ai practice no graphic or plastic arts, except for carving and decorating implements used in gren mahé. Houses and ritual sites are unadorned. The principal medium of creative artistic expression is a complex and highly developed ritual language. Ritual language, which employs a recondite lexicon and special grammar, is marked by an aesthetic poiesis by which lines of four words form couplets or quatrains in which each word in one line is paired semantically and in parallel with the word in the same position in the complementary line.

Medicine. Illness and misfortune are the result of individual acts contrary to hadat, the classificatory order encoded in the parallelisms of ritual language, the largely unarticulated organon of tradition, mores, etiquette, and proper relations that guides and legitimates relations of individuals to others, groups to groups, and human beings to the world of nature, ancestors, spirits, and the deity. Acts not in accord with hadat lead to confoundings of categories with consequences detrimental both to human beings and to the world itself. Curing, which is the correction of such acts, is accomplished by a simple rite in which the curer seeks, in ritual language, the "source and origin" of illness in the past acts of the afflicted person. Having detected the cause of illness, the curer prescribes a simple sacrifice to correct the past wrong action, thereby effecting a cure.

Death and Afterlife. The living and their ancestors are bound together in a relationship of mutual dependence and service. The living perform the rituals by which ancestral spirits advance through three stages of the afterlife. Ancestors reciprocate by providing the living community with the power of fertility and animation on which life depends. The spirit of the newly dead, nitu maten, is "hot" and must be "cooled" in ritual. The cooling of the dead takes place in three stages. The first is burial, before which the nitu maten is confused, volatile, and potentially dangerous to the living. Between burial and the second-stage mortuary ritual of likon, the spirit paces the boundary between the house yard and the forest, and, by its presence, guards the members of the house from harm. After likon, the spirit reenters the house. Several years later, the final mortuary rite frees the spirit from its house, whereupon it takes up residence in the forests of the domain as a guna déwa spirit. Guna déwa no longer possess individual identity but can be summoned by their descendants when their assistance is required.

See also Ata Sikka

Bibliography

Lewis, E. D. (1982). "The Metaphorical Expression of Gender and Dual Classification in Tana 'Ai Ritual Language." *Canberra Anthropology* 5:47–59.

Lewis, E. D. (1988). "A Quest for the Source: The Ontogenesis of a Creation Myth of the Ata Tana 'Ai." In *To Speak in Pairs: Essays on the Ritual Languages of Eastern Indonesia,* edited by James J. Fox. Cambridge: Cambridge University Press.

Lewis, E. D. (1988). *People of the Source: The Social and Ceremonial Order of Tana Wai Brama on Flores.* Verhandelingen van het Koninklijk Instituut voor Taal-, Land- en Volkenkunde 135. Dordrecht and Providence, R.I.: Foris Publications.

Lewis, E. D. (1989). "Why Did Sina Dance? Stochasm, Choice, and Intentionality in the Ritual Life of the Ata Tana 'Ai of Eastern Flores." In *Creating Indonesian Culture,* edited by Paul Alexander. Oceania Ethnographies, 3. Sydney: Oceania Publications.

Lewis, E. D. (1990). "Word and Act in the Curing Rituals of the Ata Tana 'Ai of Flores." *Bijdragen tot de Taal-, Land- en Volkenkunde* 146:1–12.

Wurm, Stefan A., and Shiro Hattori, eds. (1983). *Language Atlas of the Pacific Area.* Part 2. Canberra: Australian Academy of the Humanities.

E. DOUGLAS LEWIS

Atoni

ETHNONYMS: Atoin Pah Meto, Atoin Meto, Timorese; Orang Timor Asli (in Indonesian)

Orientation

Identification. Atoni live in the central mountainous part of western Timor, Indonesia, bounded to the east by the Tetum and to the west by the sea or by Rotinese and other immigrant lowland groups around Kupang Bay and Kupang City, the capital of the Province of the Eastern Lesser Sundas (Propinsi Nusa Tenggara Timur). Atoni have been Indonesian citizens since 1949, when the Republic of Indonesia succeeded the Netherlands East-Indies. Atoni wholly occupy the two administrative districts of North-Central Timor and South-Central Timor, part of Kupang District, and the former Portuguese enclave of Oe-cussi in West Timor, claimed and occupied by Indonesia since 1975 though not recognized by the United Nations. The name "Atoni" means "man, person" and is short for "Atoin Pah Meto" (People of the Dry Land) or "Atoin Meto" (Dry People) ("Atoin" being "Atoni" in metathesis). Europeans called them "Timorese," and Indonesians of Kupang may refer to them as "Orang Timor Asli" (Native Timorese) in contrast to immigrant Rotinese, Savunese, and other settlers around Kupang who come from nearby islands.

Location. Atoni are found at approximately 9°00′ to 10°15′ S and 123°30′ to 124°30′ E in mountainous central regions and rarely by the malarial coasts with their poor soils. Timor is mountainous throughout with only modest coastal lowlands and few river plains. The climate is marked by an intense westerly monsoon rainy season (January to April) and a long easterly monsoon dry season (May to December) when only modest localized rains may occur. Large rocky hills and some natural savannas mark the west Timor landscape.

Demography. Census counts are not accurate, but Atoni are estimated to number about 750,000 and are the largest ethnic group in western Timor.

Linguistic Affiliation. Atoni speak an Austronesian language of the Timor Group that is not mutually intelligible with languages of their neighbors on the island or nearby islands. No written language is used, although some church books were prepared before World War II by a Dutch linguist in a romanized script. The Indonesian national language is now used in town offices, businesses, town and rural schools, the media, and some churches; a related dialect, Kupang Malay, was used by traders for centuries.

History and Cultural Relations

Timor has been settled for many thousands of years, and certainly received migrants over its history, but nothing is known of the genesis of the Atoni people. They have been distinguished linguistically from their neighbors since the arrival of Portuguese and Dutch observers in the seventeenth century. Atoni were probably involved in the sandalwood trade for the past one or two millennia, mediated by Malays, Makassarese, and later Europeans. They were raided for slaves by outsiders. Though a swiddening people relatively isolated in their mountain homes, Atoni developed princedoms before European contact in the late sixteenth century. Timor was contested between Dutch and Portuguese in the seventeenth and eighteenth centuries, and they were to divide the island between them, taking west and east respectively. The Dutch remained in Kupang, however, and the Atoni interior only came under direct Netherlands-Indies government administration after 1912.

Settlements

Most Atoni live in small dispersed settlements of twenty to forty houses in mountainous areas, and some live along the only main road that runs from Kupang to Atambua. Traditional houses are beehive-shaped and made from forest products, with roofs coming near the ground; many Atoni are now adopting rectangular walled houses with windows, made from either wood or concrete, particularly in areas nearer markets and the road. Settlements are not marked by central common grounds, stone plazas, or public buildings, which may be found in some other areas of eastern Indonesia. Modest wooden churches are increasing in number.

Economy

Subsistence, Commercial Activities, and Trade. Atoni are primarily swidden cultivators of maize and some dry-land rice who, because of inadequate farming conditions, have been drawn into a money economy through the sale of forest products (such as palm sugar and wild honey) and livestock (chickens and Bali cattle). The latter are sold in roadside or small town markets, usually to non-Atoni middlemen linked to small interior towns and to Kupang's export facilities. Cattle were introduced by the Dutch and now outnumber people in western Timor, contributing to ecological pressure while providing a money income for owners. Over the past 20 years some Atoni have also moved to Kupang for unskilled work.

Industrial Arts. Atoni produce fine woven cloths for male and female dress, together with basketry and ropes in great varieties for daily and ceremonial use. They do not work metal and must import both tools and the silver and gold jewelry that they value. Woodworking is now limited to house and some furniture construction. Wooden utensils made in the past are no longer found, nor is wooden statuary (except in some funeral contexts).

Division of Labor. Men and women engage in a variety of planting and harvesting activities in fields, orchards, and gardens, and both can be found in markets selling produce. Men mainly build and repair swidden fences and corrals, manage cattle, and hunt, while women tend small animals, gather wild plants, and have primary responsibility for the children.

Land Tenure. Atoni are primarily swidden cultivators of maize and rice fields who have rights of usufruct on land over which clans and territorial groups hold long-term rights. Orchards are held by the families of the planters and may be inherited. Land is not, in general, a commodity. The nuclear family is the primary farming unit, working its own plot alone or with some near kin.

Kinship

Kin Groups and Descent. Atoni belong to named, exogamous patrilineal descent groups, or "name groups" (_kanaf_), which may be extensive in size and widely distributed within a territory but which are not corporate. Localized lineages of the same "name group" (some of which may in fact use different names) are the cooperative units for ritual, economic, legal, or marriage activities. Atoni place importance on continuing affinal alliance ties between lineages that stand in complementary relationships as wife givers and wife takers.

Kinship Terminology. Atoni have a Dravidian type of kinship terminology that clearly distinguishes affines from agnates in Ego's generation and the first ascending and descending generations. In the second ascending and descending generations, agnates and affines are merged terminologically in many Atoni areas, though in some areas the distinction is maintained. Consistent with an Atoni ideal of symmetrical marriage exchange, mother's brother's daughters and father's sister's daughters are called by the same term.

Marriage and Family

Marriage. Marriage, an ideal and norm that marks adult status, is viewed as establishing or maintaining alliances between local lineages. Marriages may be arranged to continue old alliances, or an individual may choose a spouse and their marriage will then establish new alliances. In either case, parents and lineage-mates are involved because marriage establishes continuing relationships between wife givers and wife takers that are important in daily and ritual life. Bride-wealth is paid over time and goods are exchanged between affinal allies at subsequent life-cycle ceremonies. The amounts and the duration of payments vary in different Atoni territories and, within the same territory, by social status as well as by the type of alliance made. In general, marriages to persons more closely related through previous marriages, or to persons from the same or nearby villages, require lower payments than marriages to more distant persons. Postmarital residence is normally virilocal, though it may be temporarily uxorilocal. Divorce and remarriage are possible though not frequent and may entail bride-wealth repayment depending upon determination of fault.

Domestic Unit.   The domestic unit is normally a nuclear family of about five persons (extended families are uncommon), and occasionally includes "borrowed children" from other families or widows/widowers. Widowed or divorced persons, however, often live alone or with a child or grandchild in a separate domestic unit, usually near close relatives.

Inheritance.   Atoni may distinguish between inherited property, which remains within a patrilineage and normally goes to sons, and property acquired in a marriage, which may be inherited by a spouse and/or male and female children. The former category, not extensive, may involve heirlooms or orchard land. The latter may include orchards, livestock, or money. There is pressure to keep property within patrilineages or close affinal groups.

Socialization.   Children are socialized mainly within the nuclear-family-based domestic unit or by mother's brothers (the primary wife givers), and they participate in the work of the parents. Gender differences are marked early in life. Both parents socialize and educate young children through public verbal and physical affection and discipline. Corporal punishment of children by parents, of younger siblings by older siblings, and of females by males is considered acceptable. As children grow toward adolescence, they must show public deference to all elders, including parents, although they may be closer to their mother's brothers and father's sisters than to other elders. There are no initiation rites nowadays outside church christening ceremonies, although warfare played a role in that regard in the past for young males. From 1970 to 1990, school education expanded considerably for young people.

Sociopolitical Organization

Social Organization.   Formerly Atoni had noble, commoner, and slave classes, but society is increasingly egalitarian. Slavery was abolished by the Dutch and princedoms were eliminated by the Indonesian government in the 1970s, though former noble families may still have more access to resources than do commoners. Society is rooted in clan membership and affinal relationships between clans, and village leadership is often passed down in patrilines (as was true in the princedoms). There are no other formal groups in village society, though churches form the basis for social interaction in many villages.

Political Organization.   Until the early 1970s, Atoni were subjects of many self-governing princedoms. After 1912 these were organized by the Netherlands-Indies government into three districts, headed by Dutch administrators. After 1950 these districts (*kabupaten*) were headed by Indonesians. In the 1970s the princedoms became subdistricts (*kecamatan*) of the Indonesian state bureaucracy, some headed by former

princes, others not. Elected headmen now serve the government, though many are from leading local patrilines of the past. At the village level, informal dual headmen may be found, one to deal with government matters and another to handle customary issues. Recognized clan elders from the past princedoms may serve informal leadership roles within the subdistricts as well.

Social Control.   Conflict may arise over inheritance, marriage, and other domestic disputes, theft of orchard products and animals, or personal offenses. Disputes are settled primarily at village level between agnates and affines of those concerned, or by customary village heads, with compensation being the primary means of settlement. In the past princes were ultimate courts of appeal, and now problems may be carried to local Indonesian subdistrict authorities. Moral or ritual missteps and infractions are believed to be punished by ancestors, by curses supported by transcendental justice, and, among Christians, by God.

Religion and Expressive Culture

Religious Beliefs.   Christianity (Catholic in North-Central Timor and Protestant in South-Central Timor and Kupang Districts) has spread rapidly during the past two decades. Previously most Atoni followed traditional beliefs in Lords of the Sky and Earth, ancestral rewards and punishments, ghosts, and spirits of places and things. Magical complexes associated with warfare and headhunting are now gone, and certain other institutions are fading, such as sacred houses of clans, sacred clan regalia, and propitiatory stones and posts. Belief in ancestral power, spirits, transcendental justice, and the power in life-cycle rituals remain, however, and traditional beliefs and Christianity are combined in complex ways.

Religious Practitioners.   Specialists in the supernatural (*mnane* or *meo*) still may divine sources of affliction privately, propitiate Lords of the Sky and Earth, and deal with spirits regarding illness, sorcery, and other afflictions, while Christian leaders seek to integrate Christian belief into Atoni daily life and also assist people in dealing with afflictions. Officiants who propitiated for the princedom's welfare and triumph in war no longer practice, and masters of clan ritual are less important.

Ceremonies.   Apart from ubiquitous Christian home and church services to deal with the life cycle and affliction, public ceremonies involving agnates and affines focus on marriage and death (which bring together these basic social groupings and include village mates). Less public local lineage ceremonies still concern birth and agriculture (planting and harvesting), though these too are more marked by Christian prayer.

Arts.   Dances and gong-and-drum music associated with traditional religious ritual have declined with the advance of Christianity and the reduction of patronage once received from princes, as has the formalized and poetic speaking ritual, important to nobles. Material arts are few, other than fine tie-dye weaving by women and ornamental basketry made by both sexes.

Medicine.   Illness may have natural or supernatural causes. Herbal medicines for the former are widely known. Some Atoni have medicine for the latter, but there are recognized specialists (mnane or meo) who deal with the supernatural. Birth is natural, aided by knowledgeable women, not specialists. Biomedical facilities are limited to some towns and rural health posts, and thus are not easily accessible to most Atoni.

Death and the Afterlife.   Atoni funeral ritual separates the deceased from living agnates and ensures that the spirit joins ancestors and does not wander on earth. Funerals require that the wife-giving affines of the deceased—who are responsible for an Atoni's soul throughout his/her lifetime—lead a cortege (and carry the front of the coffin) from the house of the deceased to the burial ground. Death is the major life-cycle ritual and calls for attendance by many agnates, affines, and hamlet mates, and the exchange of formal gifts. In the past, funerals, marriages, and annual tribute offerings of princes were the major ceremonial events binding the subjects of a princedom together. Today Christian ceremonial plays an increasing part in Atoni funerals.

Bibliography

Cunningham, Clark E. (1973). "Order in the Atoni House." In _Right and Left: Essays on Dual Symbolic Classification_, edited by Rodney Needham, 204–238. Chicago: University of Chicago Press.

McWilliam, Andres R. (1989). "Narrating the Gate and the Path: Place and Precedence in South West Timor." Ph.D. Thesis, Department of Anthropology, Research School of Pacific Studies, Australian National University, Canberra.

Ormeling, F. J. (1956). _The Timor Problem: A Geographical Interpretation of an Underdeveloped Island._ Groningen and Bandung: J. B. Wolters.

Schulte Nordholt, H. G. (1971). _The Political System of the Atoni of Timor._ The Hague: Martinus Nijhoff.

Sherlock, Kevin (1980). A _Bibliography of Timor._ Research School of Pacific Studies, Aids to Research Series, no. A/4. Canberra: Australian National University.

CLARK E. CUNNINGHAM

Bagobo

The Bagobo (Manobo, Manuvu, Obbo, Obo) may be thought of as several groups of people, each of whom speak one of three Bagobo languages; these languages belong to the Manobo Family. Until sometime in this century, there were two major groups, which were distinguished from each other by geographic separation and by several cultural distinctions. The upland Bagobo live in the very mountainous region between the upper Pulangi and Davao rivers on Mindanao in the Philippines, whereas the coastal Bagobo once lived in the hills south and east of Mount Apo. The coastal Bagobo were influenced by Christianity, plantations, and resettlement among coastal Bisayans; they now reside either with the upland Bagobo or with the Bisayans and do not exist as a separate group.

Upland Bagobo numbered 30,000 in 1962. Their traditional subsistence is derived approximately 75 percent from swidden fields that yield rice, maize, sweet potatoes, and other crops. Twenty-five percent of their diet comes from hunting, fishing, and gathering. Some villages consist of only a few families on a hilltop and are impermanent owing to the needs of swidden farming. In larger valleys, up to 100 families may live together in more permanent villages. They are organized by bilateral kindreds that work together to pay bridewealth, for wergild, and to form vengeance groups. Bilateral kinship reckoning, a strict incest prohibition, and small villages together make most villages exogamous. Residence is matrilocal. Until World War II, villages were autonomous and were governed by one or more _datus_, who were wealthy legal authorities and negotiators. After World War II, a single datu gained control over the entire area, in response to intrusions by loggers and Christian Filipinos.

The Bagobo believe in a supreme being who inhabits the sky world, as well as a deity who brings sickness and death to incestuous couples. The Bagobo are also known for their long epic poems, _tuwaang_.

Bibliography

Manuel, E. Arsenio (1975). "Upland Bagobo (Manuvu)." In _Ethnic Groups of Insular Southeast Asia_, edited by Frank M. LeBar. Vol. 2, _Philippines and Formosa_, 47-50. New Haven: HRAF Press.

Bahnar

ETHNONYMS: Alakong, Bonom, Ho Drong, Jo Long, Kon Ko De, Kontum, Krem, Tolo, To Sung

A group enumerated at 136,859 in 1985, located in southeast Lai-Cong Tum province in Vietnam. The Bahnar have considerable contact, including intermarriage, with neighboring groups such as the Sedang, and were closely aligned with the French colonists. As with many other Mon-Khmer Language groups, Bahnar villages are characterized by centrally located, large, well-built communal or men's houses. Each village is governed by a headman, with a number of neighboring villages aligned into an administrative unit called a *toring*. There is some evidence of a class structure in traditional Bahnar society, consisting of freemen, debtors, foreigners, and slaves. The traditional religion is based on the direct relationship between an individual and the spirits and ghosts that influence daily affairs.

See also Muong

Bibliography

Mole, Robert L. (1970). *The Montagnards of South Vietnam.* Rutland, Vt.: Charles E. Tuttle.

Bajau

ETHNONYMS: Badjaw, Bajau Laut, Bajo, Luwa'an, Pala'au, Sama, Sama Dilaut, Turijene'

Orientation

Identification. Variants of the Malay term "Bajau" (e.g., Badjaw, Badjao, Bajo, etc.) are applied to a variety of predominantly maritime Sama-Bajau-speaking peoples whose scattered settlements are found throughout a vast region of islands and coastal littorals, extending from the southern Philippines to the northern and eastern coasts of Borneo, and eastward over much of eastern Indonesia, from Sulawesi to Timor. In Malaysia and Indonesia the term "Bajau" is applied to both boat-nomadic and sedentary populations, including some land-based, primarily agricultural groups with no apparent history of past nomadism. In the southern Philippines the term "Bajau" is reserved exclusively for boat-nomadic or formerly nomadic groups, while more sedentary Sama speakers are referred to as "Samal," a name applied to them by the neighboring Tausug, but used also by Christian Filipinos (see Samal). In eastern Indonesia the Bajau are called "Bajo" by the Bugis and both "Bajo" and "Turijene'" (people of the water) by the Makassarese. The most common term of self-designation is "Sama" or "a'a Sama" (a'a, "people"), generally coupled with a toponymic modifier to indicate geographical and/or dialectal affiliation. Historically the Bajau have lacked overall political cohesion and primary loyalties are generally with these smaller subgroupings. In Sulu and southeastern Sabah, boat-dwelling groups and those with a recent history of boat-nomadism identify themselves as "Sama dilaut" or "Sama mandilaut" (sea Sama). They are referred to by other Sama speakers as "Sama pala'au" (or "pala'u") and by the Tausug as "luwa'an." Both names have pejorative connotations, reflecting the pariah status generally ascribed to boat-nomads by those living ashore. In Malaysia and Indonesia nomadic or formerly nomadic groups are known as "Bajau Laut" or "Orang Laut" (sea people).

Location. In Sabah (Malaysia) the Bajau are present along both the eastern and western coasts of the state and in the foothills bordering the western coastal plains, from Kuala Penyu to Tawau on the east. In eastern Indonesia the largest numbers are found on the islands and in coastal districts of Sulawesi. Here, widely scattered communities, most of them pile-house settlements, are reported near Menado, Ambogaya, and Kendari; in the Banggai, Sula, and Togian island groups; along the Straits of Tioro; in the Gulf of Bone; and along the Makassar coast. Elsewhere settlements are present near Balikpapan in East Kalimantan, on Maratua, Pulau Laut, and Kakaban, and in the Balabalangan islands off the eastern Borneo coast. Others are reported, widely scattered, from Halmahera through the southern Moluccas, along both sides of Sape Strait dividing Flores and Sumbawa; on Lombok, Lembata, Pantar, Adonara, Sumba, Ndao, and Roti; and near Sulamu in western Timor. In Sabah, boat-nomadic and formerly nomadic Bajau Laut are present in the southeastern Semporna district, while Sulu-related groups are found in the Philippines in small numbers from Zamboanga through the Tapul, western Tawitawi, and Sibutu island groups, with major concentrations in the Bilatan Islands, near Bongao, Sanga-Sanga, and Sitangkai.

Demography. Boat-dwelling groups have never, from the earliest historical evidence available, constituted more than a small fraction of the total Sama-Bajau-speaking population. However, their numbers have declined rapidly in the last century, and today they probably amount to fewer than 10,000. In eastern Indonesia, the Bajau as a whole, including both nomadic and sedentary groups, number between 150,000 and 200,000, and in Sabah, approximately 120,000, including at least 30,000–40,000 recent Philippine migrants.

Linguistic Affiliation. All of the scattered populations variously referred to as "Bajau" are Sama-Bajau speakers. However, not all Sama-Bajau speakers are Bajau. A member of the Hesperonesian Branch of Austronesian, the Sama-Bajau Language Family includes some ten languages, the majority of which are spoken almost exclusively in the Philippines, by a variety of people including the Yakan, Samal, and others not ordinarily known as "Bajau." In eastern Indonesia the Bajau speak what appears to be a single language, characterized by only minor dialectal differences, known as Indonesian Bajau. In the eastern coastal districts of Sabah, at least two closely related varieties of Bajau are spoken, known as Central and Southern Sama. In Sabah the two are frequently classed together as East Coast Bajau. Both are divided into a variety of local dialects with close links to allied dialects spoken by Samal groups in the neighboring Sulu Archipelago of the Philippines. A separate language, known as West Coast

Bajau, is spoken in the northern and western coastal districts from Kuala Penyu to Terusan, with some overlap with East Coast Bajau in northern Sabah. Recent linguistic studies show that the boat-nomadic Bajau Laut are not a linguistically homogeneous population, nor are they linguistically distinct as a group from the shore-based Sama-speaking communities present around them. Those living in Semporna and southern Sulu speak Southern Sama, while those in western Tawitawi and central and northern Sulu speak varieties of Central Sama. Except for the division in Sabah between East and West Coast Bajau, locally contiguous dialects, whether spoken ashore by settled land-based groups or at sea by boat-nomadic or partially nomadic communities, are usually mutually intelligible, in most areas grading into one another without sharply defined language boundaries.

History and Cultural Relations

A variety of local legends traces the original dispersal of the Bajau to the loss or abduction of a princess, a mythic event variously associated with the different early sultanates of the region: Johore, Malacca, Brunei, Sulu, Luwu, or Bone. In more prosaic terms, linguistic evidence suggests that the Proto-Sama-Bajau-speaking ancestors of the present Bajau began to spread from an original homeland located in the northeastern islands of Sulu, southwest of Mindanao, sometime early in the first millennium A.D. The principal movement was southwestward, through the Sulu Archipelago of the Philippines, to the eastern Borneo coast. From Sulu and eastern Borneo, subsequent migrations carried Bajau speakers eastward through the Straits of Makassar to coastal Sulawesi and from there southeastward into the Moluccas. By the early seventeenth century, Dutch accounts of Sulawesi record the presence of large numbers of Bajau around Makassar. Following Makassar's defeat by Dutch and Bugis forces in 1669, many of these communities are said to have dispersed to other islands in eastern Indonesia. By the early eighteenth century, fleets of Bajau were voyaging on fishing and _trepang_-collecting expeditions as far south as Roti and Timor. Some of our fullest descriptions of the Indonesian Bajau come from this period. Most are described as strongly maritime people, sea-going dependents of either Bugis or Makassarese patrons. The outward spread of the Bajau from Sulawesi appears to have been closely linked to the development of a maritime trade in trepang (sea slug or _bêche-de-mer_), a Chinese culinary delicacy, and to the associated expansion of Bugis and Makassarese political and commercial influence. For almost 200 years the Bajau acted as the principal gatherers of trepang throughout the eastern islands of Indonesia. In northern Borneo, the Bajau were already well established when Captain Thomas Forrest first visited the western and northern coasts of what is now Sabah in 1773. In western Sabah, the Bajau were under the loose suzerainty of the Brunei sultanate and in some areas, notably Tempasuk, maintained close ties with small Illanun enclaves; some of them, during the eighteenth and nineteenth centuries, staged settlements for slave-raiding voyages into other parts of Southeast Asia. On the southeastern coast of Sabah, the Bajau were historically part of the Sulu zone, a maritime sphere of political and commercial interests dominated by the Sulu sultanate and its Tausug rulers. Here the principal seat of power was at Jolo, in the central islands of the Sulu Archipelago. In 1878 the territory now comprising Sabah was ceded by the sultans of Sulu and Brunei to the British North Borneo Chartered Company, while in 1915 the Sultan of Sulu relinquished all secular power over his former territories to American colonial authorities in Manila. The subsequent colonial period saw the breakdown of traditional patterns of administered trade and formal hierarchy, the abolition of slavery, the emergence of Chinese and European commercial interests, and the partial suppression of traditional forms of piracy and raiding. In Sabah, the Mat Salleh Revolt (1894–1900), which was the first major uprising against European rule, was led by a leader of Bajau-Sulu ancestry. Since 1963, when Sabah gained independence within Malaysia, and throughout most of the postcolonial period, the Bajau, as the largest Muslim minority, have played a decisive role in state politics, disproportionate to their numbers. In Indonesia change has been equally rapid since independence. Here Bajau communities have been under official pressure to abandon boat-nomadism and nearly all are now shore-based, living in coastal villages, characteristically dependent on fishing, trade, and other maritime pursuits for their livelihood.

Settlements

Local communities take a wide variety of forms. At one extreme, among Bajau Laut boat-dwellers, local communities consist of scattered moorage groups made up of families whose members regularly return, between intervals of fishing, to a common anchorage site. Such communities tend to be fluid in makeup and are characteristically organized around smaller family alliance groups (_pagmundah_). The latter are comprised of anything from two to six closely related boat-dwelling families whose members regularly fish and anchor together, often sharing food and pooling labor, nets, and other gear. Intermoorage relationships are maintained through intermarriage, frequent exchange of visits, and the movement of families from one group to another. Such relations, and a similar status as clients of surrounding shore people, reinforce a wider sense of identity. Somewhat less extreme are pile-house villages made up of families whose members regularly move between the village and extended periods at sea as boat-dwelling family fishing crews. Houses in such communities are often small and poorly constructed; some of them are too low to permit their occupants to stand upright inside. Such communities are generally those of recently settled boat-nomads. More typical are well-established pile-house villages. Here village members fish largely in all-male crews, on a daily or overnight basis, returning to the village for meals and to sleep. Such settlements generally consist of densely clustered houses built in close association with nipa and mangrove forests, where village members find seasonal employment as thatch- or woodcutters, particularly during the northwest monsoon when squalls and high seas prevent open-sea fishing. Houses usually consist of a single unpartitioned room, raised on piles 1 to 2 meters above the ground or highwater mark. Most are fronted by an open porch or platform, often serving as a common work area, with an attached kitchen at the rear. Finally, at the opposite extreme are land-based villages built inland from the immediate shoreline. Here individual houses are generally separated by house compounds, fruit trees, and gardens. Houses, both ashore and in tidal settlements, are individually owned, with the house owner generally acting as the household head or spokesman. Households are grouped into clusters (*tumpuk* or *ba'anan*). Most clusters contain between two and five closely related and physically adjacent households, although a few headed by especially wealthy or effective leaders may be considerably larger, attracting the allegiance of more distant kin and affines. Household spokesmen and other core-cluster members are most often related as married siblings, spouses of siblings, or members of closely related sibling sets. Because of the tendency to uxorilocal residence, ties between married sisters generally predominate. One household head is looked to as the cluster spokesman. A cluster may coincide with a parish, a group of households affiliated with a single mosque. More often, however, a parish contains more than one cluster, with one cluster spokesman, typically the mosque owner or sponsor, acknowledged as the principal parish leader. A parish might comprise a village, or be larger or smaller. In villages containing more than one parish, one parish leader, having the support of the majority of household spokesmen, acts as village headman.

Among boat-nomadic groups, the boats used as family dwellings vary in size and construction. Those of northern and central Sulu are basically small dug-out vessels with double outriggers, while farther south, in southern Sulu and southeastern Sabah, boats are generally larger, averaging 10 meters with a beam of between 2 and 2.5 meters, lack outriggers, and are plank-constructed with solid keel and bow sections. All are equipped with a roofed living area made of poles and *kajang* matting and a portable earthenware hearth used for preparing family meals, usually carried near the stern.

Economy

Subsistence and Commercial Activities. For many groups, although by no means all, fishing is the principal source of livelihood. In Sabah, where the Bajau comprise less than 20 percent of the population, they make up over two-thirds of the state's fishermen. However, except for the Bajau Laut, other communities are economically flexible, adopting farming where land is available, or taking up other occupations. In western Sabah, most Bajau settlements are located inland from the immediate coastline, chiefly along the lower rivers draining the western coastal plains. Here the majority practice farming, engage in trade, and rear water buffalo, cattle, and horses. In addition, some travel inland annually to join interior communities in rice harvesting in return for a share of the crop. For agricultural or partially agricultural groups, the main crops grown are rice, cassava, maize, bananas, and, as cash crops, copra and fruit. Fishing communities are characteristically located close to areas of coral reef, submerged terraces, bays, channels, or stretches of inshore water sheltered by fringing reefs, islands, or coastal headlands. The marine life exploited by Bajau fishermen is diverse, including over 200 species of fish, large varieties of shellfish, crustaceans, dolphins and other sea mammals, sea turtles (taken for their shell, eggs, and egg sacks), sea urchins, and edible algae. Fishing equipment includes driftnets, liftnets, spears, spearguns, handlines, longlines, traps, harpoons, explosives, lures, jigs, and poisons. Since the 1950s, major technological changes have included the introduction of manu-

factured nylon netting, explosives, and motorized fishing vessels. Fishing activity varies with tides, monsoonal and local winds, currents, migrations of pelagic fish, and the monthly lunar cycle. Most driftnetting is done on falling tides, with favored periods coinciding with the new, full, and "dark" or late-rising phases of the moon. During moonless nights, fishing is often done with lanterns, using spears and handlines. Catches include skates, cuttlefish, and squid. Ebb tides are important for gathering, diving for shellfish, and inshore and beach netting. In exposed areas, monsoon winds often require seasonal shifts in fishing grounds and occasional suspension of fishing during high seas. Today fishing is primarily for market sale. Most fish are preserved by salting or drying. In villages located close to urban areas, landings may also be sold directly to retail vendors or to local middlemen for export sale. In the Philippines the introduction of agar-agar aquaculture in the mid-1970s dramatically affected the local economy of southern Sulu. Together with secessionist conflict and rapid population growth, it has led to a massive influx of newcomers, mainly Tausug and Samal from central Sulu, who have tended to displace Bajau Laut populations from their traditional fishing grounds in the southern Sibutu and Tawitawi islands, forcing many to migrate as refugees into southeastern Sabah. Here their numbers are swelling an already burgeoning fishing population. As a result, the rich coral reefs of the region, which for centuries provided protein and local trading wealth, are under increasing threat of destruction.

Industrial Arts. Shore- and land-based groups tend to specialize in different lines of trade and craft production; some communities, for example, act as centers of boat building, pottery making, weaving, blacksmithing, or interisland trade and transport. Other specialized crafts include the manufacture of kajang mats and roofing; pandanus mats, sunhats, and food covers; shell bracelets, tortoise-shell combs and other ornaments, lime and salt making, and skilled carpentry and woodcarving.

Trade. Trade occupies a central place in the Bajau economy. Historically, the Bajau were highly valued by the traditional trading states of the region for their specialized seafaring skills. European accounts of the seventeenth and eighteenth centuries attest to their local importance as suppliers of marine commodities, boat builders, seamen, and occasionally pirates and slave raiders. Bajau in western Sabah historically traded with inland Dusun communities, exchanging dried fish, salt, lime, shell ornaments, and other coastal products for rice, fruit, tobacco, and forest and agricultural goods. Out of this trade evolved a network of periodic markets, known as *tamu*, held at from five- to twenty-day intervals. Today, along both sides of the Philippine border, smuggling provides a lucrative living for those with the necessary capital and commercial connections.

Division of Labor. Both men and women participate in farm work. Smithing, boat building, and interisland trade are male occupations, while women weave and make and market pottery. Except for boat-nomadic groups, fishing is carried out by all-male crews, with women and children engaging in inshore gathering.

Land Tenure. Among boat-dwelling and other strongly maritime groups, fishing grounds are available for common exploitation. For the Bajau Laut, fishing areas typically overlap, making possible cooperation between families from neighboring moorage groups, particularly during large-scale fish drives. Among more settled fishermen, fish-trap and liftnet sites and artificially constructed fish corrals are subject to individual ownership; otherwise, as with other groups, fishing grounds are unowned. Historically, boat-nomadic communities were without land or other property ashore, except for small burial islands. Here the dead of several neighboring moorage groups were buried. In addition, community members were allowed access to sources of fresh water, usually a well or spring, and the use of the immediate shoreline (which provided certain supplies, such as bamboo for masts and poles), in return for their economic services as clients. Among shore- and land-based groups, virtually no form of corporate ownership exists, and houses and both residential and farm land are held and inherited under individual rights of tenure.

Kinship

Despite marked differences of economic orientation and settlement, the basic features of social organization are essentially similar. Kinship is bilateral, genealogical reckoning is generally shallow, and kin groups with corporate functions are lacking.

Kin Groups and Descent. Among the Bajau Laut, close kindred are distinguished from both kin generally, whether the relationship between them is traceable or not (*kampong*), and nonkin, or "other people" (*a'a saddi*). Among a person's *kampong*, individual descent lines (*turunan*) are recognized, each leading back to a particular ancestor; close kindred (*dampalanakan* or *dampo'un*) constitute, minimally, those sharing descent from common grandparents (*mbo'*), such as Ego's cognates traced bilaterally through first cousins. Descent as such, however, is of little social significance and the principal emphasis is on collateral ties. Between an individual's dampalanakan, mutual assistance is considered obligatory unless relations are ruptured by formal enmity (*bantah*), and applies in a variety of situations (i.e., life-crisis rites, illness, economic distress, litigation, and conflict). Close kindred characteristically form the core of multifamily households, household clusters, and parish groups.

Kinship Terminology. Terminology emphasizes generation, lineality, and relative age. Cousin terms are of the Eskimo type.

Marriage and Family

Marriage. Kin are favored as marriage partners. Exceptions are the children of brothers and those nursed by the same mother or nursemaid. Marriage is either parentally arranged or initiated by elopement or abduction. Arranged marriages are the ideal, but elopement is frequent. Marriage negotiations are normally set in motion by the man's family, often with the help of a go-between. After a proposal is accepted, the bride's father designates one of his kinsmen to act as his daughter's guardian (*wakil*). The man chosen formally receives bride-wealth from the groom's family and represents the woman's side during the wedding ceremony. The religious component of the rite is conducted by an imam. Weddings usually take place in the guardian's house, to which the cou-

ple is conducted in separate ceremonial processions, often with music and dancing. Divorce is frequent during the first two or three years of marriage and remarriage is relatively easy for both partners. After that, divorce tends to be infrequent. Following marriage, a couple is expected to set up its own household within two or three years, except for one child, usually the youngest, who normally remains to look after the parental couple in their old age. New houses are generally built close to the natal household of the bride. Polygyny is permitted but infrequent.

Domestic Unit. Domestic organization is variable. Among boat-dwelling groups, each boat typically shelters a nuclear family, plus often one or two additional kin, averaging, in all, five or six persons. Here the family is both a domestic group and an independent economic unit. Among groups whose members divide their time between village residence and dispersal at sea, domestic organization is characteristically complex. While the nuclear family functions independently at sea, its members are frequently incorporated, upon their return to the village, into larger, multifamily households. The members of these larger groups share a common hearth, meals, and residence within a single village pile house; they are identified by name with its owner, as his *tindug* (followers). Among settled, shore- and land-based groups, households are often large. Although the majority are reported to contain a single stem or nuclear family, larger groups, consisting of the families of two or more married siblings, are not uncommon. Each household has an acknowledged head. The latter, usually the house owner, is most often a man still actively engaged in making a living.

Inheritance. Inheritance is generally bilateral. Many forms of property, however, are associated through their use with one sex or the other. Such property ordinarily passes from father to son, or from mother to daughter. Examples of traditional male property are cattle, farmland, suspended gongs, and fishing boats; female property includes household furnishings, cooking utensils, jewelry, and *kulintangan* (stationary gongs). In addition, the Bajau distinguish between property acquired in the course of marriage and property inherited separately, to which the owner's spouse acquires no claim.

Socialization. Preadolescent children traditionally undergo ritual haircutting (*maggunting*), followed by prayers, weighing (*magtimbang*), and a public distribution of foodstuffs. At puberty boys are circumcised, while in most communities girls undergo partial clitoridectomy between the ages of 2 and 6. Unlike male circumcision, the latter is a small private rite witnessed only by women. For one or two years, most children receive a course of Koranic instruction. Those who complete their studies undergo a "graduation" ceremony (*magtammat*) sponsored by their parents. Today, in addition, most children attend public school, although few complete more than three or four years of primary education.

Sociopolitical Organization

Social Organization. Boat-dwelling and strongly maritime communities tend to be internally egalitarian. Others, particularly those closely linked in the past to the trading polities of the region, developed systems of stratification much like those of the dominant Tausug, Maguindanao, Bugis, and others, comprised of nobles, commoners, and slaves. During the eighteenth and nineteenth centuries, slave raiding was characteristic of most areas of Bajau settlement and local populations absorbed large numbers of slaves, most of them captives from other areas of the Philippines and Indonesia, many of whom eventually gained their freedom, some rising to positions of prominence and wealth.

Political Organization. In Sulu and southeastern Sabah, the sultan of Sulu historically claimed proprietary rights over all boat-dwelling Bajau. Outside of Jolo these rights were generally delegated to regional leaders acting locally as the sultan's representatives. In practice, proprietorship was expressed in patron-client relations. As patrons, local shore leaders asserted "ownership" over individual moorage groups. Implied was a willingness to defend the rights entailed from outsiders. The relationship involved privileged trade, boat-dwelling clients supplying their patron with fish and other sea products, formerly including trade commodities like mother-of-pearl and trepang, in return for assurances of physical security, a moorage site, and agricultural foodstuffs. Should a patron fail to protect his clients, or impose oppressive terms of trade, a boat group might quit its former anchorage site and seek out a rival leader willing to take the place of its former patron. Thus mobility and competition for clientage among shore leaders checked abuses of the relationship and assured the Bajau Laut a considerable degree of political autonomy. However, boat-dwelling groups traditionally lacked parish organization, and therefore had no formal representation in the state except through their patrons. In contrast, shore and land-based groups have always had their own parish, village, and regional leadership, with personal authority operating largely through leader-centered coalitions. While the power of individual leaders is locally based, each historically owed allegiance to the sultan or local head of state. The position of more powerful regional leaders was legitimized through their investiture with titles. Thus the sultan incorporated local communities into the larger polity by appointing proven local leaders to act in his name as representatives of the state. In return for tribute and political fealty, titleholders were granted rights to conduct and regulate trade, levy taxes, maintain order, and administer the law. Today regional leaders operate largely in the context of electoral politics or through state appointment and serve generally as links between community leaders and the national administrative structure in any of the three countries involved.

Social Control. Responsibility for resolving disputes falls chiefly on house elders and parish and village leaders. Above the village level, factional rivalries tend to be pervasive.

Conflict. Boat-dwelling Bajau Laut see themselves, in contrast to their neighbors, as nonaggressive people who prefer flight to physical confrontation; in the past, individual moorage groups looked to their patrons ashore to insulate them from the endemic feuding and competition for power occurring around them. As a consequence, the politically dominant groups of the region have historically viewed the Bajau Laut with disdain as timid, unreliable subjects. Among shore groups vendettas occur, sometimes resulting in long-term enmity, but endemic armed conflict is generally lacking. In the past, many groups engaged in slave raiding, often in conjunction with trade, and were recruited from time to time by the regional states of the area as a naval fighting force.

Religion and Expressive Culture

Religious Beliefs. The Bajau are Sunni Muslims of the Shafi school. Claims to religious piety and learning are an important source of individual prestige, and persons considered descendants of the Prophet (*salip*) are shown special deference. Perceived differences in degrees of Islamic practice are also associated with the relative status of different Bajau groups. Those most closely identified with the historical trading states of the region are generally regarded as the most orthodox, with the Bajau Laut, as the most peripheral group, seen by others as living outside the faith, as non-Muslims. Owing to their boat-nomadic way of life, Bajau Laut moorage groups lack mosques. For those ashore, the mosque represents the primary focus of community leadership and religion. In adopting settled village life, the members of Bajau Laut communities normally construct a mosque in addition to individual houses, and so undergo not only ethnic assimilation but also overt Islamization. Sedentarization is thus marked by a change of religious status (which is often contested, but generally acknowledged in time), and by the emergence of newly recognized positions of community leadership.

God (Tuhan) is the creator of heaven and earth, of the first man (Adam) and woman (Hawa), and of Iblis, or Satan, who leads people to evil. God is also the creator of good, as revealed by the Prophet, the traditions, and law (*sara'*). All events ultimately occur by the will of God. In this world, however, human purposes may also be thwarted or furthered by the actions of spirits or the agency of human evildoers. These latter forces are dealt with mainly by charms, amulets, offerings, mediumship, and divination.

Religious Practitioners. Except for boat-nomadic groups, every parish is served by a set of mosque officials. These include an imam, who leads parish members in prayer; a *bilal*, who performs the call to prayer; and a *hatib*, who gives the Friday mosque reading. The imam also officiates at life-crisis rituals, counsels parish members in religious and legal matters, and leads them in prayer during minor rites of thanksgiving. In times of misfortune or crises, other religious practitioners may also be consulted, including midwives, herbalist-curers, spirit mediums, and diviners.

Ceremonies. The annual Islamic calendar includes: a month of fasting (*puasa*); Hari Raya Puasa, a feast to celebrate the end of Ramadan; Hari Raya Haji, a feast of sacrifice observed during the month of Jul-Hadj; *tulak bala'*, a ritual bathing performed to cleanse away evil during the month of Sappal; and Maulud, the birthday of the Prophet. Among boat-dwelling and formerly boat-dwelling groups, community spirit mediums are assembled at least once a year for a public séance and nightly trance-dancing (*magigal jin*). In times of epidemic illness, they are also called on to set a spirit-boat (*pamatulikan*) adrift in the open sea beyond the village or anchorage site in order to remove illness-causing spirits from the community.

Arts. Bajau craftsmen have traditionally created ornaments of shell and turtle shell, and embellished houses, boats, house furnishings, and grave markers with carved designs. Pandanus mats are made by women for both sale and home use. In the Tempasuk area of western Sabah, Bajau women weave several types of textiles. The most important are *kain mogah*, long cloths of small, somewhat somber design, used mainly as trade cloth and for house hangings, and _destar_, square headcloths worn by men, woven mainly in rectangular design elements, using brighter dyes and often incorporating figurative motifs. Music and dance are richly elaborated. Musical instruments include the kulintangan, an idiophone of between seven and nine knobbed gongs suspended horizontally in a wooden frame. The kulintangan, providing the main melodic line, is played by women, together with suspended gongs and drums, the latter played by male musicians, either alone or in accompaniment to dance. The _gabbang_, a wooden xylophone, normally of seventeen keys, is also played by women, either as a solo instrument or in accompaniment to singing and dancing. The main dance form that employs the gabbang is the _daling-daling_, performed usually at weddings or betrothals, in which male and female dancers exchange improvised verses of song.

Death and Afterlife.   Death rites follow Islamic practice. The body is bathed and shrouded and buried in a grave niche with its head facing Mecca. If death occurs in the morning, the body is ideally buried before nightfall; if at night, before noon the following day. After a grave is filled, it is often covered with sand or crushed coral and is marked with a stone or wooden marker. Burial is accompanied by a period of vigil lasting up to seven nights. Additional commemorative rites may be held on the 20th, 40th, and 100th day and on the first anniversary of death. Following a period of atonement, an individual's soul is believed to ascend to heaven, while the body descends to hell, where it suffers punishment in proportion to the misdeeds the person committed in life. Spirits of the dead are thought to remain in the vicinity of their graves, at times requiring offerings and other signs of remembrance. Some graves, particularly those of ancestors who possessed extraordinary spiritual or physical powers, may acquire the status of _tampat_, sites of wonder-working power, and be visited by persons in search of special favors.

   See also Samal; Sea Nomads of the Andaman; Selung/Moken

Bibliography

Fox, James J. (1987). "Bajau (Indonesia)." In _Muslim Peoples: A World Ethnographic Survey_, edited by Richard V. Weekes, 80–81. Westport, Conn.: Greenwood Press.

Nimmo, H. Arlo (1972). _The Sea People of Sulu_. San Francisco: Chandler.

Sather, Clifford (1978). "The Bajau Laut." In _Essays on Borneo Societies_, edited by Victor T. King, 172–192. Oxford: Oxford University Press.

Sather, Clifford (1985). "Boat Crews and Fishing Fleets." _Contributions to Southeast Asian Ethnography_ 4:165–214.

Sopher, David (1977). _The Sea Nomads_. Singapore: National Museum.

Warren, James (1971). _The North Borneo Chartered Company's Administration of the Bajau, 1878–1904_. Athens: Ohio University Center for International Studies, Southeast Asia Program.

                                    CLIFFORD SATHER

Balantak

ETHNONYMS: Kosian, Mian Balantak

Numbering about 30,000 in 1982, the Balantak inhabit the most easterly end of the east-central peninsula of Sulawesi Island, Indonesia. Balantak is classified in the West Indonesian Group of the Austronesian Language Family. Rectangular raised houses are scattered among the swidden fields, with small clusters around the local chief. Domestic animals include dogs, fowl, and goats. Swidden production includes rice, yams, taro, and millet. Descent is bilateral. Formerly, the Balantak were ruled by local chiefs and integrated into the Ternate Sultanate. Traditional religious beliefs centered on ancestor worship. Since 1900 Islam and Christianity have been prominent.

   See also Banggai

Bibliography

LeBar, Frank M. (1972). "Balantak." In _Ethnic Groups of Insular Southeast Asia_, edited by Frank M. LeBar. Vol. 1, _Indonesia, Andaman Islands, and Madagascar_, 138–139. New Haven: HRAF Press.

Balinese

ETHNONYMS: none

Orientation

Identification.   The Balinese live on the island of Bali, in the archipelago nation of Indonesia. Both their language, Balinese, and religion, Balinese Hinduism, reflect a Malayo-Polynesian culture influenced by Buddhism and Hinduism.

Location.   Bali is located between 8° and 8°50′ S and 114°20′ and 115°40′ E. The area is 5,580 square kilometers. The climate is tropical with two seasons, rainy between October and March and dry between April and September.

Demography.   In 1989 the population of Bali was about 2,782,038, of which perhaps 5 percent were Chinese, Muslim, and other minorities. The annual population increase was 1.75 percent. Denpasar, the capital, had a population of 261,263.

Linguistic Affiliation.   Balinese is an Austronesian language of the Malayo-Javanic Subgroup. Despite phonological similarity with the languages of eastern Indonesia, Java has been a stronger linguistic and literary influence. Balinese was influenced by Indian languages both directly and through contact with Javanese. The earliest (eighth century A.D.) inscriptions found in Bali are in both Sanskrit and Old Balinese. Balinese has levels of speech that require speakers to adjust vocabulary to their relative caste position and reflect feelings about both the person spoken to and the subject matter spoken about. These levels are most elaborate when discussing the human body and its functions, with nine levels of vocabulary for some lexical items. Balinese script was derived from the Pallava writing systems of southern India.

History and Cultural Relations

Archaeological remains, inscriptions, and literary and oral historical accounts indicate that an indigenous population in Bali came into increasing contact with travelers from Java after the fifth century A.D. These outsiders brought Hindu and Buddhist ideas of religion, language, and political organization. It is not known whether the travelers were themselves from the subcontinent, Indianized inhabitants of Java, or both. In the eleventh century A.D., Airlangga, son of a Balinese king and a Javanese queen, became the first ruler to unite Bali with an eastern Javanese kingdom. For the following three centuries the Balinese were intermittently ruled from the east Javanese kingdom of Majapahit, which fell to Islamic forces in 1515. Court officials then fled to Balinese kingdoms where they strengthened the Indianized literary and statecraft traditions that endured in Bali, which was not influenced by Islam. For the next three centuries Bali had small kingdoms, several of which periodically dominated one or more of the others. The Dutch colonial government largely ignored Bali, which had no good harbor on the northern trade route, until the middle of the nineteenth century. In 1855 the first resident Dutch official arrived in north Bali and colonial control over the island increased thereafter until absolute direct governance was imposed by defeating the southern kingdoms militarily in 1906 and 1908. Direct Dutch colonial rule lasted until the Japanese occupied the island from 1942 to 1945. After World War II there was fighting in Bali between those who supported Indonesian independence and forces attempting to reestablish Dutch colonial rule.

Settlements

The Balinese define a village as the people who worship at a common village temple, not as a territorial unit. In fact, inhabitants almost always live in a contiguous area and both colonial and national governments have sought to redefine the village as a territorially based administrative unit. Settlements are centered on the village temple and public buildings, which are usually situated at the intersection of a major and minor road. Both the village and the house yards within it are ideally laid out, with the most sacred buildings in the area nearest Mount Agung, the abode of the gods, and the profane structures nearest the sea, the region of more ambivalent spiritual beings. Families live in house yards that are open, walled areas containing buildings, including a family temple facing the direction of Mount Agung, one or more pavilions for sleeping and sitting, a kitchen, and a refuse area where pigs are kept. Wealthy families have large yards with brick, tile-roofed buildings decorated with fine carvings in stone and wood. Poor families have smaller yards with buildings and walls being made of mud and wattle.

Economy

Subsistence and Commercial Activities. For centuries the Balinese have been wet-rice farmers whose irrigation system regulates planting on mountain slopes and seaside plains. Yearly double-cropping is common and the national government supports the introduction of several strains that permit three annual crops in certain areas. Small mechanized plows can be used only in level areas. More commonly, water buffalo pull plows in small family fields, often steep terraces on the mountainsides. Although the volcanic soil is naturally rich, multiple-crop schemes require chemical fertilization. The government protects the rice price and buys all excess harvest for redistribution. In the west of the island there is a profitable coffee-growing region and in the north oranges are a cash crop. The local Balinese economy is based almost entirely on agriculture and government employment in offices and schools. Although Bali has a large tourist trade, most local households do not participate in this kind of economic activity.

Industrial Arts. There is no heavy industry in Bali and little light manufacturing. In tourist areas, carvers and painters produce objects for sale to visitors, often on consignment from art shops.

Trade. In towns, goldsmiths, tailors, and other merchants provide consumer goods. Each town has a market for vegetables, fruit, packaged and other foodstuffs, and animals such as pigs and chickens. Such markets are also held on a rotating basis in some villages. Villagers, often women, bring agricultural items to sell and return home with manufactured goods to peddle either door-to-door or in small shops. Alternatively, merchants may go to the village to buy agricultural goods or to sell such items as cloth, patent medicines, or soap. Men sell cattle in a central market.

Division of Labor. In agricultural activities men plow and prepare the fields. Men and women plant and harvest manually in large groups, while weeding is done by family members. Women keep the gardens, care for the pigs, and keep small snack stalls; they often control the income they gain from these activities. Men care for the cattle that are kept in garden areas. Women care for the children, assisted by the husband or other family members. Although men and women replace each other in domestic and agricultural chores when necessary, there is a stricter distinction between men's and women's ritual work. Men are the priests and women make the elaborate offerings used in rituals.

Land Tenure. Legally, rice and garden land are owned and registered in the name of an individual man, although his sons may be working his holdings. Villagers consider land to belong to a patrilineal descent group with the current owner inheriting the right to use, or dispose of, the land. Royal families formerly had large holdings.

Kinship

Kin Groups and Descent. Balinese distinguish different types of kinship relationships. Each type, from the smallest to the most inclusive, is described as a group of men, related through a common ancestor, who worship with their families at a common ancestor temple. The group is organized around the performance of rituals twice a year at these temples. The household has a temple in the house yard. The men (and their families) who divide an inheritance have a larger local ancestor temple. These inheritance groups can be joined into larger putative kin groups, which assert, but cannot trace, descent from a common ancestor. A family may be active only in a small, local ancestor group or they may see themselves as part of a series of nested groups with alliances in other parts of the island. Larger kin groups are likely to form and be strong in factionalized areas and times. Kin-group membership is reckoned patrilaterally but matrilateral kinship is also remembered.

Kinship Terminology.   Kin terms are Hawaiian or generational with all men of father's generation bilaterally referred to as "father," and so on with mother, cousins, grandparents, and children. Individuals have a teknonym that indicates their gender, caste, and birth order. Children are called by this teknonym and adults are called "father of . . . " or "mother of . . . " after the birth of their first child. Old people are known as "grandfather or grandmother of. . . . "

Marriage and Family

Marriage.   Residence after marriage is patrilocal. Although men may have more than one wife, most marriages are monogamous. Ideally women should not marry men of lower caste or kinship group; a family acknowledges inferiority toward their daughter's husband's group. To avoid such an admission in areas where kin groups are strong and opposed, there is a preference for ancestor-temple group endogamy. In other areas most marriages are village-endogamous with wealth and personal attraction playing an important part in marriage choice. Divorce rules vary but generally a woman married less than three years returns to her father's home with nothing. If she has been married more than three years, and is not adulterous, she receives a percentage of what the couple has earned after the marriage, but none of her husband's inheritance. Children of a marriage remain with their father. When a woman has been chosen by her father as his heir, the divorce rules are applied in reverse.

Domestic Unit.   The domestic unit consists of people who eat from the same kitchen. The household includes the husband, wife, children, patrilateral grandparents, and unmarried siblings.

Inheritance.   The Balinese inherit patrilineally. A man without sons may choose a daughter to inherit or allow his brothers to divide his property. The family house yard is inherited by the oldest or the youngest son, who is then responsible for any old people or siblings still living there.

Socialization.   Children are cared for by their parents, grandparents, and older siblings. They are treated with great affection. Boys are taught to be lively and capable, while girls are encouraged to be responsible and attractive.

Sociopolitical Organization

Social Organization.   Balinese individuals and kin groups identify themselves as being members of one of four hereditary caste groups. These groups are said to have in the past corresponded to occupational categories, although this is no longer the case. Ninety percent of the population is Sudra, the group said to have been farmers and considered to be of lower caste. Certain ritual activities are reserved to priests of the Brahman caste and the former rulers who were of the Ksaytria and Wesia castes, but other members of these groups are, and were, farmers and merchants. Families belonging to the three higher castes are more likely to be part of supravillage ancestor-temple groups.

Political Organization.   Bali is one of the twenty-eight provinces of the nation of Indonesia. The province is divided into seven regions (_kabupaten_), each of which is subdivided into districts (_kecamatan_). Districts are divided into villages (_desa_), which are composed of subunits (_banjar_). The units above the village level carry out regional and national policy. The village-level officials are elected by the village council, which is made up of male heads of household. These leaders execute governmental policies such as registration of land sales, births and deaths, and also organize local projects including the repair of facilities and the holding of local elections.

Social Control.   Above the village level there is a police force. In the village there is a system of fines for residents who do not attend meetings or group work projects. However, informal control mechanisms such as gossip and group pressure are used more frequently.

Conflict.   The Balinese avoid the open expression of conflict. Villagers who have protracted quarrels such as legal disputes over inheritance usually try to avoid each other. Supravillage conflict formerly led to warfare.

Religion and Expressive Culture

Religious Beliefs.   Balinese Hinduism mixes Hinduism with animistic traditions. Each temple congregation holds periodic rituals to placate and please the supernaturals and thereby protect the group's peace and prosperity. The Balinese make offerings to their ancestors, spirits connected to places, and other supernaturals, some with Indic names.

Religious Practitioners.   The larger ceremonies are conducted by Brahman priests. Lower-caste priests care for temples and perform local ceremonies.

Ceremonies.   Rituals are performed on several cycles, the most important being the six-month cycle. Every six months there are islandwide ceremonies, and each temple has an anniversary ritual every six months. There are also life-cycle rituals arranged by families, the most important being the cremation.

Arts.   Rituals, whether family or village, may include music, dance, drama, and shadow-play performances. In ritual context artistic performance has a sacred association. Stone and wood carving in home or temple indicates high prestige for the owner or congregation. Royal and wealthy people have supported artistic performances and productions, in part as a display of their prestige. Tourist art includes paintings, carvings, and shortened secular performances.

Medicine.   Government medical care is widely available and used. Indigenous medicine holds that illness or other misfortunes can be caused by angry spirits or ancestors, witchcraft, or imbalance in the bodily humors.

Death and Afterlife.   A person's caste, wealth, and prestige are reflected in the size and elaborateness of his or her funeral. Living descendants must perform rituals that move the deceased souls through the afterlife to rebirth in a younger member of the family. Neglect of these rituals may cause the dead ancestor to make family members ill.

Bibliography

Belo, Jane (1949). *Bali: Rangda and Barong.* Monographs of the American Ethnological Society, 16. Seattle and London: University of Washington Press.

Belo, Jane (1960). *Trance in Bali.* New York: Columbia University Press.

Geertz, Clifford (1980). *Negara: The Theatre State in Nineteenth Century Bali.* Princeton N.J.: Princeton University Press.

Geertz, Hildred, and Clifford Geertz (1975). *Kinship in Bali.* Chicago: University of Chicago Press.

Swellengrebel, J. L., et al. (1960). *Bali: Life, Thought, and Ritual.* The Hague: W. van Hoeve.

Swellengrebel, J. L., et al. (1969). *Bali: Further Studies in Life, Thought, and Ritual.* The Hague: W. van Hoeve.

ANN P. McCAULEY

Banggai

ETHNONYMS: Aki, Mian Banggai, Mian Sea-Sea

A people numbering about 86,000 in 1979, the Banggai inhabit the Banggai Archipelago, off the tip of the east-central peninsula of Sulawesi, Indonesia. The Mian Sea-Sea and Mian Banggai are two subgroups of the Banggai. Both groups speak dialects of Aki, which is classified in the West Indonesian Group of Austronesian languages. Traditionally, houses were scattered among the swidden fields. Under Dutch rule, nucleated villages became the norm. Subsistence is based on yams, taro, maize, sago, bananas, and vegetables. Coconuts are produced for export. Descent is bilateral. Traditional beliefs in ancestral spirits are held alongside Islam and Christianity. Formerly, the ruler of the Banggai principality was appointed by the sultan of Ternate.

See also Balantak

Bibliography

LeBar, Frank M. (1972). "Banggai." In *Ethnic Groups of Insular Southeast Asia,* edited by Frank M. LeBar. Vol. 1, *Indonesia, Andaman Islands, and Madagascar,* 139–140. New Haven: HRAF Press.

Batak

ETHNONYMS: Batak subsocieties include Angkola-Sipirok, Dairi-Pakpak, Karo, Mandailing, Simelungun, and Toba

Orientation

Identification.   The Batak subsocieties are closely related, rapidly modernizing ethnic monority groups whose rural home regions are in the rugged highlands and plains near North Sumatra's Lake Toba. The word "Batak" may have originally been an epithet used by Muslim lowlanders to refer to the mountain peoples in a derogatory way, as "primitives." Today the term is much less stigmatic and is used in some subsocieties, such as the Toba, as an everyday ethnic designation. Some of the groups along the borders of the Batak regions (e.g., Karo, Mandailing) eschew the label "Batak" in favor of their subsociety designations. Although the Batak societies share close dialects and similar social structural patterns, they never have had any significant political unity. During Dutch colonial times they were loose tribal confederations, with some chiefdom formation in border areas. Ethnic boundaries shift often and ethnic identity is labile. Today, with large numbers of city migrants and greater political power in multiethnic competition, many Batak are reemphasizing their Batak ethnic character, and inventing "ancient Batak village traditions" through their use of the mass media and by staging lavish rituals.

Location.   The Batak home regions surround Lake Toba in North Sumatra, spanning the large highland region between the Acehnese and Gayo-Alas peoples to the north and the Minangkabau to the south. The home regions include heavily forested mountains, now crosscut with passable roads, and wide, fertile plains, laid out into rice paddies and grazing land. The Batak farm areas straddle the Bukit Barisan, Sumatra's main northwest-southeast mountain chain. North Sumatra has a distinct rainy season (September-December) and a pronounced hot, dry period (May-August).

Demography.   North Sumatra had a 1989 population of 10,330,091. Most of this population is Batak, with smaller numbers of Javanese, Indonesian-Chinese, Acehnese, and Minangkabau. There is also a large Batak diaspora population in multiethnic cities such as Jakarta, Bandung, and Surabaya. Many Bataks moved to Javanese cities in the 1920s and 1930s for employment as clerks, teachers, and newspaper writers and editors (the Bataks were one of Outer-Island Indonesia's first deeply literate peoples). This migration pattern has continued, augmented by Bataks from poorer families seeking jobs in the army and transportation.

Linguistic Affiliation.   The Batak dialects are Western Austronesian languages closely related to Malay, Javanese, and Tagalog. The Toba, Angkola, and Mandailing dialects are quite similar and mutually intelligible, while Karo, Kairi-Pakpak, and Simelungun are generally not understood outside their home areas. No Batak language is mutually intelligible with the national language, Bahasa Indonesia, although the latter is widely known throughout the Batak home regions. Batak languages have a conversational level and a more esoteric oratory level, used in *adat* (ancient custom) ceremonies. Genres of speech here include verse-form verbal duels, mythic chants, dirges, and clan genealogies. Literacy in the Latin alphabet is widespread (introduced in Dutch colonial public schools and mission schools, beginning in the 1850s in Angkola and Mandailing). There was also an old Batak script, a syllabary based on Sanskrit-derived court-writing systems from west or south Sumatra. Little used or even known today, the Batak script was once a runic code for divination and spells, for village priests.

History and Cultural Relations

Despite the relative inaccessibility of the highlands, the Batak groups have been deeply shaped by influences from neighboring cultures. Many words for Batak political leaders and religious concepts show Indian influence, as do Batak divination and astrological lore. Border areas such as Karo and Mandailing model their traditional political systems on the nearby state societies, Aceh and Minangkabau. Islam was introduced to the southern Batak lands from Minangkabau in the 1820s, on the eve of the Dutch incursion into the area. By the 1850s, they had established a civil administration in the southern Batak areas, a region they hoped to use as a buffer between Muslim Aceh and Muslim Minangkabau. The Dutch gradually extended their control northward through Toba, encountering armed resistance from the charismatic warrior chief, Sisingamangaraja XII. By 1910 all Batak areas were under Dutch control, schools had been established in Toba, Angkola, and Mandailing, and missionary Christianity was thriving in Toba. By the 1920s, literate Batak had established a cosmopolitan city culture of newspapers and book publishing in Medan and Sibolga; writers were turning their attention to nationalist and anti-Dutch concerns. North Sumatra was occupied by the Japanese from 1942 to 1945. Since the Indonesian national revolution of 1945–1949, the region has remained an economically vital part of the Indonesian state. Owing to population pressure on over-used farmland, out-migration to cities continues.

Settlements

Village size varies greatly by subsociety: some Toba rice-farming villages have only 4 or 5 houses, while some Mandailing and Angkola villages have 100 to 200 houses. Market towns dot the highlands too, serving as hubs for large numbers of mountain villages. In Karo and Toba, some traditional villages remain, with Great Houses (carved, high-peaked, adat houses, for several families linked through clanship and marriage alliance). More common today are Malay-style houses, divided into rooms and roofed with zinc, not thatch. Throughout the Batak areas the "complete" village is both a small model of the cosmos and a replica of the entire social order, with all its requisite interlocking parts. These consist of the village founders and their close lineage mates, their traditional wife givers (who have provided the founders with brides and blessings over many generations), and their traditional wife receivers, who marry the founders' daughters and provide the village with labor services and physical protection. Cosmic as well as social order is maintained, it is thought, if all three partners mutually support each other and keep the "flow of blessings" circulating through human society and the agricultural realm. Similar patterns of thought are found throughout eastern Indonesia.

Economy

Subsistence and Commercial Activities. All regions are rice-cultivation areas, combining dry fields with extensive, terraced paddies. One rice crop per year is typical in some of the less fertile uplands, although wide plainlands sometimes support two crops. Government development projects are spreading green-revolution varieties of high-yield rice throughout the province. Cash crops (coffee, tobacco, cloves, cinnamon) have been grown since colonial times; market gardening also supplements rice production (peppers, cabbage, tomatoes, beans). Government projects encourage the cultivation of peanuts and fish farming. Traditional forest products such as camphor and incense are still collected, as is forest rubber. Karo is a major fruit and vegetable exporter. Domestic animals include chickens, ducks, water buffalo, goats, and (in non-Muslim areas) pigs. Outside the agricultural sector, Batak work in the transportation industry, in cloth sales, and in Sumatra's ubiquitous markets.

Industrial Arts. Market towns typically have mechanics, carpenters, house builders, tailors, and road-pavement crews, while village men make fish nets and women weave ceremonial textiles and make rattan baskets. In larger towns, shops and repair businesses are owned by Indonesian-Chinese entrepreneurs.

Trade. Since at least early colonial times, the highlands have been crosscut by trade routes for salt, salted fish, dried hot peppers, and cooking oil—the basic ingredients, with rice and greens, of the standard village meal. Since the 1950s, paved roads and crushed stone roads have been extended to many village areas, augmenting the old colonial main routes between market centers. Bus transport to Medan and Padang is dependable and frequent.

Division of Labor. Farm families tend to share household tasks and field labor among the men, women, and children. Heavy planting and harvest tasks are often done by larger work groups, recruited by age (groups of adolescents) or clan and marriage-alliance ties to the farm family in question. Some wealthier village families hire poorer relatives to work their land, on a sharecropping basis. In pre-Dutch times southern Batak high chiefs had slaves who worked as their house servants and field laborers.

Land Tenure. In the ideal situation, family rice land is not to be bought and sold but should pass to sons and their households, with a smaller share going to daughters. In practice, some families do sell paddy land, for school tuition or other pressing needs; in addition, the establishment of new villages east of the traditional Batak lands has opened up new farming territory. Traditional houses and lineage heirlooms pass down through the patriline. Parents often circumvent the strict patrilineal inheritance rules for land by bestowing land gifts on favored daughters at their weddings or on the birth of their first child.

Kinship

Kin Groups and Descent. The Batak peoples have kinship systems similar to the Kachin of highland Burma. They have patrilineal clans, divided into localized lineages (often centered on ancestral houses and tombs). Lineages of different clans are linked together through asymmetrical marriage alliance—Lineage A will get its wives from Lineage B of another clan. Lineage B will thus serve as the politically and ritually superordinate alliance partner to A, showering it with fertility blessings, good luck, and supernatural protection. Lineage A in turn will give its daughters in a second direction to C, of still another clan. Lineage C will then become A's own subordinate alliance partner. Lineages of varying time-depths are the operative units in this marriage system. Today, many lineages have members in several villages as well as in migrant communities in the multiethnic cities. Clans are very large, never meet corporately, and in fact often straddle two ethnic subsocieties such as Toba and Angkola. Some Batak peoples imagine that all clans originated in a Toba ancestral home, and spread outward from there because of ancient clan wars. Much adat ceremonial activity is directed toward contacting lineage ancestors and securing their blessings.

Marriage and Family

Marriage.   As noted, the ideal marriage involves a young man and a young woman from two linked lineages that have a long-standing alliance relationship. In practice, many marriages forge bonds between lineages with no previous alliance; that situation is usually accepted as a means "to widen the sphere of kin-term usage" and to provide more alliance partners for support. When families are conforming to the ideal, however, a man would marry his exact mother's brother's daughter. This marriage would repeat the marriage his father made in the previous generation: both the older man and his son would have obtained brides from the same house in the same traditional wife-giver lineage. Elaborate gift exchange accompanies marriage in many subsocieties. The bride brings ritual textiles and various foods (identified with femininity) to her new house, while the bridegroom's family gives countergifts of bride-wealth payments, jewelry, and livestock. Such exchange is conceptualized as part of a complementary opposition scheme in which wife givers and wife receivers work together to produce a fertile marriage, which in turn empowers the village. Residence is ideally with or near the new husband's parents for several years, after which the new couple formally split off to set up their own household. In prenational times some areas such as Karo and Toba had large, multifamily houses, with a full complement of wife givers and wife takers. Lower-class people never had such large and complex houses. Divorce, much discouraged in the adat oratory, is possible under Islamic law and Indonesian civil law. For wealthier families, given the fact that marriage alliance carries so many larger political implications, divorce is shameful. When Batak migrant men marry women from other, non-Batak ethnic groups, a new bride is sometimes adopted into a lineage as her groom's mother's brother's daughter.

Domestic Unit.   There are several household types: (1) older married couples living with married sons and their other unmarried children; (2) new couples just separated from such parental households; (3) young married couples with children; and (4) older couples with several unmarried relatives sharing the same house. Many migrants from the cities move back to their home villages temporarily and live with relatives, so household structure is extremely fluid. Multifamily wife giver/wife receiver "complete" households have been rare in recent decades.

Inheritance.   Sacred property such as old rice land, lineage heirlooms, and the ancestral house should pass down the patriline, whereas bride-wealth goods circulate among houses linked through marriage alliance. Daughters can obtain rice land as bridal gifts from their fathers. In some areas, the eldest son and the youngest son get the larger share of heritable goods, and the youngest son and his wife are obligated to care for his aged parents.

Socialization.   Attendance at public school or at Muslim school is compulsory and dominates children's lives today. The national schools stress Indonesian patriotism and "modern values." At home, older siblings have a large role in the care of younger brothers and sisters, frequently carrying them around in tight cloth slings. Young children are rarely scolded or even reprimanded; children are cajoled into obeying with small food or cash gifts.

Sociopolitical Organization

The Batak subsocieties are part of the multiethnic nation of Indonesia, centered in the capital of Jakarta and dominated by the Javanese. North Sumatra is a province of the nation, and all Bataks are citizens. The civil servants who administer the area are, for the most part, Batak themselves.

Social Organization.   Like other Southeast Asians, Batak tend to pay great attention to social hierarchy. In this area, this is phrased in terms of traditional social-class background (aristocrat, free commoner, or slave descendant), closeness to the founder lineage of a person's home village, and occupation prestige (with farm labor at the bottom and salaried office work at the top). Using a system of indirect rule, the Dutch rigidified the old Batak class systems, strengthening the hand of the traditional nobles. Poorer families looked to the colonial schools as a means for their children to escape class discrimination in farm villages.

Political Organization.   Each Batak area has a dual political organization today: the bureaucracy of the national Indonesian government extends from the province of North Sumatra down to the village level (with civil officials, a police force, and a judiciary), while Batak villages have their councils of elders, their chiefs (*rajas*), and their chiefs' councils, selected according to genealogical position in each area's founder clans. Village clusters and larger chieftaincy domains are organized according to both marriage alliance and descent ties, in a pattern reminiscent of traditional social organization in eastern Indonesia. The chiefs and their councils supervise adat ceremonials and some points of inheritance law and marriage, and serve as the prestigious, morally upright "old guard" of their villages. The government officials, for their part, control the secular political sphere.

Social Control.   Violent crime and business law are under the control of the national government and their police force, while traditional councils exercise some moral control over everyday village social order. Adat leaders can exact fines for disallowed marriages; they also supervise the payment of bride-wealth, a major source of tension. In some areas fear of witchcraft and sorcery is common and articulates with factional disputes. Poisoners are often thought to lurk just over the next hill (a common ethnic boundary-maintenance device).

Conflict. Until Dutch pacification efforts in the mid-1800s, intervillage warfare and lineage-to-lineage feuding were quite common, given severe pressure for the farmland. After the colonial era, this legacy of intense intergroup rivalry took new forms: conflict within the Protestant church, conflict among lineages to see which one can put on the most lavish ancestor-commemoration ceremony, and conflict over access to modern jobs. At the village level factionalism is bitter, constant, and quick-changing, based on competition for land and, today, government favors.

Religion and Expressive Culture

Religious Beliefs. Virtually all Batak have converted to Islam or Protestant Christianity over the last 170 years, although in some areas beliefs that spirits can infest people and make them ill remain strong. An older Batak pantheon of creator deities and mythical clan founders has largely been eclipsed by the world religions. Batak converts often speak of an older "Age of Darkness" before their forefathers found out about "true religion." The southern Batak areas of Angkola-Sipirok and Mandailing converted to Islam starting in the 1820s; these are markedly pious, learned areas today, with many hajji and Quranic schools. Toba is a similarly serious, well-schooled Christian area, with many ministers and religious teachers. Karo is a region of much more recent conversions: pagan areas remain, and some villagers and townspeople converted to world religions in 1965, to avoid being labeled Communist sympathizers in the national unrest attending the establishment of the Suharto regime.

Each area has a varying syncretic blend of Islamic or Christian figures with indigenous spirits; the latter are a very minor part of the system of thought in long-converted areas. With increasing literacy, the old creator deities and the figures of myth have generally been demoted to the status of folklore figures.

Religious Practitioners. All areas have the standard religious personnel of world Islam and Christianity, as well as curer-diviners who contact supernaturals through trances and perform exorcisms.

Ceremonies. Most areas have split off adat, or custom, from _agama_, or true religion (that is, Islam or Christianity). This stratagem allows Batak to remain pious monotheists and to maintain an elaborate round of adat ceremonies, with ritual speeches, dances, processions, and gift exchange. Adat ceremonies focus on lineage ancestors, births in the lineage, and marriage alliance (with long, contentious weddings).

Arts. Nineteenth-century European missionaries discouraged carving and ritual dirges and dances, fearing these were blasphemous. This eliminated much of Toba's magnificent traditional sculpture and masked dances. House architecture in the old Great-House style has become too expensive to maintain today; few "Cosmic Houses" remain. Batak textile arts still thrive, as these cloths are still a vital part of marriage and mortuary exchange.

Medicine. Modern, scientific medicine is practiced by a thin network of government health workers, based in clinics, while curer-diviners practice alongside them, concentrating now on "spirit infestations" and some aspects of childbirth and poison control.

Death and Afterlife. Resilient beliefs in powerful lineage ancestors exist in some areas in tandem with the afterlife theories of Christianity and Islam. Adat's ceremonial speeches can be used to invoke the blessings of long-dead lineage ancestors. Masked dancers once served as mediums for ancestors to interact with living persons, but such performances have now been redefined as quaint customs.

See also Gayo

Bibliography

Carle, Rainer, et al. (1987). _Cultures and Societies of North Sumatra_. Berlin: D. Reimer Verlag.

Cunningham, Clark N. (1958). _The Postwar Migration of the Toba-Bataks to East Sumatra_. Yale University Southeast Asia Studies, Cultural Report no. 5. New Haven.

Kipp, Rita Smith, and Richard Kipp, eds. (1983). _Beyond Samosir: Recent Studies of the Batak Peoples of Sumatra_. Ohio University Papers in International Studies, Southeast Asia Series, no. 62. Athens.

Siagian, T. P. (1966). "A Bibliography of the Batak Peoples." _Indonesia_ 2:161–185.

Singarimbun, Masri (1975). _Kinship, Descent, and Alliance among the Karo Batak_. Berkeley and Los Angeles: University of California Press.

Vergouwen, J. C. (1933). _The Customary Law of the Toba Bataks of Northern Sumatra_. The Hague: Martinus Nijhoff.

SUSAN RODGERS

Baweanese

ETHNONYMS: Bawean Islanders, Boyanese, Oran Boyan, Orang Babian, Orang Bawean, Orang Boyan

The Baweanese are the inhabitants of Bawean Island, located at 5°50′ S and 112°40′ E north of Java in the Java Sea. This island is part of Indonesia. The original Baweanese migrated there from Madura at the end of the fourteenth century and today the Baweanese speak a dialect of Madurese, although they consider themselves to be a distinct ethnic group. Their number is estimated at about 60,000. In addition to the Baweanese, the island population includes Diponggo, Bugis, Kema, and Madurese. The first three have been essentially assimilated into Baweanese society, while the Madurese have remained separate and are today economic rivals with the Baweanese.

The island economy is centered on fishing and the growing of maize and rice. Mat weaving, once a highly developed art, has declined in importance. The Baweanese are Sunni Muslims and strict observers of religious practice.

The most notable aspect of Baweanese culture is *merantau*, the migration of men (today, more often entire families) to other parts of Indonesia. In the past, men generally migrated to find work in Singapore and the west coast of Malaya; today Riau Archipelago south of Singapore is also a major migration site. In the past also, Singapore was seen as a stopping-off point to earn money for the trip to and from Mecca. Today, migration off the island for employment is a goal in and of itself.

Bibliography

Koentjaraningrat (1972). "Bawean Islanders." In *Ethnic Groups of Insular Southeast Asia*, edited by Frank M. LeBar. Vol. 1, *Indonesia, Andaman Islands, and Madagascar*, 59. New Haven: HRAF Press.

Vredenbregt, Jacob (1964). "Bawean Migration." *Bijdragen tot de Taal-, Land- en Volkenkunde* 120:109–137.

Vredenbregt, Jacob (1984). "Baweanese." In *Muslim Peoples: A World Ethnographic Survey*, edited by Richard V. Weekes, 126–130. Westport, Conn.: Greenwood Press.

Bilaan

ETHNONYMS: Balud, Baraan, Bilanes, Biraan, Blann, Buluan, Buluanes, Tagalagad, Takogan, Tumanao, Vilanes

Together, the Koronadal and Sarangani Bilaan numbered about 175,000 in 1981. They live in south-central Mindanao, in the Philippines. Bilaan is classified in the Hesperonesian Group of Austronesian languages. Houses are dispersed and built adjacent to gardens. Rice, maize, and millet are grown in swidden gardens; sugarcane, bananas, and tubers are grown in kitchen gardens. Domestic animals include chickens, pigs, and dogs. Descent is bilateral.

Bilaanland was divided into several districts or domains, each ruled by a local *datu*. The datu was both judge and defender of his followers. War captives were taken as slaves and for human sacrifice. Bilaan religion was pantheistic.

Bibliography

LeBar, Frank M. (1975). "Bilaan." *In Ethnic Groups of Insular Southeast Asia*, edited by Frank M. LeBar. Vol. 2, *Philippines and Formosa*, 61–62. New Haven: HRAF Press.

Bisaya

ETHNONYMS: Besaya, Bisayah, Jilama Bawang, Jilama Sungai

Orientation

The name "Bisaya" is applied primarily to those people living on the middle reaches of rivers in Sabah and Sarawak draining into Brunei Bay on Borneo. The Bisaya are culturally diverse; in mainland Sabah, they are primarily Muslims engaged in wet-rice cultivation, but in Sarawak most are neither Muslim nor Christian (though one large group, the Limbang, are now converted to Christianity). The Bisaya live in small groups interspersed among other peoples, and have adapted many of their cultural features from these peoples. The Bisaya language belongs to the North Indonesian Branch of the Austronesian Family. In 1983, the Sarawak Bisaya numbered 4,000; in 1960 the Brunei Bisaya numbered approximately 7,000, and in 1970 the Sabah Bisaya population was 14,000.

Little is known of Bisaya history. Presently, their contact with the Malays gives them access to buffalo, boats, and fish. Some Bisaya gain prestige by paying Malays to slaughter buffalo at ceremonial feasts.

Settlements

Villages have between 30 and 200 people, and though they have centers, they also stretch alongside riverbanks. In addition, there are sometimes temporary encampments in the interior. There are no public buildings, but there are rice granaries. Villages are permanent, and contain at least one longhouse with at least four apartments (*lobok*). Longhouses are rectangular and are built on pilings 3 to 4.5 meters high; they may be as much as 60 meters in length. They are bisected lengthwise, and there is a closed veranda for ceremonies. Longhouses may have as many as seven apartments, though they formerly had more.

Economy

The Bisaya staple food is rice, which is grown by both wet and dry horticulture in swiddens. Because of declining fertility, disputes, and omens, wet-rice swiddens rarely are used for more than two years. The Bisaya use a dibble stick rather than the plow. Rice swiddens also produce the following crops (raised between rice plants) for sale: chilies, corn, cucumbers, gourds, pumpkins, yams, and others. Fruits raised are bananas, breadfruit, coconut, and jackfruit. Hunting is much more important than fishing; game includes wild pigs, wild buffalo, deer, and pheasants, which are killed with guns, spears, and blowguns. Bisaya women (and some men) gather ferns, amaranths, and fruits for food, as well as medicinal plants, honey, camphor, and gutta percha. The Bisaya also raise buffalo, pigs, and chickens. Though they are accomplished carpenters, the Bisaya never learned to smelt or forge metal or to weave cloth. (Before they traded for cloth, clothing was made of bark.) They trade primarily with the Chinese (and formerly with Malays), receiving cloth, metal goods, and pottery items. All property belongs to one of the following classes: ancestral property, personal property, marital property, and house-group property. Real property rights are inherited ambilineally. Once land is abandoned, however, it becomes available for use by anyone living in the village.

Kinship

The Bisaya kinship terminological system is bilateral with Eskimo cousin terminology. Descent is ambilineal, without corporate descent groups; descent group affiliation is used to establish land rights and figures in the payment of respect to influential people. A major kin group is the apartment family (_sanan lobok_), which shares food and has a common hearth and common prayers for horticulture. Another kin group is the house family (_sanan alai_), which shares some ceremonial objects, the performance of some rituals, and the chores of house repair.

Marriage and Family

The most desirable marriages are to kin, in the following order of preference: second or third cousins, first cousins, and fourth or fifth cousins. Only parents or siblings are forbidden as marriage or sexual partners. Polygyny is allowed but is rare because of the expense. Sororal polygyny is forbidden. Parents often arrange first marriages, sometimes making matches with children as young as 8 years of age. Residence is ambilocal, and the newlyweds must live in the same apartment as the parents; only when the couple has a child does it move to live in its own apartment. Inheritance is ambilateral with no preference for either gender.

Sociopolitical Organization

Government-selected headmen were first appointed in 1930; before that there were no headmen, but rather a council of elders. Presently, the Limbang Bisaya are headed by three officials appointed by the federal government. Status is based on wealth, but there are no social classes. The wealthy must give feasts, which serve to redistribute wealth. Gossip and ridicule are the major forms of social control; feuding is practiced. Warfare is defensive, and the Bisaya do not hunt heads.

Religion and Expressive Culture

The Bisaya religion is animistic; there are shamans and diviners. Illness is caused by soul loss, and a spirit medium is used for retrieval. The dead are revered, but there is no true ancestor worship. Spirits of the dead can be dangerous if not properly mourned. The wealthy give large amounts of food for the "crocodile" or harvest ceremony, the main agricultural ceremony.

Bibliography

Peranio, Roger D. (1972). "Bisaya." In _Ethnic Groups of Insular Southeast Asia_, edited by Frank M. LeBar. Vol. 1, _Indonesia, Andaman Islands, and Madagascar_, 163-166. New Haven: HRAF Press.

Punchak, Sylvester Sarnagi (1989). "Bisaya Ethnography: A Brief Report." _Sarawak Museum Journal_ 40:37-48.

DANIEL STROUTHES

Bolaang Mongondow

ETHNONYMS: Bolaang-Mongondo, Boolaang-Mongondonese, Mongondou, Mongondow

A 1983 estimate places the population of the Bolaang Mongondow at over 1.5 million. They live on the northern or Minahassa peninsula of Sulawesi, Indonesia. They are a coastal group who merged with the inland Mongondow. Bolaang Mongondow is classified in the Hesperonesian Group of Austronesian languages. Villages are strung along roads, mostly on the upland plateaus. Subsistence is based on wet rice, sago, yams, and cassava. Domestic animals include pigs, cattle, buffalo, goats, and chickens. Islam dates to 1830, and about 90 percent of the people are Muslims. The other 10 percent are mainly Protestant. Descent is bilateral. Bolaang Mongondow society was traditionally divided into nobles, commoners, and slaves, with each group having many subdivisions.

Bibliography

LeBar, Frank M. (1972). "Bolaang Mongondow." In _Ethnic Groups of Insular Southeast Asia_, edited by Frank M. LeBar. Vol. 1, _Indonesia, Andaman Islands, and Madagascar_, 127–128. New Haven: HRAF Press.

Bonerate

ETHNONYMS: Orang Bonerate, Salayar, Selayar

Orientation

Identification. Bonerate live on the island of Bonerate, which is situated in the middle of the Flores Sea in Indonesia. They call themselves "Orang Bonerate" and are referred to by the same term by their neighbors. Westerners have grouped them with both Bugis and Selayar people. They speak the Bonerate language and, according to official records, are all Sunni Muslim.

Location. Bonerate is situated at approximately 7° S and 121° E. The area belongs to the moist deciduous monsoon forest zone. The rainy season normally starts in the latter part of December and lasts through February. Showers also occur quite often in March and April. The rest of the year is dry, but occasional showers may appear any time. Bonerate, meaning "flat sands," has two minor hills, the higher of which reaches less than 200 meters above sea level. The island is formed from corals, is almost circular in shape, fringed by extensive reefs, and covers about 70 square kilometers. The soil is of poor quality. Where fields are cleared, seeds are sown between coral-limestones. There are no rivers or creeks, and water is a scarce resource during the dry season. Water for human consumption is fetched from village wells. During the dry season the water in the villages located close to the shore is often of poor quality and brackish.

Demography. The island's total population is approximately 5,500 (1978), which includes people of various origins and affiliations. The largest ethnic group is the Bonerate, who are regarded as descendants of the original population and early Butonese immigrants.

Linguistic Affiliation. The Bonerate language is spoken in all villages and is the language of local market communication. All over South Sulawesi, different languages have been in prolonged and often intimate contact with each other. This blurs the distinction between dialect and language. The reference to a Bonerate "language" is based on the knowledge that the tongues spoken on the neighboring islands and Bonerate are not mutually understandable. This does not mean, however, that the inhabitants of the different islands are unable to communicate verbally. First, Bonerate individuals master more than the local "language"; they are bi- and even trilingual. Second, a significant number of the islanders have some knowledge of Bahasa Indonesia (the national language), which is also the language of the schools. According to Bonerate people, their language shares many similarities with Butonese. The Bonerate language has been included with the Muna-Butung Group.

History and Cultural Relations

Accounts of Bonerate history and traditional culture are few, and interisland variation in this area is significant. We do, however, know that in the past a combination of trading, slaving, and piracy formed the base of the economy. There are strong indices pointing to the probability that the island was never able to feed a large population solely from domestic resources. Population pressures seem always to have been somewhat relieved by the customary period men spend at sea. During the nineteenth and early twentieth centuries there were reports of some export of deer antlers and hides. But approximately 30 years ago, dogs were introduced for hunting and the deer were driven into the sea; they are now extinct. Another economic enterprise that has ceased is the growing of cotton for spinning and weaving. As late as the beginning of this century textiles were being exported from Bonerate. Bonerate materials, however, could not compete with modern factory-made textiles from Java. Orang Bonerate have a long-standing tradition and reputation for being particularly skilled builders of the local type of *prahu* (sailship). In earlier times, Bonerate had a stratified society with sharply defined classes: kings, queens, and their descendants; nobility; commoners; and slaves. Today, this social division is of almost no importance in everyday interaction.

For centuries and up to the present men from the South Sulawesi mainland, especially of Bugis affiliation, Butung, and Flores have settled and married at Bonerate. Immigrant men far outnumber immigrant women. The cultural impact of these relations can be observed both in ritual and everyday village life. Orang Bonerate have close, ancient, and lasting relations with Bajau people (also known as sea nomads). In earlier times this interaction may have had the character of a symbiotic relationship. At the present the relationship would more correctly be described as an ecologically based cooperation in which Bajau fetch water at Bonerate and barter fish and other sea products for cultivars grown on Bonerate.

Settlements

Orang Bonerate live in ten villages, the populations of which vary from approximately 20 to 1,000 residents. Seven of the villages are seashore communities; the remaining three are situated in the interior of the island. When the residents from the latter want marine foods, they barter for them in the coastal villages, or they purchase them at the market at the island capital (*ibu kota*). This survey of Bonerate's settlements would not be complete without the mention of an eleventh village that was emerging in 1978. People from two inland villages cooperated in building new houses and developed swiddens at a virgin inland location. The people who periodically lived at the new site gave the growing scarcity of land around their home villages as the reason for moving there. At that time no children had yet been born there. The development of the new village was based on local initiative, not sponsored by the island's civil servants.

Most houses on Bonerate have bamboo or rough wood walls and roofs of thatched coconut-palm leaves, and are built on poles. The size is highly variable from small, one-room all-thatch huts to houses with a veranda, bedrooms, and a separate firehouse/kitchen.

Economy

Subsistence and Commercial Activities. Orang Bonerate regard themselves first of all as agriculturalists. They practice a system of slash-and-burn subsistence agriculture. Owing to a lack of water, only one crop is possible per year. Primary forest is absent from the island. Secondary forest and bush land are cleared in the preparation of swiddens. Fields are usually cultivated for up to three years and then lie fallow from six to ten years. The technological level is low; a long-bladed bush knife and a digging/weeding iron rod are the only agricultural implements in use. Corn is the staple crop, backed by cassava. In addition, pumpkins, watermelons, and such vegetables as peas and beans are grown. Some fruits, such as bananas, papaya, breadfruit, and coconuts are also grown for local consumption. Domesticated animals are few, but include goats, ducks, hens, dogs, and cats. Most animal proteins in the diet derive from fishing and the gathering of marine animals such as worms and mollusks. At the island capital some men have specialized as shipbuilders. During the 1980s they managed to shift from the construction of sailships to motor vessels suited for local interisland commercial traffic. The boats are built on contracts for clients all over South Sulawesi and other parts of Indonesia. Most men in the age group of 19 to 30 years are absent from the island from six to ten months yearly, while they are sailing as crew members on Bonerate boats engaged in the copra and spices trade between the Moluccas and Java. The major effect of this trade has not been economic, in terms of the wages earned by the sailors. Only ship owners and captains make a profit, and few households are involved at this level. Rather, the most important effect of this trade is that the absentees reduce the pressure on food, which is yearly in short supply during parts of the dry season.

Industrial Arts. Except for the building of boats, which is carried out at a remarkably low technological level and without blueprints, the island has few artisans. One blacksmith resided on Bonerate in 1978.

Trade. Bonerate has one market, which is open once every week. There are a few small stores in the larger villages.

Division of Labor. With the exceptions of boat building, a few fishing activities, and the sailing of boats, division of labor by gender is poorly developed at Bonerate. Men and women engage in some fishing activities, and work together at the swiddens. The traditional home tasks are usually assigned to women, but men also cook, tend babies, fetch water, and wash clothes.

Land Tenure. Agricultural land is collectively owned by the villagers; plots for cultivation are allocated by the village headmen. Fishing and collecting of beach and shore resources are open to all.

Kinship

Kin Groups and Descent. Formerly kin groups were closely knit to a rigid system of social rank. Today kin groups exceeding the household units, based on core families, have relatively little significance. Moral support may, however, be sought from relatives recognized through both male and female links. Bilateral relatives are also recruited for occasional communal tasks such as ritual activities and agricultural work.

Kinship Terminology. The Bonerate kinship system is clearly bilateral. Kin terms are the same whether the linking relative is one's mother or father. It is a generational system; all members of each generation are grouped terminologically. In the generation of Ego, relative age and the distinction between siblings and cousins are emphasized. Thus, elder siblings are referred to as *ikaka* and younger as *yaisu*. Gender is marked by adding the suffix *moane* (male) or *vovine* (female). Parallel and cross cousins are named *sapisa*. In the parent generation *ina* (mother) and *ama* (father) are identified; all other members of that generation are *tuha*, with the exception of the in-laws, who are *davo*. Grandparents and grandchildren are named *ompu*. One's children are *anak*. In everyday encounters, however, parents are referred to with teknonymic terms by the name of the eldest son.

Marriage and Family

Marriage. When people marry, social prestige is at high risk. Orang Bonerate stress that fathers and mothers gain prestige through their daughters. Men try to move up the social ladder by marrying socially important women. According to what people say, a woman does not lose in rank by marrying down, but her husband will always be seen as inferior in comparison with his in-laws. Most weddings are arranged by the parents of the bride and groom. Wealthy parents of Bonerate girls find it natural to donate money to the family of the groom. This is done to enable them to pay a substantial bride-price. Residence is generally uxorilocal. Polygyny is possible, but almost absent from Bonerate. Marriages tend to be stable, and divorce is rare.

Domestic Unit. The nuclear family, which may include one or more married daughters and grandparents, is the most significant family and residential unit. Egalitarianism between the sexes, particularly between husband and wife, is a striking feature of Bonerate social organization, which should be regarded as matrifocal.

Inheritance. Bonerate sons and daughters inherit equal shares of their parents' estate and other belongings. There is only one exception to this rule of even distribution of inheritance. The parental house, which is actually the mother's house, and all household equipment, belong to the youngest daughter. If there are no daughters, the house belongs to the youngest son.

Socialization. The absence of the father is experienced by most infants and children for prolonged periods when fathers are at sea. Otherwise both parents take part in the socialization of their children. Also, child care by young caretakers is an institutionalized custom. The caretakers may be siblings, but not necessarily so. In socialization emphasis is placed on emotional control, that is, the concealment of expressions of love, joy, and anger from public exposure. Orang Bonerate seldom praise their children, nor do they use physical punishment in child rearing. Children seem to direct aggression toward themselves and culturally acceptable targets such as animals and strangers. Puberty rites are staged for both girls and boys.

Sociopolitical Organization

Bonerate belongs to the Kabupaten Selayar in the province of South Sulawesi. It is the administrative center of the district of Pasirmarannu, which means that the *chamat*, or head of the district civil administration, is located here together with police and military personnel. Authority lines follow the rules laid down by the modern republic of Indonesia.

Social Organization. The traditional stratified social organization of the Bonerate has generally lost its social relevance, but is expressed for instance during occasions of ritualized dances. A new elite based on economic success seems to be emerging among the islanders.

Political Organization. Bonerate society is a hierarchical system organized by locally recruited headmen for the island (*kepala desa*), settlements (*kepala linkung*), and neighborhood (*kepala kampung*). These headmen cooperate with, and carry out, the policy of the civil servants, who are recruited from areas outside Bonerate. The local headmen, and the islanders in general, have little influence in political issues above the restricted *kampung* level.

Social Control. Internal island conflicts are generally avoided and aggression is directed toward outsiders, but nowadays no action is carried out. When necessary, headmen at the different levels mediate when potential conflicts appear.

Conflict. In the past Bonerate men were renowned pirates. Today any serious conflict is taken care of by police or military personnel. At the village level, minor conflicts are solved within the community by strategies of ridicule, gossip, and reference to normative respect toward elders.

Religion and Expressive Culture

Religious Beliefs. Orang Bonerate regard themselves as Muslims, but they do not follow the Quranic prescriptions strictly. Most villages have a mosque, but except during

Ramadan these are poorly frequented. Imams are present only in the largest village. The local religion is syncretistic: many traditional customs, such as the belief in supernatural beings, are integrated into its belief system. Iblis is the deity to whom many Orang Bonerate make offerings at small altars. Some people refer to Seta as a synonym for Iblis. "Seta" is commonly used to denote spirits and ghosts in much of Indonesia. The villagers' preference for the Arabic-derived term "Iblis" may reflect the strong desire to appear Islamized and thus blur the connections to a traditional religion of spirit worship.

Religious Practitioners. There are no full-time traditional ritual experts on Bonerate. Minor rituals are carried out by both women and men.

Ceremonies. On special occasions, a possession-trance ritual is staged. The ritual is led by two women dressed as male sea captains. A medium dances until she enters a state of trance. At this point she walks on live embers and thus proves her authentic role as a medium. Then Iblis, who has taken possession of the medium's body, speaks, and the message is interpreted by the ritual leaders. Only women can be possessed in this way at Bonerate. Other rituals also are staged, some of which are in concord with Quranic prescriptions, such as the first haircut for boys.

Arts. At ritual occasions, highly stylized war and other dances are performed, accompanied by flutes and drums. Ornamental arts are poorly developed.

Medicine. Severe illness is generally attributed to "soul loss" and an imbalance of elements in the body. Accidents and injuries may also inaugurate illness. Resort to local healers, both men and women, is common; they apply few local remedies but trust in blowing on water, which the patient drinks, or blowing at the chest and upper back to restore the body's balance. Modern medicines are obtained from "barefoot doctors" and at the island health station.

Death and Afterlife. The funeral is not elaborated and is regarded primarily as a matter of household and close-family concern. Graves are not attended. Ritual crying is carried out at the time of death. Before the corpse is buried, ideally before the next sunset, Orang Bonerate take some precautions such as not taking part in fishing or other activities that bring them in close contact with the sea. Concepts of afterlife are influenced by Islam, but also show traditional traits. After death the soul sets out on a voyage through the dark before it reaches the site of final rest.

Bibliography

Broch, Harald Beyer (1985). "'Crazy Women Are Performing in Sombali': A Possession Trance Ritual on Bonerate, Indonesia." *Ethos* 13:262–282.

Broch, Harald Beyer (1985). "Resource Utilization at Miang Tuu, a Village on Bonerate Island in the Flores Sea." *Contributions to Southeast Asian Ethnography* 4:5–29.

Broch, Harald Beyer (1987). "Ethnic Differentiation and Integration: Aspects of Inter Ethnic Relations at the Village Level on Bonerate." *Ethnic Groups* 7:19–37.

Kriebel, D. J. S. (1920). "Het Eiland Bonerate." *Bijdragen tot de Taal-, Land- en Volkenkunde* 76:202–222.

HARALD BEYER BROCH

Bontok

ETHNONYMS: Bontoc, Bontoc Igorot, Guianes, Igorot

The Bontok are located in the steep gorge country of the upper Chico River system in Central Mountain Province of northern Luzon, the Philippines. The 1960 census listed the Bontok population at 78,000. The number of western and eastern Bontok speakers was estimated at 30,000 and 6,000 respectively in the mid-1980s. The Eastern and Western Bontok languages are closely related to Kankanai (Lepanto), a part of a subgroup within the northern Luzon Group of Philippine languages.

The Bontok economy involves agriculture, hunting, fishing, the domestication of animals, industrial arts, and trade. Fields are irrigated by carrying water in pots, diverting streams, or by constructing dams and wooden troughs. All people involved in the use of the water participate in the construction of the irrigation systems. Dogs are used to hunt the wild buffalo that are important for marriage feasts. Pigs are trapped in pits. Pig raising is also an important part of the culture. Cocks, cats, and birds are snared. Fishing is done by diverting streams and driving the fish into nets or traps. The Bontok have domesticated water buffalo, pigs, chickens, dogs, and cats. The Bontok are also familiar with metal working; they use double-piston bellows and charcoal to forge spear blades. Each village specializes in a particular craft, and there is thus trade between the villages for spear blades, pipes, baskets, hats, beeswax, pottery, salt, fermented sugarcane juice, and breech cloths. Handfuls of rice are used to pay for imported cotton cloth, brass wire, clothing, blankets, and axes.

The Bontok culture is noted for village wards (*ato*). Each village has between six and eighteen ato, each of which contains between fourteen and fifty houses. The ritual center of the ato consists of a stone platform that was the original site of headhunting ceremonies, an unmarried girls' dormitory, and an unmarried men's dormitory that also serves as a club house and council house. Each ato is governed by a council of elders.

In the traditional religion, which remains strong, spirits of the dead are of extreme importance. The *anito* inhabit a spirit world located in the mountains and it is just like the world in which the Bontok live. Spirits are consulted on all important matters, and answers are given through bird calls. Lumawig is the supreme being, the creator, the personification of all forces of nature. The *patay* are hereditary clans of priests who conduct ceremonies to honor Lumawig. Healing ceremonies can be performed by the patay or by old people. The healing ceremonies do not include singing or dancing, and the priests do not enter a trance. Minor rituals may be performed by the head of the household.

See also Sagada Igorot

Bibliography

Birket-Smith, Kaj (1952). "The Rice Cultivation and Rice Harvest Feast of the Bontoc Igorot." _Det Kongelige Danske Videnskabernes Salskab, Historisk-filologiske Meddeleser_ 32:1–22.

Cawed-Oteyza, Carmencita (1965). "The Culture of the Bontoc Igorots." _Unitas_ 38:317–377.

Himes, Ronald S. (1964). "The Bontok Kinship System." _Philippine Sociological Review_ 12:159–172.

Reid, Lawrence (1961). "Ritual and Ceremony in Mountain Province." _Philippine Sociological Review_ 9:1–82.

PATRICIA ANDREUCCI

Brao

The Brao (Lave, Love), who numbered about 18,000 in 1984, are swidden rice cultivators located over a fairly large area from 14° to 16° N and 106° to 108° E in northeast Cambodia and southeast Laos. Brao is a Mon-Khmer, Austroasiatic language. The Brao language is closely related to Krung and Kravet spoken in Cambodia, and if speakers of these languages are counted with the Brao, the total number is about 30,000.

Bru

The Bru, also known as the Baru, B'ru, and Leu, are a group numbering about 50,000 in 1985 with 40,132 in Vietnam and the remainder in neighboring Laos. They are linguistically and culturally related to the nearby Kalo (Ca Lo, Ka Lo) and some experts suggest that the Kalo are best classified as a Bru subgroup.

Bibliography

LeBar, Frank M., Gerald C. Hickey, and John K. Musgrave, eds. (1964). _Ethnic Groups of Mainland Southeast Asia_, 138. New Haven: HRAF Press.

Buddhist

The Buddhists of Southeast Asia are not considered here in a detailed article, since many of the longer articles in this volume deal with specific Buddhist cultural groups. Buddhism is, after all, a world religion with several hundreds of millions of adherents; and so, as with any other major and widespread faith, considerable diversity may be found in cultural practices.

The form that Buddhism has taken in Myanmar (Burma), Thailand, Cambodia, Laos, and the delta of the Mekong, as in Sri Lanka, is called Theravada. Vietnam, on the other hand (except for the Mekong delta), can be grouped with China, Korea, Japan, Tibet, and Mongolia, all countries that follow the Mahayana form of Buddhism, a form that derives from the late Indian schools of Buddhism and their interaction with Tantrism. All forms of Buddhism of course take their origin from the teachings of Gautama the Buddha (also called Sakyamuni, c. 560–480 B.C.).

Buddhism was slow to spread to Southeast Asia. By the middle of the third century B.C. it had reached Sri Lanka, and from there, after some centuries, it was carried to Burma, at the latest by the fifth century A.D. In Thailand there is little trace of the religion before the thirteenth century A.D., while in Cambodia it can be traced back to the third century A.D. But this was probably not, in the latter case, Theravada Buddhism, but rather another form called Sarvastivada. It was only in the fourteenth century A.D. that Theravada appeared in Cambodia and Laos. For some centuries following the third century A.D. other parts of Southeast Asia were Buddhist, although they have not been so in recent centuries. Java and Sumatra, in particular, were strong centers of the faith, as were, to a lesser extent, Malaya and Borneo. Buddhism remained in much of this insular area until the massive conversion to Islam in the fifteenth century. A vast canon of the text in Pali, collectively known as the Tripitaka and covering a span of nearly two millennia, forms the basis for the Theravada sect. These texts and commentaries contain the orthodox doctrine and rules for the highly important monastic life, which can be traced back to the first Buddhist schism of the fourth century B.C., and the "doctrine of the elders" that was formulated, if not written down, at the time. This doctrine recognized three alternative paths for the devotee: (1) _arahat_; (2) _paccekabuddha_; and (3) fully awakened Buddha. An arahat was a worthy one who had achieved the goal of Buddhist life by gaining insight into the true nature of things; a paccekabuddha is one who, having gained enlightenment, lives alone as an "isolated Buddha" without trying to teach others. The cult of Theravada Buddhism broke away from Brahmanic ritual and also from Mahayana forms.

The Mahayana sect, though at one time present in Cambodia, alongside Hinduism, in modern Southeast Asia occurs only in Vietnam, and then not in the southernmost parts. This sect had its origin around the first century A.D., and entailed a reinterpretation of the Theravada discipline for monks, which in turn freed them to travel freely and even settle in distant lands. As a result it was the Mahayana form of Buddhism that reached China, Japan, Korea, and Vietnam. One important feature of Mahayana doctrine was the concept of _bodhisattva_, essentially an idea that certain almost heavenly personages have the potential to become future Buddhas. This idea allowed for the assimilation of numerous popular local cults in the countries just mentioned, and goes a long way toward explaining why Mahayanists are very much more numerous than Theravadists in Asia.

Returning to the Theravada sect, we must note the importance of the monastery (often called a pagoda). In former times all adolescent Buddhist boys were expected to spend some months there; many still do. The monastery was a central institution, to be found in very many of the Buddhist towns and villages. It was attached to a temple (called a *vihara* or pagoda), which contained several statues of the Buddha. Local forms of the temple were architecturally diverse. Other buildings commonly found within the precincts of a temple were a prayer hall, perhaps a school or library, and huts or cells for the monks, students, and some other elderly residents.

The monastic community was a moral community, bound together by its observance of the five basic commandments (Panch Sila) of Buddhism; but monks and nuns would observe three (sometimes five) additional restrictions. Some monks would remove themselves from the main community of their monastery to live in caves or remote huts as hermits, either alone or as a small group. Those more active in the community would teach the youths and young monks, or might preach to the faithful, study texts, or simply meditate.

Even within the Theravada sect, there was no overarching theocratic structure, and certainly no person analogous to a pope or Dalai Lama. In keeping with the fact that in each country of Southeast Asia Theravada Buddhism had a distinct history, the organization of the sect does not reach beyond a national level. Local temples and monasteries are essentially self-sufficient, for they depend on their own lands and the offerings of the faithful. Property belongs either to the community or, to a lesser degree, to the Buddha or to the monks.

The broad appeal of Buddhism throughout history can be attributed to the strongly universalistic content of its ethical teachings, which were first expounded and elaborated upon by the Buddha himself in a lifetime of sermonizing. The essence of these teachings is summarized as the "Noble Eightfold Path," which prescribes: (1) right understanding, (2) right aspiration or purpose, (3) right speech, (4) right bodily action, (5) right means of livelihood, (6) right endeavor, (7) right mindfulness, and (8) right concentration. Against this were set the five proscriptions, or Panch Sila: (1) refrainment from injuring any living things; (2) refrainment from taking that which has not been given; (3) refrainment from excessive sensuality; (4) refrainment from false or harmful speech; and (5) refrainment from any drink or drug that clouds the mind. Perhaps overlooked in these dual formulations is the great Buddhist emphasis on generosity, especially the giving of alms. Overall it must be admitted that Buddhism provided a code of conduct, a direction to both one's thoughts and one's actions, that could pervade the entire fabric of a peaceable society. If the perfect Buddhist society has not yet emerged, it is still a fervent hope for hundreds of millions in East and Southeast Asia.

Bibliography

Bareau, André (1976). "Le bouddhisme à Ceylan et dans l'Asie du Sud-est." In *Histoire des religions,* edited by Henri-Charles Puech. Vol. 3, 330-352. Encyclopédie de la Pléiade. Paris: Éditions Gallimard.

Lafont, Pierre-Bernard (1976). "Le bouddhisme vietnamien." In *Histoire des religions,* edited by Henri-Charles Puech. Vol. 3, 353-370. Encyclopédie de la Pléiade. Paris: Éditions Gallimard.

Spiro, Milford E. (1970). *Buddhism and Society: A Great Tradition and Its Burmese Vicissitudes.* New York: Harper & Row.

PAUL HOCKINGS

Bugis

ETHNONYMS: Boegineezen, Buginese, To Bugi, To Ugi', To Wugi'

Orientation

Identification. The Bugis are the predominant ethnic group inhabiting the southern peninsula of the island of Sulawesi (formerly Celebes) in Indonesia. They speak a distinct language also called Bugis, although linguistically and culturally they are closely related to the neighboring Makassarese who are dominant in the southern tip of the peninsula. Their ethnic autonym—"To Ugi'"—derives from a village formerly on the Cenrana River. Other Indonesian ethnic groups often call them "To Bugi," while the Indonesian label is "Bugis."

Location. Within the province Sulawesi Selatan, Bugis are concentrated along the coasts of the southwestern peninsula and in the rice plains of its interior, north of the city of Ujung Pandang and south of the mountains of Tana Toraja (roughly between 5° and 4° S along a peninsula spine at 120° E). The region is composed of several agroclimatic zones. The west coast has its highest rainfall in December, while the east coast is wettest around May. Intermediate areas (e.g., interior rice plains) have a bimodal distribution with two dry seasons. Bugis have settled throughout the Indonesian archipelago as traders, fishermen, and farmers, especially in eastern Sumatra and the Riau Archipelago and along the entire shoreline of Sulawesi, as well as in coastal areas of Kalimantan, Buru, Ambon, Flores, and most of the islands of eastern Indonesia. The rhythm of both agriculture and trading has been affected by the prevailing monsoon seasons in all these settlements.

Demography. Extrapolating proportions from the 1930 census, the last to itemize ethnic groups, estimates of Bugis in South Sulawesi in the 1970s ranged around 3.2 million speakers. Given continuing population growth and the many Bugis outside the homeland, a current estimate of over 4 million is not unreasonable. Within the 72,781 square kilometers of the province, Sulawesi Selatan's 1990 population is projected at 7,082,118, with an average population density of 91 persons per square kilometer and an annual growth rate of 1.74 percent. Continual out-migration keeps the growth rate below the national average; the sex ratio of 96 indicates the preponderance of males in this out-migration.

Linguistic Affiliation. Bugis, Makassarese, Mandar, Sa'dan Toraja, Pitu Ulunna Salo, Seko, and Massenrempulu (Duri) form a distinct South Sulawesi Subbranch within the Western Indonesian Branch of Austronesian languages. Sa'dan Toraja speakers are the closest linguistic relatives of the Bugis, while the speakers of Central Sulawesi languages to the north represent an indigenous population whose occupation preceded that of the South Sulawesi peoples. Bugis and Makassarese share a common script based on an Indic model. In this syllabic script, each of twenty-two symbols stands for a consonant, sometimes prenasalized, plus the inherent vowel *a*. The five other vowels are indicated by adding diacritics. One further symbol stands for a vowel without a preceding consonant. Writing was developed around 1400, but probably does not derive directly from Javanese *kawi*.

History and Cultural Relations

Reconstruction of proto-South-Sulawesi suggests the lower course of the Sa'dan River as the homeland from which Bugis dispersed, moving up the Sa'dan Valley and across to the Gulf of Bone, settling in the Palopo area and then expanding to the south. Luwu', centered at the head of the Gulf of Bone, was the first great kingdom. Although Luwu' was based on control of trade, especially iron and nickel, by the fourteenth century the rise of complex chiefdoms based on wet-rice agriculture among Bugis to the south had led to its eclipse. After the sixteenth-century rise of Makassar to commercial preeminence, the Makassarese realms of Goa and Tallo achieved overlordship over most Bugis areas by the mid-seventeenth century. The Bugis realm of Bone allied with the Dutch to overthrow Makassar in 1667 and became the most powerful of the South Sulawesi kingdoms thereafter, a position maintained more or less throughout the colonial era. Refugees from Bugis realms, especially Wajo', formerly allied with Makassar, began the great diaspora of Bugis throughout the archipelago in 1670. Bugis mercenaries attained positions of power in Johor, the Riau Archipelago, Aceh, and elsewhere (including Thailand), while in later migrations Bugis opened settlements in Jambi and elsewhere in eastern Sumatra. Many Bugis nobles associated themselves with twentieth-century Indonesian independence movements. Thus they and their descendants have retained considerable prestige and power by occupying positions of influence in the bureaucracy of modern Indonesia.

Settlements

The national government has consolidated Bugis settlements into municipal villages (*desa*) that range in size between 2,000 and 10,000 inhabitants in rural areas. The centers of these desa are located along main roads, with the majority of the population in dwellings clustered along both sides of thoroughfares. However, desa also include more remote hamlets of several houses clustered among rice fields and gardens, reachable by minor roads or tracks. Each desa usually contains between two and five hamlets. During growing seasons some family members may reside in field huts dispersed among fields. Most Bugis have retained their traditional forms of stilted houses, sometimes 3 meters or more off the ground, with plank walls and floors. Only the very poorest have thatch walls. Roofs are now almost always made of corrugated iron. The number of tiers appearing on the front gable indicates the rank of the householder.

Economy

Subsistence and Commercial Activities. South Sulawesi serves as the rice bowl for eastern Indonesia, and its wet-rice plains form the heartland of the Bugis. Government rice-intensification programs have converted farmers to miracle rice varieties in almost all areas, with heavy inputs of fertilizer and pesticides. Mechanization has been more sporadic, with some farmers still using water buffalo and oxen to plow and harrow their fields, while others resort to minitractors. Besides large livestock, most households keep chickens; young boys herd ducks as an ancillary occupation. The sickle has replaced the finger knife (*ani-ani*) for harvesting all but ritually important glutinous rice varieties. Although groups of relatives and friends still gather to harvest communally in some areas, harvesting is increasingly being performed by itinerant bands of landless Makassarese, as well as Mandarese and migrant Javanese. The latter two groups are also hired as planting teams. Coastal Bugis also work as fishermen in boats plying the Strait of Makassar and Gulf of Bone, as well as engaging in pond-fish cultivation. Bugis outside the homeland are known for opening wet-rice fields, but have also developed stands of coconut palms, clove trees, pepper plants, and other cash crops.

Industrial Arts. Tailors, mechanics, and other specialists sometimes reside and practice in villages, but more often are clustered in towns and cities. Bugis women are expected to be proficient at weaving silk sarongs, which is carried on as a cottage industry. Chinese perform many commercial and industrial roles in the cities, and make the intricate filigree silverwork for which the area is known.

Trade. Bugis are famed as traders throughout the archipelago and successfully continue to transport cargoes of bicycle tires, wood, household accessories, and other goods in small ships of traditional design (e.g., *pinisi* and *paduwakang*), though now motorized. In many remote interior areas, from Sulawesi itself to Irian Jaya, Bugis run the only village kiosks. As itinerant peddlers, Bugis also sell cloth, costume jewelry, and other goods. Although Chinese control distribution of more capital-intensive goods such as electronics in city shops, Bugis are the major vendors of fish, rice, cloth, and small goods in the stalls of urban and rural markets. Women are often the vendors of such goods, especially foodstuffs, in rotating rural markets.

Division of Labor. Men perform most stages of work in the rice fields, but harvesting teams are composed of both sexes. Women and children sometimes perform minor tasks in fields, such as protecting against birds. Besides domestic tasks such as cooking and child care, women also are expected to weave silk sarongs for sale. Many Bugis women serve as vendors of foodstuffs and other goods in markets, and have control over the income derived from their own sales. Women, often divorcées, may also be itinerant peddlers.

Land Tenure.   Although smallholder plots of less than 1 hectare are still found in areas of intensified rice cultivation, modernization has resulted in increasing landlessness. Many farmers resort to sharecropping (*téseng*) arrangements allowing them to keep a portion of the harvest, with better lands (e.g., with technical irrigation) yielding a higher proportion to the landowner. Such arrangements continue the tradition of landed nobles granting the use of fields to their followers. Landlessness has resulted in increased circular migration to cities and out-migration to wilderness areas outside South Sulawesi, where fields can be opened.

Kinship

Kin Groups and Descent.   The Bugis exhibit a general Eskimo kinship organization with bilateral descent. Personal kindreds function as occasional kin groups and are often referred to by the term *siajing*. The *kapolo* of Luwu' has been described as an ambilateral ramage, but this type of group, although centered on a core of related noble kin, also includes nonconsanguineally related members. It is thus better considered an entourage of followers, invoked on such occasions as marriages of noble leaders.

Kinship Terminology.   Eskimo cousin terms are used. While cousin terms are not differentiated, same-sex sibling terms are differentiated as elder and younger, while opposite-sex sibling terms are also distinguished. Neither father's nor mother's siblings are distinguished by sex, nor from each other; the same is true for siblings' and cousins' children. Grandparent and grandchild terms can be further specified reciprocally as from the lap, knee, calf, instep, and "scraping interface" as the generational difference moves from 2 to 7 (e.g., *eppo ri uttu*, "grandchild of the knee" = great-grandchild). The importance of rank is evident in the divergent usage of address terms by nobles and commoners. Nobles of higher generation or greater age in the same generation are addressed as "lord" (*puang*). Where generation and age are incongruent, a combination of terms is often used. Commoners may extend kin terms to nonkin, and usually use teknonyms to address and refer to fellow commoners.

Marriage and Family

Marriage.   Marriages are traditionally arranged by parents or noble patrons. Nobles tend to favor marriages among close relatives, with first-cousin marriage especially preferred. Marriage is hypergamous, with the bride-price received for daughters and sisters the clearest marker of family status. As a matter of family honor, a young girl should be married off as soon as possible after menarche. By Islamic law, men may have up to four wives, but polygyny, even among nobles, is increasingly rare, although a few decades ago the highest nobles sometimes had dozens of wives. Among commoners, immediate postmarital residence is uxorilocal, but among nobles a lower-status wife may move to the residence of her higher-status husband. Divorce is common, especially among couples originally united in arranged marriages.

Domestic Unit.   The developmental cycle is based on the stem family, although most domestic groups reside neolocally in nuclear family residences at some point in the cycle. Often the youngest daughter remains or is called back to provide for elderly parents. Households frequently contain retainers, often poor relatives but sometimes unrelated children of clients, who perform household chores for room, board, and (in cities) schooling expenses.

Inheritance.   In accordance with Islamic law, women receive half the inheritance portion of their brothers. But intervening factors such as which child (often a daughter) has remained to take care of the parents influence inheritance shares, especially of the parental house. Both men and women may inherit rice land.

Socialization.   Both parents are involved in the upbringing of children, and elder siblings, especially sisters, often act as caretakers. Fathers often administer corporal punishment, encouraging sons to act aggressively by taunting and mock fighting. Cross-sex sibling ties are especially strong, while the same-sex sibling relation can be full of tension and opposition. Allowing elderly and childless relatives to raise some of one's children is common, as is the practice of allowing children living with urban relatives to attend higher levels of school.

Sociopolitical Organization

Social Organization.   Consciousness of rank differences pervades all activities. All traditional domains recognized a basic division into nobles, commoners, and slaves, but the composition and perquisites of intermediate ranks varied across domains. As descendants of heavenly beings, nobles are believed to possess white blood, increasingly diluted by intermarriage with lower ranks. However, an ethos of enterprise complements this hierarchy, allowing social mobility based on economic, military, and political achievement. Although recognition of nobility continues, slavery has been abolished, though descendants of slaves are still readily identified. Hierarchical relations are seen as supportive and caring, while relationships among putative peers are competitive and oppositional.

Political Organization.   Traditional realms were governed by the nobility, who constituted a unitary intermarrying class that transcended the domain boundaries. Leader-follower groups, entourages around noble cores, provided the basis of political allegiance. Although patron-client relations of this sort persist, penetration of the national government has produced changes at the local level. The province is divided into twenty-three regencies (*kabupaten*), in twelve of which Bugis are the predominant ethnic group, while two others are transitional between Bugis and Makassarese occupation. These regencies roughly correspond to former realms with government-appointed leaders often chosen from local noble families. However, the government is increasingly appointing former military personnel, often from outside the area, as heads of regencies, as well as at the lower district (*kecamatan*) and municipal village (desa) levels. Many of these appointees claim noble status, as part of the general trend to "title inflation." Each desa has a headman, as do the hamlets of which a desa is composed. Increasingly, headmen are being converted to employees of the national government (*pegawai negeri*). Both within the government hierarchy and in informal contexts, dispensing patronage to lower-status followers remains a crucial element of local politics.

Social Control. A value system emphasizing deference to leaders of higher rank provides one basis of social control, although such leaders traditionally had to validate their leadership by military exploits and the distribution of largesse to followers. A sharp sense of personal honor/shame (_siri'_) continues to motivate much social behavior, especially in such contexts as the elopement (_silariang_) of a daughter or sister, where family status must be defended by pursuit and punishment of the couple. Islamic functionaries or respected nobles act as mediators in such cases. Even the provincial government seeks the validation of local experts in customary law (_pallontara'_), who sanction development programs at large public meetings.

Conflict. In the past, considerable conflict was generated by succession disputes, in which nobles led their entourages against fellow claimants backed by other neighboring realms. Migrant Bugis were active as mercenaries throughout the colonial period, and often determined the balance of power in such areas as the Riau Archipelago and the Kutei Sultanate of East Kalimantan. South Sulawesi's 1950–1965 secessionist uprising against the Republic of Indonesia was carried out under the aegis of Islam, but its leader also attacked the privileges of indigenous nobility. The increasing role of the military in local governance since that time has precluded large-scale conflict. Nevertheless, the provincial capital has witnessed riots against local Chinese.

Religion and Expressive Culture

Religious Beliefs. Almost all Bugis adhere to Islam, but there is great variety in the types of Islam practiced. Most Bugis identify themselves as Sunni Muslims, but their practice, influenced by Sufi tenets, is a syncretic blend that also includes offerings to spirits of ancestors and deceased powerful personages. However, reformist Islamic organizations, especially Muhammadiyah, have gained many adherents in some areas and have established their own educational institutions. The I La Galigo literature preserved in ancient manuscripts (_lontara'_) describes a cosmology involving an upperworld and an underworld, each of seven layers, and a host of heavenly beings from whom nobles trace descent, but knowledge of details of this literature is not widespread among commoners. The To Lotang, a group of non-Muslim Bugis in Sidrap regency, continue to adhere to an indigenous belief system based on the lontara' and similar to that of the Toraja to the north, but has had to affiliate with the national Hindu movement to retain legitimacy as a religion. The extent to which Hindu-Buddhist notions have influenced Bugis religious and sociopolitical notions is currently a matter of debate.

The I La Galigo literature presents a pantheon of deities (_dewata_) from whom nobles trace descent, but contemporary Bugis argue that this literature basically recognizes a single great God (_Dewata Seuwa é_) in accord with the monotheism of Islam. Despite this, some of the other deities (e.g., the rice goddess) are still given offerings, even by Muslims. Village Bugis also recognize a panoply of local spirits associated with the house, the newborn, and sacred sites; they are variously termed "the ethereal ones" (_to alusu'_), "the not-to-be-seen" (_to tenrita_), "evil spirits" (_sétang_), etc. In fact, every object is thought to have its own animating spirit (_sumange'_), whose welfare must be catered to in order to insure good fortune and avert catastrophe.

Religious Practitioners. In addition to Islamic judges (_kali_), imams serve as local leaders of the Muslim community; they conduct Friday worship services, deliver sermons, and preside at marriages, funerals, and local ceremonies sanctioned by Islam. Small numbers of transvestite priests (_bissu_), traditionally the guardians of royal regalia, still, though rarely, perform rituals involving chants in a special register of Bugis directed to traditional deities recognized in the lontara'. Curing and consecration ceremonies are conducted by _sanro_, practitioners with arcane knowledge and expertise in presenting offerings and prayers to local spirits.

Ceremonies. Besides the celebration of calendric Islamic holidays (Lebaran, Maulid, etc.), Bugis of syncretic orientation perform many domestic consecration ceremonies (_assalamakeng_) involving offerings to local spirits, guardians of the house, supernatural siblings of the newly born, and other such spirits. Some districts and regencies also sponsor festivals marking planting and harvesting, although some of these have become more civic spectacles than religious celebrations. Especially among nobles, weddings are major occasions for the display of status and often involve presentations of local culture, including processions. The bissu rituals, however, increasingly are restricted and performed without large audiences.

Arts. Regional dances (e.g., _padendang_) are still performed at some ceremonies for the harvest and other occasions, as well as at government-sponsored festivals, but some (e.g., bissu dances) are now rarely performed. Young men enjoy practicing Indonesian martial arts (_pencak silat_) and the traditional sport of maintaining a woven rattan ball (_raga_) in the air with one's feet and other body parts, excluding the hands. Traditional Bugis houses still abound, and are used as the basis of modern architectural designs, but figurative art is meager in keeping with Islam. Bugis music is also heavily influenced by Middle Eastern models. Music performed on flute (_suling_) and lute (_kacapi_) similar to that in West Java is common. Epic songs of traditional and contemporary martial heroes are still composed and performed, even on radio. Amulets, especially of Middle Eastern origin, are in demand, while Bugis _badik_, daggers with characteristically curved handles, are prized heirlooms. Gold ornaments and gold-threaded _songket_ cloths are paraded at weddings. Royal regalia are now on display in some local museums.

Medicine. While Western medicine has made inroads with the government-established rural medical health centers (_puskesmas_), many illnesses are seen as specifically Bugis and curable only by indigenous practitioners (_sanro_) who use such techniques as extraction of foreign objects, massage, use of bespelled or holy water, and blowing on the patient after the utterance of prayers. Illness may be due to one's spirit leaving the body when subjected to sudden shock, and certain therapies are directed to its recovery. Invulnerability magic is much prized, with the shadow playing an important protective role. Certain illnesses and misfortunes are inflicted by specific spirits associated with each of the four major elements—fire, air, earth, and water.

Death and Afterlife.   Islamic notions of heaven and hell are now most influential, although among syncretic Bugis local spirits are still identified as the spirits of deceased rulers and other formerly powerful individuals. Funerals follow Islamic rites, and are not occasions for major redistributions, as among the neighboring Toraja. Memorial gatherings for prayer and a shared meal may be performed at such intervals as forty days after a death.

See also Makassar

Bibliography

Andaya, Leonard (1981). *The Heritage of Arung Palakka: A History of South Sulawesi (Celebes) in the Seventeenth Century.* Verhandelingen van het Koninklijk Instituut voor Taal-, Land- en Volkenkunde. The Hague: Martinus Nijhoff.

Errington, Shelly (1989). *Meaning and Power in a Southeast Asian Realm.* Princeton: Princeton University Press.

Hamonic, Gilbert (1987). *Le langage des dieux: Cultes et pouvoirs pré-islamiques en pays bugis Célèbes-Sud, Indonésie.* Paris: Centre National de la Recherche Scientifique.

Millar, Susan Bolyard (1989). *Bugis Weddings: Rituals of Social Location in Modern Indonesia.* Berkeley: University of California at Berkeley, Center for South and Southeast Asia Studies.

Pelras, Christian, et al. (1975). *Archipel: Études interdisciplinaires sur le monde insulindien,* no. 10. Special issue devoted to South Sulawesi.

GREG ACCIAIOLI

Bukidnon

ETHNONYMS: Binokid, Binukid, Higaonan, Higaunen

Orientation

Identification.   The Bukidnon people of the southern Philippines speak the Binukid dialect within the Manobo Language Family. "Bukidnon" is a Bisayan word for "people of the mountains," first used by Bisayan-speaking settlers of Mindanao's north coast, on whom its negative connotation for non-Hispanicized (i.e., "non-civilized") mountain people was not lost. The Spanish, who had referred to all upland peoples simply as *monteses,* adopted it in the late nineteenth century to distinguish Binukid speakers from the Manobo living directly to their south. The nonindigenous origin of the term has occasioned some controversy in recent years, with Bukidnon influenced by PANAMIN, the Philippine government agency formerly in charge of tribal peoples, adopting the name "Higaonnan" (derived from the Binukid *gaon* for "away from the water") as an alternative. This, however, has not caught on with most Binukid speakers who, grown used to "Bukidnon," steadfastly continue to call themselves by this name.

Location.   Bukidnon today is the name of a Philippine province measuring 8,294 square kilometers landlocked in north-central Mindanao. The Bukidnon people for the most part live north of the eighth parallel on the grassland plateau 300–900 meters in elevation that is dominated by Kitanglad Mountain, the second-highest (after Mt. Apo) Philippine peak at 2,938 meters. Rivers rush from Kitanglad and other mountains, cutting precipitous gorges through the adtuyon clay soil. The Cagayan and Tagoloan river systems empty into Macajalar Bay to the north; the Pulangi, which originates in northeast Bukidnon, sweeps south into Cotabato where it becomes the Rio Grande of Mindanao. The plateau's average mean temperature is 23° C and rainfall averages 274.3 centimeters annually. September is the wettest month; the driest period is in March and April.

Demography.   The Bukidnon people have been a diminishing minority in the province that bears their name ever since Filipinos from elsewhere in the archipelago began settling there in growing numbers after World War II. Many have intermarried with these newcomers, and their children have grown up speaking Cebuano-Bisayan, the province's lingua franca today, with 65.9 percent of the population now listing it as their mother tongue. In contrast, only 71,007, or 13.3 percent of the province's population of 532,818 in 1975, reported Binukid as their mother tongue, and only 3,351 of these reside in urban areas. Binukid speakers can be found today mainly in small *barangay* in the northern municipalities of the province. Few possess either wealth or political power.

Linguistic Affiliation.   According to the linguist Richard Elkins, Binukid and its sister languages, Kinamigin and Cagayano, represent the first branch in the family tree of Manobo languages within the Malayo-Polynesian language category. Dialects include Banuaon (Banuanon), spoken along the Agusan border, southern Bukidnon Manobo, and Higaonan in the northern reaches of the province.

History and Cultural Relations

Bukidnon trace their origins to a pre-Islamic, Proto-Manobo-speaking population located along the southwestern coast of Mindanao, perhaps near the mouth of the Rio Grande. According to their oral epic known as the *Ulagina,* or *Olagina,* the central event in their history involved their journey away from the coast and the trials they endured in the wilderness as they followed their great culture hero named Agyu. They settled on the plateau and developed trade ties with both the Islamicized Maguindanao to their south and the Hispanicized Visayans to their north. They remained relatively uninfluenced by Spanish rule until the 1880s and 1890s when Jesuits baptized over 8,000 of the 20,000 people whom they estimated to comprise the Bukidnon population, and persuaded most of these to settle in towns built on the model of the Philippine plaza complex. Bukidnon also became more and more closely tied to the Philippine economy as producers of cash crops like abaca, cacao, coffee, and tobacco. The American colonial government created a special province called Agusan in 1907, with Bukidnon as one of two subprovinces whose "non-Christian" population came directly under American governance. Bukidnon became a full province in 1914, but as an area predominantly of "non-Christians" and hence still a Special Province, it remained directly under American control. Americans initiated a flourishing cattle industry on the plateau, which employed a number of Bukidnon men as cowboys. They also opened a pineapple plantation, which involved still more Bukidnon in the new cash economy. Guerrillas and Japanese soldiers destroyed the cattle herds during World War II, leaving the land open for thousands of farmers who migrated to Bukidnon in the 1950s and 1960s, thus raising the province's population from 63,470 in 1948 to 194,368 in 1960, and to 414,762 in 1970. During this time of rapid population growth, the Binukid-speaking population remained comparatively stable. Today they may be divided into three principal categories. First, some continue to reside in very remote settlements near the headwaters of the Pulangi or high up on the slopes of Mount Kitanglad or Mount Kalatungan. A second category, comprising the majority of Bukidnon who reside in small barangay spread out across the plateau, is more acculturated. Finally, a third and much smaller category embraces those living in Malaybalay and other towns along the highway, most of whom have ceased to regard themselves as culturally different from their Bisayan neighbors.

Settlements

Bukidnon once lived in or near _tulugan_ (communal houses with appended individual quarters) in groups of usually fewer than fifty related families presided over by a head _datu_ (chief) and lesser datus. By the turn of the century, thanks to the efforts of Spanish priests and American colonial officials, all but a few of these had been replaced by settlements of single-family houses located for the most part along the main north-south road or along feeder roads. Today some Bukidnon continue to live in small, rather dispersed strip settlements located along trails and logging roads far from the highway. Houses in these remote villages are usually made of bamboo and thatch, and many are raised above the ground with floors of bamboo strips. More Bukidnon live in barangay along the highway or feeder roads, where small general stores are typically made of wood and cinder-block, as are some of the homes, and corrugated iron is the preferred material for roofing. Finally, a minority of the Bukidnon people live in towns like Malaybalay, Impasugong, and Valencia where their housing is indistinguishable from that of their migrant (usually Bisayan) neighbors.

Economy

Subsistence and Commercial Activities. The Bukidnon have always been farmers, and with 95 percent still living in rural areas they remain primarily farmers today. Maize and rice are their principal crops. Until the turn of the century they cultivated these entirely in swidden plots along the edge of the plateau. As they were persuaded to settle in towns and villages on the grasslands, they began plow agriculture in small plots near their homes. Nevertheless, it is still common for Bukidnon, especially in remote villages, to practice slash-and-burn farming while also maintaining a garden plot around their home. Few possess mechanized means for plowing. They use a water buffalo or bullock to pull their plow and they harvest by hand. Other subsistence crops common in Bukidnon communities include nangka, camote (sweet potato), gabi, cassava, beans, banana, and coconut. In recent years many farmers have invested in coffee growing as a commercial substitute for abaca, which for decades was their principal cash crop. While agriculture remains the foundation of the Bukidnon economy, many young Bukidnon have gained employment with mining and logging companies in the province, usually as guards rather than miners or loggers. In all of these cases, Bukidnon represent an impoverished or at best marginal economic group. The exceptions to this rule are the Bukidnon civil servants (usually teachers or clerks) who represent a significant minority of the Binukid-speaking population, especially in urban areas.

Industrial Arts. Some Bukidnon families supplement their meager income by mat making, basketry, and embroidery. But other traditional arts such as pottery and wood carving have been virtually lost.

Trade. Few Bukidnon have ever been traders. Today some farmers transport their produce as far as Cagayan de Oro, but most sell at the nearest mill. There are a number of local Bukidnon cooperatives and Bukidnon-owned general-merchandise stores, but these are the exception in a trading world dominated by Tagalogs, Ilocanos, Cebuanos, other migrants, and Chinese. Bukidnon, as a rule, are just too poor to become economically competitive.

Division of Labor. Bukidnon women have enjoyed a degree of power and respect, especially those with salaried jobs such as teaching. But the division of labor continues to place them at a disadvantage because they also are expected to cook, clean, rear the children, and launder. In agriculture they do the planting (although men assist) and weeding, and they help with the harvest. They also earn some supplementary income through their mat making, basketry, and embroidery work, and by serving as washerwomen for more affluent families. When not engaged in preparing the soil for planting and other agricultural tasks, men may work at carpentry, construction, stripping abaca, and transporting crops to market.

Land Tenure. In Bukidnon Province over 60 percent of the farms are under title to their resident farmer, although tenancy rates have been rising since 1960. The Bukidnon people worked their land under usufructory arrangements rather than as private property until the present century. Today most do not own any land. Those who do own very small farms of less than 5 hectares, and many of these do not have a secure title. In remote areas, where swidden agriculture is still common, they slash-and-burn unused land without any title at all. Whether swidden or plow agriculturalists, smallholders or tenants, Bukidnon tend to be, at best, poor subsistence farmers, and many do not have sufficient land or tenancy rights to be self-sufficient at all.

Kinship

For Bukidnon, descent is traced bilaterally. Their kin group consists of consanguineous relatives on both their father's and their mother's sides, and affinal relatives by marriage. Today they live in nuclear-family households, but there are usually kindred living in the same barangay to whom they can turn for help and support, and, like other Filipinos, they maintain a relationship based on ties of reciprocity with relatives wherever these may be.

Marriage and Family

Marriage. Bukidnon marriages are monogamous, although in the past datus took more than one wife if they could afford to do so, a custom still practiced by a few datus in remote areas today. Child betrothal, studied by Cole in 1910, is a thing of the past. Marriages, which used to be initiated by the bridegroom's father and arranged by parents of both bride and groom who used go-betweens to negotiate an appropriate bride-price, are now typically based on freedom of choice. While one can marry either within or outside one's community, brothers and sisters, and cousins on both sides, are forbidden to wed. After marriage it is still common for the new couple to live with and work for the wife's parents for at least a few months before they move to a house of their own. Some Bukidnon still conduct two marriage ceremonies, one following their ancient customs and presided over by datus, and a second within the Roman Catholic church. Divorce is rare. Where it happens, common property is divided equally, and if the wife has any property in her own name she may take this with her.

Domestic Unit. In contrast to the past when large extended families lived in tulugan, today few Bukidnon households are larger than mother, father, children, and perhaps grandparents. When the families of married sons and/or daughters are dwelling in the same household, this is usually only a temporary arrangement.

Inheritance. When her husband dies, a wife without children will inherit all the family property. If she has children, she will inherit half the property, and her children (male and female) will split the other half equally.

Socialization. The mother, with help from her older children, has primary responsibility for child rearing. Bukidnon children are socialized to be generous in their treatment of others, to avoid or minimize interpersonal conflict by being sensitive to others' self-esteem, and to be respectful of their natural environment.

Sociopolitical Organization

Social Organization. Bukidnon today are so intermixed and intermarried with non-Bukidnon that, while they remain cognizant of the ethnolinguistic identity of other residents in their barangay, they cannot be said to maintain a separate social organization. Like other Filipinos, their social circle consists of a mosaic of personal alliances that each Bukidnon weaves with non-Bukidnon as well as with other Bukidnon out of real kinship ties, ritual kinship relations, relationships based on special debts of gratitude, market-exchange partnerships, patron-client bonds, and friendships. One's place in this circle is not determined by rank at birth. Those who receive greatest respect from other Bukidnon tend to be those living in towns who have, by virtue of their educational level, obtained salaried civil-service jobs. It follows that the Bukidnon tend to place extraordinary importance on education, for this has been their ticket to success. This relatively open social system, however, represents a marked change from the past. Until the turn of the century, Bukidnon society remained hierarchically organized, crowned by the tribal head datu whose *sakop* (followers) included his first wife and other wives and their children, lesser datus and their families, families of freemen without a datu as their head, and slaves by

debt bondage or capture—although even then, and with the exception of slaves, rank depended less on birth than on talent. Sakop worked the land designated for them by the head datu, protected the community from would-be slavers, and served the head datu on request.

Political Organization. Despite recent efforts by the Philippine central government to organize and employ datus in a Higaonan Datu Association, political unity continues to elude the Bukidnon people. Before the Spanish began resettling them in villages on the plateau, they may have recognized regional chiefs known as *masalicampo*. But there is no evidence that they were ever united under a single leader possessing the stature of a sultan or raja, and they have never regarded themselves as anything like a nation.

Social Control. As is the case with other Filipinos, Bukidnon stress skills that enhance smooth interpersonal relations and minimize interpersonal conflict. When a difference of opinion arises, in order not to injure another's self-esteem, they will seek out a go-between, employ euphemism rather than open criticism, or just go along (at least superficially) with the situation. In the old datu system, if a go-between succeeded in settling disputes without arousing hard feelings on any side, he soon came to be called "datu" for dispute settling; this involved not only fairness and acquaintance with customary law, but generosity in using one's own resources (plates, jars, animals, money) to assuage the bad feelings of a disputant. Today Bukidnon continue to seek out leaders who can arbitrate their disagreements and thereby help them circumvent the more expensive and formal legal system of the Philippines.

Conflict. Bukidnon generally seek not to engage in fighting but rather to avoid it. This, however, was not always the case, and there have been important exceptions to this rule in recent history. Cole reported that until the twentieth century *bagani* (warriors) would frequently raid Manobo or other Bukidnon settlements for slaves and personal prestige. They produced only very crude weapons themselves, depending on trade with Moros for their best knives and spears. They did not practice headhunting, but did on occasion engage in the ritual sacrifice of a captured enemy. In the last two decades acts of violence have become more and more commonplace as Bukidnon have lashed out against loggers, migrant settlers, the personnel of large sugar and pineapple corporations, and others whom they blame for their general loss of land and power. The most serious of many such incidents occurred in 1975 when hundreds of Bukidnon joined the Rizalian revitalization movement in the remote region of Miarayon between Mounts Kitanglad and Kalatungan. At least 34, and perhaps as many as 200, were killed in the fighting that ensued between them and the Constabulary.

Religion and Expressive Culture

Religious Beliefs. Today, Bukidnon in the major towns worship no differently than their non-Bukidnon neighbors, but those in more distant villages have accepted Christianity more selectively. They continue to believe in a vast hierarchy of invisible supernatural beings led by Magbabáya, "most powerful of all." These spirits possess human characteristics and, while most are beneficent, they have to be won over with sacrifices of food and drink. Christian images, novenas, crucifixes, celebrations, and saints have simply been substituted for the old amulets, ceremonies, and guardian spirits, and the primary purpose of worship remains one of short-term gain rather than long-term salvation. Some Bukidnon in the vicinity of Malaybalay have converted to Protestant churches. Others, in remote regions of the province, have become Rizalians. In the traditional Bukidnon pantheon there are six categories of spirits. Highest of these are the great spirits of sky, earth, and the four cardinal points, including Magbabáya. Second are the guardian spirits of certain activities (farming) and things (water, animals). Then come the localized nature spirits of whom the _busao_ are malevolent. Each Bukidnon has his/her personal guardian spirits. Finally, there are the _gimokod,_ or multiple souls within one's body, which may leave and have to be called back by an intermediary (_baylan_) to avert death.

Religious Practitioners. Catholic priests are the principal religious figures to whom Bukidnon turn today. But in villages where priests are not resident, and especially in those that are visited by priests only once a month or less, the baylan still plays an important role as the one who can communicate with spirits. Both men and women can be baylan. One who wishes to do so simply studies with an established baylan to learn how to ascertain the cause of illness by identifying which spirit is involved, and how to perform the precise actions and intone the exact invocations called for in ceremonies intended to summon and please the spirit in question. Baylan claim to be intermediaries, not mediums. A few have become millennarian leaders. They have never formed a priesthood, and they have no temples or churches.

Ceremonies. _Pamuhat_ is the generic term for ceremonies propitiating the spirits through prayers and sacrifices of food and/or drink. The principal Bukidnon celebration was _kaliga_ (_kaliga-on_) at harvest time, but today the fiesta serves as a substitute.

Arts. The arts have declined in both quality and quantity throughout this century. Today Bukidnon women still make and sell grass mats and grass or abaca-fiber baskets. Also, the annual celebration since 1974 of Kaamulan in the provincial capital of Malaybalay has helped revive the art of appliqué in the creation of bright red, white, blue, black, and yellow Bukidnon outfits. Owing to the popularity of Western songs played loudly over the radio, few Bukidnon sing the old songs (_sala_ and _limbay_) or play the old instruments (flutes: _lantuy_ and _pulala;_ Jew's harp: _kula-ing;_ stringed instrument: _dayuray;_ gong; and drum). Dances, some of which are mimetic of birds or animals, are limited to the Kaamulan festival and, where kaliga-on is still celebrated, to that harvest festival.

Medicine. Today Bukidnon everywhere know the value of modern medicine and medical practices, and when seriously ill will spare no effort to obtain treatment in a clinic or hospital. But because even common drugs are too expensive for most Bukidnon, they will utilize home remedies and medicinal herbs, and may also call upon a baylan, before seeking help from trained medical personnel.

Death and Afterlife. Few Bukidnon today think of death or the afterlife any differently than do their non-Bukidnon neighbors, and their funeral ceremonies are also identical. In villages far from the highway, some Bukidnon continue to believe that one's soul goes to Mount Balatukan regardless of one's conduct in life, and these people will bury with the deceased a few of his/her belongings for use in that terrestrial abode of the dead. Otherwise Christian burial is practiced.

Bibliography

Cole, Fay-Cooper (1956). _The Bukidnon of Mindanao._ Volume 46 of Fieldiana: Anthropology. Chicago: Field Museum of Natural History.

Edgerton, Ronald K. (1982). "Frontier Society on the Bukidnon Plateau, 1870–1941." In _Philippine Social History: Global Trade and Local Transformations,_ edited by Alfred W. McCoy and Ed. C. de Jesus. Honolulu: University Press of Hawaii.

de Guzman, Alfonso, and Esther M. Pacheco, eds. (1973). _Bukidnon Politics and Religion._ Quezon City: Institute of Philippine Culture, Ateneo de Manila University.

Lao, Mardonio M. (1985). _Bukidnon in Historical Perspective._ Musuan, Bukidnon: Central Mindanao University.

Madigan, Francis C. (1969). _Mindanao's Inland Province: A Socio-Economic Survey of Bukidnon._ Book 1, _Bukidnon Province as a Whole._ Cagayan de Oro City: Research Institute for Mindanao Culture, Xavier University.

RONALD K. EDGERTON

Bunun

ETHNONYMS: none

Orientation

Identification. The Bunun of Taiwan use the term "Bunun" to refer to all Bunun; it means "person." Their language is also called Bunun. The Bunun are known to have been divided into six named subgroups (Isbukun, Takebaka, Takebanuan, Takepulan, Taketodo, and Takevatan), each characterized by differences in dialect and culture. There are no longer any Bunun who identify themselves as belonging to the Takepulan subethnic group, and scholars have suggested that the Takepulan have been assimilated into other subgroups. The largest of the remaining subethnic groups is the Isbukun.

Location. The Bunun are scattered in the mountainous area of central Taiwan between 23° and 24° N and at about 120°30′ E, an area that includes Yu-shan Mountain, the highest mountain in Taiwan. The climate is subtropical. Annual rainfall is about 200 centimeters. Most rain falls in the summer months from July to September, when typhoons are frequent.

Demography. In 1978, the estimated population was 32,000, or 0.3 percent of the total population of Taiwan. There were 18,113 Bunun reported in a 1932 census, so their numbers have been slowly increasing. There are now some temporary migrants in the cities, but most Bunun still live in the "reservation area."

Linguistic Affiliation. Historical linguists classify the Bunun language as belonging to a Branch of Proto-Northern Indonesian, which is a Branch of Proto-Hesperonesian. The latter is thought to belong to the Proto-Western Austronesian Language Family, which is in turn a branch of Proto-Austronesian.

History and Cultural Relations

There are few written documents with which to trace Bunun history. Oral history indicates, however, that the Bunun lived in the Puli plain in the eighteenth century, and thereafter were forced by Han Chinese immigrants and Plains Aborigines to move to their current location. Most Bunun now regard Yu-shan as their ancestral homeland. Before 1895, the Bunun territory in central Taiwan had expanded east and south from the Yu-shan area as a result of population growth, in the process coming into contact with other aboriginal peoples such as Atayal, Tsou, Ami, Puyuma, Paiwan, and Han Chinese. The Japanese colonial government also had some impact on the Bunun during its occupation (1895–1945). After World War II, the Republic of China (R.O.C.) government and Christianity have been influential. The extent of the impact of neighboring ethnic groups, the Japanese government, the current Han Chinese-dominated government, and Christianity is difficult to establish, but it is clear that the Bunun have been reinventing their culture and society in response to these external contacts.

Settlements

The Bunun population is the third largest of the Taiwan aboriginal groups, and they occupy the second-largest area. They have been the most successful of Taiwan Aborigines in the expansion of their territory through migration. The average Bunun settlement size is quite small compared to other Taiwan aborigines. A 1938 survey reported an average settlement size of 111.22 persons. Also, the Bunun are located in the higher elevations of Taiwan. A 1929 survey by T. Kano reported that 68.2 percent of Bunun settlements were located above 1,000 meters. Bunun settlements can be divided into three types that are localized in different parts in Taiwan: (1) large settlements with strict clan organization in the north; (2) smaller and more isolated settlements in the east and the center; (3) scattered and isolated settlements in the south which, except for state-imposed administrative divisions, lack clear boundaries.

Economy

Subsistence and Commercial Activities. Like many other Taiwan aborigines, the Bunun lived until the end of World War II on a "traditional" subsistence diet of maize and sweet potato produced by shifting cultivation. This subsistence economy overshadowed commercial activities, though commerce has long been present. The Japanese government successfully forced the Bunun to cultivate wet rice instead of maize before the end of World War II. When the Bunun began to cultivate cash crops about 1970, wet rice was given up. These crop substitutions have contributed to an increase in other commercial activity to obtain food and other consumables.

Industrial Arts. Many new technologies from the Han Chinese and the Japanese have been accepted by the Bunun, and the traditional industrial arts of textiles, house building, and metallurgy have all but disappeared.

Trade. Lacking their own industries, the Bunun are heavily dependent on trade, which, in turn, has bound the Bunun increasingly closely with the wider Taiwan society. Economic exploitation of the Bunun by Chinese middlemen has led to serious interethnic conflict.

Division of Labor. Traditionally, men were in charge of hunting, and women and children were responsible for food gathering. Women performed everyday agricultural tasks, but men performed the heavier work of clearing land and harvesting crops. Men also assumed the important traditional sociopolitical roles (such as military leader and public shaman); women performed domestic work. This traditional division of labor gradually has given way in the face of increasing social differentiation. The market economy has reinforced the preexisting traditional value placed on personal performance. Capable women can now take any job or occupy any social status.

Land Tenure. Traditionally, the Bunun classified land into three categories: for hunting, for planting, and for housing. Each type was controlled, respectively by the patriclan, household, and settlement. These categories might sometimes overlap when the same parcel of land could be controlled by different social units for their separate functions. This traditional classification no longer exists. First, the R.O.C. government carried out a land survey with the explicit intention of imposing a "modern" concept of ownership. Second, land has become valued as part of Bunun entry into the wider market economy of Taiwan.

Kinship

Kin Groups and Descent. In comparison with other Taiwan aborigines, Bunun are noted for their complex clan system. The smallest unit is the subclan (*gauduslan*). Each subclan is distinguished from other subclans by name. Subclan names are now used as surnames. All members of a subclan are descendants of a common patrilineal ancestor, although the exact genealogical relationship is sometimes unknown. The subclans are organized into clans (also called gauduslan). All clan members are descendants of a common though unknown patrilineal ancestor. The subclans of a clan are hierarchically ordered on the basis of the birth order of the various focal ancestors of the individual subclans. Each clan is identified by a unique clan origin myth describing the birth order of the focal ancestor of each subclan. Clans are organized into another higher level called *gavian*. Only some gavian are named, and the genealogical relations between the clans may be either assumed or mythical. Kin groups thus emphasize a centripetal solidarity with their assumed or mythical patrilineal descent and birth order, which are inborn or ascribed. Egalitarian and competitive tendencies, however, also are manifest: status is achieved and individually manipulable.

By his own achievement, any male can split the original sub-clan and found a new one if he can attract enough followers. Sometimes he can reorder the hierarchical birth order in a clan, or switch his clan's gavian association. Also, the concept of "person" supports and is more fundamental than patrilineal ideology. The concept of "person" is grounded in _hanido_ (spirit) beliefs, where a person's spirits are derived from the father and a person's body from the mother. Since the end of World War II, this clan system has gradually lost most of its social functions. Kin relations, however, still conform to the Bunun concept of person.

Kinship Terminology. The Bunun are noted for their Omaha kinship terminology insofar as males of a mother's patrilineal subclan tend to be addressed by the same kin term as the mother's brother. T. Mabuchi suggests that the use of this single kin term is based on the Bunun belief in the spiritual predominance of the mother's brother over his sister's children.

Marriage and Family

Marriage. Bunun often remarry after losing a marriage partner, but otherwise observe strict monogamy. Residence is traditionally patrilocal and descent patrilineal, and, since the end of World War II, both have been strengthened by Han Chinese influence. Marriage is in principle arranged by parents, though in practice a person has some latitude of choice. Before the end of World War II, there was a preference for settlement endogamy and prohibitions on the following types of marriage: (1) within the same gavian, (2) with the mother's patriclan member, (3) with people whose mothers were from one's mother's patriclan. With an average of 111.22 people per settlement, the number of gauduslan and gavian in any one settlement was limited. Preferential settlement endogamy and clan proscriptions left so few choices in marriage that, in Mabuchi's opinion, proscriptive marriage rules acted in practice as prescriptive ones. With the increase in external contacts since the end of World War II, marriages outside the settlement, including with other ethnic groups, have increased, but the traditional clan proscriptions have strengthened.

Domestic Unit. Bunun refer to their domestic group as _lumah_, which includes both the house and all members of the domestic unit regardless of kin ties. Earlier studies emphasized the "extended family" as a major feature of the Bunun. Recent studies have found, however, that the domestic unit is not necessarily a kin unit, but instead has its own logic allowing inclusion of members who lack consanguineal or affinal ties. Traditionally, the domestic unit and the settlement were homologous in structure but complementary in function. The relations between the domestic unit and settlement and between the spatial structure and the material of the house have also changed in response to external forces.

Inheritance. The property of the domestic unit traditionally was inherited by its members according to past contribution to the domestic unit, without taking consideration of kin relations or ascribed status. This made it possible for domestic-unit property to be inherited by nonpatrilineal members. However, the strengthening of patrilineality through external Han Chinese influence has resulted in disputes and lawsuits between members of the same domestic unit.

Socialization. Without age grades or age sets, Bunun socialization traditionally was carried out by the domestic unit and settlement as a normal part of everyday life. The presence of the church and Christianity, and of the state educational system and state ideology, have diluted, or even replaced, some original Bunun cultural ideas. As a consequence, Christianization and Sinicization now also play a role in socialization.

Sociopolitical Organization

Social and Political Organization. The settlement was traditionally an important and autonomous sociopolitical unit. Beyond the settlement, there were only temporary alliances among settlements for defense against their common enemy. The domestic unit was the basic social unit within the settlement, and there was no formal intermediate institution connecting the two levels. There were two formal sociopolitical offices through which some people could take charge of the social order: the _lisigadan lus-an_ and the _lavian_. The lisigadan lus-an was in charge of the social order within the settlement; the lavian dealt with relations with other Bunun settlements and other tribes. Both offices could be attained through the practical achievements of an individual, and thus were not ascribed. Still, the members of a settlement's dominant clan had a better chance of obtaining such offices. The Bunun lacked a formal process for denominating these offices. Succession was earned through successful practice as confirmed by settlement consensus. Differences within a settlement about who would be a more capable leader usually resulted in the splitting of the settlement. Since the end of World War II, however, the traditional political system has been replaced by the R.O.C. political system and the settlement has completely lost its traditional political autonomy. The new administrative offices (such as village head) can only deal with other settlements, or with higher-level bureaucratic units. Within a settlement, church leaders now play, to a limited extent, the traditional role of the lisigadan lus-an.

Social Control and Conflict. Traditionally, intra- and intersettlement conflicts were resolved by the lisigadan lus-an and the gavian. In fact, this mechanism was grounded in common beliefs and customs, through which a consensus could be created by way of social pressure on the deviant. The presence of Han Chinese immigrants and merchants who do not share Bunun beliefs and customs has weakened this form of social control, and generates conflict in the course of competition for their respective economic benefit. The R.O.C. government has taken a large part in resolving this kind of social conflict. Thus, not only has the mechanism of social control changed, but so has the nature of social conflict. Social conflict between the Bunun and the Chinese has become more serious.

Religion and Expressive Culture

Religious Beliefs and Supernaturals. The traditional religious beliefs of the Bunun are based on the concept of "hanido"—the spirit of any animate creature or inanimate natural object. The hanido of any natural object has its own special innate power. The strength of hanido power varies among living beings or objects of the same category. The hanido spirit leaves and is transformed or disappears when a living being dies or an object vanishes. Human beings are like other living beings and objects, except that humans have two hanidos instead of one, a good hanido of the right shoulder and a bad hanido of the left shoulder. A person's hanidos determine what a person wants to do, and the final outcome of any activity depends on the hanidos having the strength to overcome the strength of another living being's or object's hanido. By this kind of belief, Bunun can explain general problems in everyday life. Another important religious concept is *dehanin*. Dehanin refers to the sky, although its meaning is more ambiguous. It traditionally referred to the power of various celestial phenomena such as wind, rain, thunder, lightning, moon, sun, star, and so on. Because the power of dehanin was inactive in ordinary life, attention was paid to dehanin only during times of disaster. Traditionally, rituals had to be held to express gratitude to the celestial bodies or dehanin for relief from disaster. Today, Christian beliefs have been accepted by being assimilated to the traditional beliefs in dehanin and hanido. "Dehanin" is now used to refer to the Christian God, and "hanido" to evil or Satan.

Religious Practitioners and Ceremonies.   Traditionally, any person could perform a ceremony for himself or herself or for others if his or her hanido had enough power. In this sense, a religious practitioner was not a special social category, and potentially any person could serve in any ritual role. Traditional ceremonies can be classified into two categories: life-cycle rituals and calendrical rituals. The former continue to exist with a Christian color, but the latter have been abandoned with the demise of shifting cultivation.

Death and Afterlife.   Traditionally, kin buried the body of a dead person in different places depending on the cause of death. Violent and accidental deaths were regarded as bad deaths (*ikula*), and the body was immediately buried on the spot. The hanido of persons who died violently or accidentally were harmful to human beings. Death at home from illness or natural causes was a good death (*idmamino madai*). Kin buried the body of such dead persons in their house. If the dead person had made a major contribution to the society, he or she would be buried near the door of the house so that the hanido of the dead person could protect the surviving members of the domestic unit. The hanido of such persons would go to *maiason*, where their great ancestors lived forever. With Christianization, the dead are now buried at the entrance to the settlement. The same distinction between good and bad deaths is maintained, however, and "maiason" now refers to paradise. Other traditional taboos and customs related to death are still observed.

See also Taiwan Aborigines

Bibliography

Huang, Ying-Kuei (1988). "Conversion and Religious Change among the Bunun of Taiwan." Ph.D. dissertation, University of London.

Mabuchi, T. (1974). *Mabuchi Toichi Chosaku-shu*. 3 vols. Tokyo: Shakai Shiso-Sha.

YING-KUEI HUANG

Burakumin

ETHNONYMS: Eta, Hinin (historic, derogatory); Hisabetsumin; Outcaste; Shin-Heimin (historic, often derogatory); Tokushu Burakumin (often derogatory)

Orientation

Identification.   It is important to note that neither historic outcastes nor Burakumin are racially distinguishable from the majority of Japanese, despite some common beliefs and academic writings that propose non-Japanese racial origins for Burakumin. Although in the historic period the mainstream Japanese subjected outcastes to strict dress codes and often required them to wear pieces of leather on their outer garments to signify their status, in contemporary Japan there is little to isolate the Burakumin from the majority population. Except for their reported informality of dress code, language, and behavior, Burakumin do not differ from the Japanese majority in appearance, language, and most other cultural practices.

Burakumin exclusively or dominantly occupy many small communities or areas in a community; indeed, their culture name means "hamlet or community people." (In this article, "Burakumin" is used to designate the people, "buraku" to designate their communities.) The names "Eta" and "Hinin" were used through the Middle Ages to refer to outcastes of various sorts. Eta was derived from the Japanese word for leatherworker, a name that was later spelled differently in Chinese characters to mean "plenty of defilement," which suits the popular perception of their occupation. Hinin means "nonhuman." After the abolition of caste in 1871, these words were replaced by Shin-Heimin (new commoners), Hisabetsumin (discriminated people), Tokushu Burakumin (special community people), or Burakumin.

Since the Burakumin look and behave much like the majority population, others most commonly identify Burakumin by their place of origin. Although Burakumin may choose to "pass" as non-Burakumin to avoid various forms of discrimination, they risk having their identity scrutinized if others discover their place of birth and original residence. Local people know certain areas in a locality to be buraku, and they see any connection to such areas as signifying outcaste origin. Even when a person from a buraku moves to a different region in Japan, background investigation or accident may reveal his or her origin, and this discovery often results in stigmatization of the person's professional, social, personal, and emotional life.

Location.   Burakumin communities are more heavily distributed in western Japan, particularly in the prefectures of Hyōgo, Okayama, Hiroshima, Ehime, and Fukuoka. Urban centers in western Japan, such as Kyoto and Osaka, have large numbers of buraku. In contrast, the Tokyo metropolitan area, situated in eastern Japan, has a surprisingly small number of buraku.

Demography.   There are some arguments about how many buraku and Burakumin exist in Japan today. The General Affairs Agency census in 1985 reported that there were then 1,163,372 Burakumin and 4,594 buraku in Japan. Independent scholars of the Burakumin issue criticize these figures as much too small and say they do not reflect the reality of the

Burakumin situation. Their estimates suggest that 2 to 3 million Burakumin and approximately 6,000 buraku currently exist in Japan.

The Burakumin are heavily concentrated in the western part of Japan. According to the above-mentioned statistics, Hyōgo has the largest number of Burakumin (153,236), followed by Osaka (143,305), Fukuoka (135,956), Nara (62,175), and Okayama (56,687). In eastern Japan, Saitama, Gumma, and Tochigi prefectures have relatively high numbers of Burakumin. There are no known Burakumin in the northernmost prefecture of Hokkaidō.

Before the 1920 census no comprehensive demographic data existed; however, some regional records were available. The population survey of Kyoto in 1715 recorded 11 outcaste communities with a population of 2,064; in 1800 4,423 outcastes were reported in Osaka; the National Census of 1871 counted 261,311 Eta, 23,480 Hinin, and 79,095 other categories of outcastes. The 1920 census reported that there were 4,890 buraku and 829,675 Burakumin in Japan; by 1935, the number of buraku had increased to 5,367 and that of Burakumin to almost 1 million.

As a general tendency the Burakumin population was increasing faster than the general population of Japan in the last century. The official abolition of outcaste status and assimilation efforts seem to have had no influence over the persistence of Burakumin. Continuous recruitment of new members by marriage and high birthrates in Burakumin communities account for this tendency.

Linguistic Affiliation. The linguistic affiliation of the Burakumin is identical to that of mainstream Japanese. Some ethnographic reports indicate that their speech tends to be more informal and colloquial than that of the mainstream Japanese. In contemporary Japan, where most Burakumin children are educated in the same formal schooling system as other Japanese children, any community or occupational jargon Burakumin may have developed historically is bound to decrease or even to disappear.

History and Cultural Relations

The history of outcastes in Japan dates back to its early historic period, beginning in the eighth century A.D. (Nara period). Under the centralized bureaucratic government with imperial leadership, clan-based groups called Uji and Kabane became associated with often exclusive occupational guilds, or be. These guilds included leatherworkers, caretakers of the dead and tombs, and butchers—the traditional occupations of later outcastes.

The practitioners of these occupations gradually became separated from the majority society through the ancient to early feudal periods as unclean, undesirable, lowly, and less than human, and Japanese society denied them rights granted to its mainstream members. In addition to encompassing the traditional occupational groups, the outcaste community absorbed people who dropped out of the social systems because of poverty or criminal behavior, as well as those who failed to be an integral part of the stable society, for instance, runaway peasants, flood-plain dwellers, and itinerant entertainers of all sorts.

Toward the end of the twelfth century the failing economic system based on peasantry and heavy taxation helped cause the decline of imperial power and the rise of the military class, which marked the beginning of the feudal age. The consequent political instability and poverty affected commoners most severely, and a large number of peasants lost their financial means and social affiliation and were forced out of their homes and their assigned land. Because all peasants of the time were legally bound to their land and it was illegal for them to leave it, there was no place for them in the social system, and they became a transient population. Together with all other kinds of people who were excluded from the socioeconomic system, they joined traditional outcastes, to form the medieval outcaste population.

Historic evidence indicates that the medieval outcastes' occupation and residence varied. They engaged seasonally in work ranging from street performing, street sweeping, and leatherworking to unauthorized religious practices, changing their residence to accommodate their seasonal occupation.

This fluid population of outcastes gradually evolved into more specialized occupational groups throughout the feudal age. In the period of continuous military confrontations, from the fifteenth to the sixteenth century, warlords invited outcaste leatherworkers to their territories in order to secure the supply of military gear. The increasing demand for leather goods required a large number of outcastes in the industry and accelerated the occupational differentiation of outcastes.

In the seventeenth century the Tokugawa shogunate consolidated the systematic and legal discrimination against outcastes in Japan. After conquering warlords in most of the territory known today as Japan, the Tokugawa government set out to establish a strict administrative system that ensured social and economic stability for nearly three centuries. Incorporation of the outcaste below the rigidly divided castes of warriors, farmers, artisans, and merchants was a strategy for detracting from the dissatisfaction of lower castes: no matter how difficult their lives may have been they were still better than those of the "nonhuman" outcastes.

Eta and Hinin were two major categories of outcaste in this period. The most crucial differences between the two were the terms of their status and the areas of their occupational specialization. The Eta inherited their status and tended to engage in farming, craftwork, and community services. Hinin were usually those who had been degraded to outcaste status as a punishment and who could be reinstated to other castes; their occupations were usually unskilled or transient. Entertainers also fell into this latter category.

Although outcastes in the Tokugawa period varied in occupation and worked as leatherworkers, basket and sandal makers, temple caretakers, crematory workers, butchers, entertainers, laborers, and farmers, others commonly treated them as nonhumans and forced them into hard labor, economic difficulties, and poor living conditions. Outcastes lived in designated segregated districts or separate communities, and occupational necessity determined their access to the public areas. Government-imposed dress codes prohibited any ornaments and narrowly defined types and quality of garments allowed for outcastes.

Their services and the products of their labor belonged to the government authority, and until later in the period there was no direct compensation for their work; instead, the government allowed them the "privileges" of begging and gathering from the commoners who benefited from the outcastes' services. This practice led to the common but untrue belief that outcastes were "beggars" and not a productive part of society, and it strengthened the discriminatory perception of and behavior toward outcastes.

Toward the end of the nineteenth century, a major political change occurred. The shogunate failed in economic reforms and mismanaged the inevitable contacts with foreign countries. After negotiations among political leaders, the emperor was restored in 1868 as the sole political power of Japan, supported by low-rank warrior-class technocrats. The new government's priority was to modernize and Westernize the then "backward" nation. In 1871 the government emancipated the outcastes as a part of this modernization effort.

This emancipation brought no real change in the discrimination against outcastes. Discriminatory practices against Burakumin persisted in almost every aspect of life, and the government made little effort to enforce its declaration of "equality." In the municipal house registration government officials recorded former outcastes as "Shin-Heimin" (new commoners), thus clearly distinguishing them from the traditional commoners. Segregated residence also continued, although there were no more legal restrictions. The only change that occurred was a negative one: the industries that outcastes had traditionally dominated were now open to everyone, and nonoutcaste investors began to venture into leatherwork and other crafts, threatening the small-scale former outcaste manufacturers and placing a heavy economic strain on many Burakumin. In addition, rapid political and economic changes caused financial difficulties to common people, and their frustration often found outlets in "Eta-gari" (an outcaste hunt).

Many political and cultural movements characterize the struggle of former outcastes or Burakumin throughout modern history. Reconciliation and assimilation movements represent one side of their efforts, which argues that the poverty and different life-style of Burakumin caused the persisting discrimination and that the improvement of Burakumin living standards and cultural assimilation into the mainstream society are essential to eliminate the discrimination. The other side of the scale is the more aggressive political movement that defines the Burakumin situation as a class issue and the result of victimization rooted within the mainstream society. People who support this position assert the responsibility of the larger society for positive changes in Burakumin issues. These movements, aided by the democratic constitution instituted after World War II, the Law for Special Measures for Dōwa Projects (1969), and the Law for Special Measures for Regional Improvement (1982), have succeeded in improving the Burakumin situation and reducing discrimination to a certain extent.

More than a hundred years after emancipation, however, the deep root of discrimination against Burakumin is far from dead; indeed, it is finding a new soil in the complex social problems of contemporary Japan. While subtle forms of discrimination and vague but definite prejudice against Burakumin are the most common problems, some recent incidents show that hostility between the majority population and Burakumin still exists. A group of teenagers in Yokohama beat and killed homeless people in the 1980s, and day laborers from buraku participated in an outbreak of street riots in Osaka in 1991. The Law for Special Measures for Regional Improvement expired in March 1992, and the Japanese legislature concluded that there was no more need for this antidiscrimination law and decided not to renew it. The future development of the Burakumin movement under the new legal conditions is uncertain.

The long, continuing history of outcaste/Burakumin discrimination contains certain underlying ideas that have developed and supported the structure of discrimination and segregation in Japanese society. The most well-argued aspect of this discrimination centers on religious beliefs about the protection of ritual cleanliness. Teachings of Shintoism, the native religion of Japan, place a strong emphasis on ritual cleanliness as the essential part of righteousness, which is to be strictly guarded from contamination by death and blood. The introduction of Buddhism in the sixth century, and its recognition as a state religion from the eighth century onward, added to this view of death and blood as taboo, as the imperial and shogunate governments fully embraced the Buddhist doctrine against killing in their official policies. Thus the Japanese considered occupations that dealt with death or bloodshed "unclean" and contacts with them defiling. (This view that outcastes and their descendants are "unclean" is strong even today among many Japanese.) Still, the society needed to care for the dead properly according to the religious requirements, dispose of animal carcasses, and produce leather goods; the solution to this dilemma was the segregation of people who engaged in such occupations from the general population.

Furthermore, at the heart of the outcaste existence, which has served the contradictory needs of Japanese society, is the connection between the outcastes' continuing economic importance and their lack of access to political power. For instance, Hijiri priests in ancient Japan were extremely important religious figures, as they were knowledgeable in the agricultural calendar and counseled farmers with the proper timing for seasonal activities. The Yamato clan, the politicoreligious power in the early historic period, saw them as competition and eventually made them outcastes. The Hijiri priests thereafter played the same economic role in agricultural communities but were devoid of political influence.

In the feudal age, repeated civil wars increased the demand for leather goods, and thus it was very important for feudal lords to have outcaste leatherworkers, called "Kawata" or "Eta," under their control. In the later feudal age, lords often assigned outcastes to the cultivation of marginal land, used them as virtual slaves in various enterprises to improve the local cash economy, or placed them in dangerous situations such as those of guards and low-status detectives. In spite of the crucial roles they played in the feudal society, their ascribed outsider status effectively prevented them from gaining any political power. In the later Tokugawa period some of the outcastes became quite affluent and influential. A legend from this period depicts the defensive reaction of the government: an Eta was killed in Edo (later Tokyo), and the head of the outcastes in Edo appealed to the magistrate; he ruled that an Eta was worth one-seventh of a regular person, and therefore one regular person had to murder seven Eta before he could be convicted.

In modern industrial Japan, Burakumin workers supply cheap, disposable labor to industry as part-time workers or day laborers. Burakumin also work more often than mainstream Japanese for small businesses and factories that belong to the lower stratum of the hierarchical industrial structure of modern Japan. Thus they frequently suffer from having unstable incomes and few benefits.

Some theorists also have postulated that the existence of outcastes is a reincorporating mechanism of sociocultural deviation. The outcaste population has been increasing constantly, largely because of the continuous flow of new members from mainstream society, either directed by authority or pressured by economic failure or loss of social affiliations. Japanese culture holds it as ideal to be average and to keep to one's place in society, and deviation from the norm is strongly discouraged from early childhood. This cultural emphasis has successfully incorporated most of the population most of the time, thus creating a largely homogeneous society. However, there were people throughout history who were excluded from the majority society, and students of discrimination issues have discovered the historical systematic segregation of those who failed to be normative or who lost legitimate status in society. Existence of outcastes may be the way Japanese culture coped with unwanted segments of society, keeping them usefully under control yet isolated from others.

These three factors—the perceived need for ritual cleanliness juxtaposed with the economic need for "unclean" occupations; the desire to keep those with economic power from having political power; and the need to purge mainstream society of undesirable elements—together have established, supported, legitimized, and, most important, depoliticized the discrimination issues. Many mainstream Japanese still accept arguments that postulate non-Japanese origins, inherent inferiority, and ritual uncleanliness of outcastes; thus, the differential treatment of Burakumin seems almost "natural" to them. There is no evidence, however, to support such hypotheses. It is rather, as summarized above, a political, economic, and ideological manipulation throughout Japanese history that has created discrimination against Burakumin.

Settlements

Both historic outcastes and Burakumin have lived in segregated communities of one sort or another. In the feudal age their segregation was strictly enforced and people of outcaste status were forced to live in undesirable locations, often on the outskirts of or completely outside a mainstream community. The modern Japanese officially have abolished such segregation, but it continues to exist in the form of de facto ghettos, recognized as "Tokushu Buraku" (special community), or simply buraku. The term "Dōwa Chiku" (assimilation district) is often used in the same fashion.

The conditions in buraku are typically poor, characterized by inferior sanitation, insufficient space and privacy, old housing structures, poorly maintained streets, and a lack of public and recreational areas. Improvement of living conditions has been a great concern for Burakumin. The government has made efforts over the last several decades to improve the living environment and educational opportunities in buraku. Roughly half of Burakumin live in Dōwa Chiku, which are designated target areas for the assimilation projects. In these districts, government-funded programs are being executed to improve housing, sanitation, and public services so as to match the living standard of buraku to that of mainstream communities.

Yet the reality of the buraku is less than ideal. Economic hardship and discrimination deeply rooted in Japanese people, both mainstream and Burakumin, are probably two major reasons for the slow change and persistence of age-old issues regarding the buraku.

Economy

Outcastes traditionally specialized in leatherwork, basketry, sandal making, temple caretaking, street sweeping, butchering, street performance, tenant farming, and unauthorized religious practices. Until the end of the feudal age, outcastes dominated these occupations; at the time of their emancipation, nonoutcaste businesses began to operate in some of these trades, and often drove former outcastes out of business.

Today some Burakumin still are involved in the traditional crafts and trades, but many of them work as factory hands, day laborers, and all sorts of unskilled laborers. In general, their wage levels are low, and their economic struggle in the face of the overall affluence of the Japanese is striking. Many Burakumin work for small businesses, earn minimum wage with few work benefits, and suffer from insufficient and unstable incomes. The comparison of average annual income per household in 1984 reveals that the Burakumin household average was then approximately 60 percent of the national average. The percentage of fully employed Burakumin is significantly lower than that of the overall Japanese labor force. Lower educational achievement and occupational discrimination further hinder the economic advancement of Burakumin. As a consequence a significant number of Burakumin rely on government welfare to survive.

Industrial Arts. Outcaste leatherworkers of the feudal age made beautiful horse gear and armor, some of which still survives. Basketry and sandal making are among the most important—and rapidly forgotten—craft traditions in which historic outcastes and traditional Burakumin produced essential items for the common people.

Kinship

Burakumin kinship practice generally follows that of the mainstream Japanese. (See the article on Japanese for a description.)

Marriage and Family

Marriage and Domestic Life. Burakumin marriage practice and family life are similar to those of the mainstream Japanese, except for certain minor differences reported in ethnographic literature. Marriage and sexual relationships in buraku tend to be more informal and unstable. Extramarital relationships are not uncommon, and, because of the frequency of unstable marriage alliances, they are socially accepted in many cases. An unmarried household head is very common, and many households consist of a single parent and (often illegitimate) children. Economic situations and the mobility of spouses influence postmarital residence; it may take many forms that mainstream society considers irregular. Because of discrimination and long-lasting segregation, endogamy within buraku has been dominant, but the younger generations increasingly are opting for intermarriage with non-Burakumin.

Inheritance. Observers have reported that Burakumin inheritance practice is more informal than that of the mainstream Japanese, presumably because of the flexible and often unstable Burakumin family structure. Ultimogeniture, which is very rare among the mainstream Japanese, is not uncommon among Burakumin.

Socialization. Reflecting the informality of buraku life, socialization of Burakumin children is generally less strict than that of mainstream Japanese. Economic hardship and unstable family structure force many Burakumin parents to leave their children for long hours with their relatives, with neighbors, or sometimes at home without adult supervision. Some children were raised in family craft shops beside the working parents. The educational standard is generally lower among Burakumin than among mainstream Japanese. Analysts believe that economic difficulties, discrimination, and a lack of motivation and role models are the main causes of this problem.

Sociopolitical Organization

Social Organization and Social Control. Although Burakumin as a whole are situated in the lowest stratum of Japanese society, there is a distinct socioeconomic differentiation within Burakumin communities. The higher level of their stratification mainly consists of better-educated, financially more secure, lower-middle-class small-business owners and administrators who now often work outside buraku. The first Burakumin leadership came from this class. A typical Burakumin of the lower level, however, would be undereducated, marginally employed, and often on a government relief program because of insufficient or unstable income. Migrant workers, day laborers, and some factory hands belong to this group.

The upper-class Burakumin are constantly at odds with the lower-class Burakumin, since they do not necessarily share the strong sense of alienation common among the lower-class Burakumin. Assimilation into mainstream Japanese society is a historically popular theme among them, and some even view lower-class Burakumin as a "burden" to their effort to eliminate discrimination through self-improvement.

The *oyabun-kobun* relationship is an important factor in the internal organization of buraku. Oyabun-kobun is a traditional concept of hierarchical relationship between a superior who acts as a parent figure (oyabun) and an inferior who takes the role of a child (kobun). Ordinary people and also criminal organizations (*yakuza*) commonly have adopted this informal hierarchy. Buraku oyabun are very influential in the community, and they often act as job-placement agents or middlemen between Burakumin manufacturers and non-Burakumin buyers. In this relationship of mutual interests and dependency, an oyabun is expected to supply a fair share of steady jobs to kobun and to negotiate with outside buyers or employers, and a kobun is obliged to accept an oyabun's offers and to complete the assignment satisfactorily. However, since the oyabun is in a dominant position, the relationship is not symmetric and so a kobun may follow an oyabun unwillingly for fear of losing jobs or being ostracized.

Political Organization. As citizens of Japan, Burakumin today participate in the Japanese political system through voting. As a strong interest group, Burakumin regularly send their representatives to the Diet and the local legislatures.

The current situation is the achievement of a long politi-

cal struggle since the 1871 emancipation. Burakumin formed their first organization, Bisaku Heimin Kai (Bisaku Common People's Association), in 1902 in Okayama Prefecture, in reaction to the harsh discrimination that continued after emancipation. A year later they founded Dai Nippon Dōhō Yūwa Kai (Greater Japan Fraternal Conciliation Society), the first nationwide organization of Burakumin. Their movement was called the Yūwa (reconciliation) movement, and their goals were to eliminate discrimination against Burakumin through self-help and through the improvement of living conditions, educational standards, and economic conditions in buraku. In 1919, Burakumin leaders gathered for the first time with government officials, representatives from the aristocracy, and scholars at Dōjō Yūwa Taikai (Sympathetic Reconciliation Convention) to discuss the discrimination issue.

In the 1920s, many Burakumin leaders became dissatisfied with the Yuwa movement, which was not seeking positive changes in awareness among the majority Japanese. It was also a time of social radicalism in Japan, and Burakumin activists started the "leveling" movement to eliminate all inequalities and discrimination through political channels. They formed the Zenkoku Suiheisha (National Levelers' Society) in 1922. Their slogan was "tetteiteki kyūdan" (thorough denunciation): when they found a discriminatory behavior or statement, they summoned the person responsible for the incident and demanded a public apology. Although this method was successful in some cases of discrimination, both the mainstream society and the moderate sector of Burakumin movements viewed it as violent and so resisted the campaign.

At the same time, the radical branch of Suiheisha was becoming increasingly critical of the denunciation method, and it began to insist on a more radical, even anarchistic approach to the issue. By 1925 the internal differences were becoming too large to reconcile, and in 1926 radical segments formed separate organizations. The moderate group established the Nihon Suiheisha (Japan Levelers' Society) to continue the policies of the original Suiheisha movement.

Although Burakumin movements saw a brief moment of victory in 1935 and 1936 when they succeeded in sending their own representatives to the Fukuoka Prefectural Assembly and to the House of Representatives, Japan's increasing militarism and patriotism began to interfere with their political activities. In 1940 Suiheisha was dissolved and its members decided to support Yamato Hōkoku Undō (Japan Patriotic Movement), which was founded to coordinate the patriotic efforts of Burakumin.

Burakumin movements, which were virtually nonexistent during World War II, quickly revived at the end of the war with the support of the new constitution, which guaranteed freedom of expression and equal rights to all citizens. In 1947 Burakumin formed the Buraku Kaihō Zenkoku Iinkai (National Committee for Buraku Liberation). In 1955 the organization changed its name to Buraku Kaihō Dōmei (Buraku Liberation League, or BLL). However, Communist influence began to split the organization from inside, and more radical Communists separated from BLL and formed the Buraku Liberation League Normalizing Liaison Association, which aimed to redirect the Liberation League by introducing a more Marxist-oriented position.

Throughout the postwar period Burakumin organizations have been successful in a number of legal battles and in denunciation of discriminatory publications and behavior. They also have made remarkable advances in education, including the improvement of educational opportunities for Burakumin and the introduction of antidiscrimination education programs in public schools.

Conflict. Both Burakumin and the historic outcastes have been scapegoats in times of social unrest and economic difficulties. Numerous reports of riots and associated Eta-gari (outcaste hunts) after the political transition in the late nineteenth century demonstrate how violence toward Burakumin became the outlet for insecurity and frustration among commoners at the time. Burakumin did not have much protection against this aggression, but the hardship accelerated their effort to form an organized movement against discrimination. Today the Buraku Liberation League's denunciation program is a popular tool for correcting discriminatory behavior and thinking, but some scholars and Burakumin activists question its legal basis and actual effectiveness.

Religion and Expressive Culture

Religious Beliefs. (See also the article on Japanese for a general description.) Historically most Buddhist sects rejected outcastes, as most outcastes violated the Buddhist taboos against death and killing through their occupations. The Jōdo Shinshu or Shinshu sect, whose founding philosophy roughly translates as "restoring righteousness in evil men," and the Nichirenshu sect, which preached the salvation of common people, were the only sects that accepted outcastes, and even today they are the most common Buddhist sects to which Burakumin belong. Outcaste members were, however, subject to segregation within the religious organization, as was apparent in the Tokugawa period practices of *eta-dera* (temples exclusively for a outcastes) and *eta-za* (segregated seating for outcastes when they attended the same temples as regular people).

In the modern period Christian missionaries took special interest in the buraku's social problems, and their belief in the equality of human beings before God attracted many Burakumin to this religion.

Religious Practitioners. In addition to training institutionalized priests like those in the mainstream Japanese society, outcaste communities produced many unauthorized practitioners of Shintoism, Buddhism, and various folk religions. Hijiri priests, diviners, and ceremonial performers are the most prominent examples. They served the religious and ceremonial needs of commoners who could not afford the services of authorized priests or who sought alternatives to the institutional religions.

Arts. (See also the article on Japanese for a general description.) The traditional occupational specializations of outcastes included those of performing artists, such as actors, singers, dancers, and street entertainers. Founders of two of the most important theatrical traditions in Japan were outcastes. The dancer/actress Ōkuni performed the earliest form of Kabuki play on the floodplain in Kyoto. Kanami and Zeami, a father and son who began the Noh play in the fourteenth century, were also of outcaste origin, and at the height of their success they performed for the shogun of the time and enjoyed considerable prosperity and political influence.

Medicine. Burakumin medical practices roughly follow those of the mainstream Japanese. Historic outcastes and Burakumin may have developed their own folk medicine because of difficulty in obtaining medical services, but there is no documentation of this.

Death and Afterlife. Burakumin beliefs about death and the afterlife are similar to those of the mainstream Japanese. The rejection and hardship they have experienced may have affected their thoughts on the subject. The dominant Buddhist sect among Burakumin, Jōdo Shinshu, advocates introspective prayer and promises well-being in the next life regardless of one's status in this life.

See also Japanese; Kolisuch'ŏk

Bibliography

Brameld, Theodore (1968). *Japan: Culture, Education, and Change in Two Communities*. New York: Holt, Rinehart & Winston.

Buraku Liberation Research Institute, ed. (1977). *Discrimination against Buraku, Today*. Osaka: Buraku Kaihō Kenkyūsho.

Buraku Liberation Research Institute, ed. (1985). *White Paper on Human Rights in Japan*. Osaka: Buraku Kaihō Kenkyūsho.

De Vos, George A., and Hiroshi Wagatsuma (1966). *Japan's Invisible Race: Caste in Culture and Personality*. Berkeley and Los Angeles: University of California Press.

Donoghue, John D. (1977). *Pariah Persistence in Changing Japan*. Washington, D.C.: University Press of America.

Kawamoto, Shoichi (1985). *Hisabetsu Buraku no Kōzō to Keisei*. Tokyo: Sanichi Shōbō.

Miyoshi, Shoichiro (1980). *Hisabetsu Buraku no Keisei to Tenkai*. Tokyo: Kashiwa Shōbō. Rev. ed. 1991.

Neary, Ian (1989). *Political Protest and Social Control in Prewar Japan*. Atlantic Highlands, N.J.: Humanities Press International.

Takagi, Masayuki (1991). "A Living Legacy of Discrimination." *Japan Quarterly* (July–September): 283–290.

Wolferen, Karel von (1989). *The Enigma of Japanese Power*. New York: Knopf.

Yoshino, I. Roger, and Sueo Murakoshi (1977). *The Invisible Visible Race*. Osaka: Buraku Kaihō Kenkyūsho.

SAWA KUROTANI BECKER

Burmese

ETHNONYMS: Burmans, Myanmarese

Orientation

Identification. The Burmans speak Burmese (a Tibeto-Burman language) and live in the central plain of Burma, in the Union of Burma, which was renamed Myanmar in 1990. "Burman" is the name of the people of this region, while "Burmese" refers to the language and culture of these people and to other citizens of Myanmar. The Burmans are overwhelmingly adherents of Theravada Buddhism.

Location. Myanmar lies between India and China and also borders Thailand. The central plain formed by the Irrawaddy River and the Salween River is the home of the Burman, while the hill country around the plain is populated by Karen, Kachin, Chin, Shan, and some smaller tribal groups. The climate is dominated by the monsoon, which brings a rainy season lasting from June to October, followed by a brief cool season, and then a four- or five-month hot and dry season.

Demography. In 1992 the population of Myanmar was estimated at 42.6 million. The official count, at last census estimate (1988), was 33 million. Population growth is estimated at about 3 percent per year. Burmese speakers are about 70 percent of the national population.

Linguistic Affiliation. Burmese is a part of the Tibeto-Burmese Family, a Subfamily of the Sino-Tibetan Family. Outside the Sino-Tibetan Family—which includes Kachin, Chin, and several tribal languages on the China border—Tai (various dialects in the Shan states), Mon-Khmer (lower Burma), and some Indian languages on the western frontier are spoken in Myanmar.

History and Cultural Relations

The Burmans apparently migrated south from Yunnan, along with several other linguistic and cultural groups, more than 3,000 years ago. The Mons, the Tai, and the Burmans, the predominant population, were all of the same physical type called southern Mongoloid. The history of Burma begins with King Anawratha in 1057, when the king conquered the Mons in southern Burma and brought back, according to legend, a complete copy of the three books of the Pali canon, the basis of Theravada Buddhism.

Anawratha proceeded to make Theravada Buddhism the official religion of his kingdom, driving out other varieties of Buddhism and attempting to suppress and regulate forms of animism. This dynasty reigned for about two and one-half centuries.

The conquest of Yunnan by Kublai Khan shook the Burmese throne along with the rest of mainland southeast Asia, and after the fall of the capital at Pagan various principalities under shifting Tai, Mon, and Burman rulers held sway in various parts of the country. A new Burmese dynasty arose in Pegu and later shifted to Ava as its capital, giving an inland central-valley orientation to this and future Burmese regimes.

European trade and frontier squabbles led to three Anglo-Burman wars; the peacock throne was toppled and the last king Thibaw and his queen were sent into exile. Under British rule Burma became a province of India. Lower Burma was turned into one of the world's largest exporters of rice, while teak, rubies, and other products continued to enter world markets. A sort of ethnic division of labor took place with Europeans at the economic and political top, and most of the Burmans locked into the lower spaces of the classic plural or export economy. This export economy was hard hit by the world depression of the 1930s, and a rising nationalism combined with hard times led to the Saya San rebellion, suppressed by the British.

In World War II the Japanese occupied Burma and granted it nominal independence. The Japanese trained the "Thirty heroes" who became the military leaders of the independence movement called the "Thakins." Burma received independence in 1948 and proceeded to attempt to rebuild a war-ravaged country.

Upon its founding, the Union of Burma was plagued by ethnic unrest from separatist movements among the Karens (KNDO was the name of the armed insurgency) and various Communist and other insurgent groups, as well as vicious political in-fighting among the Thakins and other Burmese leaders. The hero of the independence movement, Aung Sang, and members of his cabinet, were assassinated by opponents. U Nu was elected prime minister, but the troubles with separatists, insurgents, and political disunity continued, leading to a caretaker government of the army under the command of General Ne Win. U Nu won another election, but in 1962 the army again took control, and a single-party government under Ne Win, as of 1990, runs Myanmar, despite a recent election which gave a majority to the opposition party.

Settlements

Villages are the predominant form of human settlement. Over 65,000 villages make Myanmar a mainly rural country. Villages are of three kinds. In Upper Burma the village surrounded by a palisade or a fence is common. Ingress and egress are through a village gate, and the fence or palisade is often manned by village guards. There are also clustered villages without a boundary fence. These villages do not have regular plans and usually lack public buildings. The only major difference between houses is that some have one story, others two. Monasteries are always placed outside the bounds of the village. Fields lie beyond the village, usually within walking distance, but houses are set among trees and fruit crops. The third settlement type is a line village strung out along a road or river bank. Towns and cities are found near or on major rivers and waterways, indicating both irrigation centers and transport networks. Yangon (formerly Rangoon) is now a major Burmese city and the nation's capital; Mandalay is the home of former kings and the cultural capital.

Economy

Subsistence and Commercial Activities. Wet-rice cultivation dominates agricultural activity. Most of that crop is now consumed domestically because the export industry has shriveled under the centralized control of the military powers. Upland, rain-fed rice is common in Upper Burma above the 100-centimeter rain line, and in the hill country slash-and-burn agriculture (swidden agriculture rather than crop rotation) is practiced. Cotton, maize, peanuts, onions, and other crops are produced. Logging, especially of teak for export, is still an important industry. There is an active fishing industry in Burmese waters, and dried shrimp and fish are important components in the diet. Mining of rubies and the export of jade are successful industries. Drilling for and refining oil are on a small scale, hardly for export. Among Burmese handicrafts, lacquer ware is distinctive. Wood carving, stone sculpting, and brass casting are local industries. Tobacco, cheroots, and cigars are produced. There is a small livestock industry, some jute processing, and a little tin and tungsten mining. The economy, however, remains overwhelmingly agricultural and extractive.

In the sector of industry and mining, technology is slightly obsolete but appropriate; in agriculture, on the other hand, most of the technology is geared to the small rice producer. A wooden plow with metal share yoked to a pair of bullocks, the wooden-toothed harrow, the sickle, the metal-bladed hoe, a long knife, ropes and twine of various grasses, and the forked stick comprise the long-standing farming kit. Bamboo and wood items are ubiquitous, and iron and metal nearly so. Modern technology is represented by the sewing machine, the loudspeaker and amplifier, the battery-run transistor radio, some guns, and an occasional vehicle. In the cities an assortment of machines and vehicles dating from World War II predominates.

Kinship

The kinship system counts relatives on both the mother's and father's side, and there are no kinship-based groups beyond the family. It is not the category of kinship that is important, but rather the personal relations cultivated, relative age, generation, and the sex of persons who are linked. Age, sex, and generation, in fact, are the major axes for ordering most social relations. Beyond the nuclear family, terms of address reflect relative age, seniority, and respect rather than the degree or category of kinship.

Marriage and Family

Most marriages are monogamous. Marriages are not a sacramental affair and are arranged by families, but usually on the request of one or the other of the potential marriage partners. Divorce is easy, informal, but infrequent after the arrival of children. Families tend to be nuclear and to live in their own compound, but many households (the really effective unit) are made up of extended families or compound families. This results in part from the normal cycle of family formation and dissolution rather than from a preference for larger than nuclear families. The strongest bond in the family is the mother-daughter relationship, which is lifelong. There is no strong domestic division of labor; men cook and tend babies, and women are barred only from the monkhood.

Sociopolitical Organization

Myanmar is made up of fifteen states and divisions, all centralized under a single bureaucracy run by the army and its mass organization, the Lanzin party. This was constitutionally set up in 1974. Below this formal structure are the villages, linked by various agencies in a hierarchy reaching from the village to the prime minister's office. The village has an elected headman and he is the link between the bureaucracy and the party. There are agencies of the central government in contact with the villagers, but it is chiefly the army and the mass party that impinge on the local organization, which tries to settle its disputes at the local level.

Religion and Expressive Culture

Buddhism is a pervading force in Burmese society. The hillsides dotted with pagodas, the hosts of saffron-robed monks, and innumerable monasteries all proclaim the breadth and depth of Buddhist belief and practice in Myanmar. Almost all Burmans (more than 95 percent) are Buddhist. There are also Christians, chiefly among the Karen, Kachin, and Chin, and a sprinkling of Muslims and Hindus. Buddhism is Theravada, although this distinction is only meaningful to the learned or sophisticated monk or abbot. The religion of the ordinary Burman is _boda batha,_ the way of the Buddha.

Burmese Buddhism is characterized by consensual elements of knowledge, belief, and practice that are separate from the more specialized knowledge of the Pali Canon and the commentaries known to some learned monks. The ideas of _kan_ (related to karma) and _kutho_ (merit) underlie religious practice. Kan is the moral nucleus earned throughout many lives that goes on from life to life in the never-ending chain of rebirth, until the very remote end of nirvana, when rebirth ends. Rebirth, in form and place, is determined by the accumulated merits and demerits earned in previous existences. A person can be reborn in one of the three levels of existence: this world, the hells below, or the various heavens above. The whole worldview of Buddhism is summed up in the continually heard refrain: _aneiksa_ (change, the impermanence of everything), _dokhka_ (life is suffering), and _anatta_ (no self, the ego is an illusion). The next most common summary of the belief system is the repetition of the triple jewel: I take refuge in the Buddha, I take refuge in the teaching, and I take refuge in the monkhood. The monkhood (_sangha_) is loosely organized into two principal sects without significant doctrinal splits. Monks (_pongyi_) are highly honored, and most Burmese boys spend some time in a monastery after an induction ceremony (_shinbyu_) mimicking the Buddha's renunciation of secular life.

Supplementary to the Buddhist worldview are belief systems involved with crisis management, prediction, and divination. _Nats_ are the most important of these systems. These spirits are mainly malevolent and must be propitiated at stated times and places to avoid harm and evil. There are also ghosts, demons, spirits, and goblins in the forest, caves, and natural features capable of causing trouble to people.

Alchemy, astrology, and horoscope casting are employed in attempts to read the future disposition of forces toward the affairs of individuals. There is a system of curing and healing depending on notions of a balance of elements in the patient.

Arts. The _pwe_ (a play, or a song and dance performance), often lasting several days and nights, often accompanies the ritual calendar.

Bibliography

Nash, Manning (1973). _The Golden Road to Modernity: Village Life in Contemporary Burma._ Chicago: University of Chicago Press.

Spiro, Melford E. (1970). *Buddhism and Society: A Great Tradition and Its Burmese Vicissitudes.* New York: Harper & Row.

Shway Yoe [James George Scott] (1882). *The Burman, His Life and Notions.* Reprint. 1963. New York: W. W. Norton & Co.

Steinberg, David (1980). *Burma's Road Toward Development, Growth, and Ideology under Military Rule.* Boulder, Colo.: Westview Press.

Tinker, Hugh (1959). *The Union of Burma: A Study of the First Years of Independence.* London and New York: Oxford University Press.

MANNING NASH

Butonese

ETHNONYMS: Orang ("people") Buton, Orang Butung, Orang Butuni

Orientation

Identification.   Before 1960 the people living in the sultanate of Buton were called Butonese. To this sultanate belonged the main islands of Buton (Butuni or Butung), Muna, and Kabaena, the Tukangbesi Islands and two regions on the southeastern part of the island of Sulawesi (Rumbia and Poleang). In 1960 the more-than-four-centuries-old sultanate was dissolved and the two already existing regencies (*kabupaten*) were fully incorporated in the Indonesian nation. The kabupaten of Muna is in the northern parts of Muna and Buton, and the kabupaten of Buton comprises the other parts of the former sultanate. This means that it is difficult to designate exactly who the Butonese are. It depends on time and situation. Today, most of the people of Muna will not accept being called Butonese.

Location.   The area of the former sultanate is located between 4° and 6° S and 122° and 125° E. The total area is 11,300 square kilometers. The islands are formed from raised coral reefs, and are rather mountainous. Clayey plains are especially found in north and east Muna, northeast Buton, and Rumbia. The easterly monsoon is from May to December and the westerly monsoon from December to April.

Demography.   In 1878 the population of the sultanate of Buton was estimated at 100,000; in 1980, the population of both kabupaten together was estimated at 491,144 (316,759 in Buton, 174,385 in Muna). The population density was about 44 per square kilometer and the population must be growing at the rate of about 2 percent per year.

Linguistic Affiliation.   The language situation is complicated. Two main groups of languages can be distinguished: the Bungku-Mori Group, which is closely related to the languages of southeast Sulawesi, is used on the island of Kabaena, in the north and northeast of Buton, and in the area of Rumbia/Poleang on the mainland of Sulawesi, and the Buton-Muna Group is used in the other part of the former sultanate. To the latter group belong four languages or subgroups of languages. The first is the Wolio language. Wolio is the language spoken in the center of the former sultanate by the nobility (*kaomu*) and the second estate (*walaka*), who lived mainly in the center (Kraton Wolio), and some villages in the neighborhood. It is still spoken in that area, including the present capital of the kabupaten, Baubau. The total number of Wolio speakers does not surpass 25,000. The second language of this group is the Muna language spoken on Muna and the northwest coast of Buton. The third is the subgroup of south(east) Buton, and the fourth is the subgroup of the languages of the Tukangbesi Islands. All these languages belong to the Indonesian Branch of Austronesian. Formerly only Wolio, for which Arabic characters were used, was a written language. It is falling into disuse as a written language because the schools now teach the national Indonesian language using roman characters.

History and Cultural Relations

According to their own tradition, migrants from Johore established the kingdom of Buton, probably in the beginning of the fifteenth century. The kings (raja) had relations with the Hindu kingdom Mojopahit on Java and probably were also Hindu. The sixth raja converted to Islam in 1540, and so became the first sultan. Under his reign the whole kingdom was formally converted to Islam. It is clear from western records that Buton lay at a strategic point on the route from Java and Makassar (South Sulawesi) to the Moluccas, the heart of Indonesian spice production. Especially in the first half of the seventeenth century it was difficult for Buton to maintain its independence in the power struggle between the two Indonesian sultanates of Makassar and Ternate (North Moluccas), in which the Dutch East India Company, VOC, also played an important role. In 1613 Buton entered into the first contract with the VOC, during a meeting between the fourth sultan, La Elangi, and the first Governor-General, Pieter Both. With this contract Buton sought support for its independence from Makassar and Ternate. Only after the sultanate of Makassar had been subjugated by the VOC in the years 1667–1669 did Buton become free from this power struggle. From then on Buton formed part of the territory administered under the Pax Neerlandica. During the seventeenth, eighteenth, and nineteenth centuries the sultanate of Buton managed to remain an independent kingdom. The government of the Netherlands-Indies was not really powerful enough in the nineteenth century to intervene effectively. But this changed at the beginning of the twentieth century. A new contract was imposed in 1906, which stated that the government could interfere in the sultanate's internal matters. Although it was "self-governing," Buton was then definitely part of the colonial system. The foundations were laid for entirely new sociocultural and economic developments, especially in connection with government, education, health services, and the economy. It was one more step toward complete integration in the sociopolitical system of the Indies, and after 1949 in the state of Indonesia. This integration, or incorporation, culminated in 1960 with the dissolution of the sultanate a few months after the death of the last sultan.

Settlements

At the beginning of the twentieth century appoximately 50 percent of the settlements counted less than 500 inhabitants, 35 percent between 500 and 1,000, and 15 percent more than 1,000 inhabitants. The residence pattern was either very concentrated or very dispersed. Both types were the result of the threat of attacks of pirates who ravaged the islands of the sultanate. Many villages, especially on the east coast of Buton and on the Tukangbesi Islands, were strongholds with thick and high stone walls around the settlement. Even a village like Rongi, in the center of the southern part of Buton and 30 kilometers from the coast, was a real stronghold. Villagers unable to build a fortress on a hill lived in a very dispersed way so as not to attract the attention of pirates, or to make it difficult for pirates to surprise a whole village. The colonial government and the Indonesian government tried to consolidate and concentrate the villages. In 1980 50 percent of the villages in the kabupaten of Buton had between 1,000 and 2,000 inhabitants, 32 percent less than 1,000, and 18 percent more than 2,000 inhabitants. In the kabupaten of Muna the percentages were respectively 63, 17, and 20. Baubau, the capital of Buton, had 17,879 inhabitants and Raha, the capital of Muna, 13,593 inhabitants. The houses in the villages on the islands are raised off the ground about 1.5 meters and are often sturdily built with balks and planks, a few windows, and a roof of small planks, *atap* (sago palm leaves), or corrugated iron.

Economy

Subsistence and Commercial Activities. The main subsistence crops are maize, tubers, and dry (*ladang*) rice. Which is the real staple crop depends on the area. In Rongi maize is the main crop and rice the second. On the Tukangbesi Islands tubers are the main crop and maize the second. When there is a surplus these crops are also sold, but the main cash crops are tobacco, peanuts, and, recently, cashew nuts. In the villages on the coasts, fishing plays an important role. Surpluses are sold at markets. From time immemorial the Buton people have been renowned as the seafarers of the Eastern Archipelago. They were traders and transporters, using their *praus* with a carrying capacity of up to about 50 tons. The slave trade was very important for Buton in the seventeenth and eighteenth centuries. At the beginning of this century the total number of praus in the sultanate was estimated at 300. In 1981 the island of WangiWangi, one of the Tukangbesi Islands, had 220 sailing praus registered, 150 of which were still in use. A decline in use of sailing praus was paralleled by the increase in motorized sailboats, of which 37 were registered on that island, with a capacity varying between 10 and 20 tons. Because of mobility in Butonese society and the lack of economic opportunities in the area, many Butonese migrate to other parts of Indonesia, especially to the Moluccas. This is in part seasonal migration for the gathering of cloves on the Moluccan islands.

Industrial Arts. Most villages along the coasts have part-time specialists as boat builders. All villages have part-time specialists as performers of rituals, addressing such things as agriculture, house building, and curing of illnesses. Around the capital, Baubau, near the old center (*kraton*) of the sultanate, some industrial arts involving, for instance, brass, pottery, and silver, still exist. In all villages, women weave silk or cotton sarongs, although this activity is declining. Peddlers, small stores, and markets are found throughout the Buton area. Present in the capitals Baubau and Raha are shops for all kinds of consumer goods, and bigger markets than those found in the villages.

Division of Labor. Seagoing was and is the work of men, as was governing the sultanate. Work in the fields is mainly the task of the men, but women assist when there is much work. Pottery and weaving are women's work, brass and silver manufacturing is men's work. Blacksmiths and boat builders are men. Preparing meals and most of the work within the household is done by women. They also keep the money that is earned by men and are involved in all the decisions about spending household money.

Land Tenure. Traditionally, rights to the land around the villages belonged to the community, and formally to the sultan. Every household had the right to use a part of this land, which was distributed by the village council. When the land was abandoned for a long time, it again became fully communal land. In accordance with present Indonesian law, land tenure rests with the individual. Most Butonese still have rights to land; only the descendants of former slaves, who became free after 1906, may still be landless.

Marriage and Family

Marriage. Polygynous marriages occurred especially among the kaomu and the walaka. The sultan, in particular, had many wives, for reasons of state integration. Most marriages today are monogamous even though Islamic law allows polygyny. Although parents are much involved in the arrangement of the marriage, freedom of partner choice was always a part of Buton culture. Cousins in the first, second, third, and sometimes fourth degree are distinguished by special kinship terms. In most villages marriages with the first cousin are forbidden, except for the nobility. In some villages marriages to second or third cousins are preferred, in order to keep possessions within the family. After marriage the man stays in the house of his bride's parents until he can build his own house.

Domestic Unit. The nuclear family is the usual domestic unit, forming a household in which it cooks and eats meals around the same hearth. After a wedding the newlywed couple often lives with the bride's parents. Old people, especially widows, often live in the household of one of the children, usually one of the daughters. Orphans usually live in the household of near kin. If a widow lives in her own house, one or more grandchildren often live with her.

Inheritance. Property is usually divided equally among the surviving children. Some goods, however, such as the *keris* (a ceremonial knife), are inherited only by men, and others only by women. The house is usually inherited by the child who stayed with the parents, after marriage, to care for them; usually this is the youngest daughter. In the kraton, more elaborate rules of inheritance existed than in the villages.

Socialization. Infants are now raised by both parents. Because Buton society was divided into four classes, the children of each class were socialized according to the norms of those classes. The girls of the kaomu and the walaka had to stay in seclusion between first menstruation and marriage; no men were allowed to see them. After World War II this custom disappeared. As in all of Indonesia, the opportunities for education are the same for both sexes.

Sociopolitical Organization

The former sultanate of Buton is now divided into two kabupaten, which form a regular part of the province of Sulawesi Tenggara.

Social Organization. In the former sultanate four classes were distinguished: 1) the kaomu, from whom the sultan was chosen and for whom certain positions were reserved; 2) the walaka, who also belonged to the ruling elite: the representatives of the walaka chose the sultan; 3) the *papara*, the inhabitants of the villages, living in rather autonomous communities; and 4) the *batua*, slaves, usually working for the kaomu or the walaka. After 1906 the slaves became free, but only slowly has their position improved. During and after the struggle for independence (1945-1949) the distinction between the different classes was no longer as socially and politically acceptable, but informally it continued to play a role, especially with marriages. Clearly distinct socioeconomic classes are not (yet) present in Butonese society. Thanks to the widespread education system, considerable social mobility exists.

Political Organization. The former sultanate included four small vassal states (*barata*) which had their own ruler and council (*sarana*) but which had to pay tribute to the sultan and to support him in conflicts. At the beginning of the nineteenth century the influence of the Buton state in the internal affairs of the principality of Muna was very weak. In the area that fell directly under the sultan and the sarana Wolio (the council of the state Wolio, or Buton), the people were organized in villages (*kadie'*) that were more or less autonomous regarding internal affairs; each had its own sarana, which operated under the supervision of one of the members of the sarana Wolio. The kadie' had to support the sultan and the sarana Wolio with contributions of money, food, and manpower, according to written regulations. With the incorporation of the sultanate into the state of Indonesia the whole society is now organized according to general state laws. The two kabupaten are divided into several subdistricts (*kecamatan*). The head of the subdistrict (*camat*) is an appointed official. The head of the regency (*bupati*) is chosen by the council of the kabupaten and appointed by the government. The subdistricts are divided into villages (*desa*), with a chosen village head (*lurah*), recognized by the government. In several villages in the Buton area an official of the office of the subdistrict was appointed as village head. In some villages the traditional village council (*sarana kadie'*) is still functioning alongside and in cooperation with the "modern" village administration, as was the case in 1981 in the village Rongi. In other villages the traditional organization has completely disappeared. The present villages consist of one or more former kadie'. The Indonesian government provides a wide range of services including school, police, courts, health services, tax collection, and registration of vital information.

Social Control. Informal social control is still strong in the villages within the context of kinship relations, traditional village organizations (if still existing), and the religious organizations.

Conflict. Warfare with neighboring states ended after the Pax Neerlandica was established in the second half of the seventeenth century. In the past, internal conflicts might arise from disputes over succession to the position of sultan, or over the misbehavior of the sultan or high office holders. Sultans could be dismissed by the representatives of the walaka (the *siolimbona*), who also had the right to choose the sultan. Since the incorporation into the colonial state in 1906, conflicts were suppressed first by the colonial power and then by the state of Indonesia.

Religion and Expressive Culture

Religious Beliefs. Islam is dominant in this area, although in the southern part of Muna there lives a small number of Christians (Roman Catholics), and in the regions (kecamatan) of Rumbia and Poleang, among the roughly 40,000 inhabitants Protestant Christianity is dominant. Because of the way Islam was adopted by and disseminated from the center to the villages, the knowledge of Islam in the villages is rather limited. It was the policy of the elite to spread the religious knowledge to the villages in a limited way, so as to keep them dependent. In the center itself Islam was accepted in the form of mysticism, or Sufism, which flowered in the beginning of the seventeenth century in Aceh, and from there apparently influenced Buton. Probably Sufism was rather in accordance with the Hinduistic beliefs that preceded Islam here. One remarkable feature of this Sufism in the center of the sultanate Wolio was a belief in reincarnation, which still exists in the present Buton, especially in the center. In the villages the belief in reincarnation was not very strong and was considered to be an official part of Islam as disseminated from the center, according to J. W. Schoorl. Nowadays a more orthodox form of Islam is disseminated throughout Indonesia, via instruction in the state schools by official teachers, and by the provision of sermons (*chotbah*) to all the villages for reading during the Friday service.

Various supernatural beings play a role in village life, including guardian spirits of houses, praus, and villages; harvest beings; possession spirits who cause illness; and helpful spirits who provide guidance. The spirits of deceased kin, the *arwah*, still play an important role in the life of the Butonese. They can help their still-living relatives, but can also cause illnesses when they are disturbed by the behavior of these relatives.

Religious Practitioners. In the former sultanate, the religious council (*sarana agama* or *sarana hukumu*) was in charge of all religious matters as far as they were associated with Islam. The council had its seat in the central mosque (*mesydid agung*) in the kraton of Wolio. This council still existed in 1981 but in a limited form, and its main function, the close cooperation with the center of power, the sultan, and the sarana of Wolio, for the well-being of the sultanate, was lost after 1960. In former times there was also an integration of Islam and traditional *adat*. So four of the twelve *moji* (or *modin*—those who call for prayer) were called *bisa* and had the special task, accomplished through inner strength obtained by asceticism (*beramal*), to safeguard the kingdom against natural disasters and attacks by enemies. In this work they cooperated closely with the sultan, who had the same task. The mosque in the capital Baubau is now the official center of Islam in the kabupaten of Buton. Officials and most of the Islamic people living in Baubau attend Friday prayers and the Islamic ceremonies in this mosque. In the Muslim villages there are village mosques (the *langgar*), and the religious officials needed to organize the Friday prayers and some of the ceremonies, insofar as they are known in the villages. In Rongi there still was a religious council (the *sarana agama*). In addition to Islam, there are the traditional beliefs in supernatural beings and forces; several types of people with special knowledge of this supernatural world play a role in Buton society as mediators between those beings and the common people in cases of illness and uncertainty.

Ceremonies. In the Muslim towns and villages the main Muslim holidays are celebrated, although in the villages knowledge of these ceremonies is less than complete. In the center, most of the ceremonies contain elements of traditional Butonese religion. In the capitals and the Christian villages, the Christian feasts and ceremonies are held in the way that is usual in Indonesian churches.

Arts. With the dissolution of the sultanate, most of the court arts disappeared. Today, some efforts are being made to revive the old court dances. Butonese culture was not rich in traditional forms of art.

Medicine. Traditional healers (*pande'* or bisa in Rongi) still play an important role, especially in villages that are iso-lated from the capitals of the subdistricts (kecamatan), where at present there are clinics (*puskesmas*) with modern medical personnel. The traditional healers usually find supernatural causes for the illnesses and prescribe prayers, offerings, or other rituals to neutralize these causes. The Butonese had an extensive knowledge of medicinal herbs and leaves.

Death and Afterlife. For Muslims, funerals follow Muslim rites mixed with some traditional elements. On the one hand the Butonese Muslim knows and more or less believes Muslim teachings about the last day (*hari kiamat*) and the weighing of the good and the bad, going to heaven and hell. On the other hand there is still a strong belief in reincarnation, and many Butonese can tell into which child a grandfather, grandmother, or other deceased relative has returned.

Bibliography

Anceaux, J. C. (1988). *The Wolio Language.* Leiden: Verhandelingen KITLV.

Ligtvoet, A. (1878). "Beschrijving en Geschiedenis van Boeton." *Bijdragen tot de Taal-, Land- en Volkenkunde* 4, pt. 2:1–112.

Schoorl, J. W. (1985). "Belief in Reincarnation on Buton." *Bijdragen tot de Taal-, Land- en Volkenkunde* 141:103–134.

PIM (J. W.) SCHOORL

Central Thai

ETHNONYMS: Khon Thai, Siamese Tai, Syam, Tai, T'ai, Thai

Orientation

Identification. The Central Thai speak the Central Thai (Tai-Shan) dialect, live in central and southern Thailand, and are predominantly of the Buddhist faith. The Thai name for their country is "Müang Thai," meaning "the free country," and their self-name is "Khon Thai," meaning "the free people." The terms "Siam" and "Siamese" were used mainly by Westerners; "Siam" was the official name of the country from about 1825 until 1930.

Location. Thailand is located between 6° and 21° N and 98° and 106° E. The Central Thai primarily occupy the central alluvial plain dominated by the Chao Phraya (Menam) River. This river basin covers approximately one-fifth of the total area of the country. The monsoon winds bring on a rainy season that lasts from May or June to October or November.

Demography. In 1992 the population of Thailand was estimated as 57,200,000. The population density averages 111.5 persons per square kilometer and the population is growing at the rate of 3 percent per year. Tai-speaking peoples constitute approximately 80 percent of the population of Thailand. Approximately 13 million of the nation's population speak the Central Tai dialect. Speakers of other dialects of Tai are the Tai-Yuan of the north, the Tai-Lao of the northeast, and the Pak-Tai of the south. Malay-speaking Muslims constitute approximately 4 percent of the population of Thailand, and Chinese, who live primarily in the cities, constitute roughly 14 percent. Bangkok, the capital city, had an estimated population of 5,832,843 in 1989.

Linguistic Affiliation. Scholars have not reached a consensus on the affiliation of the Tai language. Tai has traditionally been considered a branch of the Sinitic Family (which includes various Chinese languages and Tibetan), but there seems to be substantial evidence that there are relationships between Tai, Kadai, and Indonesian subgroups and that these three languages should be classified together as a branch of the Proto-Austric Family (which includes the languages of the Philippines, Melanesia, Polynesia, Micronesia, and Indonesia). Tai is also related to Laotian and Shan. It is monosyllabic and tonal. The Thai script has forty-four consonants, thirty vowels, and nine tonal signs.

History and Cultural Relations

The original home of the Thai people was in the Chinese province of Yunnan. They are believed to have migrated south in successive waves, beginning perhaps as early as about A.D. 1050. The first Thai capital in the area now known as Thailand was established in 1280 at Sukothai. The capital was moved from there to Ayuthia, to Tonburi, and finally, in 1783, to Bangkok, where it has remained. The Kingdom of Thailand has never been colonized by any Western nation, but some territory was lost to the British and French empires when Europeans entered the rice and teak markets during the nineteenth century. The opening of the commercial rice market changed the Thai economy from one of subsistence to one of cash, producing profound economic, demographic, and social changes during the twentieth century. Thailand's absolute monarchy became a constitutional monarchy after a revolution in 1932. In spite of the king's loss of political power, the monarchy has retained its prestige and symbolic value, especially among rural Thai. Political trends since the revolution include a pro-Western foreign policy coupled with very deliberate efforts toward modernization, authoritarian government (in spite of the constitutional veneer), and encouragement of nationalism embodied in the phrase "king, country, religion."

Settlements

Villages range in size from about 300 to 3,000 persons. Some villages are spatially distinct while others are administrative subdivisions in an area of continuous settlement. There are three major village types: strip, clustered, and dispersed. In the strip pattern, houses are strung along both sides of a waterway or road, with open fields stretching behind. In the cluster pattern, houses are built in a roughly circular pattern among fruit trees, coconut palms, or rice fields; the settlement is connected to the main road by a path or cart track. In the dispersed pattern, each nuclear family lives on its own land, surrounded by its rice fields or orchards. Houses are connected by waterways or paths, and much travel is by boat. Prominent in villages are the temple compound and the school, with a few shops scattered nearby. Two styles of housing are common throughout Thailand. The first, for the more affluent, is the sturdy, paneled or clapboard-walled house of teak or mahogany, raised off the ground, with planked floor, a few windows, and a roof of attap palm, tile, or corrugated iron. The second type of house is a low-pitched gabled house on a bamboo frame with a roof and perhaps a porch, thatched with palm or grass, and with sides of the same or of woven bamboo or matting, and earthen floors.

Economy

Subsistence and Commercial Activities. Wet-rice agriculture dominates the Thai economy, with about 80 percent of Thailand's population living in rural agricultural communities. Ordinary rice is produced both as a dietary staple and for cash sales. Agriculture is not widely mechanized in spite of development efforts, and plowing is still done mainly with a single metal-shod plow drawn by bullocks or water buffalo. The crop is harvested by hand. Thai farmers also grow maize, yams, chilies, cassava, eggplant, and beans. Commercial crops beyond rice include sugarcane, tobacco, rubber, coco-

nut, and cotton. Each household catches fish, an important source of food, using nets, scoops, spears, baskets, and hooks. Domestic animals include pigs, chickens, ducks, cattle, and water buffalo.

Industrial Arts. Most villages have part-time or seasonal specialists such as sewing-machine operators, blacksmiths, and boat builders. In some areas there are brass, pottery, and charcoal manufacturers and silk- and cotton-weaving home industries. For the most part, though, industrial and commercial tasks are performed by the Chinese, while the Thai farm and govern.

Trade. Small stores, peddlers, and markets are found throughout rural Thailand. Women bring home-grown produce to the market for sale or to supply other merchants.

Division of Labor. The Central Thai are notable for the near absence of a division of labor by sex. Theirs is one of the few cultures in the world where women as well as men plow and harrow. Both sexes also fish. The traditional home tasks are assigned to women, but men also cook, tend babies, clean house, and wash clothes.

Land Tenure. Since the emergence of the commercial rice market in the mid-nineteenth century, the population has grown steadily. The amount of land devoted to rice cultivation has increased, although there has been little modernization of agricultural technology. The combination of population growth and the increasing production of rice has resulted in landlessness for growing numbers of people. The nonavailability of land has produced a class of laborers who cannot expect to gain their subsistence from the land. Since traditional Thai culture is based on self-sufficient rice agriculture or individually owned land, this situation is producing major changes in Thai society, including permanent or seasonal migration of men to the large cities for wage labor.

Kinship

Kin Groups and Descent. Three types of kin group have been described: (1) multihousehold compounds that share productive equipment and have cooperative work teams; (2) hamlet clusters that contain independent households of kindred joined either by work reciprocity or by the domination of one wealthy household; and (3) linked hamlets of kin who live at a distance from each other but who are joined by shared life-cycle rites, provision of help to visiting kin, and assistance in securing shelter and employment for migrating kin. Descent is bilateral.

Kinship Terminology. Hawaiian-type cousin terms are used. The social emphasis on age is reflected by the fact that most kinship terms indicate the relative ages of people.

Marriage and Family

Marriage. Although polygynous marriage has long been part of Thai culture, most marriages today are monogamous. Marriages are theoretically arranged by the parents, but there is quite a bit of freedom in the choice of marriage partners. Since fellow villagers are often considered relatives, marriages are usually locally exogamous. Marriage with second cousins is allowed. The independent family household, established soon after marriage, is the ideal. More often, though, the couple resides for a short time with the wife's family. Residence with either the wife's or the husband's family on a more permanent basis is becoming more frequent. Divorce is common and is effected by mutual agreement, common property being divided equally.

Domestic Unit. Those people who cook and eat meals around the same hearth are considered a family. This group, averaging between six and seven persons, not only lives and consumes together, but also farms cooperatively. The nuclear family is the minimal family unit, with grandparents, grandchildren, aunts, uncles, co-wives, cousins, and children of spouses added on. Membership in the household unit requires that one perform an acceptable amount of work.

Inheritance. Property is divided equally among surviving children, but the child who cares for the parents in their old age (often a younger daughter) ordinarily receives the homestead in addition to her share.

Socialization. Infants and children are raised by both parents and siblings and, in recent times, by other household members. Emphasis is placed on independence, self-reliance, and respect for others. The Central Thai are notable for almost never using physical punishment in child rearing.

Sociopolitical Organization

Thailand is a constitutional monarchy with a king as head of state and a prime minister as head of the government.

Social Organization. Thai society is hierarchically organized on the bases of age, occupation, wealth, and residence. The rural farmers stand below the artisans, merchants, and government officials of the cities. The clergy stand as a group apart from society. Social classes, in the sense of stable, ranked statuses, are absent in the presence of considerable social mobility. Many interpersonal relationships, however, are hierarchical, and patron-client relationships are common.

Political Organization. Thailand is divided into seventy-three provinces (_changwat_). The provinces are divided into districts (_amphoe_), and these into municipal areas and communes (_tambon_). Each tambon is composed of several numbered hamlets (_muban_), which appear to be primarily administrative divisions. Tambon seem to range in size from 1,400 to 7,000 people. Each muban has a headman (_phuyaiban_) and the head man of the tambon, the _kamnan_, is chosen from among the phuyaiban. The muban, and probably the tambon as well, are groups whose functions appear to be purely administrative, since only occasionally do the natural communities coincide with them. Thus a village may be composed of people from two different tambon and several different muban. They constitute a community in the sense that all the people of the village recognize the village temple and the government school. There does not appear to be a native Thai term for such a "natural" community and if asked the name of his or her village, the average inhabitant would probably refer to the temple that serves it. The Thai government provides a wide range of services including schools, police, courts, health services, tax collection, and the registration of vital information. District governments maintain the highways, canals, bridges, schools, and irrigation systems.

Social Control. To a large extent, social control is maintained by a Buddhist value system, which places a premium on avoiding conflict and fleeing rather than fighting. Gossip is an important informal source of social control. Because the natural community has no administrative structure, the temple committee, made up of monks and lay people, often concerns itself with village issues as well as temple affairs.

Conflict. In the past, warfare generally arose from disputes over succession to the throne, misbehavior of a vassal, and conflicts with neighboring states. Since the late 1880s a national military establishment on the European model has existed. Since the 1930s military personnel have taken an increasingly active role in politics.

Religion and Expressive Culture

Buddhism is a central and unifying force in Thai society. There are over 31,000 temples and the Thai regularly give gifts to the temple, attend festivals, and have their sons ordained.

Religious Beliefs. Theravada Buddhism is the official religion of Thailand (95 percent of the population); there are also Muslims (4 percent), and small numbers of Christians, Hindus, Confucians, and animists. Various supernatural beings play a role in village life. They include the guardian spirits of houses and villages, harvest beings such as the Rice Mother, possession spirits who cause illness, and helpful spirits who provide guidance.

Religious Practitioners. About 85 percent of Thai men are ordained priests, although only a small minority makes the priesthood its life work. The head priest at each temple maintains the basic rules of the monastic order. Priests read sermons, sing blessings, and participate in life-cycle rituals. They often also play a central role in village government. In addition to priests there are exorcists, spirit doctors, and diviners who mediate between humans and the spirit world through incantations, charms, possession, and sympathetic action.

Ceremonies. The religious calendar includes the New Year's Festival in April; the day of birth, enlightenment, and death of the Buddha in May; Lent from July to October; and the Festival of Lights in November. In addition, there is an annual fair and days set are aside for presenting robes and food to the priests.

Arts. Although now discouraged by the government, the tattooing of men is still common. Both art and architecture are characterized by subtlety of design and form, with considerable use of amulets, mystical drawings, and both public and private statuary. Traditional musical instruments such as gongs, clappers, wooden blocks, and the long drum are used alongside Western instruments such as saxophones, flutes, and horns. Dance dramas, repartee performances, and shadow plays are a common form of theatrical entertainment in rural villages.

Medicine. Illness is attributed to fright, prolonged adversity, spirit possession, and an imbalance of elements in the body. Locally purchased home remedies and the services of healers are commonly used.

Death and Afterlife. The funeral is the most important life-cycle event because it signifies the launching of the deceased into his or her next existence. Rebirth occurs after a stay in purgatory, the length of which is determined by one's sinfulness. The older and more prestigious the deceased, the more elaborate the funeral rites. The formal mourning period is seven days, after which the body is taken to the house or a morgue where it may be kept for days or even years until it is cremated.

See also Pak Thai; Shan; Tay; Yuan; Dai in volume 6

Bibliography

Donner, Wolf (1978). The Five Faces of Thailand: An Economic Geography. New York: St. Martin's Press.

Phillips, Herbert P. (1966). Thai Peasant Personality: The Patterning of Interpersonal Behavior in the Village of Bang Chan. Berkeley and Los Angeles: University of California Press.

Sharp, R. Lauriston, and Lucien M. Hanks (1978). Bang Chan: Social History of a Rural Community in Thailand. Ithaca, N.Y.: Cornell University Press.

Terwiel, Berend J. (1975). Monks and Magic: An Analysis of Religious Ceremonies in Central Thailand. Lund: Studentlitteratur; London: Curzon Press.

M. MARLENE MARTIN AND DAVID LEVINSON

Cham

ETHNONYMS: Kiam, Nguoi Cham-pa, Tchame, Tchams, Thiame, Tscham, Tsiam

Orientation

Identification. The Cham are a Malay people who represent the remnant of a once large and powerful kingdom (Champa) that was dominant in the Vietnamese coastal region from about A.D. 200 until its demise in A.D. 1471. In 1901 they were on the verge of extinction. It is believed that the original home of the Cham was Java. There they adopted a number of Indian cultural elements (particularly in the religious and artistic spheres) before their migration to Indochina.

Location. Vietnam and Cambodia are the locus of Cham culture. The Cham are found in south-central Vietnam and in the Tonle Sap and Chau Doc areas of Cambodia.

Demography. In 1910 there were 15,389 Cham in Annam and 30,000 living in Cambodia. In 1981 there were 155,000 Cham reported living in Cambodia and Vietnam.

Linguistic Affiliation. Cham is a branch of Malay that contains elements drawn from several language families. Some of its more important elements are those from Malayo-Polynesian languages, Khmer, Vietnamese and Chinese languages, Indochinese languages, Sanskrit, and Arabic.

History and Cultural Relations

Leuba demarcates three periods in Cham history. In the first of these, the Cham were at war with China (from the second to the tenth centuries A.D.). During the second period the Cham were engaged in armed conflict with the people of Annam (tenth to fifteenth centuries A.D.). The end of this period witnessed the destruction of the kingdom of Champa by the Annamese emperor Thanh ton (in 1471 A.D.). Attempts to throw off the yoke of Annamese subjugation failed, and a gradual decline of Cham culture took place from the sixteenth century onward. During this third period, the decline of the kingdom precipitated an exodus from Champa to Cambodia by a number of Cham dignitaries and persons of noble birth. The last descendant of the Cham royal line died early in the twentieth century at Palei Chanar. The early 1900s witnessed a decline in the Cham population, but subsequent times have witnessed their resurgence. The ancient Cham were known for their seafaring skills, agricultural inventiveness, and construction of temples and religious monuments. The culture of the Cham in more recent periods has had little of the flavor of its ancient progenitor, relative poverty having replaced the grandeur of its ancient past.

Settlements

Cham villages are extremely poor. Leuba has noted that they convey a sense of impermanence. Homes are made of split bamboo and are elevated above ground level (by the use of pilings) to protect against flooding. The space beneath the house serves frequently as a shelter for water fowl (e.g., ducks). The typical home has few adornments and domestic utensils. The structure may contain several rooms separated by walls. Access to these rooms is by means of a hallway running along the side of the house or by doorways in the walls separating the rooms.

Economy

Subsistence and Commercial Activities. Although agriculture figures prominently in the everyday life of the Cham, animal domestication, hunting, and fishing are also a part of their cycle of subsistence. Crops grown include rice (by means of wet and dry cultivation), cotton, maize, tobacco, castor-oil plants, manioc, peanuts, ferns, and vegetables. An alternative to wet cultivation (used for the growing of rice) is that of ray cultivation (the Cham variety of slash-and-burn agriculture). Mangrove and other trees are also cultivated for profit. Buffalo, goats, dogs, poultry, and ducks are domesticated. Eggs are also collected. Animals and their by-products are used for a variety of purposes (i.e., for food, sacrifice, and agricultural assistance). Hunting (with nets, beaters, dogs, and traps) and fishing (with nets) is also engaged in.

Industrial Arts. Basic tools used by the Cham include pots, bowls, chopsticks, looms, spinning wheels, mortars (for rice pounding), baskets, jars, ashtrays (for torches), trays, calabashes, baskets, jars, ladles and spoons (made of coconut shells), cooking spoons, combs, rope, and a small quantity of iron implements. Low wooden beds are also manufactured for domestic use. Bedding (of cotton, wood, and matting) also is used. Little furniture is made, and luxury industries are scant.

Trade. Leuba reported the existence of a trade relationship between the Cham and the Moi. The Moi trade spices, cereals, and poultry to the Cham in exchange for iron bells, dried fish, and silk garments. The Moi also work as hired laborers for the Cham.

Division of Labor. Men and women share labor-related responsibilities. However, Cham women play an important role in the subsistence cycle and in the management of family affairs. They are responsible for household chores, the socialization of children, textile manufacture (e.g., the carding, spinning, and weaving of cotton), vegetable cultivation, burden bearing, grain preparation (i.e., threshing, husking, and milling), and water drawing.

Land Tenure. Both individual and village ownership of land seems to occur in certain Cham villages.

Kinship

Kin Groups and Descent. Cham kinship practices represent a fusion of Hindu and pre-Hindu elements. LeBar cites Maspero's observation that the Cham had a matrilineal clan system that predated their Hinduization. The system also is said to have been totemic. Of these clans, the two that are reported to have struggled for dominance are the coconut-tree clan and the areca-nut-tree clan. Succession to the office of king was patrilineal (perhaps showing Hindu influence) rather than matrilineal.

Kinship Terminology. Hawaiian kinship terminology is employed for first cousins.

Marriage and Family

Marriage. Once females reach the age of consent, they are allowed a considerable degree of freedom in mate selection. They are permitted to choose mates (from their own religious faith or others) and to initiate the mate-selection process. Polygynous unions are permitted (with the consent of the first wife) and the first wife is the agent responsible for the introduction of subsequent spouses into the household. Divorce is permitted and is usually initiated by the wife. Economic factors are a determinant in marital form, polygyny being limited to more wealthy Cham. Postmarital residence is matrilocal.

Inheritance. Inheritance of property, succession rights, and prerogatives related to ancestral worship is through the female line.

Socialization. Cham women are the chief agents of socialization.

Sociopolitical Organization

Political Organization. The Cham village is made up of several hamlets and is governed by elected officials numbering from five to fifteen. These officials are charged with safeguarding the public, the distribution of community funds, and tax collection. Each village is also governed by a mayor. All officials, with the exception of the mayor, are subject to individual taxation. A larger administrative division is made up of groups of eight to twelve villages. These groups are governed by a group leader. Three to four of these village groups compose the highest administrative division, the _huyen_.

Social Control. Social control is maintained by a combination of regulations derived from indigenous and national (i.e., governmental) sources.

Conflict. Conflict between the Cham and their immediate Vietnamese neighbors was characteristic of early Cham history. After their defeat at the hands of the Vietnamese, many Cham fled to Cambodia. Subsequent contact between the two groups has improved over the years to the point where the Cham have adopted many aspects of Vietnamese culture. No Cham military structure has existed since the fall of the Champa empire.

Religion and Expressive Culture

Religious Beliefs. Two religious systems are followed by the Cham: Islam and Hinduism. The adherents of Islam are known as _cham bams_ (sons of religion) or _cham aclam_ (Cham of Islam). Those who follow Hindu practice are called _cham jat_ (thoroughbred Cham), _cham kaphirs_, or _akaphirs_ (infidels). A substratum of indigenous religious practice is to be found in the syncretized form of Islam and Hinduism practiced by the Cham. The Chams of Cambodia, most of whom are Muslim, are members of the Shiite branch of Islam. The Cham of Vietnam, who are almost exclusively Hindu, practice a form of Shaioita Brahmanism.

Religious Practitioners. The chief religious functionary of the Muslim Cham is the imam, the congregational leader. Other Muslim officials include the _ong-grou_ (high priest of the mosque), the _katip_ (assistant to the ong-grou), and the _mo'duo'n_ (censor). Among the Hindu Cham, the most important religious officials are the priests who belong to the _basaih_ caste. This caste elects three high priests (_po adhia_) who serve in this capacity for life. From the age of ten, children of this caste are taught appropriate sacerdotal rituals and activities. Other practitioners include the _camenei_, the _kathar_, and the _paja_ (celibate priestess/prophetess), the _kain yan_, the _rija_, and the Hindu _mo'duo'n_. The camenei, who form a caste inferior to that of the basaih, are responsible for temple upkeep. The kathar are cultic musicians who sing hymns and play instruments for ceremonial observances. The paja officiates at domestic ceremonies. The kain yan (assistant to the paja) presents offerings to the paja and performs ceremonial dance. Finally, the rija (family priestess) also officiates at certain family-based magicoreligious rites. The Hindu mo'duo'n is a celebrant at certain magicoreligious observances.

Ceremonies. The calendar of the Hindu and Muslim Cham contains a number of ceremonial occasions that are marked by magicoreligious rites. Many of these contain indigenous elements that have been blended with elements of Islam and Hinduism. Two major feasts are observed by the Hindu Cham: Bon Kate (September-October), observed on the fifth day of the fifth month, and Bon Cabur (January-February), held on the first day of the ninth month. The spirits of the departed are honored on these occasions. A festival meal is shared and five days of celebration accompany each of these feasts.

Arts. The visual arts of the Cham are not well developed. Music (instrumental and vocal) is, however, highly developed, though musical instruments are of the most rudimentary type. The Cham literary corpus includes a number of songs and hymns, prayers, rituals, folktales, and lists of divinities.

Death and Afterlife.   Muslim Cham bury their dead twice (provisionally and then permanently). Several commemorative ceremonies are carried out near the tomb during the year following the death of an individual. The bones of the deceased are exhumed when the final ceremony takes place, and are carried to a permanent resting place in the area that serves as the people's common cemetery. Here the bones, along with the deceased person's rings, are buried. The Hindu Cham, by contrast, cremate the deceased after ceremonial preparation of the body. The remains are placed in a family sepulcher.

Bibliography

Cabaton, Antoine (1901). *Nouvelles recherches sur les Chams*. Translated by Human Relations Area Files, Inc. Paris: E. Leroux.

Hickey, Gerald C. (1964). "Cham." In *Ethnic Groups of Mainland Southeast Asia*, edited by Frank M. LeBar, Gerald C. Hickey, and John K. Musgrave, 245–249. New Haven: HRAF Press.

Leuba, Jeanne (1923). *Un royaume disparu: Les Chams et leur art*. Translated for Human Relations Area Files, Inc. Paris: G. Van Oest.

Maspéro, Georges (1928). *Le royaume de Champa*. Paris and Brussels: G. Van Oest.

Olivier, G., and H. Chagnous (1951). "Anthropologie physique des Chams." *Bulletin de la Société des Études Indochinoises* 26:271–318.

HUGH R. PAGE, JR.

Chaobon

Also known as the "Niakuoll" and sometimes erroneously called the "Lawa," the Chaobon are a group of about 14,000 (1984) living in settled wet-rice agricultural villages in central and northern Thailand. "Niakuoll" is their self-name. They are called "Chaobon" by the Thai, meaning "hill people." Extensive contact with the neighboring Thai and Central Thai has resulted in a close resemblance between Chaobon villages and those of these dominant groups, and traditional animistic beliefs have been largely replaced by Buddhism.

Bibliography

Seidenfaden, Erik (1958). *The Thai Peoples*. Bangkok: Siam Society.

Chinese in Southeast Asia

ETHNONYMS: Huaqiao, Huaren, Sangley (in the Philippines), Tangren (Mandarin)

Orientation

Identification.   The Chinese in Southeast Asia once referred to themselves as "Huaqiao" (Chinese sojourners) but now describe themselves as "Huaren" (Chinese people). Another common ethnonym for Chinese, "Zhongguo ren" (people of the Central Kingdom), is avoided in Southeast Asia because it holds overtones of political allegiance to China: the Overseas Chinese live outside the political boundaries of China and are citizens or permanent residents of a variety of Southeast Asian nations. The southern Chinese, who form the core of immigrants to Southeast Asia, also refer to themselves as "Tangren" (people of Tang), alluding to the fact that their ancestors migrated to southern China at the demise of the Tang dynasty in the tenth century A.D. In the Philippines they are called "Sangley," from a Southern Min word referring to "[those who] do business."

Location.   Overseas Chinese are found in cities throughout Southeast Asia, and although populations may be found in rural areas, the Chinese are overwhelmingly urban. In Southeast Asian cities they are visible in their capacity as merchants, with shops sometimes clustered in distinctive "Chinatowns."

Demography.   Migration to Southeast Asia originated primarily in the coastal area of southeastern China, in particular Fujian, Guangdong, and Hainan, and reached its peak in the second half of the nineteenth century, spurred by new opportunities created by the opening of treaty ports after the First Opium War. The only predominantly Chinese population in Southeast Asia is that of Singapore, where an estimated 2 million Chinese form 76 percent of a population of 3 million. In Malaysia, the Chinese form a large minority, currently estimated at 34 percent of a population of 18 million. In Indonesia, where the Chinese are only 3 percent of the total population of 195 million, there are 5 to 6 million Chinese; in Thailand, the Chinese population has been recently estimated as 5 to 6 million or more in a total population of 57 million; in the Philippines there are 600,000 in a population of 62 million; in Cambodia, 300,000 in a population of 8.5 million; in Laos, 25,000 in a population of 4 million. In Vietnam in the mid-seventies there were perhaps 2 million Chinese, but many have since become refugees. Demographic statistics do not always reveal the extent of the Overseas Chinese presence, since partially assimilated Chinese may not be counted as "Chinese" in a census report even though they maintain Chinese identity.

Assimilation.   Chinese who settled in Southeast Asia before the mid-nineteenth century were likely to intermarry and become assimilated to local populations, or to develop new social forms syncretized from elements of Chinese and local cultures. Examples include the mestizos of the Philippines, the Peranakans of Indonesia, and the Baba of Singapore and Malaysia. In contemporary Indonesia and Malaysia, cultural assimilation is now less common: the practice of Islam is now an important expression of ethnic and national identity for "peoples of the soil," and this tends to form an obstacle to intermarriage and full assimilation. By contrast, Chinese have tended to assimilate more readily in the Buddhist countries of mainland Southeast Asia. In Thailand, for example, assimilation has been relatively easy for Chinese; at the same time a population of "Sino-Thai," who have maintained distinctively Sinitic cultural practices while adopting the Thai language and Thai names, has persisted. On the one hand, assimilation has resulted from the relative absence of barriers to intermarriage into a population that shares a common world religion in Buddhism, and on the other hand it is the result of government policy, which since 1948 has restricted Chinese-language instruction in formerly Chinese-medium educational institutions. In Vietnam, it was once axiomatic that Chinese found low barriers to assimilation, since Vietnam had been deeply influenced by Sinitic culture, adopting Chinese characters, Mahayana Buddhism, and for a time a bureaucratic structure of government in which candidates for high office were selected through an examination system modeled on that of imperial China. However, colonial rule and its political aftermath have had an impact on the position of Chinese populations in Southeast Asia. For example, in the period of French colonial rule, French regulations discouraged Vietnamese but encouraged Chinese participation in commerce, and in 1970 it was estimated that while Chinese Vietnamese were only 5.3 percent of the total population, they controlled 70–80 percent of the commerce of Vietnam. In the aftermath of the Vietnam War, the Chinese Vietnamese became a political target, and many fled or were driven out of Vietnam. The Chinese Kampucheans were labeled urban "exploiters" by Pol Pot, and it is estimated that 200,000 perished between 1975 and 1979.

Linguistic Affiliation.   Overseas Chinese speak a variety of Sinitic regional languages, drawn from three language groups that are not mutually intelligible. Major regional languages include Min (Northern and Southern), Yue, and Hakka. Within Overseas Chinese communities, Chinese also identify themselves by their topolect of origin (misleadingly termed a "dialect"). Topolects of Southern Min include Fujian (Hokkien, Fukien), Chaozhou (Chaochow, Taechew, Teochew), and Hainan. Topolects of Northern Min include Fuzhou (Foochow, Hockchew), Xinghua (Henghua), and Fuqing (Hockchia). Speakers of Yue (Cantonese, Guangfu, Yueh) and Hakka (Hokka, Ke, Kechia, Kejia, Kek, Kheh) are also widely found in Southeast Asia. A single urban community in Southeast Asia might include speakers of eight or more Sinitic topolects, and in such situations, one topolect tends to become the lingua franca for that community. For example, the Fujian topolect of Southern Min (Hokkien) is dominant in many Overseas Chinese communities in Malaysia, Singapore, Indonesia, and the Philippines, whereas another Southern Min topolect, Chaozhou (Teochew), dominates in Thailand. There are also long-resident Chinese populations who speak Southeast Asian languages as the language of the home: an estimated 65 percent of Chinese Indonesians speak Indonesian in the home; an estimated 80 percent of Chinese Thai speak Thai. In some cases, Chinese has been creolized with Southeast Asian languages: Baba Malay, formed from Hokkien and Malay, is spoken in Singapore and Malaysia; Peranakan Indonesian, formed from

Indonesian, Javanese, and Hokkien, is used in Indonesia. The Chinese regional languages share a single written language, which was once learned through diverse literary registers of the regional languages. Since the Republican Revolution of 1911, the written language has been learned through Mandarin-medium education, which was for a time a force for Chinese nationalism in Southeast Asia as well as in China. With the exception of Singapore, Southeast Asian governments have in the postcolonial era promoted national languages at the expense of Chinese-medium education, thus eroding one important base for the continuation of Sinitic culture in Overseas Chinese communities. For example, the Indonesian government promotes Bahasa Indonesia as the medium of education and public discourse, and it has restricted Chinese-medium education and the Chinese-language press. In Malaysia, mastery of the national language, Bahasa Melayu, is increasingly indispensable to public life. However, Mandarin Chinese continues to be a medium of instruction in Chinese-medium primary schools and private secondary schools, and the Chinese-language press has persisted. In the Philippines, Chinese-language instruction has been restricted since 1973, and the new generation of Chinese Filipinos is considered more Filipino than Chinese in outlook. The command of Chinese languages is useful in business, and allows Chinese to maintain ethnic ties across national boundaries; this is one important motive for the maintenance of Chinese-language ability in the context of Southeast Asia.

History and Cultural Relations

Chinese Buddhist monks paid early visits to Southeast Asia, but regular trading visits did not begin until the fourteenth century. Chinese were drawn to the rich entrepôts of Malacca, Manila, and Batavia as trade developed between Europe and Asia in the following centuries, and they were also attracted in considerable numbers to work in Ayuthia, Thailand. In 1842, Great Britain and China signed the Treaty of Nanking, which ceded the island of Hong Kong to Britain and opened five treaty ports to British trade and residence, including Xiamen (Amoy) and Fuzhou (Foochow) in Fujian Province. Labor migration was encouraged, and a thriving "coolie trade" brought many Chinese men (and a much smaller population of Chinese women) from these ports to work in parts of the world where labor was needed, including colonial Southeast Asia. The coolies met with varied fates: some returned to China after their sojourn in Southeast Asia; some perished under arduous working conditions and ill treatment; and some stayed, the most successful prospering greatly under the protective umbrella of European colonial rule. In the colonial period, Overseas Chinese were frequently middlemen between the European colonists and Southeast Asian producers or consumers. In the Federated Malay States and the Straits Settlements, for example, Chinese bid for contracts to manage the lucrative opium farms and controlled opium distribution on behalf of the British. In Indonesia, Chinese farmers collected taxes and worked as labor contractors for the Dutch; they were also moneylenders and dominated internal trade. The legendary successes of a few who amassed great wealth reinforced the stereotype of Chinese migration as a form of economic colonialism that exploited Southeast Asian resources and the Southeast Asian "peoples of the soil."

Settlements

In urban Southeast Asia, opulently decorated temples, *kongsi* (collective ancestral halls), dialect associations, and Chinese chambers of commerce are among the most impressive expressions of Chinese cultural identity and presence. A common form of construction combines place of work and residence in shop-houses, connected and fronted by a 1.5-meter covered veranda. Businesses frequently cluster: for example, fabric sellers, jewelry dealers, and sellers of ritual paraphernalia each will have a territory within the business district. Where allowed, food is hawked on every corner; also common are Chinese restaurants, in which large groups can be entertained at wedding or festival banquets. In Singapore and elsewhere, development and modernization have created new settlement forms that stand beside the old: many Chinese now reside in high-rise apartments or suburban housing estates, and shops and restaurants cluster in malls as well as in rows of shop-houses.

Economy

Subsistence and Commercial Activities. Overseas Chinese have found their economic niche primarily in commerce, though in the context of the modern state they have diversified into a variety of occupations. The family-run business is common and describes a range of undertakings, from modest ventures involving the cooperation of husband and wife (with children sometimes providing labor) to multinational firms run by family members trained in the latest management techniques and employing nonfamily members. Increasingly, employees in Chinese-managed firms are multiethnic rather than exclusively Chinese.

Trade. Overseas Chinese have historically been traders and middlemen in Southeast Asia. Chinese business networks are legendary for the extent of their international linkages, which often follow family or ethnic networks.

Division of Labor. Husband and wife frequently cooperate in running family firms. Household work is primarily managed by women, and children often assist in this work. Unmarried children also frequently help out in small family businesses.

Kinship

Kin Groups and Descent. In Chinese society, descent is patrilineal, and each child is given his or her father's surname, one of the Chinese "100 surnames." With the exception of Singapore and Malaysia, Chinese in Southeast Asia have been urged or required to adopt non-Chinese names as a step toward identification with the nations in which they live. Many surname groups have kongsi that maintain genealogical records for that surname, though the importance of this aspect of identity has waned somewhat.

Kinship Terminology. The extensive and detailed Chinese kinship terminology distinguishes members of the patrilineage from matrilateral kin, as well as marking generation and birth order. Maintenance of the Chinese kinship termi-

nology is a fundamental aspect of a claim to Chinese identity for creolized Chinese such as the long-resident Baba community of Melaka (Malacca), Malaysia.

Marriage and Family

Marriage. Urban Chinese generally marry in their twenties or thirties, and residence after marriage is often with the husband's family. It is common to marry across subethnic ("dialect") group boundaries; Overseas Chinese tend toward a high degree of religious tolerance, and religious differences are in general not a barrier to intermarriage. Chinese have intermarried with members of local Southeast Asian populations; however, intermarriage with a Muslim entails conversion to Islam and so, to some extent, loss of Chinese identity—thus the rate of intermarriage has been lower in Malaysia and Indonesia than elsewhere in Southeast Asia. Divorce in traditional Chinese society was difficult: a woman who left her husband would give up her children who, as members of her husband's patrilineage, would remain with their father's family. This is no longer the case; women have a much higher likelihood of getting custody rights under modern laws than they did in the prewar period. With the increasing economic independence of women, and with residence in extended families often replaced by nuclear-family residence, divorce is no longer as strongly discountenanced as it once was.

Domestic Unit. The extended patrilineal family persists, and at the most developed phase in the cycle a family may include parents, unmarried sons and daughters, and married sons with their wives and children. The nuclear family, however, is increasingly the norm, and young couples who can afford to do so establish independent residences.

Inheritance. Property is passed from the husband to his wife and children upon death; however, the patrilineal custom of leaving property to sons persists. Men, while living, may give property and financial support to persons who are not legal heirs (such as "little wives" and their children), who may be helped with gifts, support in achieving educational goals, or loans to aid them in business ventures.

Socialization. Child-rearing responsibilities fall primarily to the mother, though grandparents or other relatives sometimes tend children, freeing the mother to seek employment. Children are taught to respect their elders by using the appropriate terms of address and, ideally, to show deference to authority by not defending themselves when criticized. Education follows the standard of the country in which children reside: Chinese-medium education has been restricted throughout Southeast Asia (except in Singapore and in Malaysia, where the constraints are relatively moderate), and government-designed curriculums attempt to orient the younger generation toward identification with Southeast Asian national cultures. Chinese cultural forms are often transmitted outside the educational system by community-based cultural and recreational clubs.

Sociopolitical Organization

Social Organization. Chinese society in Southeast Asia tends to be stratified, with relative wealth or poverty definitive of social status. At the same time, Overseas Chinese maintain crosscutting links between classes through membership in associations that link members through bonds like those of "dialect" group and shared surname. The leaders of associations such as the Chinese chamber of commerce may be called upon to represent the interests of the Chinese community and to promote community aims. With the exception of Singapore, at the national level Overseas Chinese continue to tend to exercise economic rather than political power and influence.

Social Control.   Overseas Chinese live in modern states, and are subject to the legal and political systems of those states. Within their communities, concern with "face" or reputation promotes acts of public-spirited generosity. Chinese culture is imbued with ethical ideas drawn from Buddhism, Taoism, and Confucianism, and celebrates heroic figures who embody these ideals; the notion of karma gives hope of superior rebirth to those who are moral in their present lives.

Conflict.   Overseas Chinese came to Southeast Asia with a tradition of self-policing. In the nineteenth century, secret societies (_tongs_) maintained forces of fighting men, and violent confrontation between rival secret societies was common, as was fighting between members of different subethnic groups (Cantonese against Hokkien, for example). In contemporary Overseas Chinese communities, a minority of Overseas Chinese are involved in the "underground economies" of the area, and illicit business activities such as prostitution, the drug trade, and illegal gambling have their own "police force" in the form of gangs that provide protection to those involved in these activities. Conflict between Chinese and majority populations has occasionally erupted into violence in Southeast Asia. Outbreaks of anti-Chinese violence are often ascribed to resentment of the favorable economic position of the Chinese, a position that is, to some extent, the legacy of European colonial rule.

Religion and Expressive Culture

Religious Beliefs.   Chinese religious culture is syncretic, and Chinese "popular" religion is comprised of elements of Buddhism, Taoism, and Confucianism. The practice of Chinese religious culture involves performing the rituals of ancestor worship and participation in the cycle of public festival events: both are coordinated by the rhythms of the lunar calendar. Some Chinese are also active in the support of such world religions as Mahayana Buddhism, Theravada Buddhism (Sri Lankan and Thai), and Christianity.

Chinese religious culture is polytheistic and involves worship and placation of a variety of hierarchically arranged supernatural beings. The most basic division is that between heaven and earth. At the top of the heavenly hierarchy are spiritual beings who transcend human life, like the Lord of Heaven; next are the spirits of human beings who have, through their spiritual cultivation and perfection, transcended the human cycle of death and rebirth to become Buddhas, Bodhisattvas, or Immortals; next are the venerated spirits of human heroes. Earth, by contrast, is associated on the one hand with gods of the earth, who are territorial protectors, and on the other with the "prison of earth," or hell, which is governed by an appointed bureaucracy modeled on the courts of the district magistrates of prerepublican China. Ghosts are thought to be potentially malevolent beings who may cause human suffering when provoked.

Religious Practitioners.   Buddhist monks and Taoist priests contribute to Chinese religious culture by performing funeral rituals and the rites associated with public festivals. Buddhism functions as a world religion as well as serving the needs of religious culture. Buddhist monasteries offer education and retreats for lay Buddhists. Buddhist monks and Taoist priests ideally base their authority on spiritual self-cultivation and on mastery of the traditional texts chanted in ritual performance. Spirit mediums by contrast are ordinary persons whose special abilities belong to the spirits who possess them. Spirit mediums engage in ritual performances and folk healing, and they are frequently consulted for aid when Chinese encounter medical or personal problems that do not resolve themselves and thus are thought to have a spiritual cause. Christian missionaries were active during the colonial period in establishing schools and promoting conversion to a variety of Christian religions; Christianity also has a presence among the Chinese of Southeast Asia. While women may become Buddhist nuns or spirit mediums, Chinese women do not tend to become religious practitioners, in part because they are considered ritually impure as the result of menstruation and childbirth.

Ceremonies.   Participants in Chinese religious culture perform the rites of ancestor worship, offering food, drink, and incense on a family altar on the first and fifteenth days of the lunar month. Offerings are also made at this time to the Lord of Heaven, a select number of gods on the family altar, and the gods of the earth. In addition, major ancestral offerings are made during the Qing Ming festival on the fifth day of the fourth lunar month, on the fourteenth or fifteenth day of the seventh lunar month, and on the twenty-second day of the twelfth lunar month. Festivals are celebrated to honor or placate a range of deities, and community members worship in the temple during the festive period and enjoy the Chinese opera or stage show performed in the deity's honor. Religious practitioners are frequently involved in the celebration of festivals; Buddhist monks or Taoist priests may be engaged to perform elaborate rituals, in particular during the Hungry Ghosts festival; spirit mediums perform dramatic rituals such as firewalking or "washing" in hot oil in the festivals that honor their patron deities.

Arts.   Chinese art forms are frequently linked with the affirmation of cultural identity in the Southeast Asian context. They include traditional music, Chinese opera and puppet theater (most commonly performed at temple festivals), Chinese dance, painting, calligraphy, and literature, including works written in Chinese and English as well as in a variety of Southeast Asian languages. Overseas Chinese also engage in a variety of crafts, including gold- and silversmithing, furniture making, and the design and manufacture of batik textiles.

Medicine.   Modern medicine is used side by side with Chinese medicine. Overseas Chinese consult acupuncturists, bonesetters, herbalists, and Chinese traditional doctors as well as modern medical practitioners. Certain illnesses and mental disturbances (including anxiety) are ascribed to "collisions" with members of the spirit world or to the action of black magic. When such causation is suspected, the ill person is frequently taken to visit a spirit medium, who diagnoses the cause and offers a magical cure.

Death and Afterlife.   Funeral rituals draw kin together with members of the groups in which the deceased participated to perform the ceremonies that transform the deceased into an ancestor, represented on the family altar with a spirit tablet. Funerals may express the social status of the deceased both through the scale of ritual performance and the scale of events such as the funeral cortege that transports the coffin to the grave or crematorium. Rituals of salvation may be performed by Taoist priests or Buddhist monks or nuns. The Taoist ceremonies performed forty-nine days after the death dramatically depict the soul's journey through the courts of hell, where it is given a potion of forgetfulness and sent on to a new rebirth. This ceremony offers the soul paper models of goods that the soul is thought to need in its new life (a house, money, servants, a car), and these are burned at the conclusion of the ritual.

Bibliography

Coughlin, Donald (1960). *Double Identity: The Chinese in Modern Thailand.* Hong Kong: Hong Kong University Press.

Cushman, Jennifer, and Wang Gungwu, eds. (1988). *Changing Identities of the Southeast Asian Chinese since World War II.* Hong Kong: Hong Kong University Press.

DeBernardi, Jean (1992). "Space and Time in Chinese Religious Culture." *History of Religions* 31:247–268.

Halpern, Joel Martin (1964). *Economy and Society of Laos: A Brief Survey.* Monograph Series, no. 5. New Haven: Southeast Asian Studies, Yale University.

Lim, Linda Y. C., and L. A. Peter Gosling (1983). *The Chinese in Southeast Asia.* Vol. 1, *Ethnicity and Economic Activity.* Vol. 2, *Identity, Culture, and Politics.* Singapore: Maruzen Asia.

Pan, Lynn (1990). *Sons of the Yellow Emperor: The Story of the Overseas Chinese.* London: Mandarin Paperback.

Purcell, Victor W. W. S. (1965). *The Chinese in Southeast Asia.* London: Oxford University Press.

Skinner, G. William (1957). *Chinese Society in Thailand: An Analytical History.* Ithaca, N.Y.: Cornell University Press.

Somers Heidhues, Mary F. (1974). *Southeast Asia's Chinese Minorities.* Camberwell, Australia: Longman.

Suryadinata, Leo (1989). *The Ethnic Chinese in the ASEAN States: Bibliographic Essays.* Singapore: Institute of Southeast Asian Studies.

Tan Chee Beng (1988). *The Baba of Melaka: Culture and Identity of a Chinese Peranakan Community in Malaysia.* Kuala Lumpur: Pelanduk.

Wee, Vivienne (1988). *Who Are the Chinese?* Working Paper no. 90. Singapore: National University of Singapore, Department of Sociology.

Wickberg, Edgar (1965). *The Chinese in Philippine Life, 1850–1898.* New Haven: Yale University Press.

Wilmott, Donald (1960). *The Chinese of Semarang: A Changing Minority Community in Indonesia.* Ithaca, N.Y.: Cornell University Press.

Wilmott, William E. (1967). *The Chinese in Cambodia.* Vancouver: University of British Columbia Press.

JEAN DeBERNARDI

Chong

The Chong (Xong) are a group estimated at 5,500 in 1984, located along the Cambodia-Thailand border at about 12° N and 103° E and in the Cardamom Mountains. The Chong are closely related to the Pear and Saoch, who also speak Mon-Khmer languages and are classified as Southwest Upland Groups. The Chong now are largely assimilated into Khmer society.

Chrau

The Chrau are a group of about 20,000 (1981) located in Dong Nai Province in Vietnam. Known subgroups include the Ro, Bajieng, Mru, Jre, Buham, Bu-Preng, and Bla.

Cotabato Manobo

ETHNONYMS: Dulangan, Tudag

Numbering 10,000 to 15,000 in 1981, the Cotabato Manobo inhabit the central portion of the southwest highlands of Cotabato on Mindanao Island in the Philippines. Through contact with the neighboring Magindanao and Christian Filipinos who have settled in the region, much of the traditional culture has disappeared. Cotabato Manobo is classified in the Hesperonesian Group of the Austronesian Language Family. Settlements are generally composed of five to eight households. Houses are usually of bamboo and thatch, rectangular in shape, and raised 3 to 6 feet on piles. Major crops include rice, maize, bananas, sweet potatoes, taro, and vegetables. Agriculture is supplemented by trade, fishing, and hunting. Leadership is achieved, not ascribed at birth. The Cotabato Manobo believe in a high god and hold rituals honoring the rice spirit; many of the people have converted to Christianity.

Bibliography

Maceda, Marcelino N. (1975). "Cotabato Manobo." In _Ethnic Groups of Insular Southeast Asia_, edited by Frank M. LeBar. Vol. 2, _Philippines and Formosa_, 45–46. New Haven: HRAF Press.

Duane

Like the Jeh, Menam, Noar, and the Sayan, the Duane are considered by some a distinct ethnic group in central Vietnam and Laos, although little is known about them.

Dusun

ETHNONYMS: Idäan, Kadazan, Kalamantan, Kiaus, Piasau Id'an, Saghais, Sipulotes, Sundayak, Tambunwhas (Tambunaus), Tuhun Ngaavi

Orientation

Identification. The Dusun live in northern Borneo and speak several regional dialects of a language belonging to the Austronesian family. The Dusun name for themselves, in the Penampang regional dialect, is "Tuhun Ngaavi" (the people). Dusun commonly have recognized differences among themselves through the use of geographic designations (e.g., Tambunan, Penampang, Tempassuk, etc.) and on the basis of dominant subsistence activity in rice agriculture, employing the descriptors _tuhun id ranau_ (people of the wet rice fields) or _tuhun id sakid_ (people of the hill rice fields) to note a distinction between subsistence based on irrigated rice and on swidden rice cultivation. The term "Dusun" has been used by

Cua

Also known as "Khua," the Cua are a group of about 10,000 to 15,000 (1973) settled in Gia Lai-Cong Tum Province in central Vietnam.

Europeans, who, in the nineteenth century, adopted the colloquial Malay language usage, _orang dusun_ (people of the orchards) as a standard reference term. The recent ethnological literature refers to this population as "Dusun," or has grouped the culture with a larger entity, the Kalimantan nation, which includes the Kalabit, Milanau, and Murut peoples of northern Borneo. In the years following the inclusion (on 16 September 1963) of the former British colony of North Borneo into the new nation of Malaysia as the state of Sabah, the Dusun people began to employ the term "Kadazan" to refer to themselves and to distinguish their culture and society from other indigenous populations in Sabah. Today many Dusun view the name "Dusun" as a legacy of European colonial domination and as a disparaging ethnic identification that discounts their long cultural history and knowledge as a people well-adapted to a demanding local environment.

Location. The Dusun population is found in the Malaysian state of Sabah, which comprises an area of 73,710 square kilometers on the northern tip of the island of Borneo between 4° and 7° N and 115° and 119° E. Dusun communities are located along Sabah's narrow eastern and northern coastal plains and in the central mountain interior ranges and valleys, with a few communities located in the headwater areas of the Labuk and Kinabatangan rivers. Sabah's climate is marked by a high average annual temperature (27° C) and humidity, seasonal heavy rains, gusty winds, and bright sunshine. These climatic factors vary somewhat with altitude and location in Sabah. Annual rainfall in the two yearly monsoon seasons (May to October, November to April) may total between 254 and 520 centimeters, depending on local topography. There may be dry periods of two to four weeks each year when the monsoon winds change direction. Monsoon rainstorm winds sometimes blow at gale force, while heavy rainfall often brings widespread flooding, particularly in Sabah's low-lying areas. The monsoon seasons are characterized by a period of several months when days have hot, sunny, and humid mornings followed by afternoon thunderstorms.

Demography. The 1960 census of North Borneo conducted by the British colonial government reported a total population of 454,421 persons with 306,498 individuals noted as members of "indigenous tribes." The Dusun were the most numerous of the twelve indigenous groups counted in that census, totaling 145,229 persons or approximately 47 percent of the indigenous population and 32 percent of the total population. A 1980 government census notes a total Sabah population of 955,712 persons. However, the census does not provide specific figures for the twenty-eight groups listed under the heading of *pribumi* or "indigenous" peoples, totaling 742,042 persons. It is possible to estimate, however, that in 1980 the Dusun population comprised at least 101,000 more persons than in 1960, based on an average annual rate of growth in Sabah of approximately 4 percent. A more accurate estimate of the 1980 Dusun population, based on a higher rate of population growth (approximately 6 percent annually) would place the total Dusun population at approximately 319,750 persons, or 43 percent of the Sabah pribumi population at that time. A reasonable estimate of the Dusun population in 1989, based on a 6 percent annual rate of population increase between 1980 and 1989, would be a total of about 492,400 persons. In 1989, the Dusun were the largest ethnic group in Sabah, followed by the Chinese.

Linguistic Affiliation. The Dusun language is classified as part of the Northwestern Group of Austronesian languages and is related to languages spoken in Borneo, Indonesia, the Philippines, Taiwan, and Madagascar.

History and Cultural Relations

The origin of the Dusun population is uncertain at present. Existing archaeological and physical anthropological evidence, considered with the results of historical and comparative studies, suggests that the Dusun are descendants of populations migrating into northern Borneo in successive waves some time about 4,000 to 5,000 years ago (and possibly earlier). They brought with them a Neolithic, or food-producing, way of life, based on swidden cultivation supplemented by hunting and foraging. Change in Dusun life, derived from contacts with other cultures, has been taking place for a long period. The historical record indicates contact, particularly in coastal communities in western and northern Sabah, between Dusun and Indians, Chinese, Malays, and Europeans. Thus, beginning after the seventh century B.C., Indian traders and travelers en route by boat to and from south China stopped briefly along the western and northern Borneo coasts to replenish supplies or seek shelter from severe South China Sea weather. These Indian travelers included various types of craftsmen and Brahman and Buddhist teachers and priests. During the time of the Western Han Empire (202 B.C. to A.D. 9), Chinese traders and religious pilgrims traveling to and from India also were in contact with the coastal peoples of western and northern Borneo, seeking local products. Chinese trade with India, with stops by ships along the coasts of Borneo, expanded several times until A.D. 1430, and included the establishment of some trading settlements, such as the one founded in A.D. 1375 at the mouth of the Kinabatangan river in the eastern part of north Borneo by a Chinese trader (Wang Sen-ping). These contacts between northern Borneo native peoples and Chinese traders and travelers over many centuries introduced a wide range of Chinese cultural forms to Bornean populations, and brought them the techniques and tools of irrigated rice agriculture using the water buffalo as a principal source of power in field preparation. Between the ninth and thirteenth centuries A.D. the early Malay Buddhist kingdom of Srivijaya, centered in the area of the present-day city of Palembang, Sumatra, dominated the southern and southwestern coasts of Borneo. Representatives of this kingdom made contact with people along the coasts of western and northern Borneo. Then the powerful Hindu kingdom of Majapahit, located in Java, exercised state power in the same coastal areas of Borneo beginning in the early fourteenth century A.D. Islamic influences and cultural forms spread to the area as the state of Malacca, ruled by a Muslim prince, exerted its domination in the fifteenth century A.D. Some European cultural influences reached the western and northern Borneo coasts as traders sought local products, particularly spices, following the conquest of Malacca by a Portuguese fleet in A.D. 1511. Regular and intensive contacts between Europeans and the coastal peoples of Borneo did not begin until after the mid-nineteenth century A.D., as the British sought to establish protectorates to maintain the safety of trade routes through the South China Sea. In northern Borneo, a private chartered company was established by British investors in 1881, which ruled the area as a sovereign entity until 15 July 1946, when British North Borneo became a British colony. British colonial rule continued for seventeen more years, until North Borneo became the state of Sabah in Malaysia in September 1963. Thus the Dusun were in regular contact with British cultural and social forms for eighty-two years, during which power, authority, and law were usually imposed unilaterally and with little regard for Dusun tradition. These contacts brought Dusun to realize they were citizens of a Malaysian state, and also brought them into regular contact with a new national language (Bahasa Melayu) and an emphasis by the national government on Muslim religious traditions, values, and social practices.

Settlements

Dusun communities traditionally number (as of 1959) about 300 to 400 persons and range from a low of about 100 persons to over 1,000 persons. Most Dusun communities are distinct, compact, or nucleated entities set in the center of, or directly adjacent to, food-producing areas. Dusun settlements employing swidden cultivation have a "longhouse" type of dwelling, or a series of nuclear-family apartments built on one level, fronted by a common veranda and covered by a common roof. Some Dusun swidden communities have several longhouses grouped closely together. Dusun communities basing their food production on irrigated rice agriculture often contain a number of separate nuclear-family dwellings grouped closely together in a type of "divided longhouse" form (e.g., family apartments no longer fronted by a common veranda or covered by a common roof) and are arranged along the length of a footpath, often on a rise or bluff overlooking nearby rice fields. Coconut palms, fruit trees, and other useful plants are grown near the houses in compact Dusun settlements using irrigated rice farming. In both types of Dusun community, family members move out at the beginning of the day to tend fields, perform various tasks connected with agriculture, or forage and hunt in nearby jungle areas. Structures in both kinds of Dusun community traditionally have hardwood support posts with split-bamboo sides and floors and either a bamboo-tile or *atap* palm-thatch roof.

Economy

Subsistence and Commercial Activities. Today irrigated rice agriculture is the dominant food-producing activity in Dusun communities. The rice is grown for use as a meal several times a day. The irrigated rice crop is set out initially as seedlings in nursery plots, then hand transplanted into small plots, less than a hectare in size, that are prepared by both women and men. Field preparation involves repair of the low earthen dikes used to retain the water that flows across the fields, as well as the repair of the irrigation systems employed by Dusun to bring water from nearby streams and rivers. The irrigation systems often involve transporting water across ravines through bamboo or wooden conduits and call for considerable practical knowledge of hydrodynamics, especially in leading water to fields located at a distance from a stream. Dusun wet-rice agriculture traditionally involves breaking the soil with a hoe and plowing the field with a flat-board harrow that has wooden teeth attached to the underside, pulled by a water buffalo wearing a woven rattan harness. The rice crop is harvested by hand and initially winnowed in fields on woven, split-bamboo mats. Further winnowing of the rice crop may occur near grain storehouses where any surplus is held until required for food or trade. The irrigated rice cycle is divided into eleven named phases, each associated with a specific kind of work activity and associated with ritual and ceremonial activities, including a communitywide harvest celebration. Dusun families also plant and tend small gardens near their houses, where they may grow some twenty-five types of foodstuff, including the sweet potato, greater yam, manioc, bottle gourd, various types of bean, squashes, chilies, and a wide variety of other garden crops. The borders of garden areas are used to cultivate trees and shrubs bearing coconuts, bananas, breadfruit, mango, papaya, durian, limes, and other fruits that supplement the daily rice diet. A half-dozen plants also are cultivated near Dusun houses or garden plots for use in manufacturing tools, shelter, and clothing. These plants include bamboo, kapok, betel palms, indigo, and derris. Dusun also eat the shoots of bamboo plants. A variety of domestic animals provide food, power, and raw materials for the Dusun. Chickens and ducks are common fowl, and geese are sometimes kept. Pigs and water buffalo both are used by Dusun as food; the buffalo is employed as a power source in rice agriculture. Pigs and water buffalo also play an important role in ritual activities that are a vital part of Dusun life. Dogs and cats are kept as domestic animals in most households, the dogs serving as hunting companions and the cats reducing the rat population in houses and rice-storage structures.

Industrial Arts. Dusun communities usually have part-time and seasonal male and female specialists expert in the making and repair of tools and implements used in agriculture and hunting and foraging activities. They also make and repair buffalo harnesses and plows and weave rattan fish traps and split-bamboo baskets of various kinds, rice-sifting trays, and other implements used in everyday storage and the carrying of foodstuffs. Metal tools, ceramic containers, and cloth traditionally have been obtained by Dusun from Chinese traders or merchants.

Trade. The Dusun have depended for centuries upon these traders for manufactured goods. In addition, weekly markets exist in most Dusun areas of Sabah. Here Dusun women bring local produce for sale or barter. Such markets are also places for buying various manufactured goods.

Division of Labor. Traditional household tasks are assigned to Dusun females, although males are expected to undertake household work if their wives are ill, in the late stages of pregnancy, or absent from the community for a time. Dusun men perform the heavy labor associated with house and storehouse building and getting wood and bamboo supplies for this purpose. Men and women work together in most swidden rice agricultural tasks, including field repair, planting, harvesting, and weeding. Men undertake the clearing and firing of fields in the preparation of swidden rice cultivation because these activities are considered too dangerous for women. The construction and repair of irrigation channels used in wet-rice agriculture tend to be the task of men, although women often participate. Men are expected to participate in infant and child care. Dusun women do not hunt, are not skilled in the weapons used in the hunt, and have little knowledge of hunting lore. The weaving of split-bamboo mats, field hats, and sifting trays are the exclusive domain of women; males have scant knowledge or skill in such work.

Land Tenure. Irrigated wet-rice agriculture is based on a set of cultural beliefs concerning the use and inheritance of land. Individual ownership and the inheritance of irrigated fields by descendants of landowners form the cornerstones of this system of land tenure. A steadily increasing population has placed significant pressure on the ownership and inheritance of irrigated rice lands and has resulted recently in the growth of a group of young Dusun unable to own land. This has caused migration of many young people to the towns and cities of Sabah to seek wage-labor incomes. Thus Kota Kinabalu, the Sabah state capital, grew from 21,719 persons in 1960 to 108,725 persons in 1980.

Kinship

Kin Groups and Descent. Descent in Dusun culture is bilateral. Ego-oriented kindreds also are present and are active in celebration of important events in the life of an individual. For Dusun, a kindred is a group of relatives recognizing their relationship to a particular individual without regard to whether the relationship is traced through a male or female relative. Dusun also have specific social groups, all members of which are descendants of a particular founding ancestor, whose activities are told in legend and folktale on special occasions of ritual feasting and ceremony, and in whose name some land and moveable property are owned. These ancestor-oriented kin groups conventionally have regulated marriage between members through insistence on the practice of endogamy.

Kinship Terminology. Dusun traditionally employ Eskimo cousin terminology. They also emphasize the relative ages of unrelated persons through use of special kin terms.

Marriage and Family

Marriage.   Marriages are typically monogamous, although polygynous marriage is permitted between older, wealthy males and younger females believed capable of producing healthy infants. Dusun commonly prohibit marriage with any first or second cousin and view marriage with third cousins as distasteful. There is some freedom in choosing marriage partners, within limits set by Dusun culture. Following an arrangement to marry between a man and a woman, often made in secret, formal discussions concerning marriage are initiated by the man's father, paternal grandfather, or a father's brother with the woman's father, paternal grandfather, or a father's brother. Marriage involves direct and substantial payment by a groom to the father of the bride. Marriages tend to be locally exogamous. Following marriage, couples routinely establish independent family households close to both their families, although a newly married couple may reside initially with the groom's father and occasionally with the bride's father while working to accumulate enough wealth to establish an independent household. Termination of marriage, other than through death of a spouse, requires initial arbitration by a community leader, then a formal hearing if the effort at reconciliation fails. A ritual fine may be required of an individual found to be at fault in the dissolution of a marriage.

Domestic Unit.   The nuclear family is the minimal family unit occupying a household. Some relatives may be added to the nuclear family as the need arises to support them, particularly if they are aged, ill, or handicapped. These relatives are expected to assist in some way in the household unit.

Inheritance.   The Dusun traditionally follow the general principle that all children should receive a fair share of the estates of their parents. A child who cares for an aged parent before death may receive some special additional consideration in property inheritance. A husband has little control over the property brought to a marriage by his wife. The Dusun have developed and use a traditional system for deciding complex questions concerning the distribution of property.

Socialization.   Parents tend to share the care of infants and young children. Older siblings often care for infants and young children when parents are away from the household at work. The process of cultural transmission traditionally provides for a long period of freedom from most tasks for maturing children, with few restrictions on their behavior. Then, at about 11 or 12 years of age, children are expected to begin to participate in daily work activities and to be responsible members of their families and community. Prior to this age children are considered by parents to be naturally inclined to noisiness and illness, somewhat temperamental, easily offended, quick to forget, and prone to wandering away from home. Dusun parents try to shape this nature through use of a wide variety of specific physical and verbal rewards and punishments. Because infants and young children are not viewed as competent humans until they reach about 11 or 12 years of age, they are not judged harshly or punished by parents when they misbehave.

Sociopolitical Organization

The Dusun jurisdictional hierarchy is traditionally organized at the level of the local community. In the past they have given no attention to larger sociopolitical entities such as parish, district, province, or a political state. Their communities are led by males selected through an informal, community-wide consensus, who hold formal office as "headmen" (*mohoingon*) with wide powers. This office is viewed by Dusun as nonhereditary in its succession.

Social Organization.   Society is traditionally organized about several territorially based divisions that serve as a focal point for the performance of certain ritual and ceremonial activities. These territorial divisions may contain one or several mutual-aid groups whose members assist each other in heavy work (for example, house building or field clearing). Dusun society is also organized on the basis of age, sex, personal and family wealth, and the region of residence. Seniority in age, for both females and males, plays an important part in social life. Women are widely respected for their specialized craft, ritual, and ceremonial knowledge.

Political Organization.   Dusun are citizens of the nation of Malaysia, a federal parliamentary democracy based on the British model. Malaysia contains thirteen states, each with an elected assembly and headed by a chief minister. In Sabah, the state assembly has forty-eight seats. The chief minister, Mr. Joseph Pairin Kitingan, a 49-year-old Dusun, is a Christian and the first Dusun to qualify as a lawyer in Malaysia. First elected to office in 1985 in an upset victory over the candidates of two Muslim-led political parties, Mr. Kitingan's political party (PBS, or Parti Bersatu Sabah—Sabah United Party) gained control of the state government by winning a majority of seats in the assembly. Following state-court challenges by members of the previous state government and their allies, Mr. Kitingan called another assembly election in 1986. During the two-month election campaign there were violent incidents that included rioting and bombings by political activists supporting the main opposition party, Bersatu Rakyat Jelata (Sabah People's Union or Berjaya). The PBS party of Mr. Kitingan increased its majority in the Sabah state assembly in the elections held in May 1986, and Mr. Kitingan continued in office as chief minister. In June 1986 the PBS party became part of the Barisan Nasional (National Front) political party, an alliance of thirteen parties that presently is the ruling party in Malaysia. Thus, the Dusun now live in a complex nation-state political setting organized significantly beyond their traditional sociopolitical concerns. A head of state with the power of constitutional oversight, a prime minister directing a national government and substantial internal security and defense forces, and a bicameral parliament—all these are distant democratic forces affecting daily Dusun life through executive and legislative decisions.

Social Control.   Social control in Dusun communities is maintained largely through informal sanctions, including shame, mockery, gossip, and ridicule, with some use of shunning behavior. The Dusun have also developed more formal means of dealing at the community level with individuals accused of serious violations of the norms and mores of traditional life. Dusun have several techniques for litigating complaints against individuals. Litigation occurs in the context of a body of abstract principles that are imbued with an aura of tradition, or *koubasan*, which provides a moral and ethical authority that binds all persons involved in litigation to that body of abstract principles. Litigation in Dusun communities is conducted by a village leader (the mohoingon) who functions in ways that establish facts in a case and who may administer one or several tests of truth. The leader also has the power to levy various fines and several kinds of punishment against persons found guilty of violating traditional behavior. Litigation is a public process.

Conflict. Dusun traditionally have engaged in conflict between communities, with organized raiding parties of men seeking to engage in hand-to-hand combat persons, social groups, or communities believed to have caused an imbalance of personal or community fortune (_nasip tavasi_) and luck (_ki nasip_). Such armed conflict usually arose from an effort to restore the fate or luck of individuals or a community that had been made bad (_aiso nasip, talat_) through the real or supposed acts of some individual, group, or other community. The objective of combat was to secure trophies for a display that publicly symbolized a full restoration of good fortune and luck. Among such trophies were the severed heads of individuals vanquished in close combat. Head trophies were given special care, often stored in particular places, including house eaves, and formed an integral part of special rituals and ceremonies held periodically in Dusun communities to note formally that community and individual luck and fortune remained in balance. Following 1881, the Chartered Company acted vigorously, but until near the time of World War II with limited success, to suppress head-taking combat. Such conflict has not subsequently been a feature of Dusun life.

Religion and Expressive Culture

The Dusun traditionally are animists, believing there is a direct and continuing relationship between the events of daily life and a complex world of good and evil supernatural beings and unseen forces. Dusun also believe that proper ritual and ceremonial acts can be interposed between humans and supernatural beings and forces in an attempt to modify, or even to control, events that cause humans to fall ill, be uncertain, lose their luck, feel pain, or become fearful.

Religious Beliefs. Dusun conceptions of the universe include a variety of malevolent supernatural beings and forces believed to be responsible for the personal crises of human life, including accidents, illness, and death. These harmful beings include entities and forces that have existed since the time of the creation of the world, as well as the souls of the dead doomed by the creator being to an eternity of wandering and cannibalism because of evil deeds performed while alive. A group of beneficial spirit beings and forces is also believed to be important in keeping order in the universe and in daily human life. The most important of these supernatural beings and forces in everyday life is the "spirit of the rice," a female entity who serves as the guardian of the rice crop and rice storehouse and in whose name specific rituals are performed at times of rice planting and harvest. In addition, Dusun traditionally believe in the existence of a specific class of named supernaturals whose attributes and powers are known and used by ritual specialists as they seek to divine and control events leading to life crises. A creator force, personified into a being called "Asundu," who has a legendary history and is possessed of awesome powers, is said to have shaped the universe and to direct the destiny of all its inhabitants. A specific power of the creator, believed to be derived from the inexhaustible store of the power of this being, is said to provide for the curative and restorative powers of female and male ritual specialists. Objects, geographic locations, and persons are said to be imbued with considerable amounts of this power and must be treated with respect or avoided if possible. A special designation (_apagun_) and carved symbols are used by Dusun to "wall off" such locations or objects from inadvertent human contact. Today, large numbers of Dusun have become Christians and so reject many animistic beliefs and practices. Some have also become Muslims.

Religious Practitioners. Some male and female individuals in each Dusun community are specially knowledgeable in the many ritual and ceremonial acts used to mediate between humans and the supernatural world. These rituals and ceremonies involve spirit possession, use of symbolic objects, recitation of lengthy sacred verses, and often center upon specific individuals, places, or crops afflicted with a disease or ill fortune. The effectiveness of a ritual or ceremony is said to depend upon precisely following correct procedures and the accurate recitations of verses. Female ritual specialists tend to concentrate on curing and divination regarding individual illness and bad fortune. Male ritual specialists tend to concern themselves with alleviation or prevention of a worldwide scope. The verses recited by female and male ritual specialists are often expressed in an archaic form of the Dusun language not known or widely used in a community; they are learned through long apprenticeship to senior ritual specialists.

Ceremonies. Public performances of ritual acts, many concerned with the annual swidden and irrigated rice agricultural cycle, are a regular feature. Ceremonies marking individual life-cycle stages or transitions (for example, birth, marriage, and death) are also important.

Arts. Art and house architecture are imbued with forms and designs common to other native Bornean peoples. Many of these art forms are believed by Dusun to express a "spiritual" (_id dasom ginavo_) intent or quality, and are said to exhibit their deep understanding, or _ginavo_, and respect for Dusun tradition, or _koubasan_. Traditional musical instruments include a bamboo mouth harp, a bamboo-and-gourd wind instrument, and gongs of various sizes obtained in the past from Chinese traders. Dusun men have traditionally practiced tattooing of their necks, forearms, and shoulders with intricate designs of deep spiritual meaning.

Medicine. Personal illness is believed by Dusun to derive from bad fortune, various actions taken by harmful supernatural beings and forces, and the malign intentions of human adversaries. A wide range of medicinal remedies, derived from various plant and animal products and made into different lotions and poultices, is used to help alleviate and cure illness. Special importance is attached to a variety of a swamp-plant root that is believed to have magical and curative powers and is used by female specialists when seeking to divine and cure personal illness.

Death and Afterlife. The Dusun believe that following death the spirit of an individual proceeds to the supernatural world. There the spirits of the dead are said to rest near the creator being in a world similar to the human world but lacking disease, bad fortune, failed crops, and combat, where all things are new and never in need of replenishment. Some spirits of the dead are believed not to reach the place of the dead since they are captured en route by harmful spirits or eaten by cannibal spirits. A period of formal mourning, which includes a number of ritual and ceremonial actions, is intended to ease the transition of the dead to their new life in the afterworld.

Bibliography

Evans, I. H. N. (1922). *Among Primitive Peoples in Borneo.* Philadelphia: Lippincott.

Evans, I. H. N. (1953) *The Religion of the Tempasuk Dusuns of North Borneo.* Cambridge: Cambridge University Press.

Hurlbut, H. M. (1985). "Social Organization and Kinship among the Labuk Kadazan People." *Philippine Journal of Linguistics,* no. 15 (December 1984)–16 (June 1985), pp. 55–70.

Rutter, O. (1922). *British North Borneo.* London: Constable & Co.

Rutter, O. (1929). *The Pagans of North Borneo.* London: Hutchinson & Co.

Williams, T. R. (1965). *The Dusun: A North Borneo Society.* New York: Holt, Rinehart & Winston.

Williams, T. R. (1969). *A Borneo Childhood: Enculturation in Dusun Society.* New York: Holt, Rinehart & Winston.

THOMAS RHYS WILLIAMS

Endenese

ETHNONYMS: 'Ata Ende, 'Ata Jaö, Orang Ende

Orientation

Identification. The most popular word in the literature for the people around the central part of Flores has been the "Endenese" or (in Indonesian) "Orang Ende." The people who can be referred to as "Endenese" may be divided into two groups in terms of culture and religion. One is the coastal Endenese, who have been under the influence of Islam. Their culture is an amalgam of traditional features and foreign elements. The other is the mountain Endenese. It is with these people that this cultural summary mainly deals.

Location. The Endenese live in the central part of the island of Flores in eastern Indonesia. The administrative division in which they reside, Kabupaten Endeh (or Ende Regency), is located between 8° and 9° S and between 121° and 122° E. Flores is one of the three biggest islands in Nusa Tenggara Timur (the eastern Southeast Archipelago), Sumba and Timor being the other two. Roughly speaking, the mountain area that runs along an east-west axis through the island divides central Flores into two parts: the north coast and the south coast, a division that is also pertinent to the cultural geography of the people. Flores is located in one of the typical monsoon regions. The wet west monsoon (with northwest wind) begins around December or January and ends in March or April. The dry east monsoon (southeast wind) begins in May or June and ends in October or November. The west monsoon brings rain, which, however, rarely amounts to more than 200 centimeters annually in the central part of Flores. The dry season is also marked by relatively few clouds, yet in the transitional period from the west to the east monsoon (i.e., between May and July) there are abundant clouds (*kubhu kuu*). The western part of Flores (Manggarai, Ngada) is the wettest, and the north coast tends to be drier than the south coast. The average annual rainfall in Endeh (on the south coast) in the years from 1879 to 1928 was 113.8 centimeters (ninety-one rainy days) and the average rainfall in Maumere (on the north coast) in the same years was only 95.4 centimeters (sixty-seven rainy days).

Demography. In view of the small area they occupy, the coastal Endenese are relatively numerous, with an approximate population of 43,000. A rough estimate of the mountain Endenese population would be 20,000.

Linguistic Affiliation. The language of central Flores belongs to the Bima-Sumba Group of Western Austronesian.

History and Cultural Relations

Before the arrival of the Portuguese in the sixteenth century, the island of Flores already had been used as a trading port by the Javanese (especially for the sandalwood derived from Timor). The Portuguese arrived at Melaka (Malacca) in 1511 and the first bishop in Melaka sent three missionaries to Solor, a small island off the east coast of Flores. Between the sixteenth and seventeenth centuries, Islam is said to have come to Ende. Thus, in the sixteenth century, the island of Flores was a battlefield between the Islamic forces and the Portuguese. Then in the seventeenth century, a third force came onto the scene; namely, the Dutch East India Company, which was established in 1602. In 1613, a Dutch fleet under the command of Apollonius Scot sailed through the islands in the eastern part of Indonesia. Before arriving at Kupang, Scot went to Solor and attacked the fortress there, taking it from the Portuguese. In the decades between 1610 and 1640, the Portuguese in Larantuka and the Dutch on Solor played a kind of seesaw game, which in the long run turned in favor of the Dutch. The fortress on Pulau Ende had been destroyed in the 1620s. After that incident the city of Endeh, where the rajadom of Ende may already have formed itself, replaced Pulau Ende as a focal point in central Flores. Around this time the Portuguese influence over the area was waning. The Dutch East India Company selected Ende as a rajadom and concluded a formal contract in 1793. The company's involvement in eastern Indonesia ended in 1799 when its charter expired and was replaced by Dutch colonial rule. Prior to 1907, the Dutch principle of government had been minimal direct involvement. In 1907, military reinforcement came from Kupang, and the whole land of Flores was pacified by military force.

Settlements

One mountain Endenese village, in general, consists of ten to twenty houses, each of which used to include one extended family (married brothers, adopted daughter-in-law—the would-be wife of a son—and dependents such as those who could not pay their bride-wealth). Today, each house contains only a nuclear family. Houses are constructed around the village yard (_wewa_). Ideally, a village has an altar or a set of altars, called _tubu musu ora nata_, in the center of the yard; but today few Endenese villages have tubu musu ora nata. Also ideally, one village is occupied by one patrilineally related group, but in most villages there are many outsiders.

Economy

Subsistence and Commercial Activities. The Endenese are mostly slash-and-burn agriculturalists. Wet-rice fields are not popular in the area because of the shortage of water. Generally speaking, the staple is a combination of cassava (_'uwi 'ai_), rice (_'aré_), and maize (_jawa_). The most important cash crop has been coconut (_nio_). Livestock is reared only for consumption and gift exchange. Households have an average of three pigs, and some chickens. The goat population is much smaller than the pig population. Only a few households in a village have cattle, horses, or water buffalo.

Division of Labor. There is no clearcut division of labor between sexes except that men tend to do work that needs more physical strength, such as cutting trees. Everyday cooking is done by women. On ceremonial occasions men cook meats and women cook rice.

Trade. People on the southern part of the island sometimes go to the northern coast to get cheap salt. A few people descend to a coastal village to buy fish to sell in their mountain villages. Except for these sporadic trading activities, the mountain Endenese do not engage in much commerce.

Land Tenure. Each ritual community, _tana_, whose members are supposed to have originated in an ancient village and be patrilineally related, has ritual rights over the land named after that community. These rights express themselves in a ritual called the "yam ritual" (_nggua 'uwi_), which marks the beginning and end of certain prohibitions concerning agricultural activities. Individual land tenure is also recognized by the inhabitants, based on the ritual transference of a parcel of land from wife giver to wife taker, especially from mother's brother to his sister's child. This institution is known as _pati weta ti'i 'ané_, "giving to a sister, offering to a sister's son."

Kinship

Kin Groups and Descent. Descent is traced patrilineally. The Endenese ideological framework for kin groups consists of only one word, _waja_, which means, literally, "an old one." When used in the context of kin grouping, it means "patrilineal descendants of an old one (named)." Thus "waja Juma," for example, means patrilineal descendants of Juma.

The generational depth is, at the deepest, four to five. A waja is supposed to possess a characteristic ritual (_nggua_) attached to their ritually owned parcel of land.

Kinship Terminology. The Endenese kinship terminology can be said to represent roughly the ideology of unilineality and asymmetric alliance (matrilateral cross-cousin marriage). In other words, the terminology does not contradict the ideology much. Unilineality is expressed in such equations as that between (1) father and father's brothers (_'ema_) and (2) mother and mother's sisters (_'iné_) and in such distinctions as that between father's sisters (_noö_) and mother's sisters (_'iné_). Asymmetry is expressed in such equations as that between wife's father and mother's brother (_mamé_), and such distinctions as those between (1) mother's brothers (_mamé_) and father's sister's husband (_aki noö_) and (2) mother's brother's daughters (_'ari_ or _kaë_) and father's sister's daughters (_weta_). The term _'éja_ is an exception in that it can denote both wife's brother and sister's husband.

Marriage and Family

Marriage. Marriage is preferred with one's mother's brother's daughter. However, this matrilateral cross-cousin marriage (a marriage type called _mburhu nduu wesa senda_) is not regarded as a prestigious marriage. A marriage with a girl with whose group one has no previous alliance (a marriage type called _'ana 'arhé_) is the most prestigious one. Considerable bride-wealth (_ngawu_) is demanded from the side of the bride. The amount varies from one type of marriage to another. If a man can pay only a small portion of the bride-wealth demanded, he has to stay with his father-in-law. Otherwise the bride should go to the groom's village, where they may stay with the groom's father or build a new house.

Domestic Unit. Nowadays the domestic unit corresponds to a nuclear family. Married sons tend to build a new house near their parents' house. Residence is virilocal once the prescribed bride-wealth has been paid.

Inheritance. In accordance with the ideology of patrilineality, inheritance is, in most cases, through the patrilineal line. The eldest son is supposed to inherit everything from his father. Exceptions occur where bride-wealth is concerned. Though never stated clearly as a rule, it seems to be the case that rights over bride-wealth for a sister are assumed only by her full brothers. Thus the eldest brother cannot have a say over the bride-wealth paid for his half-sister.

Socialization. Fathers as well as mothers take care of children. According to older informants, there used to be some initiation rites for children, such as filing of teeth and cutting of hair, but these practices no longer exist.

Sociopolitical Organization

Social Organization. The ideological unilineal descent group, waja, has no social function. There are scarcely any terms for religious/social functions in Ende. People are regarded as more or less equal to each other in their religious/social status. Some informants hint at the existence of the status of a slave (_o'o_). Yet there is no public mention of someone's being (or having been) a slave.

Political Organization. Some older people are respected because of their reputed greater knowledge of "history/

genealogy" (*susu 'embu kajo*) and play eminent roles in discussion (*mbabho*) to resolve disputes, and especially in negotiation of bride-wealth.

Social Control. There is no formal mechanism to control conflict, except for the Indonesian administrative functionaries such as *kepala desa* (village chiefs), who are usually coastal Endenese living beyond the social world of the mountain Endenese. Parties to a dispute come together and discuss (mbabho) the matter in question with some outside observers. Even though people seldom reach agreement, after the discussion they tend not to raise the matter again for the time being.

Conflict. Most serious conflict occurs in relation to land ownership. Whoever speaks aloud and fluently about the history (especially the history of the parcel of land in question in relation to kinship idioms such as pati weta ti'i 'ané) is regarded as a winner. But because of the lack of a formal mechanism for resolving such a conflict, the losing party raises the same matter again and again after a due interval. In effect, no Endenese community can be said to be socially harmonious—there is always some litigation going on over land in a community.

Religion and Expressive Culture

Religious Beliefs. A "supreme being" or "god" in Ende is called *nggaë*. Nggaë is, however, seldom invoked. In everyday life, the people are more intimate with the ancestors (*'embu kajo*) and spirits (*nitu*). They are invoked in the prayers at any agricultural ritual and are asked to bring a good harvest. Witches (*porho*) are believed to live among the ordinary people. They are believed to do harm to people upon the slightest excuse.

Religious Practitioners. A person who falls ill and decides that the illness is caused by a witch's attack sometimes seeks a famous practitioner (*'ata marhi*). These practitioners are ordinary people who are known to have some special knowledge; no specialization is involved.

Ceremonies. The yearly agricultural activities are marked at both the beginning and end by a communal ritual of yam eating (*kaa 'uwi*). This yam ritual is held once a year by each village. The order in which participating villages do this remains the same every year.

Arts. In marriage ceremonies and funerals (and occasionally at kaa 'uwi) people dance a traditional dance called *gawi naro*. Spontaneous songs are "ad-libbed" by a singer at the center of the circle of dancers.

Medicine. Traditional medicines are called *wunu kaju*, literally "leaves of trees." There are two kinds of medicine: those used by practitioners (*'ata marhi*), which need esoteric spells, and those that do not. Only occasionally do people go to the coast or the town of Endeh to get modern medicines.

Death and Afterlife. At a funeral, a set of valuables called *'urhu* (head) should be given to the brother of the mother of the deceased. He is the first to dig the grave for the corpse. The deceased is believed to go to Mount Iya, near the town of Endeh. No elaborate myth or legend is narrated as to the origin of death or of the afterlife on Mount Iya.

Bibliography

Kate, H. F. C. ten (1894). "Verslag eener reis in de Timorgroep en Polynesië." *Tijdschrift van het Koninklijk Nederlandsch Aardrijkskundig Genootschap*, 2nd ser. 11:659–700, 765–823.

Nakagawa, Satoshi (1984). "Endenese." In *Muslim Peoples: A World Ethnographic Survey*, edited by Richard V. Weekes, 251–253. Westport, Conn.: Greenwood Press.

Nakagawa, Satoshi (1988). "The Journey of the Bridegroom." In *To Speak in Pairs: Essays on the Ritual Languages of Eastern Indonesia*, edited by James J. Fox. Cambridge: Cambridge University Press.

Roos, S. (1877). "Iets over Endeh." *Tijdschrift voor Indische Taal-, Land- en Volkenkunde* 24:481–580.

Van Suchtelen, B. C. M. M. (1921). "Endeh (Flores)." *Mededeelingen van het Bureau voor de Bestuurszaken der Buitenbezetting, Bewerkt door het Encyclopaedisch Bureau* (Afleverin XXVI). Weltevreden: N.V. Uitgev. -Mij. "Papyrus."

Van Suchtelen, B. C. M. M. (1922). *De ruine van het out-Portugeesche fort op Poeloe Ende (Zuid-Flores)*. Den Haag: N.V. Boekdrukkerij Voorheen Firma T.C.B. Ten Hagen.

SATOSHI NAKAGAWA

Filipino

In its broadest sense, "Filipino" (fem. "Filipina") refers to citizens of the Republic of the Philippines, a grouping that numbered an estimated 62,380,000 people in 1992. "Filipino," however, is often used in a more restricted sense to refer to Christian Filipinos, who comprise 93 percent of the population. Muslims (4 percent) and others, including animists ("pagans"), comprise the remaining 7 percent. Relations between Christian Filipinos and Muslims (who live mainly on Mindanao Island) are troubled, with the former often viewing the latter as violent, warlike, and backward. Efforts by Muslim political groups to achieve independence continue. Roman Catholicism was introduced to the Philippines by the Spanish in the 1500s and 84 percent of the population is now

Roman Catholic, with another 9 percent Protestant. The major Christian ethnic groups, ranked according to their estimated population in 1962–1963, are the Cebuan (6,529,800), Tagalog (5,694,000), Ilocano (3,158,500), Panayan (2,817,300), Bikolan (2,108,800), Samaran (1,488,600), Pampangan (875,500), and the Pangasinan (666,000). Smaller groups include the Ibanag (314,000), Aklan (304,000), Hantik (268,000), Sambal (72,000), Ivantan (11,800), Itawas (11,800), and Isinai (11,500). Bisayan is a generic label that encompasses Cebuans, Panayans, and Samarans.

Many Filipinos distinguish among the different Christian Filipino groups on the basis of stereotypical perceptions of these groups. Thus, Tagalogs are seen as proud, boastful, and talkative; Pampangans as independent, self-centered, and materialistic; Ilocanos as hard-working, aggressive, and with an eye toward the future; and Bisayans as musical, passionate, fun-loving, and brave. Identification with one's group is strong and remains a marker of social identity even in overseas communities.

Christian Filipinos live mainly in coastal lowlands and valleys, primarily on Luzon, Samar, Leyte, Cebu, Bohol, Siquijor, Panay, and Negros Islands. Most Christian Filipinos on Mindanao are recent immigrants.

Philippine languages are grammatically and phonetically similar to one another and all are classified as Austronesian. Filipino (Pilipino), based on Tagalog, is the national language, with English an important second language. Despite the Spanish influence, the Spanish language was never widely spoken.

The Philippines were probably settled initially through many small migrations from mainland Southeast Asia. Chinese influence was felt early and was substantial. With the exception of Mindanao and other islands in the south, influence from the islands that now form Indonesia was minimal. Spanish contact began with Magellan's visit in 1521 and officially ended in 1898 when Spain ceded control to the United States. In addition to Roman Catholicism, which made the Philippines the only predominantly Roman Catholic nation anywhere in Asia, the Spanish brought the roman alphabet, private ownership of land, the Gregorian calendar, and various New World plants such as cassava, maize, and sweet potatoes. The American period (1898–1946) saw the introduction of national public education, the English language, and agricultural and industrial development. During World War II the country was occupied by Japan, and in 1946 it became an independent republic.

The economy continues to center on agriculture, especially rice, sugarcane, and hemp. Foresting has long been an important industry, and deforestation is now a growing problem. Industrial activity is mainly around Manila and focuses on the processing of agricultural products.

The nuclear family, one's kindred and personal alliances, and godparenthood (_compadrazgo_) are the central features of family life and social relations. Much attention has been paid to the "familial" nature of Filipino society and the emphasis placed on the family as compared to the individual.

Filipino Roman Catholicism is a synthesis of the Roman Catholicism brought by the Spanish and some animistic beliefs of the traditional cultures. Especially important among the latter are beliefs in spirits of the land and ancestors' souls who influence the lives of the living.

See also Tagalog; Visayan

Bibliography

Hart, Donn V. (1975). "Christian Filipinos." In _Ethnic Groups of Insular Southeast Asia_, edited by Frank M. LeBar. Volume 2, _Philippines and Formosa_, 16-22. New Haven: HRAF Press.

Kurian, George T. (1987). "Philippines." In _Encyclopedia of the Third World_. 3rd ed., 304–307. New York: Facts on File.

Schirmer, Daniel B., and Stephen Rosskamm Shalom, eds. (1987). _The Philippines Reader: A History of Colonialism, Neocolonialism, Dictatorship, and Resistance_. Boston: South End Press.

Steinberg, David (1982). _The Philippines: A Singular and Plural Place_. Boulder, Colo.: Westview Press.

Gaddang

The Gaddang (Gadan, Ga'dang, Gaddanes, Iraya, Pagan Gaddang, Yrraya) live in the middle Cagayan Valley in northern Luzon, the Philippines. "Gaddang" refers to both the Christianized Gaddang who are now largely assimilated into Ilocano or general Filipino society and the Pagan Gaddang. In the 1960s, there were about 2,500 Pagan Gaddang and 25,000 Christian Gaddang. Their combined number in 1975 was estimated at 17,500, suggesting continuing assimilation into mainstream Filipino society.

Bibliography

Wallace, Ben J. (1969). "Pagan Gaddang Spouse Exchange." _Ethnology_ 8:183–189.

Gayo

ETHNONYMS: Gajo, Utang Gayó

Orientation

Identification.   The Gayo live predominantly in the central highlands of Aceh Province in Sumatra, Indonesia, and are Sunni Muslims. Gayo refer to themselves as "Urang Gayo," meaning "Gayo people," primarily on grounds of command of *basa Gayo,* the Gayo language.

Location.   The Gayo homeland lies across the Bukit Barisan Range in Aceh Province, between 4° and 5° N and 96° and 98° E. The range divides the homeland into four plateaus, each with a river system along which Gayo have settled. The largest concentration of settlement is the town of Takèngën (Takengon) by Lake Lauttawar. The area gradually declines in elevation from about 1,500 meters in the north to about 500 meters in the south. Northeast trade winds bring heavy rains in a four-month period between October and March; the southeast trades can bring a lighter rainfall between April and September.

Demography.   The 1980 population of the district of Central Aceh was 163,339, of which about 140,000 were Gayo speakers. In the 1980s about 45,000 Gayo resided in other districts in the Aceh highlands and about 25,000 lived elsewhere in Indonesia, giving a total population of about 210,000 Gayo.

Linguistic Affiliation.   The Gayo language belongs to the Western Indonesian Branch of the Austronesian Family and lexically is most closely related to the Batak Subfamily. The presence of Mon-Khmer loanwords suggests early coastal contacts with some Mon-Khmer-language-speaking societies. The earliest known writing in Gayo used the Jawi script (Arabic letters) but since the 1950s most Gayo have used standard Indonesian orthography. By the 1980s most Gayo had at least minimal competence in the Indonesian language.

History and Cultural Relations

Substantial written references to the Gayo only begin in the late nineteenth century. It is likely, however, that the Gayo homeland belonged to the Islamic kingdom of Aceh in the seventeenth century and that Islamization of the area had begun by that time. At the outbreak of the Aceh-Dutch war in 1873, Gayo possessed a strong sense of ethnic distinctiveness but recognized a nominal Acehnese suzerainty. Some Gayo continued to resist the Dutch after the invasion of the highlands in 1904. During Dutch occupation (1904–1942) Gayo developed a thriving cash-crop economy in vegetables and coffee, attained a relatively high level of basic education, and participated in the movements of Islamic modernism and Indonesian nationalism. Gayo fought to maintain Indonesian independence (declared in 1945) and participated in the provincial Darul Islam rebellion against the central government (1953–1962). Gayo took part in the postcoup massacres (GESTAPU) of 1965–1966 and, unlike most of Aceh, voted for the government party, GOLKAR, in the 1970s and 1980s.

Settlements

In the 1980s Gayo lived in isolated households, small mountain hamlets, larger clustered villages, and in towns and cities. Villages ranged in population from one hundred to several thousand persons. Precolonial villages consisted of one or more longhouses, which were raised on stilts and divided into kitchens and sleeping rooms for three to nine nuclear or extended families. Houses were clustered together for protection, often on a hill. Gayo began to replace longhouses with low, single-family dwellings in the 1920s; some longhouses remained in the south in the 1980s. A single-family house has a roof of palm leaf or corrugated iron, a front public room and rear kitchen with a raised eating platform, and sometimes a sleeping room.

Economy

Subsistence and Commercial Activities.   In 1980 about 70 percent of the residents of Central Aceh (and perhaps 80 percent of Gayo residents) were engaged in farming. Others engaged in trade or civil service. Most Gayo farmers grow rice (usually with irrigation) or coffee. Most rice farmers puddle their fields with the hooves of water buffalo, and transplant, weed, and harvest local varieties of rice by hand. A few plows, but no tractors, are in use. Gayo also grow tobacco, yams, cassava, soy beans, potatoes, avocados, and a range of citrus fruits. Hard cakes of sugar are made from the sap of the sago palm (*Arenga pinnata*). Many Gayo fish in the rivers and in Lake Lauttawar, using nets and hooks. Water buffalo, goats, chickens, and ducks are kept.

Industrial Arts.   Gayo manufacture fishing equipment, embroider designs onto manufactured cloth, and work as tailors. Gayo also own and operate village rice hullers and, in Takèngën, several large coffee-processing plants.

Trade.   Sundry and eating shops are found throughout the region, and Gayo traders carry goods overland to the most remote communities. Sugar, rice, coffee, oils, other foodstuffs, and clothes are marketed within the homeland, while horses and water buffalo are driven to the coasts for sale. Coffee exports are largely controlled by Acehnese and Chinese, although in the 1970s Gayo traders became more active.

Division of Labor.   In rural settings women and men jointly perform many of the major agricultural tasks either as a household unit or in mixed-sex labor groups. Plowing, puddling fields, fishing, and long-distance trade journeys by foot are undertaken only by men. Most child care, firewood gathering, cooking, and weeding is performed by women. Women often control household budgets, operate shops, and trade in cloth and foodstuffs. In Takèngën, women as well as men work in the civil service.

Land Tenure.   Individuals control plots of agricultural land. Villages hold residual rights and once could block sales, but in the 1960s individuals used the courts to gain the right to sell land outside the village. The amount of available rice land has grown only slowly, but in the 1970s and 1980s large forest areas were cleared by smallholders for coffee growing. Forest clearing has produced problems of fire damage and soil erosion in the region.

Kinship

Kin Groups and Descent. Two major combinations of social units appear in the homeland: (1) a village divided into distinct kin categories, each associated with a different village office, and (2) kin categories that extend across several villages and are centered in a mother village. In both cases membership in the category can be traced through males or females, but claims to uniquely patrifilial ties carry weight in intravillage political matters.

Kinship Terminology. An Iroquois system was in use throughout Gayoland, but a generational system without a cross/parallel distinction has been used increasingly since the 1970s, reflecting changing marriage patterns and the Islamic bilateral ideology.

Marriage and Family

Marriage. The village and the supravillage kin categories are exogamous. Although marriage between second cousins is permitted, most Gayo consider a third-cousin relation to be the proper minimal distance. Polygynous marriages, though permitted, are rare. In rural areas most marriages are between couples who already were acquainted. The two major marriage forms followed in the 1980s were: (1) virilocal marriages with bride-wealth and a counterpayment of bride goods that established a lasting exchange relation between two kin categories, and (2) uxorilocal marriages with little or no payment that obliged the couple to support the wife's family. Although the choice of the couple's village of domicile was fixed by the marriage form, nearly all virilocally married couples and many uxorilocally married couples left the parents' household after an initial period of residence. As the clearing of new lands for cash cropping grew more attractive in the 1970s, more marriages were contracted without specifying domicile. Divorce once meant that the party who had married into a village left with no property, but since the legal reforms and economic changes that began in the 1960s, most divorcing couples divide common property equally.

Domestic Unit. Households vary in size from single persons to three-generation extended families. Households generally eat together, but adolescent boys often sleep as a group in the village prayer house. The household is the basic unit of production and consumption, and has a common household budget.

Inheritance. Prior to independence (1945) households passed on property to children who remained in the village after marriage, and favored the child who had cared for the aged parents. In the 1960s individuals began to petition the newly established Islamic court to redivide estates along the lines of Islamic property law. The success of these requests, and broader changes in religious education, led many Gayo, particularly those living in and around Takèngën, to apply Islamic law in dividing their own estates.

Socialization. Parents, resident grandparents, and siblings raise children. Care givers emphasize the importance of a sense of shame (kemèl) and respect for others according to kin relation. Physical punishment is rare.

Sociopolitical Organization

Social Organization. Kin relations and village structure play an important role in organizing everyday interactions. In the precolonial and colonial periods the highest-level rulers could claim prestige and high social status, but Gayo society before and after independence has been characterized by basically egalitarian sociopolitical relations among individuals and among villages.

Political Organization. The Gayo homeland has been part of the republic of Indonesia since independence in 1945. Most of the Gayo homeland lies in the district (kabupaten) of Central Aceh in the province of Aceh. The homeland also includes parts of three other districts. Each district has a head, under whom serve the heads of subdistricts (kecamatan) and villages (desa). For the most part the village corresponds to the basic Gayo political unit, the sarak opat, meaning "four elements" and referring to the three village officials plus the remaining villagers. In the precolonial period the homeland was divided among six domains, each with a domain lord (kerjurun); the authority and prestige of these lords varied greatly.

Social Control. The importance placed on avoiding embarrassment and shame exerts a strong guiding and restraining influence on conduct, as does the role of the kinship system in organizing respect, avoidance, and cooperation. The Indonesian police and army maintain a presence in all subdistrict capitals and exercise their police powers readily.

Conflict. In the precolonial system conflicts between villages were settled by public-resolution sessions and sometimes were mediated by a third party. The colonial and Indonesian governments assumed jurisdiction over all criminal matters.

Religion and Expressive Culture

Religious Beliefs. Gayo have been Muslims at least since the seventeenth century. Beginning in the late 1920s, modernist Muslims (kaum mudë) sought to purge religious practices of "improper" elements. They focused on rituals of propitiation, the form of worship (salat, semiyang), and marriage exchange. Other religions are represented in the town of Takèngën by Chinese (Christianity, Buddhism, Confucianism) and a small number of Batak residents (Christian). In rural areas Gayo communicate with guardian spirits, ancestors, and prophets, as well as spirits sent to cause illness. In the modernist town environment such activities are less common, but healing through exorcism is widely practiced.

Religious Practitioners. Each Gayo village has a religious official (imëm) who assists at weddings, funerals, and religious festivals, but every Gayo man and woman carries out duties as a Muslim, including burying the dead, bringing children into the world, and worshipping God. Healers exorcise illness-causing spirits from patients. Associated with each mosque is a sermon giver and one or more attendants. Government-appointed officials register marriages, divorces, and reconciliations under Islamic law. A district branch of the national Council of Ulama delivers opinions on religious matters.

Ceremonies. Gayo observe a number of festivals according to the lunar Muslim calendar, most notably the prophet Mohammed's birthday (Molud, Arabic Maulud en-nabi), the

Mohammed's birthday (Molud, Arabic Maulud en-nabi), the feast after the fasting month (Reraya, Arabic Id al-fitr), and the day of sacrifice during the pilgrimage events (Reraya Haji/ Korban, Arabic Id al-adhal). The life cycle is marked by ritual events. Seven days after birth the child is ritually bathed, introduced to the natural and spirit worlds, and given a name. Circumcision (boys) and incision (girls) takes place at varying times during youth. Wedding celebrations include the Islamic ritual (nikah) and formal exchanges of speeches and goods between the two parties. Most ritual or ceremonial events center on a ritual meal (kenduri).

Arts.   Gayo art is largely verbal. The didong, sung poetry, once involved a single performer, but since the 1950s has pitted two teams of men and boys against each other. The teams trade songs and insults throughout the night. Saèr, religious poetry, was an important instrument of religious change in the 1930s and 1940s. Saman is a series of songs and chants, usually with religious content, that is performed by a line of kneeling boys and resembles dhikir religious chanting. Although Gayo once built water vessels, wove, and carved, these skills became obsolete because of the availability of cheap imported goods; in the 1970s and 1980s, only the art of embroidering Gayo designs remained.

Medicine.   Gayo utilize spiritual healing, local knowledge of leaves and roots, and the medicines available through the local polyclinics. Healers attribute illness to the activities of malevolent spirits.

Death and Afterlife.   At least since the late 1920s Gayo have differed among themselves about the nature of death, with some holding that postmortem communication with the dead is possible and morally important for the deceased's well-being, and others arguing that such attempts deny the act of God that took the person out of this world and thus represent the illegitimate supplication of spirits. Postmortem chanting (sammadiyah) sends blessings to the deceased, and graves of important ancestors sometimes are visited as part of the healing process.

Bibliography

Bowen, John R. (1991). Sumatran Politics and Poetics: Gayo History, 1900–1989. New Haven: Yale University Press.

Bowen, John R. (1993). Muslims through Discourse: Religion and Ritual in Gayo Society. Princeton: Princeton University Press. Forthcoming.

Snouck Hurgronje C. (1903). Het Gajoland en Zijne Bewoners. Leiden: E. J. Brill.

JOHN R. BOWEN

Gorontalese

ETHNONYMS: Gorontalo, Holontalo, Hulontalo

Numbering around 500,000, the six subgroups who comprise the Gorontalese occupy much of northwestern Sulawesi Island, Indonesia. The six subgroups are the Gorontalo, Suwawa, Limbotto, Bolango, Atinggola, and Boelemo. The languages spoken by the latter four groups have now disappeared, with only Gorontalo and Suwawa still spoken, although they are now being replaced by Bahasa Indonesia. The Gorontalese are swidden-rice farmers, growing both wet and dry rice supplemented by maize, yams, and millet. Coconut is grown commercially. Groups along the coast supplement farming by fishing.

Nearly all Gorontalese are Sunni Muslims, although many of their life-cycle ceremonies and religious beliefs have survived in syncretic form.

Bibliography

LeBar, Frank M. (1972). "Gorontalo." In Ethnic Groups of Insular Southeast Asia. Vol. 1, Indonesia, Andaman Islands, and Madagascar, edited by Frank M. Lebar, 128–129. New Haven: HRAF Press.

Nur, S. R. (1984). "Gorontalese." In Muslim Peoples: A World Ethnographic Survey, edited by Richard V. Weekes, 290–294. Westport, Conn: Greenwood Press.

Halang Doan

A group of about 2,000 swidden-rice cultivators in Attopeu Province in Laos and Dac Lac Province in Vietnam. There is some question as to whether the Halang Doan are a distinct group or a subgroup of the Jeh.

Hanunóo

The 7,000 Hanunóo (Bulalakao, Hampangan, Hanono-o, Mangyan) live in an area of 800 square kilometers at the southern end of Mindoro Island (12°30′ N, 121°10′ E), in the Philippines. They speak an Austronesian language, and most are literate, using an Indic-derived script that they write on bamboo. The Hanunóo were largely out of contact with schools and missions at least as late as the early 1950s. They trade with coastal Filipinos for metal, European-made glass beads, and salt, and they act as wholesalers for their interior neighbors, the Buhid, who supply the Hanunóo with clay pottery.

Hanunóo live in single-family dwellings of wood, bamboo, and thatched roofs. These structures are built on pilings, often in rows so that their verandas join end to end. Granaries resemble houses, but they are smaller and lack verandas. Settlements are semipermanent and autonomous, and have no more than fifty residents; they vary in size from two to twelve houses, with an average of between five and six. The Hanunóo choose as sites for their villages valley slopes overlooking streams, and they name them after the nearest geographic feature. The social group that lives in the village, however, goes by the name of one of the eldest members.

The Hanunóo rely primarily on swidden horticulture for their food. In a previously unused (primary) swidden they plant first corn and then rice. Shortly before the harvest, they plant corn, beans, and sugarcane among the rice. They plant sweet potatoes and other tubers in previously used (secondary) swiddens. Although the Hanunóo sometimes then plant bananas and papayas, they let most swiddens lie fallow after two years. The Hanunóo trade surplus crops with lowland peoples for the goods already mentioned. Fishing is an important source of food as well, though in the past hunting—done with poisoned arrows, spears, traps, dogs, and fire surrounds—was more important. The traditional game included wild pigs, deer, monkeys, and wild water buffalo. The Hanunóo eat the meat of domesticated pigs, chickens, and humped cattle on festive occasions.

The Hanunóo manufacture baskets. In addition, women pick, gin, and weave cotton into clothing and blankets; men import scrap iron and forge it into knives and other tools using bamboo double-piston bellows. Individuals can own trees, but they may have merely usufructory rights to land.

Hanunóo have bilateral descent, and kindreds are important. Their only corporate group is the nuclear family; it works together in legal, economic, and horticultural matters. In most cases, the named village group is an exogamous group composed of a man, his wife or wives, their unmarried children, and their married daughters and their families. Nuclear families may change residence but they always stay close to either the husband's or wife's kindred.

During the major *panludan* feasts, boys and girls court by exchanging love songs. Accompanied by fiddles, guitars, nose flutes, and Jew's harps, the boy first sings a verse appropriate to the circumstance, and then the girl answers in song; large numbers of love songs are preserved on bamboo. The marriage takes place with the agreement of both families. There is bride-service but no ceremony, bride-price, or gift exchange. Sometimes, however, couples simply elope. Most couples reside matrilocally. Although the Hanunóo believe that one should never marry a blood relative, in practice they are essentially endogamous within fairly small regions. Thus many people marry others they know to be kin, and this requires ritual cleansing. Inheritance is bilateral.

There is very little social stratification; what there is is based on age and skill at weaving or blacksmithing (though there are no full-time specialists). There is no significant accumulation or concentration of wealth.

The local village group is autonomous, and there are no chiefs. The eldest relatives of parties to a dispute adjudicate the dispute; most sanctions involve the payment of glass beads as a fine. Sometimes an ordeal by hot water is used to establish the truth in judicial proceedings. In cases of murder, the close kin of the victim avenge him or her. The Hanunóo do not practice warfare.

The Hanunóo have major named deities whom they associate with creation, but these hold little significance in daily life. Nevertheless there are numerous important spirits, including the ghosts of the dead and guardian spirits (*kalag*), as well as the spirits of nature who watch over mountains, rocks, forests, etc. The guardian spirits require propitiation, and they like to see that people follow *adat* (customary legal rules). The Hanunóo propitiate spirits through feasts and rituals, and they offer the spirits food (rice, pig blood, or betel quids) and especially strings of glass beads.

Should the people neglect either propitiation or the observance of adat, these kalag may become angry and allow evil spirits (*labang*) to harm humans. The labang may cause illness or death by attacking a human's soul. To treat illness, the Hanunóo have massage specialists, herbalists, and mediums (*balyanan*). The balyanan have control over spirits who live in stones, which they guard carefully; they send these spirits to attack the evil spirits that cause the illness.

Hanunóo bury their dead and then exhume their bones one year after death. The Hanunóo greatly fear the suffering that the ghosts of the dead (who are usually kalag) may cause the living, and so they treat the bones of the dead very well. The Hanunóo bundle them up, talk to them, feed them, consult them about the future, and dance with them at the elaborate and expensive panludan festival. For this festival, the Hanunóo erect special dance houses, bone houses, and offering houses. Following the ceremony, they put the bones in a niche in a cave.

Bibliography

Conklin, Harold C. (1954). "The Relation of Hanunóo Culture to the Plant World." Ph.D. dissertation, Yale University.

Conklin, Harold C. (1957). *Hanunóo Agriculture: A Report on an Integral System of Shifting Cultivation in the Philippines.* United Nations, FAO Forestry Development Paper no. 12.

LeBar, Frank M. (1975). "Hanunóo." In *Ethnic Groups of Insular Southeast Asia*, edited by Frank M. LeBar. Vol. 2, *Philippines and Formosa*, 74–76. New Haven: HRAF Press.

Hmong

ETHNONYMS: Man, Meo, Miao, Mong

Orientation

Identification. The Hmong have migrated to Southeast Asia from the mountainous parts of southwestern China, where many still remain. They have settled in the mountainous regions of northern Laos, northern Vietnam, and northern Thailand, and there are small groups of Hmong in Myanmar (Burma) near the Chinese border. Since the ending of the Indochina wars large numbers of Hmong refugees from Laos have been resettled in Western countries, including the United States. There are two main cultural divisions of the Hmong in Southeast Asia, marked by differences of dialect and custom, between the White Hmong and the Green Hmong (who pronounce their name as "Mong"). Hmong religion is based on domestic ancestral worship and shamanism, and they speak dialects of the Miao Branch of the Miao-Yao Language Family.

Location. Southwestern China, Myanmar, and northern Indochina form a unified geographical zone characterized by four main mountain ranges outcropping from the eastern Himalayas and the Tibetan plain, with a semitropical climate and dense tropical rain forest in some areas. At around 1,000 meters deciduous trees give way to evergreen forest. Mountain peaks range from 2,535 meters in Thailand to 7,470 meters in southern China. North-south–running mountain ranges separate fertile alluvial river valleys united in the past only by a network of caravan routes.

Demography. There are some 2 million Hmong speakers in China, approximately 200,000 in Laos, 300,000 in Vietnam, and 50,000 in Thailand. More than 30,000 others are in refugee camps along the Thai border with Laos. More than 100,000 have been resettled in Western countries.

Linguistic Affiliation. Hmong forms part of the Western Branch of the Miao languages, which also include Hmu and Kho Xyong. Miao is related at its upper levels to the Yao dialects, from which a Proto-Miao-Yao can be reconstructed. No relationship to other languages has been firmly established, although the whole group has been influenced strongly by Chinese. The Miao-Yao languages are usually classed as Sino-Tibetan, although some scholars disagree with this. Hmong has eight tones and a complex phonology.

History and Cultural Relations

The Miao were first recorded in Chinese annals as a rebellious people banished from the central plains around 2500 B.C. by the legendary Yellow Emperor (Huang Di) of China. Because the Hmong today retain traces in their culture of the earliest known forms of Chinese social organization, some specialists have considered them the aboriginal inhabitants of China, predating the Han. Their legends, however, have led others to speculate that they may have originated from a northern polar region. Records exist of the Miao in China from 1300 to 200 B.C.; from then until A.D. 1200 they were subsumed under the generic Chinese term for southern barbarians (Man). There are, however, good records of the Miao

from 1200 to the present, and we can be fairly certain that they refer to the ancestors of the Hmong. Most focus on the many uprisings of the Miao against the Chinese state, bearing witness to a long historical displacement of the Hmong and other southern Chinese minority people from the centers of power as the Han Chinese population slowly expanded southward. Hmong began migrating into Southeast Asia around 1800. The last major Miao rebellions in China were in 1856.

In Vietnam and Laos, the Hmong fell under the authority of the French colonial government. A major Hmong rebellion against excessive levies on opium production broke out in Laos in 1919; it took the authorities several years to suppress the revolt, which assured the Hmong of a measure of self-representation. During the Indochina wars, Hmong loyalties were severely fragmented among the royalists, neutralists, and opposition in Laos, and large numbers fled to Thailand when the Pathet Lao gained control of their country in 1975. In Thailand a similar polarization occurred as a result of the 1959 ban on opium production; the ban failed to suppress opium production, giving rise to a government policy of tolerating an illegal practice. Many Hmong supported the armed rural struggle of the Communist Party of Thailand against the government in the 1960s and early 1970s, which has now largely ended. Policies of tolerance toward opium production have also now ended, and this may facilitate Hmong acceptance of the many programs targeted at replacing opium-poppy cultivation with alternative cash crops.

Settlements

Houses are usually built directly on the ground rather than on piles. They were traditionally made out of upright wooden shingles notched together or bound with hemp rope and creepers without the use of nails, and thatched with teak leaves or cogon grass. In some parts of China the Hmong live in houses made out of adobe or stone after the Chinese fashion; in Laos and Thailand some have adopted the Thai style of housing. Richer households may be able to invest in zinc or polystyrene roofing, while poorer families may have to construct their houses entirely out of pieces of split bamboo and rough matting. The traditional village numbered only about seven houses, but today, owing to reasons of security and the need for intensive cultivation of the land, villages of between seven and fifty households are more common. They are often arranged in a horseshoe pattern just beneath the crest of a mountain, and are, if possible, sheltered by a belt of forest and located close to a source of water. New villages are carefully sited according to the principles of a geomantic system aimed at ensuring a fundamental harmony between man and the forested environment. Water is often piped down the mountain to the village through a series of semitroughs formed out of lengths of split bamboo, and is collected, usually by women, in wooden or metal buckets. In some areas wells are maintained, or tap systems have been constructed. Usually tall clumps of cooling bamboo, peach, or banana are maintained near the village, while the neighboring slopes are devoted to herbal gardens. Raised wooden granaries are constructed near each house to protect against scavengers; small chicken coops or stables may also be built. Pigs traditionally are not penned but left free to clear the village of refuse. In some villages shops are maintained, often by Chinese traders.

Economy

Subsistence and Commercial Activities. The Hmong economy is based on the integrated cultivation of dry rice, maize, and opium poppy as a cash crop. Rice forms the staple diet in most of Southeast Asia, where maize is primarily used as animal fodder, but in southern China and at higher elevations the cultivation of rice for subsistence is replaced by that of maize, millet, or buckwheat. Hunting and gathering play subsidiary parts in the economy, while the domestic husbandry of pigs and chickens provides the main source of protein. In certain areas the Hmong have surrendered the shifting cultivation of dry rice in favor of intensive irrigated rice cultivation on permanent terraced fields laboriously constructed on the flanks of mountains.

Maize and poppy form an integrated cycle because they can be planted successively in the same fields. Maize is usually planted in the fifth or sixth month, after the rice has been planted, and it is harvested in the eighth or ninth month, allowing opium poppy to be planted in the same fields for harvest after the New Year, at the end of the twelfth month. Forests must be burned off for the shifting cultivation of dry rice early in the year, and dried out before rice can be dibbled in the fields fertilized by the nitrogenous ashes. While rice fields can only be used for two to three years, maize fields can be continually replanted for some eight years. It has been argued that the increasing overpopulation of the hill areas of Thailand has led to increases in the length of time the same parcel of land is kept under cultivation, resulting in declining rice yields that force the Hmong to produce opium as a cash crop to buy rice from lowland traders. Opium is the best crop to grow because it adapts well to harsh soil conditions and there is a ready market for it. Many Hmong families are indebted to traders (who tend to be of Yunnanese origin) for their rice, and so must continue to produce opium in order to survive.

Industrial Arts. The Hmong do not produce their own pottery, but are famous for their silverwork, and in most villages there are blacksmiths specializing in the production of farming tools and weapons. Chinese silversmiths also often are employed; there are no full-time craft specialists among the Hmong. Women, however, spend a large proportion of their time spinning, weaving, and embroidering hemp and cotton in the intricate needlework of traditional Hmong clothing.

Trade. The most significant trading activity is that of opium for cash or rice. This takes place on an individual household basis, with organized paramilitary groups whose representatives visit villages on a regular basis, through itinerant traders who travel to the villages after the opium harvest to make their purchases, or through the medium of shopkeepers settled in the villages. There are no full-scale regional markets among the Hmong communities, although individual Hmong may visit lowland markets occasionally to make important purchases and sometimes to sell forest products or vegetables.

Division of Labor. There is no full-time occupational specialization in traditional Hmong society, all adult members of which are farmers. Individuals, however, may specialize as wedding go-betweens, blacksmiths, or funeral specialists. The most prestigious specialization is that of the shaman, whose duties are to cure illness and prevent misfortune. The main division of labor in agricultural work is between men and women. Women take most of the responsibility for housework and child care but also play a crucial part in agricultural activities. Child labor is also important in agricultural work.

Land Tenure. As traditional shifting cultivators, the Hmong have, in general, lacked permanent titles to land and, often, citizenship rights in the countries in which they are settled. Attempts have been made by the Thai government to encourage permanent settlement by issuing land-use certificates, but these remain limited. However, in some areas where the Hmong have turned to permanent forms of rice agriculture, they have obtained land-use rights. In general, land-use rights in shifting cultivation belong to the one who first clears the land, and lapse after an indeterminate period of noncultivation.

Kinship

Kin Groups and Descent. Hmong society is divided into a number of named exogamous patrilineal clans similar to the Chinese surname groups. The ideal number of these, when they are referred to in ritual discourse, is twelve, but there are in fact more than this, some having been founded by inmarrying Chinese males. Within the clans, the lineage is the basis of Hmong social organization, and the local segment of the lineage acts as the major corporate ritual and political body at the village level. Major lineage differences within a clan are distinguished by variations of ritual at household and funeral ceremonies.

Kinship Terminology. Hmong kinship terminology is more generative than inclusive, distinguishing relatives on the basis of generation, sex, and relative age, and above all between affinal relatives and relatives by descent. As in the Chinese system, patrilateral parallel cousins (having the same surname) are distinguished from all other cousins by a special term. It has been suggested that the system was once a bilateral one that has been considerably influenced by the Chinese system.

Marriage and Family

Marriage. Polygyny is permitted and two or three cowives may inhabit the same house. Owing to the high bride-wealth demanded at weddings, however, it is only the richer men who can afford to take a second wife. On marriage a woman is completely incorporated into her husband's descent group and will be worshiped by his descendants as an ancestor, retaining only her original clan name. The levirate is practiced among the wives of elder brothers. Marriages can be arranged by parents but are more often the result of the free choice of the spouses. Premarital sex is allowed, and marriages often take place at the first pregnancy. A rare form of marriage by capture also exists, usually in the case of parental disapproval of a match. On marriage a woman moves to her husband's home, except in uncommon instances where a family has only daughters or the groom cannot afford to pay the bride-wealth, in which case uxorilocal residence occurs. Divorce, which is very rare, is almost always initiated by men. The fact that the wife's natal family may be unwilling to return her bride-wealth acts as a sanction against divorce. Suicide may be the only recourse left to an unhappy wife, yet the threat of suicide can itself prove a powerful sanction.

Domestic Unit.   The household is the main unit of economic cooperation and also the most fundamental unit of ritual worship. Households vary in composition from nuclear and stem to more extended types, since usually some time after marriage, or at the birth of a child, a son will move out with his family to form a new household. These may range in size from one to twenty-five members, including, for example, the children of several living or deceased siblings, and unmarried women of several generations. Such large households, however, are rare.

Inheritance.   Shifting cultivation means that there is no land to inherit and little other heritable property. What wealth a family possesses will usually be divided equally among its sons. The house and its belongings, however, will usually go to the youngest son, who is expected to remain in the house to care for his aged parents.

Socialization.   Literacy remains uncommon despite state efforts to educate Hmong children in Thai, Lao, Vietnamese, or Chinese. Attendance at rituals provides an important occasion for young boys to learn their traditional customs, while women are educated in the skills of embroidery and singing by their mothers or elder female siblings and friends. Fathers play a large part in teaching young children to speak, and other local languages are often acquired individually at a later stage. Participation in agricultural work by all capable members of the household leads to an early familiarization with subsistence skills.

Sociopolitical Organization

Social Organization.   Hmong social organization is based on the kinship system, divided into patrilineal clans that define affinal relations, and subdivided into local lineages formed out of individual households. The ritual head of the lineage is its oldest living member; ranking within the lineage is on the basis of age seniority, but is largely egalitarian.

Political Organization.   There is no political organization above the village level in traditional Hmong society. An assembly of male lineage elders makes local decisions and discusses problems or arbitrates disputes. At these assemblies women also take informal part. The ritual head of the lineage and its shamans enjoy the most prestige and authority in decision-making activities. In many areas local headmen of villages are appointed to deal with external affairs. These men do not necessarily enjoy full authority over their own lineages and cannot represent other lineages in the same village, but tend to be those most skilled in dealing with outsiders.

Social Control.   Social control is largely maintained through the importance attached to traditional customs that distinguish the Hmong from other ethnic groups and affirm the unity of the lineage. The knowledge of these customs tends to be the preserve of lineage elders and shamans. Gossip and occasionally accusations of witchcraft also act as mechanisms of social control. The authority of a father (who controls bride-wealth payments) over his sons, and of men over women, is a fundamental feature of this system.

Conflict.   Any member of the lineage has the right to summon the lineage to war, although in practice it is the views of the eldest that will be the most respected. In case of conflicts with other ethnic groups or emergencies, the Hmong send out scouting parties in pairs from each village to report on the situation. Conflicts within Hmong society generally take place between local lineages and rarely involve related clan members. The great majority of these disputes concerns marriages and bride-wealth payments, children born out of wedlock, and extramarital affairs. Conflicts over land and the adoption of Christianity also occur, but these are rare.

Religion and Expressive Culture

Religious Beliefs.   The Hmong otherworld is closely modeled on the Chinese otherworld, which represents an inversion of the classical Chinese bureaucracy. In former times, it is believed, humans and spirits could meet and talk with one another. Now that the material world of light and the spiritual world of darkness have become separated, particular techniques of communication with the otherworld are required. These techniques form the basis of Hmong religion, and are divided into domestic worship and shamanism.

Religious Practitioners.   Every male head of a household practices the domestic worship of ancestral spirits and household gods represented at different sites in the architecture of the Hmong house. Particular rituals must be performed by him in honor of these spirits, most during the New Year celebrations. Whereas domestic worship is conducted for the benefit of individual households by their heads, shamanism is only practiced by a few men in each lineage, and is for the benefit of others since its primary purpose is to cure illness. Illness is often diagnosed by the shaman as the result of soul loss; his task is to recall the wandering soul and so restore health.

Supernaturals.   The two malevolent Lords of the otherworld are Ntxwj Nyug and Nyuj Vaj Tuam Teem. Saub is a kindly deity who periodically comes to the rescue of humanity, and Siv Yis was the first shaman, to whom Saub entrusted some of his healing powers to protect humankind from the diseases with which Ntxwj Nyug afflicted them. Household and ancestral spirits (*dab*) are distinguished from the tutelary spirits of the shaman (*neeb*). Within the household there are special altars to the spirits of wealth and sickness, of the bedroom, the front door, the loft, the house post, and the two hearths.

Ceremonies.   The major calendrical ceremony is New Year, when the household spirits are renewed, the ancestral spirits honored, and the shamanic spirits dispatched temporarily to the otherworld. New clothes are donned, parties of villagers visit other villages, antiphonal songs are sung by courting couples, and courting games of catch are played. Each household sacrifices domestic animals and holds feasts. Weddings are also celebrated with great display.

Arts.   Needlework, embroidery, and the chanting of love songs are particularly esteemed artistic skills. The playing of the reed pipes, the notes of which are said to express the entirety of Hmong customs, is an art that takes many years to acquire. New dances, song forms, and pictorial arts have appeared in the context of the refugee camps.

Medicine. Herbal medicine is a specialty of many women who maintain special altars to the spirits of medicine. Forms of massage and magical therapy are also used. Shamanism remains the primary medical and therapeutic technique, although modern medicines are employed extensively.

Death and Afterlife. The ritual specialist at death is not necessarily a shaman, whose business is to preserve life. The purpose of the funeral and mortuary rites is to ensure the safe dispatch of the reincarnating soul to the otherworld. Funerals last a minimum of three days, attended by all local male kin within the household of the deceased. The reed pipes are played each day and a special song is sung to guide the reincarnating soul on its journey. Cattle must be slaughtered. The corpse of the deceased is inhumed in a geomantically selected site. On the third day after burial the grave is renovated, and a special propitiatory ritual is performed thirteen days after death for the ancestral soul, which will protect the household. A final memorial service to release the reincarnating soul, held a year after death, is somewhat similar to the funeral; and some years after death, in the case of severe illness or misfortune, a special propitiatory ritual may be performed for the same spirit.

On the way back to the village of its ancestors, the reincarnating soul must collect its "coat," or placenta, buried beneath the floor of the house. The dangers and pitfalls of this journey are pictured in the poetic geography of the funeral song, which parallels the long historical journey of the Hmong from a country probably to the north of China. The song describes the creation of the first couple, the deluge, and the first drought, and represents a historical journey back to the origins of humanity, to which the deceased must return before being reborn.

Bibliography

Cooper, Robert G. (1984). _Resource Scarcity and the Hmong Response: Patterns of Settlement and Economy in Transition._ Singapore: Singapore University Press.

Geddes, W. R. (1976). _Migrants of the Mountains: The Cultural Ecology of the Blue Miao (Hmong Njua) of Thailand._ Oxford: Clarendon Press.

Hendricks, Glenn L., Bruce T. Downing, and Amos S. Deinard, eds. (1986). _The Hmong in Transition._ Minneapolis: University of Minnesota; Center for Migration Studies.

Lemoine, Jacques (1972). _Un village Hmong Vert du Haut Laos: Milieu, technique et organisation sociale._ Paris: Centre National de la Recherche Scientifique.

Lin Yüeh-Hwa (1940). "The Miao-Man Peoples of Kweichow." _Harvard Journal of Asiatic Studies_ 5:261–345.

Ruey Yih-Fu (1960). "The Magpie Miao of Southern Szechuan." In _Social Structure in South-East Asia,_ edited by George P. Murdock, 143–155. Viking Fund Publications in Anthropology, no. 29. Chicago: Quadrangle Books.

NICHOLAS TAPP

Hre

Sometimes also called the Da Vach or Davak, the Hre are a group enumerated at 94,259 in the 1985 census of Vietnam. They are located in the mountainous area of central Vietnam. The official Vietnamese spelling is H.Rê.

Ibaloi

The Ibaloi (Benguetano, Benguet Igorot, Ibaloy, Igodor, Inibaloi, Inibaloy, Inibiloi, Nabaloi) inhabit central and southern Benguet province and western Nueva Vizcaya Province, Luzon, the Philippines. In 1975 they numbered nearly 89,000. Ibaloi is classified in the Hesperonesian Group of the Austronesian Language Family. Contact with neighboring groups and Christian missionaries and involvement in the national economy have produced considerable local variation in Ibaloi culture.

Houses, generally scattered in fields or on hillsides, are raised about two meters on posts and covered with a pyramidal thatched roof. Subsistence is based on wet rice, tubers, beans, and maize, supplemented occasionally with the meat of pigs, dogs, chickens, water buffalo, horses, and cattle. Descent is bilateral. There is marked differentiation between the rich and the poor, with a considerable concentration of power and influence in the hands of the former. The traditional Ibaloi religion centered on ancestor worship.

Bibliography

Barnett, Milton L. (1967). "Subsistence and Transition of Agricultural Development among the Ibaloi." In _Studies in Philippine Anthropology,_ edited by Mario D. Zamora, 299–323. Quezon City: Alemar-Phoenix.

Iban

ETHNONYMS: Dayak, Dyak, Sea Dayak

Orientation

Identification. The name "Iban" is of uncertain origin. Early scholars regarded it as originally a Kayan term, *hivan*, meaning "wanderer." The use of the name by those Iban in closer association with Kayan gives support to this possibility. Other Iban, of Sarawak's First and Second Divisions, used the name "Dayak," and even today consider "Iban" a borrowed term. The participation of a few Iban in alliances with Malays for coastal piracy in the nineteenth century led to their being called "Sea Dayaks."

Location. Iban are to be encountered in all of the political divisions of the island of Borneo, but in the largest numbers in the Malaysian state of Sarawak, on the northwest coast. They have lived predominantly in the middle-level hills of the island, and during the last 150 years, fully half have moved onto the delta plains. Within the past 25 years, 20 percent of Sarawak's Iban have moved into the state's urban centers.

Demography. There were approximately 400,000 Iban in the state of Sarawak in 1989 (368,208 in 1980). Reliable figures for Kalimantan, the Indonesian part of the island, are unavailable.

Linguistic Affiliation. The Iban language is distinct from other Bornean languages, and though it shares a limited number of words with Malay it is not a Malay dialect.

History and Cultural Relations

The Iban trace their origins to the Kapuas Lake region of Kalimantan. With a growing population creating pressures on limited amounts of productive land, the Iban fought members of other tribes aggressively, practicing headhunting and slavery. Enslavement of captives contributed to the necessity to move into new areas. By the middle of the nineteenth century, they were well established in the First and Second Divisions, and a few had pioneered the vast Rejang River valley. Reacting to the establishment of the Brooke Raj in Sarawak in 1841, thousands of Iban migrated to the middle and upper regions of the Rejang, and by the last quarter of the century had entered all remaining divisions. The most dramatic changes in the past three decades have been abandonment of longhouses and permanent settlement in Sarawak's towns and cities. Iban have lived near other ethnic groups with whom they have interacted. The most important of these societies have been the Malays, Chinese, Kayan and, during the Brooke Raj and the period of British colonialism, Europeans. The dynamic relations between Iban and these societies have produced profound changes in Iban society and culture.

Settlements

Iban settlements are still predominantly in the form of longhouses. During the time when headhunting was endemic, the longhouse provided a sound strategy of defense. It continues to be a ritual unit, and all residents share responsibility for the health of the community. A longhouse is an attenuated structure of attached family units, each unit built by a separate family. The selection of different building materials and the uneven skills of Iban men who build their own houses are apparent in the appearance of family units, some with floors of split bamboo, others with planed and highly polished hardwood floors. The average width of a family unit is 3.5 meters, but the depth, that is, the distance from front to back, varies widely. A longhouse may include as few as 4 families with 25 residents in a structure less than 15 meters long, or as many as 80 families with 500 residents in a house about 300 meters long. Access to a longhouse is by a notched-log ladder or stairs. At the top of the ladder is an uncovered porch (*tanju'*) on which clothing, rice, and other produce may be dried. Inside the outer wall is a covered veranda (*ruai*), which is the thoroughfare for traffic within the house, where women and old men sit during the daytime weaving or carving, and where families gather in the evening to recount the day's events or to listen to folklore told by storytellers. Beyond the inner wall is the family apartment (*bilik*), where the family cooks and eats its meals, stores its heirlooms, and sleeps. Above the bilik and extending halfway over the ruai is a loft (*sadau*), where the family's rice is stored in a large bark bin and where unmarried girls sleep. The longhouse is constructed with its front to the water supply and preferably facing east. The core of each longhouse community is a group of siblings or their descendants. Through interethnic marriages, members of other societies may become part of Iban settlements and are assimilated as "Iban" in a generation or two. Until the past quarter-century, all Iban lived in or were related to longhouse settlements. Life in the longhouse was considered "normal," and those few people who lived in single-family dwellings apart from the longhouse were thought to be possessed by an evil spirit. Within the past 25 years, through a process of social and economic differentiation, many affluent Iban have built single-family houses. In the towns to which Iban are moving, they live scattered among Chinese and Malays in squatters' communities.

Economy

Subsistence and Commercial Activities. The primary activity of a majority of Iban is rice farming. In the hills, farmers practice swidden cultivation of fields averaging one hectare. Each family maintains its own seed bank of rice, and plants between one dozen and two dozen varieties in any year. At the center of its field they plant their sacred rice (*padi pun*), a gift of some spirit to an ancestor, which has been retained over generations to recall the origins of that family. Given the uncertainties of rice farming in the hills, dozens of ritual acts are performed to ensure a successful crop. At the end of April, the head of the house holds a meeting of all family heads to discuss farm sites and an approximate date for the first rites. The meeting ensures that all residents coordinate their activities and that the rice matures at about the same time. Simultaneous maturation is critical because it helps reduce the losses of any one family to insects, birds, and wild animals, who spread themselves over several fields rather than concentrate on just one. It also permits families to coordinate their harvest rituals. Auguries are taken in June, farms are cleared in June and July, and burned over in August or September. When the rice has ripened, it is informed through ritual that it is to be harvested and transported back to the longhouse. On the last day of harvest, farmers make an offering to the final stand of rice to ensure that the soul of the rice will return to the house with them, and not remain behind in the ground. In the plains, farmers practice farming of wet rice in permanent fields. Introduction of herbicides, pesticides, and commercial fertilizers has permitted Iban to remove vegetation, control weeds and insects, and increase the yields of their farms. With much greater control over the success of their efforts, farmers rely much less on ritual. In addition to rice, farmers plant gourds, pumpkins, cucumbers, maize, and cassava. Rice is complemented with a variety of jungle vegetables and fruits collected by men and women for consumption with the evening and morning meals. Fishing has provided the principal source of protein in the Iban diet, but logging and the consequent silting of many streams and rivers have greatly reduced the numbers of fish. Techniques of fishing are sophisticated and adjusted according to the conditions of the waters. Fish traps are placed in constricted streams, and large nets are inclined over larger streams. Fish are taken with a seine or with hooks. Hunting of wild pigs and deer, using dogs, traps, and nets, varies from community to community, according to the region, forest conditions, and animal population. Almost all families keep chickens and pigs, and every longhouse has dogs. Chickens, pigs, and water buffalo are used in sacrifices, and eggs are an essential ingredient of any offering.

The most important commercial activity for the largest number of Iban men has been the institutionalized *bejalai,* or journey to work for wages. In some longhouses almost all able-bodied men are away at any given time, working for a distant logging company or in the oilfields of northern Borneo. Wage earning enabled men to buy jars, gongs, and other valuables for their families. Rubber and pepper have provided an unstable source of income, as has cocoa, a recent introduction. The attraction of salaried jobs is one of the principal reasons for Iban urban migration. Iban are employed in every major occupational category in Sarawak's cities.

Industrial Arts.   Iban women are superb weavers using the backstrap loom. Most men are skilled in the use of the piston bellows. In addition to weaving blankets and other cloths, women weave mats and baskets.

Trade.   Iban collect bamboo and rattans for their own use or for sale. Natural rubber and the illipe (*Bassia* sp., the Indian butter tree) nut, which is available about every fourth year, are other important collectibles. Ironwood, sawed as logs or cut as poles, is becoming increasingly scarce.

Division of Labor.   Domestic chores, such as cooking and tending the bilik, are performed primarily by women. Both men and women collect wild foods for family consumption and, among Iban living near towns, for sale. Men fell trees and do the heavier farm work, fish, hunt, and take on contracts with logging and oil companies. In urban contexts, both men and women perform office jobs.

Land Tenure.   Rights to land are established by clearing and farming it, or by occupying it. Rights to the use of farmland are vested in the bilik-family, and are held in perpetuity. These rights are maintained in the living memory of the residents of each longhouse. Boundaries are indicated by landforms or trees, or are marked by planting a row of bamboo. Except for the land overshadowed by the eaves of the long-

house, there is no land to which a community holds rights. With the introduction of surveys and titles to land in the early 1900s, Iban who lived closer to government centers obtained titles to their land, under which rights of individual familes to land could be verified. As a result of increased population and the commercialization of land, some Iban have bought land for investment and speculation.

Kinship

Kin Groups and Descent.   The fundamental unit of Iban society is the bilik-family, a group of five or six persons defined by kinship and affinity. Depending upon negotiations at a couple's marriage, there is an almost even chance that their children will be born into the family of either the wife or the husband. Iban families are part of a widely ramifying kinship system that developed in response to Iban mobility. The *suku juru* and *kaban belayan* correspond to the kindred. The former connotes kin ties originating with one's grandparents and includes persons to the degree of first cousin. The latter is any group of people who share rights of reciprocity with an Iban, and may include nonkin and even non-Iban. More inclusive groups include "the brotherhood" and "food sharers," made up of distant kin who would be invited to one's festivals, or whose festivals an Iban would attend. Attachment is ambilateral and descent is ambilineal. Although some Iban are capable of reconstructing genealogies up to fifteen generations in depth, such reconstructions are selective and illustrate the Iban practice of "genealogizing" so as to establish ancestral ties with strangers.

Kinship Terminology.   Terms of reference are Eskimo and the terms of address are Hawaiian.

Marriage and Family

Marriage.   Preferred and proscribed marriages are commonly recognized. Though parents prefer to arrange their children's marriages, especially educated young people would rather choose their own mates. Marriage is preferably with a person between the degree of first and fifth cousin. Distinctions are made between parallel and cross cousins; marriages between the former are avoided. Although most Iban marriages are monogamous, isolated instances of sororal and nonsororal polygyny occur. Marriage between a man and a woman who are related as members of adjacent generations is not approved, but propitiatory rites can be performed if, for example, an aunt and nephew insist on marrying. Marriage within the kin group is preferred to protect property rights and to avoid union with a descendant of slaves or a person of ill fortune. Residence is ambilocal or neolocal. Divorce may be initiated by either partner and, with mutual consent, is relatively easy.

Domestic Unit.   The bilik-family is an autonomous unit, able to join with other units of a longhouse or to detach itself. Iban become members of a family through birth, adoption, marriage, or incorporation. The family is responsible for construction of its own unit, production of its own food, and management of its own affairs. In a sample of 1,051 families, 60 percent were comprised of parents and children, 40 percent included grandparents. The family is a kin-based, corporate group that holds in trust land, sacred rice, sacred charms, ritual formulas, taboos, and heirloom gongs and jars. Traditionally, one son or daughter remained in the bilik to ensure continuity over time. With urban migration and mail service making possible postal remittances, an increasing number of parents have no adult child residing in the bilik with them.

Inheritance. Male and female children share equally in rights to real and other property so long as they remain members of their natal bilik. Children who move out of the bilik at marriage or for any other reason receive a small portion of the family estate, and in theory relinquish all rights to family land. In fact, however, they retain the right to request land for farming at the annual meeting commencing the agricultural year.

Socialization. At birth an infant becomes the center of attention and the subject of numerous rituals. Weaning is casual and discipline relaxed. During the farming season, children are left in the care of older people. By age 5, children wash their own clothes and by 8, girls help with domestic chores. Traditionally adolescent males would undertake "the initiate's journey," a trip of several months or years, from which they were expected to return with trophies. Adolescent females demonstrate their maturity with diligence and in the weaving of ceremonial cloths, baskets, and mats.

Sociopolitical Organization

Social Organization. Each longhouse, as each bilik, is an autonomous unit. Traditionally the core of each house was a group of descendants of the founders. Houses near one another on the same river or in the same region were commonly allied, marrying among themselves, raiding together beyond their territories, and resolving disputes by peaceful means. Regionalism, deriving from these alliances, in which Iban distinguished themselves from other allied groups, persists in modern state politics. Essentially egalitarian, Iban are aware of long-standing status distinctions among themselves, recognizing the *raja berani* (wealthy and brave), *mensia saribu* (commoners), and *ulun* (slaves). Prestige still accrues to descendants of the first status, disdain to descendants of the third.

Political Organization. Prior to the arrival of the British adventurer James Brooke there were no permanent leaders, but the affairs of each house were directed by consultations of family leaders. Men of influence included renowned warriors, bards, augurs, and other specialists. Brooke, who became Rajah of Sarawak, and his nephew, Charles Johnson, created political positions—headman (*tuai rumah*), regional chief (*penghulu*), paramount chief (*temenggong*)—to restructure Iban society for administrative control, especially for purposes of taxation and the suppression of head-hunting. The creation of permanent political positions and the establishment of political parties in the early 1960s have profoundly changed the Iban.

Social Control. Iban employ three strategies of social control. First, from childhood, they are taught to avoid conflict, and for a majority every effort is made to prevent it. Second, they are taught by story and drama of the existence of numerous spirits who vigilantly ensure observation of numerous taboos; some spirits are interested in preserving the peace, while others are responsible for any strife that arises. In these ways, the stresses and conflicts of ordinary life, especially life in the longhouse, in which one is in more or less constant sight and

sound of others, have been displaced onto the spirits. Third, the headman hears disputes between members of the same house, the regional chief hears disputes between members of different houses, and government officers hear those disputes that headmen and regional chiefs cannot resolve.

Conflict. Major causes of conflict among Iban have traditionally been over land boundaries, alleged sexual improprieties, and personal affronts. Iban are a proud people and will not tolerate insult to person or property. The major cause of conflict between Iban and non-Iban, especially other tribes with whom Iban competed, was control of the most productive land. As late as the first two decades of the twentieth century, the conflict between Iban and Kayan in the upper Rejang was serious enough to require the second rajah to send a punitive expedition and expel the Iban forcefully from the Balleh River.

Religion and Expressive Culture

Religious Beliefs. Religious beliefs and behavior pervade every part of Iban life. In their interpretations of their world, nature, and society, they refer to remote creator gods, who brought the elements and a structured order into existence; the bird-god Sengalang Burong, who directs their lives through messages borne by his seven sons-in-law; and the popular gods, who provide models for living. Iban religion is a product of a holistic approach to life, in which attention is paid to all events in the waking and sleeping states. The religion involves an all-embracing causality, born of the Iban conviction that "nothing happens without cause." The pervasiveness of their religion has sensitized them to every part of their world and created an elaborate otherworld (Sebayan), in which everything is vested with the potential for sensate thought and action. In Iban beliefs and narratives trees talk, crotons walk, macaques become incubi, jars moan for lack of attention, and the sex of the human fetus is determined by a cricket, the metamorphosed form of a god.

Though the gods live in Panggau Libau, a remote and godly realm, they are unseen, ubiquitous presences. In contrast to the exclusive categories of Judaism and Christianity, "supernaturals" and "mortals" interact in all activities of importance. In contrast to the gods who are more benevolently inclined towards mortals, Iban believe in and fear a host of malevolent spirits. These spirits are patent projections onto a cosmic screen of anxieties and stresses suffered by Iban: the menacing father figure, the vengeful mother, the freeloader, and becoming lost in the forest. Iban strive to maintain good life and health by adherence to customary laws, avoidance of taboos, and the presentation of offerings and animal sacrifices.

Religious Practitioners. There are three religious practitioners: the bard (*lemambang*), the augur (*tuai burong*), and the shaman (*manang*). Individually or in teams, bards are invited to chant at all major rituals. They are highly respected men, capable of recalling and adapting, as appropriate, chants that go on for hours. The augur is employed for critical activities such as farming or traveling. The shaman is a psychotherapist who is consulted for unusual or persistent ailments.

Ceremonies. Iban rituals (*gawa, gawai*) may be grouped into four major categories: (1) one dozen major and three dozen minor agricultural festivals; (2) healing rituals, performed by the shaman, commencing in the bilik and progressing to the outer veranda; (3) ceremonies for the courageous, commemorating warfare and headhunting; and (4) rituals for the dead. Iban of all divisions perform rituals of the first two categories. Ceremonies to honor warriors have assumed greater importance in the upper Rejang, and rituals for the dead have been much more elaborated in the First and Second divisions of Sarawak.

Arts.   The Iban have created one of the most extensive bodies of folklore in human history, including more than one dozen types of epic, myth, and chant. Women weave intricate fabrics and men produce a variety of wood-carvings.

Medicine.   Though they have a limited ethnopharmacology, Iban have developed an elaborate series of psychotherapeutic rituals.

Death and Afterlife.   Life and health are dependent upon the condition of the soul (_samengat_). Some illnesses are attributed to the wandering of one of an Iban's seven souls, and the shaman undertakes a magical flight to retrieve and return the patient's soul. Boundaries between life and death are vague, and at death the soul must be informed by a shaman that it must move on to Sebayan. Crossing "The Bridge of Anxiety," the soul is treated to all imaginable pleasures, many of which are proscribed for the living. After an undetermined period of revelry, the soul is transformed into spirit, then into dew, in which form it reenters the realm of the living by nourishing the growing rice. As rice is ingested, the cycle of the soul is completed by its return to human form. Gawai Antu, the Festival of the Dead, may be held from a few years to 50 years after the death of a member of the community. The main part of the festival occurs over a three-day period, but takes months or even years to plan. The primary purpose of the festival is to honor all the community's dead, who are invited to join in the ritual acts. The festival dramatizes the dependence of the living and dead upon each other.

See also Kalimantan Dayaks

Bibliography

Freeman, Derek (1970). _Report on the Iban._ Monographs on Social Anthropology, no. 41. London: London School of Economics. [Issued in 1955]

Jensen, Erik (1974). _Iban Religion._ Oxford: Clarendon Press.

Sutlive, Vinson H. (1978). _The Iban of Sarawak._ Arlington Heights, Ill.: AHM Publishing Corp. Reprint. 1988. Prospect Heights, Ill.: Waveland Press.

VINSON H. SUTLIVE, JR.

Ifugao

ETHNONYMS: Ifugaw, Ipugao, Yfugao

Orientation

The Ifugao are a rice-growing people who live in a mountainous region of Luzon in the Philippines. The Ifugao homeland of Ifugao Province (17° N, 121° E) occupies less than 750 square miles in the center of northern Luzon. Of the 106,794 Ifugao in 1970, 25,379 lived outside the province of Ifugao. Population density may reach 400 per square mile. The Ifugao language is Austronesian and is most closely related to Bontok and Kankanai.

History and Cultural Relations

The renowned Ifugao system of terraced rice growing appears to have developed indigenously over a period of at least four centuries. Ifugao contact with the outside world was mainly with American military officers and schoolteachers early in this century. Later, transportation improved and allowed people to travel to earn wages. After World War II, the production and sale of wood carvings became important.

Settlements

Hamlets (_buble_) of eight to twelve dwellings, housing a total of thirty or more people, are built on hillocks on the sides of valleys. The houses (_bale_) are built on terraces close to rice fields. They and the granaries are made of timber and rest on four posts, with thatched roofs; the only difference in design between the two is that houses are larger and have hearths. There are also temporary buildings, such as houses for the unmarried, which are built on the ground. Houses once had a shelf for the skulls of enemies taken in battle. The typical household consists of the nuclear family; once children are old enough to take care of themselves, they go to live in boys' houses and girls' houses.

Economy

The Ifugao depend greatly on their wet-rice pond fields. The majority—84 percent—of their diet is derived from agriculture, most of it from the wet fields; 10 percent is from the fish, clams, and snails living in those wet fields. The Ifugao grow taro, cotton, beans, radishes, cabbage, and peas in those same fields, but they raise sweet potatoes and corn elsewhere in swidden fields. A man's status depends on his rice fields. Irrigation is accomplished by dikes and sluices. Pond fields range in size from just a few square meters to more than one hectare, the average size being 270 square meters.

Kinship

Kinship terminological categories are relatively few; several types of relationship are described by the same term. For example, all kin of Ego's generation are known by the same term. A second term applies to one's child, nephew, or niece, and a third to one's mother and one's parents' sisters. Bilateral kinship relationships are the most important social ties. Every individual is a member of an exogamous bilateral kindred that extends to one's great-great-grandparents and third cousins. It is responsible for the welfare of its members, and formerly the Ifugao activated it in times of feud. One's kindred becomes allied with one's spouse's kindred at marriage.

Marriage and Family

Monogamy is the norm, but the wealthy sometimes practice polygyny. The incest prohibition extends to first cousins; more distant cousins may be married only on payment of livestock penalties. Ifugao courtship takes place in the girls' houses (*agamang*). Before a wedding, temporary trial marriages sometimes occur. Wealthy parents arrange marriages through intermediaries, and they make decisions concerning their children's use and inheritance of property. Families exchange gifts and maintain close relations following marriage. Divorce may occur by mutual consent, or with the payment of damages if contested. Grounds for divorce include bad omens, childlessness, cruelty, desertion, and change of affections. There is a vast difference in property allocation if the couple has children. Childless partners each take whatever they brought individually into the marriage through inheritance and then divide commonly acquired joint property equally; if there are children, all property goes to the children. A widow or widower may marry again only after making a payment to the deceased spouse's family; the payment is reduced if the second spouse is of that same family. Postmarital residence is typically close to the largest rice field acquired by either partner, but newlyweds may initially spend some time with the parents of either the groom or the bride. Both sexes may inherit property and debts from both parents, although the firstborn receives the greatest share. An illegitimate child has the right to receive support from his or her natural father's family but no right to inherit from his estate.

Sociopolitical Organization

Traditionally, social differentiation has been based on wealth, measured in terms of rice land, water buffalo, and slaves. The wealthy aristocrats are known as *kadangyan*. The possession of a *hagabi*, a large hardwood bench, secures their status symbolically. They maintain their high status by giving feasts and by displaying their heirlooms, including hornbill headdresses, gold beads, swords, gongs, and antique Chinese jars. Kadangyan tend to class endogamy. The less wealthy are known as *natumok*; they have little land, which forces them to borrow rice from the kadangyan at high interest rates. Because of these high rates, it is nearly impossible for natumok to rise to kadangyan status. The poor, *nawatwat*, have no land; most of them work as tenant farmers and servants to the kadangyan.

The Ifugao have little by way of a formal political system; there are no chiefs or councils. There are, however, approximately 150 districts (*himputonā'an*), each comprised of several hamlets; in the center of each district is a defining ritual rice field (*putonā'an*), the owner (*tomona'*) of which makes all agricultural decisions for the district.

Bilateral kinship obligations provide most of the political control. Beyond local areas, in which people are controlled largely by kinship behavior, are areas that are more and more unfriendly the farther outward one goes; at a certain point one reaches what was formerly known as a "war zone," within which Ifugao once fought head-hunting battles.

Social control is a combination of kinship behavior and control by a *monbaga*, a legal authority whose power rests on his wealth, knowledge of customary legal rules (*adat*), and especially a large supporting group of kin who stand behind his decisions. The monbaga's main sanctions are death and fines. The degree of wealth of the offender or the degree of his or her kinship relatedness mitigate the severity of the punishment; the less wealthy or the more distantly related the offender, the more likely that death is the sanction. However, the monbaga could not control feuding between kin groups within the larger group and warfare with outsiders. Feuds were often of long duration; if they ended at all, they were most often concluded by intermarriage between the feuding groups. Warfare often took the form of raiding, with up to 100 men in a war party. Raiders not only collected heads for display on the skull shelves of expedition leaders, but also took slaves for sale to lowlanders. Blood feuds and warfare ended with the U.S. occupation of the Philippines, headtaking by mid-century.

Religion and Expressive Culture

The complexity of Ifugao religion is based in part on the complex Ifugao cosmology. The Ifugao divide the universe into the known earth, *pugao* (the people refer to themselves as "I-pugao," or "inhabitants of the known earth"); the sky world, *kabunian*; the underworld, *dalum*; the downstream area, *lagod*; and the upstream area, *daiya*. Each of these five regions has large numbers of spirits. The spirits have individual names and each belongs to one of thirty-five categories, among them hero ancestors, celestial bodies, natural phenomena, and diseases. In addition, the Ifugao have deities; these figures are immortal, are able to change form or become invisible, and are mobile.

Ifugao priests are men who take their positions voluntarily and after a period of apprenticeship. Their job is to serve the members of their kindreds by invoking the spirits of deceased ancestors and deities. Priests do not make their living from their priestly activities, although they are compensated with meat, drink, and prestige.

Rituals and ceremonies—for the purposes of augury, omenology, hunting success, agricultural abundance, prestige feasts, etc.—typically make use of as many as fifteen priests. Priests recite myths to give them power over the deities and hero ancestors named in them, by way of inviting them to possess their bodies. Invoking deities may involve chanting for more than five hours. Once in the priest, a deity is given an offering (which may be betel, chicken claw, pig, chicken, etc.) and is fed rice and wine (through the body of the priest). Finally, an exhortation is made to the deity.

Illness is caused by deities taking souls in cooperation with ancestors. Priests treat illness through divination and curing rituals, in an effort to have the deity return the soul. If the deity does not do so, the sick individual dies. A corpse is washed, its orifices are plugged, and it is placed in an honorary death chair (corpses of kadangyan people are given insignias). There the body lies in state guarded by a fire and a corpse tender, and it is "awakened" each night; the wealthier the deceased, the longer this period lasts (up to thirteen days). Burial is in a family sepulcher or in a coffin that is placed either in a mausoleum or under the house. Sometimes secondary burials take place three to five years later, especially if the deceased is unhappy and causing illness among the living. Some Ifugao groups bury males and females separately and inter children in jars.

Bibliography

Barton, Roy Franklin (1919). "Ifugao Law." _University of California Publications in American Archaeology and Ethnology_ 15:1–186.

Barton, Roy Franklin (1922). "Ifugao Economics." _University of California Publications in American Archaeology and Ethnology_ 15:385–446.

Barton, Roy Franklin (1930). _The Half-Way Sun: Life among the Headhunters of the Philippines._ New York: Brewer & Warren.

Barton, Roy Franklin (1946). "The Religion of the Ifugaos." _American Anthropological Association Memoir_ 65:1–219.

Conklin, Harold C. (1980). _Ethnographic Atlas of Ifugao: A Study of Environment, Culture, and Society in Northern Luzon._ New Haven: Yale University Press.

Lambrecht, Francis (1932). "The Mayawyaw Ritual, 1. Rice Culture and Rice Ritual." _Publications of the Catholic Anthropological Conference_ 4:1–167.

Lambrecht, Francis (1955). "The Mayawyaw Ritual, 6. Illness and Its Ritual." _Journal of East Asiatic Studies_ 4:1–155.

Ilanon

Numbering about 65,000, the Ilanon (Ilano, Ilanum, Ilanun, Illanun, Iranon, Lanon) inhabit the area surrounding and inland from Polloc Harbor, on Moro Gulf, Mindanao, the Philippines. Ilanon is classified in the Hesperonesian Group of the Austronesian Language Family. Subsistence is based on wet rice and maize. The strategic location of Ilanon villages along the harbor and rivers' shores made them major recipients of trade goods flowing from Malaysia. The Ilanon are best-known for their former role as raiders and pirates throughout greater Malaysia. Fleets of Ilanon boats rowed by slaves raided the Central Philippines, as well as islands and shipping from Sumatra to New Guinea. The Ilanon are closely related to the Maguindanao to the south, although the former consider themselves to be a distinct group.

See also Maguindanao

Bibliography

Mednick, Melvin (1975). "Ilanon." In _Ethnic Groups of Insular Southeast Asia_, edited by Frank M. LeBar. Vol. 2, _Philippines and Formosa_, 35. New Haven: HRAF Press.

Ilongot

ETHNONYMS: Ibilao, Ibilaw, Ilungut, Ilyongut, Lingotes

Orientation

The Ilongot live in Nueva Vizcaya Province of Luzon in the Philippines. They numbered about 2,500 in 1975. The name "Ilongot" is Tagalog and Spanish, and is derived from "Quirungut" (of the forest), one of the people's own names for themselves. The Ilongot language is Austronesian, and there are three dialects: Egongut, Italon, and Abaka. They use Ilocano and Tagalog in trading. The Ilongot are culturally conservative and unsubjugated. They live as an enclave and resist incursions into their territory.

Settlements

Ilongot live in thirteen named dialect groups each with an average population of 180. Each of these groups includes several settlements, which in turn are made up of four to nine households (five to fifteen nuclear families, forty to seventy people). When people move to a new area, their houses are built in clusters, but as farther, more widely spaced new fields are cleared, houses are built near the new fields, and the settlement pattern becomes dispersed. Where there is missionary influence, houses are built clustered near runways. Houses sit on pilings up to 15 feet above the ground, and have walls of grass or bamboo. There are no inside walls; each nuclear family (there are one to three per house) has its own fireplace. There are also temporary field houses.

Economy

The Ilongot depend primarily on dry-rice swidden agriculture and hunting, as well as fishing and gathering. They burn and plant new fields each year, growing maize and manioc among the rice. Fields that already have produced one rice crop are planted in tobacco and vegetables, and fields that are in their last productive service are used to grow sweet potatoes, bananas, or sugarcane. Fields made from virgin forest are in use for up to five years, then lie fallow for eight to ten years. Fields are abandoned after a second use, and the group farming them leaves to find new virgin forest. Men in groups hunt several times a week with the aid of dogs; the meat acquired is shared equally among all households and is consumed immediately. Sometimes hunts of three to five days take place, and the meat from these trips is dried for trade or for bride-price discussions. Individuals who hunt keep their meat for trade. Fish are taken by nets, traps, spear, or poison. The Ilongot gather fruits, ferns, palm hearts, and rattan from the forest. They keep domesticated dogs for hunting, and pigs and chickens for trade. Men forge their own knives, hoes, and picks, and make rattan baskets, whereas women weave and sew. The items noted above as destined for trade are exchanged for bullets, cloth, knives, liquor, and salt. Most trade within Ilongot society occurs during bride-price payments and gift giving. Real property belongs to whoever clears it; personal property belongs to the individual as well.

Kinship

Above the level of the nuclear family, the be:rtan, or ambilaterally reckoned allegiance, is important. Generally, males prefer to become members of their father's be:rtan, and females members of their mother's, although in cases in which a man's parents pay his bride-price, all of his children become members of his be:rtan. This term is used polysemically to refer in the first sense to kin to whom one is linked during discussions of various social situations, as well as the thirteen mutually exclusive local dialect groups. The names of be:rtan are geographical names, plant names, place names, or color terms. Kin terminology is of the Hawaiian type. Affinal terminology applies only to Ego's generation.

Marriage and Family

Young men are expected to engage in a successful headhunt before marriage. Young men and women select each other as marriage partners and form couples prior to marriage. Such a relationship includes casual field labor, gift giving, and sex. Later, there are formal discussions and marital exchanges. These discussions are used to settle disputes with the family of the potential spouse. Premarital pregnancy causes the marriage process to speed up under threats of violence, and disputes are usually ended with marriage. Marriage with closely related cousins (especially second cousins) is preferred, because community leadership is held by sets of male siblings. Levirate and sororate are common upon the death of a spouse. Marriage is monogamous, and matrilocal for some years after the wedding; married couples may return to the husband's natal village only when bride-price payments are complete.

Sociopolitical Organization

There is no formal leadership. Informal leadership resides in sets of brothers, especially those with oratorical (puruN) skills and knowledge of genealogy; women claim to be unable to understand puruN. The leader cannot apply sanctions, but can orchestrate consensus. In cases of dispute requiring an immediate resolution, the offended party may require that the alleged offender undergo an ordeal to establish innocence. Warfare is practiced in the form of headhunting. The reasons for headhunting are an unsettled feud, a death in one's household, and the obligatory requirement of a young man to kill before marrying. A pig is sacrificed when the headhunters return. Warring groups may establish peace through negotiations and exchanges.

Religion and Expressive Culture

Until the 1950s, when Protestant proselytizers arrived, the Ilongot had had no contact with major world religions. The traditional belief system includes supernatural beings who are both helpful and dangerous. Illness is conceived to be caused by supernaturals who lick or urinate on the individual, by deceased ancestors, or by supernatural guardians of fields and forests who become angered by human destruction of what they guard. There are a few shamans who treat disease, and anyone so cured can use a portion of the shaman's spiritual power to cure; otherwise, spiritual curing power comes from illnesses and visions. The individual's spirit, which travels at night during his life, continues on after death. Since this spirit is dangerous to the living, it is forced away from habitations by sweeping, smoking, bathing, and invocation.

Bibliography

Barrows, David P. (1910). "The Ilongot or Ibilao of Luzon." Popular Science Monthly 77:521–537.

Keesing, Felix M. (1962). The Ethnohistory of Northern Luzon. Stanford, Calif.: Stanford University Press.

Rosaldo, Renato (1970). "Ilongot Society: The Social Organization of a Non-Christian Group in Northern Luzon, Philippines." Ph.D. dissertation, Harvard University.

Tugby, Donald J. (1966). "A Model of the Social Organization of the Ilongot of Northeast Luzon." Journal of Asian and African Studies 1:253–260.

DANIEL STROUTHES

Indonesian

Indonesia is essentially an equatorial country that stretches from 11° S to 4° N, a location that gives its climate a certain unity. It is a very large country, spanning from west to east more than 4,800 kilometers between 95° E and 141° E. Of its myriad islands at least 6,000 are inhabited by people we call "Indonesians." They have also been called "Maylay Islanders," "Malaysians," or "East Indians." The term "Indonesian" was invented by James Richardson Logan in his study The Languages and Ethnology of the Indian Archipelago (1857).

Although this name is applied today to any of the 195,300,000 citizens of the Indonesian nation-state (1992 estimate) and not to any one culture, there is a certain unity to the Indonesian people, which can be recognized in physical features, language, economy, and religion. (What follows, on the other hand, hardly applies to the approximately 1,600,000 Papuans on the half-island of Irian Jaya, also called Irian Barat or western New Guinea. These people, being Melanesians, were more appropriately covered under various headings in volume 2, Oceania. See also the article on Irianese.)

Indonesians are typically short in stature (males being in the range of 1.5–1.6 meters), with wavy black hair and medium-brown complexion. As their location at the southeastern tip of Asia suggests, the present population must represent an earlier mingling of southern Mongols, Proto-Malays, Polynesians, and, in some areas, Arabs, Indians, or Chinese. All speak languages related to Malay (i.e., the Austronesian Family), except in New Guinea and the northern half of Halmahera. The economy of most Indonesian cultures is based on intensive cultivation of irrigated rice, although for many communities plantation crops or trade are also very important pursuits. Some 87 percent of Indonesians are Sunni

Muslims, a widespread religious adherence that presents another unifying factor. About 9 percent are Christians, and there are some Hindus (mainly Balinese) and Buddhists (mainly some 3 million Chinese).

Indonesia has had a long history of colonial contact. After some early intercourse with the Portuguese, Spanish, and English, the entire area of Indonesia fell under Dutch colonial rule from 1627 to 1942. Throughout this very long period the Dutch were interested primarily in developing commerce and plantation crops, and did relatively little to modernize society or propagate Christianity. The Japanese invasion in 1942 ultimately led to national independence in 1949. Up to that time the country had variously been known in the literature as the Netherlands Indies, Dutch East India, the Malay Archipelago, Malaysia, or the East Indies (also Hinterindien, Insulinde, Malaiischer Archipel, or Niederländisch-Ostindien in German; Nederlandsch-Indië or Tropischen Holland in Dutch); the name "Indonesia" was favored by anthropological writers because it paralleled the names given the neighboring culture areas of Micronesia, Melanesia, and Polynesia.

The small adjoining islands of Java, Madura, and Bali, which together make up barely 7 percent of Indonesia's land area, are disproportionately prominent in the country, both politically and economically, because together they are home to more than 63 percent of the total national population, contain the national capital and the most intensive area of rice production, and are the center of the modern tourist industry.

One might very loosely categorize the cultures of Indonesia under three headings: Hinduized societies practicing rice cultivation, Islamized mercantile cultures on some coasts, and remote tribal groups that engage in a variety of economic activities. (For further details, see the Introduction to this volume.)

Several dozen distinct Indonesian cultures are discussed in separate articles in this volume. A total enumeration of such cultures would probably exceed 300, depending on the ethnolinguistic criteria employed.

See also Balinese; Javanese; Madurese

PAUL HOCKINGS

Irianese

This new term is sometimes used for the inhabitants of Irian Jaya or West Irian, which is the most easterly province of Indonesia; it was known in colonial times (until 1963) as Dutch New Guinea. While the territory has been part of Indonesia since then, its inhabitants are culturally, linguistically, and racially separate, for they are Papuans and belong to the Melanesian culture area. Specific groups in the region are covered in Volume 2, _Oceania_.

Isneg

The Isneg (Apayao, Isnag, Isned, Kalina', Mandaya, Payao) are a group in northern Luzon, the Philippines. In 1981 their population was estimated at 12,000. The Isneg are slash-and-burn cultivators of hillside rice; they also grow yams, taro, sweet potatoes, maize, sugarcane, and bananas. Their small hamlets average about eighty-five people each.

Bibliography

Keesing, Felix M. (1962). "The Isneg: Shifting Cultivators of the Northern Philippines." _Southwestern Journal of Anthropology_ 18:1–19.

Itneg

Itneg is a general term that refers to speakers of Itneg languages who reside on Luzon in the Philippines. The Summer Institute of Linguistics lists four Itneg languages: Binongan (Tinggian, Tinguian, Tinngguian), Inlaod, Masadiit, and Southern. In 1975 the total number of Itneg speakers was 50,000, although almost all were bilingual in Ilocano. Itneg-speaking groups have been in contact with various neighboring groups such as the Bontok, Kalingas, Overseas Chinese traders, and Ilocano for some time, and today are assimilated into Ilocano society.

Bibliography

LeBar, Frank M. (1975). "Tinggian" and "Apayo." In _Ethnic Groups of Insular Southeast Asia_, edited by Frank M. LeBar. Vol. 2, _Philippines and Formosa_, 95–100. New Haven: HRAF Press.

Japanese

ETHNONYMS: Nihonjin, Nipponjin

Orientation

Identification. The Japanese people, the majority of whom live in the archipelago known as Japan, which lies off the eastern coast of the Asian continent, speak the Japanese language. Japan, the most technologically advanced society in the world today, officially was transformed from a feudalistic country to a nation-state in 1871. It remains a homogeneous society in that less than 1 percent of the population is classified as non-Japanese and immigration to Japan is regulated carefully. A considerable amount of emigration has taken place since the end of the last century, largely to the United States, Canada, and South America. The indigenous religious system is Shinto; Buddhism was brought to Japan from China via Korea in the sixth century. The majority of Japanese people today classify themselves as both Shinto and Buddhist, and just over 1 percent as Christian. A large proportion of the population is, however, effectively secular in orientation. The Japanese identify themselves in terms of what is taken to be a shared biological heritage, birth in Japan, and a common language and culture. Although Japan is a postindustrial society and has, particularly since World War II, been thoroughly exposed to North American and European cultures and values, the sense of a shared past and unique cultural heritage remains central in creating a modern Japanese identity.

Location. Japan consists of four main islands—from north to south, Hokkaidō, Honshū, Shikoku, and Kyūshū—in addition to a number of island chains and a thousand smaller islands. It occupies less than 0.3 percent of the world's land area and is about one twenty-fifth the size of the United States. Japan lies in the temperate zone, at the northeastern end of the monsoon region, and has four distinct seasons. Rainfall is abundant. Japan is subject to numerous earthquakes and, in late summer, to typhoons. Rugged mountain chains, several of them containing active volcanoes, account for more than 72 percent of the total land area, and numerous swift, shallow rivers flow from the mountains to the sea. Relatively little land is available for agriculture, just over 14 percent today; dwellings and roads occupy another 7 percent, leaving most of the countryside covered by dense, cultivated forests.

Demography. The population of Japan is just over 123 million people, with a density of 326 persons per square kilometer in the habitable areas, making it one of the most densely populated countries in the world. About 76 percent of the Japanese people live in cities; well over half of urban dwellers reside in one of four metropolitan areas made up of the sixteen prefectures around Tokyo, Ōsaka, Nagoya, and Kitakyūshū. The Tokyo megalopolis is comprised of about 30 million people and contains the administrative unit known as the Central Tokyo Metropolitan Area—approximately 11 million people, a population on the decline because of a small but steady exodus of families who favor suburban residence.

Life expectancy at birth is 75.91 years for men and 81.77 years for women, the longest in the world for both sexes. In 1935 the average life expectancy was 47 for men and 50 for women, and thus it has increased by about 30 years in just over half a century, an extremely rapid rate of change. The proportion of those aged 65 and over is increasing rapidly. At present the elderly comprise about 15 percent of the population, but this figure is expected to rise to more than 23 percent early in the next century. At the same time the birthrate is falling; it is estimated at present to be 1.37 live births per 1,000 population per year, insufficient to replace the current population.

In 1721 the feudal government instituted regular, nationwide census taking with surveys repeated every six years. It is estimated from these records that Japan's population remained stable at about 30 million from the early eighteenth century until the latter part of the nineteenth century. From 1872 to 1975 it grew threefold, and Japan now ranks seventh in the world in terms of population.

Linguistic Affiliation. Japanese is a polysyllabic, highly inflected language. It is usually assigned to the Altaic Group of languages, which includes Korean, Mongolian, and Turkish languages and is not related to Chinese. The indigenous peoples of Japan were most probably the Ainu, a very small number of whose descendants now live in the northernmost island of Hokkaidō. It is widely accepted that the Ainu and Japanese languages are unrelated and that the Japanese of today are primarily descended from peoples who migrated long ago from the Asian mainland and displaced the Ainu, driving them northward.

It is estimated that Proto-Korean and Proto-Japanese separated from each other about 6,700 years ago, sometime after the first distinctive society, known as the Jōmon, was established in Japan. However, pottery dating back about 12,000 years, the oldest known in the world, indicates that a well-developed social organization (possibly that of the Ainu) was present before the arrival of peoples from the Asian mainland. Although Japanese is predominantly an Altaic language, it has some similarities to Austronesian, a linguistic group associated with Micronesia, Melanesia, and Southeast Asia; it is usually assumed that continuous cultural contact and possibly repeated migrations from these areas to Japan over many centuries account for these similarities.

From about 300 B.C. the Jōmon culture was gradually transformed and largely replaced by the vital Yayoi culture, whose archaeological remains give clear evidence of sustained contact with China. With the establishment of the Yayoi culture the foundations for the present-day Japanese language were clearly established.

Written Japanese is complex because it makes use of Chinese characters (*kanji*), of which approximately 2,000 must be used just to read a newspaper. The reading of Chinese characters in Japanese texts is particularly formidable because most have more than one reading, usually depending on whether they appear singly or in combinations. In addition, two separate forms of phonetic syllabic script, both derived originally from Chinese characters, are used together with the Chinese characters. One, *katakana*, is used largely to express words of foreign origin; the other, *hiragana*, is reserved principally for inflectional endings and suffixes, which are extensively employed in Japanese but which do not exist in Chinese. In addition many technical words, acronyms, and so on are expressed today in roman letters.

Both syllabic scripts were developed by the eighth century, but at first they were not integrated with the Chinese script. At that time hiragana was used for personal correspondence and classical Japanese poetry: it was known as "women's hand." Early Japanese literature was set down entirely in what was thought of as this "pure" Japanese style, while Chinese characters were used for official and religious documents.

History and Cultural Relations

The most comprehensive record of early Japan that remains was written by the Chinese some time before A.D. 300. It portrays the Japanese as law-abiding people, fond of drink, concerned with divination and ritual purity, familiar with agriculture (including wet-rice cultivation), expert at fishing and weaving, and living in a society where social differences were expressed through the use of tattooing or other bodily markings. Among the early rulers of Japan some were women, the most famous of whom is Himiko of Yamatai. Current mythology reconstructs the first Japanese state as created around a "divine" emperor, a direct descendant of the sun goddess Amatarasu, in about 660 B.C., in what is now known as the Kinki region. Historical records dating to about the fifth century A.D. can be accepted as reasonably reliable. Early historical society was tribal in organization, divided into a large number of family groupings established as agricultural, craft, and ritual-specialist communities, some of which were exceedingly wealthy. In the early seventh century Chinese-style centralized bureaucratic rule was adopted; later, with the Taika reform in the mid-seventh century, many more Chinese institutions were embraced, followed by the building of the Chinese-style capital city of Nara in the eighth century. Although all authority theoretically was concentrated in the hands of the emperor, throughout Japanese history until the late nineteenth century, in contrast to China, emperors were usually dominated by a succession of court families and military rulers.

After the transfer in A.D. 794 of the capital to Heian-kyo, later to become Kyōto, a period of artistic development took place until the early twelfth century. During this period contacts with China were disrupted, allowing Japan to develop its own distinctive cultural forms. The world's first novel, *The Tale of Genji* by Murasaki Shikibu, was written at this time together with other major literary works; Buddhism not only was consolidated as a religion but also became a political force to reckon with. A succession of civil dictators, all members of the Fujiwara family, manipulated successive emperors in order to control the country. Under them taxation of peasants became oppressive, but at the same time the state entered into opulent decline, leading to an eventual loss of power over the outlying regions. Competing dominant families, notably the Minamoto and the Taira, who had been thrust temporarily into the background by the Fujiwara, returned to Kyōto to impose military control there. The Taira ruled for thirty years but eventually succumbed to Minamoto Yoritomo, who ousted them and took firm control of Japan. Yoritomo went on to establish a military government in Kamakura in eastern Honshū and persuaded the emperor to grant him the hereditary title of shogun; thus began an era of military rule that lasted for seven centuries. It was at Kamakura that the samurai code of discipline and chivalry was con-

ceived and developed, while the imperial household remained in Kyōto, producing a succession of puppet emperors.

The groundwork for feudalism, built on the ruins of the centralized Chinese-style bureaucratic state, was laid down during the Kamakura shogunate. On the whole, the lot of the Japanese peasants was better than that of European serfs in that they often retained some rights over land and largely were protected from crippling taxes. During the fourteenth century there was a short-lived restoration of imperial rule, followed by a new military government established by the Ashikaga family in Kyōto, which lasted for two centuries. This was a time of prosperity and the full flowering of Bushidō (the way of the warrior), including the aesthetic and religious expression of this discipline. The Portuguese Jesuit Francis Xavier first arrived in Kyūshū during the sixteenth century, followed by other Christian missionaries and then traders. Toward the end of the century a plague of civil wars broke out in Japan, which continued until order finally was restored by the military leader Hideyoshi Toyotomi in 1590. The pacification and unification of the country was completed by the first of the Tokugawa shoguns, Ieyasu, who then moved the seat of the shogunate to Edo, now Tokyo. As part of the process of consolidation, the shogunate virtually isolated Japan from the outside world, a situation that lasted for more than 265 years. Ieyasu and his son persecuted foreign missionaries and Japanese who had converted to Christianity. All contact with foreigners was restricted to the island of Deshima off the coast of Nagasaki.

Japanese feudalism reached a final, centralized stage under the Tokugawas, and neo-Confucianism, with its hierarchical ordering of society, was made a central part of the ideology. Strict class divisions were enforced between samurai, peasants, merchants, and artisans. Respect and obedience were the code of the day. During this period literacy and numeracy became widespread, and the foundations for a modern society were well established. A self-conscious cultivation of indigenous Japanese traditions, including Shintō, took hold among certain samurai, who would become politically active in the eventual restoration of the emperor. At the same time Japan came increasingly under pressure to open its shores to the outside world, and the resulting internal turbulence led to the collapse of the shogunate. This was followed by the Meiji Restoration of 1868, in which the emperor once again gained full sovereignty and set up the imperial capital in the city that was known from then on as Tokyo.

During the Meiji era a modern nation-state was firmly consolidated, a constitution was promulgated, a central government was established, the Tokugawa class system was abolished, a national system of education was put in place, a modern legal code was adopted, and a formidable military and industrial machine was assembled. The entire country threw itself into the process of modernization, for which purpose European—and, to a much lesser extent, American—models were initially emulated. Japan's victories in both the Sino-Japanese War of 1894–1895 and the Russo-Japanese War of 1904–1905 and its annexation of Korea in 1910 established Japan as a world power. Its place in the modern world order was further consolidated at the end of World War I, which Japan had entered on Britain's side under the provision of the Anglo-Japan Alliance of 1902. During the 1920s the worldwide recession affected the Japanese economy, most particularly because of its great dependence on foreign trade.

By 1925 most small industries had been crushed by the monopolies of the giant corporations headed by extremely wealthy and powerful families. Faltering confidence in the government was reinforced by the exposure of a number of scandals. The military, which was suspicious of both the giant corporations and politicians, seized the moment and thus helped propel Japan toward World War II, although undoubtedly the freezing of Japanese assets by the United States and the embargo placed by the Americans on oil shipments to Japan triggered an already inflammatory situation.

The Japanese finally surrendered after two atomic bombs had been dropped, one on Hiroshima and another on Nagasaki. During the American occupation, which lasted from 1945 to 1951, Shintō was abolished as a state religion; elections, in which women could vote for the first time, were held; new political parties were established; and a new constitution was formulated. Under Prime Minister Shigeru Yoshida the country made formidable strides towards democratic self-government. Japan soon entered a phase of rapid economic growth, which has since been transformed into a low-growth economy geared to "internationalization." Today the Japanese are trying to integrate economic success with what they describe as a "humanistic" and more "spiritually" oriented life-style.

Settlements

The history of housing in Japan reflects two primary influences: the indigenous influence of climate, land formation, and natural events (typhoons and earthquakes); and the external influence of foreign architectural design. Traditional Japanese architecture is made of wood with deep projecting roofs as protection against the monsoon rains. By the sixteenth century the typical Japanese house with a joined-skeleton frame of post-and-beam construction and elaborate joinery was common. The floor is raised above the ground, its posts resting on foundation stone, which allows the entire structure to bounce during an earthquake. This type of house is still dominant in rural settings and remains also in urban areas, usually squeezed among concrete buildings today.

In cities, most people live in apartments or housing corporations; land prices and taxes are exorbitant, making the buying of homes nearly impossible in the city centers. The suburbs have encroached ever deeper into the countryside, where house prices are a little cheaper, and many people commute for as many as four hours to and from work each day. The required coordination between government and the private sector makes city planning extremely difficult in Japan. Nevertheless, recent years have seen the emergence of policies systematically designed to develop larger-scale housing and industrial projects in regional areas rather than a simple restructuring of the megalopolis.

Economy

Subsistence and Commercial Activities. The postwar economy of Japan is based on a competitive-market, private-enterprise system. Less than 8 percent of the population remains fully occupied with agricultural production, although many families retain farming as a secondary occupation. The most usual pattern is that the wife works the farm while the husband is employed full-time in business or industry. Rice remains the principal crop, although its production is strictly controlled and there are financial incentives for diversification. Over the past forty years there has been a steady reallocation of labor from agriculture and a large number of relatively inefficient small-scale industrial and service occupations to highly productive, technologically sophisticated enterprises. The majority of the population is occupied today in manufacturing, business, financing, service, and the communication industries. Japan consistently has kept its unemployment rate at 2.5 percent or lower—by far the lowest in the industrialized nations. Most businesses are privately owned, and demand for goods and services determines what will be produced and at what prices. The role of government in the economy is indirect, largely through close cooperation with business, wide dissemination of information to shape incentives, and provision of research and development funds.

Despite the steady reallocation of labor, not all production is concentrated in giant companies. Small units of production remain very prevalent; for example, more than half the workers in manufacturing are in enterprises with fewer than 100 workers. Japan is an exceedingly wealthy country, with the second-largest gross national product (GNP) in the world. There is a reasonably good distribution of income across the population; abject poverty is virtually nonexistent.

Industrial Arts. Throughout Japanese history the production of ceramics, cloth, silk, paper, furniture, metal implements, and so on has been carried out by individuals in extended households, by professional artisans, and in cottage industries. Techniques were usually passed on from one generation of specialist families to another, sometimes over hundreds of years. A few such families remain in existence, although it has become increasingly difficult to find successors. Distinguished craftspeople are sometimes recognized by the government as "national treasures." Today the bulk of industrial arts is mass-produced, and workers are trained in an apprenticeship system or in technical schools, but handmade crafts continue to be highly valued and play a major role not only in the art world and the tourist industry but also in daily life.

Trade. Most trade in Japan is organized and conducted by the nine very large, highly diversified commercial houses known as *sōgō shōsha*, which structure and facilitate the flow of goods, services, and money among client firms. These trading houses operate both within Japan and internationally. The total sales of these nine firms account for about 25 percent of Japan's GNP, and the imports and exports handled by them amount to about half of foreign trade. These companies originated in the Meiji period, and today maintain a system of domestic offices linked by the latest communication techniques to a worldwide network of overseas offices. Japan's trade is characterized by the export of finished products and the import of raw materials, of which oil is perhaps the most strategic. At present the nation has an enormous trade surplus with most of its international trading partners.

Division of Labor. Since 1945 Japan has adopted a comprehensive legal framework dealing with labor conditions including labor relations, labor protection, and social security. Labor conditions are managed largely by the Ministry of Labor. The Labor Standards Law of 1947 contains a "bill of rights" for individual workers and guarantees minimum wages, maximum hours of work, and so on. Many white-collar workers are nevertheless required to put in long hours of overtime work. About one-third of Japanese workers are unionized; almost all Japanese unions are organized at the level of the enterprise, and they include in their membership blue- and white-collar workers and, often, low-level managerial personnel. Branch unions often form an enterprisewide federation, which in turn may participate in a national industrywide federation. Most union activity takes place, however, at the level of the enterprise.

The school system is designed to be egalitarian and, in theory, entrance into the work force is based on educational merit. In practice, graduation from certain schools provides a greater guarantee of entry into the top universities, graduation from which facilitates entry into the professions and high-ranking civil service jobs. Employment based on personal connections is still prevalent in Japan. A provision for equal wages for equal work regardless of gender was adopted in 1947, but discrimination against women in the workplace continues to the present time. In April 1986 the Equal Employment Opportunity Law, designed to eliminate gender inequalities, was passed, followed in 1988 by the Labor Standards Law. These laws remove many of the restrictions placed on working women—in particular, the number and timing of the hours they can work each day. In practice, considerable social pressure remains for a woman to give up work during her first pregnancy. When they return to work, women are very often hired as part-time employees, although their working hours are long, and many of them work a six-day week. Employers are not required to pay benefits to such employees, who can be hired and fired easily during economic cycles of expansion and contraction.

Land Tenure. At the end of World War II, nearly 50 percent of the population still lived in rural surroundings. At that time 36 percent of the farm families owned 90 percent or more of their land; another 20 percent owned between 50 and 90 percent; 17 percent owned 10 to 50 percent; and 27 percent owned less than 10 percent. Tenants paid rent in kind. Landholdings were, and remain, small (1 hectare on average). Land reform was carried out during the Allied occupation, including the transfer to the government of all land owned by absentee landlords. Today 90 percent of the farmland is owned and worked by individual families. Of urban land area, over 77 percent is residential, nearly 11 percent industrial, and just over 12 percent commercial. Urban residences are small and prohibitively expensive, on average more than three times the cost of housing in the United States. Many families live in apartments for years until they can afford a down payment on a house. Approximately 65 percent of the families in Japan own their home, but in the metropolitan areas this number falls below 30 percent.

Kinship

Kin Groups and Descent. The most usual living arrangement in Japan today is the nuclear family—more than 60 percent of the households are of this type, and the number has increased steadily throughout this century. Another 16 percent are single-person households. Just over 20 percent of households are extended, most of which are in rural areas. This type of household, known traditionally as the *ie,* is thought today to have been typical of living arrangements in Japan until well into this century, although in reality there

was always considerable regional and class variation in connection with household composition. The ie usually was comprised of a three-generation household of grandparents, parents, and children; it was not extended laterally under one roof. In many regions of Japan in prewar years more than one household could comprise the ie, and households existed in a hierarchical grouping known as the *dozoku,* composed of one senior household and "stem" or branch households situated nearby. The traditional ie, a corporate economic unit, was patrilineal and patrilocal, and the head of the household was held responsible for the well-being and activities of all family members. The household, rather than individual family members, was taken as the basic unit of society, a situation that still applies for many purposes today.

Kinship Terminology. The kinship system is bilateral, and includes relatives connected to both husband and wife. Cognates and affines are addressed by the same terms. In this system horizontal ties are usually stressed over vertical ties, and hence the kinship system is ideally complementary to the hierarchical lineage system. Honorifics are built into the terms used to address or refer to grandparents, parents, and older siblings within the family. Terms for brothers and sisters are differentiated according to age. When referring to one's own family members beyond the confines of the family, however, the honorifics are dropped and the terms are changed.

Marriage and Family

Marriage. Marriage in Japan until the Meiji period had been characterized as an institution that benefited the community; during the Meiji period it was transformed into one that perpetuated and enriched the extended household (ie); and, in postwar years, it has again been transformed—this time into an arrangement between individuals or two nuclear families. Today marriage in Japan can be either an "arranged" union or a "love" match. In theory an arranged marriage is the result of formal negotiations involving a mediator who is not a family member, culminating in a meeting between the respective families, including the prospective bride and groom. This is usually followed, if all goes well, by further meetings of the young couple and ends in an elaborate and expensive civic wedding ceremony. In the case of a love marriage, which is the preference of the majority today, individuals freely establish a relationship and then approach their respective families. In response to surveys about marriage customs, most Japanese state that they underwent some combination of an arranged and love marriage, in which the young couple was given a good deal of freedom but an official mediator may have been involved nevertheless. These two arrangements are understood today not as moral oppositions but simply as different strategies for obtaining a partner. Less than 3 percent of Japanese remain unmarried; however, the age of marriage is increasing for both men and women: early or mid-thirties for men and late twenties for women are not unusual today. The divorce rate is one-quarter that of the United States.

Domestic Unit. The nuclear family is the usual domestic unit, but elderly and infirm parents often live with their children or else in close proximity to them. Many Japanese men spend extended periods of time away from home on business, either elsewhere in Japan or abroad; hence the domestic unit often is reduced today to a single-parent family for months or even years at a time, during which period the father returns rather infrequently.

Inheritance. Freedom to dispose of one's assets at will has been a central legal principle in Japan since the implementation of the Civil Code at the end of World War II. Inheritance without a will (statutory inheritance) is overwhelmingly the case today. In addition to financial assets, when necessary, someone is named to inherit the family genealogy, the equipment used in funerals, and the family grave. The order of inheritance is first to the children and the spouse; if there are no children, then the lineal ascendants and spouse; if there are no lineal ascendants, then the siblings and the spouse; if there are no siblings, then the spouse; if there is no spouse, procedures to prove the nonexistence of an heir are initiated, in which case the property may go to a common-law wife, an adopted child, or other suitable party. An individual may disinherit heirs by means of a request to the family court.

Socialization. The mother is recognized as the primary agent of socialization during early childhood. The correct training of a child in appropriate discipline, language use, and manners is known as *shitsuke*. It is generally assumed that infants are naturally compliant, and gentle and calm behavior is positively reinforced. Small children are rarely left on their own; they also are not usually punished but instead are taught good behavior when they are in a cooperative mood. Most children today go to preschool from about the age of 3, where, in addition to learning basic skills in drawing, reading, writing, and mathematics, emphasis is on cooperative play and learning how to function effectively in groups. More than 94 percent of children complete nine years of compulsory education and continue on to high school; 38 percent of boys and 37 percent of girls receive advanced education beyond high school.

Sociopolitical Organization

Social Organization. Japan is an extremely homogeneous society in which class differences were abolished at the end of the last century. An exception was the *burakumin*, an outcaste group, the majority of whom are descendants of ritually "unclean" people (leatherworkers, butchers, grave diggers). Although discrimination against burakumin was made illegal after the war, many continue to be severely stigmatized, and most of them live close to the poverty line.

Japan is widely recognized as a vertically structured, group-oriented society in which the rights of individuals take second place to harmonious group functioning. Traditionally, Confucian ethics encouraged a respect for authority, whether that of the state, the employer, or the family. Age and gender differences also were marked through both language and behavioral patterns. Women traditionally were expected to pay respect first to their fathers, then to their husbands, and finally, in later life, to their sons. Although this hierarchy is no longer rigidly enforced, it is still very evident in both language and interpersonal behavior.

Social groups of all kinds in Japan frequently are described as "familylike"; a strong sense of group solidarity is fostered consciously at school and work, leading to a highly developed awareness of insiders and outsiders. Competition between groups is keen, but the vertical structuring of loyalty, which overarches and encompasses the competing entities, usually ensures that consensus can be obtained at the level of whole organizations and institutions. The finely tuned ranking order that pervades Japanese organizations today is modeled on fictive kinship relationships characteristic of superiors and their subordinates in the traditional workplace. These relationships are often likened to bonding between parents and children and are present not only in the labor force but also in the worlds of the arts and entertainment, in gangster organizations, and so on. Despite the pervasiveness of hierarchy, institutional affiliation is recognized as more important than social background in contemporary Japan. This preference combined with the existence of a highly uniform educational system leads, paradoxically, to a reasonably egalitarian social system.

Political Organization. The 1947 postwar constitution proclaimed the Diet as the highest organ of state power and the sole law-making authority of the state. The Diet is divided into two elected chambers: the lower chamber, or the House of Representatives, where a term of office lasts for four years; and the upper chamber, or the House of Councillors, whose members serve a six-year term. Of the two, the House of Representatives holds more power. Much of the business of each house is conducted in standing committees to which special committees may be added as the need arises. Executive power resides in the cabinet, at whose head is the prime minister. The cabinet is directly responsible to the Diet. The House of Representatives chooses the prime minister, who then selects the cabinet. The power of the prime minister is curbed severely by rival intraparty factions, and cabinet posts are reshuffled frequently, both of which processes influence decision making. The judiciary is, in theory, independent of the government, and the supreme court has the power to determine the constitutionality of any law, regulation, or official act. However, supreme court judges are appointed by the cabinet and in turn influence the appointment of other judges.

Throughout the postwar years the authority of the central government has been consolidated. The relatively conservative Liberal Democratic Party has been repeatedly reelected to power ever since its formation in 1955, a situation brought about in part by its close connection with wealthy interest groups, a highly effective and far-flung bureaucracy, and an electoral system imbalanced in favor of votes from rural areas. Since the 1960s a series of active citizens' movements interested in consumer and environmental issues has repeatedly challenged the ruling party, resulting in some policy changes. Japan is frequently described as a society where a preponderance of political power that takes precedence over all other social activities exists at every level of society. Furthermore, the implementation of power is designed above all to carry forward group objectives rather than individual rights or interests.

The emperor presently is described in the constitution as the "symbol of the people and the unity of the nation" but holds no formal political power. On New Year's day 1946 the then Emperor Hirohito formally announced that he was an ordinary human being, thus breaking the tradition, which had existed since prehistory, of attributing semidivine status to Japanese emperors. Nevertheless, at the enthronement of Hirohito's son in 1991, Shintō ceremonies were performed, including rituals involving divinities. The lives of the imperial family remain very secluded and carefully controlled by the Imperial Household Agency; their existence provides, among other things, a focus for nationalistic sentiment, which at times is strongly expressed.

Social Control. Law enforcement is carried out by a police system organized into prefectural forces and coordinated by a National Police Agency. Public safety commissions supervise police activities at both the national and prefectural levels. Particularly at the local level, the police force enjoys wide public support and respect, although this is tinged with a certain ambivalence because the police remain strongly associated with prewar authoritarianism. Local police are required to visit every home in their jurisdiction twice a year to gather information on residents; this activity is generally regarded positively by citizens. Police are also required to participate actively in community organizations and activities, and they maintain close links with local governments. The crime rate in Japan is exceptionally low for an urban, densely populated society, in part because segments of each community cooperate actively with the police in crime-prevention activities.

Conflict. Serious conflict in Japan is dealt with under the rubric of the legal system, which is organized so that out-of-court resolutions are by far the most usual. Compromise and conciliation by third-party mediators are widely practiced. Japan has relatively few lawyers and judges, and cases that go to court take an exceptionally long time to reach settlement.

Religion and Expressive Culture

Religious Beliefs. There are more than 200,000 religious organizations in Japan, the majority of them either Shintō or Buddhist in orientation. Since neither of these religions is exclusive, a situation of religious pluralism has existed for more than ten centuries and today most of the population claims to be both Shintoist and Buddhist, with about 1 percent being Christian. Shintō is the indigenous animistic religion of Japan. Known as the "way of the *kami* (deities)," it is both a household and a local-community religion. The doctrine is largely unwritten, religious statuary is uncommon, and Shintō shrines are simple but elegant wooden structures usually situated in a sacred grove of trees, entry to which is gained through an archway known as a *tōri*. The divine origin of the imperial family is one of the basic tenets of Shintō; after the Meiji Restoration and particularly during World War II, Shintō came to be regarded as a state religion with the emperor as its head and was intimately associated with nationalism. State Shintō was abolished under the postwar constitution, but as a community religion it does still play a very important role in many aspects of Japanese ceremonial and symbolic life, in particular with childhood ceremonies and weddings.

Buddhism was introduced to Japan from India via China and Korea in the middle of the sixth century. By the eighth century it was adopted as the state religion, but practitioners still turned to China as the source of authority. From the ninth century Buddhism spread throughout the population in Japan and gradually took on a distinctive Japanese form associated particularly with the Pure Land, Nichiren, and Zen sects. From the seventeenth century, for more than 250 years, Buddhism enjoyed political patronage under the Tokugawa shogunate, but with the restoration of the emperor and the establishment of state-supported Shintō in the second half of the nineteenth century, there was a movement to disestablish Buddhism. In the postwar years, most of the population has become essentially secular, and Buddhist priests are contacted almost exclusively for funerals and memorial services. The tourist industry is now a major source of support for the better-known temples and shrines.

Neither Confucianism nor Taoism constitutes a separate religion in Japan, but these traditions have contributed deeply to Japanese life and have influenced both Shintō and Buddhism. Confucianism, largely in the form known as Neo-Confucianism, provided the foundation for ethical relationships in both government and daily life, particularly from the seventeenth century onward. Although no longer officially sanctioned, its tenets continue to influence daily life. Religious Taoism, like Confucianism, was imported from China to Japan and actively supported from the sixth century. It has had a long-lasting influence on popular religious beliefs, particularly in connection with sacred mountains, firewalking, and purification rituals of all kinds. All of these religious traditions have contributed to a greater or lesser degree to the following features that characterize Japanese religious principles: a veneration for ancestors; a belief in religious continuity of the family, living and dead; a close tie between the nation and religion; pluralism in religious beliefs; a free exchange of ideas among religious systems; and religious practice centered on the use of prayer, meditation, amulets, and purification rites.

Religious Practitioners. Any male may train for the priesthood, but in smaller temples and shrines the position of head priest is often passed on from father to son or adopted son. Celibacy is not required, and the wives of priests often receive some formal training and participate in the running of the temple. Larger temples take in acolytes who, after years of discipline, may be assigned to subsidiary temples. Buddhist priests are often very accomplished at traditional arts, in particular calligraphy. In Shintō shrines young women, often daughters of priests and supposedly virgins, assist with many shrine activities.

Ceremonies. Religious activities at a Shintō shrine reflect the seasonal changes and are associated particularly with the planting and harvesting of rice. These celebrations are still held in many shrines, together with important purification ceremonies at the New Year and midyear to wash away both physical and spiritual pollution. The major festival days are the New Year's festival, on the first day of the first month, the girls' festival on the third day of the third month, the boys' festival on the fifth day of the fifth month, the star festival on the seventh day of the seventh month, and the chrysanthemum festival on the ninth day of the ninth month. These festivals are celebrated both in the home and at shrines. A newborn child is usually dedicated to the service of a deity at a shrine on his or her first trip out of the house, and at ages 3, 5, and 7 children are again presented at the shrine dressed in traditional clothes. Marriage is also associated with the Shintō shrine, but most people, although they often use traditional dress replete with Shintō-derived symbolism, have secular marriages. Public ceremonies at Buddhist temples are less frequent, the most important being the annual *bon* ceremony, in which the dead are believed to return for a short while to earth, after which they must be returned safely to the other world. Some temples occasionally hold healing ceremonies, conduct tea ceremonies, or participate in *setsubun*, a purification ceremony to welcome spring.

Arts. Prehistoric artifacts, such as the *haniwa* figures found in the tombs of the Yamato rulers of early Japan, are often thought to represent a purity and simplicity of design that has remained characteristic of Japanese art until the present day. Art of the early historical period is dominated by Buddhist statuary, which reveals a mastery of both woodwork and metalwork. During the Heian period a distinctive style of literature and art associated with the court was developed, including long, horizontally rolled narrative scrolls and a stylized form of painting that made use of brilliant color and a formalized perspective. The mid-fourteenth to the mid-sixteenth centuries are considered to have been the formative period for all the major Japanese art forms that survive to the present time, including ink painting and calligraphy, the Nō drama, ceramics, landscape gardening, flower arranging, the tea ceremony, and architecture that makes extensive use of natural wood and subordinates the building to its natural surroundings. The Tokugawa period was characterized by the emergence of literature and art forms associated with the newly emerging urban classes, which flourished side by side with earlier forms of religious and ruling-class artistic expression. Extensive use was made of the wood-block print by urban residents of feudal Japan as a medium for portraying daily life at that time. Since the middle of the nineteenth century Japanese art has come under the influence of both Europe and North America. Traditional art forms still flourish and change in a society that today produces some of the most sophisticated and innovative art, photography, architecture, and design in the world.

Literature and poetry (of which the haiku and the tanka are perhaps the most famous forms) have both flourished throughout Japanese history. The Kabuki theater, for popular consumption, in which the performers are all male, first appeared in the Tokugawa period, as did Bunraku, the puppet theater. The modern Japanese novel took form in the middle of the last century and is particularly well known for its introspection and exploration of the concept of self, together with a sensitivity to minute details.

Medicine. Japan has a complex, pluralistic medical system that is dominated today by a technologically sophisticated biomedicine. The earliest references to healing are recorded in the chronicles of mythological and early historical times. Shamanistic practices were present from at least A.D. 400 together with the use of medicinal-plant materials. Two theories of disease causation were dominant at this time: contact with polluting agents, such as blood and corpses; and possession by spirits. The secular, literate Chinese medical tradition was first brought to Japan in the sixth century by Buddhist priests. Grounded in the philosophical concepts of yin and yang, in which a harmonious relationship between the microcosm of the human body and the macrocosm of society and the universe is central, this system, known in Japan as *kanpo*, makes use of herbal material together with acupuncture, moxibustion, and massage as therapeutic techniques. It remained dominant until shortly after the restoration of the emperor in 1867, at which time European medicine was adopted as the official medical system.

The Japanese government established a national health-insurance system in 1961, becoming the first Asian country to do so. Today, Japan has a well-supplied, reasonably efficient modern health-care system. Nevertheless, healing practices conducted by religious practitioners, both Shintoists and Buddhists, remain prevalent, and there has been an extensive revival of kanpo. The practice of herbal medicine is limited today to qualified physicians, and acupuncturists and other traditional practitioners must be licensed; some of these practitioners work within the national insurance system. Many ordinary physicians make use of herbal medicines in addition to synthetic drugs.

Death and Afterlife. In Japan death is believed to take place when the spirit is separated irrevocably from the body. Between life and death is an interim stage of forty-nine days in which the spirit lingers in this world until finally it is settled peacefully in the realm of the dead. Annual memorial services must be held for the dead and it is not until the thirty-third or fiftieth year after death that the spirit loses its individual identity and is fused with the spirits of the ancestors. Most Japanese do not adhere closely to this tradition today, but they still retain some sensitivity to these ideas. Yearly Buddhist observances in August at the bon festival for the souls of the dead continue to remind people of the links between the living and the dead, and of the possibility of spirits of the dead returning to earth. There is also a widely shared Buddhist-derived belief that one can attain a form of eternity or enlightenment while still in this world through the realization of one's full potential on earth. This tradition is associated particularly with the martial arts, the tea ceremony, and other forms of traditional arts and crafts, as well as with meditation.

See also Ainu; Burakumin

Bibliography

Beardsley, Richard K., John W. Hall, and Robert E. Ward (1959). *Village Japan.* Chicago and London: University of Chicago Press.

Bestor, Theodore C. (1989). *Neighborhood Tokyo.* Stanford, Calif.: Stanford University Press.

Boscaro, Adriana, Franco Gatti, and Massimo Raveri, eds. (1990). *Rethinking Japan: Social Sciences, Ideology, and Thought.* 2 vols. Folkestone, Kent: Japan Library; New York: St. Martin's Press.

Embree, John F. (1939). *Suye Mura, a Japanese Village.* Chicago: University of Chicago Press.

Gluck, Carol (1985). *Japan's Modern Myths: Ideology in the Late Meiji Period.* Princeton, N.J.: Princeton University Press.

Hardacre, Helen (1989). *Shinto and the State, 1868–1988.* Princeton, N.J.: Princeton University Press.

Jansen, Marius B. (1980). *Japan and Its World: Two Centuries of Change.* Princeton, N.J.: Princeton University Press.

Nakane, Chie (1970). *Japanese Society.* Berkeley and Los Angeles: University of California Press.

Norbeck, Edward (1976). *Changing Japan.* 2nd ed. New York: Holt, Rinehart & Winston.

Okimoto, Daniel I., and Thomas P. Rohlen (1988). *Inside the*

Japanese System: Readings on Contemporary Society and Political Economy. Stanford, Calif.: Stanford University Press.

MARGARET LOCK

Javanese

ETHNONYMS: Orang Djawa, Tijang Djawi, Wong Djawa

Orientation

Identification. The Javanese are Indonesia's largest ethnic group and the world's third-largest Muslim ethnic group, following Arabs and Bengalis. "Wong Djawa" or "Tijang Djawi" are the names that the Javanese use to refer to themselves. The Indonesian term for the Javanese is "Orang Djawa." The term *djawa* has been traced to the Sanskrit word *yava*, "barley, grain." The name is of great antiquity and appears in Ptolemy's *Geography.*

Location. The Javanese primarily occupy the provinces of East and Central Java, although there are also some Javanese on other Indonesian islands. Java, one of the largest islands of Indonesia, is located between 6° and 9° S and 105° and 115° E. The climate is tropical, with a dry season from March to September and a wet season from September to March. Mountains and plateaus are somewhat cooler than the lowlands.

Demography. The Javanese population was 2 million in 1775. In 1900 the population of the island was 29 million and in 1990 it was estimated to be over 109 million (including the small island of Madura). Jakarta, the capital city, then had a population of about 9.5 million people. Some areas of Java have close to the highest rural population density in the world: the average density is 1,500 persons per square mile and in some areas it is considerably higher. In 1969 Jay reported a population density of 6,000–8,000 persons per square kilometer in residential areas of rural Modjokuto. Population growth combined with small and fragmented landholdings has produced severe problems of overcrowding and poverty.

Linguistic Affiliation. The Javanese are bilingual. They speak Bahasa Indonesia, the Indonesian national language, in public and in dealings with other ethnic groups, but at home and among themselves they speak Javanese. The Javanese language belongs to the West Indonesian Branch of the Hesperonesian Subfamily of the Malayo-Polynesian Family. Javanese has a literary history dating back to the eighth century. The language has nine styles of speech, the uses of which are determined by principles of etiquette. There is a trend toward simplification of speech levels.

History and Cultural Relations

Wet-rice agriculture and state organization were present in Java before the eighth century. Indian influence between the eighth and fourteenth centuries produced a number of petty Shaivite/Buddhist kingdoms. The Madjapahit Empire flourished near the present city of Surabaja during the fourteenth and fifteenth centuries, during which time Indian Muslims and Chinese dominated international trade. When the center of power shifted to port towns during the sixteenth century, Indian and Malay Muslims dominated trade. The aristocracy adopted a form of Islam that had been influenced by south Indian religious beliefs, and Islam spread.

The Mataram Kingdom rose in the sixteenth century and flourished until the middle of the eighteenth century. First the Portuguese, and later the Dutch, dominated trade during this period. The Dutch East India Company divided Mataram into several vassal states around 1750 and later these states came under the rule of the Dutch colonial government. Except for a brief period of British rule, Java remained under Dutch rule; it was opened to private Dutch enterprise after 1850. A nationalist movement arose in the early twentieth century and communism was introduced. There was an unsuccessful revolution in the late 1920s. After Japanese occupation during World War II, Indonesia declared its independence. The Dutch transferred sovereignty to Indonesia in 1949 after four years of warfare.

Settlements

High population density imparts an urban quality to all of Java, including the rural areas. The majority of the population lives in small villages and towns and approximately 25 percent lives in cities. Population is evenly distributed and villages are often separated by no more than a few hundred meters. Villages are never more than 8 kilometers from a town. Although there are a number of towns and cities in Java, the only cities with true urban and industrial characteristics are Jakarta, Surabaja, and Semarang. Landholdings are small and fragmented.

The typical village house is small and rectangular. It is built directly on the ground and has a thatched roof. The inside has earthen floors and its small compartments are divided by movable bamboo panels. House styles are defined by the shape of the roof. Village houses that reflect urban influence have brick walls and tiled roofs. Large open pavilions at the front are typical of houses of high-ranking administrative officers and members of the nobility.

Economy

Subsistence and Commercial Activities. Java has a dual economy with industrial and peasant sectors. The Dutch established plantations based on a Western model of business organization. This segment of the economy is now concerned with estate agriculture, mining, and industry. It is highly capitalized and it produces primarily for export. Wet-rice agriculture is the principal activity of the peasant economy; fishing is important in coastal villages. Animal husbandry is not developed for want of space. A number of dry-season crops are produced for sale, and there are also some small-scale cottage industries and a local market system.

Industrial Arts. Small-scale industries are not well developed because of problems in capital, distribution, and marketing. Cottage industries in Central Java Province are silver work, batik, handweaving, and the manufacture of native cigarettes.

Trade. There are local markets, each servicing four to five villages throughout rural Java. The retailers are usually women.

Division of Labor. Javanese are primarily farmers, local traders, and skilled artisans. Intermediate trade and small industry are dominated by foreign Asians, and the large plantations and industries are owned by Europeans. In precolonial Java, the population was divided between royalty, with its court and the nobility, and the peasantry. Two more classes emerged under colonialism and with the development of administrative centers. These classes are landless laborers and government officials, or *prijaji*. The prijaji are generally urban and there are several statuses. In rural areas farming remains the predominant occupation. Some people engage in craft specializations and trade but these occupations are usually part-time. The majority of everyone's time is spent on farming. In rural areas learned professionals such as teachers, spiritual leaders, and puppeteers are usually people from affluent families. These latter occupations have considerable prestige but they are also practiced only part-time. Local and central government officials have the highest prestige.

Land Tenure. Traditionally much of the land was held communally and communities recruited corvée (unpaid labor) for the king, the nobility, or the colonial government. Even today, communal land is reserved for schools, roads, and cemeteries and for support of the village headman and his staff. The corvée consisted of a group of villagers (*kuli*), who constituted the productive labor force of the village. Communal land was allotted for usufruct as compensation to the kuli. In some places the kuli became a hereditary status included with the inheritance of the land. In addition, many Javanese villages have tracts of communal land allotted to the population for usufruct on a rotating basis. Individual holdings are small.

Kinship

Kin Groups and Descent. Descent is bilateral and the basic kin group is the nuclear family (*kulawarga*). Two kindredlike groups are recognized by the Javanese. One is the *golongan*, an informal bilateral group whose members usually reside in the same village and who participate together in various ceremonies and celebrations. The *alur waris*, the second kindredlike group, is a more formal unit involved in caring for the graves of ancestors.

Kinship Terminology. Four principles govern Javanese kinship terminology. First, the system is bilateral; that is, the kin terms are the same whether the link is the father or the mother. The second principle is generational; that is, all the members of each generation are verbally grouped. The third principle is seniority, a principle that subdivides each generation into junior and senior categories. Finally, the fourth principle is gender. There is a slight distinction made between nuclear-family relatives and others.

Marriage and Family

Marriage. Individuals usually choose their own spouses, although parents sometimes arrange marriages. Marriage is prohibited between members of the nuclear family, half siblings, and second cousins. Several types of marriage are disapproved of but people can avoid the supernatural sanctions associated with them by performing protective rituals. The idea of preferred marriages is not widely known.

Marriage formalities include a gift to the bride's parents from the groom's relatives, a meeting of the bride's relatives at her house the night before the ceremony, civil and religious ceremonies and transactions, and a ceremonial meeting of the couple. Divorce is common and is accomplished according to Muslim law.

Most marriages are monogamous. Polygyny is practiced only among the urban lower class, orthodox high-ranking prijaji, and the nobility.

There is no fixed postmarital residence rule, although the ideal is neolocal. Uxorilocal residence is common in southern Central Java Province. High-ranking prijaji and the nobility tend toward residence in either of the parents' homes. Urban prijaji are neolocal.

Domestic Unit. The Javanese term for "household" is *somah*. Peasants and the average urban prijaji live in monogamous nuclear-family households with an average population of five to six. High-ranking prijaji and the nobility have polygynous uterolocal extended families and are larger.

Inheritance. Dwellings and their surrounding garden land are inherited by a married daughter or granddaughter after a period of coresidence. Fruit trees, domestic animals, and cultivable land are inherited equally by all the children, while heirlooms are usually inherited by a son.

Socialization. Children are treated indulgently until the age of two to four when inculcation and discipline begin. The most common methods of discipline are snarling, corporal punishment, comparison to siblings and others, and threat of external disapproval and sanctions. The latter type of discipline encourages children to be fearful and shy around strangers. Mothers are the primary socializing agents, as well as sources of affection and support, while fathers are more distant. Older siblings often take care of young children. First menstruation for girls is marked simply by a *slametan*, or communal meal, while for boys circumcision, occurring between the ages of 6 and 12, is an important and dramatic event.

Sociopolitical Organization

Social Organization. Javanese social classes have a long history. During the time of the Mataram Kingdom, peasants were ruled by a landed nobility or gentry representing the king. The king allotted land to some people in an appanage system. Merchants lived in coastal and port towns where international trade was in the hands of Chinese, Indians, and Malays. The port towns were ruled by princes. This pattern prevailed until the colonial period. During that period, in addition to the peasantry, two new classes arose, nonpeasant laborers and the prijaji. The prijaji, descendants of the precolonial administrative gentry, were "white-collar" workers and civil servants. There was a class of nobles (*ndara*) who could trace their descent from the rulers of the Mataram Kingdom.

During the twentieth century, there has been a trend toward an egalitarian social system and a drive to make upward mobility available to all. By the middle of the twentieth century, peasants comprised the largest class and there was a growing class of landless agricultural laborers.

Political Organization. Indonesia is an independent republic and the head of state is President Suharto. The capital of Indonesia is Jakarta and the ministries of the national government are located there. The ministries have branches at various levels from which they administer services. There are three provinces (*propinsi*) in Java. In addition, the Special Region of Jogjakarta, or Daerah Istimewa Jogjakarta, has provincial status. There are five residencies (*karésidènen*) in each province. Each residency contains four or five districts (*kawédanan*) and each district has four or five subdistricts (*katjamatan*). There are ten to twenty village complexes (*kalurahan* in Javanese, *desa* in Indonesian) in each subdistrict. The smallest unit of administration is the *dukuhan* and each kalurahan contains two to ten of them. Some dukuhan contain a number of smaller villages or hamlets also called desa. The kalurahan or desa is headed by an official called a *lurah* and the dukuhan is headed by a *kamitua*.

Social Control. In rural areas the neighborhood exerts the greatest pressures toward conformity with social values. The strongest sanctions are gossip and shunning. Kin seem to have less force than the neighborhood in exerting social control.

Conflict. Interpersonal conflict, anger, and aggression are repressed or avoided in Javanese society. In Java it is difficult to express differences of opinion. Direct criticism, anger, and annoyance are rarely expressed. The major method of handling interpersonal conflict is by not speaking to one another (*satru*). This type of conflict resolution is not surprising in a society that represses anger and expression of true feelings. Concern with maintaining peaceful interactions results in not only the avoidance of conflict and repression of true feelings, but also in the prevalence of conciliatory techniques, particularly in status-bound relationships. One source of antagonism is between adherents of different religious orientations; this is related to class differences, prijaji versus *abangan* villagers (see under "Religious Beliefs"), and has much to do with rapid social change.

Religion and Expressive Culture

Religious Beliefs. Virtually all Javanese are Muslims. In reality, the religion of the Javanese is syncretic, with Islam being laid over spiritual and mystical beliefs of Hindu-Buddhist and indigenous origins. The difference in degree of adherence to the doctrines of Islam constitutes a dichotomy that pervades Javanese culture. The *santri* are strict in their adherence to Islam while the abangan are not. This dichotomy has class and political-party implications.

The peasant abangan knows the general structure of Islam but does not follow it to the letter. The abangan religion is a blend of indigenous beliefs, Hinduism-Buddhism, and Islam. In addition to Allah, abangan believe in several Hindu deities and numerous spirits that inhabit the environment. Abangan also believe in a form of magical power that is possessed by the *dukun*, who is a specialist in magical practices, a curer, and/or a sorcerer.

The prijaji abangan religious practice is similar to that of the peasant abangan but it is somewhat more sophisticated. It has an elaborate philosophy of fate and is quite mystical.

Asceticism and the practice of meditation are characteristic of prijaji abangan religion. Sects under the leadership of gurus are typical.

The santri are present among all social levels but they predominate in the commercial classes. The santri diligently comply with Islamic doctrine. They perform the required prayers five times a day, attend communal prayers at the mosque every Friday, fast during the month of Ramadan (Pasa), do not eat pork, and make every effort to perform the pilgrimage to Mecca at least once.

Religious Practitioners. There are several types of religious practitioner in Islam. There are sects consisting of a guru or *kijaji* (teacher) and *murid* (disciple) dyads that are hierarchically organized. Individual kijaji attract students to their *pondoks* or *pesantren* (monasterylike schools) to teach Muslim doctrines and laws. In addition to the dominance of Islam, magic and sorcery are widely practiced among the Javanese. There are many varieties of dukun, each one dealing with specialized kinds of ritual such as agricultural rituals, fertility rituals, etc. Dukun also perform divination and curing.

Ceremonies. The communal meal, the slametan, is central to abangan practice and is sometimes also performed by santri. The function of the slametan is to promote *slamet*, a state of calmness and serenity. The slametan is performed within a household and it is usually attended by one's closest neighbors. Occasions for a slametan include important life-cycle events and certain points in the Muslim ceremonial calendar; otherwise it is performed for the well-being of the village.

Arts. Geertz (1964) describes three art "complexes," each involving different forms of music, drama, dance, and literature. The Javanese shadow play, the *wajang*, is known worldwide and is central to the *alus* (refined) art complex. The wajang uses puppets to dramatize stories from the Indian epics, the Mahabharata and the Ramayana, or from Java's precolonial past. Wajang performances are accompanied by *gamelan* (percussion orchestras), which also have achieved worldwide fame. Another art form associated with the alus complex is batik textile dyeing. The alus art complex is classical and traditional and is largely the domain of the prijaji. The other two art complexes are more popular, nationally shared, and Western-influenced.

Medicine. Doctors practicing scientific medicine are present and are consulted in Java, especially in urban areas, but curers and diviners continue to be important in all of Javanese culture. In addition to the dukun who perform magic rites, there are many dukun who cure illnesses. These latter dukun include curers who use magic spells, herbalists, midwives, and masseurs. It is said that even urban prijaji who regularly consult medical doctors may also consult dukun for particular illnesses and psychosomatic complaints.

Death and Afterlife. Funerals are held within hours of death and they are attended by neighbors and close relatives who are able to arrive in time. A coffin is built and a grave is dug quickly while a village official performs rituals. A simple ceremony is held at the home of the deceased followed by a procession to the graveyard and burial. A slametan is held with food provided by neighbors. Javanese funerals are marked with the same emotional restraint that characterizes other social interactions. Graves are visited regularly, especially at the beginning and end of the fasting month, and they are tended by relatives. The Javanese believe in continuing ties with the dead and especially ties between parents and children. Children hold a number of slametans at intervals after death with the last held 1,000 days after the death. There are varying beliefs about life after death, including the standard Islamic concepts of eternal retribution, beliefs in spirits or ghosts who continue to influence events, and belief in reincarnation, the last sternly condemned by the orthodox Muslims.

Bibliography

Dewey, Alice G. (1962). *Peasant Marketing in Java*. New York: Free Press of Glencoe.

Geertz, Clifford (1964). *The Religion of Java*. New York: Free Press of Glencoe.

Geertz, Clifford (1975). *The Social History of an Indonesian Town*. Westport, Conn.: Greenwood Press.

Geertz, Hildred (1961). *The Javanese Family: A Study of Kinship and Socialization*. New York: Free Press of Glencoe.

Jay, Robert (1969). *Javanese Villagers: Social Relations in Rural Modjokuto*. Cambridge and London: MIT Press.

Williams, Linda B. (1990). *Development, Demography, and Family Decision Making: The Status of Women in Rural Java*. Boulder, Colo.: Westview Press.

M. MARLENE MARTIN

Kachin

ETHNONYMS: Dashan, Jinghpaw, Khang, Singhpo, Theinbaw

Orientation

Identification. "Kachin" comes from the Jinghpaw word "GaKhyen," meaning "Red Earth," a region in the valley of the two branches of the upper Irrawaddy with the greatest concentration of powerful traditional chiefs. It refers to a congeries of Tibeto-Burman–speaking peoples who come under the Jinghpaw political system and associated religious ideology. The main people of this group are the Jinghpaw; their language is the lingua franca and the ritual language of the group. In Jinghpaw, they are called "Jinghpaw Wunpaung Amyu Ni" (Jinghpaw and related peoples). The Singhpo are their kin in the Hukawng Valley and in northeasternmost India, closely associated with the Ahom rulers of that part of Assam from the thirteenth century. "Theinbaw" is the Burmese form. "Khang" is the Shan word for Kachin, whom the Chinese used to call "Dashan." Other than Jinghpaw (Chinese spelling, Jingpo), the Kachin are comprised of Maru (own name, "Lawngwaw"), Atsi (Szi, Zaiwa—the majority Kachin population in Yunnan), Lashi, and speakers of the Rawang language of the Nung group, Achang (Burmese term, "Maingtha," meaning "people of the [Shan] state of Möng Hsa"), and some in-resident communities of Lisu speakers (Yawyin, in Burmese). Lashi and Atsi-Maru (and smaller groups akin to Maru) are called "Maru Dangbau" (the Maru branch) in Jinghpaw.

Location. Kachin are located primarily in the Kachin State of Myanmar (Burma) and parts of the northern Shan State, southwestern Yunnan in China, and northeasternmost India (Assam and Arunachal Pradesh), between 23° and 28° N and 96° and 99° E. The Maru Dangbau are found mainly along the Myanmar-China border in this range. It is a region of north-south ranges, dissected by narrow valleys. In the val-leys there are also Shan (Dai, in Yunnan) and Burmans, and those Kachin who are more heavily influenced by Shan culture. In the far north there are peaks as high as 5,000 meters but the Kachin settlements and swiddens normally range between 1,200 and 1,900 meters or so, while the two main towns in Myanmar's Kachin State (Myitkyina and Bhamo, originally a Burman and a Shan town respectively) are about 330 meters in elevation. Snow is always found on the highest northern peaks, and the upper elevations are subject to cold-season frosts. There are more than 50 days of frost a year at higher elevations. Rainfall occurs mainly in the monsoon season (between June and October) and is between 190 and 254 centimeters on average. Temperatures are substantially lower on the high eastern slopes over the China border and in the northern Shan State. The forest cover is mixed evergreen/deciduous broadleaf monsoon forest, with subtropical forest at lower elevations, including teak (*Tectona grandis*).

Demography. There are no reliable census reports from recent decades from Myanmar. Projections from the estimates of the 1950s (then about half a million in all) suggest a total Kachin population of perhaps a million or more, of which Yunnan contains over 100,000 and India but a few thousand. Average population density is uneven. Because of the relatively poor growing conditions of the eastern zone and the adjacent northern Shan State, there was a greater tendency for Kachins to incorporate valley areas originally belonging to the Shan, as well as to practice swiddening on grassland rather than on forested slopes. In the intermediate zone along the north-south part of the Myanmar-China border, however, the relative density was especially high, owing to profitable concentration along the Chinese caravan trade routes there; the associated high incidence of raiding caused some villages to practice high-slope terracing of wet-rice fields rather than rely exclusively on swiddening. These historical conditions restricted access to enough forested upland to permit rotation cycles that were long enough for fallow fields to revert to natural cover. Even in the more fertile zone of the west, conditions of warfare and trade sometimes led to high density and resulted in grassland rather than forest swiddening, with associated tendencies toward erosion. Overall, many villages had twenty houses or fewer, with more than five persons each, on average.

Linguistic Affiliations.   All the Kachin languages are of the Tibeto-Burman Family. Jinghpaw and its dialects (chiefly Sinli, in the south, which is the Standard Jinghpaw of the schools based in the towns of Bhamo and Myitkyina; Mungun in Assam; Gauri [Hkauri] in the east; and Hkaku in the north and west [known as the Red-Earth country]) are an autonomous branch of the family, while the languages of the Maru Dangbau are in the Burmese-Lolo Branch, akin to Burmese. Nung is less certainly placed in Tibeto-Burman, while Lisu is a Loloish language in the Lolo-Burmese Branch.

History and Cultural Relations

There are Chinese mentions of Kachin in Yunnan going back to the fourteenth or fifteenth century, and there are obscure references to what must be Singhpo clients in the chronicles of the Ahom Kingdom in Assam, dating as early as the thirteenth century. There are similar mentions in the chronicles of some Khamti Shan principalities from the Upper Chindwin, while Leach argues that the prototypical Kachin chiefly (Gumchying Gumtsa) domains of the Red-Earth country may have arisen in the context of Khamti conquest of the area and displacement of Tibetan traders from the region of Putao (Hkamti Long). However, the first historical light on them comes from the end of the eighteenth and the start of the nineteenth century. Their spread was connected with the spread of the Shan (and Ahom) Tai-speaking peoples of the region's valleys, with whom Kachin have had a symbiotic relation. There are more Shan borrowings than any other in the Jinghpaw lexicon, and Shan-Buddhist ideas (and terms) are found in the ideological rhetoric associated with the Gumlao version of their political system ("Gumlao" means "rebellious aristocrats"; see below). Most of the ethnography comes from the work of American Protestant and European Catholic missionaries, who started work in the Bhamo area in the late nineteenth century, and later extended to the Kachin areas in the Shan States and northward to and beyond Myitkyina, which the railway reached in 1899. The rest of what we know, aside from professional ethnography, comes from the records and diaries of British colonial officers and associated traders. There are Chinese sources for the Yunnan Kachin, only now becoming available outside China, and these show a long-standing place for Jinghpaw in the Tusi system of imperially appointed political-cum-customs agents in this borderland of Southeast Asia, the Kachin chiefs being subordinate to local Shan princes in this context. There was an expansion of Kachin settlement toward the east and south from late in the eighteenth century, in which the Kachin followed the growth of the Chinese overland caravan trade, especially with the rise and spread of commercial opium growing. This led to a flowering of the Gumlao political system, owing to the injection into Kachin politics of new sources of wealth from involvement in the trade and from the levying of tribute on the caravans. It also led to more confrontation of Kachin with Shan, and to instances of Kachin taking over minor Shan valley principalities. There is also indication that a much earlier period saw a similar development of centers of political power in the Red-Earth country, when the chiefs there were able to collect tribute from the annual influx of itinerant Tibetan pack traders going to Burma and even Siam and wintering in Kachin territory, where they gathered forest products for sale farther on. In the Third Anglo-Burmese War of 1885, while the British were taking Mandalay, the Kachin were also trying to take advantage of the collapse of royal Burma, and it was thought that, had the British failed to reach Mandalay when they did, the Kachin (and Shan?) might have reached it first. During the British imperium in Burma and India most of Kachinland was under the Frontier Administration, but the Triangle, north from Myitkyina, between the two branches of the Irrawaddy, was largely unadministered until just before the Japanese invasion of 1942. The Kachin State has been a constitutent of the Union of Burma (now Myanmar) since that country regained independence in 1948, and the President-elect on the eve of the socialist military coup of 1962 was a Kachin chief, the Sama Duwa Sinwa Nawng. Since the coup, however, the Kachin have been a major element in the multiethnic insurgency against the Myanmar government throughout the mountains of the Myanmar-China-Thailand border region, which has led to the extension of Kachin communities into northern Thailand. In 1953 a Jingpo Autonomous Region was established in southwestern Yunnan in China; the Peoples' Republic of China has proved a magnet and refuge for some of the insurgent leaders from Myanmar. Kachins have served prominently in Burma's armed forces (as also in British times), and some hundreds served, some in Europe, during the First World War.

Settlements

Traditional Kachin villages usually had far fewer than 100 households; the larger villages existed for defense, but the requirements of swidden agriculture led to segmentation of villages. In the old days many were stockaded. Houses were built on piles. There were three sorts of houses. In regions with strong hereditary chiefs ruling multivillage tracts, the chief's house was sometimes up to 30 meters long (10 meters wide), occupied as a single dwelling by the extended household of the chief. These were generally on steep mountain terraces. This form of dwelling served to symbolize the ownership of the tract by the lineage of the chief. Since livestock were considered individual household property rather than lineage property, they were not kept under the "longhouse." In some pioneer Gumlao settlements there were real longhouses, composite structures with separately owned individual household apartments along a corridor. Again, livestock were kept separately. These longhouses symbolized the cooperative nature of the Gumlao political order.

The rest of the Kachin lived and continue to live in individual household dwellings. Water supply was a critical factor in village size and placement, but villages that were high up for defense purposes were often distant from their water supply. Most villages were entered through a sacred grove marked by posts serving to elicit prosperity from the gods, and by shrines to the spirit of the earth, where community sacrifices were held.

The other kind of building that exists today is the household granary. The house posts and beams are made of wood, floors and walls of woven split bamboo, roof thatched with grass. Domestic tasks like weaving and rice pounding are done under the overhanging front gable of the house, under which the larger animals are also kept. Inside, the house is partitioned lengthwise. The left (up-slope) side consists of sleeping apartments; the right side is left open for cooking, storage, and entertainment. At the end of the apartments is a space for the household spirit and ancestral spirits not yet sent to the land of the dead. In front of the house are altars to spirits and large X-shaped posts to which cattle are bound during sacrifices aggrandizing the household. The main external decoration is the pair of hornlike ornaments over the front roof peak on important aristocratic houses. Inside chiefs' houses there are various symbolically carved boards and posts signifying the ritual claim to spiritual sources of general prosperity in the sky world and the nether world, and a head of a buffalo sacrificed at the construction.

Economy

Subsistence and Commercial Activities.   Traditionally, all Kachins were farmers and there was no full-time occupational specialization. Save where Kachin settlements have encroached on Shan valley principalities, there is swidden farming. The main staple crop is rice, and the burnt-over swidden is cultivated with a short, heavy-handled hoe and planted with a planting stick, the crop being reaped with a knife or sickle. Swiddens, especially in the colder, less well rain-fed eastern zone, are also planted with maize, sesame, buckwheat, millet, tobacco, and various species of pumpkin. Vegetables and fruits are planted in house-yard gardens. People also raise some cotton and opium poppy. As one goes east into the Dehong of Yunnan, cultivation is a mixture of upland wet-rice terraces, monsoon swiddening, and grassland swiddening. Rice farming starts in February or March, and the cut slopes are burnt over and planted before the onset of the monsoon in June; harvesting is in October. Grain, which is threshed by being trampled by buffalo, is stored by December. Kachins do not generally use a swidden for more than three years at a time. Fallowing ideally takes at least twelve years, but field rotation does not usually require moving the settlement; villages often last half a century or more.

Fishing with traps and poison is common, but economically insignificant. Hunting with traps, snares, deadfalls, pellet bows, and guns is especially common in the agriculturally slack cold season between December and February. Cattle, buffalo, pigs, dogs, and fowl are bred for sacrifice but generally not for eating. Pigs are fed cooked mash in the evening but scavenge during the day. Some dogs are used in hunting, and some horses are kept.

Boiled rice with a vegetable stew and sometimes meat or fish are eaten three times a day. There is an aversion to eating cats, dogs, horses, monkeys, sheep, and goats. Tobacco and betel are commonly chewed. Opium smoking has been widespread in the last century or so. Rice beer is prepared, the malted mash also being taken during heavy work and on journeys, while the liquor is also distilled. These drinks are essential to hospitality and to ritual sacrifice.

Industrial Arts.   Most metalware is obtained from Shan and Chinese, but in some northern regions there are lineages of blacksmiths who smelt ore. No pottery making is reported, though earthenware pots are common. Bamboo, cane, and grass are used to weave mats, baskets, and house walls. Woodworking and carving are not elaborate. Women weave on the belt loom, producing elaborate, largely floral-geometric designs, with some embroidery.

Trade.   Trade is mainly with Shan and Chinese (and Burmese) for salt, metalware, and the prestigious heirloom wares exhibited by aristocratic lineages. Kachins attend the markets held every five days in Shan towns, where they sell small amounts of garden and forest produce. The extent of Kachin involvement in opium growing and trading is in dispute, but the poppy was commonly cultivated in the area, though perhaps mainly by non-Jinghpaw. Trade with the Chinese caravans that came through the region carrying, among other things, opium, was a major source of wealth for the settlements of the intermediate zone; chiefs extracted considerable revenue from traders in their domains.

Division of Labor.   Men clear and burn the swiddens, hunt, go on raids, and assume most political and religious roles. Women have full responsibility for weeding, harvesting, transporting, and threshing; both men and women cook and brew from the crops, marketing any surplus. Women fetch water and firewood; they prepare raw cotton for weaving their own clothing and make their husbands' (largely Shan-style) clothes from commercial cloth.

Land Tenure.   Forest lands in a tract are village property and there is no private property in swidden land. Chiefs or the joint rulers of a Gumlao community have the sole right to allow people to live in a village and the sole right to dispose of land to those wishing to use it, but may not refuse any resident household use of swidden lands. Deciding when and where to shift swidden sites and assigning swidden plots are the prerogative of the chief and the elders. Irrigated lands can be inherited and sold to a fellow villager, but never to an outsider; this right follows the rule that a cultivator may not be dispossessed from a plot while it is in use.

Kinship

Kin Groups and Descent.   Descent is agnatic and there are eponymous clans with fixed correspondences between clan names in the different languages. The five aristocratic clans are descended from the sons of Wahkyet-wa, youngest brother among the ancestors of the Shan, Chinese, and other peoples. These brothers were descendants of Ningawn-wa, eldest brother of the Madai nat, chief of the sky spirits. The aristocratic clans are, in order of precedence, Marip, Lahtaw, Lahpai, N'Hkum, and Maran. The clans are divided into major lineages and these into lesser segments and local lineage groups, and it is especially to the last that exogamy strictly applies, although all the clans are exogamous in theory. In some regions a form of marriage called *hkau wang magam* is practiced, which prohibits marrying into a lineage from which a wife has been taken until the fourth generation, and requires a marriage with a mother's brother's daughter's daughter's daughter (MBDDD). In such cases the MBDDD may turn out to be in one's own lineage, and the requirement must still be met. Some traditional lineage genealogies recited by bards are very long, though the number of generations back to the common ancestor seems to be a fixed number (i.e., genealogical telescoping). Clans are sometimes spoken of as if they were tribes because major chiefly domains have a majority of their residents in the chief's clan, which owns the village tract. In Jinghpaw proper, the wife acquires no membership in her husband's clan and lineage, but in Gauri she acquires it to some extent, and this difference corresponds to differences in the ease of divorce and in the recovery of marriage payments in such cases; in Jinghpaw proper, recovery is made from the wife's family, while in Gauri it is made mainly from her seducer, if any.

Kinship Terminology.   Kinship terminology is bifurcate-merging, with Omaha-type cousin terminology. The members of the lineage from which wives are taken and given, respectively, are referred to (by male speakers) with affinal terms (save that in the second descending generation the members of one's wife-taking groups are called by grandchild terms and the members of the second ascending generation of the wife-giving group are given grandparent terms). On the other hand, the wife takers of one's wife takers are all "grandchildren" and the men of one's wife givers' wife givers are all "grandfathers," regardless of generation. Furthermore, a male Ego calls the men in his own generation, whether wife giver or wife taker, by the same "brother-in-law" term (*hkau*); he calls the women in nonascending generations and men of descending generations of his wife-giving group "wife's younger sibling" (*nam*); and he calls the members of the three central generations of his wife takers, exclusive of the men of his own generation, by the term *hkri*, meaning "sister's children." Women of ascending generations of one's own lineage are "aunts by consanguinity" (*moi*) and the men of corresponding generations of wife takers are "uncle-by-marriage" (*gu*); women of the three central generations of wife givers' wife givers are *ni*, etymologically an "aunt" term, which has primary reference to the wives of classificatory mother's brothers (*tsa*, first ascending male wife giver). There are terms for actual husband and wife, and real/classificatory siblings are distinguished by age relative to the speaker.

Marriage and Family

Marriage.   Traditionally premarital sex was allowed; adolescents used to gather in the front apartment of a house evenings for singing, recitations of love poetry, and lovemaking. These relations need not, and some of them could not, lead to marriage. Fines are levied in favor of a girl's family for fathering a bastard. Parents try to arrange marriages to ally with other lineages, but negotiations are turned over to go-betweens. Bride-price is paid by the groom's father and the latter's lineage mates and may involve lengthy negotiations with payments extending over many years; there may also be a year or two of bride-service. The bride's family provides her with a dowry and helps defray the wedding costs. Polygyny, not common, is allowed, and often arises from the obligation to take on the widow of a real or classificatory brother. Some chiefs have several wives, some of them Shan or Burmese, and these cases arise from the need for marriages of state. Exogamy is more theoretical than strict, and it is quite possible to marry even a somewhat distant consanguine (*lawu-lahta*). This follows from the two principles of asymmetrical marriage alliance and lineage segmentation. The first has a single rule: one may not take wives from the same lineages to which one gives wives; the reversal of an alliance is a major offense against the whole social order. Since wife givers (*mayu* in Jinghpaw) outrank their wife takers (*dama* in Jinghpaw) ritually and in rights and duties to one another, wife givers can extort a great deal from their wife takers, from which derives the auxiliary principle of diversification of alliances. Far from its being a rule that one should normally marry a woman from a wife-giver lineage, it is often thought strategic to negotiate a new alliance. This possibility reinforces the tendency for lineages to segment (or fission) when they become too large and have to compete for limited social and economic resources. It follows that one's distant lineage mates may well have separated themselves and have their own marriage networks, in which case each has effectively become a distinct unit of marriage alliance, and hence can intermarry. In Kachin ideology, however, exogamy and marriage-alliance relations are fixed once and for all among the five aristocratic clans, with the result that this ideological model of the system has the five clans marrying in a circle (e.g., Lahtaw, Marip, Maran, N'Hkum, Lahpai, Lahtaw, each being wife giver to the next). This is consistent with the rules. Wife giver–wife taker relations, and the restrictions against reversing them, are not transitive. They extend only to certain of the wife givers of one's own immediate wife giver (and of the wife taker of one's own immediate wife taker) because a woman's lineage brothers hold a sort of lien on the children, so that her husband's lineage must pay off that lien (to the natal lineage of her actual mother) along with paying the marriage price to her lineage. In principle the rank distinction between aristocrats and commoners (*du ni* and *darat ni* respectively) is rigid, but for the same reasons that clan exogamy is only a fiction, so is this. The politics of marriage alliance combined with the tendency for local lineage segments to constitute separate entities occasionally allows a rising commoner lineage of wealth and power to get a major wife from a lineage in an aristocratic clan that may have fallen on hard times, if the alliance is suitable to the two parties and the prices paid are appropriately inflated. There are, however, some clans that figure as unequivocal commoners (not merely darat ni but *darat daroi*, "utter commoners"); an example is the clan Labya, properly called Labya *mi-wa*, indicating that it is of Chinese origin and has been included fairly recently in the Kachin system.

Domestic Unit.   Ideally, residence is virilocal, but uxorilocal marriage is not notably uncommon. This is especially true in the case of a noninheriting son, whose claims on the assistance of his real or classificatory mother's brother, whose daughter is a preferential wife, may be greater than those on his own father.

Inheritance.   Usually the youngest son (*uma*) inherits his father's house and office, if any, while much of the movable property may go, in the father's lifetime, as dowry to his daughters and as marriage settlements on the older sons. The youngest son in return is expected to support the parents in their old age and arrange their funerals. A childless man's estate reverts to his brothers or lineage mates and their heirs. The principle of ultimogeniture is modified by the fact that an eldest son is thought to succeed in some measure to the powers of the "mother's brother" or wife-giver line and in any case is next in line after the youngest in succession, so that the position of an eldest son of a youngest-son line is especially important. This may be an idea associated with the Gumlao political order, but compare the mythical genealogy of the chiefly clans.

Sociopolitical Organization

Social Organization.   See under "Settlements" and "Marriage and Family"

Political Organization.   There are several versions of the system. Gumchying Gumtsa chiefs are the ritual models of chiefdom and the base for this kind of organization is the Red-Earth country. Their authority derives from their monopoly of priests and bardic reciters of genealogical myths, through which ritual specialists they control access to the spirits who make human occupancy of the land possible. They claim the right to various services and dues from their subjects, notably a hind quarter of all animals (wild and domestic) that are killed in the tract, and so are called "thigh-eating chiefs." Gumlao communities reject on principle the hereditary privileges of chiefs. In particular, they believe that all aristocrats of the community are equal, that is, all householders who can get someone to sponsor the essential Merit Feasts and sacrifices. It is a mistake to call this a "democratic" system, since its principle is wider access by aristocrats to chieflike privileges (though they reject the thigh-eating dues); a Gumlao man is called *magam*, which signifies an aristocrat though not a chief (*duwa*) by strict succession. Gumlao is based on the idea that a noninheriting son who can find wealth and a place to set himself up may try to get an important Gumchying Gumtsa chief to sponsor him in a feat that will raise him to standing as a full chief; but first he must temporarily renounce all claims to standing (*gumyu*, which literally means "to step down from privilege") while he awaits the sponsoring rites. When local and historical circumstances conspire to make wealth more generally accessible, there are aristocrats who will not bother with sponsorship at all, since sponsorship becomes expensive and has to be postponed proportionally to the demand for it. They simply assume the ritual attributes, although not the thigh-eating privileges, of chiefdom. This seems to be the root of the Gumlao movement. Not surprisingly, as conditions ease there will be *gumlao magam* who again seek sponsorship as full chiefs, at which point Gumlao tracts turn again into Gumchying Gumtsa domains. The oscillation is fueled by a perennial ideological debate about the allowable sources of ritual privilege, as well as by the combined effects of the principle of lineage segmentation and the tendencies toward disaffection brought about through primogeniture. When a Kachin chief in close contact with Shan becomes more like a Shan prince (*sawbwa*, or *tsao-fa*), often because he has taken over lowland Shan territories or because he desires political recognition on the part of other sawbwas, he will try to assert even greater power over his "subjects" and may even abandon Kachin priestly services and the closely connected reliance on upland farming. Such a chief is called "Gumsa duwa," a Gumsa chief. In tending toward becoming Shan and asserting a sharp distinction between "rulers" and "subjects" incompatible with the claims and intricacies of the Kachin marriage-alliance system (a Shan prince, of course, simply takes and gives wives as tribute), and in giving up the ritual basis of his authority, he will tend to lose the allegiance of the Kachin manpower on which his real power depends. The alternative is the compromise status of Gumrawng Gumsa (pretentious chiefs), who claim exclusive right over a village and maintain enough upland swiddens to satisfy the Kachin priests who must serve them, but remain unconnected with the hierarchy of Kachin authority deriving from the rules of strict succession and sponsorship, have no authority outside the village, and are not recognized outside the village as thigh-eating chiefs. Traditional Kachin chiefs, not being absolute rulers, rarely acted apart from the wishes of the council of household elders. In Yunnan, where Kachin chiefs have long had a place within the Tusi system in the context of Shan principalities, it is not unknown for agents (*suwen*, probably a Chinese title) to usurp much of the power of the chiefs, even though these administrative agents may be commoners.

Conflict.   Suppressed upon the extension of British rule, Kachin warfare was mainly guerilla action, raiding, and ambush, with sporadic instances of cannibalism and head-hunting reported.

Religion and Expressive Culture

Christian missionaries have already been mentioned. At present most, if not all, Kachin communities are Christian, and the social rift between Catholic and Protestant communities sometimes is quite deep. Recent years have also seen some Government-sponsored Buddhist-missionary activity among Kachins in Myanmar.

Religious Beliefs.   One class in Kachin religion includes the major deities, named and common to all Kachin, remote ancestors of commoner and aristocrat alike. These Sky Nat (*mu nat*—the word "nat" means a spirit Lord) are ultimately children of the androgynous Creator (Woishun-Chyanun), whose "reincarnation" is Shadip, the chief of the earth nats (*ga nat*), the highest class of spirit. The youngest sky nat (senior by ultimogeniture) is the Madai Nat, who can be approached only by chiefs, whose ultimate ancestor was his eldest brother and dama, Ningawn-wa, who forged the earth. A direct daughter of Madai Nat was the wife of the first Kachin aristocrat. Below all these in rank are the *masha nat*, the ancestor nats of lineages; that of the uma, or youngest-son line of thigh-eating chiefs, has special importance. There is also a vague sort of "High God," Karai Kasang, who has no myths (except that he seems to have something to do with the fate of the souls of the dead) and who Leach thinks is a projection of the Christian God of the missionaries; this spirit's name makes no sense in the Kachin language. Below all these are minor spirits such as household guardians and the spirits of immediate ancestors, witch spirits (*hpyi*) who possess those accused of unconscious hereditary witchcraft, and the *maraw*, unpersonified "fates" to be placated; they can upset the best laid plans and the boons granted by higher deities. Beyond these are the uniformly hostile ghosts and spirits, whose evil works are not, as Leach claimed, man's punishment for infraction of proper obligations.

Religious Practitioners.   There are mediums and diviners; a medium works by trance and is inexplicably chosen for his or her calling, while divination is a learned skill. These are basically private practitioners. There are also priests (*dumsa*) who officiate at sacrificial rites, and the rather scarce *jaiwa*, or bards, who preserve and recite genealogies and associated myths at great Merit Feasts (*manau*) in which chiefs and other high aristocrats proclaim and validate the ancestral sources of their authority. These are all learned offices, never hereditary, and they are essential to the ritual practices of aristocracy and chiefdom. Priests have two sorts of sacrificial assistants (ritual butchers). Of all these offices, only that of medium may be exercised by women. Priests, bards, and sacrificers are paid with a portion of the sacrifice. Priests also can work as sorcerers. The main work in treating illnesses is intercession with spirits by some or all of these officiants. The chief has the ritual duty of declaring sabbaths from all work at the time of rites held for recurrent or exceptional communal times of crisis such as plagues or junctures in the agricultural cycle (e.g., just before the first sowing the chief and his priests make offerings to the spirit of the earth, which is followed by a four-day sabbath).

Death and Afterlife. One cause of death is said to be that the cord that the Creator holds, thus sustaining the soul, is eventually gnawed away by spirits. Spirits can also entice the soul from the body, and death ensues if the soul cannot be found and enticed back home. Ultimately myth has it that death came to Kachin mankind because human beings originally had to attend ceremonies of the sky-spirit people, and, as dama, had to contribute costly gifts. This cost so much that Sut Wa Madu, the ancestor who founded the _sut manau_ (Feast of Merit, a major ritual connection between the two worlds), decided to hold a mock funeral, thus enticing the sky people to attend and bring gifts. The female sun spirit (Jan nat, one of the Sky Nats) felt that this compromised the asymmetrical relations between mayu and dama, and she decreed that if there were to be human funerals, then men would have to suffer death—not so much as a punishment as in order to restore the net balance of the relationship with a quitclaim payment of men's souls. This tale expresses the ultimate paradox of an asymmetrical alliance relation; for the net circulation of the system is impossible to maintain asymmetrically when there are fewer than three parties to the relationship. On the one hand, with payments going all one way, the system lacks completeness, or closure. On the other hand, payments in an asymmetrical relation cannot go both ways. Burial is a week after death; this interval is used to try to ensure the separation of the spirit of the deceased from the world of the living, a task aided by a priest, who makes offerings to the ghost and asks it to go away. The final obsequies may be postponed for as much as a year on account of the expense. Then the priest recalls the soul from its temporary limbo and tells it the route to the land of the dead. If thereafter divination shows that the spirit has not gone, it will be installed in the household altar, which had been temporarily removed from the house at the time of the death and is now reinstalled.

Bibliography

Carrapiet, W. J. S. (1929). _The Kachin Tribes of Burma._ Rangoon: Superintendent of Government Printing and Stationery.

Friedman, Jonathan (1979). _System, Structure, and Contradiction._ Copenhagen: National Museum of Denmark.

Gilhodes, Charles (1922). _The Kachins: Religion and Customs._ Calcutta: Catholic Orphan Press.

Hanson, Olaf (1913). _The Kachins: Their Customs and Traditions._ Rangoon: American Baptist Mission Press.

Leach, Edmund R. (1954). _Political Systems of Highland Burma._ Cambridge: Harvard University Press; London: G. Bell & Sons.

Leach, Edmund R. (1961). _Rethinking Anthropology_ (chapters 2, 3, and 5). London: Athlone Press.

Lehman, F. K. (1977). "Kachin Social Categories and Methodological Sins." In _Language and Thought: Anthropological Issues_, edited by William McCormack and Stefan Wurm, 229–250. The Hague: Mouton.

Lehman, F. K. (1989). "Internal Inflationary Pressures in the Prestige Economies of the Feast-of-Merit Complex." In _Ritual, Power, and Economy: Upland-Lowland Contrasts in Mainland Southeast Asia_, edited by Susan D. Russell, 89–102. Occasional Paper 14. DeKalb: Northern Illinois University, Center for Southeast Asian Studies.

Lintner, Bertil (1990). _Land of Jade: A Journey through Insurgent Burma._ Bangkok: White Lotus.

Maran, LaRaw (1967). "Towards a Basis for Understanding the Minorities of Burma: The Kachin Example." In _Southeast Asian Tribes, Minorities, and Nations._ Vol. 1, edited by Peter Kunstadter, 125–146. Princeton, N.J.: Princeton University Press.

F. K. LEHMAN

Kalagan

There are aproximately 8,000 Kalagan (Calagan, Kagan, Karagan, Laoc, Saka, Tagakaolo) living on the island of Mindanao in the Philippines. They are located in the area between the interior uplands and the western coast of the Davao Gulf. Kalagan are Tagakaolo who have converted to Islam, either through intermarriage or contact with the Maguindanao. Islamization is a relatively recent development among the Tagakaolo and many older Kalagan still retain traditional beliefs. Kalagan speak Tagakaolo, a subgroup of the Central Philippine Language Group. Some Kalagan are swidden agriculturalists, while others are involved in wage labor. Maize is the major crop, and is harvested two or three times a year. Coastal Kalagan are also fishermen, and some work as plantation laborers.

See also Maguindanao

Bibliography

Gowing, Peter G. (1984). "Kalagans." In _Muslim Peoples: A World Ethnographic Survey_, edited by Richard V. Weekes, 367. Westport, Conn.: Greenwood Press.

Kalibugan

"Kalibuga" (Kolibugan) means "mixed breed" and refers to the Subanun of the Philippines who have intermarried with the Tausug and Samal. Kalibugan, who number about 15,000, live in villages on the coast in western Mindanao. Most have converted to Islam. Their culture shares elements with those of Subanun, Tausug, and Samal.

See also Subanun

Bibliography

Gowing, Peter G. (1975). "The Growing List of Filippino Muslim Groups." *Danalan Research Center Reports* 1:5–6.

Kalimantan Dayaks

ETHNONYMS: Biadju, Bidayuh, Dajak, Daya

The category "Kalimantan Dayaks" includes several groups of indigenous peoples in southern and western Kalimantan in both Malaysian and Indonesian parts of the island. They may be distinguished from the Malay population by the fact that they are not Muslim, and from the Penan (or Ot) by the fact that they are settled rather than nomadic. They are further characterized by their practices of living along river banks; growing rice in swiddens; gathering forest products; bilineal inheritance and bilateral kinship reckoning; uxorilocal residence; political unity rarely above the level of the village; absence of social stratification (although slavery is or was practiced by some groups); multifamily dwellings (often including longhouses); and, in most cases, secondary burials. The Dayaks speak a number of related Austronesian languages, and there are, in addition, many more dialects. Owing to great linguistic and cultural variation, as well as to the political autonomy of the large numbers of villages, the categorization of Dayak peoples by culture and by social group has been problematic, and there are differences of opinion as to how this should be done; we rely here on linguistic, cultural, and geographic factors. In addition to the four ethnic groups discussed below, there are others, including the Lawangan, Tundjung, Tamuan, Lamadau, Arut, Delang, Mamah Darat, and Kebahan (an Islamic Dayak or Orang Melayu group). Distinctive or salient features of four major groups follow; all groups are linguistically united, with the exception of the Land Dayaks.

The Ngadju Dayaks are the largest central Kalimantan group; they live in the area from the Barito drainage to Kotawaringin, and from the south coast to the Mahakam Valley. This group lives along the larger rivers, and uses two or three family houses rather than longhouses. The Ngadju regard the Ot Danum as their cultural ancestors. They rely a great deal on fishing, and less on hunting. Ngadju villages are sometimes politically united as subtribes under chiefs. Slavery is practiced, and slaves are killed at the funerals of chiefs. Ngadju culture includes tattooing and tooth filing.

The second ethnic group is the Ot Danum Dayaks, who live on the headwaters of rivers, and who speak dialects of the same language, which is closely related to Ngadju. The Ot Danum number approximately 30,000. They gather or raise fruit, rubber, and lumber for sale, and make dugout canoes that they trade downriver. The Ot Danum raise dogs, pigs, and chickens; cattle are raised for celebrations. Iron forging is important, and is done with bamboo double-piston bellows. Land is owned individually, but may be sold only to another member of the village.

A third ethnic group is known as the Maanyan Dayaks, a society of approximately 35,000 people who live in the Patai river drainage and share a single language. They had lived in a single village until external influences caused their society to fragment. Presently, the Maanyan Dayaks live as distinct subgroups each having a name and a common set of cultural rules (*adat*), and residing in a group of several villages. The Maanyan do not have longhouses; their dwellings are built to house one nuclear or extended family. Each nuclear family has its own swiddens and field house, in which they live while tending crops. Ambilineal descent groups (*bumah*) hold usufructory rights in village lands. Shamans cure through spirit possession and trance, function as priests at funerals and entertain as dancers. They also act as repositories of group knowledge; they memorize creation myths, history, and the genealogies of important families. One of the subgroups of the Maanyan, the Padju Epat, cremates the bones of its dead; this practice was once followed by all Maanyan.

The fourth group is known as the Land Dayaks (or Bidayuh), and this very heterogeneous group of people inhabits western Kalimantan and southern Sarawak. They had a population in southern Sarawak of 104,885 in 1980, and in western Kalimantan of approximately 200,000 in 1942 (more recent figures are not available). Though Land Dayak villages are large by comparison to other Dayak villages, often containing 600 or more people, the population lives in just one or a few longhouses. In contrast with the other groups, the Land Dayaks speak more than one language. This largest Dayak group is also the most culturally distinctive; though they now live alongside streams, they once lived on fortified hilltops. That feature which most distinguishes the Land Dayaks from other Dayaks is their long and pervasive contact with the Chinese, who came to trade, and with the Dutch and the Malay, who came as both traders and colonizers. Another distinctive feature is the headhouse, which serves as a men's house, a council house, and a ceremonial facility; it gets its name from the fact that the heads of captives are stored beneath it.

See also Iban

Bibliography

Avé, J. B. (1972). "Kalimantan Dyaks." In *Ethnic Groups of Insular Southeast Asia*, edited by Frank M. LeBar. Vol. 1, *Indonesia, Andaman Islands, and Madagascar*, 185–187. New Haven: HRAF Press.

DANIEL STROUTHES

Kalingas

ETHNONYMS: Calinga, Kalingga, Kinalinga

Orientation

Identification. Largely celebrated in the popular literature for their invidious headhunting, the Kalingas are surrounded by other Philippine peoples who are equally famous for their headhunting, including the Apayaos to the north, the Bontoks to the south, and the Ifugaos farther to the southeast. In 1914 the Kalingas were described by Dean Worcester, the first American administrator in their mountainous area, as "a fine lot of headhunting savages, physically magnificently developed, mentally acute, but naturally very wild." Actually the Kalingas themselves did not traditionally use the term "Kalinga," which probably meant simply "enemy" in the language of neighboring lowland peoples and which was used by the early Spanish explorers to refer to everyone in the mountains of northern Luzon. Politicians, administrators, and anthropologists have nevertheless come to apply the word ethnolinguistically to a people fairly well distinguished from their neighbors by a network of mutually intelligible dialects and by similar customs, personal names, ballads, ceremonies, and epic poems.

Location. The Kalingas live in the North Luzon Highlands (sometimes referred to as the Cordillera Central), a rugged and sharply dissected block of mountains stretching north from approximately 16° N for about 320 kilometers and averaging about 65 kilometers wide, between 120° and 122° E. This massive mountainous area, the largest in the Philippine archipelago, boasts several peaks higher than 2,740 meters in its southern range. Located in the north-central section of these highlands, Kalinga territory extends perhaps 30 kilometers north to south and 80 kilometers east to west around 17° N—where the peaks reach about 2,470 meters—and includes the middle drainage area of the northward-flowing Chico de Cagayan River and its tributaries, especially the larger eastward-flowing ones, such as the Mabaca, Saltan, Bananid, and Pasil Rivers, and the northward-flowing Tanudan River.

Demography. Demographic information is at once scarce and unreliable, but some regional studies have been made and there are informed estimates. The most recent figure approaching accuracy on the number of ethnic Kalingas dates to 1972, when the population was estimated at 72,500. Based on a 1.2 percent population-growth rate from a regional study in the mid-1970s, their 1990 population should have been around 92,000.

Linguistic Affiliation. Linguists supply several classifications of languages in the Philippines. Most agree that all these languages belong to the larger Austronesian Family, and most agree that the Kalinga language belongs to a northern Luzon grouping. The most recent classification follows a line from Austronesian (formerly Malayo-Polynesian) through (the new) Malayo-Polynesian (along with Atayalic, Tsouic, and Paiwanic) to Western Malayo-Polynesian to Northern Philippine, and Kalinga may belong to what is sometimes called the North Cordilleran Cluster.

History and Cultural Relations

Although available evidence indicates that at least one major migration route for most peoples of the North Luzon Highlands was from South China through Taiwan and into northern Luzon by way of the Cagayan River Valley, any statements on prehistory must be understood as speculation. Accuracy begins only with the Spanish contacts. Ferdinand Magellan discovered the Philippines for Spain in 1521, and the first Spanish contact with Northern Luzon was in 1572 when Juan de Salcedo, the grandson of Miguel de Legazpi (who occupied the Manila area in 1565) explored the Ilocos coast. He learned about the gold mines in the North Luzon Highlands, which initiated the Spanish interest in the southern areas of the mountains. These areas are, however, quite far from Kalinga territory. Their experience with the Spaniards came from the Spanish posts first established in 1598 in the province of Abra to the west of Kalinga territory. In 1614 the first missionary, Fr. Juan de Pareja, went into Western Kalinga (Tinggian) territory, but not much missionary work was done until the 1800s when the Augustinian Order established missions among the Apayaos—the Kalingas' northern neighbors—and the Western Kalingas. The primary interest of the Spaniards, however, centered on the gold and copper mines in the southern North Luzon Highlands, though in 1668 they finally gave up the notion of direct occupation. Thereafter, one of the main reasons for Spanish interest in the North Luzon Highlands was control of highlander trade with the lowlanders to protect the Spanish tobacco monopoly. The Spaniards were not very successful in this endeavor either. After the tobacco monopoly was abolished in 1882 the Spaniards paid little attention to the highlands. Soon the Americans took over as colonial masters of the Philippines and set up their civil government in 1902. The bulk of the North Luzon Highlands fell administratively into a division known as Mountain Province. Within this province Kalinga Subprovince was created in 1908 by an act of the Philippine Commission, as a part of an overall reorganization of the North Luzon Highlands. In 1967 the Philippine government created four new provinces out of the old Mountain Province, one of which was Kalinga-Apayao. Beginning in the mid-1970s the Kalingas were brought into sudden, direct, and brutal contact with the Philippine nation-state as a result of government attempts to build four major dams on the Chico River, two of them in Kalinga territory. In April 1980 a squad of Philippine army soldiers gunned down Macli-ing Dulag, an outspoken Kalinga opponent of the dams. In June 1984 more than 3,000 government troops launched a major military assault on the Kalingas, including indiscriminate bombing and strafing of villages. People were raped and tortured. The World Bank dissociated itself from the projects, and the government of President Corazon Aquino, which was installed in February 1986, has "permanently postponed" work on the dams.

Trade is carried on between Kalinga groups and with cultural groups outside Kalinga territory. Kalingas also trade with lowlanders, especially through the lowland provincial market in Tabuk. Although interethnic marriage is rare, some Kalinga men have married Bontok women, who have a reputation as hard workers.

Settlements

Most of the villages, which range from five to fifty households, contain a crowded cluster of huts and are often located for defense on fairly inaccessible lower ridges and usually marked by groves of coconut trees. The larger villages typically contain a central plaza where public rituals of birth and death and other events are celebrated. All houses are raised above the ground on posts, with steps or a ladder leading up to a single entrance. The majority of the houses are square, single-room dwellings, though some of the older houses were octagonal. The walls are commonly made of split and plaited bamboo. Roofs are pitched, made of strong reeds, and thatched with thick grass. Split bamboo mats resting on a grating of small beams make up the floors. Each dwelling has a fire pit that consists of a square box about a meter wide and a couple of hands high filled with sand and accumulated ash and located toward the back of the room. This is the hearth around which all the activities of the household revolve, including the cooking of the daily meals. Above it is a rack for drying food, wood, and wearing apparel.

Economy

Subsistence and Commercial Activities. Subsistence is based on a rice staple raised both in permanent irrigated rice terraces and in swiddens. In addition to rice, a variety of tubers, legumes, and vegetables is grown in the swiddens. Maize, sugarcane, tobacco, and coffee are also raised. The meat of domesticated pigs and water buffalo supplies most of the animal protein, though in the heavily forested areas a variety of wildlife, such as deer, wild pigs, bats, lizards, and birds, is hunted.

Industrial Arts. Many people engage in craft work, particularly in the manufacture of wood utensils and tools. Ironworking, basketry, and pottery making are also widespread.

Trade. Traditionally trade was quite limited because of the fear of losing one's head, but the pacification activities of the American administration led to the opening of trade routes. Traditional trade was carried out under the aegis of the pacts that the nearly sovereign territorial units set up independently with each other, and was largely controlled by regional elites. Open-air markets such as exist in the lowlands are unknown, and trade is conducted between households.

Division of Labor. Although more egalitarian than most Southeast Asian groups and certainly more egalitarian than modern Western societies, the Kalingas are nevertheless patriarchal. In general, men do the strenuous, brief work, such as clearing the forest, building fences, and plowing, and women do the time-consuming, boring work, such as planting, weeding, and harvesting. Women do, however, inherit important political offices, such as interregional pact stewardships, and they are the shamans. In addition, women are responsible for the formation of the reciprocal work groups upon which the success of individual households depends.

Land Tenure. Along with family heirlooms—generally ancient Chinese beads, jars, plates, and gongs—irrigated rice terraces, house sites, and livestock are the most valued property. Landlessness was nonexistent in the past and is still very rare. Only user rights are recognized for swidden plots, and most regions still have communal land.

Kinship

Kin Groups and Descent. The descent system is bilateral and characterized by merging of collateral with lineal kin, use of reciprocal terms, primary importance of the generation principle, and rarity of sex-differentiation in terms of reference. Kindred are of prime importance and consist of the eight pairs of great-great-grandparents, siblings, first cousins, second cousins, third cousins, and the ascendants and descendants of all these categories. There are no corporate descent groups, but in the major town, Lubuagan, the former capital of Kalinga Subprovince, there are wealthy families that seem to be showing the beginnings of patrilineal corporate descent groups; the fathers in these families are arranging marriages for their children with second- and third-degree cross cousins in other wealthy families.

Kinship Terminology. The terminological system generally fits the Eskimo type but emphasizes the kindred rather than the nuclear family.

Marriage and Family

Marriage. Marriages follow rules of regional endogamy and result in the creation of demes. Within these demes marriage between relatives closer than third cousins is forbidden. The demes range from 60 to 1,000 households, and the whole of the Kalinga territory is composed of perhaps 70 to 80 of these demes. The postmarital residence rule is matrilocal. Polygyny is allowed but is practiced by only a few of the wealthy men.

Inheritance. When children marry, they all inherit nearly equal shares of the patrimony. In fact, land and other property are not actually "owned" but held in trust for one's children. In practice, the best land goes to the oldest son, and the house goes to the youngest daughter.

Socialization. Children generally live in a house with their parents, but they come into contact with a relatively large number of adults who are usually related to them in some way in the intermarried deme and who may discipline and train them. Socialization is generally by example and corporal punishment is rare.

Sociopolitical Organization

Social Organization. Most sociopolitical decisions are made by elderly men who command respect through their prestigious deeds. In the past such prestige was gained in headhunting but today arises mainly from men's ability as public speakers. Kalingas act as autonomous individuals, and households exercise a great deal of autonomy. Even children enjoy much independence in their decision making, and it is rare that anyone directly orders anyone else to do anything.

Political Organization. Political structure is based on the residential settlement and the deme. These larger units are organized in the same way as among most other mountain groups in Southeast Asia, and the most common word used in the anthropological literature to described this type of organization is "loose." Whatever decisions need to be made on a village or regional basis are arrived at through discussion and consensus. Although each deme is a politically and socially sovereign entity and each can make treaties with others governing trade, conflicts, and territorial boundaries, the household and, indeed, individuals, are largely autonomous. Naturally, modern governmental units established in Manila have come to act as a template over the traditional processes, but recent experiences of the Kalingas with the Philippine government have not been happy ones and these "foreign" political mechanisms are not easily accepted.

Social Control. Disputes are usually resolved by discussion among kindreds. Severe infractions of customary law may result in a hearing at an informal gathering presided over by village or regional elders. In consultation with competing kindreds these elders may levy fines. In recent disputes some have tried to use the Philippine court system to gain legal title to land, but the public reaction against them has been strong.

Religion and Expressive Culture

Religious Beliefs. As a pragmatic, present-oriented people, Kalingas have a saying, "Nothing happens that does not start from the hearth"; in other words, the household is the center and the focal point of the world. Then comes the kindred, and then the deme. Also, in concert with the other peoples of the North Luzon Highlands, the Kalingas traditionally have had a concept that the universe consists of five areas: the Earth, the Skyworld, the Underworld, the Upstream Area, and the Downstream Area. The Skyworld is geomorphic and is occupied by the creator-god Kabunyan and some of the other high gods. Many of the great adventures of the gods take place in this distant cosmic land. The other areas of the cosmos have their own characteristics. The highest order of deities are Kabunyan and the other high gods, the *pinain,* and the *alan.* The second group is composed of the deities of dead ancestors and relatives. The third group consists of mythological creatures and culture heroes who were once humans but whose origins are too ancient to trace. The pinain inhabit the forests, river banks, brooks, swamps, pathways and large trees. The alan are generally malevolent. Christian missionaries have made some slight inroads into the belief system, but for the most part the people retain their traditional religion.

Religious Practitioners. This religion is clearly of the shamanic type, and the shaman is typically a woman. She receives a "call" and serves an apprenticeship. She has her own spirit helpers, paraphernalia, and chants, and most of her shamanic duties relate to the manipulation of spirits to cure illnesses. She sacrifices chickens and sometimes pigs. In community ritual she also serves as an entertainer, dancing and singing; she also admonishes people about proper behavior.

Ceremonies. While some of the ceremonies may take only a few minutes, most last four to six hours and some may go on for several days. They usually focus on the life cycle, agriculture, headhunting, and animal hunting. Most of the life-cycle ceremonies concentrate on the first few years of life. Various food taboos are observed, and their violation is thought to be the primary cause of illness, death, or other misfortunes.

Arts. Musical instruments include bamboo nose flutes and clappers, ancient bronze gongs traded from China, various stringed instruments that are strummed, and bamboo trumpets. The communitywide rituals include an enormous amount of dancing.

Medicine. Modern Western medical practitioners are rare, and the people rely mostly on traditional cures. The most common diseases are measles, bronchopneumonia, tuberculosis, goiter, and disorders of the skin, eyes, and intestines, especially diarrhea. Endemic goiter is related to iodine-deficient soils, which are common in mountainous areas. Cholera and malaria are now rare.

Death and Afterlife. Behavior on earth does not affect existence in the hereafter. A corpse is smoked, and a funeral may last for several days with the sacrifice of various livestock depending on the status and wealth of the household. The body has been buried in different ways, in a jar in the distant past, in a mausoleum in the recent past, and currently in the ground.

See also Bontok; Ifugao; Sagada Igorot

Bibliography

Bacdayan, Albert S. (1967). "The Peace Pact System of the Kalingas in the Modern World." Ph.D. Dissertation, Cornell University.

Barton, Roy F. (1949). *The Kalingas: Their Institutions and Custom Law.* Chicago: University of Chicago Press.

Billiet, Francisco, and Francis Lambrecht (1970). *The Kalinga Ullalim.* Baguio City: Catholic School Press.

Deraedt, Jules (1970). "Myth and Ritual: A Relational Study of Buwaya Mythology, Ritual, and Cosmology." Ph.D. Dissertation, University of Chicago.

Dozier, Edward P. (1966). *Mountain Arbiters: The Changing Life of a Philippine Hill People.* Tucson: University of Arizona Press.

Lawless, Robert (1977). *Societal Ecology in Northern Luzon: Kalinga Agriculture, Organization, Population, and Change.* Papers in Anthropology 18 (1). Norman: University of Oklahoma, Department of Anthropology.

Lawless, Robert (1987). "The Kalingas: People of the North Luzon Highlands." *World and I* 2(4): 476–489.

Magannon, Esteban T. (1972). *Religion in a Kalinga Village.* Quezon City: Community Development Research Council, University of the Philippines.

Takaki, Michiko (1977). "Aspects of Exchange in a Kalinga Society, Northern Luzon." Ph.D. dissertation, Yale University.

ROBERT LAWLESS

Kankanai

The Kankanai (Central Kankanaey, Igorot, Kakanay, Kankanaey, Kankanay, Southern Kankanai) are a group numbering around 110,000 in 1981 in northern Benguet Province, southwest Mountain Province, and southeast Ilocos Province, Luzon, the Philippines. Kankanai is classified in the Hesperonesian Group of the Austronesian Language Family. The Central Kankanai are closely related linguistically to the Lepanto, or Northern Kankanai, and are culturally similar to the Ibaloi. Kankanai settlements are generally scattered.

See also Bontok; Ibaloi; Sagada Igorot

Bibliography

LeBar, Frank M. (1975). "Kankanai." In *Ethnic Groups of Insular Southeast Asia*. Vol. 2, *Philippines and Formosa*, edited by Frank M. LeBar, 90–92. New Haven: HRAF Press.

Karen

ETHNONYMS: Kareang, Kariang, Kayin, Pwo, Sgaw, Yang

Orientation

Identification. Historically, the written Burmese term "Karen" probably came from the word "Kayin," referring to the particular group of peoples in eastern Myanmar (Burma) and western Thailand who speak closely related but different Sino-Tibetan languages. The Central Thai or Siamese word for Karen is "Kariang," presumably borrowed from the Mon term "Kareang." The Northern Thai or Yuan word "Yang," the origins of which may be Shan or from the root word *nyang* (person) in many Karen languages, is applied to the Karen by Shans and Thais. The designation "Karen" in fact includes several different subgroups, each with its own language and name. The largest, Sgaw and Pwo, have differences of dialect within their languages. The Sgaw or Skaw refer to themselves as "Pwakenyaw." The Pwo term for themselves is "Phlong" or "Kêphlong." The Burmese identify the Sgaw as "Bama Kayin" (Burmese Karen) and the Pwo as "Talaing Kayin" (Mon Karen). Thais sometimes use "Yang" to refer to the Sgaw and "Kariang" to refer to the Pwo, who live mainly south of the Sgaw. The word "Karen" was probably brought to Thailand from Burma by Christian missionaries. The term "White Karen" has been used to identify Christian Karen of the hill Sgaw. Other important subgroups include the Kayah and Pa-O. Prior to Burmese independence the Burmese term for the Kayah was "Kayin-ni," from which the English "Karen-ni" or "Red Karen" derived; Luce identifies them as "Eastern Bwe" or "Bghai." The Burmese term for the Pa-O is "Taungthu," adapted by the Shans as "Tong-su." Karennet (Kayin-net, or Black Karen) were listed in the 1911 census. Luce's classification of minor Karen languages listed in the 1931 census includes Paku; Western Bwe, consisting of Blimaw or Bre(k), and Geba; Padaung; Gek'o or Gheko; and Yinbaw (Yimbaw, Lakü Phu, or Lesser Padaung). Additional groups listed in the 1931 census are Monnepwa, Zayein, Taleing-Kalasi, Wewaw, and Mopwa. Scott's *Gazetteer* of 1900 lists the following: "Kekawngdu," the Padaung name for themselves; "Lakü," the self-name of the Bre; "Yintale" in Burmese, "Yangtalai" in Shan, for a branch of Eastern Karenni; the Sawng-tüng Karen, also known as "Gaung-to," "Zayein," or "Zalein"; Kawn-sawng; Mepu; Pa-hlaing; Loilong; Sinsin; Salon; Karathi; Lamung; Baw-han; and the Banyang or Banyok. These early sources are often inconsistent and lack adequate references for further research or clarification.

Recently anthropologists have remarked on the limitations of identifying the Karen primarily on the basis of language or name, noting that the complex and fluid Karen group identity is a cluster of traits that includes, among other things, language, political and social organization, religion, and material culture. Populations of Karen speakers may differ in these traits. Hinton and stresses economic and political interests as more significant to Karen identity than cultural features or "ethnic" distinctions. Some contemporary writings on the question of Karen identity place more importance on the belief of the Karen in the distinctiveness of their language as a cultural marker than they do on the objective linguistic distinctiveness of Karen languages. Other writings emphasize the contemporary Thai-Burmese political-economic context in which Karen ethnic identity is forged.

Location. Until the mid-eighteenth century the Karen lived mainly in the forested mountainous regions of eastern Burma, where the hills are divided by long narrow valleys running north to south from the Bilauktaung and Dawna ranges along the Salween River system to the broad high plateau of the Shan uplands. Today Karen reside in both Myanmar and Thailand, within the area between 10° and 21° N and between 94° and 101° E. Karen settlements are found in the hills along the border between the two countries along the length of Tenasserim into the Shan plateau from 10° N as far as 21° N. Most Karen inhabit Myanmar, in both lowland rice-growing plains and hill regions, with large numbers in the central Irrawaddy Delta, in the Irrawaddy and Sittang valleys from the coast to about 19° N, and in the northern part of Tenasserim. In Thailand most of the Karen settlements are along the hilly western border and range northward and eastward to the Mekong from approximately 12°00′ N to 20°30′ N. Karen villages are located in three distinct physical environments: the lowland plains of the Irrawaddy, Sittang, and Salween deltas and the coast of Tenasserim; the Pegu Yoma, a hilly range between the Irrawaddy and the Sittang; and the Shan upland, which varies geographically from a rolling high plateau (1,000 meters in elevation on average) in the Shan State to the north-south hills and narrow valleys of the Kayah and Karen states and interior Tenasserim to the south. These hill regions are covered with tropical rain forest that contains great varieties of vegetation, ranging from towering hardwoods to dense bamboo and vines that fires burn off during the hot dry season. The tropical-monsoon climate has two seasons, the monsoon from mid-May through September and the dry season from October through April. It is cold from November to February and becomes extremely hot in March and April, before the advent of the cooling monsoon rains. The precipitation range is from less than 200 centimeters annually in the southwestern Shan State to more than 254 centimeters in the central Irrawaddy Delta and more than 500 centimeters in Tenasserim.

Demography. Karen are the largest "tribal" minority in both Myanmar and Thailand. Although recent census figures for Myanmar are unavailable, their population there, projected from 1,350,000 in the 1931 census, is estimated at more than 3 million. Karen in Thailand number approximately 185,000, with about 150,000 Sgaw, 25,000 Pwo Karen, and much smaller populations of B'ghwe or Bwe (about 1,500) and Pa-O or Taungthu; together these groups comprise about 56 percent of the highland minority people of Thailand. Approximately one-third of the Karen population in Myanmar lives in the Karen State or administrative division. The Sgaw Karen, with a population of over 1 million, have settlements in the mountainous Karen State, in the Shan uplands, and to a lesser extent in the Irrawaddy and Sittang deltas. The Pwo Karen (approximately 750,000) inhabit primarily the Irrawaddy Delta. The Pa-O live mainly in southwestern Shan State. The approximately 75,000 Kayah, or Red Karen, live almost entirely in Kayah State, the smallest state in Myanmar. Political and economic circumstances have affected demographics. Since the early 1980s between 10,000 and 20,000 Karen from Burma have been living in refugee camps in Thailand. Outside Myanmar and Thailand, there is a growing community of Karen immigrants in Bakersfield, California.

Linguistic Affiliation. Despite the linguistic and numerical importance of the Karen, surpisingly few studies of Karen languages have been conducted in recent times. There continues to be controversy concerning the linguistic affiliation of the Karen group of languages, although it is widely accepted that within the Sino-Tibetan Stock all Karen linguistic subgroups are related to each other. Pwo and Pa-O form one subgroup, with Sgaw and several related languages forming another. Lehman and Hamilton cite André Haudricourt's view that Karen falls in the Tibeto-Burman classification. Benedict and Shafer both positione Karen as a distinct Sino-Tibetan Division, the Karenic. Luce and to some extent Jones, on the other hand, argue that Karen is linguistically related to Thai. The most generally accepted view is that the Karen languages are a divergent subfamily of the Tibeto-Burman Language Family. Matisoff notes the similarity in phonology and basic vocabulary of Karen dialects to Lolo-Burmese, the other major Tibeto-Burman Language Subgroup in Thailand with similar tone systems, the same paucity of final consonants, and a comparably rich set of vowels. He points out that syntactically Karen's atypical placement of the object after the verb may be the reason some linguists have set it apart genetically from the other Tibeto-Burman languages.

History and Cultural Relations

The early history of the Karen remains problematic, and there are various theories regarding their migrations. It appears that Karen peoples originated in the north, possibly in the high plains of Central Asia, and emigrated in stages through China into Southeast Asia, probably after the Mon but before the Burmese, Thai, and Shan reached what is now Myanmar and Thailand. Their slash-and-burn agricultural economy is an indication of their original adaptation to hill life. Eighth-century A.D. inscriptions mention the Cakraw in central Burma, who have been linked with the modern Sgaw. There is a thirteenth-century inscription near Pagan bearing the word "Karyan," which may refer to Karen. Seventeenth-century Thai sources mention the Kariang, but their identity is unclear. By the eighteenth century, Karen-speaking people were living primarily in the hills of the southern Shan states and in eastern Burma. They developed a system of relations with the neighboring Buddhist civilizations of the Shan, Burmese, and Mon, all of whom subjugated the Karen. European missionaries and travelers wrote of contact with Karen in the eighteenth century. During the turmoil among the Burman, Yuan, and Siamese kingdoms in the second half of the eighteenth century, the Karen, whose villages lay along the armies' routes, emerged as a significant group. Many Karen settled in the lowlands, and their increased contact with the dominant Burman and Siamese led to a sense of oppression at the hands of these powerful rulers. Groups of Karen made numerous mostly unsuccessful attempts to gain autonomy, either through millenarian syncretic religious movements or politically. The Red Karen, or Kayah, established three chieftainships that survived from the early nineteenth century to the end of British rule. In Thailand Karen lords ruled three small semifeudal domains from the mid-nineteenth century until about 1910. British and American Christian missionaries arrived in Burma after the British annexation of lower Burma in 1826. The Karen, many of whom had converted to Christianity, had a distinctive though ambiguous relationship with the British, based on shared religious and political interests; prior to World War II they were given special representation in the Burmese Legislative Assembly. Christian missionary activity may have been the most important factor in the emergence of Karen nationalism, through the development of schools, a Karen literate tradition, and ultimately an educated Karen elite whose members rose in the ranks of the British colonial service. In 1928 the Karen leader, Dr. Sir San C. Po, argued for an autonomous Karen state within a federation. During the war, the Karen remained loyal to the British after the Japanese occupation; there was increased antipathy between the Karen and Burmans, who were backed by the Japanese. After the war, the British prepared for Burma's independence. The Karen National Union (KNU) promoted Karen autonomy, but after Aung San's assassination in 1947 hopes for an independent Karen state were shattered. Since Burmese independence in 1948, the Karen relationship with Burma has been primarily political. The old Karen-ni states formed Kayah State, and in 1952 the Burmese government established Karen State with Pa-an as its capital. During the 1964 peace negotiations, the name was changed to the traditional Kawthoolei, but under the 1974 constitution the official name reverted to Karen State. Many Karen, especially those in the lowland deltas, have assimilated into Burmese Buddhist society. In the hill regions many resist Burmese influence and some support, directly or tacitly, the insurgent KNU movement, which has been at war since 1949, in its efforts to achieve independence from Burmese rule. It is currently in a coalition with other ethnic groups and Aung San Suu Kyi's party, the National League for Democracy, which supports the formation of a union of federal states. The Kawthoolei (the name for the KNU territory) government has the difficult task of interacting with the Karen revolutionary military hierarchy and with the heterogeneous Karen population, which consists of both nonhierarchical traditional hill Karen and more educated delta Christian Karen who have joined them. Movement back and forth across the Thai-Myanmar border continues as Karen villagers cross to cut swiddens and Karen political refugees arrive in increasing numbers in Thailand's Mae Hon Son Province. In Thailand the Karen are facing assimilation into Thai society through mass education, the economic necessity of engaging in wage labor for Thai employers, and the assimilation of highland Karen into a generalized "hill tribe" category generated by Thai and foreign tourists.

Settlements

Contemporary Karen settlement patterns vary considerably as a result of geographical diversity and cultural contact. Research in the past twenty years has focused on Thai Karen; no comparable research has been done in Burma. Traditional Karen villages, compact and stockaded, consist of houses and granaries. Population figures for Thai highland Karen indicate an average of twenty-three houses in a village (Kunstadter 1983), a figure similar to those reported in the 1920s by Marshall for Karen hill villages in Burma. In upland and lowland Pwo Karen villages matrilineal kin arrange their houses together; this practice may derive from the traditional Karen longhouse. Stern (1979) includes David Richardson's description of Karen villages on the upper Khwae Noi in 1839–1840 containing three to six longhouses, each holding several families with a separate ladder for each. Sgaw Karen village names often reflect their pattern of settlement in valleys at the headwaters of streams. The history of Karen settlement indicates the importance of the village as a community, as village sites are frequently moved but continue to retain their name and identity.

The predominant village unit is the house, usually inhabited by five to seven family members. Anderson and Marshall in the 1920s described villages in which longhouses were characteristic (and in some cases the only structure), accommodating twenty to thirty families. Both longhouses and separate houses in the hill villages are made from bamboo, sometimes in combination with wood timbers; they have thatched roofs and require reconstruction in a new location every few years. Houses in upland valleys are generally more substantial, made of wooden posts with plank floors and walls, although bamboo is often used. Today roofs of teak leaf or grass thatch, which must be rethatched annually, are being replaced by corrugated iron sheets by those who can afford them in both hill and valley villages. In the plains Karen villages of Myanmar, the housing follows lowland-Burmese style. Traditionally and still today, most Karen houses in Myanmar and Thailand are raised above the ground with the multiple purposes of protection from floods or wild animals and shelter for domestic animals.

Economy

Subsistence and Commercial Activities. Traditionally hill Karen were subsistence cultivators practicing swidden agriculture. Today, their economy is mainly subsistence-oriented, requiring two sectors to produce enough food for survival: an agricultural sector based on swiddening and wet-rice cultivation, and a cash or market economy. Most hill Karen have taken up wet-rice agriculture only within the past generation, and the annual ritual cycle is still associated with the longer swidden rice-growth cycle. Swidden rice fields are generally burned and planted at the beginning of the wet season (March–April); rice is harvested in October, threshed in November, and stored in granaries. Swidden cultivators may harvest tea and cultivate maize, legumes, yams, sweet potatoes, peppers, chilies, and cotton. Tobacco, betel leaves and nuts, and fruits including bananas, durians, and mangoes are grown in the valley bottomlands. Plains and valley Karen are wet-rice agriculturalists who follow the same cycle as the Burmese and Mon. Village Karen of all ages participate in hunting and gathering. Hill Karen males still hunt for subsistence, pursuing birds, squirrels, lizards, deer, and wild pigs. They use crossbows, slingshots, snares, traps, and guns. Gathering, a more important food supplement than hunting, is done also for trade; women and children may collect roots, leaves, bamboo shoots, herbs and bark for medicinal purposes, wild fruits, frogs, small lizards, insects, paddy crabs, ant larvae, honey, beeswax, mushrooms, firewood, weeds for pig food, stick lac, and snakes. Both plains and hill Karen fish for consumption or trade. Plains Karen follow Burmese techniques. Hill and valley Karen techniques include pond fishing, bamboo poles with lines and hooks, throw nets with lead weights made by male villagers, bamboo fish traps, surrounds using jute rope, and paddy fishing with baskets.

Hill Karen generally keep water buffalo, oxen, pigs, chickens, and dogs. Water buffalo are used in wet-rice production, and oxen for pulling carts. Some buffalo and oxen are raised to be sold for profit. Traditionally pigs were used in ceremonies such as weddings, funerals, and lineage rituals. Although pigs are still used for these purposes today, in the Thai hills they are more often raised for sale to the Thais. Christian Karen raise pigs for their own consumption or for trade. Chickens are also used ceremonially, and chickens and eggs are sold at market. Cattle are usually corralled, whereas pigs and chickens are allowed to forage by day and sleep at the household by night. Buddhist plains Karen keep cattle and buffalo. Karen occasionally trap elephants in the wild and are noted as elephant handlers; most mahouts in Myanmar and Thailand are Karen.

Industrial Arts. Weaving, almost exclusively the domain of women, is done in both plains and hill Karen households, but it is more important in the hills. Hill Karen use only the traditional belt loom, whereas plains Karen use either the belt loom or the Burmese fixed-frame loom. In the past, cotton was ginned, whipped, spun on a wheel, dyed, and woven at home. At present some hill Karen still grow and spin their own cotton thread, but much of the thread is bought in local markets. Dye, which was derived from plants or minerals, is now often purchased, bringing new variations in the traditional colors. Articles including clothing, blankets, and highly prized shoulder bags are woven in the traditional Karen symbolic and decorative patterns unique to each subgroup, for household use and for markets as far away as Chiengmai and Toungoo. Bamboo baskets and mats are made by highland women for household use or for sale. Men make most of the tools and implements for agriculture, fishing, hunting, and construction. The machete is the most common tool.

Trade. The cash or market sectors of Karen subsistence economies are important but vary greatly. Traditionally Karen have traded cotton cloth, forest products, game, and domestic animals to Burmese and Mon in exchange for rice, pottery, salt, and fish paste. Hill Karen carry on trade in Burmese, Shan, and Thai markets, whereas lowland Karen are tied into the Burmese economy. The hill Karen studied by Hinton (1975) were engaged in raising livestock and selling them to the Northern Thai, wage labor in the city, renting out elephants to timber contractors, and sale of forest products. Hamilton, Kunstadter, and Rajah described hill Karen participation in lowland wage-labor, trade, and cash-market economies as consisting of the picking and selling of tea and the sale of livestock, forest products, household-manufactured tools, and woven goods. Tourism has become a significant source of income for Thai hill Karen.

Division of Labor. Women gather foods, medicinal plants and herbs and firewood, and engage in paddy fishing; they raise pigs and chickens, carry water, prepare rice for cooking, prepare alcoholic drinks, raise cotton, spin, and weave. Men hunt, tend the buffalo and oxen, plow, build houses, cut timber, and make mats and baskets. Fishing, sowing, reaping, threshing, winnowing, and some cooking are done by both men and women.

Land Tenure. Land use and rights to swiddens vary depending on local politics, ecological stability, and population demands on resources. Usufructuary rights to swiddens and fallow swiddens are common. Traditionally each village had its accepted farming areas in which community members were free to use what they needed as long as they selected plots within swiddens designated by the village chief and elders. Today the need to remain on a site permanently in order to own the paddy fields for wet-rice cultivation has forced many hill Karen, particularly in Thailand, to give up swiddening or to overwork and thus lower the productivity of nearby swidden fields.

Kinship

Kin Groups and Descent. There is much scholarly controversy regarding the Karen kinship system, which is probably best characterized as a cognatic or bilateral system with matrilineal descent. Marshall described a group of matrilineally related persons participating in certain rituals for their ancestral spirit. The leader was the oldest living female of the line. Iijima, Hamilton, and others have observed these ancestral rituals taking place among both Sgaw and Pwo Karen matrilineages.

Kinship Terminology. Hamilton notes that the Karen bilateral system of filiation does not result in a descent group, but a set of statuses for structuring relationships. Matrilineal descent, on the other hand, indicates a person's genealogical connection to his or her mother's relatives. A Karen man and woman who are directly related to each other through a pair of sisters, for example, should not marry because they are members of the same matrilineage, although if there is even one male in the descent chain they may marry. Karen kinship terminology is overall quite similar among subgroups. A person equates his or her father's brother with his or her mother's brother. For grandparents and great-grandparents, male collaterals (maternal or paternal) of the same generation are equated, as are females. There are separate terms for generations, equating all children in each generation. Ego calls siblings only by birth-order terms, and may add a suffix to denote gender. The Sgaw term _dau'pywae_ (_dang phu vwi_ in Pwo) refers to the sibling set. Ego equates all cousins, but may add one of two suffixes to distinguish lineage members from nonmembers. People distinguish their own children from their brothers' children and their sisters' children, whom they equate with the children of their cousins. Birth order is important, but is usually used only in the first ascending and descending generation.

Marriage and Family

Marriage. A Karen may marry anyone who is not closely related (i.e., anyone except siblings, first cousins, and lineage mates). Among Pwo and Sgaw Karen there are proscriptions against certain matrilineal and intergenerational marriages. Patrilateral parallel second cousins may marry, but matrilateral parallel cousins of any degree may not because the latter are of the same lineage or of the same female spirit. Marriage is monogamous. Courting takes place on social occasions such as weddings, funerals, and communal planting and harvesting. Proposals, which require parental approval, are made by the young man or woman, although a go-between is often used. Premarital sex is prohibited, and 15 to 20 percent of bridegrooms pay a fine for having broken the rule. The marriage ceremony involves rituals to the Lord of Land and Water (see under "Religion and Expressive Culture") marking the union of the new couple and the husband's incorporation into the bride's parents' household. The ritual and wedding feast in the bride's village can last three days. After marriage the bride gives up her long white dress for the black embroidered blouse and red-and-black tubular sarong of married women; men continue to wear the traditional red fringed shirt.

Residence is usually matrilocal. Up to 30 percent of Karen marriages are village-exogamous. The groom moves to the house of the bride's father and eventually may establish a new household in that village. Postmarital residence depends as much on availability of agricultural land resources as on ideal uxorilocal pattern, binding villages in an interdependent net of relationships.

Domestic Unit. The normal domestic unit is the nuclear family, made up of husband, wife, and unmarried children. In the hills each nuclear family traditionally occupied either an apartment in a longhouse or a separate house in the village.

Inheritance. Property is generally divided into three shares, with equal parts going to the eldest (_a' vwi shiae_ in Pwo Karen) and youngest children (_a' oe dae_) and slightly smaller shares to middle children (_a' oa 'klae_). Inheritance takes place ideally before the death of the parents, to avoid disputes and the bad luck brought by personal property containing the dead person's _k'la_ (_kala_), or spirit. The youngest child, preferably a girl, cares for the parents until their deaths and controls their property. Widows retain control of their property until remarriage.

Divorce is discouraged and rarely occurs: 5 to 6 percent of marriages in the Thai hills, and about double that in lowlands and towns, end in divorce. Divorce may be initiated by either partner and is granted upon payment of compensation to the divorced party. The wife keeps the house and the children; other property is divided equally, except for any paddy land that was previously owned by one of the partners.

Socialization.   There has been little research on traditional Karen childbirth and socialization practices. Karen women fear complications in childbirth, knowing this to be a common cause of death. There are dietary restrictions and other taboos that pregnant women must observe. To ease the birth, midwives cast magical spells and conduct ceremonies to placate spirits. Traditionally a mother sits by the fire for three days after the birth of her child; during this period rituals are held and amulets are used to protect and purify both mother and child. There is a naming ceremony when the child is one month old. Children are taught to emulate the same-sex parent. Young girls and boys both carry water, collect firewood, and care for younger siblings; both transplant rice in paddy fields, although boys do so less frequently than do girls. By puberty children do only the work that is appropriate to their gender. Education for Karen in Burma was formalized in missionary schools, which devised a Karen script based on Burmese and also taught English and Burmese. The Burmese and Thai governments have promoted the establishment of government schools in tribal villages or towns, to which Karen children are sent to live. The Karen National Union runs its own school system in Kawthoolei, where they teach English and Karen.

Sociopolitical Organization

Social Organization.   Traditional Karen social organization is based on the residential units of the household, the lineage segment, the village, and the village complex. Several nuclear households are linked together through matrilineal descent and matrilocal residence to form a lineage segment. The village structure forms around one or more lineage segments linked by marriage and/or descent. The village may split, with one or more segments separating to form daughter villages, resulting in a village complex that shares kin and spirit connections. Several more or less related village complexes make up a local subgroup. Each of the four residential units, the household, the lineage segment, the village, and the village complex, performs specific ritual, social, political, or economic functions. Nonresidential matrilineages may crosscut an area. Lineage rites (*oxe chuko* in Sgaw; *oxe pgo* in Pwo) require the presence of all descendants of the matrilineal group (*dopuweh*) regardless of which village they live in; attachment is to the line, not to the locality. Karen society is generally undifferentiated and unstratified, although status is accorded to wealth and age. Wealth is counted in livestock and rice, with elephant owners enjoying the highest status. The young are expected to defer always to elders in the family and to members of the village council of elders, as well as in intervillage and lineage-segment relationships. Karen ethnic identity, despite geographic and ecological diversity, social and cultural differentiation, a large gap between the illiterate and the well-educated elite, and a variety of religions ranging from traditional animism to Buddhism, Protestantism, and Catholicism, seems to maintain itself in the context of dominant social groups.

Political Organization.   The village is the most important political unit. It is headed by a chief or headman (*dang khaw* in Pwo) and a council of elders. Chieftainship is hereditary in the male lineal or collateral line. Traditionally the chief had both secular and religious functions, and his authority rested as much on his personal influence as it did on his institutional role. As the spiritual link to the village spirits, he is vested with the power to act on behalf of the village. Kunstadter (1979) has noted the contrast in authority structure between inherently unstable Thai Karen hill villages and long-established, relatively stable valley villages. In the hills, the ambiguity of the inheritance principle by which authority can be established when there is no clear heir has led to frequent fission of villages. The subsequent rapid dispersal of the Karen population has helped them succeed in their demographic and geographic competition with other highland peoples. In contrast to the autonomy and egalitarian political structure at the traditional village level, Karen have lived for generations under the authority of other peoples: Mon, Shan, Siamese/Thai, Burmese, and British. The institution of the elected or appointed headman, separate from the traditional chief, has been imposed by British, Burmese, Thai, and now Kawthoolei authorities to deal by consensus with the bureaucracies of national or colonial governments. The Free Karen State of Kawthoolei is democratic, with an electoral system consisting of village, township, district, and national representatives.

Social Control.   Traditionally any disputes were solved through the village headman and council of elders. As both spiritual and political leader, the village headman might deal with behavioral problems through social sanctions and/or spirit propitiation. For example, there are strong sanctions against adultery, which is seen as an affront to the Lord of Land and Water; he must be assuaged by ritual sacrifice by the guilty parties, and possibly even their banishment, to avert a natural disaster striking the community. Today traditional village authority exists in the contexts of Thai, Burmese, and Kawthoolei authority, each with its own political and administrative structures to which villagers must respond regarding criminal complaints, taxation, the recording of marriages, births, and deaths, and so on.

Conflict.   Historically intervillage raids and Karen slave raids into Shan territory were common prior to British intervention. Weapons included spears, swords, guns, and shields. Today the primary conflict, which affects both sides of the Thai-Myanmar border, is the ongoing war between the Burmese military and the Karen National Union.

Religion and Expressive Culture

Religious Beliefs.   Indigenous Karen religion is animistic, rooted both in nature and in the ancestral matrilineage. It is based on belief in cosmogonic deities and several important supernatural powers, which are propitiated by specific rituals and ceremonies. This indigenous religious system includes the concepts of k'la (*kala*), or life principle, which is possessed by humans, animals, and some inanimate objects, and *pgho*, an impersonal power. Many Karen in the plains of Burma and in the highlands of Thailand embraced Buddhism through contact with Burman, Mon, Shan, and Thai Buddhists. In 1828 Ko Tha Byu became the first Karen to be converted by Christian missionaries, beginning conversions on a scale unprecedented in Southeast Asia. This is often explained by the striking parallels between Karen cosmogonic myths and the Old Testament. By 1919, 335,000, or 17 percent of Karen in Burma, had become Christian. In some areas Karen religion was syncretic, incorporating Buddhism and/or Christianity into indigenous religious practices. This sometimes took the form of a millennarian cult with a powerful leader and with elements of Karen nationalism envisioning a new order on Earth in which the Karen would be powerful. The data in Thailand indicate that of Pwo Karen, 37.2 percent are animist, 61.1 percent Buddhist, and 1.7 percent Christian; of Sgaw Karen, 42.9 percent are animist, 38.4 percent Buddhist, and 18.3 percent Christian (1977). Although current figures are unavailable for Myanmar, it is estimated that most Pwo and Pa-O Karen practice Buddhism and animism, that many Sgaw Karen are now Christians, mainly Baptist, and that most Kayah are Catholic.

The Karen cosmogonic myth tells of Y'wa, a divine power who created nature, including the first man and woman, and of Mü Kaw li, the basically feminine deity, who in serpent form teaches them their culture, including rice production, the identity of the ancestral spirit (*bgha; ther myng khwae* in Pwo), rites of propitiation of various spirits, and methods for securing k'la. Y'wa gives the Karen a book, the gift of literacy, which they lose; they await its future return in the hands of younger white brothers. The American Baptist missionaries interpreted the myth as referring to the biblical Garden of Eden. They saw Y'wa as the Hebrew Yahweh and Mü Kaw li as Satan, and offered the Christian Bible as the lost book. Bgha, associated mainly with a particular matrilineal ancestor cult, is perhaps the most important supernatural power. The other significant supernatural power, called the "Lord of Land and Water" or "Spirit of the Area" (Thi Kho Chae Kang Kho Chae), protects the well-being of the people in the village with which he is associated. There are also local deities associated with elements of nature such as trees and rivers, or with agriculture (e.g., the rice goddess).

Religious Practitioners. The two major traditional religious practitioners are the village headman, who is the ritual specialist who leads the ceremony to the Lord of Land and Water, and the eldest woman of the senior line of the matrilineage, who officiates at the sacrificial feast for the ancestral spirit, bgha. There are people endowed with pgho, the impersonal supernatural power, including prophets (*wi*) and medicine teachers (*k'thi thra*); some Karen possessing pgho became leaders in syncretic millennial religious movements. There are also witches or "false prophets" (*wi a'bla*) who put their power to evil purposes.

Ceremonies. The most significant traditional ceremony is probably the propitiation of the bgha by all the matrilineally related kin, led by the eldest and most senior woman. A sacrificial feast is held at least annually to prevent the bgha from consuming the k'la of kin-group members. Iijima suggests this collective ritual expresses the essence of traditional Karen identity. Rites of sacrifice to the local Lord of Land and Water, held each year for territorial protection, are officiated over by the village headman. In addition, agricultural and lifecycle rituals are conducted, local spirits are supplicated with offerings or minor ceremonies, and k'la is secured by ordinary people or specialists.

Arts. Weaving (discussed above), with embroidery and seed work embellishing many woven garments, is the most notable Karen art. Karen make jewelry from silver, copper, and brass; ornaments of wool or other materials; beads; rattan or lacquered-thread bracelets; and traditionally earplugs of ivory or silver studded with gems. In the Thai hills, males are still tattooed for adornment. Music, both vocal and instrumental, is performed with nearly all traditional religious rituals, and Karen ballads and love songs are sung on many occasions. Karen ceremonial bronze drums, crafted by Shan artisans, are treasured as ritual objects by Karen householders—as well as by art collectors in Bangkok and abroad. Karen Christians have developed music that combines traditional Karen, church, and Western popular music.

Medicine. The causes of illness and death are traditionally spiritual. Marlowe notes that for Sgaw Karen, illness is the system through which the spirits of places (*da muxha*) and spirits of the ancestors (*sii kho muu xha*) signal their displeasure or their desire to be fed. K'la can become detached from human bodies during vulnerable times such as sleep or contact with the k'la of a person who has died, and must be ritually secured to the body to avoid illness or even death. Divination using chicken bones, feathers, eggs, or grains of rice is often employed to find the spiritual origin of a disease. In the case of k'la or soul loss, a shaman may be summoned to perform a soul-calling ceremony. There are rites of propitiation for various nature and ancestor spirits that cause illnesses. Karen also use herbal and animal-derived medicines.

Death and Afterlife. Karen have two categories of death: "natural" death resulting from old age and certain diseases, and "violent" death resulting from accidents, magic, attacks by spirits, childbirth, and murder. Some non-Christian Karen believe in an afterlife in a place of the dead, which has higher and lower realms ruled over by Lord Khu See-du. The k'la leaves the body at death; eventually it will be reincarnated in a proper body but, as a ghost, it can possess the body of another person. In traditional villages family and friends gather to sing eulogies and make music (today this may take the form of amplified pop music) to send off the newly liberated spirit and ensure that it does not remain in the place of the living, thus bringing bad luck. The dead person's possessions, which emanate the owner's k'la, may be removed from the village. The dead body is washed, dressed in the finest clothing, and buried in a coffin or mat. On their return from the burial ground villagers erect obstacles to prevent the k'la of the deceased from following. Animist and Buddhist funerals may be extensive rites involving the slaughter of many animals, whereas Christian funerals are much simpler.

Bibliography

Benedict, Paul (1972). *Sino-Tibetan: A Conspectus.* Cambridge: Cambridge University Press.

Bradley, David (1983). "Identity: The Persistence of Minority Groups." In *Highlanders of Thailand*, edited by John McKinnon and Wanat Bhruksasri, 46–55. Kuala Lumpur: Oxford University Press.

Burling, Robbins (1969). "Proto-Karen: A Reanalysis." *Occasional Papers of the Wolfenden Society in Tibeto-Burman Linguistics*, no. 1:1–116. Ann Arbor, Mich.

Falla, Jonathan (1991). *True Love and Batholomew: Rebels on the Burmese Border*. Cambridge: Cambridge University Press.

Hamilton, James W. (1976). *Pwo Karen: At the Edge of Mountain and Plain*. American Ethnological Society Monographs, no. 60. St. Paul, Minn.: West Publishing.

Hinton, Peter (1979). "The Karen, Millennialism, and the Politics of Accommodation to Lowland States." In *Ethnic Adaptation and Identity: The Karen on the Thai Frontier with Burma*, edited by Charles F. Keyes, 81–98. Philadelphia: Institute for the Study of Human Issues.

Hinton, Peter (1983). "Do the Karen Really Exist?" In *Highlanders of Thailand*, edited by John McKinnon and Wanat Bhruksasri, 155–168. Kuala Lumpur: Oxford University Press.

Iijima, Shigeru (1979). "Ethnic Identity and Sociocultural Change among Sgaw Karen in Northern Thailand." In *Ethnic Adaptation and Identity: The Karen on the Thai Frontier with Burma*, edited by Charles F. Keyes, 99–118. Philadelphia: Institute for the Study of Human Issues.

Jones, Robert B. (1961). *Karen Linguistic Studies: Description, Comparison, and Texts*. University of California Publications in Linguistics, vol. 25. Berkeley and Los Angeles.

Keyes, Charles F. (1977). *The Golden Peninsula: Culture and Adaptation in Mainland Southeast Asia*. New York: Macmillan.

Keyes, Charles F. (1979). "The Karen in Thai History and the History of the Karen in Thailand." In *Ethnic Adaptation and Identity: The Karen on the Thai Frontier with Burma*, edited by Charles F. Keyes, 25–62. Philadelphia: Institute for the Study of Human Issues.

Klein, Harold (1991). "The Karens of Burma: Their Search for Freedom and Justice." Manuscript.

Kunstadter, Peter (1979). "Ethnic Group, Category, and Identity: Karen in Northern Thailand." In *Ethnic Adaptation and Identity: The Karen on the Thai Frontier with Burma*, edited by Charles F. Keyes, 119–164. Philadelphia: Institute for the Study of Human Issues.

Kunstadter, Peter (1983). "Highland Populations in Northern Thailand." In *Highlanders of Thailand*, edited by John McKinnon and Wanat Bhruksasri, 15–45. Kuala Lumpur: Oxford University Press.

Lehman, F. K. (1979). "Who Are the Karen, and If So, Why? Karen Ethnohistory and a Formal Theory of Ethnicity." In *Ethnic Adaptation and Identity: The Karen on the Thai Frontier with Burma*, edited by Charles F. Keyes, 215–253. Philadelphia: Institute for the Study of Human Issues.

Lewis, Paul, and Elaine Lewis (1984). *Peoples of the Golden Triangle*. London: Thames & Hudson.

Luce, Gordon H. (1959). "Introduction to the Comparative Study of Karen Languages." *Journal of the Burma Research Society* 42(1): 1–18.

Luce, Gordon H. (1959). "Old Kyaukse and the Coming of the Burmans." *Journal of the Burma Research Society* 42(1): 73–109.

Marlowe, David (1979). "In the Mosaic: The Cognitive and Structural Aspects of Karen-Other Relationships." In *Ethnic Adaptation and Identity: The Karen on the Thai Frontier with Burma*, edited by Charles F. Keyes, 165–214. Philadelphia: Institute for the Study of Human Issues.

Marshall, Harry Ignatius (1922). "The Karen People of Burma: A Study in Anthropology and Ethnology." *Ohio State University Bulletin* 26(13).

Matisoff, James (1983). "Linguistic Diversity and Language Contact." In *Highlanders of Thailand*, edited by John McKinnon and Wanat Bhruksasri, 56–86. Kuala Lumpur: Oxford University Press.

Po, San C. (1928). *Burma and the Karens*. London: Elliot Stock.

Rajah, Ananda (1986). "Remaining Karen." Ph.D. dissertation, Australian National University.

Scott, J. George, and J. P. Hardiman (1900). *Gazetteer of Upper Burma and the Shan States*. Pt. 1, vols. 1–2. Rangoon: Government Printing.

Shafer, Robert (1955). "Classification of the Sino-Tibetan Languages." *Word* 11:94–111.

Stern, Theodore (1979). "A People Between: The Pwo Karen of Western Thailand." In *Ethnic Adaptation and Identity: The Karen on the Thai Frontier with Burma*, edited by Charles F. Keyes, 63–80. Philadelphia: Institute for the Study of Human Issues.

NANCY POLLOCK KHIN

Kasseng

The Kasseng (Kaseng) are a group of about 6,000 (1981) swidden rice cultivators located in the Boloven plateau region of southern Laos.

Bibliography
Hoffet, J. (1933). "Les Moïs de la chaîne annamitique." *Terre, Air, Mer: La Géographie* 59:1–43.

Kattang

The Kattang (Katang) are a group of about 10,000 (1981) swidden rice cultivators and wet-rice agriculturalists in the Muong Nong area of southern Laos.

Bibliography

Hoffet, J. (1933). "Les Moïs de la chaîne annamitique." _Terre, Air, Mer: La Géographie_ 59:1–43.

Katu

The Katu (Cò Tu, Kato, Ka-Tu) are a group of swidden rice, maize, and cassava cultivators located primarily along the Laos-Vietnam border in central Vietnam. The 1985 census of Vietnam enumerated 36,967 Katu. Katu means "savage" and is a term of reference used by outsiders. The Katu name themselves after specific villages where they live.

Kédang

ETHNONYM: Édang

Orientation

Identification. The Kédang speak "the language of the mountain" (_tutuq-nanang wéla_), as opposed to the Lamaholot of their neighbors on the small eastern Indonesian island of Lembata. Most are Roman Catholic, many are Muslim, and a few retain the traditional religion.

Location. Kédang lies between 8°10′ and 8°20′ S between 123°35′ and 124° E, at the east end of the island of Lembata (known on most maps as Lomblen) in the Indonesian province of Nusa Tenggara Timur.

Linguistic Affiliation. The language belongs to the Central Malayo-Polynesian Subgrouping of Austronesian.

Demography. According to the 1980 census there were 28,677 persons living in Kédang. The average population density was 108 persons per square kilometer. There were 81 males per 100 females, compared with 99.6 for the province as a whole. This low figure results in part from out-migration of men seeking employment elsewhere. The ratio among the age group 15 to 24 years, for example, is 53 males per 100 females.

History and Cultural Relations

Little is known of the history of Kédang prior to the closing decades of the nineteenth century. In the 1870s, with Dutch military assistance, the raja of the neighboring island of Adonara secured political control over Kédang. The Dutch did not themselves enter the area in force until 1910, when they disarmed and registered the population of the entire island. From that time on Kédang history was submerged in that of the Dutch East Indies and the Republic of Indonesia. Catholic missionaries began working there in the 1920s, but Islamic conversions kept pace with those of the Catholics.

Culturally, as well as linguistically, the people of Kédang are closely allied with their neighbors to the west, the Lamaholot, with whom they share features of social structure and religious ideas. There are also similarities with speakers of Bahasa Alor on the islands of Pantar and Alor to the east. Bahasa Alor may be regarded as a dialect of Lamaholot. They are not culturally or linguistically related to the more numerous populations of Alor and Pantar who speak non-Austronesian languages.

Settlements

Villages of a few hundred persons, made up of named hamlets, have been reorganized by the Indonesian government into "administrative" villages of 1,000 to 2,000 inhabitants, sometimes consolidating two or more older villages. Village government consists of an elected head, treasurer, and secretary. During the wet monsoon, when there is much continuous work on the fields, many people spend extended periods living in field huts several miles away from their villages. The traditional house is a simple bamboo structure, with a grass- or palm-leaf-covered roof supported on house posts. These buildings are carefully oriented according to traditional religious ideas and the Kédang conception of space. Increasingly, with encouragement from the government and the Catholic mission, brick houses with corrugated iron roofs are being erected.

Economy

Subsistence and Commercial Activities. Most of the population depends on subsistence swidden agriculture, although in recent years mining has provided some local employment. The staple crop is maize, supplemented by dry rice, tubers, vegetables, and spices. Cotton is grown for local use. Palms are exploited for innumerable purposes, including the provision of food and building materials. Copra, tamarind, and candlenuts are sold to dealers to raise cash for various purposes, including payment of taxes. A small amount of coastal fishing takes place. Among domestic animals are pigs, chickens, goats, and dogs. Schoolteachers earn wages.

Industrial Arts. Traditionally Kédang women were prohibited from weaving, although today many do weave cloth for everyday wear. They must never, however, weave in the ritually important ancient village centers. The Kédang proper lack the skills of pot making, smithing, weaving, and dyeing of fine _ikat_ cloths, although local residents deriving from neighboring groups do provide these goods and services to a limited extent.

Trade. Some coastal peoples engage in petty trading. There are weekly local markets where inexpensive commodities and produce may be purchased for cash. Young men increasingly travel from Kédang seeking employment as far away as Malaysia. Small stores, mostly in Chinese hands, are found in a few of the larger villages.

Division of Labor. Men fish, hunt, and carry out the extended negotiations attendant on marriage and the giving of marriage gifts. A very few women also hunt. Cooking, except at feasts, is primarily a task for girls and women. Both sexes clear, plant, weed, and harvest fields.

Land Tenure. Originally, rights in land were vested collectively in the village, represented by the descent group that was regarded as "lords of the land," usually thought to be the first or oldest existing inhabitants. Permission to use the land was obtained from them successively by other descent groups. Individual rights of usage were established by clearing and maintaining fields. Since World War II, the government has overseen the opening of fields in areas previously made uninhabitable by warfare and piracy and has encouraged a shift toward private, individual conceptions of property.

Kinship

Kin Groups and Descent. Each village or hamlet includes a number of named patrilineal clans, linked to one another by a series of asymmetric marriage alliances.

Kinship Terminology. The relationship system is ordered by the rule of patrilineal descent and the prescription to marry a man or woman in the category of *mahan*, which includes the mother's brother's daughter and the father's sister's son, both cross cousins.

Marriage and Family

Marriage. Most marriages now involve at least one person who is Catholic or Muslim, and the formal ceremony of that religion is followed. Formerly there was no wedding ceremony, although marriage entailed and still entails an elaborate series of exchanges over a period that may exceed the lifetimes of the husband and wife. These exchanges correspond in pattern to prescribed asymmetric marriage alliance. This rule gets its clearest expression in social classification, ritual, and behavior of the linked families rather than in the overall configuration of actual marriages. The Kédang distinguish wife-giving allies from wife-taking allies. The former are superior to the latter. The mother's close male relatives exercise control over the health and well-being of her children and are regarded by them as divine. Alliance gifts are typically gongs and elephant tusks for the wife givers and fine *ikat* (tiedyed) cloths returned to the wife takers. Polygyny is permitted to non-Catholics and has a small but regular incidence. Divorce occurs with some regularity among non-Catholics. It is expected that a newly married couple will reside with the wife's parents for a few months to a year. Thereafter the couple establishes an independent household. When the man and woman come from different villages, they usually settle near the husband's patrilineal kin, but there are many exceptions.

Domestic Unit. Households generally consist of husband, wife and children, plus, at various stages, elderly parents, daughters' husbands, and occasionally grandchildren. Naturally, demographic happenstance varies the pattern.

Inheritance. Wealth objects, buildings, and alliance obligations pass down through the male line.

Socialization. Children are cared for both by parents and by other relatives, and are rarely subjected to physical punishment. Parents observe restrictions regarding their movements, use of water, and cutting of hair following a child's birth. There are no rites of passage (except those of Islam and Catholicism) associated with maturation and aging from the ending of this period of restriction until youth and early adulthood, when the teeth sometimes are filed and blackened. Teeth blackening is now disappearing. Age is characteristically associated with authority. An elder must be shown respect. Elders within the clan supervise its affairs. Those in the mother's clan have an authority colored by their lifegiving attributes and spiritual influence.

Sociopolitical Organization

Social Organization. Class lines are blurred in Kédang. In the past, Kédang may well have been a source of slaves, but little information is available on the subject. Until recently, certain families of the village Kalikur could have been described as a nobility of sorts.

Political Organization. The present government of the Republic of Indonesia has virtually eliminated grass-roots political activity in rural villages outside the confines of its political organization, GOLKAR. Historically, clans of the village of Kalikur had political and military ascendancy at certain periods over the rest of Kédang, and this was given formal recognition under the Dutch in the appointment of the *rian-barat* ("great and heavy"), a sort of subraja. Today Kédang is divided into the two districts (*kecamatan*) Omesuri and Bujasuri, and is included in the Regency of Flores Timur.

Religion and Expressive Culture

Religious Beliefs. The 1980 census indicates that 52 percent of the population was Muslim and 48 percent Roman Catholic, but these numbers deliberately disguised the portion who have converted to neither religion. In 1970, according to local records, 45 percent of the population was Muslim, 28 percent Catholic, and 27 percent retained the traditional religion. These numbers do not, of course, give any idea as to the nature and degree of individual religious commitment. The increase between 1970 and 1980 of avowed Catholics is, however, in keeping with the direction of change in the regency as a whole. Even Muslims and Catholics sometimes participate in traditional rituals, and some villages have revived communal rituals that had once lapsed because of noncooperation by adherents of Islam and Christianity. As in other eastern Indonesian communities, the traditional name for God is made up of the words for moon and sun (Ula-Loyo). In Kédang there is no equivalent of the neighboring Lamaholot inclusion of the earth in a unitary Godhead.

In addition to "Moon-Sun," other indigenous names for God include "Great Sun" (Loyo Rian), "White Sun" (Loyo Buyaq), "Morning Star-Sun" (Lia-Loyo), and "Great Morning Star" (Lia Rian). To a degree, the moon and sun can be seen as contrasted aspects of divinity. The sun is male, primarily controls eternally constant changes, and is creative. The sex of the moon is indeterminate. Mythically it is unproductive, but it is otherwise closely associated with the calendar, biological processes, and physiological changes. Pleiades and the morning star are also aspects of divinity. There are also guardian spirits of individuals, villages, fields, houses, and springs. Various kinds of free spirits are recognized, and there are witches.

Religious Practitioners. Increasing numbers have become Muslim religious leaders (_hajjis_) and Catholic priests or nuns. In traditional culture, priests who were expert at divination and who performed community and individual rituals (_molan-maran poan-kémir_) can be distinguished from those adept at healing and traditional medicine (_molan-maran potaq-puiq_).

Ceremonies. In addition to Muslim and Catholic services and prayer, there are ritual observances at birth and death. Some villages once again hold an annual ceremony for purifying the village at the beginning of the rainy season in December. In the dry season there were formerly village-wide ceremonies for the harvest, principally associated with beans. Today there are still such ceremonies held by descent groups. Individual guardian-spirit ceremonies are held in response to misfortune. Very occasionally a rain-making ceremony might be held. Feasts are often associated with the exchange of marriage prestations and funerals.

Arts. Although skilled in the use of bamboo and wood for producing buildings, tools, and musical instruments, the Kédang are notable for their lack of such arts as painting, decorative carving, sculpture, and weaving.

Medicine. Some modern medicine is now available from government-established clinics. Otherwise care is in the hands of traditional healers.

Death and the Afterlife. Unusual, particularly violent, or sudden forms of death are distinguished from ordinary deaths. The only "good" death occurs at a great age. The universe is constructed of levels, and the inhabitants of this world have already gone through seven levels, being reborn and then dying on each in succession before reaching this one. People who die normal deaths are eventually reborn and cycle through the remaining five levels before, on their final death, their bodies become fish in the sea and their souls return to God. The souls of those who have died a "bad" death cease to cycle, but take their abode at the horizon and return periodically on the wind to cause misfortune to the living.

See also Lamaholot

Bibliography

Barnes, Robert H. (1974). _Kédang: A Study of the Collective Thought of an Eastern Indonesian People._ Oxford: Clarendon Press.

Barnes, Robert H. (1980). "Concordance, Structure, and Variation: Considerations of Alliance in Kédang." In _The Flow of Life: Essays on Eastern Indonesia_, edited by James J. Fox, 68–97. Cambridge: Harvard University Press.

Barnes, Robert H. (1982). "Number and Number Use in Kédang, Indonesia." _Man_ 17:1–22.

R. H. BARNES

Kenyah-Kayan-Kajang

ETHNONYM: Bahau

Orientation

"Kenyah-Kayan-Kajang" is a term referring to a complex of riverine culture groups living in Sarawak. The Kenyah and Kayan are the main groups, whereas the Kajang consist of a number of small groups that are assimilating to one or the other of the other two. There are numerous subgroups as well. The Kayan live in the central portions of major central Borneo rivers (Kayan, Mahakam, Kapuas, Rajang, and Baram); the Kenyah live in the Apo Kayan drainage. The complex as a whole occupies an area within 1° to 3° N., and 113°00′ to 116°30′ E. In 1980, the population of Kenyah and Kayan was 28,925. Kenyah and Kayan are closely related Austronesian languages.

History and Cultural Relations

Kenyah and Kayan people consider the head of the Kayan River their point of origin. The Kenyah seem to have inhabited central Borneo for a considerable length of time, whereas the Kayan, a mobile and conquering group, came relatively lately from the south and east. The Kayan enslaved and assimilated the Murut and other groups in the area. In the early twentieth century, the Brooke regime put an end to the headhunting and warfare practiced by these peoples.

Settlements

Among the Kenyah, the village consists of one longhouse. Among the Kayan, a village (which may have from 30 to 1,148 inhabitants) consists of a group of longhouses. Each village has a section of river as its own territory. As a result of soil degradation, a village will move along the river, returning after 12 to 15 years. The Kayan longhouses are impressive for their size and durability. They are raised on pilings (originally as part of a defense strategy), are constructed of ironwood planks, and may be as long as 300 meters; they may house 500 people each (although the average is 200–300). Each family owns the planks and beams that make up its part of the longhouse. Unmarried older boys and men sleep on the veranda, while unmarried girls, women, and female slaves live with their respective families.

Economy

Rice, raised in swiddens, is the staple; corn, yams, pumpkins, cucumbers, and tobacco are also raised. In some Kenyah groups, rice cultivation is controlled by women. Fishing, which is more important to the diet than is hunting, is accomplished primarily by poisoning with tuba root. Hunting is mainly done with dogs and blowguns, and the most important game is the wild pig. Goats, dogs, pigs, and chickens are raised domestically, the latter two for sacrifice. The Kenyah and Kayan are skilled woodworkers, metalworkers, and canoe builders. They trade their knives and swords, which are famous throughout central Borneo. For the Kenyah, rubber has become the most important cash crop. A Kayan individual who clears primary forest land has undisputed ownership of it.

Marriage and Family

Kayan and Kenyah marry within their own classes. Marriage among commoners is often within the longhouse community, and first-cousin marriage is prohibited; bride-price is usually optional in lieu of bride-service. Residence is ambilocal. Among the aristocracy, marriage is usually outside the longhouse, and there is no bar to first-cousin marriage. An aristocrat male marries first an aristocrat female; after this he is free to marry polygynously a woman from any class. The children produced by such a marriage are of an intermediate class. Male offspring inherit gongs, weapons, and canoes; females inherit beads, though the value of shares is equal among all offspring.

Kinship

Kinship terminology is bilateral, reflects generation, and has an Eskimo-type cousin terminology. Descent is bilineal or ambilineal. Villages tend to be made up of people related consanguineally and affinally. Among the Kayans, each village (*uma*) has its own aristocratic genealogy.

Sociopolitical Organization

Kenyahs, Kayans, and Kajangs live in highly stratified societies. Aristocrats (*ipun uma* or *keta'u*) are politically dominant and allied with each other through marriage over an area that crosses tribal and linguistic boundaries. Their wealth is in gongs, beads, and jars. They control the use of bird's nest caves (where swallows' nests, used for food, abound), and because they own slaves they are able to grow much more food than can commoners. Middle-class commoners (farmers and craftsmen) are known as *panyun*. Slaves (*lupau* or *lepen*) are the descendants of prisoners of war. Within the village, each longhouse has a headman, who is an aristocrat. In villages having more than one longhouse, one of the longhouse headmen is also a village headman. There is no political unity above the level of the village, although in the past large war parties composed of the men of several villages were organized. Kayan headmen also receive free agricultural labor from village members.

Religion and Expressive Culture

A central feature of the life of these peoples was the *mamat*, or head feast, which is now rare owing to Christian influence. The mamat required a new head; its purposes included ritual purification, marking the end of a period of mourning for a deceased kinsman, or the ritual completion of a new longhouse.

Bibliography

LeBar, Frank M. (1972). "Kenyah-Kayan-Kajang." In *Ethnic Groups of Insular Southeast Asia*, edited by Frank M. LeBar. Vol. 1, *Indonesia, Andaman Islands, and Madagascar*, 168–173. New Haven: HRAF Press.

Sagan, Jacob Dungau (1989). "The Kenyah People of Sarawak." *Sarawak Museum Journal* 40:119–141.

Uyo, Lah Jau (1989). "Kayan People of Sarawak." *Sarawak Museum Journal* 40:56–88.

DANIEL STROUTHES

Kerintji

Numbering around 170,000 as of 1977, the Kerintji people (Corinchee, Corinchi, Corinchia, Kerinchi, Kinchai, Koerintji, Korinchi, Korinci, Korintji, Kurintji) live in the fertile, high-elevation "Kerintji Basin," two degrees south of the equator in West Sumatra, Indonesia. Kerintji is classified in the Hesperonesian Group of the Austronesian Language Family. The people live in longhouses composed of adjoining family apartments. The dietary staple, rice, grown in irrigated fields, is supplemented by fish from Lake Kerintji. Matrilineages are the corporate landholding groups. Considerable importance is still attached to the inherited status of chief, accompanied by titles of rank. Many Kerintji are now Muslim; the pre-Islamic religion contained elements of ancestor worship, animism, and Indic pantheism.

Bibliography

Jasper, M. A. (1972). "Kerintji." In *Ethnic Groups of Insular Southeast Asia*, edited by Frank M. LeBar. Vol. 1, *Indonesia, Andaman Islands, and Madagascar*, 29–30. New Haven: HRAF Press.

Khmer

ETHNONYMS: Cambodian, Kampuchean, Khmae

Orientation

Identification. The term "Khmer" designates the dominant ethnic population (and the language) of Cambodia. The term "Cambodian" is also used for inhabitants of the country, including some non-Khmer ethnic groups. Khmer often refer to their nation as *srok khmae*, the country of the Khmer, and to themselves as "Khmae" (Khmer). The English designation "Cambodia" (or French "Cambodge") are Westernized transliterations of Kambuja, a Sanskrit name used by some ancient kingdoms in this region. From 1975 to early 1989 the country was called Kampuchea but was subsequently renamed Cambodia.

Location. Cambodia is situated between approximately 10° and 15° N and 102° and 108° E. The country's interior is largely a lowland plain, rising to low mountains in the southwest and northwest, and high plateaus in the northeast. Running roughly north to south are two major waterways: the Mekong river in the eastern part of the country, and the Tonle Sap, a huge lake and river in the west, the two rivers converging at the capital city of Phnom Penh. Many smaller rivers and streams crosscut the lowlands. The climate is mainly hot and humid, with a rainy season from about June to November.

Demography. Population figures are only approximations, given the absence of any census since 1962. In 1992 Cambodia had about 8.5 million people, with estimates of population increase ranging from about 1.5 to 3.0 percent per year. The current population is much smaller than it might otherwise have been because of tremendous mortality under conditions of warfare, revolution, and famine between 1969 and 1980. The death rate was particularly high during the Democratic Kampuchean regime between 1975 and 1979, with estimates ranging from one to two million deaths from illness, starvation, or execution. At the time, men had a higher mortality rate than women, thus creating a skewed sex ratio in which females constitute 60–80 percent of the adult population in some communities. Other ethnic groups in Cambodia are Vietnamese, Chinese, the Muslim Cham (also called the Khmer Islam, although their language and religion are distinct from those of the Khmer), and various highland "tribal" groups collectively known as the Khmer Loeu ("upland Khmer," although their languages and cultures differ from those of the lowland Khmer). All of these minorities comprised about 15 percent of the total population in the early 1970s, but many fled or died during the subsequent turmoil and they are now estimated to be about 10 percent of the total population.

Linguistic Affiliation. Khmer belongs to the Mon-Khmer Family that some linguists place within a larger Austroasiatic Language Stock. It is related to the languages of the Mon people in Burma and to a number of other Mon-Khmer-speaking groups in various parts of mainland Southeast Asia and India. Khmer is nontonal and largely disyllabic, and has a special vocabulary to speak to and about royalty and Buddhist monks. The Khmer script is derived from an ancient south Indian writing system.

History and Cultural Relations

The prehistoric origins of the Khmer are not clear. After the first century A.D., complex polities emerged in this region. Ancient Khmer civilization reached a peak during the Angkor period (A.D. 802–1432), when the famous Angkor Wat and other monumental structures were built, and Khmer kings ruled an irrigation-based empire extending beyond the boundaries of present-day Cambodia. Khmer power subsequently declined, and the kingdom was subject to periodic encroachments by the neighboring Thai and Vietnamese. In 1864 Cambodia became a protectorate under French colonial rule, and in 1887 Cambodia, Laos, and Vietnam were designated the Union of French Indochina. After World War II (during which the country was occupied by the Japanese), Cambodia was granted independence from France, in 1953. Until 1970 the country was a constitutional monarchy with a figurehead king and real political power vested in a prime minister, assembly, and ministries. The major political leader during this time was Norodom Sihanouk (who again became head of state in 1991). In 1970 a military coup by Lon Nol overthrew Sihanouk, abolished the monarchy, and established the Khmer Republic. In the early 1970s the country was in turmoil with internal problems, repercussions from the war in Vietnam that precipitated U.S. bombing of Cambodia, and civil war between the government and Communist revolutionaries commonly known as the Khmer Rouge. In 1975 the Khmer Rouge triumphed and renamed the country Democratic Kampuchea (DK). Under the leadership of Pol Pot, the communistic DK regime attempted to restructure Cambodian society and culture radically: it evacuated people from urban centers into rural areas; reorganized the population into communes and work teams with collectivized ownership, production, and distribution; suppressed Buddhism; and imposed harsh living conditions and discipline that led to many deaths from lack of food, exhausting work loads, illness, and executions. In late 1978 the Vietnamese entered Kampuchea to combat DK incursions into Vietnam, and by early 1979 they drove the Khmer Rouge out of the country. The Vietnamese installed a new government, named the People's Republic of Kampuchea (PRK), with Khmer officials and Vietnamese advisers and occupying troops. The Vietnamese advisers and soldiers gradually withdrew, and the country was renamed the State of Cambodia (SOC) in 1989, although it retained officials from the PRK. The PRK/SOC government was opposed by so-called resistance forces composed of three factions: a Sihanouk group; supporters of a former prime minister named Son Sann; and die-hard Khmer Rouge who had fled to the northwest region bordering on Thailand. In late 1991 the contending groups negotiated a political settlement that called for a temporary governing council composed of representatives from the current government and resistance groups, with United Nations peacekeeping forces and teams to supervise eventual open elections. At this time it was not yet clear what the precise nature of the new government would be, though Sihanouk was again recognized as head of state.

Settlements

Village size ranges from a few hundred to over a thousand people. Rural settlements are of three basic types: houses may be strung out in a linear fashion along a roadway or stream, arranged in a relatively compact cluster, or dispersed among rice fields. Among the houses are trees, shrubs, and kitchen gardens, with rice paddies around or alongside the settlement. A community may have its own Buddhist temple compound (_wat_), and possibly a school.

The traditional Khmer-style house is gable-roofed, rectangular, and raised on piles, with access by stairs or ladder. Depending on a family's means, a house may have thatch or wooden walls, a thatch or tile roof, bamboo or wooden floors, and wood or concrete pilings. During the DK period, however, most of the population had to live in small thatch houses built directly on the ground, and many people continue to have such homes because they cannot afford to build houses in the traditional style. The interior of poorer homes is basically an open space with cloth, thatch, or wooden partitions; and there are minimal furnishings apart from wooden platforms used for sitting and sleeping. More prosperous homes have several rooms and more furniture. Kitchens are often partitioned off, although some households cook beside or beneath the house. City dwellers may live in Western-style houses or apartments.

Economy

Subsistence and Commercial Activities.   Cambodia has a predominantly agricultural economy. Most Khmer are rural peasants with smallholdings who grow wet rice for subsistence and sometimes for sale. River-bank dwellers, however, often emphasize fruit and vegetable production (*chamkar*). Mechanized agriculture is very rare, and cultivation is carried out with relatively simple implements: a metal-tipped wooden plow pulled by draft animals, a hoe, and hand-held sickles. Irrigation systems are not widespread, and most cultivation depends on rainfall. Villagers obtain additional food from trees and kitchen gardens that produce a variety of herbs, vegetables, and fruits (e.g., basil, pepper, beans, cucumbers, sweet potatoes, mangoes, bananas, coconuts, sugar palms, etc.), and from fishing with poles, scoops, or traps in flooded rice paddies or local waterways. (There are also fishing villages along large rivers and Lake Tonle Sap, though the inhabitants may be non-Khmer.) It should also be noted that villagers are part of a larger market economy requiring money to buy various necessities. They therefore commonly engage in various side pursuits (e.g., temporary menial labor in the city, making palm sugar for sale) to earn cash. Cambodia's main exports are rubber (grown on formerly French plantations), beans, kapok, tobacco, and timber. The most common domestic animals are cattle, water buffalo, pigs, chickens, ducks, dogs, and cats.

Industrial Arts.   Most villagers can do basic carpentry and make certain items such as thatch, baskets, and mats. There are also part- or full-time artisans who engage in home production of various goods (e.g., cotton or silk scarves and sarongs, silver objects, pottery, bronzeware, etc.). Industrial manufacturing and processing of goods are very limited.

Trade.   Except for the DK period when money and trade were abolished, there have long been peddlers, shops, and markets in both the countryside and urban centers. The PRK government initially advocated a semisocialist economy, but the SOC has openly espoused a capitalist market system. Prior to 1975 commerce was primarily in the hands of Chinese or Sino-Khmer; at present, there are still Chinese merchants but more Khmer may be moving into trade. Khmer villagers sell surplus produce or vend other items to one another, to itinerant merchants, or in local or urban markets.

Division of Labor.   While there is some gender division of labor, a number of tasks may be done by either sex. The current shortage of males in the adult population means that women must sometimes undertake activities that were customarily performed by men. Men plow fields, collect sugar-palm liquid, do carpentry, and purchase or sell cattle and chickens. Women sow and transplant rice and have primary responsibility for such domestic activities as cooking, laun-

dry, and child care, although men can also do these if necessary. Women control household finances and handle the sale or purchase of rice, pigs, produce, and other goods.

Land Tenure.   Prior to 1975 most Khmer peasants owned small amounts of land for cultivation; landlessness and absentee landlordism were not widespread but did exist in some regions. During the DK regime, communal ownership replaced private property. In the PRK, after an initial period of partial collectivization, land was redistributed to individuals and private property was formally reinstated in 1989. Land, like other property, is owned by both males and females.

Kinship

Kin Groups and Descent.   There are no organized kin groups beyond the family, but an individual recognizes a kindred or circle of relatives (*bong p'on*) by blood and marriage on both paternal and maternal sides of the family. Ideally there should be affection and mutual aid among kin; discord between relatives is thought to be punished by ancestral spirits. There is usually considerable interaction among kin, but an individual may have close ties with certain relatives and not others. Descent is bilateral.

Kinship Terminology.   Formal terms of reference for cousins are Eskimo, but terms of address are Hawaiian. Kin terms denote relative age in Ego's generation and distinguish among parents' siblings according to age relative to one's parents. Kin terms are often used to address nonkin of the same or lower social status.

Marriage and Family

Marriage.   Marriages are predominantly monogamous. Before 1975 polygyny was legal but not common; it was forbidden by the DK regime and remains so under the present-day government. With the current shortage of males, however, there are reports that some men have multiple if informal "wives." A young man may initiate a marriage proposal by asking his parents to send a go-between to negotiate with a young woman's parents; the woman and her parents may then accept or reject the proposal. In other cases, parents themselves arrange marriages for their children. The groom's family customarily gives a monetary gift to the bride's parents to help defray wedding expenses borne by her family. There are no rules of community endogamy or exogamy, and cousin marriage is permitted. A married couple may live in its own household, with either the wife's or husband's family, or possibly with other relatives. Residence with the wife's family, especially in the early years of marriage, is common but not a strict rule. Choice of residence depends on circumstances, and a couple may shift residence over time as situations change. Divorce can be initiated by either husband or wife on various grounds. Each person takes back whatever individual property was brought to the marriage, while any common property is divided.

Domestic Unit.   Households may be either a nuclear family of parents and unmarried children, or some sort of extended family. The latter is commonly a three-generational unit composed of parents, a married child and his or her spouse and children, but extended families can include various other kin. Because of the high mortality rate during the DK period, during which many families were decimated, present-day households may consist of varying combinations of relatives; there has also been an increase in the number of single-parent families (with usually a widow). Members of a household commonly share work, resources, and produce.

Inheritance. Inheritance is bilateral, and transmission of property occurs either at the time a child marries or when parents die. Parents ideally try to give each child some sort of equitable inheritance (whether land, money, or goods), but in practice some children may get more than others because of individual needs or parental favoritism.

Socialization. Children have various caretakers in addition to parents: elder siblings, grandparents, and other older relatives. Child rearing is generally permissive. Children are instructed primarily by word and by example, and physical punishment was rare in pre-1975 village life. Youngsters are, however, expected to display proper behavior and learn essential skills as they grow older.

Sociopolitical Organization

In 1992 the State of Cambodia was headed by a president/ head of state, a prime minister, a council of ministers, and an elected national assembly.

Social Organization. Pre-1975 Cambodia was hierarchical, although some social mobility was possible. Several socioeconomic strata were differentiated on the basis of relative wealth and prestige: an elite of Khmer aristocrats and high-ranking officials; a middle stratum of urban people in commerce, professions, and white-collar occupations (many of whom were Chinese or Vietnamese); and a bottom layer of peasants and workers. Theravada Buddhist monks constituted a separate social category and received enormous respect. Within a village some families were more prosperous than others, but economic differences were not great. Individuals were given differential prestige and authority based on age, religiosity, or personal qualities. The DK regime attempted to level social classes and create an egalitarian society by making virtually everyone live like peasants, but a new social hierarchy emerged with the DK cadre at the top. After 1979 Cambodia experienced several years of generalized poverty, but recent economic revival is stimulating the reemergence of socioeconomic differentiation.

Political Organization. Cambodia is comprised of eighteen provinces (_khayt_) that are further divided into smaller administrative units of districts (_srok_), subdistricts (_khum_), and finally towns and villages (_phum_). Each province, district, subdistrict, and village has its own administrative personnel who oversee matters concerning the territorial unit and are responsible to the next higher level of government.

Social Control. At the community level, social control is maintained through socialization from childhood into norms of proper conduct and through use of informal sanctions such as gossip or ostracism. Individuals seek to avoid the "embarrassment" or "shame" of improper behavior, as well as to earn religious merit by following the major Buddhist rules of conduct (do not lie, steal, drink alcoholic beverages, fornicate, or kill living creatures). Certain kinds of misbehavior are thought to bring punishment from supernatural beings, usually in the form of illness. Although police and law courts exist, many people avoid using them except when absolutely necessary.

Conflict. Within the community, open confrontation between individuals is rare because cultural norms discourage aggressive anger and conflict. On the larger societal level, governments since the time of the ancient kingdoms have maintained military forces to deal with internal unrest and conflict with other polities. Cambodia has experienced several decades of warfare since the late 1960s: repercussions from the war in Vietnam, civil war between government troops and Khmer Rouge Communist rebels in the early 1970s, conflict between DK and Vietnam in the late 1970s, and continued fighting through the 1980s between the government and "resistance forces" consisting mainly of Khmer Rouge.

Religion and Expressive Culture

Theravada Buddhism is the dominant religion of Cambodia, but Khmer religion actually combines Buddhism, animistic beliefs and practices, and elements from Hinduism and Chinese culture into a distinctive blend.

Religious Beliefs. Theravada was the official state religion from about the fifteenth century. Buddhism and other religions were crushed during the DK period. Buddhist temples were destroyed or desecrated, monks were killed or forced to leave the holy order, and Buddhist observances were forbidden. After 1979 Theravada gradually revived, and it was once again officially recognized by the state in 1989. Relatively few Khmer are Christian. The Cham (Khmer Islam) minority group is Muslim, while the Khmer Loeu or upland tribal peoples traditionally had their own distinctive religions.

A variety of supernatural entities populates the universe. These include spirits in the natural environment or certain localities, guardian spirits of houses and animals, ancestral spirits, demon-like beings, ghosts, and others. Some spirits are generally benign and can be helpful if propitiated, but others can cause sickness if they are displeased by lack of respect or by improper behavior.

Religious Practitioners. Each Buddhist temple has resident monks who follow special rules of behavior, conduct religious observances, and are accorded respect as exemplars of the virtuous life. A man can become a monk for a temporary period of time, and prior to 1975 many Khmer males did so at some point in their lives. Some men remain monks permanently. The practice continues, but there are now fewer temples and monks than before 1975. In addition to monks, the _achar_ is a sort of lay priest who leads the congregation at temple ceremonies and presides over domestic life-cycle rituals. Other religious specialists deal more with the realm of spirits and magical practices: _kru_, who have special skills such as curing sickness or making protective amulets; mediums (_rup arak_), who communicate with spirits; and sorcerers (_tmop_), who can cause illness or death.

Ceremonies. There are many annual Buddhist ceremonies, the most important of which are the New Year celebration in April, the Pchum ceremony honoring the dead in September, and Katun festivals to contribute money and goods to the temple and monks. Life-cycle ceremonies marking births, marriages, and deaths are conducted at home. Weddings are particularly festive occasions. There are also rituals connected with healing, propitiation of supernatural spirits, agriculture, and other activities, as well as national observances such as boat races at the Water Festival in Phnom Penh.

Arts.   Music and dance are important elements of Khmer culture that occur in ordinary village life as well as in formal performances in the city. Traditional instruments include drums, xylophones, and stringed and woodwind instruments, although popular music incorporates Western instruments. There are classical, folk, and social dances, traditional and popular songs, and theater. Literature includes folktales, legends, poetry, religious texts, and dramas. Artistry is also expressed in architecture, sculpture, painting, textiles, metalware, or even the decorations on a rice sickle.

Medicine.   Illness may be explained and treated according to Western biomedicine, and/or attributed to other causes such as emotional distress or supernatural spirits. Treatment for the latter can include folk medicines, Chinese procedures such as moxibustion, and rituals conducted by kru healers. Traditional and biomedical procedures may be combined to cure illness.

Death and Afterlife.   Funerals are one of the two most important life-cycle ceremonies. Cremation is customary and is carried out, along with attendant rituals, as soon as possible after death. Pieces of bone that remain after cremation are put in an urn kept at home or placed in a special structure at the Buddhist temple. According to Buddhist doctrine an individual goes through successive reincarnations, and one's position in the next life will be determined by meritorious and virtuous conduct in this life. Only exceptional persons similar to Buddha might achieve *nirvana* and release from the cycle of reincarnations.

See also Cham

Bibliography

Chandler, David C. (1983). *A History of Cambodia.* Boulder, Colo: Westview Press.

Ebihara, May (1968). *Svay: A Khmer Village in Cambodia.* Ann Arbor, Mich.: University Microfilms.

Ebihara, May (1984). "Revolution and Reformulation in Kampuchean Village Culture." In *The Cambodian Agony,* edited by David Ablin and Marlowe Hood. Armonk, N.Y.: M. E. Sharpe.

Vickery, Michael (1986). *Kampuchea: Politics, Economics, and Society.* London: Frances Pinter; Boulder, Colo.: Lynne Rienner Publishers.

MAY EBIHARA

Khua

Khua number about 5,000 (1981) and live in northern Vietnam and east-central Laos.

Kmhmu

ETHNONYMS: Kammu, Khamu, Khmu, Kho' Mu, Kmhmu', Lao Theung; also Kha, Kha Che, Xa Cau, which are pejorative

Orientation

Identification.   The Kmhmu are the indigenous inhabitants of northern Laos prior to the southwestward migrations of Tai-speaking peoples. They have expanded within the last two centuries to bordering areas of Thailand, China, and Vietnam, and since 1975 to the United States, France, and Canada. In the Kmhmu language, "Kmhmu'" means "person, human"; they were formerly known by the pejorative term "Kha" or "Xa" (from Tai languages), meaning "slave, serf." Kmhmu are divided into a number of local groups known as *tmooy* (guest or stranger); the word refers to people who are like us but unknown to us, and may even include members of other neighboring Mon-Khmer ethnic groups. Another term, *jĕ'*, refers to people who are not like us (for instance, Lao, Tai, and Hmong). The tmooy groups are believed by some scholars to be the remnants of ancient political divisions, although it is more likely they are simply differentiated by geography. The Tmooy Ou are those living near the Ou river; the Tmooy Yuan are those who formerly paid tribute to the Tai Yuan overlord; the Tmooy Cvaa are those living in the Luang Prabang region, formerly Muang Cvaa. People also may be distinguished by which negative particle they use: Tmooy Al are speakers of a northern dialect and Tmooy Am speakers of a southern one.

Location.   Kmhmu traditionally lived at the lower elevations of mountain ridges in northern Indochina. They once centered on the valleys of the Nam Ou, Nam Tha, and Nam Beng rivers and their confluence with the Mekong river. Following Tai migrations into this area, Kmhmu were dispersed in every direction, often absorbing smaller related ethnic groups. They inhabit tropical forests watered by monsoons, with a rainy season that extends from May or June to September or October.

Demography.   The largest number of Kmhmu live in the Lao People's Democratic Republic, numbering 400,000 in the 1985 census; they comprise 10 percent of the country's population and constitute the largest single minority ethnic group. Kmhmu in Thailand number from 5,000 to 50,000; in China there are approximately 2,000; and in Vietnam there were 32,000 in 1979. In mountainous regions the population density is very low; there are also small urban populations in cities such as Luang Prabang, Vientiane, Lampang, and even Bangkok. Some 3,000 Kmhmu now live in North America, and approximately 750 live in France.

Linguistic Affiliation.   Kmhmu speak a number of mutually intelligible dialects of the Kmhmu language, which is the largest member of the Khmuic Group of the Northern Mon-Khmer Branch of the Austroasiatic Language Family. Their territory is surrounded by groups speaking smaller languages of the Khmuic Family; in many cases these people also speak Kmhmu itself. Kmhmu are almost all at least bilingual, speaking their mother tongue and whatever is the locally dominant

Tai language (Lao, Northern Thai, Tai Dam, Lue). The contemporary vocabulary includes a large proportion of Tai loanwords, many borrowed centuries ago and others borrowed more recently. Kmhmu in Vietnam, the United States, and France also speak the languages of those countries as a third language. Their own language includes two main dialect groups: Southern Kmhmu dialects maintain a historical distinction between voiced and voiceless initials, whereas Northern Kmhmu dialects have replaced this with a distinction between low tone and high tone.

History and Cultural Relations

The Kmhmu once were masters of the domain of Muong Cvaa (or Muong Sua), centered on what is now the city of Luang Prabang. Following their conquest in the thirteenth century by Lao people, the Kmhmu were driven into remote mountain ranges or became serfs to a Lao aristocracy. In places, however, the Kmhmu retained a good deal of autonomy and local authority, sometimes even governing over local Lao and Tai populations. The Kmhmu were recognized as older brothers of the Lao and Tai in coronation ceremonies and other court rituals in Luang Prabang and Nan, and in oral traditions of the Lao and Kmhmu. In the nineteenth and twentieth centuries, Kmhmu frequently rebelled against the local Tai and Lao feudal lords and French colonial authorities, in millennarian rebellions that were called Sôk Cheuang (Cheuang's Wars), after the mythical or legendary culture hero Cheuang. From 1945 until 1975, Kmhmu were in the forefront of the Lao independence revolution, making up the largest part of the Neo Lao Hak Xat (Pathet Lao) military forces. A smaller segment of the Kmhmu population supported the United States and Royal Lao Government; many of them fled as refugees following the establishment of the Lao People's Democratic Republic in 1975.

Kmhmu share many cultural traditions with their Lao and Tai neighbors, and with other neighboring ethnic groups including the Lamet (Rmeet), Hmong, and Thin (Mal-Pray). These may include subsistence technology, crafts and material culture, music and song, and clothing. There are nevertheless cultural traditions unique to the Kmhmu, or borrowed from them by their neighbors. Intermarriage with members of other ethnic groups is not infrequent; in some cases non-Kmhmu people (especially those from smaller ethnic groups) marry into a Kmhmu village, adopting Kmhmu language and traditions, while in other cases Kmhmu marry out, taking on the language and traditions of another group (especially the larger Lao or Tai culture).

Settlements

Kmhmu mountain villages range from 15 to 150 households, and from 100 to 1,000 people. The larger the village, the more prosperous it is likely to be; small villages usually have less territory available for farming and villagers are less able to accumulate wealth or material possessions. Often situated alongside a mountain stream that can provide drinking water, the village is surrounded by land used for swidden agriculture. In places, Kmhmu villages also have adjoining rain-fed or irrigated rice paddies; some now have tea plantations or groves of commercial trees. Houses are built on stilts or pilings, and are made from bamboo, wood, or both. A prosperous villager will have a house with wooden walls and a metal or wood-shingle roof; a poor villager will have a house with plaited bamboo walls and a thatched roof. The arrangement of houses in the village is determined by the contours of the terrain; the village chief's home (or a communal men's house, where that tradition is preserved) is located near the center, along the path or road entering the village. A typical traditional house includes three chambers, each with a hearth: a front area for receiving guests, a central area for the family's cooking and eating, and a rear area where the ancestral altar is maintained. In urban areas of Laos or Thailand, or in North America and France, Kmhmu live in houses or apartments, often clustering together with other Kmhmu families when possible.

Economy

Subsistence and Commercial Activities. The dominant aspect of Kmhmu life is the cultivation of dry rice in swidden fields on mountain slopes. Traditionally they practice a sustainable swidden system in which fields are cleared, burned, and planted for one or two years, then left to regenerate as long as possible—ideally a dozen years or so. Where the land available for a village's cultivation is restricted by terrain or the proximity of other villages, it may be necessary to practice a shorter cycle, requiring longer use of a field and shorter periods of regeneration. This results in rapid depletion of the soil and requires villagers to seek fields farther from the home village. Governmental efforts in recent years have been directed toward sedentarization, discouragement of swidden agriculture, and the introduction of irrigated rice agriculture; these efforts have had only mixed success where they have not indeed been harmful. The sloping swidden fields are not plowed but planted with a dibble or planting stick. Maize, legumes, gourds and squash, taro and yams, chili peppers, eggplants, and herbs are sown among the rice plants. Pigs, water buffalo, goats, chickens, and ducks are kept for meat or eggs. A large part of the traditional diet, especially during the season when new fields are being planted and rice stocks are depleted, is filled by plants gathered in the forests and by fish, birds, and small game captured with nets, snares, and crossbows.

Industrial Arts. Kmhmu are well known to their neighbors as specialists in the crafting of baskets of all kinds, snares, and traps, all of bamboo. Women in some regions spin cotton and weave small shoulder bags using a backstrap loom, but in general Kmhmu are not known for textiles and have no broadcloth weaving. Clothing was traditionally acquired from neighboring Tai peoples, and is now most likely to be mass-produced in Western style. In certain regions Kmhmu may practice blacksmithing of knives, swords, and agricultural implements, or may make jewelry, but these are not prominent traditions.

Trade. Kmhmu live in close proximity to other ethnic groups and engage in frequent, albeit small-scale, trade with their neighbors. These trade relations are symbolized in certain ritual exchanges incorporated into court ceremonies, where Kmhmu provide beeswax, resins, stick lac, honey, and other products gathered in the forests, in exchange for metal goods, cloth, and industrial products. In China and northwestern Laos, Kmhmu controlled several salt mines and engaged in trade with others wanting this precious commodity. Historical accounts also describe Kmhmu as providing rice to their lowland neighbors, the Lao or Tai.

Division of Labor. There are few daily tasks that are restricted to one gender; under circumstances of necessity almost any task can be performed by either gender. Tasks associated with men are hunting and trapping, felling trees, blacksmithing, and long-distance trade that requires sleeping away from the village. Tasks associated with women are planting rice, carrying water, gathering forest plants, feeding animals, and trade with nearby villages. Both men and women perform most agricultural tasks of clearing brush, cultivating, weeding, harvesting, and carrying; either may cook, although men are said to be better and are responsible for butchering large animals. Child care is generally women's work, although men frequently carry their infants.

Land Tenure. The land surrounding a village is generally recognized by others as belonging to that village. Rights of usufruct ensure that those who have cleared a field and cultivated it have the right to its use in the future. The historical primacy of the Kmhmu is acknowledged by the Lao and other Tai groups in court rituals in which they pay tribute to the Kmhmu as the ancestral owners of the territory. Decades of war and the Socialist economic system of the Lao People's Democratic Republic led to massive dislocations and to collectivization efforts, both of which disrupted traditional land-tenure relations. More recently, efforts to sedentarize Kmhmu and discourage swidden agriculture have also changed the bases of land tenure.

Kinship

Kin Groups and Descent. Kmhmu kinship is characteristically a gens triplex system of prescribed marriage with the matrilateral cross cousin. There are three *jeua* (lineages) each comprising one or more *snta'* (totemic clans): the quadruped lineage may include the civet, tiger, gaur, monkey, squirrel, and bear clans; the bird lineage may include the forktail, hornbill, mynah, kite, and kingfisher clans; the plant lineage includes the fern clan. Descent is patrilateral in some regions, bilateral in others. Lineage A takes wives from Lineage B and husbands from Lineage C; Lineage B takes wives from Lineage C and husbands from Lineage A; Lineage C takes wives from Lineage A and husbands from Lineage B.

Kinship Terminology. Kmhmu kinship terminology reflects the asymmetrical-alliance system. The members of the lineage related to Ego as wife givers/husband takers are referred to as *éém* and the members of the lineage related to Ego as wife takers/husband givers are referred to as *kheey*. Kinship terminology distinguishes kin and affines, parallel cousins, and cross cousins. Kin are distinguished terminologically by gender (except for members of the grandchild and great-grandchild generations). Relative age is marked terminologically for kin of the same gender as Ego.

Marriage and Family

Marriage. Although marriages are traditionally arranged through negotiation between the two families involved, individuals have substantial influence over their choice of spouse as long as they choose within the prescribed kinship system. Adolescent girls receive nocturnal visits from suitors, who make use of a Jew's harp to send verbal messages of love to the girl. If she reciprocates the boy's affection, she responds by playing on a flute. Premarital sexual activities are accepted, although they should not result in pregnancy. Marriage is negotiated between the two families, and formalized through ceremonies hosted by each side. Where the boy's side meets the bride-price expected by the girl's side, the new family may reside near the boy's family. Where the boy is unable to meet the bride-price, he will indenture himself to his father-in-law for a period of service, during which the new family resides with the girl's parents. Divorces are formalized through negotiation between the two sides; they may require a refund of the bride-price (for instance if the match does not produce offspring, or the wife is unfaithful) or a fine (if the husband has abandoned or mistreated the wife). Polygyny is sometimes practiced by more prosperous men.

Domestic Unit. The household is the primary domestic unit, comprised of a nuclear family as its core and sometimes including grandparents, grandchildren, siblings, children-in-law, and others. Young unmarried men may reside for some period in the communal men's house or *joong*, or they may live together away from the village in an urban area where they have gone as temporary laborers.

Socialization. Infants are raised by both parents and by older siblings, aunts, or cousins. A father can perform most parental responsibilities. Infants are usually carried by adults in slings on the chest or back; when carried by a child they may be held on the hip. Adolescent males traditionally reside together in a communal men's house, where they learn techniques of hunting, trapping, and material culture.

Sociopolitical Organization

Social Organization. Kmhmu villages are not highly stratified, and relative prosperity or poverty depends more on individual circumstance than on heredity. Older people are generally accorded respect, and those with special knowledge of herbal medicine or special talents for song or musical performance are recognized as experts. Ritual specialists and shamans are known as such, although in daily life they work just as others do (observing certain special ritual prohibitions and obligations). Young men reside temporarily in the joong but do not constitute an age-set; there are no initiation ceremonies.

Political Organization. The political structure of the ancient Kmhmu domain of Muang Cvaa is unknown, although tales and legends speak of Kmhmu kings. More recently, Kmhmu were incorporated into the civil and political administration of their Lao and Tai neighbors; the degree of their subservience varied from region to region. Village chiefs (*naay baan*) of monoethnic Kmhmu villages were always Kmhmu; a mixed Lao-Kmhmu village might have a chief from either group. In certain places Kmhmu could serve as *naay phong* or *tasseng* (two levels of local chief), in some cases even having authority over Lao villages within the phong or tasseng. More often, however, Kmhmu could not exercise authority over members of other ethnic groups. Until the independence revolution, Kmhmu could not aspire to higher positions such as *chao muang* (district chief) or *chao khoueng* (province chief), but in contemporary Laos Kmhmu can be found at every level of government.

Social Control. Within a household, the father exercises most authority, although the mother is in charge of money. Social control is usually expressed through subtle means: either by gossip about someone else or through an indirect or veiled reference, heuristic tale, or parable. In times of stress, turmoil, or personal misbehavior, the concerned party might be the focus of a communal ceremony intended to encourage them to do right by demonstrating the community's concern and solidarity. An informal assemblage of village elders may be convened to arbitrate disputes between families, to discipline unruly or disruptive members, or to make decisions for the village as a whole. Unreconciled disputes or unresolved grievances may separate families or lead to the fissure of the village.

Conflict.   Conflict in traditional village life can often be avoided through compromise, acquiescence, or flight. One of the most important things affecting the lives of contemporary Kmhmu was the three-decade-long war of independence from 1945 to 1975; this conflict was one in which Kmhmu were profoundly implicated, although they had little control over its course.

Religion and Expressive Culture

Religious Beliefs.   Kmhmu traditional religion is marked by belief in a pantheon of _hrôôy_ (spirits) who include ancestor spirits, household spirits, village spirits, locality spirits, rice spirits, and spirits associated with natural phenomena, animals, and dragons. Each person has _hrmaal_ (soul-spirits) who are inclined to flight at times of turmoil or transition. For at least the last century, Kmhmu villages have adopted Buddhism, often without completely forgetting their traditional religion. Protestants undertook missionary activity from the nineteenth century, and Catholics from 1945; adherence to Christianity usually required giving up most traditional beliefs. Kmhmu who have migrated to the United States and France usually practice Christianity, although some maintain those beliefs that can still be practiced in their new circumstances.

Religious Practitioners.   Most Kmhmu are able to perform common ceremonies and some rituals; more elaborate rituals require the expertise of a specialist. Shamans who have undergone elaborate long-term training may diagnose spirit-caused illnesses and perform shamanic ceremonies to cure them.

Ceremonies.   Ceremonies and rituals are required to honor the hrôôy spirits, to forestall the danger they might cause if offended, to pacify spirits when they are angered, and to restore harmony when the spirits create trouble. Wrist-tying ceremonies and other ceremonies of reintegration are required to call a hrmaal back to the body or prevent its flight.

Arts.   Kmhmu have rich traditions of verbal art, including myths of the origin of the group and of each totemic clan, humorous and heuristic tales, prayers, riddles, play languages, and sung verse. Kmhmu song features an elaborate poetic structure of reverse parallelism that is ubiquitous among the Kmhmu and rarely known among other groups. Kmhmu music features a number of flutes, reed flutes, mouth organs, Jew's harps, and percussion instruments, almost all made of bamboo. The bronze drum is important as a symbol of wealth and status, in ceremonies and rituals, and as a musical instrument.

Medicine.   Knowledge of traditional medicinal plants and herbs is widely held; they are gathered in the forests or may be cultivated in village gardens. Shamanic healing is practiced only by highly trained specialists.

Death and Afterlife.   After death, a long narrative song is sung by the survivors, guiding the deceased's spirit to its resting place. If this cannot be done properly, or the spirit is hungry, it may return to haunt the survivors with its plaintive demands. The spirits of those who die accidentally are especially likely to return to trouble their survivors.

See also Hmong; Lamet; Lao

Bibliography

Dang Nghiem Van (1973). "The Khmu in Vietnam." _Vietnamese Studies_ 36:62–140.

Lindell, Kristina, Hakan Lundstrom, Jan-Olof Svantesson, and Damrong Tayanin (1982). _The Kammu Year: Its Lore and Music._ London: Curzon Press.

Lindell, Kristina, Jan-Ojvind Swahn, and Damrong Tayanin (1977–1989). _Folk Tales from Kammu._ 4 vols. London: Curzon Press.

Proschan, Frank (1989). "Kmhmu Verbal Art in America: The Poetics of Kmhmu Verse." Ph.D. dissertation, University of Texas at Austin.

Roux, Henri, and Tran Van Chu (1927). "Les Tsa Khmu." _Bulletin de l'École Française d'Extrême-Orient_ 27:169–222.

FRANK PROSCHAN

Kolisuch'ŏk

ETHNONYMS: Hwach'ŏk, Paekchŏng, Yangsuch'ŏk

Orientation

Identification.   These ethnonyms (and also some others: Such'ŏk Kwangdae, Chaein, and so on) refer to members of the little-known but significant (in terms of both numbers and economic impact) social minority that comprised distinctive "outcaste" communities throughout much of Korean social history. Distinctive Korean outcaste communities are no longer extant. Their stigma initially derived from a proclivity to pursue rude and peripatetic lifestyles at a time when the majority Korean culture was becoming settled, agricultural, and Buddhist; it was then fixed by a rigid social system into an inherited occupational trait-complex that centered on butchering cattle.

The position of Korean outcastes in relation to the three major social classes of Yi-dynasty Korea (A.D. 1392–1910) can be thought of in terms of a pyramid. At the apex was the scholar-gentry class (_yangmin_). Commoners (_sangmin_) comprised the numerical majority, and were principally free-born farmers. At the base of the pyramid were the low-born (ch'ŏnmin), mainly slaves. The outcastes were also at the bottom and were not only low-born but separate from the main body of Korean society (and therefore not -min, or "nonhuman"); they were truly extrasocietal. In addition to butchering, outcastes also mastered and monopolized a constellation of satellite industries and occupations, together with complex networks of skills and services, upon which the Korean majority society, in peace and at war, depended. Outcaste communities were known by different ethnonyms that correspond roughly with the successive dynastic periods in Korea: the Unified Silla period (Kolisuch'ŏk, Yangsuch'ŏk, A.D. 660–935); Koryŏ (Hwach'ŏk, Such'ŏk, Chaein, 935–1392); and Yi, or Chosŏn (Paekchŏng, Kwangdae, 1392–1910). Prolonged spatial and social marginalization of indigenous Koreans into an outcaste social minority promoted the development of some distinct ethnic characteristics in their communities. Accordingly, their everyday lives became secretive and unknown to majority Korean society, which anyway found them repulsive and uninteresting. Owing to the rapid and near total assimilation of outcastes into mainstream Korean society during the latter half of the twentieth century, the opportunity to develop any detailed and balanced picture of their community life has passed.

Location.   Korea is an extremely mountainous peninsula extending southward from the Manchurian plain of Eurasia, projecting over 8° of latitude into the Pacific basin, and creating there a partial bridge between the continent and the western Pacific island arcs near Japan. Summers throughout most of the peninsula are humid and hot, and winters are cold and dry. This seasonal climate encourages farming, but steep terrain limits agricultural production to merely one-fifth of the land surface.

Demography.   Outcastes may have originated as small bands of protohistoric riverine migrants. If so, their activities dispersed away from, and back into, a multitude of river valleys according to the cycle of seasons. Little effort was made to enumerate the outcaste minority during subsequent dynastic times. As polluting and untouchable "nonpeople," outcastes were administered "at a distance," and went uncounted during many censuses. Owing to their successful economic niche and accessibility to meat protein, their numbers increased during the dynastic period. Some dramatic population and economic gains for outcaste communities coincided with the Mongol invasion beginning in 1231, when non-Buddhist meat eaters and their allies, including exotic butchers and entertainers from central Asia, entered and occupied the entire peninsula for nearly a century, thereby enriching the skills and gene pool of the indigenous Korean outcaste society. A registration of outcaste peoples toward the end of the nineteenth century placed their number at approximately 50,000. During the middle of the Japanese occupation period (1910–1945) Korean Paekchŏng were estimated at over 40,000 individuals comprising 8,000 households and inhabiting as many as 350 distinct settlements. This estimate is considered low. The Paekchŏng were widely distributed throughout the peninsula at that time, with their largest numbers in the southern provinces of the land. The changing distribution of outcaste communities throughout the peninsula during past times was influenced by spatial changes in the demand for their inherited industrial monopolies and the service specialties and goods they supplied. Except for troubled times of famine, war, and political upheaval, when their reliance on the nomadic life-style had some adaptive value, service nomads of the Unified Silla period in general became more sedentary during the Koryŏ and Yi periods as the class structure solidified. Early on the outcastes' numbers were small and their distributions dispersed out from, and contracted into, a multitude of river valleys according to the cycle of seasons. To the extent that the outcastes were armorers and camp followers, their distributions varied with the fortunes of war. For example, in response to the increasing threat of land invasions during the Koryŏ dynasty, many outcastes were relocated by the government into the northern provinces. Many returned to itinerancy and marauding toward the end of the Koryŏ period. Later, these unruly outcastes became temporarily fixed in space when coerced by the early Yi government into abandoning their inherited itinerant ways to become farmers. This opportunity to assimilate into majority Korean society was short-lived. The economic trade-off for respectability was unpopular with the outcastes. More important, majority society vehemently and successfully resisted their assimilation, which threatened to "pollute" both its class system and village living space with the erstwhile untouchables. Thereafter, itinerancy remained a popular option in the outcaste community's occupational trait complex, and the widespread distribution of outcastes on the peninsula was guaranteed.

Linguistic Affiliation.   Korean was the language of the outcastes. However, distinctiveness in speech and gesture is noted in some accounts. A dialect would be one outcome of this indigenous minority's long history of extreme social marginalization, ghettoization, and exclusive economic monopolies.

History and Cultural Relations

As indicated, Korea's outcaste communities could have evolved from the early marginalization of indigenous bands of riverine migrants, principally hunter-gatherer basketmakers, by sedentary agriculturalists. In this scenario, the village-dwelling Korean majority came to require and then demand the specialized goods and services of itinerant Korean "outsiders," but were wary of them on account of divergent lifestyles. Over time, prejudice led to hostility. Vague reasons for suspicion became rationalized with the successful introduction of Buddhism on the peninsula after A.D. 372. After several centuries, concepts of "pollution" and "untouchability" became institutionalized under Korean Buddhism. As time progressed further, a rigid class structure that totally excluded the outcastes was implemented and enforced by the majority society. This oppressive system solidified during the middle Yi dynasty. The beginning of egalitarian social reform did not begin to erode this system until 1894, when revised laws freed outcastes from inheriting inferior status in Korean society. Some related laws, however, deprived them of their inherited occupational monopolies, which resulted in increased economic hardships. Although the occupations of the erstwhile outcastes were no longer tainted and open to anyone, prejudice against them hardly diminished for the next fifty years. In the general opinion of the majority society during this period, successive centuries of untouchable status had tainted their bloodlines; Paekchŏng were considered polluted no matter what they did. Examples of some of the more degrading aspects of outcaste relations with majority Korean society during the Yi dynasty offer some insight into the evolution of an ethnic underclass on the peninsula. Most significant, marriage laws restricted outcastes to selecting mates from their own communities, isolating their gene pool. Perhaps this is why non-Koreans were acceptable for assimilation into outcaste society. Dress codes made outcastes immediately recognizable, whereupon a multitude of oppressive interpersonal social conventions were set into motion, designed to perpetuate by law the tremendous spatial and social gap that existed between a submissive minority and a dominant majority. Korea's untouchables, for example, were not permitted to wear the leather shoes they manufactured, but were restricted to straw sandals. They could not wear horsehair hats, nor travel by horseback, nor even cross the threshold into a "respectable" person's courtyard. Moreover, prevailing etiquette permitted children of the high-born to "speak down" to adult outcastes. This oppressive regime was only tolerable to outcastes because they enjoyed important legal rights of economic interaction with the members of majority society. These rights of access, however much circumscribed by humiliating conventions, protected the economy of the outcastes and promoted their livelihood and collective destiny. For example, settled outcastes were entitled to (and eventually licensed to) territorial rights to perform at local weddings and funerals and to butcher for village festivals. And, when slaughtering, the choicest morsels belonged to the butchers. In addition, outcastes were paid an annual tribute in rice by villagers for their entertainment and ceremonial services. Whatever pent-up resentment the degraded outcastes held toward the dominant majority society no doubt gained some release whenever an outcaste was called upon to torture and execute one of its members.

Settlements

Physical marginalization of sedentary outcaste communities isolated them in hamlets just beyond the periphery of most Korean villages. This peripheral location kept them available and controlled, and spared sensitive Buddhists and Neo-Confucians the cries and odors of animal slaughter. Modifications in their living space to accommodate the special requirements of their industries and occupations distinguished outcaste settlements from majority Korean settlements. No matter how prosperous, outcaste families were forbidden tiled roofs on their homes; a uniformity of straw roofs became characteristic of the outcaste settlement.

Economy

Subsistence and Commercial Activities.   The price paid by outcastes for their secure niche in Korean economic history has always been their dignity. Their inherited occupational trait complex, viewed over the long term, has centered on the butchering of cattle. This specialized economic niche was guaranteed to them in A.D. 525 when a law was enacted that required everyone to adopt the strictures of Buddhism, and especially forbade the killing of animals for food. There are numerous additional occupations and industries monopolized by outcastes—many itinerant in nature—that seemingly are unrelated to sedentary butchering. For example, an old Korean maxim relates that "a butcher dies with a willow leaf in his mouth." This offers some insight into the evolution

of a variegated outcaste economy: another name for the earliest hunting-gathering Kolisuch'ŏk was "Yangsuch'ŏk," meaning "willow-basket wanderers." Among all indigenous Korean communities, these itinerants were most open to accepting orphans and outsiders into their society. This would have accelerated their marginalization by the more conservative indigenous majority on the peninsula. With the introduction of Buddhism, marginalization of the Kolisuch'ŏk began to become more institutionalized. Rather than just some unsubdued wandering tribes of the past, vaguely defined, the Kolisuch'ŏk communities were observed from the Buddhist perspective to survive by willingly breaking two of Buddhism's eight commandments, and for these transgressions they were "unclean," "untouchable," and despised. These two commandments prohibited the killing of living things and having frivolous economic pursuits (e.g., singing, dancing, acting). Outcaste industries and occupations were therefore either degrading (involving pain, blood, and death) or diverting (involving frivolity). Historically, this covered a wide array of goods and services that were unavailable, impractical, or forbidden to the "respectable" members of majority Korean society, who nevertheless demanded them. Moore cites seven classes of outcaste occupations from the Yi period: servants of the sheriff who beat people, etc.; buffoons, or traveling singers; butchers; basketmakers; sorceresses (female shamans); dancing girls; and makers of leather shoes. We can find a lowest common denominator in the hunting, butchering, executing, and basketmaking outcastes, in their peculiar—for Buddhist Korea—disregard for life. We can also identify a skill complex common to all of these occupations, one that centers on the knife as a symbolic artifact for the outcaste community. Once marginalized, the Kolisuch'ŏk were predisposed to expanding their economy into butchering, the marketing of animal skins, and the manufacture of leather footwear. The recurring exigencies of warfare on the peninsula rewarded basket-making leatherworkers, who manufactured woven shields sheathed in hides. We also observe the considerable overlapping of the degrading occupations and the diverting occupations, as ritual slaughter, music, and dancing all become monopolized over time by the outcaste minority; for example, outcaste jugglers sometimes tossed balls they had crafted from the organs of animals. Although early Yi government attempts to settle and assimilate outcastes as farmers were unsuccessful, by the early twentieth century many Paekchŏng, lately deprived of their hereditary monopolies and guaranteed income, had finally turned to agricultural pursuits, at least on a part-time basis. Remnants of the traditional itinerant outcaste economy and community persisted even into the early 1980s in some tiny, family-operated traveling circuses and medicine shows. These are but a shadow of conditions a scant century ago, when the outcaste economy thrived, and _dosa_ (butchers), _u'pa_ (dancing and singing troupes), _ch'anggi_ (retired female entertainers and prostitutes), _chup'a_ (female wine sellers), _necha_ (puppeteers), _macho_ (gamblers), and _hwarang_ (comic magicians) itinerants traversed the peninsula. Female sorcery has more recently become co-opted and romanticized by the Korean government as part of its tourism and folklore industry, but is clearly dissociated from the Korean Paekchŏng tradition, which apparently embarrasses everyone and is never mentioned. The butchering of cattle remains a ubiquitous industry in Korea and is still distasteful to many Koreans, yet proceeds today without social stigma.

Industrial Arts.   In addition to assorted leather manufacturing and basketwork, metalworking eventually became an outcaste industry but was never their exclusive domain.

Division of Labor.   Men killed and butchered cattle, and stripped bark from the willow (a process that Buddhists equated with animal slaughter). Dog catching and butchering occupied both young and old males. Women's tasks may have included some killing of small animals, for example the sacrifice of a chicken by a sorceress (*mudang*). Bartering baskets became primarily a female specialty. Increased door-to-door peddling of basketwork provided outcastes with opportunities to experiment with other sources of income: entertainment, healing, and exorcism, for example. A tendency evolved in Korean majority society to attribute sacred powers to the mudang, and this parallels the gradual stereotyping of Gypsy women in the West. Among all outcastes, female entertainers and prostitutes achieved closer physical (as contrasted with social) contacts with members of the male "respectable" classes, and this perhaps best illustrates subtle differences between Hwach'ŏk-type (degraded; male; "untouchable") and Chaein-type (frivolous; female; "touchable") categories of outcastes that have always existed.

Land Tenure.   The Korean outcaste economy has been characterized as productive but nonagricultural. Many outcastes were itinerant, or semi-itinerant, so questions of land tenure are inappropriate for them. If successful sedentary communities of outcastes ever accumulated substantial capital and property during the dynastic era, these quantities and their distribution are unknown. Known Paekchŏng-owned agricultural lands of the early twentieth century were subsequently vacated, owing to a rapid dissipation of most Paekchŏng culture bearers into mainstream urban-industrial society, facilitating their search for anonymity.

Kinship, Marriage, and Family

Kin Groups and Descent.   Compared to the majority Korean society, knowledge of outcaste kin-group structure and organization is minimal. Outcastes were unmotivated to embrace a tradition of memorizing or writing genealogies (*chokpo*) like "respectable" peoples.

Marriage and Family.   Insufficient data preclude any meaningful discussion of marriage customs and domesticity for Korean outcastes as distinct from majority Korean society. In view of their "special" status and peculiar inherited rights and obligations, however, the socialization of outcastes must have differed significantly from the Korean social norm. In their nonagricultural, landless economy, inheritance centered more on the transfer of skills than of property. This helped to facilitate a rapid readaptation of settled outcastes to itinerant lifestyles, as necessary.

Sociopolitical Organization

Outcaste communities were internally self-governing, but detailed descriptions are unavailable.

Religion

The original Kolisuch'ŏk riverine migrants were no doubt animists. Throughout the past millennium outcastes were anathema to Korean Buddhists, Taoists, and Neo-Confucians. At the same time, their contributions in the service of these religions were significant, as outcastes were the longtime purveyors of incantations, charms, occult services, and sacrificial meat to the general public. Outcaste slaughtering for village ceremonies was sometimes preceded by swordplay and sword dancing. This suggests some convergence of ritual sacrifice and entertainment during the past. Their own prevailing religious convictions during most of the dynastic period (for example, whether or not outcastes practiced an ethnic religion) are unclear. They were especially attracted to Christianity when this opportunity finally arose toward the very end of the Yi period, but many "respectable" Korean Christians even then resented their involvement.

See also Burakumin; Korean

Bibliography

Chang, D. H. (1974). "A Study of the Korean Cultural Minority: The Paekchŏng." In *Traditional Korea: Theory and Practice*, edited by A. C. Nahm, 55–87. Kalamazoo: Western Michigan University Center for Korean Studies.

Moore, S. F. (1898). "The Butchers of Korea." *The Korean Repository* 5:127–132.

Passin, Herbert (1956–1957). "The Paekchŏng of Korea." *Monumenta Nipponica* 12:195–240.

Rao, A., ed. (1987). *The Other Nomads: Peripatetic Minorities in Cross-Cultural Perspective*. Cologne and Vienna: Bohlau.

Soon, M. R. (1974). "The Paekchŏng: Untouchables of Korea." *Hong Kong Journal of Oriental Studies* 12:30–40.

DAVID J. NEMETH

Korean

ETHNONYMS: Chosŏn, Han'guk

Orientation

Identification.   Because Korea is an ethnically homogeneous nation, there are no ethnonyms per se. There are, however, several alternative names used by outsiders as well as natives, all of which come from the names of previous states or dynasties. The name "Korea" comes from the Koryŏ dynasty (918–1392). "Han'guk" is an abbreviation of "Taehan Min'guk" (Republic of Korea), which is used exclusively by South Koreans. Its origin can be traced to "Taehan Che'guk" (Great Han Empire), the new name of the Yi dynasty (1392–

1910) chosen in 1897. "Chosŏn" originated from Old Chosŏn (2333–194 B.C.), the first Korean state that possessed a bronze culture. The Yi dynasty was also named "Chosŏn" and North Korea prefixed it for the name of its regime, "Chosŏn Minjuju-ŭi Inmin Konghwa'guk" (Democratic People's Republic of Korea). From "Chosŏn," meaning "morning calm and freshness," Korea acquired the epithet by which it is known, the "land of the morning calm."

Location. The Korean Peninsula and its associated islands lie between 33°06′ and 43°01′ N and between 124°11′ and 131°53′ E. Of the entire peninsula's area of 219,015 square kilometers, South Korea is 98,477 square kilometers, including islands and excluding the 1,262 square kilometers of the Demilitarized Zone (DMZ), about 45 percent of the entire peninsula. Korea is geomorphologically characterized by abundant hills and mountains, which occupy nearly 70 percent of its territory. Low hills, plains, and basins along the rivers are located in the south and the west, whereas the eastern slope is steep with high mountains and without significant rivers and plains. Winter is long, cold, and dry. January is the coldest month, and its average temperatures range from about 2° C in southeastern Korea to about −21° C in parts of the northern mountainous region. Summer is short, hot, and humid, with late monsoon rains. In the hottest month, July, temperatures average between 21° C and 27° C. Annual rainfall varies from year to year, and ranges from 50 centimeters in the northeastern inland region to 140 centimeters on the southern coast. About 70 percent of the annual rainfall occurs from June through September.

Demography. The population of South Korea has grown rapidly since the birth of the republic in 1948. Accelerating between 1955 and 1966, it reached 29.2 million, with an annual average growth rate of 2.8 percent; but the growth rate declined significantly during the period of 1966 to 1985, falling to an annual average of 1.7 percent. Thereafter, the annual average growth rate was less than 1 percent. As of 1 January 1989, the population of South Korea was slightly over 42.1 million. The population of North Korea for 1989 is unavailable, but it was estimated to be over 21 million in 1987. South Korea's Economic Planning Board estimates that its population will increase to between 46 and 48 million by the end of the twentieth century, with growth rates ranging between 0.9 and 1.2 percent. Since Korea is one of the world's most homogeneous nations ethnically and racially, the population of other national origins is negligible and the legal status of such aliens is mostly temporary. However, as of 1988 nearly 4 million ethnic Koreans live outside the peninsula: 1.7 million in China; 1.2 million in the United States and Canada; 680,000 in Japan; 85,000 in Central and South America; 62,000 in the Middle East; 40,000 in western Europe; 27,000 in other Asian countries; and 25,000 in Africa.

Linguistic Affiliation. Although the remote origins of the Korean language are disputed among linguists, it is generally believed that the prototype of the Korean language belongs to the Ural-Altaic Language Group and specifically to the Altaic Language Family, which includes Turkish, Mongolian, Japanese, Korean, and others. Modern Korean is descended from the language of the Silla Kingdom (57 B.C.–A.D. 935). The prolonged political and cultural influence of the Chinese upon Korea had a profound impact upon the written and spoken Korean language, especially from the Confucian classics.

The Japanese attempted to stifle the Korean tongue completely toward the end of their colonial rule (1910–1945), but they failed to leave more than a minimum trace of their language on Korean. Prior to the invention of Han'gŭl in 1446, Korean borrowed Chinese characters, using either the sounds or the meanings of certain Chinese characters. Even today, Koreans use Chinese characters alongside their own written language, as the Japanese do. Although the Korean language displays some regional variations both in vocabulary and pronunciation, there are no mutually unintelligible dialects. Variations are recognized between North and South Korea, resulting from a prolonged separation of the two Koreas.

History and Cultural Relations

Recent archaeological evidence has revealed that Paleolithic humans began to inhabit the Korean Peninsula some 40,000 to 50,000 years ago. It is not yet known, however, whether the contemporary Korean people are the descendants of the Paleolithic inhabitants. The Korean people commonly trace their origins to the founding of the state of Old Chosŏn, which arose in the northwestern corner of the peninsula. Several kingdoms and dynasties succeeded it; by the seventh century, the peninsula was united under the Silla Kingdom. The inhabitants of the peninsula have suffered from frequent foreign intruders, and the history of Korea can be told in terms of geopolitical adversities. Because Korea is located in the middle of the Far East, it has always been vulnerable to attacks from neighboring states. In addition to invasion and domination by Chinese dynasties over the centuries, nomadic northern tribes have continually intruded on Korea. The rise and fall of Chinese dynasties has had a profound impact on the security of Korea. Two full-scale Japanese invasions into Korea in the sixteenth century devastated the Korean Yi dynasty. Taewŏn'gun (1821–1898) of the Yi dynasty adopted a policy of isolationism in direct response to Western incursion, but in the mid-nineteenth century Japan, China, Russia, some European nations, and the United States pressured Korea to open its doors to outsiders in the name of modernization. Competing foreigners clashed on Korean soil, which led to the Russo-Japanese War (1904–1905). Victory in this conflict provided Japan with a firm base for sole control of the peninsula, which it annexed in 1910 and maintained as a colony until 1945. Despite persistent foreign threats, invasions, and incursions, the peninsula has been united since the seventh century, except in rare and temporary instances, and has remained undivided, protected on its northern border by two rivers, the Yalu and Tumen.

The peninsula was, however, divided in 1945 along the 38th parallel by the United States and the Soviet Union at the start of the cold war. This division eventually led to the fratricidal Korean War (1950–1953), as a result of which the existing demarcation at the 38th parallel was broadened to form the DMZ. Since the peninsula has been divided, the two Koreas have taken distinctly different paths. Whereas South Korea is evolving into a liberal democracy after years of authoritarian and military rule, North Korea has emerged as a committed Communist society. By 1992, North Korea was one of very few Communist countries remaining in the world. Beginning in 1971, there has been a continuing series of inter-Korea talks, although these discussions have alternated between dialogue and tension. Nevertheless, despite a prolonged division, a civil war, and the differences in ways of life, all Koreans share a strong common belief that they are the same brethren (*tong'jok* and *min'jok*).

Settlements

Before recent economic growth and industrialization accelerated urbanization, most Koreans lived in the countryside. In 1910 when Japan colonized Korea, the urban population of Korea was no more than 3 percent of the total population. Traditionally Korean villages were located along the southern foothills, and many Koreans believed that an ideal site for a house or village must have a hill behind it and a stream in front.

In some villages the population consists solely of members of one lineage; other villages have many different lineages. The size of villages varies, ranging from 10 to 150 households. Most of the housing consists of one-story structures made of stone or homemade bricks. Formerly, some of the houses had thatch roofs, which have been replaced by tile or slate roofs as part of the New Village movement that began in 1970. Traditionally, rooms were heated by the *ondol* method, and hot air from burning wood outdoors warmed the stone floor. Now coal, oil, and electricity are replacing wood.

Rural settlement patterns have been altered significantly by a massive migration from rural to urban to industrialized areas beginning in the mid-1960s. In this period, at least 9 million farmers and their families, nearly a quarter of the total population, are estimated to have left their farms and moved to cities. In 1988, the urban population reached over 78 percent. In mid-1989, the population of Seoul, the capital, was more than 10.5 million, nearly one-fourth of the entire South Korean population, with a population density of 17,365 persons per square kilometer. Construction of large numbers of high-rise apartment complexes in Seoul and other cities has alleviated housing shortages to some extent and has determined the major settlement pattern of urban Korea.

Economy

Subsistence and Commercial Activities. Before the 1900s, Koreans lived as subsistence farmers of rice, barley, sorghum, and other crops and satisfied most of their basic needs through their own labor or through barter. Fishery products in the coastal villages were popular. The Japanese introduced some heavy industries, locating them in the north, and improved Korean infrastructure for obvious reasons. In the meantime, the south remained mainly agricultural, with some light industry. Division of the peninsula made it impossible for Koreans to exchange products between northern industries and southern farms. The Korean economy lost its balance.

A drastic transformation of the Korean subsistence economy took place after the mid-1960s as South Korea adopted a policy of economic modernization, emphasizing export-oriented industrialization and growth. A series of five-year economic plans beginning in 1962 has exceeded the goals originally set, and growth rates have been phenomenal. Real growth was 12.5 percent between 1986 and 1988, and 6.5 percent in 1989. South Korea became the world's tenth-largest steel producer by 1989 and began exporting automobiles, ships, electronic goods, textiles, shoes, clothing, and

leather products. Because of South Korea's emphasis on industrialization, the relative importance of the agricultural sector has steadily declined. By January 1989, agriculture, fishing, and forestry employed approximately 13 percent of the total industrial work force and generated 10.2 percent of gross domestic product. At the same time, farmers increased their income (by 24.4 percent in 1988) by raising cash crops, thus increasingly becoming commercial farmers.

Industrial Arts. A variety of implements and objects of industrial arts is available. Most popular are manufacturing replicas of the Koryŏ and Yi dynasty celadons. Lacquerware and items with mother-of-pearl inlay are popular. "Knots" with silk thread for accessories are another product, manufactured using ancient arts. Most of these are sold domestically, but some limited quantities are made for export.

Trade. Since Korea's economic modernization has become oriented toward industrialization and growth, Koreans place a great emphasis on export. Annual trade in 1988 was more than $900 billion, and South Korea became the world's tenth-largest trading nation. Main export items include textiles, clothing, electronic and electric equipment, footwear, machinery, steel, rubber tires and tubes, plywood, and fishing products. Major import items are machinery, electronic and electrical equipment, petroleum and petroleum products, steels, grain, transport equipment, chemicals, timber and pulp, raw cotton, and cereals. South Korea achieved a surplus of more than $4.6 billion in the balance of payment for trade in 1989.

Division of Labor. During the Koryŏ and Yi dynasties, until it was outlawed in 1894, division of labor by class was pervasive: *yangban* (nobility), mainly the scholar-officials, were largely exempt from manual labor performed by commoners. Division of labor by gender was also prominent, strongly influenced by Confucian-oriented values: men were primarily responsible for outside labor as providers, whereas women performed domestic tasks. Despite the existence of male preference in many jobs and occupational ranks, the gender gap is narrowing, especially for highly educated women in the cities. Domestic work, however, has continued to be the work of women. In the case of urban working women, their burden has become doubly onerous. In the rural villages an increasing number of women participate in agricultural work, even in the rainfall (nonirrigated) field, which was not the traditional pattern.

Land Tenure. Traditionally, the king owned all land and granted it to his subjects. Although specific parcels of land tended to remain within the same family from generation to generation (including communal land owned by clans and lineages), land occupancy, use, and ownership patterns were legally ambiguous and widely divergent. The Japanese conducted a comprehensive land survey between 1910 and 1920 as their colonization began, in order to identify landownership. Farmers whose families had farmed the same land for generations but who could not prove ownership to the colonial authorities lost their land. Those farmers either became tenants or were forced to leave the land, emigrating to the cities or overseas. At the time of liberation, almost half (48.9 percent) of farm households were landless tenants, and another 34.6 percent were part-time part-tenants, whereas only 1.4 percent were owner-cultivators. After 1945, the American occupation authorities confiscated and redistributed the land held by the Japanese colonial government, although they allowed Koreans to retain their private property. The South Korean government then carried out a land reform in 1949 whereby Koreans with large landholdings had to divest most of their land to those who actually tilled it. Land reform provided for a more equitable distribution of available land. However, by 1989, more than 30 percent of Korean farmland was cultivated by landless tenants whose numbers were estimated to be 67 percent of the total farm population.

Kinship

Kin Groups and Descent. The rule of descent in Korea was and still is patrilineal in principle, although a bilateral trend has begun to emerge. The origin of patrilineal rule may be prehistoric, but it first gained strength through Chinese influence beginning in the first half of the first century B.C. The patrilineal rule of descent gave rise to a number of elaborate kin groups, lineages, and clans. Most lineages and clans maintain written genealogical records following the patrilineal rule. There are over 1,000 clans in Korea, each of which includes scores of lineages. Some genealogies published recently tend to list female members who were already married to members of other clans.

Kinship Terminology. The influence of Chinese Confucianism has altered the original kinship terminology, especially in kinship nomenclature for reference terms among those of yangban origin. As far as the terms of address for cousins are concerned, Korean kinship can be classified as a modified Hawaiian type, although male paternal parallel cousins are favored over other cousins.

Marriage and Family

Marriage. Traditional marriages were thoroughly arranged, particularly among the noble class as a form of class endogamy. The ideal form of marriage was and is monogamy. Although arranged marriages are still popular in rural villages, an increasing number of educated and urban Koreans choose their own mates. Many of them use a compromise form between arranged marriage and free choice: parents, kin, and friends recommend several candidates equal in their qualifications and leave the final selection to the persons who are going to be married (_mat'sŏn_). Semiprofessional matchmakers are emerging in the cities; they arrange marriages between children of the newly rich and privileged class, charging high commissions for their services.

The rule of residence used to be patrilocal, but a growing number of young couples practice neolocal residence. Marital bonds have been so strong in the past that divorce was infrequent, even unthinkable. Now the number of divorces among educated, young, urban Koreans is increasing yearly. Divorce no longer carries a stigma, and remarriage does not have many guidelines.

Domestic Unit. In accordance with increasing urbanization and industrialization, the extended family is no longer a domestic unit. The predominant form of household unit, especially in the cities, is the nuclear family, although a transitional form of stem family is also common. The average number of people in households was slightly over 5 in the

1960s and 1970s, but that number had decreased to 4.1 by the mid-1980s.

Inheritance. The rule of inheritance has evolved over a long period of time. Prior to the 1600s, sons and daughters inherited equally, but since the 1800s primogeniture has been the rule, although ultimogeniture occurred in some remote mountain villages. Even after liberation in 1945 and the revision of the civil code in 1977—and despite an effort to upgrade the position of women in inheritance—the current civil code specifies the rule of primogeniture by giving 5 percent more to the eldest son than to other sons and unmarried daughters. A married daughter's share is a quarter of the allotment given to her brothers.

Socialization. In their early years children receive a great deal of affection, indulgence, and nurturing from both parents. Infants and toddlers are seldom separated from their mothers or left unattended. Parents encourage children to be dependent, obedient, and cooperative. They usually introduce prohibitive norms only as the children grow older, and they apply punishments for disobedience rather than wrongdoing. The primary agency for socialization is gradually changing from extended family to nuclear family, thus making parents more influential than grandparents, and prohibitive norms are gradually being replaced by permissive norms. Because of the influence of the Confucian heritage, Koreans have an obsession for education: they value formal education as the single most important factor for individual success and upward mobility. Currently, Korea has six years of compulsory education, and over 93 percent of the population is literate. About 35 percent of the student-age group attended colleges and universities in 1989, one of the world's highest percentages.

Sociopolitical Organization

Social Organization. When Korea was still a preindustrial and agricultural society, predominant forms of social organization were family- and kinship-centered institutions such as lineages (minimum and maximum) and clans. Kin-based organizations are still present and considered to be important. However, recent industrialization, urbanization, and massive migration have resulted in movement away from lineage- and neighborhood-based social relations toward functionally based relations. Both formal and informal social organizations are formed in factories, shops, and offices. Branches of many multinational organizations are also present. Organizations based on school ties are now pivotal.

Political Organization. Following the division of Korea, South Korea became a democratic republic, whereas North Korea remains a communist dictatorship. South Korea is in its sixth republic. The most recent constitution was approved in October 1987, effective February 1988, and mandates a strong president, elected for one five-year term, and 224 members of the 229-member National Assembly, elected by popular vote for four-year terms. Political parties appoint the remaining officials according to a proportional formula. An independent judicial branch, with the Supreme Court at its apex, administers justice. South Korea has nine provinces, which are divided into counties, cities, townships, towns, and villages, and six provincial-level cities.

Social Control. Traditionally, any conflict or dispute in a family, a village, or even among villages has been settled mainly by informal control, through the mediation of either heads of households or village elders. However, formal control mechanisms have replaced the informal social controls. In the past, Koreans were reluctant to take their grievances to the courts and even took offense at the idea, but nowadays they are not so averse to the legal process.

Conflict. The Korean Peninsula is the only remaining part of the world where a cold war remnant of ideological conflict and tension exists. Although various levels of inter-Korean talks have taken place since 1971, as of 1992 no significant progress has yet been made. Recently, in South Korea, regional conflict and resentment—especially between Chŏlla and Kyŏngsang provinces—have arisen because of the domination of South Korea's politics and business by people from Kyŏngsang Province. The three most recent presidents, all of whom were ex-generals, came from Kyŏngsang Province. The South Korean government has made a conscious effort—including the construction of a new four-lane highway between the two provincial capitals in 1984—to reduce, if not eliminate, a potentially harmful animosity between these regions.

Religion and Expressive Culture

Religious Beliefs. Koreans have been inclusive rather than exclusive in their religious beliefs, and the majority of them have opted for expressing no religious preference. Because of this, it is difficult for anyone to give an accurate religious census of Korea. Polytheistic shamanism and other animistic beliefs appear to be the oldest forms of religion, dating back to prehistoric time. South Korea has a great diversity of religious traditions, including Buddhism, Confucianism, Ch'ŏndogyo, Christianity, and as many as 300 new religious sects. Among the 1985 Korean religious population of 17 million (about 42.6 percent of the total population), over 480,000 (2.8 percent) claimed that they were Confucianists, over 8.07 million (46.9 percent) were Buddhists, more than 8.34 million (48.5 percent) claimed to be Christian (both Roman Catholic and Protestant), and the remaining 310,000 (1.8 percent) belonged to various other religions. Some estimate that by the early 1990s over a quarter of the entire South Korean population was Christian. South Korea has the highest percentage of Christians of any country in East Asia or Southeast Asia with the exception of the Philippines, and the growth rate is unusually high.

Religious Practitioners. Shamanism is performed by shamans, most of whom are women, by holding shamanic ritual, *kut*, in order to gain good fortune for clients, cure illnesses by exorcising evil spirits, or propitiate local or village gods. Shamans formerly were of low social status and were victims of discrimination. Recently, with growing nationalism, the dances, songs, and incantations of kut have been revitalized. Buddhism is experiencing a modernization movement: "mountain Buddhism" is changing toward "community Buddhism," and "temple-centered Buddhism" is turning into "socially relevant Buddhism." Accordingly, the role of monks goes beyond the religious sphere, and their worldly possessions are also modernized. Some clergymen and priests in Christian churches have become outspoken advocates of

human rights, critics of the government, and sympathizers with the union movement.

Ceremonies. Despite the strength of Christianity, most families in South Korea observe the Confucian practice of honoring their dead ancestors on the anniversaries of their death days, New Year's Day, and other holidays such as *hansik* (the 105th day after the winter solstice) and *ch'usŏk* (the fifteenth day of the eighth lunar month). The people conduct rituals and ceremonies in honor of Confucius each spring and autumn at the Confucian shrines. Shamans can hold kut at their clients' request. Buddhists pray day and night on Buddha's birthday, the eighth day of April lunar month, which is often followed by a street parade in the cities; Christians celebrate Christmas Day in their churches. Both of these days are national holidays.

Arts. Koreans have practiced the arts since prehistoric times, especially painting, sculpture, various handicrafts, and music. The walls of tombs of the Koguryŏ Kingdom (37 B.C.–A.D. 668) revealed multicolor paintings of birds, animals, and human figures. Over the centuries, Chinese art as well as Buddhism and Confucianism have influenced Korean arts: bronze images of Buddha, stone carvings, stone pagodas, and temples are influenced by Buddhism; poetry, calligraphy, and landscape paintings are influenced by Confucianism. There are many unique Korean arts, including folk paintings (*min'hwa*); Koryŏ and Yi dynasty celadons are well known. Because of their fame, many Korean potters were taken back to Japan during the Japanese invasions of Korea in the 1590s. The influence of the Western arts, especially drama, motion pictures, music, and dances, has been pronounced.

Medicine. Modern Occidental medicine is the dominant form of medical practice, and since 1991 virtually all South Koreans have had medical insurance. Traditional practice of medicine, however, is not uncommon. Shamanic rituals are performed and herbal remedies are used to cure various illnesses. Shops selling traditional medicines, including ginseng, are common.

Death and Afterlife. Christian ideas of the afterlife involve heaven and hell; reincarnation is the belief of Buddhists. Although Confucian teaching on the afterlife is uncertain and implicit, Koreans who observe ancestor worship believe that death is not a final termination but a transformation. In Korean folk belief, death means a departure from this world to the "otherworld." The otherworld is not necessarily located far away from this world but may be over the mountains. Death is thought to be a rite of passage, and the dead are generally considered to be similar to the living. Elaborate ancestor-worship rites, offering various foods as to a living person, spring out of these beliefs.

See also Kolisuch'ŏk; Koreans in Japan

Bibliography

Brandt, Vincent S. R. (1971). *A Korean Village: Between Farm and Sea.* Cambridge: Harvard University Press.

Janelli, Roger L., and Dawnhee Yim Janelli (1982). *Ancestor Worship and Korean Society.* Stanford, Calif.: Stanford University Press.

Kendall, Laurel (1985). _Shamans, Housewives, and Other Restless Spirits: Women in Korean Ritual Life._ Honolulu: University of Hawaii Press.

Kim, Choong Soon (1988). _Faithful Endurance: An Ethnography of Korean Family Dispersal._ Tucson: University of Arizona Press.

Kim, Choong Soon (1992). _The Culture of Korean Industry: An Ethnography of Poongsan Corporation._ Tucson: University of Arizona Press.

Sorensen, Clark W. (1988). _Over the Mountains Are Mountains: Korean Peasant Households and Their Adaptations to Rapid Industrialization._ Seattle: University of Washington Press.

CHOONG SOON KIM

Koreans in Japan

ETHNONYMS: Chōsenjin (North Koreans), Kankokujin (South Koreans)

At present, there are 700,000 Koreans in Japan, three-fourths of whom were born in and have grown up in Japan. Most are legally classified as "resident aliens." Koreans make up 85 percent of Japan's resident alien population. Most Koreans in Japan speak no Korean.

The historical connection between Japan and Korea is very ancient. In the seventh century, many Japanese nobles claimed Korean ancestry. Nara-period documents (A.D. 710–784) claim that the Yamato regime had control of part of Korea. Archaeological evidence, however, demonstrates an early Korean presence in Japan, but no comparable Japanese presence in Korea.

Later history reversed the trend. From the tenth through the sixteenth centuries, Japanese pirates attacked Korea extensively. In 1592 Toyotomi Hideyoshi began a seven-year war with Korea as a prelude to taking China; he failed, but managed to destroy large regions of Korea. Japan overran Korea in 1904, annexing it in 1910. Koreans were dispossessed of land so that emigrant Japanese could farm it. Koreans were forced by the threat of starvation to go to Japan; by 1930 there were 419,009 Koreans in Japan. Between 1939 and 1945 Koreans were forcibly moved to Japan, and there were 2,400,000 in Japan by the end of World War II. During that war, Koreans worked primarily in the coal mines, but they also supplied cheap factory labor. This freed Japanese to enter the military. By 1944, the need for soldiers was so acute that even Koreans were conscripted. During their occupation of Korea, the Japanese burned Korean books and forced Korean schoolchildren to learn Japanese. Following the war, most Koreans in Japan returned to Korea; the 1950 Korean-Japanese population was 544,903. It was not until 1972 that most Koreans in Japan were granted permanent residency, ending their stateless existence.

Koreans are readily identifiable to Japanese by their monosyllabic, one-character surnames, which many Japanese treat with derision. As a result, most Koreans have adopted Japanese names in addition to their Korean names; only 20 percent of Korean high-school students in Japan are registered under Korean names. Many Koreans attempt to pass as Japanese to gain better employment or to enter private schools. When discovered, however, they are quickly fired or expelled under the pretext that they are not citizens.

It is possible for those Korean Japanese whose parents were born in Japan to become naturalized citizens of Japan. To be successful, the applicant must be of "good behavior," and this precludes anyone with even the most minor of police records. On the other hand, most Koreans do not wish to become naturalized. The older Koreans still harbor hatred of the Japanese for their past actions. Many younger Koreans do not wish to be naturalized because they realize that doing so will cost them the acceptance of the Korean community but will not gain them the acceptance of the Japanese. Naturalization also requires one to "Japanize" his or her name, an emotionally difficult step for many. Intermarriage, a large step toward full assimilation, is very popular; in 1972 48 percent of Koreans marrying in Japan married Japanese. Some of these marriages were to Burakumin, who often live near Korean communities and do not discriminate against Koreans.

Although there are Korean ghettos in Osaka and Tokyo, most Koreans are spread out in many places in Japan, and this has served to make their political organizations less effective. Political organization is further divided among Koreans themselves; some 350,000 belong or are sympathetic to the Mindan (Korean Resident Association in Japan) organization and support South Korea; another 300,000 belong or are sympathetic to the Chongnyon (General Federation of Koreans in Japan) organization and support the North Korean government. Members of Chongnyon are seen by the Japanese government as citizens of North Korea, with which they have no diplomatic relations. This means that Chongnyon members have no right to the free national health insurance, to child benefits, to welfare or pensions, or to free education. Because they live in Japan, however, they pay the same taxes that Japanese citizens pay.

The Japanese government closed several Korean ethnic schools in 1949. Now, only 20 percent of Korean schoolchildren attend Korean ethnic schools, nearly all of which are operated by Chongnyon and supported financially by the North Korean government as a propaganda effort; a major part of the curriculum of these schools is "Kim Il Sung Thought." Those who attend the Chongnyon schools may complete an all-Korean education at Chōsen University, also supported by Chongnyon. Those who graduate from Chongnyon schools and who wish to attend a Japanese university have a difficult time gaining entrance. In a country in which educational achievement is an important basis for assessing personal status, this fact has tremendous consequences. Koreans in Japan rarely have good jobs; most work as manufacturers of handicrafts, as day laborers, as restaurant, bar, mine, or factory workers, or in family-operated businesses. Further, the option of working for the government is open only to Japanese citizens.

See also Burakumin; Japanese; Korean

Bibliography

De Vos, George A., William O. Wetherall, and Kaye Stearman (1983). *Japan's Minorities: Burakumin, Koreans, Ainu, and Okinawans*. London: Minority Rights Group.

Lee, Changsoo, and George A. De Vos (1984). *Koreans in Japan: Ethnic Conflict and Accommodation*. Berkeley and Los Angeles: University of California Press.

Min, Pyong Gap (1992). "A Comparison of the Korean Minorities in China and Japan." *International Migration Review* 26:4–21.

Mitchell, Richard H. (1967). *The Korean Minority in Japan*. Berkeley and Los Angeles: University of California Press.

Wagner, Edward W. (1951). *The Korean Minority in Japan, 1904–1950*. New York: Institute of Pacific Relations.

DANIEL STROUTHES

Kubu

The Kubu (Koeboe, Orang Darat) live in Sumatra and are found throughout the east-coast lowlands westward to the foothills of the Barisan Range. "Kubu" is a generic label used by outsiders for a number of scattered former hunter-gatherers in Sumatra. Kubu groups themselves prefer to be called "Orang Darat" (people of the land) or by the name of a local ethnic group. Named Kubu groups are the Mamk, Sakai, Akit, Talang, Tapung, Orang Utan, Orang Rawas, Lubu, Ulu, Rawas, Duwablas, Mountain Kubus, and Benua. In 1935, the population was approximately 25,000, and the number is probably considerably lower today. The settled Kubu are Muslims, although some traditional beliefs and practices survive. The Kubu use the language of the dominant group with which they associate, such as Riau or Djambi Malay, Minangkabau or Mandailing Batak. The Kubu now often live near Malay villages where they subsist as farmers. The traditional hunter-gatherer way of life is largely a thing of the past.

Bibliography

Keereweer, H. H. (1940). "De Koeboes in de Onderafdeeling Moesi Kir en Koeboestreken." *Bijdragen tot de Taal-, Land- en Volkenkunde* 99:357–396.

LeBar, Frank M. (1972). "Kubu." In *Ethnic Groups of Insular Southeast Asia*, edited by Frank M. LeBar. Vol. 1, *Indonesia, Andaman Islands, and Madagascar*, 46–47. New Haven: HRAF Press.

Kui

The Kui (Kuoy, Soai) are a group of more than 100,000 located in east-central Thailand, northeast Cambodia, and Laos. Some experts suggest that the Kui were settled in the area prior to the arrival of the now-dominant Thai and Lao. The Kui are closely related to the Chaobon, Chong, Pear, and other similar groups. They have been drawn into the dominant cultures in the region: the traditional religion now has largely been replaced by Buddhism, many Kui now speak Khmer or Lao, wet-rice agriculture has replaced horticulture, and there is frequent intermarriage with the Khmer.

Bibliography

Seidenfaden, Erik (1958). *The Thai Peoples*. Bangkok: Siam Society.

Lahu

ETHNONYMS: Co Sung, Co Xung, Guozhou, Kha Quy, Khu Xung, Kucong, Kwi, Laho, Lohei, Mussur

Orientation

Identification. The Lahu are one among many linguistically and culturally distinct ethnic minority peoples of the mountainous region that extends from the far southwestern part of China's Yunnan Province into Myanmar's (Burma) Shan State, northwestern Laos, northern Thailand, and northwest Vietnam. The people's own ethnonym, "Lahu" ("Laho" in some dialects), is of uncertain meaning. The old Chinese name for them was "Lohei," now dropped because of its derogatory connotations. The Tai call them "Mussur," derived from the Burmese *moksa*, "hunter." "Kucong" and "Co Sung" (also "Co Xung," "Khu Xung," and "Kha Quy") are names used in Yunnan and North Vietnam respectively for a highly divergent branch of the Lahu, traditionally forest-dwelling hunters and gatherers but in Yunnan simple swiddeners as well. Only recently have they been identified (by Chinese researchers) as belonging within the wider Lahu ethnic group. The Lahu have numerous linguistically and culturally specific subdivisions, the two most important being the Lahu Na (Black Lahu) and Lahu Shi (Yellow Lahu; called "Mussur Kwi" or just "Kwi" by the Shan). Lahu Hpu (White) is another important subdivision, especially in Yunnan, as is Lahu Nyi (Red) in Myanmar's Shan State and in north Thailand. Yunnan's Kucong also have Black and Yellow divisions; the Black Kucong reportedly call themselves "Guozhou" but are termed "Lahu Na" by their Lahu Shi neighbors, and the Yellow Kucong call themselves "Lahu Shi." Ethnic identification by color labels is widespread in Southeast Asia.

Location. About 67 percent of all Lahu live in the far southwestern tip of China's Yunnan Province, mostly near the Myanmar border in the mountains on both sides of the Lancang (Mekong) River. Outside China, Lahu communities are scattered through the federated Shan State, north Thailand, Laos's Nam Tha Province (whence some have gone as refugees to California), and far northwestern Vietnam. Their widespread settlement areas have common natural characteristics: rugged hill country cut by narrow alluvial valleys, a subtropical monsoonal climate, luxuriant natural vegetation, and mostly fertile soils. It is good country for growing rice (irrigated and dry), maize, and buckwheat, as well as cash crops like tea, tobacco, and opium. There is a wide variety of fauna, including tiger and other wild cats, bears, gaur, sambar and barking deer, gibbons, and several species of monkeys.

Demography. Lahu probably number some 600,000 people. In China (1990 census) there were 411,174 Lahu; in Myanmar, perhaps 150,000; in Laos perhaps 10,000; and in Thailand, 63,821 scattered through about 290 villages (1988 count). Vietnam's Co Sung, according to a 1984 report, numbered more than 4,000.

Linguistic Affiliation. The Lahu language (together with Lisu) belongs to the Central Loloish (or Yi) Branch of the Lolo-Burmese Subgroup of the Tibeto-Burman Family. It has close lexical affinities with the Southern Loloish Akha language. Lahu has no traditional script; the people once used notched sticks, with or without chicken feathers attached, to communicate simple messages. Three romanizations have been introduced during this century, by Protestant and Roman Catholic missionaries and by Chinese government linguists.

History and Cultural Relations

Chinese scholars count the Lahu among the ancient Qiang people of the Qinghai-Tibetan plateau. Migrating slowly southward, ancestral Lahu, along with other Qiang peoples, are said to have settled around Dali during the third to fifth centuries A.D., where they were known as the Kun or Kunming. Sometime during the next five centuries, during which they were dominated by various ruling dynasties in central Yunnan, the Lahu appear to have become consolidated as a distinct ethnolinguistic group. From the tenth century, according to Chinese sources, the Lahu began a large-scale

southerly migration, during which they bifurcated. The ancestors of the Lahu Na took a westerly route, while those of the Lahu Shi, along with the Lahu Hpu, preferred an easterly one. Eventually most Lahu came under the jurisdiction of Tai feudal overlords, recognized by the Chinese government as _tusi_, "native chiefs," holding imperial seals legitimizing their rule in the name of the Son of Heaven. During the Ming dynasty, the imperial authorities began a process of replacing native leaders by Han officials, a policy continued under the Qing dynasty, when it first affected the Lahu areas. Some Lahu areas were brought under direct Chinese control; others were administered jointly by a Chinese magistrate and a native ruler. Between the eighteenth and early twentieth centuries various sections of Lahu people (some led by warrior-priests) rebelled against these imperial authorities, Lahu fighters facing far better-armed Chinese troops with nothing but their crossbows and poison-tipped arrows. One by one, the rebellions were put down; the majority of Lahu accepted the inevitability of Chinese rule, but some fled southward into Burmese and Lao territory. Lahu were well established in the Burmese Shan States by the 1830s and in Laos by mid-century. They probably began moving into north Thailand in the 1870s or 1880s.

In recent centuries Lahu have mostly lived in mountainous areas, their villages interspersed with those of other ethnic groups, notably Wa and Hani (Akha) in the south and Yi in the north, but also many others. The rich alluvial valleys below their mountain homes have been controlled mostly by Tai peoples. Han Chinese settlers in southern Yunnan have tended to occupy lands in the foothills, above the valley bottoms but below the elevations favored by the true hill peoples. Lahu culture has been greatly influenced by its neighbors, particularly the Tai and Han Chinese.

Settlements

In the northeastern areas of Lahu settlement in Yunnan, Lahu villages resemble those of their Han and Yi neighbors. Based on irrigated-rice production, such villages are permanent settlements, some numbering over 200 households and more than 1,000 people. Houses are substantial earthen structures in the Chinese style, with roofs of thatch or wooden boards. Further southwest in Yunnan, and through Myanmar's Shan State, north Thailand, and northwestern Laos, Lahu villages tend to be much smaller and thus better suited to a predominantly swidden-farming economy. They are also less permanent, being relocated every eight to ten years. Thirty houses and 120 people are about normal, but the range is considerable. Houses are usually of bamboo, raised on wooden or thick bamboo piles and thatched with leaves or cogon grass. Averaging about 3 by 3.5 meters, they vary in size according to the number of occupants rather than family wealth. In some of the southwestern settlement areas in Yunnan, at least until the 1950s, longhouses (up to 15 meters in length) were not uncommon for extended families of 40 to 100 people, each nuclear family unit having its own apartment and cooking hearth. The settlements of the Kucong (Co Sung) reflect their hunting-and-gathering economy. These people make temporary huts, or even simpler wind shelters, by covering a bamboo or wooden frame with wild banana or bamboo leaves. They sleep on leaves next to their house fires. Such huts have to be rebuilt about once a month.

Economy

Subsistence and Commercial Activities. Probably most Lahu are still predominantly swidden farmers, cultivating dry rice as a staple, corn for their pigs, and chilies, without which no Lahu meal is considered edible. They interplant leafy and root vegetables, herbs, melons, pumpkins, and gourds with the major crops. Principal cash crops include chilies, cotton, tea, and opium poppy. Several traditionally swidden-based communities, especially in Yunnan, also have irrigated-rice lands in the foothills. Among the Sinicized northeastern Lahu, irrigated-rice farming is the mainstay, supplemented by fruit-tree silviculture, vegetable gardening, and tea cultivation. Yunnan's Kosung combine the gathering of forest products (roots, stems, leaves, and fruits) and hunting (deer, wild pigs, bears, wild cats, pangolins, and porcupines) with a rough form of swidden farming, mostly of maize but also a little dry rice. Vietnam's Co Sung have only recently taken up dry-rice swidden farming, in imitation of their Phunoi and Hani neighbors; before this they were exclusively hunter-gatherers of the forests, subsisting primarily on wild taro. Trade and barter of hill produce, both cultigens and natural, with neighboring upland and valley peoples, has long been an integral part of Lahu village life. Most Lahu farmers are familiar with the use of money, with lowland markets, and with itinerant peddlers. Some Lahu villages boast their own multipurpose provision stores, often operated by a resident Han Chinese merchant who has taken a Lahu wife.

Pigs are the most important domesticated animals, since no major festival is complete without pork. Lahu communities with irrigated-rice fields keep cattle and buffalo as draft animals. Swiddening communities sometimes keep them as capital investment, offering these animals for seasonal hire to irrigated-rice-farming lowlanders, or for sale as meat. Lahu rarely eat beef and generally abhor animals' milk. Ponies and mules are valuable pack animals, but seldom ridden. Chickens are a ubiquitous feature of Lahu villages and are frequently sacrificed. Ducks and geese also may be reared. Dogs are kept principally as guard animals; cats are less common.

Industrial Arts. Most Lahu villages boast at least one blacksmith, who forges knives, hoes, sickles, ax heads, dibble blades, opium-tapping knives, etc., from scrap iron obtained in the lowlands. Blacksmiths are usually part-time specialists, receiving payment in kind or in labor in their fields. Women spin cotton and weave cloth for clothing and shoulder bags.

Division of Labor. Division of labor is limited and based on gender and age. Men alone are the hunters and undertake the heaviest agricultural tasks. Apart from this, men, women, and children from quite tender ages cooperate in all agricultural activities. Women take major responsibility for domestic chores, collecting water and caring for the pigs and fowl. Men mostly take care of the larger animals. Men and women share gathering activities as well as cutting and collecting firewood.

Land Tenure. Among swidden communities, individual households have usufruct rights over their swiddens, and the village headman has final say in land disputes. Rights over irrigated rice fields, by contrast, are individual, permanent, and inheritable.

Kinship

Kin Groups and Descent. Although many of the Lahu in Yunnan have taken Chinese surnames (Li seems to be the most common) and patrilineage organization (for ritual purposes) is found among some Lahu groups (e.g., Lahu Sheh Leh), the traditional kinship pattern seems to be essentially bilateral, with exogamous but noncorporate cognatic kindreds. Among Lahu Nyi these include second but not third cousins. Outside the immediate family and village community, ties of kinship do not necessarily cement stronger bonds between individuals than does simple friendship. This notwithstanding, there is a pervasive notion that members of the village community should behave as "relatives" (*aw-vi aw-nyi*).

Kinship Terminology. There are some differences in terminology according to divisional affiliation and the dominant lingua franca (a Tai language or Chinese), but the underlying pattern seems fairly consistent. The Lahu Shi and Lahu Sheh Leh systems, however, have terms—absent among other Lahu divisions—to identify particular parental siblings; this usage may reflect these peoples' preference for matrilateral cross-cousin marriage. Typically, Lahu Nyi have a composite term for kin, "aw-vi aw-nyi," literally meaning "elder sibling, younger sibling." The specific (i.e., nondescriptive) kinship terminology is very simple, both in reference and address. Grandfathers on both sides are *aw-pu* (*nga* [my] *pu* in address) and grandmothers *aw-pi* (*nga pi*). Father is *aw-pa* (*nga pa*), mother *aw-e* (*nga e*). There are only descriptive terms for parents' siblings and these relatives are addressed by the terms for elder male/female sibling. There are no special terms for cousins, although these can be specified descriptively. Siblings and cousins are addressed by personal name. There are specific terms also for the next four generations. All are addressed by personal name.

Marriage and Family

Marriage. Marital unions, invariably monogamous, result from a period of courtship with minimal parental interference. Once a couple decides to marry, a go-between formally initiates negotiations between the two families. Prospective mates should not be too close; Lahu Nyi say "people related within three generations must not marry." The preference for cross-cousin marriage, common among Yi-speaking peoples, seems limited to Lahu Shi and Sheh Leh. First marriages tend to be contracted when boys are about 16 or 17 and girls 13 or 14. Wedding rites vary from one Lahu division to the next but are comparatively simple, usually involving a communal feast and the ritual participation of the village headman, priest, and elders. Christian weddings are probably the most elaborate in ritual terms. Postmarital residence is generally uxorilocal, at least initially. The groom offers bride-service to his father-in-law's household before returning with his spouse and offspring for a shorter service period in his own parental home. There is much flexibility in these arrangements, money sometimes being paid in lieu of service. Setting up an independent household, frequently in the wife's parental village, is the ultimate aim of most Lahu couples. A youngest or only child, especially if a daughter, is likely to remain permanently at home to care for the parents in their old age. Divorce (except among some Christians) is frequent and easily obtained, particularly before the birth of children. The village headman levies fines on both parties, with the side that has initiated the proceedings paying double. A short ritual publicly severs the marital bond.

Domestic Unit. The household, either nuclear and sharing one hearth, or extended with married children having their own apartments and hearths, is the basic unit of Lahu village society. Rice swiddens, livestock, food supplies, and jewelry are held by the household head on behalf of his whole household. Economic and ritual responsibilities as well as benefits are distributed among households, not individuals. The household head and his wife are jointly in charge of the domestic unit.

Inheritance. Rules for the inheritance of property can be quite complex. Among Lahu Nyi indivisible property is proportioned equally between the household and the deceased spouse's immediate nonresident relatives: parents, siblings, and children.

Socialization. The household is the principal socializing unit, with parents and siblings intimately involved. Infants and young children are treated with indulgence, seldom receiving more than a verbal reprimand. By the age of 5 or 6, girls begin to take on simple domestic chores; by 8 or 9, both boys and girls help in the fields and care for younger siblings. By their early teens, Lahu children are more or less fully socialized into adult life.

Sociopolitical Organization

Social Organization. Lahu village society is extraordinarily egalitarian. Age, not gender, fertility, or wealth, is normally the basis for what little hierarchy there is. The principal unit of village social organization is the highly autonomous household. Although ritually important patrilineages serve among Lahu Sheh Leh to link otherwise independent households, there are among most Lahu no other corporate groups between individual household and village community. Household heads agree to the leadership of one among them, who holds the title of _hk'a sheh hpa,_ "master of the village." This headman, responsible for law and order within the community, consults the village elders on major decisions. The village priest (pastor among Protestant Christians) usually has an importance in community affairs that transcends the ritual domain. Households may at any time leave and attach themselves to another community; Lahu villages are notorious for their propensity to segment. Sometimes several households move off together to set up a new village under a more acceptable leader. Beyond the individual village, it is not uncommon to find small conglomerations of villages whose leaders recognize one among them, usually the head of the pioneer community, as senior area headman. The conglomeration is frequently multiethnic, and its leader may or may not be Lahu.

Political Organization. Beyond this loose and locally based multivillage polity, one enters the domain of political relations with dominant lowland peoples. For most Lahu these traditionally have been Tai peoples. Lahu leaders often received formal recognition from their local Tai prince, to whom they pledged allegiance, supplied corvée, and paid taxes in cash and kind. As Chinese concern for political control over border areas has grown, Lahu leaders have increasingly come under Han Chinese control instead of, or in addition to, that of their local Tai lords. In modern times, Lahu have various political associations—some intense, others largely nominal—with the administrators of the nation-states in which they live.

Social Control. Village gossip and perceived supernatural sanctions are powerful constraints on deviant behavior. Within the household, the master and mistress are responsible for the good behavior of all who live under their roof. Disputes between members of different households may be brought to the village headman for judgment. Cases involving members of different villages may be taken first to the senior area headman and subsequently to the lowland authorities for settlement. Wrongdoers are usually fined, after which they may receive ritual purification. To determine unadmitted guilt, Lahu headmen traditionally have administered ritual tests of innocence.

Religion and Expressive Culture

Religious Beliefs. Differing relationships with neighboring upland and lowland peoples and degrees of exposure to evangelizing worldviews have resulted in great diversity of religious expression. Probably the majority (including some self-professed Christians and Marxists) accept the existence of a great number of spirits (_ne_) associated with natural phenomena or deceased human beings. Most spirits are thought to be essentially capricious. Even potent guardians of people, crops, and livestock (such as ancestral and locality spirits) are seen as easily offended and quick to punish. Some spirits (e.g., those of persons who have died unnaturally and those of demoniac possession) are perceived as invariably malicious. Malicious spirits are said to "bite" those who offend them, bringing sickness (often of a specific kind) to their victims. Besides such spirits, most Lahu seem to recognize, and frequently give considerable ritual importance to, a supreme and creating divinity called "G'ui-sha" (etymology obscure; Chinese scholars translate the word as "Sky Ghost"). Among Lahu Nyi, G'ui-sha is both personal deity, appropriately addressed as "Father G'ui-sha," and diffused divinity incorporating, among other supernatural beings, a female counterpart, "Mother Ai-ma." Not surprisingly, the Christian Lahu interpret G'ui-sha as the personal deity of their Judeo-Christian tradition. Lahu distinguish between physical body and metaphysical body-counterpart, the latter conceived of as comprising several distinct "souls." Nonindigenous worldviews that have profoundly affected the supernatural ideas of different groups of Lahu include a variant of Han Chinese Mahayana Buddhism first brought to them during the early eighteenth century, the Theravada Buddhism of their Tai neighbors, and Protestant and Roman Catholic Christianity introduced, in that order, by Western missionaries beginning in the 1890s. The degree to which Yunnan's Lahu have accepted a Marxist materialist worldview is difficult to determine; that many still cling to supernatural interpretations of reality is clear enough from recent Chinese publications.

Religious Practitioners. Most traditionalist Lahu communities boast spirit specialists, called _maw-pa._ These men perform propitiatory and exorcistic rites and sometimes possess shamanistic characteristics. Some Lahu communities make a sharp distinction between such spirit specialists and priests (*paw-hku; keh-lu-pa* among Lahu Sheh Leh, *to-bo-pa* among Lahu Nyi), whose primary function is to mediate between the people and their high divinity, G'ui-sha. In Protestant Christian communities, the pastor (*sa-la-pa* or *bon-ma-pa*) is the ritual leader; in Roman Catholic communities, it is the priest (*cao-bu, ca-bu*). There is a long tradition of Messianic "warrior-priests" among the Lahu peoples. Beginning as revivalist leaders, such men characteristically extend their interests into the political realm, often claiming supernatural powers and divine affiliations.

Ceremonies. All Lahu mark the major rites of passage and principal phases of the agricultural year with ritual. Much ritual also surrounds soul-recall and the propitiation and exorcism of malicious spirits. The major communal festival marks the beginning of the Lunar New Year, while the Festival of Eating the New Rice is also important. Christmas is an important festival among Christians. Several Lahu divisions have a tradition of village temples (*bon yeh* or *haw yeh*). Historical investigations suggest, if not prove, that these have evolved from the "Buddha houses" or "Buddha halls" (*fo-fang* or *fo-tang*), introduced with Mahayana Buddhism in the eighteenth century. Other significant ceremonial centers are churches and chapels in Christian villages, shrines and bamboo poles with streamers atop in honor of the village guardian spirit, and ritual dancing circles.

Arts. Cloth and basketry, embroidery and appliqué work, musical instruments (particularly gourd flutes, Jew's harps, and banjos), and domestic, agricultural, and hunting appurtenances constitute the major expressions of Lahu plastic arts; singing, dancing, and music are their principal performing arts.

Medicine. Sickness is frequently attributed to supernatural causes, and remedies are sought through propitiation, exorcism, and soul-recall. Herbal medicines are may also be administered.

Death and Afterlife. At death, prayers and ritual offerings are designed to speed the deceased's soul to the land of the dead or to the Christian heaven; after a "bad death" (by accident, violence, or in childbed) among non-Christian traditionalists, the spirit must be exorcised lest it visit a similar fate on its living kinsmen. Some Lahu groups bury their dead, others cremate. Specially appointed graveyards and cremation places are not uncommon among the more settled Lahu communities.

Bibliography

Song Enchang, et al. (1981–1982). *Zhongguo shaoshu minzu shehui lishi diaocha ziliao congkan: Lahu zu shehui lishi diaocha* (Series of survey materials relating to the social history of the minority peoples of China: A social history of the Lahu nationality). 2 vols. Kunming: Yunnan People's Publishing House.

Walker, Anthony R. (1974). "The Divisions of the Lahu People." *Journal of the Siam Society* 62:253–268.

Walker, Anthony R. (1974). "Messianic Movements among the Lahu of the Yunnan-Indochina Borderlands." *Southeast Asia: An International Quarterly* 3:699–711.

Walker, Anthony R. (1976). "The Swidden Economy of a Lahu Nyi (Red Lahu) Village Community in North Thailand." *Folk* 18:145–188.

Walker, Anthony R. (1983). "The Lahu People: An Introduction." In *Highlanders of Thailand*, edited by John McKinnon and Wanat Bhruksasri, 227–237. Kuala Lumpur: Oxford University Press.

Walker, Anthony R. (1986). "Transformations of Buddhism in the Religious Ideas and Practices of a Non-Buddhist Hill People: The Lahu Nyi of the Northern Thai Uplands." *Contributions to Southeast Asian Ethnography* 5:65–91.

ANTHONY R. WALKER

Laki

The Laki (Lalaki, Lolaki, To Laki), who numbered 125,000 in 1977, are located in the southern portion of the southeastern peninsula of Sulawesi, Indonesia. Laki is classified in the West Indonesian Group of the Austronesian Language Family. Houses are raised on stilts and since Dutch administration have been localized into villages. Rice and sago are staples, supplemented by deer hunting. Descent is bilateral. Most Laki are Muslim. Laki society is stratified into nobles and commoners; formerly there were also slaves.

Bibliography

LeBar, Frank M. (1972). "Laki." In *Ethnic Groups of Insular Southeast Asia*, edited by Frank M. LeBar. Vol. 1, *Indonesia, Andaman Islands, and Madagascar*, 142. New Haven: HRAF Press.

Lamaholot

ETHNONYMS: Ata Kiwan, Holo, Solor, Solorese, Solot

Orientation

Identification. The Lamaholot speak the Lamaholot language. The name has been applied to the ethnic group only recently and only in academic writing. The great majority is Roman Catholic, although many are Muslim and a few are

Protestant, Hindu, and Buddhist; some acknowledge no affiliation with any of these religions.

Location. The Lamaholot are found on the islands of east Flores, Adonara, Solor, and Lembata, between 8°05′ and 8°40′ S and between 122°35′ and 123°45′ E, in the Indonesian province of Nusa Tenggara Timur.

Demography. The 1980 Census inconsistently lists both 229,010 and 227,750 as the number of residents of the Regency of East Flores (homeland of the Lamaholot), omitting the ethnically and linguistically distinct Kédang. The average population density of the regency, excluding Kédang, is 81 persons per square kilometer. There were 80 males per 100 females, compared with 99.6 for the province as a whole. Some areas have suffered drastically from out-migration of young men seeking wage labor elsewhere. This problem is particularly acute in parts of north Lembata and east Adonara, where the ratio drops as low as 63 males per 100 females.

Linguistic Affiliation. Lamaholot belongs to the Central Malayo-Polynesian Subgrouping of Austronesian.

History and Cultural Relations

Islam came to the Lamaholot long before it became established on Java and elsewhere in Indonesia. There were a mosque and many Muslims on Solor in 1559, when the Jesuit Father Baltasar Diaz visited the island. The Portuguese Dominicans established a mission on Solor in 1561 and a fort in 1566. Before the arrival of the Portuguese, the Lamaholot were influenced by the Hindu Javanese. Larantuka, Flores, was said to have been conquered by a Majapahit fleet in 1357, and Solor appears in the _Negarakertagama_ as a Majapahit dependency. Some Lamaholot recognized the suzerainty of the Sultan of Ternate in the sixteenth century. The Dutch captured the Solor fort in 1613, and thereafter different Lamaholot areas were allied loosely with either the Portuguese or the Dutch until the Portuguese ceded their rights in the Solor Archipelago in 1859. The pattern of alliances with the Europeans in the seventeenth century and later roughly corresponded with indigenous feuding between villages denominated by Demonara (today simply Demon), who tended to be associated with the Portuguese, and Pajinara (today Paji), who were often Muslim and who in some cases maintained treaty ties with the Dutch. The Dutch established effective direct control through a series of military actions at the end of the nineteenth century and the beginning of the twentieth.

The Lamaholot are linguistically and culturally close to the Sikanese to the west and the Kédang to the east. There are three main dialects of Lamaholot: west (on Flores close to the border with Sika), central (east Flores, Adonara, and Solor) and east (Lembata). Bahasa Alor, spoken in enclaves on the northern coast of Pantar and the western coast of Alor, is at least partially intelligible to Lamaholot speakers.

Settlements

The government has consolidated traditional villages and hamlets into administrative units of 1,000 to 2,000 inhabitants under an elected village head, treasurer, and secretary. Bamboo houses with palm-leaf or grass roofs are being replaced with structures made of brick and cement with corrugated iron roofs. The government and the Catholic mission encourage this transformation.

Economy

Subsistence and Commercial Activities. Most people depend on swidden agriculture for subsistence. Coastal peoples often fish. Lamakera, Solor, Lamalera, and Lembata hunt whales and manta ray. Dugong are taken along protected coasts. Maize is the staple, supplemented by rice, tubers, vegetables, and spices. Cotton and indigo are produced locally. Palms have many uses in construction and food provision. Crops that are sold to traders include copra, tamarind, and candlenuts. Deer antlers, shark fins, and birds' nests are also supplied to traders for export. Domestic animals include pigs, chickens, goats, sheep, dogs, and buffalo. Deer and wild pigs are hunted. Schoolteachers are assured a regular income.

Industrial Arts. Various Lamaholot specialize in pot making, blacksmithing, and the weaving and dyeing of coarse or fine _ikat_ cloth. Some villages provide expert carpenters and boat builders.

Trade. Some of the coastal villages, particularly Lamahala, Trong, Adonara, Lamakera, and Solor regularly engage in trade of various kinds. As a general pattern, mountain dwellers trade agricultural products, coconuts, and goats to coastal villages for fish and manufactured products. Weekly markets attract inexpensive commodities and produce. Stores, mostly Chinese-owned, are found in the larger towns.

Division of Labor. Men fish, hunt, construct boats and houses, and carry on some forms of trade. Women weave, make pots, trade produce and cloth, and cook for domestic needs. Men generally assume political roles. Both sexes share in the work in the fields.

Land Tenure. In east Flores village land, usually owned by the major clan, is divided and allotted each year by the lord of the land. Elsewhere the pattern is less clear. Property tends to be associated with a village; rights of usage are established individually by clearing and maintaining fields. Under government encouragement, much previously unsafe and unused land has been cleared and concepts of individual ownership of property are being introduced.

Kinship

Kin Groups and Descent. In most areas, segmentary descent groups are ordered by patrilineal descent. In parts of Adonara, descent groups appear to have lost significance and have been replaced by the patripotestal family. In the extreme west, descent is matrilineal.

Kinship Terminology. The relationship system varies in detail from village to village. All terminologies recorded to date are ordered by patrilineal descent and a matrilateral marriage prescription.

Marriage and the Family

Marriage. Where the parties to the marriage are Catholic or Muslim, the appropriate ceremony of these religions is used. For most of the area, at least some form of asymmetric marriage alliance, involving the exchange of alliance prestations, was formerly practiced. There is great regional variation in how the alliances work and in whether or not the prestations are actually given. Catholicism generally blocks marriage between the mother's brother's daughter and the father's sister's son. Wife-giving affines are superior to wife-taking affines. The close relatives of the mother control the well-being of her children and are deemed divine by them. Alliance gifts include elephant tusks for wife givers and fine *ikat* (tie-dyed) cloths given in return to wife takers. In some places building material and cash have replaced tusks, which now are rare. Where alliance exchanges have taken place, the couple lives in the home of the husband's parents or establishes a new residence. Where no exchange has taken place, the first years of marriage are spent with the wife's family. Divorce is easily arranged, except for Catholics.

Domestic Unit.   Households include husband, wife, children, younger brothers or cousins, elderly parents, and other dependents.

Inheritance.   Homes, wealth, and alliance obligations are transmitted according to the local rule of descent, usually patrilineal. There is some variation concerning whether only the oldest brother inherits.

Socialization.   Parents and the extended network of close kin care for children. Children go through the rites of passage appropriate to their religion. Prior to the twentieth century education was available only in Larantuka, Flores. Since the 1920s, educational opportunities have expanded. Elementary education is now available to all. Junior and senior high schools and Islamic teacher-training schools are located in the regency. Some go on to higher education elsewhere in Indonesia.

Sociopolitical Organization

Social Organization.   The clans owning land are relatively powerful and wealthy. Petty nobility in various places have lost office, power, and much influence since independence. Otherwise, social distinctions based on wealth are basically not easily perceivable. Slavery, however, was formerly widespread.

Political Organization.   In east Flores the head of the original or landowning clan determines the time for planting and harvesting and directs the communal ceremonies. In some communities he grants permission to open new land. Through much of the Lamaholot region there is a system of four ritual leaders who formerly had governing powers as well. Most prominent was *kepala koten*, who assumed leadership over internal village affairs. *Kepala kelen* concerned himself with external affairs. The other two positions, *hurit* (*hurin*, *hurint*) and *marang*, were advisory. The influence of other village elders tempered the powers of these four figures. The Dutch divided the region into six administrative territories headed by rajas: Larantuka, Adonara, Trong, Lamahala, Lohayong (Lawayong), and Lamakera. Later they placed the territory of Trong under the raja of Adonara and the territories of Lamahala, Lohayong, and Lamakera under the raja of Larantuka. The Indonesian government abolished these positions. Today the Regency of East Flores (Kabupaten Flores Timur) is divided into a series of districts (*kecamatan*) under appointed heads.

Religion and Expressive Cullture

Religious Beliefs.   The census of 1980 shows that 81.9 percent were Roman Catholic, 17.3 were Muslim, and .2 percent were Protestant. There were insignificant numbers of Hindus and Buddhists, and .6 percent did not declare religious prefer-

ence. Given these figures, it might be thought that there is no longer any point in speaking about the traditional religion, even though a good deal of information has been recorded about it. These figures, however, should probably not be taken at face value.

The Lamaholot name for God is "Lera Wulan" (Sun-Moon). His female complement is called "Tana Ekan" (the Earth). Lera Wulan is now associated with the God of Christianity and Islam. Alternative names for God are Lahatala, Letala, Latala, or Lahatala Dunia (all of Arabic derivation). Lesser spirits, *nitu*, inhabit the tops of trees, large stones, springs, and holes in the ground. Also to be mentioned are Ile Woka, the god of the mountains, and Hari Botan, the god of the sea.

Religious Practitioners.   The lord of the land formerly directed communal ceremonies, usually as part of the system of four ritual leaders mentioned above. Traditional priests and healers are called *molang*. Witches (*menaka*) cause all sorts of human misfortune.

Ceremonies.   Prominent ceremonies and festivals include those associated with erecting a house or building and launching a boat, and those that take place in the clan ritual house. There are also important rituals in the fields (in connection with planting and harvesting) and on the beach (in connection with the beginning of the annual fishing cycle). Some communities maintain annual rituals purifying the village.

Arts.   The arts are largely limited to basketry, music, and the weaving of fine cloth. Decorative carving has largely disappeared. Tattooing is declining.

Medicine.   Hospitals and clinics provide some access to modern medical treatment, but not enough by any means. Traditional healers still set bones, repair sprains, and attempt to cope with more serious illness.

Death and Afterlife.   People have two souls, the *tuber* and the *manger*. While the former may leave the body, the latter may not. Upon death the tuber goes to Lera Wulan or is eaten by nitu or menaka. The manger goes to the land of the dead. The world is divided into several levels. When a person dies, he or she is reborn on the next level below. After several lives and deaths, he or she completes the cycle and begins again.

See also Kédang

Bibliography

Arndt, Paul (1940). *Soziale Verhältnisse auf Ost-Flores, Adonara und Solor*. Anthropos, Internationale Sammlung Ethnologischer Monographien, vol. 4. Münster in W.: Aschendorffsche Verlagsbuchhandlung.

Arndt, Paul (1951). *Religion auf Ostflores, Adonara, und Solor*. Studia Instituti Anthropos, vol. 1. Vienna and Mödling: Missionsdruckerei St. Gabriel.

Barnes, R. H. (1977). "Alliance and Categories in Wailolong, East Flores." *Sociologus* 27:133–157.

Barnes, R. H. (1986). "Educated Fishermen: Social Consequences of Development in an Indonesian Whaling Community." *Bulletin de l'École Française d'Extrême-Orient* 75:295–314.

Vatter, Ernst (1932). _Ata Kiwan: Unbekante Bergvölker im Tropischen Holland_. Leipzig: Bibliographisches Institut.

R. H. BARNES

Lamet

The Lamet (Kha Lamet, Le-Met) are an ethnic group numbering about 5,800 in northwest Laos. Along with the Kmhmu, the Lamet claim to be the original inhabitants of the region. Lamet is a Mon-Khmer language related to Palaung and Wa. Most adult males also speak Tai Yuan. The Lamet are in close and regular contact with the Kmhmu, Lü, Yuan, and Lao; the Kmhmu are especially influential. Slash-and-burn agriculture is the main source of food; hunting, gathering and fishing are secondary. Rice is the staple crop. The Lamet engage in trade with the Lao and Thai to obtain tools, clothing, and pottery. Some Lamet also work for wages.

See also Kmhmu

Bibliography

Hickey, Gerald C. (1964). "Lamet." In _Ethnic Groups of Mainland Southeast Asia_, edited by Frank M. LeBar, Gerald C. Hickey, and John K. Musgrave, 117–119. New Haven: HRAF Press.

Izikowitz, Karl Gustav (1951). _Lamet: Hill Peasants in French Indochina_. Etnologiska Studier 17. Göteborg: Etnografiska Museet.

Lao

ETHNONYMS: Lao Loum, Lao Meui, Lao Neua, Lao Phuan, Lao Yuon

Orientation

Identification. The Lao are a lowland people who speak the Lao language and live in Laos and parts of northeast Thailand. They are predominantly Buddhist, but also respect animist spirits. The traditional Lao name for their country is "Pathet Lao," meaning "the country of the Lao," but this name was also applied to the insurgent Communists during the Second Indochina War. The present name for the country is the Lao People's Democratic Republic.

Location. Laos extends 1,400 kilometers in a northwest-southeast direction between 14° and 23° N and 100° and 108° E. The Lao live primarily in the valleys of the Mekong River and its tributaries, at elevations below 1,000 meters. Northeast Thailand on the right bank of the Mekong is also home to many more Lao than presently live in Laos; they are called Lao (or Thai) Isan after the Thai name for that region. The north and east of Laos is characterized by rugged mountains and narrow valleys, while the terrain close to the Mekong and south of the capital, Vientiane, is more level and more heavily populated. Numerous non-Lao minority groups inhabit the upland areas of Laos throughout the country. The tropical monsoonal climate has three seasons: a warm rainy season lasting from June to November, a cool dry season from December to February, and a hot dry season from March to May.

Demography. The present population of Laos is about 4.2 million, of which about 2 million are Lao. The population density in Laos averages 17 persons per square kilometer. Separate demographic data are not available for the Lao, but national population growth is about 2.9 percent per year, and the crude birth rate is about 47 per thousand. Life expectancy at birth in Laos is about 50 years.

Linguistic Affiliation. Lao is included in the Tai Family of languages. Numerous dialects, for the most part mutually comprehensible, are spoken by different subgroups across the country and in northeast Thailand. Lao is a monosyllabic, tonal language, with numerous borrowings from Pali and Sanskrit. Orthography was simplified following the accession of the present government in 1975, and was made completely phonetic. The writing system uses twenty-six consonants and eighteen vowel symbols that can be combined to represent twenty-eight vowel sounds. There are two tone markers.

History and Cultural Relations

Original Lao settlers were part of the overall Tai migrations from southern China, beginning over 2,000 years ago. By the eighth century, Tai groups had settled through much of northern Southeast Asia, commonly in semi-independent _muang,_ or principalities, each under the leadership of a local lord. Shifting alliances and the rise and fall of petty kingdoms continued until King Fa Ngum first unified a Lao state in 1353, with its capital at Luang Prabang and encompassing all of present-day Laos and northeast Thailand. This kingdom of Lan Sang (Million Elephants) lasted about 200 years, but disintegrated under the Burmese invasions of the late sixteenth century. King Soulingna Vongsa briefly revived the kingdom during the latter half of the seventeenth century, but it again foundered and remained divided variously under Thai, Burmese, and Vietnamese influence and control until the French entered in 1893. French colonial rule served to unify the Lao provinces on the left bank of the Mekong, and reestablished the royal house of Luang Prabang under a French protectorate, but otherwise had little effect on village life. Two major periods of war (the nationalist struggle against the French between 1944 and 1954 and the Second Indochina War between 1956 and 1975) disrupted Lao villages and distorted the development of Lao towns. A Communist government took control of the present area of the Lao People's Democratic Republic in late 1975, ushering in a period of revolutionary enthusiasm, reorganization, out-migration, and consolidation. The mainly subsistence economy of Lao villages continued after 1975, but was modified by government efforts to establish collective work groups and villagewide agricultural cooperatives and to bring education and administrative oversight to rural areas. By the early 1980s the hardships of war and rapid revolutionary transformation had diminished, returning village life to approximately the same level and style as in the early 1960s. In the late 1980s, Laos gradually allowed the entry of foreign businesses and tourists, and took tentative steps toward greater political openness.

Lao and Thai have long been closely aligned culturally, and prior to 1975 the Mekong was more a communication path than a frontier. The absence of good education in Laos prompted many Lao to study in Thailand, and villages in border regions regularly participated in each other's traditional celebrations and festivals. Prior to the 1970s the Lao educational system was based on a French curriculum, and a small Lao elite was educated at French schools elsewhere in Indochina or in France itself.

Settlements

Most Lao live in villages of from ten to several hundred families. Villages are usually of the cluster type, although a number established since 1975 have been laid out in rectangular or linear patterns along a central road or a strip of public land. Few Lao villages include families of other ethnic groups. Houses are made of wood or bamboo and built on stilts above the ground. The grounds under and around the house accommodate a rice granary, family livestock and poultry, vehicles, a kitchen garden, craft equipment, and perhaps a kitchen lean-to. Towns have developed as market and administrative centers, often on the site of old muang capitals. They are ethnically diverse but few have populations over 5,000, except for some provincial capitals.

Economy

Subsistence and Commercial Activities. The Lao economy is based on subsistence rice production, usually in paddies, but also in swiddens in hilly areas. The rice-growing season extends from about June through December; dry-season vegetable crops are planted in some areas where water can be carried. A few villages with irrigation systems grow a second rice crop during the dry season. Most rural families have livestock including water buffalo, brahmin cattle, pigs, and poultry. Buffalo are the main source of farm draft power.

Industrial Arts. In the past Lao women wove most of the cloth for their family's clothing, but manufactured clothing is now steadily replacing all but the traditional woman's skirt (*pha sin*). Many villages have artisans such as blacksmiths, carpenters, or boatwrights, who are dependent on farming but practice their specialty when the need arises. Some villages specialize in activities such as pottery, charcoal, or tobacco production.

Trade. Although most Lao villages have access to market goods, trade is very limited, primarily because roads are poor or nonexistent. Traveling merchants who sold medicines and household goods, and bought farm produce and handicrafts, were strongly discouraged in the first years of the new government but are now reappearing. Rural families can also sell small agricultural surpluses and forest products at district market towns. A state marketing network buys and sells produce and dry goods on an irregular basis.

Division of Labor. Different farming and household tasks tend to be assigned to men and women, though the division is not rigid and anyone can perform any task without social disapproval. Women and girls are primarily responsible for cooking, household maintenance, carrying water, and care of small domestic animals. They also transplant rice and weed swidden fields. Men and older boys are primarily responsible for the care of buffalo and oxen, for hunting, and for plowing the paddy or clearing the swidden fields. The oldest working man in the household directs household rice production and represents the family in temple rituals and village councils. Both men and women plant swiddens, harvest, thresh and carry rice, and work in the gardens. Most Lao petty traders have been women.

Land Tenure. In the past, all land theoretically belonged to the king; now all land belongs to the state. In practice, use rights may be bought and sold, but there is little trade in land. Paddy-land holdings are relatively equally distributed, with only a few influential families owning more than 20 hectares prior to 1975. Presently paddy holdings average around 1 hectare per family, with few families controlling more than 3 hectares. Except in urban areas, almost all families have access to some farm land. Swidden fields are used temporarily by farmers who claim no permanent rights to these fields.

Kinship

Kin Groups and Descent. Descent is bilateral. Surnames have been adopted only over the last several decades. Wives usually take their husband's last name. Kin groups are defined partly by choice: siblings and immediate maternal and paternal relatives are recognized by everyone, but more distant relatives may be recognized only if the kin relationship has been cultivated. Kinship relationships are recognized and reinforced through sharing of goods and produce, labor reciprocity, and participation in family and religious rituals.

Kinship Terminology. Kinship terms differentiate by gender, by relative age (e.g., younger brother, older sister), by generation, and by side of the family.

Marriage and Family

Marriage. Marriage partners are not prescribed. Young people often marry cousins or others from their own village. Marriage partners may be proposed either by parents or by the young people, but parents of both families are generally consulted and must approve in order for traditional marriage negotiations to proceed. Bride-price varies greatly, but usually includes gold, one or more animals, and, these days, cash. The marriage ceremony itself takes place at the bride's family home and is a Brahmanic/animist ceremony. Polygyny was practiced but uncommon before 1975, but has been prohibited by the present government. Divorce is discouraged, though it may be initiated by either party. Initial residence varies, but is usually uxorilocal; patrilocal residence is also common. Most couples establish an independent residence after several years, though there is a strong tendency for the youngest daughter to continue to live with her parents to care for them in their old age.

Domestic Unit. The domestic unit is usually a nuclear family but may include grandparents and/or siblings or other relatives, often on the wife's side. The average household consists of six to eight persons. Two or more related households may farm together and store their rice in a common granary.

Inheritance. The custodial daughter and her in-marrying husband often inherit the house compound and much of the parental paddy land. Other children may receive an inheritance when they marry or leave home, with sons and noncustodial daughters receiving relatively equal shares. The content and the timing of each child's inheritance is determined by the parents. The passing on of house and field ownership to the custodial child and spouse signals the passing of authority to the next generation.

Socialization. Children learn by observation and direct instruction. Infants and very young children are indulged; older children are expected to obey their elders and help with family tasks. By age five, girls help with household work; by age nine, boys pasture cattle or buffalo. By adolescence, children can carry out nearly all adult subsistence tasks, at least with supervision. Both boys and girls attend village schools, although usually only a few boys are encouraged to continue their education in the district or provincial capital.

Sociopolitical Organization

Social Organization. Lao society lacks rigid social classes and no longer has a hereditary elite. Buddhist monks and school teachers are accorded respect, as are elders. Socioeconomic stratification is limited, particularly in rural villages where there is little or no occupational differentiation, and is based on wealth, occupation, and age. The household and extended-kin group form the basis for village social organization. Labor exchange groups for farming or other tasks are usually drawn from the entire village, or from the neighborhood, if it is a larger village.

Political Organization. Laos is a Communist state governed by the Lao People's Revolutionary Party through the party's Central Committee and the Council of Ministers. As of 1989 there was no constitution, although People's Assemblies had been elected at the district, province, and national level. Laos is administratively divided into 16 provinces (khoueng) and the municipality of Vientiane. Provinces are subdivided into districts (muang), subdistricts (tasseng) and villages (baan), although the tassengs are beginning to be abolished. Villages are "natural communities". They are governed by a locally elected headman and village council. Muang officials are appointed by the provincial or national government, and are responsible for most administrative duties such as tax collection, school supervision, and agricultural improvement; they are also the main link in communicating policies promulgated by the central government to the village. Budgetary and personnel constraints severely limit the scope of government services. Most villages have at least a one- or two-grade school, but no health services. The level and quality of education increase with proximity to district and provincial towns.

Social Control. In the village, social control is based on the need to maintain a good reputation in the community. Numerous family economic and life-cycle activities require the support and cooperation of fellow villagers, which will be withheld from those seen as dishonest, lazy, or uncooperative. In extreme cases, persons have been accused of witchcraft and expelled from a village.

Conflict. Whenever possible, open conflict is avoided in Lao society. Intermediaries are used informally to express or resolve discontent. Intervillage conflict is uncommon among Lao villages, but ethnic prejudice has led to disputes between Lao and hill-tribe villages, often over land use and animal grazing. A civil war between leftist and royalist factions continued between 1956 and 1975, and was closely tied to the war in Vietnam.

Religion and Expressive Culture

Religious Beliefs. Most Lao are Theravada Buddhists, but also practice aspects of animist worship. Small numbers have been converted to Christianity. Lao believe in spirits that inhabit certain locations, such as rivers, rice fields, or groves of trees. In addition, villages may have tutelary spirits and there is a goddess of the rice crop. Many of these spirits, especially village spirits and the rice goddess, received regular offerings in the past, but the present government has strongly discouraged such rituals. Malevolent ghosts or other spirits can possess people, and/or cause illness, which must be exorcised by a spirit doctor.

Religious Practitioners. The traditional ideal was for all men to become Buddhist monks for at least a short period. Today only a few choose to be ordained. Monks officiate at cyclical religious ceremonies and festivals, as well as at Buddhist household ceremonies and funerals. Occasionally they become active community leaders. Spirit practitioners are commonly elderly men, and there are mediums of both sexes. Practitioners are called upon to officiate at weddings, birth-related rituals, and numerous informal ceremonies, called basi or sou khouan, marking such life events as recovery from illness, departure on or return from a journey, or construction of a new home.

Ceremonies. The Buddhist lunar calendar has a festival (boun) at the full moon of almost every month. The most important calendrical ceremonies are Buddha's enlightenment in the sixth month (May), the beginning and end of Lent (July and October), and New Year (15 April). Vientiane celebrates the That Luang festival in November. Families may also sponsor Buddhist ceremonies to bless the house, gain merit, or ordain a son. Animist basi ceremonies are performed by individual households.

Arts. Classical music, dance, and literature are strongly influenced by the Hindu epics such as the Rāmāyana, and are similar to Thai and Khmer court forms. One popular form of folk music uses the khene, a bamboo-and-reed mouth organ accompanying one or two singers (mo lam) who improvise stories, banter, and courting duels. Buddhist temple architecture is characterized by steep tiled roofs, with frescoes and mosaic decorations on the walls depicting events in the Buddha's lives.

Medicine. Illness is traditionally ascribed to imbalance of the body's spirits, spirit possession, or simply to change in weather. Western notions of germs and disease are now common, however, and use of patent medicines and antibiotics rivals traditional herbal and spirit cures among families who can afford them.

Death and Afterlife.   According to Buddhist belief, death is followed by rebirth in a life appropriate to one's past karma. Following death by natural causes, the body is kept at home for one to three days, during which time villagers come to pay their respects and assist the family of the deceased during a more or less continuous wake. The body is usually cremated, but in some cases may be buried.

See also Hmong; Kmhmu; Lao Isan

Bibliography

Condominas, Georges (1962). *Essai sur la société rurale lao de la région de Vientiane.* Vientiane: Royaume du Laos, Ministère des Affaires Rurales; UNESCO.

Ireson, W. Randall, and Carol J. Ireson (1989). "Laos: Marxism in a Subsistence Rural Economy." *Bulletin of Concerned Asian Scholars* 21(2–4): 59–75.

Stuart-Fox, Martin (1987). *Laos: Politics, Economy, and Society.* London: Frances Pinter.

W. RANDALL IRESON AND CAROL IRESON

Lao Isan

ETHNONYMS: Northeastern Thai, Thai Lao

Orientation

Identification.   The Lao Isan speak the Lao dialect of the Thai language, live in northeastern Thailand, and are predominantly Buddhists.

Location.   Northeast Thailand is composed of seventeen provinces situated between 14° and 18° N and 101° and 106° E. The region is cut off from the rest of the country by two low escarpments, the Phetchabun to the west and the Phanom Dong Rak to the south. The region is dominated by the Khorat Plateau, a gently rolling area of low hills and shallow lakes drained almost entirely by the Mekong River via the Mae Nam Mun and its tributary, the Lam Nam Chi. The north and east of the region are bounded by the Mekong River, across which lies Laos. The short monsoon season brings heavy flooding in river valleys, but the dry season is long and the prevailing vegetation is sparse grass.

Demography.   Northeast Thailand is the most populated of Thailand's four regions, despite problems with farming in the area. The population for 1989 was estimated as 18.8 million, with an average density of 180 persons per square kilometer. Lao speakers constitute the majority of the population but there are sizable numbers of Central Thai speakers in the urban areas, where large Chinese or Sino-Thai populations are also found. There are Thai-speaking minorities in the re-

gion, including the Phutai, the Lao Phuan, the Saek, and the Khorat Thai, who are said to be descendants of Thai soldiers and Khmer women. In addition, the region has non-Thai-speaking populations of Khmer and Vietnamese.

Linguistic Affiliation.   Lao Isan speak a dialect of the Thai language, which is said to belong to the Tai-Kadai Family of languages. This dialect is the same as that spoken by the lowland Lao of Laos. It is a monosyllabic and tonal language with a script that is similar to Central Thai. Thai from other regions of the country are said to have difficulty understanding Lao Isan.

History and Cultural Relations

The Lao Isan live in one of the most archaeologically rich areas of Southeast Asia. Farming has been carried out in the region for approximately 5,000 years. Some of the earliest evidence of the use of bronze anywhere in the world has been found in Udon Thani Province in the northern part of the Khorat Plateau. The Lao made their presence known in the region in the fourteenth century A.D. with the founding of the kingdom of Lan Chang, which straddled both sides of the Mekong and extended its power north to Yunnan and west to the northern Thai kingdom of Chiengmai. This kingdom dissolved in the early eighteenth century into a number of competing kingdoms including Luang Prabang, Champasak, and Vientiane. The latter two kingdoms controlled parts of what is now northeast Thailand. Champasak had tributaries on the Mun and Chi rivers in what is today a part of Ubon Ratchathani and Roi Et provinces. Vientiane, meanwhile, is thought to have controlled territories in present-day Loei, Nong Khai, and Nakhon Phanom provinces. The Siamese of Ayutthaya had taken control of Nakhon Ratchasima in the seventeenth century. From the late eighteenth to the early nineteenth centuries the Siamese, from their new capital at Bangkok, fought a series of wars with Champasak and Vientiane, eventually defeating these two Lao kingdoms and absorbing the Khorat Plateau and most of Laos as outer provinces within the Siamese kingdom. Luang Prabang became a tributary vassal of the Siamese kingdom. This situation changed with the arrival of the French in Indochina, beginning with their control of Cochin China in 1862. By 1904 Siam had ceded all of the Lao areas on the left bank of the Mekong River to France and established the boundary that exists between Thailand and Laos to the present day.

During most of the nineteenth century, Siam administered the northeast as tributary outer provinces. Local politics decided the rulers of those political units and the Siamese king only asked for tribute and allegiance. With the growth of colonial powers in the region, the Siamese kingdom sought closer control over the northeast and from the late nineteenth century on replaced local "lords" with government officials appointed from Bangkok.

Settlements

The villages in the northeast tend to be clusters of houses intersected by narrow lanes. An average village contains 90 to 100 households. Villages are about 4 to 5 kilometers apart and are often connected by roads or pathways. The villages are surrounded by rice fields, swamps and ponds, grassy plains, and secondary forests. As in the rest of Thailand, locally named villages are often divided administratively by the system of districts, subdistricts, and hamlets devised by the central government. Housing is usually wooden or bamboo, with thatch or corrugated-iron roofs. As in most of Thailand, houses are raised off the ground on stilts 1.5 meters high. A village may have one or two shops selling general goods such as cigarettes, candy, matches, and produce. Now Bangkok-style cement houses can be found scattered throughout the region as money from migrant workers from the Middle East is spent on elaborate houses.

Economy

Subsistence and Commercial Activities. The northeast has the highest incidence of poverty in Thailand; 50 percent of Thailand's poor live in the northeast. The region has poor soils with low fertility and poor water-retention capabilities. Yet it accounts for approximately 36 percent of the national rice production and more than 90 percent of the kenaf, a product closely related to jute (1971/72 figures). Rice is the main crop of the region and most of this is glutinous rice, a _japonica_ variety much favored as a staple by the people of the northeast. Of all rice production in the region, 78 percent is of the glutinous variety (1970 figures). Most of the glutinous variety is consumed locally and the nonglutinous rice is marketed in Bangkok. The other major crop is kenaf, which competes with jute; its market is subject to the success or failure of the jute crop in India and Bangladesh. Kenaf is sold by the farmers in the major centers of Khon Kaen and Ubon Ratchathani, cities that are in the center of the major growing areas. Three-quarters of the kenaf is exported. The third-largest crop is maize, although it is limited by poor soils and unreliable rain. Maize is grown mainly in the provinces of Nakhon Ratchasima and Sisaket. It is marketed through Nakhon Ratchasima to Bangkok for export. Other crops in the region include cotton, sugarcane, peanuts, and cassava, but these cash crops are more productive in other parts of the kingdom.

The northeast excels, however, in the production of cattle and buffalo. A large part of the Khorat Plateau is unsuitable for crop production, but the low hills and open forests, with their abundant grass for pasture, have allowed northeastern farmers to raise cattle and buffalo for additional farm income. Approximately 40 percent of the kingdom's cattle and 55 percent of the water buffalo are raised in the northeast. Cattle are marketed through dealers who sell them to slaughter houses, 20 percent of the annual production going to slaughter houses in Bangkok. Buffalos also are sold to dealers who then sell them to slaughter houses, 60 percent of which are in Bangkok. This pattern of farmers selling to dealers and not slaughtering animals themselves is partly related to Buddhist beliefs about bad karma arising from the killing of large animals.

Manufacturing is very limited in the region. Most employment is in textile production, followed by food, beverage, tobacco, wood, and furniture production. Food (rice milling) plays a dominant role in the industrial economy.

Industrial Arts. The northeast is well known for silk and cotton textiles, woven by women. Lately these woven items have been the object of various projects seeking to revive "traditional crafts" in the region. In Nakhon Ratchasima Province there is a thriving pottery industry that probably goes back to the time of the Ayutthayan Kingdom. Today this craft is in decline. Recently, some domestic and foreign companies have moved into the region with the object of utilizing the relatively cheap labor resources for manufacturing and agribusiness projects.

Trade. Villages may have a small retail shop or two, selling manufactured items and prepared foods. Often these are operated by village families with a better-than-average income. Usually women are involved in small trading enterprises, often selling vegetables and fruits in the village or prepared food at temple fairs. In some cases, village men become involved in the cattle and buffalo trade. Larger trading operations involving rice and other agricultural products are usually carried out by Chinese or Sino-Thai traders from outside the village.

Division of Labor. Both men and women work in farming, men doing the heavier work such as plowing and clearing of forests. Generally, men and women share the other duties of farm work, such as planting, harvesting, and weeding. Women weave cloth in the off season. Typically, men fish and they build and repair housing.

Land Tenure. Despite the poverty of the region, land tenancy in the northeast is relatively low, about 10 percent of all households (1980). The vast majority of households has access to land, although land distribution is uneven and farm size is small (average 1.75 hectares). Opening new land is no longer an option, and growing populations may be absorbed by urban parts of Thailand, Bangkok in particular.

Kinship

Kin Groups and Descent. Kin groups are recruited on the basis of bilateral descent and are kindred-based. Villages are interlinked through various kinship relations and have been described as a gathering of kin.

Kinship Terminology. The terminology is classified as Hawaiian with cousin terms distinguishing relative age rather than sex. In fact, relative age for Ego is distinguished for all collaterals. Kin terms are extended to nonkin.

Marriage and Family

Marriage. Marriage in the northeast begins with a period of courtship initiated by the young couple. This may involve intervention by the parents at any point. Before the marriage takes place, the couple seeks approval from both sets of parents. Thus marriage can be interpreted as a matter of choice given the courtship pattern, but seen as arranged given the desire to have parental approval. Typically, the parents with fewer resources have less control over their children's marriage choices. Since villages are made up of kin, marriages are often exogamous with regard to the village. Ordinarily a newly married couple moves in with the wife's family and lives there until the next daughter gets married, in which case the first couple sets up its own household. Marriage is not a religious event in Buddhism, but Buddhist monks may be invited so that the couple and their relatives acquire religious merit. The event is sanctioned by the community of kin in a ritual that reinforces the importance of respect for age and the parental generation.

Domestic Unit. The family or household consists of those people who share meals and farm cooperatively; normally, they occupy a single house. The domestic cycle of matrilocal residence followed by separate residence means a family will be nuclear or extended at different points in time. Characteristically, a village will have around 65 percent nuclear households and the rest extended at any one time. But a majority of the households are participating in a cycle where married daughters bring their husbands into the family for a length of time. Eventually the last daughter, with her husband and children, lives with her parents in the natal home without setting up a separate household. In some cases, wealth (usually in land) permitting, sisters with their husbands and children live in compounds of three or four households surrounded by a wooden or bamboo pallisade. The sisters' parents remain in the natal household until their death, supplying parental leadership for the group of domestic units. Each household in the compound is a separate domestic unit.

Inheritance. Because of the pattern of setting up domestic units, in which a man moves in with his wife and her family, the parental generation tends to pass land through daughters. A son is expected to marry a woman with rights in land from her parents. Although sons may receive some land from their parents, most land is passed to women. However, as land gets scarce and the opening of new plots in uncultivated areas is virtually impossible, more land is being passed to sons because of the concern of parents about the viability of farming for the new family.

Sociopolitical Organization

Northeast Thailand is part of the kingdom of Thailand, a constitutional monarchy.

Social Organization. Village social life is threaded together by a series of hierarchical patron-client relationships. Relative age, wealth, education, and occupation all play a role in determining relative status among individuals. Because of this personal style of social organization it is difficult to form long-lasting groups in village communities that are not based on a particularly charismatic, skilled, or respected individual. Monks, especially abbots of monastic communities, can hold a particularly high status in village life. This is because villagers have respect for Buddhism and the monastic organization, and a high regard for educated persons. Abbots are usually relatively well-educated or have other skills that win respect. Such individuals can be important in the formation of groups, as many development agencies have found.

Political Organization. As in the rest of Thailand, the seventeen provinces of the northeast are divided into districts, which are made up of municipal areas and subdistricts (*tambon*). Each subdistrict is made up of numbered hamlets, which usually crosscut locally named villages. Heads of hamlets and the tambon are elected, although the process for election can vary from village to village. Both men and women are now eligible for election to these village offices. The district head is a bureaucrat appointed by Bangkok, as is every other official up to the provincial governor. Thailand has an elected form of parliamentary government, so that villagers also have the opportunity to elect representatives to the national assembly in Bangkok.

Social Control. Buddhism provides guidelines for villagers' behavior, as typified by the five precepts for the laity: refrain from taking life, from stealing, from illicit sexual activity, from speaking falsely, and from consuming inebriating substances. Gossip and clustered housing provide other means of social control. The open houses permit neighbors to be aware of each others' activities. Additionally, traditional headmen do have the prerogative to fine villagers for breaking customary regulations. These rules usually deal with unacceptable intimate contact of men with unmarried women.

Conflict. Northeast Thailand has been involved in opposition to the central authorities several times during the twentieth century. When Siam first asserted bureaucratic control over the area early in the century, there were the "men-of-merit" rebellions by politicoreligious peasant leaders. They often claimed magical powers in their opposition to Bangkok. By the 1960s, the northeast was known as a region where Communist rebels were widely popular among sections of the peasantry. In more recent times, the northeast has been part of the ongoing political conflict in Thailand typified by the gangster-style murders of political and business rivals. Thailand has the second-highest murder rate in the world. Villages in the northeast have a long tradition of acquiescence to *naklaeng*, or toughs in local gangs, who enforce political decisions made by powerful and/or wealthy community members. Villages were traditionally abused and/or protected by such gangs.

Religion and Expressive Culture

Theravada Buddhism is the dominant religion of northeast Thailand. The monastic organization in the region is linked to the central monastic authority in Bangkok. Practices are similar throughout Thailand.

Religious Beliefs. The Lao Isan differ in belief and practice from other Thai. Perhaps the most distinctive Lao Isan practice is the *bunbangfai*, the Rocket Festival. Monks and others prepare rockets to be fired off to pay respect to guardian spirits before the coming of the monsoon rains. Another major festival is that of *bunphrawes*, based on the story of the penultimate reincarnation of the Buddha. Although the story is known throughout Thailand, this festival has been the major annual festival in Lao Isan villages. As among other Theravada Buddhists, the Lao Isan gain merit by presenting gifts to the monastery and having their sons ordained as monks for short periods.

Religious Practitioners. A large majority of men become monks for some period during their lives. Ideally, ordination takes place when the man is twenty years old. This allows his parents or other close relatives to obtain the merit of this action and prepares the man for marriage and domestic life. The northeast is particularly well known for its monastery retreats for meditation. Monks from the northeast have reached the highest levels of the monastic hierarchy. Many Bangkok temples are inhabited and led by monks from the northeast. The monastic system has been an avenue for advancement for many men from the poorest part of the country. In addition to monks, there are *paahm* or Brahmans, who carry out life-cycle rituals; diviners, who are concerned with spirit-affliction; guardian-spirit mediums and intermediaries; and exorcists.

Ceremonies. The annual ritual cyle is coordinated with the agricultural cycle and is as follows: _songkran_, the New Year festival at the end of the dry season, on 13 to 15 April; _wisaka bucha_, the day of birth, enlightenment, and death of the Buddha, in May at the beginning of the rainy season; bunbangfai, the Rocket Festival, in May-June; _khao phansa_, entering the Vessa or Rain's Retreat, in July; _bun khao saak_, making merit for the spirits of the dead, in September; _ok phansa_, leaving the Rain's Retreat, in October; _kathin_, the presentation of robes to the monks, in October-November; bunphrawes, the making of merit for the recitation of the Prince Vessantara story, in February-March.

Arts. The northeast has artistic patterns similar to those in other parts of Thailand. For example, there are similarities in tattooing, architecture, design, and sculpture. There are, however, some distinctive features of northeastern art. In musical repartee, the Lao Isan have a tradition of playing the reed instrument called _kaen_. Many of the woven materials are also distinctive in the use of the _ikat_ method of resist-dye technique (_mat mii_) and supplementary weft (_phaa khit_).

Medicine. The Western biomedical system is well established in Thailand through provincial hospitals and public-health clinics. The northeast region, however, has the fewest hospitals per capita and the fewest doctors per capita. Villagers often prefer traditional herbal medicines and massage to hospital visits. Rituals such as _bai sir sukhwan_, where the soul is "tied" back into an ill or disturbed person, are important forms of healing.

Death and Afterlife. Given the importance of death in Buddhist thought, the funeral is the most important rite of passage in northeastern Thai villages. Buddhist monks officiate and it is the only rite of passage recognized as a solely Buddhist ritual. Death marks the passage of the life-force into the next life, whether that be in hell, in heaven, or on Earth as animal, spirit, or human. The funeral procession and cremation are overseen by monks. Buddhist laity participate in rituals of transferring merit to the dead, while monks chant their blessings.

See also Central Thai; Lao

Bibliography

Donner, Wolf (1978). _The Five Faces of Thailand: An Economic Geography_. St. Lucia: University of Queensland Press.

Keyes, Charles F. (1967). _Isan: Regionalism in Northeastern Thailand_. Cornell University Southeast Asia Program Data Paper no. 65. Ithaca, N.Y.

Mizuno, Koichi (1978). "The Social Organization of Rice-Growing Villages." In _Thailand: A Rice-Growing Society_, edited by Yoneo Ishii, 83–114. Honolulu: University of Hawaii Press.

Tambiah, S. J. (1970). _Buddhism and the Spirit Cults in North-East Thailand_. London: Cambridge University Press.

JOHN VAN ESTERIK AND PENNY VAN ESTERIK

Lawa

ETHNONYMS: Lava, Lavu'a, La-wor-a, Lua, Luwa

A group of about 7,000 (1987) located mainly in the Bo Luang Plateau area of northern Thailand, roughly between 18° to 20° N and between 98° to 100° E. Lawa is classified as an Austroasiatic language in either the Palaung-Wa or the Mon-Khmer Group. Degree of acculturation into Thai society varies from one locale to another, with the life-style of rural farmers in the Bo Luang area closely resembling that of their Thai neighbors. Many Lawa live in large, permanent villages based on wet-rice agriculture. In the past, iron-ore mining was an important secondary activity, although the Lawa now more often purchase iron implements from lowland communities. Acculturated villages are integrated into the national polity, primarily through the community headmen who are appointed by Thai officials. The Lawa are described as animist Buddhists; their degree of adherence to Buddhist beliefs and practices is largely a function of their degree of acculturation.

Bibliography

LeBar, Frank M. (1964). "Lawa." In _Ethnic Groups of Mainland Southeast Asia_, edited by Frank M. LeBar, Gerald C. Hickey, and John K. Musgrave, 120–121. New Haven: HRAF Press.

Lisu

ETHNONYMS: Anung, Che-nung, Khae Lisaw, Khae Liso, Lasaw, Lashi, Lasi, Le Shu O-op'a, Lesuo, Leur Seur, Li, Li-hsaw, Lip'a, Lipo, Lip'o, Lisaw, Li-shaw, Lishu, Liso, Loisu, Lusu, Lu-tzu, Shisham, Yaoyen, Yawyen, Yawyin, Yeh-jen

Orientation

Identification. The Lisu are mountain swiddeners in southwest China, northeast India, Myanmar (Burma), and Thailand. Because the Lisu are widely scattered among other peoples of many different ethnic groups, names tend to differ from one locality to another. The people refer to themselves as "Lisu" or by clan names.

Location. The main concentration of Lisu is in China's western Yunnan Province, between the Salween and Mekong rivers. Migration has scattered villages as far west as eastern Tirap (at the extreme northeast corner of India) and as far south as Kamphaeng Phet and Phitsunulok in Thailand.

Demography. In 1989, there were an estimated 481,000 Lisu in China, as many as 250,000 in Myanmar (there has never been a reliable census), about 18,000 in Thailand, and several hundred in India.

Linguistic Affiliation.   Lisu is in the Lolo (Yi) Group of Tibeto-Burman languages, closely related to Lahu, Akha, and Yi, with many Yunnanese loanwords. Most Lisu men are fluent in several languages, especially Yunnanese, Lahu, Shan, Yuan (northern Thai-Lao), and Akha. There are scripts devised by British missionaries and by Chinese, but they are little used. Some Lisu are literate in Chinese or Thai.

History and Cultural Relations

There is a Lisu tradition that their origins lie in the eastern Tibetan plateau. The Lisu are mentioned among the "Southern Barbarians" (of mountainous Yunnan and Szechwan) in the early Chinese histories and annals such as the *Man Shu* (ca. A.D. 685). The Chinese regarded them as a lesser branch of the Han, to be pacified and assimilated. This explains the derogatory names applied to them and the two trends discernible in Sino-Lisu relations: peaceful coexistence, cultural exchange, trade, and intermarriage on the one hand, and constant small-scale warfare, raids, kidnappings, banditry, enslavement, suppression, and rebellion on the other. The Chinese exchanged salt, iron, silver, and foodstuffs for beeswax, bear gall, stag horn, hides, medicinal herbs, and coffin planks. In areas closer to Chinese settlements, such as Tengyueh and to the south, Lisu were taxed, corvéed, and appointed as headmen (*tussu*) and government officers (*tumu*), perhaps as early as the Han dynasty, and certainly by the Ming. The system seldom worked well, and there were numerous grievances. After the formation of the People's Republic of China, army units and government cadres arrived to administer Lisu areas, and the Nuchiang Lisu Autonomous Zhou and other autonomous areas were formed. The abolition of slavery, land reform, and cancellation of debts were decreed in 1956. Chinese influence on Lisu culture, already considerable before 1949, has accelerated, as evidenced by the virtual end of opium growing, the introduction or extension of double cropping, manuring, irrigation and terracing, new tools, roads, bridges, medical centers, schools, economic diversification, the organization of mutual aid teams, cooperatives and communes (and their subsequent abandonment), and the development of political consciousness evident in Lisu cadres, soldiers, and Communist Party members. These changes caused great stress, particularly during times of radical change such as the Great Leap Forward and the Cultural Revolution, when "local nationalism" was criticized and rapid movement toward socialism demanded. During the lulls in Communist fervor, a continuity with the past can still be discerned: the vast majority of Lisu are still small-scale agriculturalists in remote mountain villages with few modern amenities. The movement of Lisu peoples south and east into Burma, India, and Thailand may have been related to the development of opium growing and worsening relations with Chinese administrators in the nineteenth century. Chinese pacification measures in the late nineteenth and early twentieth centuries caused large-scale movements of Lisu into Burma, and subsequently Thailand and India. Oral traditions of the Lisu in Thailand indicate that the first families arrived there from Burma between 1900 and 1930, motivated by the search for good high-elevation opium lands and a wish to escape unsettled conditions in China and Burma. The Lisu have been described as a "fine" people: robust, independent of spirit, and excellent warriors. They are also very adaptable and quick to learn the languages and ways of their neighbors. Some, especially in Myanmar and Thailand, have even intermarried with Chinese, Lahu, and Kachin, recognizing a fictitious equivalence of Lisu clans and lineages with those of neighboring ethnic groups. Chinese operate stores or caravan routes in Lisu villages, and the Lisu patronize local markets. Lisu have served in the British Burma army, the People's Liberation Army, and the Thai Border Patrol Police. Christian and Buddhist missionaries among the Lisu have not been very successful.

Settlements

With the exception of heavily acculturated valley villages in China and Thailand, Lisu villages are located on hill slopes just below the ridge line, generally at elevations between 1,300 and 3,000 meters. Sites require adequate water, usually brought in by bamboo aqueducts, since living too close to a source may invite attack by the water spirit. Defense, separation from ethnic groups with whom Lisu do not get along, good agricultural land, and cheap sources of labor (Karen, Lahu, or Yuan) are also considerations in siting villages in Thailand. There is a circulation of population among Lisu villages: individuals, families, and groups move at frequent intervals. Some villages have remained in the same location for sixty years or more, though in Thailand the average is closer to ten. Village size varies from 5 to more than 150 houses, the average in Thailand being 26. A hut for the village spirit occupies the highest elevation, and houses below should face the nearest stream, the main door thus opening downslope. Houses are built on piles or directly on the ground, the latter said to be a Chinese influence. Walls and floors are of split bamboo, roofs of thatch. A box filled with earth serves for a cooking fire. Bedrooms are in the corners for married couples; there is one for unmarried daughters and a raised sleeping/sitting platform in the main room for the unmarried sons. Animals are quartered under the house or in separate pens.

Economy

Subsistence and Commercial Activities.   Most Lisu practice swidden agriculture. In the northern areas of their settlement maize, mountain rice, barley, and millet are grown; buckwheat is also cultivated at the higher elevations, and irrigated rice on valley terraces. In Myanmar and Thailand, rice is grown at lower elevations, and maize and opium at higher elevations, either together or in separate fields. Chinese mustard, chard, beans, yams, sweet potatoes, melons, gourds, cucumbers, sunflowers, potatoes, sesame, chilies, and tobacco may be interspersed with maize. Swidden-rice fields must be shifted every two or three years; opium and maize fields are more permanent because they are intercropped and more thoroughly weeded. In former times, cotton and hemp were grown, but today most Lisu buy cloth and women sew clothing. Through government stations (*nikhom*), Border Patrol Police, and extension workers, the Thai government has persuaded a few Lisu to switch from opium to irrigated-rice agriculture, tea cultivation, or fruit or vegetable crops (peaches, potatoes). Lisu men take great pride in their ponies, which are usually the only form of nonhuman transport. Pigs and chickens are the major source of protein and are important in religious ceremonies. Every household keeps a pig or scrawny guard dogs, making it prudent for visitors to arm themselves with a sturdy staff before entering a village. Some own a few cows, oxen, buffalo, goats, sheep, or ducks. The Lisu produce and consume large amounts of liquor made from rice, maize, and millet; many in Thailand chew betel leaves and areca nuts; a few chew _miang_ (fermented tea leaves) or smoke opium; all drink tea. Men and boys hunt with crossbows, slingshots, firearms, or traps for birds, jungle fowl, barking deer, wild pigs, Himalayan bears, and rhesus macaques. Children and women catch very small fish with hooks and lines, by using commercial or plant poisons, or by diverting a stream and scooping up fish from the dry bed with small nets. They collect honey, bamboo shoots, pine nuts, berries, wild citrus, wild apples, wild mangoes, wild ginger, wild yams, mushrooms, birds' eggs, grasshoppers, and flying ants; wild orchids, parrots, and parakeets are sold to lowlanders; banana stalks, banana inflorescence, and weeds are fed to pigs. Collecting of bamboo, wood, and grasses provides raw materials for housing, fire, baskets, and making rice mortars and other tools.

Industrial Arts. All Lisu make tools from bamboo and wood (baskets, barrels for making liquor, pony saddles, winnow fans, threshing and sleeping mats). Part-time blacksmiths work iron into knives, axes, hoes, dibble blades, sickles, opium blades, opium scrapers, and horseshoes. Part-time silversmiths make jewelry from coins obtained from lowlanders. Women spin and weave cotton and hemp cloth. Even in areas exposed to great outside influence and trade, the shoulder bag is still woven using a backstrap loom, and the distinctive Lisu "tails" worn behind by women and in front by men are still laboriously hand sewn by women.

Trade. Trade is primarily with Chinese merchants, in markets, village or lowland stores, or with peddlers and caravanners. In Myanmar and Thailand, opium is the major source of income, and in recent years has allowed Lisu to buy silver coins, salt, tea, foods, cooking utensils, clothes, watches, flashlights, kerosene for lanterns, and a wide variety of other consumer goods. Trade with other Lisu or other highland ethnic groups is minimal.

Division of Labor. Every Lisu is first and foremost an agriculturalist; what little division of labor exists is the result of differences in sex, age, or special abilities. Women make clothes and share agricultural labor (except heavy clearing of forest), food preparation, and child care. Children help care for younger siblings, feed livestock, gather firewood and pine chips (for torches), wash clothes, tend fires, wash dishes, and sweep the house.

Land Tenure. Individual households have access to land based on usufruct rights. Contact with lowlanders has caused some Lisu to register land; in Thailand, land is occasionally sold. There is no recognized village territory, the fields of several villages sometimes being interspersed. Lisu in China went through the commune phase, but today most land there is once again worked by independent households.

Kinship

Kin Groups and Descent. The Lisu are divided into clans or surname groups (_zo_) that are patrilineal, exogamous, nonlocalized groups differing slightly in religious beliefs and ritu-
als, associated clan spirits, observance or timing of minor ceremonies, and the arrangement of household ritual shelves to honor patrilineal ancestors. Zo are named after flora and fauna: _bya_ (honeybee), _dzuh_ (hemp), _gwa_ (buckwheat), _ngwa_ (fish), _suh_ (wood or tree), _wu_ (bear). Certain zo are identified as Chinese clans, distinct from true Lisu clans: _cang, cu, ho, il, tao, ts'ao, wang, wu_ (different from the bear clan), and _yang_. Although a zo does not have a formal organization, never acts as a unit, and is theoretically equal in status to every other zo, the potential for clan feuds, status conflicts, and accusations of witchcraft against whole clans is always present. One seeks allies, neighbors, and hosts from fellow zo members.

Kinship Terminology. Lisu use a Hawaiian cousin terminology reflecting the importance of generational differences.

Marriage and Family

Marriage. Marriage may be with anyone who is not a member of the same clan, irrespective of residence. Cross-cousin marriage (especially patrilateral, of any degree) is preferred and often practiced, with the result that two families exchange mates over time. Polygyny is rare. Bride-payments and the nature and length of service to the wife's parents and brothers are subject to negotiation both before and after marriage. In post-1949 China, these practices have been discouraged by the authorities. After bride-service, residence is patrilocal, at first in the husband's parents' house, then in a separate house nearby. Divorces are infrequent, usually taking place before children are born; divorcées usually return to their parents' houses.

Domestic Unit. The household is the basic socioeconomic unit in village ceremonies, village assessments, village labor, and economic and ritual activities. The typical household is a nuclear or stem family, although extended families also occur. The youngest married son, together with his wife and children, normally remain in his parents' house. Frequently, one or more relatives, usually of the husband, will live with the family. The male head of the household is its spokesman, though individual members may incur debts and hold property separately.

Inheritance. All sons share in the inheritance, the youngest married son usually receiving the house and taking care of a widowed mother. Daughters receive small dowries at marriage.

Socialization. Lisu want and love children and large families. Older siblings, grandparents, and other relatives help parents care for children, often carrying them in back slings. Toilet training and weaning are lenient. As soon as able, a child begins taking part in adult activities, and by 13 or 14 is making important contributions to the household economy.

Sociopolitical Organization

Social Organization. Households form alliances based on kinship or patron-client ties for economic, social, and political purposes. When migrating, a household moves with its allies or goes to a village where fellow zo members or affines already reside. Formal request to live in a village must be made of the village headman.

Political Organization. Each village is an independent unit. Elder males provide the leadership, depending upon ability, experience, wealth, and the number of allied households that can be counted on for support. They nominate one of their own to act as headman, often only a figurehead who represents the village to the external world. Formerly, among the Black Lisu of the Upper Salween, hereditary headmen might have exerted control over several villages; class stratification (aristocrats, commoners, and slaves) existed in pre-Communist days. In Myanmar, Lisu villages are said to have owed allegiance to local Chinese or Shan *saohpa,* though this was probably more symbolic than real.

Social Control. The household is responsible for the actions of its members. The headman, acting in concert with prestigious elder males, may arbitrate disputes, levy fines, or even expel an individual from the village.

Conflict. Family feuds and personal vendettas occur, as do disputes with neighboring ethnic groups over theft or destruction of crops or livestock. Only after arbitration by elders has failed will quarrels be taken to lowland authorities.

Religion and Expressive Culture

Religious Beliefs. Religion revolves around spirit (*ne*) propitiation and ancestor worship of the two most recently deceased generations. To assure good health and good crops, a Lisu must stay on good terms with his dead ancestors and the hierarchy of other spirits. The strength of belief varies from one Lisu to the next, Chinese writers claiming that religion has greatly diminished in importance in post-1949 China. Any knowledgeable Lisu may practice divination, commonly with pig livers, chicken femurs, or bamboo dice.

Religious Practitioners. Religion is generally a male concern. Any male may become a shaman (*ne pha*) if he has the aptitude for contacting ancestors and other spirits useful in curing the sick, and if he passes initiation tests by other shamans. He has no inherent power and receives little remuneration. A village priest (*mu meu pha*), who is chosen through divination, keeps track of the religious (lunar) calendar (which frequently differs from village to village) and coordinates ceremonies for the village spirit. The Lisu observe a twelve-year cycle, similar to that of the Chinese.

Ceremonies. Most important are New Year (extending over several days in spring, and a chance to display fine clothes and jewelry, visit other villages, and seek a spouse), and the tree-renewal ceremony (held at harvest time to purify the village of bad spirits and help the guardian spirit defend the village).

Arts. The major forms of artistic expression are: clothing (especially shoulder bags worn by both men and women, embroidered with abstract designs), jewelry (worn by both men and women on wrists, neck, ears, breast, and back—the principal form of wealth), music (three-string guitars, flutes, and gourd pipes), singing (including challenge-and-response love songs between groups of young men and women), and community dancing.

Medicine. Herbal medicines are used. Sickness is a symptom of disharmony between the patient and the spirit world, so a ne pha must be consulted. In trance, he finds the spirit responsible for the sickness and the patient's family strikes a deal for the performance of a propitiating ceremony and the offering of a chicken or pig (which is afterward eaten by the patient and kin).

Death and Afterlife. When a person dies, his or her spirit is potentially dangerous for three years, after which it is invited to the altar shelf in the house of its son. Spirits of those who died without children, or who died an unusual death (homicide, suicide, strange accident) may attack people. Ancestral spirits who are honored regularly with offerings of rice, liquor or water, joss sticks, and ragweed bring good health and large crops.

Bibliography

Dessaint, Alain Y. (1972). "Economic Organization of the Lisu of the Thai Highlands." Ph.D. Dissertation, University of Hawaii.

Dessaint, William Y., and Alain Y. Dessaint (1975). "Strategies in Opium Production." *Ethnos* 17:153–168.

Durrenberger, E. Paul (1971). "The Ethnography of Lisu Curing." Ph.D. Dissertation, University of Illinois, Champaign-Urbana.

Rose, Archibald, and J. Coggin Brown (1911). "Lisu (Yawyin) Tribes of the Burma-China Frontier." *Memoirs of the Royal Asiatic Society of Bengal* 3:240–276.

ALAIN Y. DESSAINT

Loven

The Loven (Boloven, Laven) are a group of about 25,000 (1981) in the Boloven Plateau area of southern Laos. The Loven are one of the more acculturated of the local groups, through frequent contact with the Lao, Chinese merchants, and European colonists in the past. Buddhism largely has replaced traditional animistic beliefs. The traditional economy centered on swidden rice cultivation and secondary crops including maize, peppers, and yams. Irish potatoes and coffee, both introduced by the French, became important as cash crops and placed the Loven in an economic network involving Europeans and Chinese.

Bibliography

Fraisse, A. (1951). "Les villages du Plateau des Bolovens." *Bulletin de la Société des Études Indochinoises* 26:52–72.

Hickey, Gerald C. (1964). "Loven." In *Ethnic Groups of Mainland Southeast Asia,* edited by Frank M. LeBar, Gerald C. Hickey, and John K. Musgrave, 143. New Haven: HRAF Press.

Ma

Also known as the Cau Ma, the Ma are a group located in the highlands of Lam Dong, Dong Mai, and Thuan Hai provinces in Vietnam. In the census of 1985, the Ma population was placed at 25,436 with the Cho Ro (a subgroup of the Ma) enumerated at 15,022. Two other subgroups are the Cho To and Cho Sop. Some scholars consider the Sop to be a distinct group. Rice is the staple crop, grown in swiddens in the highlands and through irrigation along river banks.

Bibliography

Hickey, Gerald C. (1964). "Ma." In _Ethnic Groups of Mainland Southeast Asia_, edited by Frank M. LeBar, Gerald C. Hickey, and John K. Musgrave, 153. New Haven: HRAF Press.

Madurese

ETHNONYMS: Orang Madura, Tijang Madura, Wong Madura

Orientation

Most of the Muslim Madurese are dispersed from their home island of Madura, located off the east coast of Java. Some live in the nearby archipelagoes of Sapudi and Kangean, but nearly 8 million of the total 10.9 million Madura population live elsewhere in Indonesia (this article refers to Madurese living on Madura). The Madurese language is Austronesian, closely related to Javanese, and has two main dialects.

History and Cultural Relations

Madurese history has often been linked to that of Java. Fourteenth-century Madurese belonged to the Javanese Majapahit Empire before gaining independence. The arrival of Islam in the sixteenth century led the Madurese to develop a state organization, before they became a part of the Javanese empire of Mataram. They rebelled against the Javanese in the seventeenth century but later came under the rule of the Dutch. Presently they are governed by Indonesia.

Settlements

The vast majority of Madurese living in Madura reside in hamlets created as administrative units, rather than being organized by kinship or indigenous political units. Each hamlet may consist of between five and fifteen compounds, which are dispersed over farmland.

Economy

Unlike Java, Madura is troubled by low rainfall and poor soils. Because of the aridity, rice may be grown only once a year. For the same reason, Madurese emphasize livestock production; they raise sheep, goats, and especially cattle, some of the latter for export to Java. Further, population pressure results in small landholdings, and therefore many Madurese must work as traders and handicraft producers. Many also are fishermen, using outrigger canoes and large nets. Women work as traders and as laborers for wealthy farmers. Land is owned individually, but most villages also set aside communal land and land used to support village headmen.

Kinship

Madurese reckon kinship bilaterally. Both nuclear and extended families constitute the basic units of society.

Marriage and Family

Polygyny is allowed by Islamic law, but it is a rare man (usually a village official) who can afford to practice it. Marriage with one's first or second cousin is preferred. Marriage proposals are made by the groom's parents and include gifts. If the proposal is accepted, a bride-price including cattle is given, and the groom's parents set the date of the wedding. Wedding is by Madurese custom, but includes a Muslim religious teacher (_kiyai_). The ideal of postmarital residence is neolocal, but few newlywed couples can afford to live independently and so usually live with the bride's family. After a divorce, the property of the couple is divided by agreement. One of a couple's daughters lives permanently in her parents' house and takes care of them as they age; when they die, she inherits their house. Prior to their deaths, parents convey some of their property, including land and cattle, to their children. After death, children receive equal shares of the remaining property, in violation of Islamic law.

Sociopolitical Organization

The Madurese nobility has disappeared after centuries of foreign domination. Presently there are formal leaders, members of the village councils, as well as informal leaders, including Islamic clergy like the kiyai. The kiyai educates the children and advises adults. The authority of both types of leader depends on their ability to gain the respect of the people. Formal leaders tend to have less authority than the informal Islamic leaders; this was reflected in the 1971 elections, in which 67 percent of the Madura vote went to Nahdatul Ulama, the orthodox Islamic political party.

Blood revenge is a feature of Madurese life, especially when adultery, cattle theft, and public loss of face are involved. This is done through the practice of _carok_, in which the victim is attacked from behind with a sickle-shaped knife. The carok attack is usually fatal, and one common result of a successful attack is a blood feud between the families of the parties involved. To avoid a carok attack, one may consult a kiyai.

Religion and Expressive Culture

Most Madurese are at least nominally Sunni Muslims of the Shafi school (though a small number have converted to

Christianity). They pray five times daily, pay their *zakat* (tithe), fast during the month of Ramadan, and celebrate the Islamic holidays of Maulud and Id al-fitr (during the latter of which they visit the graves of their dead relatives). Making the pilgrimage to Mecca brings an increase in social status. The modern reform movement, Muhammadiya, which strives for adherence to the Quran and the cessation of ancestor worship, has few, if any, supporters outside the capital cities.

Madurese religion, however, is also highly syncretistic. Communal sacred meals (*kenduri*) are used when changes in life occur, for good luck. Madurese people are also known for their bullfights and bull races, during which contestants use sorcery and magic to gain an advantage over their rivals.

Bibliography

Touwen-Bouwsma, Elly (1984). "Madurese." In *Muslim Peoples: A World Ethnographic Survey*, edited by Richard V. Weekes, 458–462. Westport, Conn.: Greenwood Press.

DANIEL STROUTHES

Maguindanao

ETHNONYMS: Magindanao, Maguindanaon (recent variant), Maguindanau, Magindanaw

Orientation

Identification.   The Maguindanao speak the language of the same name, Maguindanao, live mainly on the island of Mindanao in the southern Philippines, and are the largest ethnic group of Muslim Filipinos. The names of both the people and the island on which they live refer to a large inland body of water. The ethnic designation "Maguindanao" has been translated as "people of the flood plain."

Location.   The south-central part of Mindanao, where most Maguindanao live, is located between 6° and 8° N and 124° and 126° E. This region has been known historically as Cotabato. The name is derived from the Malay for "stone fort" and apparently refers to a fort that once stood at the mouth of the Pulangi River, the main access to the interior of the Cotabato Valley. The valley is nearly surrounded by mountains, except to the west. The river, now called the Mindanao River, is a confluence of several tributaries that flow down from the mountains and snake across the valley floor before converging and emptying into the Moro Gulf on the western coast. Much of the valley floor is a vast marshland. During periods of heavy rain and flooding it resembles a large, shallow lake. Rainfall is abundant and fairly uniform throughout the year, but the wettest period is generally between May and October.

Demography.   Before this century the Cotabato Valley appears to have been only sparsely inhabited despite its large area and evident fertility. By the turn of the century there may

have been 100,000 or more Maguindanao living there. The 1948 census found 155,000 Muslims in Cotabato, nearly all of whom would have been Maguindanao. Population figures from the 1980 census are not categorized by ethnicity or religion. Those figures show that Maguindanao was the primary language spoken in 85,964 "households." Maguindanao households often include extended families and/or multiple families, so even a minimum figure of six persons per household would yield a total Maguindanao population of over 500,000. Based on field observation and previous estimates, the actual figure is probably substantially higher.

Linguistic Affiliation.   The Maguindanao language is in the Malayo-Polynesian Family. It is clearly related to many other Philippine languages including Tagalog, the predominant national language. The closest cognate language is Maranao, spoken by a Muslim group of that name living just north of Cotabato, with whom the Maguindanao have a strong cultural affinity.

History and Cultural Relations

The Maguindanao are one of many groups of "lowland" Filipinos who appear to have arrived in the islands during successive waves of migration from the Southeast Asian mainland several thousand years ago. They were well established in their present homeland by the time of the first known foreign contact around A.D. 1500. At about that time, or perhaps a bit earlier, Muslim missionaries began to arrive in this area. According to the legends of the Maguindanao, they were converted to Islam by Sarip Kabungsuwan, a Muslim prince from Johor, on the Malay Peninsula, who claimed to be a direct descendant of the Prophet Mohammed. Kabungsuwan is said to have arrived at Cotabato in a sailing ship with a small group of Samal warriors. The legends state that he won his converts peacefully by a combination of his wisdom, the appeal of his message, and certain supernatural powers that set him apart from ordinary men. The prince married a local woman who is said to have been born miraculously from a stalk of bamboo, and according to these accounts their descendants became the ruling families of both the Maguindanao and the neighboring Maranao.

The first European contact with the Philippines was in 1521, when Magellan landed in the central islands and was killed in a battle with a local chieftain. The earliest Spanish colony was founded on one of these islands in 1565, and the colonists soon learned that some of the native peoples nearby were Muslims. They identified these people with their historical enemies in Spain, the Moors. Thus they called them "Moros" and saw them as enemies to be driven away or conquered and subjugated. The armed clashes that ensued pitted the Spaniards and their local Christian converts against the Maguindanao and other Muslim peoples of the southern islands. This conflict became the long and bitter "Moro Wars," which spanned more than 300 years during the entire Spanish occupation of the islands. The Maguindanao and their Muslim allies were never fully subdued by the Spanish, but within a few years after the United States took control of the Philippines in 1898 the last major battle was fought in Cotabato, in 1905. The American forces prevailed and an uneasy peace was imposed on the region. The American colonial government encouraged people from the northern and central islands to resettle in the less populated areas of Mindanao, including Cotabato, but with limited success because of long-standing ethnic hostilities. After World War II and Philippine independence in 1946, however, large numbers of settlers moved to Cotabato. By 1970, immigrants outnumbered Maguindanao in most of Cotabato. Land disputes and other friction erupted that year into armed conflicts between Muslims and non-Muslims. Government forces intervened as the conflict escalated into civil war and spread to other parts of Mindanao and nearby islands. Most of the major fighting ended by the late 1970s, but there was continued unrest and periodic violence in Cotabato and elsewhere through the next decade. The armed conflict has been accompanied by calls for greater autonomy for the southern Philippines and the Muslim peoples there, including the Maguindanao.

Settlements

Traditional Maguindanao settlements were located mostly near the myriad waterways of their interior territory and along the extensive coast. This settlement pattern allowed relative ease of transportation and communication by boat. It also enabled the Maguindanao to dominate trade between the coast and the remote interior and mountain areas inhabited by various non-Muslim native peoples (e.g., Manobo, Tiruray, etc.). Several major trading centers were also seats of political power—even sultanates—such as the areas now known as Cotabato City, Datu Plang, and General Santos City. Other settlements along or near the waterways were controlled by _datus_ (local chieftains) and numbered hundreds or even thousands of people. The traditional homes of the datus were large wooden structures designed as multifamily dwellings, often centered in a compound with other buildings housing relatives and followers. Scattered outlying villages were comprised of smaller dwellings of wood, bamboo, and _nipa_ thatch, which also frequently housed extended families. Since the advent of American colonial rule, the traditional settlement pattern in Cotabato has been altered by the building of roads that do not follow the natural course of the waterways. Large towns have sprung up along the roads and highways, becoming new centers of commerce, while many of the older, water-oriented communities have become isolated and have languished.

Economy

Subsistence and Commercial Activities. The Maguindanao grow a variety of crops, trap fish, and obtain wild foods and other materials from the marshes for their subsistence. Wet rice is grown in the lowlands, and dry rice and corn are farmed in upland areas. Tubers, including yams and sweet potatoes, are also among the staple crops. Vegetables such as tomatoes, squash, and beans are grown, and wild greens are harvested in abundance from marshlands. Coconuts abound and are gathered at an immature stage for their tender meat and water or to be made into coconut milk for cooking. Many kinds of fruit are common, including bananas, plantains, mangoes, guavas, and durians. Freshwater fish are the main source of protein in the interior, as are saltwater fish and shellfish along the coast. Goats are raised for meat and usually are consumed on ceremonial occasions. An aged or infirm water buffalo may also be slaughtered for such events. Chickens are raised for both eggs and meat. Even today the Maguindanao produce nearly all of their own food.

Industrial Arts. Many items are hand-crafted in households from wood, bamboo, rattan, thatch, and fiber. Most of these are produced for domestic use, but some weaving, mat making, and basketry is done on a limited basis for commercial sale. In the past, the Maguindanao were known for their production of ornate brass containers, ornaments, musical gongs, etc., but brass working has become a lost art in recent times. Steel-bladed tools and weapons are still produced on a small scale.

Trade. Before this century, the Maguindanao dominated trade with people of the interior of the island and exacted tribute from them. Commodities such as salt, metal goods, Chinese pottery, cloth, beads, and other manufactured items passed inland in exchange for rice, gold, and a variety of forest products. It appears slaves may have been taken and sold as well. Trade with other islands involved many of the same items, and some Maguindanao may have been involved in piracy, which has been reported in this area for centuries.

Division of Labor. Those of highest rank in this society tend to be removed from manual labor. Among the rest, the male/female division of labor is not very pronounced. Men do the plowing, harrowing, and other heavy work of farming. Women do most domestic work, often assisted by older children. Nearly all able-bodied adults and young people join in such tasks as planting, weeding, harvesting, and threshing.

Land Tenure. Until early in this century, all land was communally owned. A person could use land if he or she could demonstrate descent from an ancestor who had cleared or used that land. In the 1920s, the American colonial government conducted cadastral surveys to determine individual landholdings. It appears many datus took this opportunity to claim the land farmed by their followers as their own, and thus acquired title to large tracts of formerly communal lands. Today there is a mixture of titled small holdings, land of uncertain title farmed on the basis of traditional claims, and "estate" lands farmed by datus or their tenants.

Kinship

Kin Groups and Descent. The Maguindanao kinship system is basically bilateral, as is common throughout the Philippines. It is unusual, however, because it is modified by a system of social rank, certain rules of descent, and distinctive marriage patterns related to these. Social rank is determined by one's _maratabat_, or social status. For those of higher rank, maratabat is based on real or imputed descent from Sarip Kabungsuwan. Higher-ranking families maintain elaborate genealogies to validate their claims to this line of descent. From the highest rank come the datus and the central political leaders who hold the title _sulutan_, or sultan. The precise social rank of those of lower status is often unclear but is said to be a factor in selecting an appropriate marriage partner. For most purposes, social rank is less important than degree of blood relationship. It is this relationship that is emphasized, and the personal kindred is the most important social group beyond the nuclear family.

Kinship Terminology. Consistent with the bilateral kinship system, terms for male and female relatives traced through either the father's or the mother's line are equivalent. Aside from the nuclear family, all members of one's kindred and often even strangers are addressed by formal male and female generational terms that may be translated as grandparent, uncle, aunt, sibling, or child.

Marriage and Family

Marriage. Monogamous marriages are the norm among the Maguindanao. Polygyny is permitted by Islamic law and local tradition, and continues to be practiced by some persons of wealth and high rank. Young people raised in the same extended household or village are considered to be too closely related—regardless of blood connection—to be married to one another. This creates local exogamy at this level. There is a strong preference, however, for marriage between related families, especially marriage of second cousins, so there is a marked tendency toward kindred endogamy. There are even some marriages between first cousins, although these are rare and are forbidden by customary law. After marriage the couple usually reside in the husband's community. Today the couple may form an independent household, whereas in the past they more often joined the man's parents in an extended household. Divorce can and does occur, especially early in a marriage. It is usually because of infertility, incompatibility, infidelity, or failure of the bride's relatives to pay an agreed bride-wealth. The marriage bond is generally strong after the birth of a child.

Domestic Unit. Households may be comprised of nuclear or extended families, the latter being more common. Even nuclear families in separate houses live immediately adjacent to relatives and share many activities with them. Extended families or multiple families living under one roof may have separate cooking hearths but often share food and socialize in ways that blur distinctions between them. In all of these cases a comparison could be made to a longhouse, or a longhouse that has been broken up into proximate living units.

Inheritance. Males and females generally inherit equally in this society. A limited exception is that among the upper class, titles and an added share of wealth are often passed on to the first-born son.

Socialization. Children are cared for and disciplined not only by their parents but by other adult members of the household. Older siblings are often assigned responsibility to care for and play with the young. When children are outside the house, any adult member of the community may gently correct or chide them, and young people are taught to address their elders by terms that mean aunt/uncle or grandparent, even if they are not related. Formal education has become common for children from families of wealth and high status. In rural areas and among ordinary people, the government-operated schools are still mistrusted as a source of disruptive outside influence. Boys may attend school for the first few grades to learn reading, writing, and simple arithmetic before being withdrawn by their parents. Many girls do not receive any formal schooling at all.

Sociopolitical Organization

Social Organization. Traditionally there have been several regions within Cotabato, each associated with a group of related families who are prominent both socially and politically. In each region are a number of important larger communities in which powerful datus reside. In these communities, status distinctions are significant in everyday life as well as on cere-monial occasions. The datu is accorded special respect and directs many of the activities of his followers. He presides over the affairs of the community and at religious celebrations or other events. Deference is shown not only to him but to his wife or wives and others of high rank who live nearby, many of whom are related to him. Central communities of this type are generally surrounded by many smaller, satellite villages, which may be some distance away. These villages usually are comprised of members of the same loosely defined kindred, possibly including remotely related relatives. Villagers recognize that they have a right to live and farm there because some of their ancestors farmed there in the past. This means they all recognize at least some degree of kinship with one another. In these villages, everyday relations are basically egalitarian. There may be a headman who represents the group in relations with outsiders. Most decisions that affect the group, however, are made by the group or by the adult males of the group. In the case of major problems or conflicts that they cannot resolve, they will turn to the datu who has authority in their area to settle the matter.

Political Organization. The highest political leaders in the past were the sultans. In the past two to four sultans reigned at any one time in different parts of Cotabato. Sometimes only one or two wielded real political power beyond their immediate area. A sultan was selected from among contenders by a council of datus, and had power only to the extent that he enjoyed their support. Today the title is honorific. Datus retain some local power, and intermarriage between families of datus extends an alliance network that continues to be politically important even in terms of national politics.

Social Control. The blood feud is one of the most serious and distinctive types of conflict in this society. It usually results from a killing that involves different families or communities. If the killer is not punished and a settlement reached quickly, a feud can be initiated and can result in seemingly interminable reprisal killings. The families of the killer and the victim try to avert this possibility by immediately negotiating through intermediaries. An effort is made to apprehend the killer and turn him over to the local datu for punishment, including death or incarceration. The families also negotiate payment of a death settlement to the family of the deceased. All members of the killer's kindred are liable for contributions to the settlement, the amount of which is supposed to depend on the social rank of the deceased. This type of serious conflict, while fortunately rare today, is mentioned as an example because of the roles played by the kindred and the datu in conflict resolution.

Religion and Expressive Culture

Religious Beliefs. The predominant religion among the Maguindanao is a form of folk Islam. Islamic beliefs and practices, which are gradually becoming more orthodox, are superimposed on a preexisting animistic belief system. People continue to believe in a variety of environmental spirits, and many tales are told of magic, sorcery, and supernatural beings. Even Sarip Kabungsuwan, who is credited with having brought Islam to this area, is described as having had powers of magic and sorcery.

Religious Practitioners. Muslim religious leaders and teachers (imam and *pandita*) preside over religious life and young schoolboys in reading and memorizing the Quran. They are the formal religious practitioners in the society. There are also other, less visible, religious functionaries who perform important services in appeasing the environmental spirits. An example is the *apo na palay*, or "grandfather of the rice," who conducts rituals and chants incantations over the rice fields at night to ensure a good harvest.

Ceremonies. Muslim religious holidays and other observances are celebrated among the Maguindanao, but in varying degrees by different communities and individuals. The most widespread ceremonies are those associated with fasting during the month of Ramadan, when virtually everyone appears to participate. Other ceremonies, such as those associated with birth, marriage, and death, tend to incorporate both Islamic and indigenous beliefs and rituals.

Arts. Arts of nearly every type are strikingly less evident in this culture than in many nearby groups. Representational art is confined mostly to weaving, basket making, and certain ornaments. Graceful dances are performed on special occasions to the rhythmic music of gongs and other instruments. Personal adornment in the forms of bright clothing, beaded jewelry, and other accessories is distinctive and colorful.

See also Maranao

Bibliography

Ileto, Reynaldo C. (1971). *Magindanao, 1860–1888: The Career of Dato Uto of Buayan.* Ithaca, N.Y.: Department of Asian Studies, Cornell University.

Saleeby, Najeeb (1905). *Studies in Moro History, Law, and Religion.* Manila: Bureau of Public Printing.

Stewart, James C. (1977). *People of the Flood Plain: The Changing Ecology of Rice Farming in Cotabato, Philippines.* Ann Arbor, Mich.: University Microfilms.

JAMES C. STEWART

Makassar

ETHNONYMS: Macassarese, Makassaren, Makassarese, Mangkasaren

Orientation

Identification. The Makassar live in the southern corner of the southwestern peninsula of Sulawesi (formerly the Celebes), Indonesia. Along with the Bugis, with whom they share many cultural features, they have been famous for centuries as seafaring traders and agents of Islam in the eastern part of the Malay Archipelago. Their name for themselves is "Tu Mangkasara'," meaning "people who behave frankly."

Location. Makassar territory is roughly between 5° and 7° S, and 119°20′ and 120°30′ E, including the island of Salayar. The Makassar inhabit the volcanic mountainous area around Mount Bawakaraeng/Lompobattang, which is traversed by a number of rivers, as well as the coastal plains, where most settlements are inhabited by a mixed Bugis-Makassar population. Except for the areas east of the volcano massif, where rainfalls are more evenly distributed over the year, the rainy season lasts from October to April.

Demography. The Makassar number about 1.8 million, with an average population density of some 245 persons per square kilometer (excluding the provincial capital Ujung Pandang). The rate of population increase in the rural areas is low today, which results from an increasing migration to the towns as well as from national birth-control projects. Makassar constitute some 72 percent of the population of Ujung Pandang (formerly Makassar), the remainder being composed of ethnic groups from all over Indonesia, including a large number of Chinese.

Linguistic Affiliation. Makassar belongs to the West Indonesian Subgroup of the Austronesian Language Family, and is most closely related to Bugis, Mandar, and several Toraja languages. It is subdivided into five mutually intelligible dialects (Lakiung, Bantaeng, Turatea, Selayar, and Konjo, the latter being classified as a separate language by some linguists), of which the "Standard Makassar," the Lakiung dialect, spoken in the western regions, is most widely used (74 percent). There are two speech levels, the higher of which is more complex in regard to morphology and lexicon. Today, few people are capable of using the high variety. The Makassar have a syllabic script comprised of nineteen characters and four additional vowel signs, which was created in the sixteenth century on the basis of Sanskrit writing and is still used, mainly by older people.

History and Cultural Relations

According to written traditions, there were a number of minor Makassar principalities in the fourteenth century. A divine princess (*tumanurung*) is said to have descended from heaven around the year 1400. She is believed to have founded the kingdom of Gowa, which was based upon a confederation of the former minor principalities. Although this and many similar myths from South Sulawesi clearly reveal an Indian influence, the impact of Hinduism on Makassar culture was comparatively slight. Among several rival Makassar kingdoms, Gowa became dominant in the sixteenth and seventeenth centuries, exercising political and economic control over the eastern part of the archipelago. Gowa's political structure was strictly hierarchical, with the king presiding over councils of subordinate rulers, ministers, and various other functionaries. Political relations with neighboring kingdoms, including those of the Bugis, were extended through intermarriage among the ruling noble families. In 1669 the Dutch captured the capital of Gowa, but rebellions and piracy continued until 1906, when the colonial troops conquered the interior regions and killed the king of Gowa. Under colonial rule as well as after Indonesia gained independence (1949), nobles were incorporated into the administrative hierarchy. Today many Makassar nobles, who are still regarded by the local population as people of a higher order, occupy prominent governmental positions in the rural regions. In the course of history the Makassar have established colonies along many coasts all over Indonesia. Principal cultural changes were brought about by the spread of Islam (which arrived on the peninsula in 1605), as well as by the growth of the town of Ujung Pandang (during the last decades of our century), where a Western-oriented life-style is now becoming dominant.

Settlements

Whereas settlements in the coastal plains usually consist of several hundred houses, villages in the interior regions are much smaller, containing from 10 to 150 houses. In some cases, the houses are clustered around sacred places; in others, they are built along both sides of a path, with the front gables oriented toward the sacred peaks of Mount Bawakaraeng/Lompobattang. Traditionally, villages were located amid the rice fields and gardens, with an average distance of some 3 kilometers from one settlement to another. In the course of current resettlement projects, many highland villages are being moved to places that are accessible by asphalt roads. In these cases, traditional settlement patterns cannot be maintained. The house is raised on wooden (formerly bamboo) piles. It is rectangular in shape and provided with a gable roof. Partitions of the gable formerly indicated the social status to which the owner belonged. No part of the house is decorated by engravings or anything similar. The interior is divided into a main room, kitchen, and (mostly only one) sleeping quarter. While formerly up to twenty people resided in a single house, nowadays most houses are inhabited by an average of five persons. Bamboo, as the traditional material for house building, has been largely replaced by wood and corrugated iron, but even in the rural locations an increasing number of houses are built of bricks. This hampers mobility, which was characteristic of the traditional local settlement pattern, since old-style houses could be moved from one place to another within a few hours.

Economy

Subsistence and Commercial Activities. While fishing is the basis of the economy along the coasts, the cultivation of rice, which is the staple food, dominates in the interior regions. Wet-rice agriculture is to be found both in the lowlands and in the mountainous regions. In the latter, dry rice, maize, and cassava are also staple crops. Other important crops are coconuts, coffee, bananas, cloves, and many kinds of fruit and vegetable. Agriculture is hardly mechanized, especially in the highlands. Only part of the wet-rice fields are mechanically irrigated, and both plowing and harvesting are done in a traditional fashion. In spite of governmental efforts to increase the production of rice (by introducing new varieties of rice, fertilizers, and pesticides), rice agriculture in the backcountry is predominantly self-sufficient. Coffee is the only product that is considered a cash crop by the peasants in these areas. Domestic animals include water buffalo and cattle (both used to draw the plow), goats, chickens, and dogs. Except for dogs, all domestic animals are eaten, but only on ritual occasions. The ordinary daily diet consists of rice, maize, cassava, vegetables, and dried fish, the latter being available in the markets.

Industrial Arts. The traditional art of weaving is no longer practiced in most regions. House building, basketry, and the production of mats are commonly considered professional activities. Blacksmiths are full-time specialists in most villages, but in general occupy very low social positions. In several places along the coast, traditional boat building has survived despite the recent emergence of motorboats.

Trade. The Makassar have for centuries been renowned for their skill as traders; seafaring trade is still very important in coastal locations. Markets, spread all over the country, are dominated in most cases by professional traders. For the majority of the population, products such as tobacco, salt, dried fish, and clothes can only be obtained in the market.

Division of Labor. In general, the division of labor is strict because of the rigid separation of the sexes in everyday life. According to tradition, home tasks are assigned exclusively to women, and female traders are found in every market. In agriculture, men do the hard work, such as plowing and carrying rice bundles after harvest, and in some regions harvest the rice.

Land Tenure. Rice fields and gardens that are part of the traditional village territory are individually owned by either men or women. In addition, everyone has the theoretical opportunity to rent or purchase untilled land, which formerly belonged to the nobility, and nowadays is governmental property. Since such land is very expensive to rent or purchase, these modes of extending control over resources are rarely practiced. In some regions most of the land is controlled by rich (mostly noble) patrons, but sharecropping among relatives is practiced everywhere.

Kinship

Kin Groups and Descent. Descent is bilateral. The inhabitants of a village or a cluster of neighboring villages consider themselves to belong to a single localized kin group, which according to tradition is endogamous. In practice, however, intermarriage between many villages is the rule, resulting in complex, widespread kin networks. Hence it is really impossible to establish any boundaries between overlapping kin groups. The proximity or distance of kin relations is defined in terms of an individual's personal kindred (*pammanakang*), which encompasses his or her consanguineal relatives as well as the latters' spouses. Although the definition of a person's kindred is very important for marriage strategy (since marriage taboos are formulated with respect to the pammanakang), the evaluation of social rank depends largely on membership in bilateral descent groups (ramages). The members of any such ramage trace their descent to a real or fictive ancestor through either father or mother. Like the village kin groups, ramages are not localized, but rather comprise countless numbers of individuals who are dispersed all over the country. Distinct terms are only applied to those ramages in which membership entitles one to succession to traditional political offices. Since all ramages are agamous, most individuals are members of two or more descent groups, which in addition are ordered hierarchically. Though descent is traced equally through males and females, patrilateral kin ties are emphasized in regard to succession to an office. On the other hand, there is a tendency to focus on matrilateral relations for the organization of rituals relating to the founding ancestors of a ramage.

Kinship Terminology. A terminology of the Eskimo type is used. Terminological differentiation of gender is confined to the terms for father, mother, husband, and wife, while in all other cases a "female" or "male" is added to the respective term of reference. Aside from the terms for "younger sibling" and "elder sibling," the age of relatives is sometimes indicated by adding a "young" or "old" to the term of reference. Teknonymy is common, though not the rule.

Marriage and Family

Marriage. In the rural locations, marriage is still arranged exclusively by the parents and/or close relatives, since according to tradition communication between unmarried young people of different sexes is strictly prohibited. Normatively, social strata are endogamous, and the groom's social rank must be higher than or at least equal to the bride's. Marriage between second cousins is preferred among the commoners, while only nobles are allowed to marry a first cousin. The bride-price is divided into "spending money" (*balanja*), which is used by the bride's family to cover the costs of the wedding feast, and a "rank-price" (*sunrang*), which is given to the bride. Both the balanja and the sunrang reflect the bride's social rank. A weak economic position of the groom's family or normative obstacles to marriage often result in elopement. There is no dominant pattern of postmarital residence. Polygyny is confined to wealthy people, because a separate household must be provided for each wife. Traditionally, divorce could be initiated only by the husband, and was fairly rare. By way of contrast, divorce is now more common, and follows Islamic law.

Domestic Unit. An average household is comprised of a nuclear family as well as close relatives who do not possess a house, in many cases including spouses of adult children. A household is considered a unit consisting of people living and consuming together; the factor of kinship is of secondary importance in this respect.

Inheritance. Sons and daughters inherit equally. If the deceased person has no children, his or her property is given to other consanguineal relatives. In case of divorce, children receive the house and the rank-price once given to the mother.

Socialization. Children are raised by both parents, elder siblings, and other relatives or household members. All adults, elder siblings, and cousins must be respected, and are addressed by honorific terms. Girls over the age of 7 traditionally were forbidden to communicate with male individuals—except for their closest relatives—until they got married. While mobility and bravery are considered important features of male behavior, girls are supposed to occupy balancing positions within the social group. Physical punishment is common.

Sociopolitical Organization

Social Organization. The most important aspect of social organization is the subtle differentiation of social rank. Makassar society is divided into nobility, commoners, and (formerly) slaves. Each of these strata is internally differentiated, with every individual ranked on a continuous social scale. A person's rank is primarily determined by that of his or her ascendants. Since descent is traced bilaterally, the definition of a person's rank depends on the different levels of rank that have been transmitted through either male or female individuals in the ramages of which he or she is a member. Marriage provides the main means for upward mobility, but low descent rank may also be compensated for by bravery, religious or secret knowledge, education, wealth, polite behavior, and (recently) occupation. Hence the boundaries between the main strata and between the various substrata are not as fixed as seems to be indicated by the comparatively few levels of marriage rank-price. Both ramages and village kin groups constitute social units for the worship of ancestors and sacred heirlooms. Owing to the principles of bilateral descent, the composition of these worship communities is flexible.

Political Organization. Traditionally, a kingdom was comprised of several principalities, each of which in turn consisted of a number of village territories. On each level the political structure was based on a myth, according to which leadership originated from a divine being (the tumanurung) who, before ascending back to heaven, left an object on earth that was henceforth believed to contain a divine spirit. Such sacred heirlooms (*kalompoang*) legitimated the political authority of noble rulers (on the levels of kingdoms and principalities) as well as that of commoner village rulers. Both noble and commoner rulers were assisted by various functionaries organized in councils. Nowadays the traditional system has been adapted to the pan-Indonesian administrative structure. In most regions, Makassar nobles hold prominent offices on the administrative levels of *kabupaten*, *kecamatan*, and *desa*, while village rulers were either installed as, or supplanted by, formal village heads. However, kalompoang and informal traditional leaders are still held in high esteem.

Social Control. The most significant means of maintaining social control is the concept of *siri'* (shame, honor, self-respect). Anyone seriously offending another person's siri' runs the risk of being killed, without any external authority being involved in the affair. Only in some cases, such as conflict over matters of land tenure or other kinds of property, are leaders requested to settle disputes. In precolonial times, the violation of marriage taboos was punished by drowning.

Conflict. Makassar claim to be looking for, rather than avoiding, conflict. Conflict arises quickly over matters of siri', which in particular relates to guarding one's own social rank and esteem, as well as that of one's female relatives. Because the local government and police now exercise control over rural communities, however, there is an increasing tendency to settle disputes peacefully.

Religion and Expressive Culture

Religious Beliefs. Islam is the dominant religion, and in the urban context various Muslim brotherhoods are very influential. On the other hand, especially in the backcountry, religious beliefs and rituals are still based largely on traditional concepts. In the traditional religion a number of deities, who are believed to dwell on the peak of the sacred mountain, occupy prominent positions. Soil, plants, and animals are considered the property of supernatural beings, which must be presented with regular offerings. In addition, the souls of the ancestors are believed to exert direct influence on the everyday life of their descendants. Owing to the increasing influence of Islam, syncretistic beliefs now prevail even in remote locations.

Religious Practitioners. In most villages, traditional priests (*sanro* or *pinati*) still perform various rituals, while Islamic functionaries (*imang*) play significant roles in official religious life. In rural locations, the position of imang is for the most part an honorary office. The imang is called upon to perform marriages, circumcisions, and death rituals, all of which imply elements from both traditional religion and Islam. Divorces in accordance with Islamic law are granted by imangs holding official positions in the local administration.

Ceremonies. Agricultural rituals are still performed in accordance with tradition, while all rites of passage nowadays include Islamic elements. Most significant are rituals centering on sacred heirlooms, which in many cases involve the making or redemption of personal vows. In addition, all periodic Islamic feasts are celebrated.

Arts. Arts play a minor role among the Makassar, and material culture is characterized by extreme plainness. There are a few dances, which now have acquired the status of mere folklore. Most musical instruments that are today considered traditional are of Indian or Arabic origin (boat-lutes, flutes, clarinets, *rebab,* and *gambus*). Elements of old Makassar music are now incorporated into Western-style popular music. Poetry and the recitation of ancient heroic legends are valued highly, although many stylistic peculiarities of the high variety of the Makassar language are liable to vanish soon.

Medicine. In case of illness, seers are commonly consulted. Illness is often attributed to a former vow that has not been redeemed yet, to sorcery and witchcraft, or to malevolent ancestor souls. Since the majority of the population cannot afford consulting a trained physician, traditional healers are still very important even in the urban context.

Death and Afterlife. In the course of the funerary rituals, the soul of the deceased is incorporated into the realm of the supernatural. Whether a soul will be benevolent or malevolent depends mainly on its former owner's behavior during life. Formerly, the community of ancestor souls was considered an integral part of the social group of the living; more recently, notions of hell and paradise (as found in Islam) have gained increasing significance.

See also **Bugis**

Bibliography

Chabot, Hendrik Th. (1950). *Verwantschap, stand en sexe in Zuid-Celebes.* Groningen and Jakarta: J. B. Wolters.

Friedericy, Herman J. (1933). "De standen bij de Boegineezen en Makassaren." *Bijdragen tot de Taal-, Land- en Volkenkunde* 90:447–602.

Rössler, Martin (1987). *Die soziale Realität des Rituals: Kontinuität und Wandel bei den Makassar von Gowa (Süd-Sulawesi/Indonesien).* Berlin: D. Reimer.

Röttger-Rössler, Birgitt (1989). *Rang und Ansehen bei den Makassar von Gowa (Süd-Sulawesi/Indonesien).* Berlin: D. Reimer.

MARTIN RÖSSLER

Malay

ETHNONYMS: Malayan, Malaysian, Melayu

Orientation

Malays live chiefly in peninsular Malaysia, where they are more than half of the population. Malays also live in East Malaysia (Sabah and Sarawak), on the coasts of Sumatra and other islands of Indonesia, extending up to the Sulu Sea of the southern Philippines. The name "Malay" is sometimes used for all of these people and refers to a cultural area called Malaysia, which ranges from southern Thailand to the Sulu Sea. This cultural sense of Malaysia never had any political unity, and "Malaysia" now refers to peninsular Malaysia (West Malaysia) and Sabah and Sarawak (East Malaysia). Malay (Bahasa Melayu) belongs to the Malayo-Polynesian Family of languages, which extend from mainland Southeast Asia to Easter Island in the Pacific. Malay is similar to modern Indonesian to about the degree that British and American English are similar, except that Indonesian shows the effects (both in structure and vocabulary) of long contact with Dutch, while Malay exhibits English influences. Malay is written in a Latin alphabet (Rumi) and a derived Indian script (Jawi).

Demography. There are more than eight million Malays in Malaysia, about 90 percent of them in peninsular Malaysia. On the peninsula, Malays tend to live in the river delta areas and the wet-rice (*padi* or *sawah*) growing regions. Towns and cities have large Chinese and Indian populations. The Malays are clustered on the east coast in the states of Kelantan, Terengganu, and Pahang. Sizable populations of Malays are also found along the west coast, in Johor, and in Singapore. The population density is about 125 persons per square mile, and the rate of increase is about 2.4 percent per year (2.8 percent in East Malaysia).

History and Cultural Relations

Malays were part of the migration southward from Yunnan and eastward from the peninsula to the Pacific islands where Malayo-Polynesian languages still predominate. Malays came in several, probably continuous, waves, pushing aside people who are now the Orang Asli (aboriginals) and the pre-Islamic or proto-Malay. Early Chinese and Indian visitors and voyagers from about 600 B.C. reported on village farming and metalusing settlements of Malays. The earliest historical date on the peninsula is about A.D. 1400. The actual history begins with the Malacca Sultanate (1402–1511), although there is mention of Malaya in the maritime empire of Srivijaya that was based on Java about A.D. 700. The trading empire based on control of the Strait of Malacca was the center of the diffusion of Islam throughout Malaysia. This spread, which was led by teachers and sufis, was peaceful. Between the 1500s and the 1800s there were struggles among competing groups such as the Acehnese, the Bugis, and the Minangkabau for dominance on the peninsula, while Melaka struggled with the Dutch and other European powers who sought to straddle the commerce in the strait. The British founded Penang in 1786, then developed Singapore and took over Melaka to form the

Straits Settlements; then they intervened on the mainland in the fratricidal wars of the Sultans and formed the Federated Malay States, and in 1909 they merged all of the above with the unfederated states to form Malaya. With the expansion of Western enterprise in tin mining, rubber, and palm plantations, Malaya imported Indian and Chinese populations to form a plural society in which Malays were just under half. With the outbreak of World War II the Japanese occupied Malaya and were expelled with the defeat of the Japanese empire. A twelve-year war called the "emergency" followed, and Malaya received its independence in 1957. For a brief time Singapore was part of the union, but is now independent. A brief war with Indonesia called the "confrontation" settled rival claims on Borneo. Civil unrest caused by communal tensions among the Malays and Chinese ushered in a period of centralized rule from 1969 to 1972, but since then Malaysia has had a working parliamentary system with coalitions among the major communal groups. Malaysia keeps close cultural ties with Indonesia and is taking a larger role in the world of Islam.

Settlements

Malay settlements tend to be strung out along the mouths of rivers, on stretches of beach, or in ribbons along a road or highway. The settlement is a village (_kampung_) made up of various houses, often built on stilts and set among orchard crops, with rice fields outside the bounds of the village. The kampung usually has no public building, unless it has a _surau_ (chapel) or a small mosque. Towns and cities are the product of immigrant populations and commercial and administrative activities, with a few cities combining the above with transport centers. Markets are held in the towns; produce flows in from the countryside via trishaw, boat, truck, bus, and train. In addition to the village patterns there are plantation line settlements. Urbanization and the formation of towns are rapidly increasing, and the cities are the fastest-growing type of settlement in Malaysia.

Economy

Wet-rice growing is the chief occupation of the Malay farmer, now often accomplished with modern irrigation systems that allow double cropping. This crop is consumed within Malaysia. The paddy farmers, who sell their rice in a market economy, are likely to be sharecroppers or tenants, not a rural proletariat. Fishing is the next-largest occupation of Malays, and this too is a small-scale commercial operation. Like most rural dwellers, the Malay peasant is engaged in smallholder rubber tapping, and just under half of the rubber production of Malaysia comes from smallholders rather than from the estates or plantations. Malays are only slightly engaged in tin mining, but they are increasingly involved in factory work and modern occupations, especially on the west coast. They are involved in transportation to and trading in the local _pasar_ markets and, increasingly, in government, professional, and town- and urban-based salary occupations. Because paddy farming is a low-paying occupation engaged in virtually by Malays only, Malay income is below that of other ethnic groups; it is government policy to reduce the income differential between Malays on the one hand and Chinese and Indians on the other. Certain Malay arts and crafts still flourish, especially on the east coast with its dense Malay occupation.

Batik cloth is woven and dyed, and silver-, brass-, and ironwork are produced and sold. Malaysia has been the fastest-growing economy of mainland Southeast Asia during the 1970s and 1980s.

Kinship

Malay kinship terminology is structured by generation, each generation having its set; by gender, male and female being differentiated within generations; and by seniority, older and younger among siblings and birth order within a family. If other status terms are available, like titles, occupations, pilgrimage or other sorts of _pangkat_, they are preferred over personal names or kin terms. There are no descent groups among the Malay, except for the matrilineages and clans among the Minangkabau of Negri Sembilan, who follow a form of customary law (_adat_) based on matrilineal descent and inheritance; this is different from the rest of the Malays, who follow bilateral norms of inheritance and descent, without formal groups. The heirs, a category called _waris_, are stipulated in Islamic usage, but equal inheritance is followed just as often.

Marriage and Family

Marriage is expected of every adult person in the society. Up to four wives are permitted under Islamic law, but the overwhelming majority of unions are monogamous. Couples are married by registering with a religious official, usually the local imam. A woman needs the consent of a male guardian to marry. Many marriages are arranged, but the consent and knowledge of the parties is sought and required. Marriage takes place after a series of gifts and counter-gifts between the families, including both bride-price and dowry. The public ceremony of marriage often takes the form of a _bersanding_, a kind of copy of a royal Hindu-style wedding. Feasting accompanies this marriage ritual. Divorce is common, simple, and frequent in an individual's life. The high rate of divorce in Kelantan and other Malay states still defies full explanation, but the ease with which a man can sever a marriage by pronouncing a verbal intention to do so must contribute to the high rate of Malay divorce. The nuclear family in neolocal residence is the preferred and most common family form; other forms of compound or extended family are but phases in a domestic cycle culminating with the nuclear family in its own compound. One common feature of Malay family life is the frequency of adoption. Childless couples may ask relatives for the opportunity to bring up one of their children, and this request is rarely refused. Adoption is partly caused by the necessity of having children to participate in the kampung-wide activities of gift exchange and feasting, from which childless couples would be barred. Children are highly valued, permissively indulged when young, but taught the proper elements of deferential behavior and speech as they grow up. A well-socialized child exhibits _budi bahasa_, the language and character of the properly raised, while ill manners are scorned as _kurang ajar_, or lacking education.

Sociopolitical Organization

Malaysia is a constitutional monarchy with a parliamentary system and a prime minister. The parliament has an upper and a lower house, and operates much like the Indian model after which it was fashioned. At the head is a king, however, chosen from the nine hereditary rulers (sultans) and serving for five years. The other two states on the peninsula are headed by governors. Below this national government with its bureaus, departments, military, constabulary, and other agencies, are the state governments with their chief ministers and departments. The day-to-day work of the government as it affects and impinges on the ordinary Malay comes through the district officer and his staff. The district officer has command of regional officers (penggawas), and this lowest level of the state civil service is in contact with local kampung headmen (penghulu), some of whom are elected, others chosen from above. With all of this formal political organization goes a system of civil courts and Islamic domestic law courts, and a flourishing political culture of competing parties and their branch organizations. Police constables and courts contain and settle disputes, and the various officers of civil government often adjudicate troubles, as does the leader of the congregation (imam). If there is a learned, pious man (alim), he will often be called in for advice on amelioration of conflict.

Religion and Expressive Culture

Malays are Muslims, and their Islamic faith is of the Sunni variety. This religion stresses the observance of the five pillars of Islam but also pays attention to the sincerity of belief by enjoining interior states of pious intent called niat. In some towns and cities Sufi brotherhoods exist. In the Malay areas of the northeast, much Islamic belief and practice is transmitted in residential boarding schools called pondok, under the tutelage of learned tok guru. Recently there has been a movement, especially among the young and in the university, to return to a more vigorous and purer form of Islam. This movement is called dakwah, from the Arabic word for a "call" back to religion. The compulsory beliefs of Islam include a severe monotheism, angels, judgment day, and Mohammed as the final prophet who received the Quran from God via the angel Gabriel. Malays should make their pilgrimage to Mecca if they are able, and there is always a waiting list of Malay pilgrims seeking passage to Mecca. The ritual calendar is geared to Islamic holidays, and the end of the fasting month of Ramadan sees the major holiday of hari raya pusa marked by feasting and visiting among relatives and friends. Underlying Islamic belief and practice are earlier beliefs and practices from Hindu and animistic sources. These hantu-hantu (as the spirits, goblins and ghosts of pre- or non-Islamic provenience are called) are mainly to be avoided, overcome, or propitiated, and are not much different from similar power in other cultures of Southeast Asia. The major venue of these spirits and forces is the curing ceremony, where a bomoh or dukun will undertake to cure a patient by an elaborate trance and body-smoking ritual. The bomoh calls on his familiar spirit from the world of spirits to remove the source of illness from the patient. There is also a large list of Malay poisons and herbal medicines used in treatment by bomohs. Bone-setting is another common form of local medical practice, and midwives still assist in the majority of deliveries.

Arts. The major form of entertainment is still the wayang kulit, the shadow play derived from the Hindu epics. The performance may cover several nights and the puppet master must be paid for his performance, either by a host or by communal contribution. Top-spinning and kite-flying contests are still part of adult entertainment. Bersilatea, the Malay

form of the martial arts, is enjoying a revival in both the countryside and the cities.

See also Singaporean

Bibliography

Firth, Raymond (1975). Malay Fishermen: Their Peasant Economy. New York: W. Norton & Co.

Ginsburg, Norton, and C. F. Roberts, Jr. (1958). Malaya. Seattle: University of Washington Press.

Nash, Manning (1974). Peasant Citizens: Politics, Religion, and Modernization in Kelantan, Malaysia. Athens: Ohio University Center for Southeast Asia Studies.

Swift, M. G. (1965). Malay Peasant Society in Jelebu. London: Athlone Press.

Wang Gungwu, ed. (1964). Malaysia: A Survey. New York: Frederick Praeger.

MANNING NASH

Manggarai

The Manggarai (Ata Manggarai) are an ethnic group located on the western end of the island of Flores, Indonesia. In 1981 their population was estimated at 400,000. Makassar and Bimanese have lived among the Manggarai for some time. Traditional villages were circular and enclosed, with a central square and ceremonial house. The Manggarai are swidden agriculturalists, growing maize and rice as their principal crops. Manggarai territory is divided into a number of dalu, small principalities that are further subdivided into glarang. The glarang are the basic landowning units and are essentially large patrilineages. Manggarai society is stratified into three classes: the dominant dalu and glarang lineages, commoners, and slaves. Although slavery no longer exists, descent from slaves remains a sign of lower status. The Manggarai are divided along religious lines, most in the west being Muslim, most in the east Roman Catholic, and those in the center still adhering to traditional beliefs. Traditional beliefs center on ancestor spirits and a supreme being called Mori Karaeng. Ata mbeko are the religious specialists. Having achieved this role through an apprenticeship, they conduct ceremonies, predict the future, and cure disease.

Bibliography

Koentjaraningrat (1972). "Manggarai." In Ethnic Groups of Insular Southeast Asia, edited by Frank M. LeBar. Vol. 1, Indonesia, Andaman Islands, and Madagascar, 81–83. New Haven: HRAF Press.

Maranao

ETHNONYMS: none

The Maranao inhabit mainly the Lake Lanao region in the northwestern section of Mindanao, the Philippines, located between 7°30' and 8°30' N and 124°00' and 125°00' E. "Maranao" means "people of the lake." The Maranao language is an Austronesian language. Closely affiliated with the Maranao is a group or subgroup possibly antecedent to the Maranao, varyingly called Iranon, Iranun, Illanun, and Ilanon. The Maranao number approximately 840,000 persons (1983), and are the second-largest Muslim group after the Maguindanao in the Philippines. Roughly 90 percent of the Maranao live in the province of Lanao del Sur, with the remainder living in Lanao del Norte and parts of Cotabato, Zamboanga del Sur, and Bukidnon. The mercantile, cultural, and educational center of the Maranao is Marawi (formerly Dansalan), the capital of Lanao del Sur.

The Maranao are primarily an inland group, comparatively isolated until recently from coastal peoples and the influence of colonial powers. Of the major Muslim groups in the Philippines, the Maranao were the last to be converted to Islam. They were a rallying point for partisan activity against the Spanish, the Americans, the Japanese, and the Republic of the Philippines, particularly during times of martial law. Many Maranao are strongly resistant to a centralized Philippines government, with some openly revolting against it. They prefer a federal form of government, with more regional autonomy, or, alternatively, secession, so as to be able to align themselves with a Muslim country or to become an independent nation.

Maranao villages are made up of a few nucleated households: several families may live under one roof in a food-sharing relationship. A typical Maranao dwelling has no partitions inside. On both walls of the house are sleeping quarters with an aisle down the center. Each family occupies one sleeping quarter. In the rear of the dwelling is a communal kitchen.

The Maranao are principally farmers and fishermen. The eastern part of Lake Lanao is fertile for rice cultivation. Fertile land has brought surpluses of maize, peanuts, sweet potatoes, coffee, citrus fruits, and exotic varieties of tropical fruits. Cottage industries such as cloth and mat weaving, wood carving, and metalwork in brass, silver, and gold are popular. Maranao are known for selling straw mats, yard goods, blankets, and metalware throughout the Philippines.

Kinship is traced bilaterally, hence membership in several villages at one time is common. Maranao conceive of villages as communities where people share a common descent instead of territory. Rank and privilege are determined by an individual's personal skills (e.g., as orator, Quran reader, or authority on law), and distinction as a leader.

The Maranao version of Islam includes many elements of pre-Islamic belief and ritual, particularly those connected with agriculture, the spirit world, and the cycles of nature. Islamic beliefs strongly reflect Sufi influence, especially in vocabulary and chants at rituals.

See also Maguindanao

Bibliography

Chaffe, Frederick H. (1969). _Area Handbook for the Philippines_. Washington, D.C.: Government Printing Office.

Majul, Cesar Adib (1973). _Muslims in the Philippines_. Quezon City: University of the Philippines Press.

Riemer, Carlton L. (1984). "Maranao." In _Muslim Peoples: A World Ethnographic Survey_, edited by Richard V. Weekes, 495–499. Westport, Conn.: Greenwood Press.

JAY DiMAGGIO

May

A group of about 1,500 (1981) living along the northern Vietnam and Laos border. They were formerly itinerant swidden cultivators, but now have become more settled.

Melanau

ETHNONYMS: A-Liko, Kelemantan, Malanow, Melano, Melanu, Milano

Orientation

Identification. The Melanau have no name to cover all Melanau-speaking people: they refer to themselves as "A-Liko X," meaning "the people of a river, a district, or a village," according to context. "Melanau," they assert, was given to them by the Malays of Brunei. The name possibly signifies "coast-dweller" in contrast to "inland-dweller."

Location. The areas of Sarawak inhabited by Melanau speakers stretch from Bintulu on the northwest coast of Borneo to the Rajang Delta in the southwest, and up the Rajang River to Kanowit. Beyond Kanowit are closely related Kajang peoples, who also are found on the River Baluy. The inhabitants of the coastal area live along rivers (Balingian, Mukah, Oya, and Igan) that run parallel to one another through dense tropical-rain-forest swamp, and frequently are referred to as the Coastal Melanau to distinguish them from Melanau speakers on the Rajang. The swampy environment, in which the only reliable food crop is the sago palm, is frequently flooded during the northeast monsoon from November to March, which virtually stops fishing from the coastal villages in January and February.

Demography. In 1980 the population of Sarawak was 1,233,103. The Melanau numbered 69,578, of whom 53,689 were Muslim; 8,486 were Christian; 1,749 were tribal; and 5,328 were registered as having no religion, which in practice means they adhered to tribal religion.

Linguistic Affiliation. Melanau is an Austronesian language of the Western Malayo-Polynesian Branch. It has no standard orthography; today individuals use their own spelling and the roman script. The Melanau language is divided into dialects, not all of which are mutually intelligible. The Coastal and Rajang dialects are linguistically related to those of the Kajang groups and groups on the coast between Bintulu and Brunei and the interior, groups sometimes referred to as Kelemantan. All Melanau people, even Muslims, speak a Melanau dialect, although today most are bilingual in Malay and Melanau.

History and Cultural Relations

Few reliable historical records of the Melanau exist before the nineteenth century, although European travelers and mapmakers placed names not unlike "Melanau" on the northwest coast of Borneo. There are also probable references to the Melanau even earlier in Chinese records. The Coastal Melanau and the Kajang groups in the interior relate that their ancestors migrated from central Borneo and founded a Kajang kingdom from which the Coastal Melanau broke away. The Coastal Melanau believe that much of their culture and many of their institutions are derived from the legendary empire of the folk hero Tugau, who was overthrown in a struggle with Brunei. Some historians suggest that these events occurred in the fourteenth century, others, as early as the seventh. In 1861 the Melanau coastal district was ceded to James Brooke, the rajah of Sarawak, by the sultan of Brunei. The Rajang Delta was already under the control of Sarawak. The cession was made to gain control of the export of sago flour to Singapore. The trade was essential for the survival of the regime of the rajah of Sarawak. So as not to disturb the flow of trade, the rajahs interfered as little as possible with the local social and political organization. During World War II the third rajah sold the country to the British government, which, until Sarawak became a part of the Federation of Malaysia in 1963, instituted a number of modernizing economic and educational changes, accompanied by further developments in representative government and administrative institutions.

Settlements

Modern villages vary in size from 300 to 1,000 inhabitants. Houses, averaging 7 by 10 meters, are built on durable wooden frames in a ribbon pattern along both banks of a river and stand some 3 meters above ground. Walls are of plank or sago bark, and roofing is of palm thatch or wooden shingles. In some areas, notably on the River Tillian at Mukah, villages were closely adjacent, and today the banks of the river are a continuous line of housing with several thousand inhabitants. Administratively the villages are still separate. Traditionally a village was made up of two, sometimes three longhouses, each with a population of about 300 people. A longhouse, consisting of separate apartments with a common veranda in front, facing the river, was essentially a fortress on ironwood piles, some 10 meters above the ground. They were often sited on the bank of the main river opposite the mouth of a tributary stream, which allowed them to see enemies approaching on the water. At the mouths of the main rivers, where representatives of the sultan of Brunei nominally held suzerainty over the river to its source, villagers had by 1830 already begun to build small separate houses, but still retained longhouses for defense. By the beginning of the twentieth century the rajah of Sarawak had successfully put an end to intertribal warfare and most longhouses were abandoned. Sago gardens were cultivated as near the village as possible, and a communal rice field was organized annually by village elders, with a strip allocated to each household.

Economy

Subsistence and Commercial Activities. Hunting and gathering, combined with the cultivation of sago gardens (normally about 4 acres in area) and the export of sago biscuit and forest products (gums, resins, rattan, timber) in exchange for metal goods, weapons, ceramics, and cloth traditionally formed the basis of the Melanau economy. The cultivation of sago gardens was supplemented by growing swamp rice (*padai paya*) and orchards on the levees of the rivers. Floods at the end of the northeast monsoon frequently ruined the rice crop, which could not be relied on for subsistence. Villages on the coast, where the water of the estuaries was too saline for extraction of flour from the sago palm, depended primarily on fishing and on the import and export trade.

Trade. During the northeast monsoon, when access to the rivers was limited and fishing was dangerous, expeditions upriver from the coastal villages with dried fish, salt, nipa palm sugar, and craft products—palm-leaf thatch, mats, baskets, and hats—were undertaken to exchange these items for sago biscuit, fruit, canoes, and timber. A similar intrariverine trade for forest products and rice was also maintained with Iban settlements in the hills beyond the swamps. Traditionally sago biscuit was exported under the auspices of aristocratic leaders from both inland and coastal villages and of Malay traders from Brunei and elsewhere. With the foundation of Singapore in 1819 and the demand from the European and American cotton industry for cheap industrial starch, the nature of the sago-export trade altered. After the conquest of the coastal district by the rajah of Sarawak in 1861, Melanau and Malay carriers and traders were replaced by Chinese immigrants, who also entered into the production of flour to the extent that they were allowed. The government, however, did not permit the sale of land to immigrants; the primary production of flour remained in the hands of Melanau villagers until after World War II, when all production was mechanized and only the gardens remained in Melanau ownership. Even though the primary production of flour remained in the hands of the Melanau until then, by 1900 the economy had become dependent on the single cash crop, and extensive changes had occurred in the social system.

Division of Labor. Male tasks include clearing the forest and planting and maintaining sago gardens, felling the ripe palm and bringing the trunk to the villages, and stripping the bark off the segments into which the stem has been cut, before rasping the pith inside into a rough sawdust. The sawdust is given to the women to wash on a platform over the river.

This rasped pith is placed on a fine-woven mat on the platform, mixed with water, and trampled by the women; the water with the flour in suspension is forced through the mat and a thin straining cloth onto draining boards leading to a trough below the platform, where the crude flour settles and surplus water is drawn away. The sale of this crude flour to a Chinese dealer is also the work of women. The proceeds of the sale are divided in various ways between the owner of the palm, the male feller, and the female trampler of the pith. This cottage industry, in which men and women controlled their own labor and profits, came to an end in the 1950s when Chinese dealers mechanized all aspects of the industry, except the growing and felling of palms. The Chinese dealer did not usually pay cash, but entered the transaction in his books and allowed goods to be bought on credit from his retail shop, thus ensuring that his clients could be kept at regular work and that he could supply his creditors with a regular and predictable supply of flour for export.

Because only Melanau are allowed to own sago land, only those with sago gardens now have any part in the production of sago. Many of the crops are mortgaged before they become mature. A large part of the male population is forced to leave the villages as migrant laborers in the lumber industry; others migrate permanently. Women are no longer economically independent.

Industrial Arts. In the cottage industry most of the necessary equipment was made locally or acquired through the intrariverine trade. Ironwork and weaving ceased with the advent of a cash economy at the end of the nineteenth century.

Land Tenure. Every village collectively owns a delimited territory that it was formerly ready to defend against all outsiders. Within that territory sago gardens and orchards, carefully delimited, are individually owned. Joint tenancy is possible, especially if a single garden is inherited by two women, for gardens are almost never subdivided. Such an arrangement is not thought satisfactory; other solutions are preferred.

Kinship

Kin Groups and Descent. Theoretically, descent is patrilineal in the allocation of rank, but is not used in the formation of groups. Three types of groups in which kinship is an important factor are found: (1) households made up of separately catering individual families, with occasional stem families (*tegen*); (2) sections of the modern ribbonlike villages largely consisting of relatives, and known as *a-sega*—a term also used for close relatives up to second cousin; and (3) ad hoc groups of kin assembled from both paternal and maternal lines of descent for specific tasks (e.g., weddings, funerals, trading expeditions).

Kinship Terminology. Kin terms are bilateral, with one term, male and female alike, for each of five generations; but the individual family is lineally set apart from other kin. In some districts seniority and gender in the parental generation and in Ego's siblings are terminologically distinguished. Kin terms are given to all relatives up to the second cousins; relatives up to fifth cousin are recognized, but connections beyond are strangers. No term is used for the kindred.

Marriage and Family

Marriage. Although polygamous marriage, with the consent of the first wife, is permitted, it is very rare and usually leads to divorce. The population of a village is divided into aristocrats (*a-menteri*), commoners (*a-bumi*), and slaves (*a-dipen*). Ideally marriage should be with a second cousin (patri- or matrilateral) within the same rank; but in small, politically independent communities the need for talent has always favored cross-rank marriages. The father of a bride is covertly permitted to choose the bride-wealth and rank he desires for his daughter through any line of descent. A wedding is the most important public occasion on which upward or downward mobility is recognized and validated. Theoretically, all first marriages are arranged by parents, but the wishes of the proposed partners are usually taken into consideration. Parents do not arrange second marriages. For a period after the wedding, uxorilocal residence is ideal, but economic advantage often overrides the ideal. One child, usually the youngest, is expected to remain with the parents. Divorce is by mutual consent, and property acquired since the marriage is divided equally.

Domestic Unit. People who cook and cater together are considered to be a family (*tegen*); but a household may consist of several separate catering and cooking units. Six or seven people constitute an average household.

Inheritance. Property is divided equally among surviving children and the offspring of any dead children. The former longhouse apartment or the contemporary house, in addition to a share of other property, is usually allotted to the child who remains with the parents. Gardens and orchards are divided as whole units and are not subdivided.

Socialization. Infants and children are reared by both parents, by siblings, and by other household members. Physical punishment is very rare; it is regarded as a debased practice of the Chinese. Individual independence is highly valued, but not at the expense of custom and respect for elderly people.

Sociopolitical Organization

Sarawak is a state in the Federated States of Malaysia; it consists of divisions, each of which in turn is divided into districts under the supervision of district officers.

Social Organization. Formerly a village was an independent unit governed by a group of self-appointed aristocrats known as *a-nyat*, or elders. The rajah of Sarawak appointed one of them as headman, answerable to the district officer. Today the influence of the elders varies with local circumstances; their power is now primarily ceremonial, concerned with validating social mobility at weddings. The suppression of endemic tribal warfare by the rajah of Sarawak allowed people other than aristocrats to acquire wealth by planting sago gardens; the gradual introduction of a cash economy permitted commoners and even slaves to acquire wealth and make claim to higher rank and even enter the group of governing elders.

Political Organization. Village headmen today are minor magistrates and try certain civil suits in addition to collecting taxes. Criminal offenses are a matter for the district officer, native officers under him, and the police. Districts vary in size and, in coastal areas, are comprised of Iban and Malay people as well as Melanau. In addition to administrative services, the state government today provides schools, dispensaries, hospitals, land surveys, and various advisory services. It also maintains highways, canals, and bridges, and subsidizes mosques and churches.

Social Control. In villages social control is largely a matter of *adat*, or custom, supervised and administered by the headmen and elders. The Coastal Melanau Adat, an attempted codification of many village adats, is followed by headmen and elders in cases of family and personal dispute, short of homicide or criminal theft, but each village claims its own version of the adat and often does not adhere to the official codification. Social control, however, is maintained primarily by a value system that places a high premium on respect for seniority, rank, and the proper order of things as embodied in the adat, any violation of which entails civil penalties imposed by the elders and automatic supernatural penalties that can be averted only by correct reparation.

Conflict. Conflict is usually seen as a disregard of proper respect, and children are brought up to avoid conflict at almost any cost.

Religion and Expressive Culture

Religious Beliefs. In 1980 53,689 Melanau were Sunni Muslim, 8,486 were Christian, 1,749 were tribal, 5,328 were listed as having no religion (but were probably all tribal), and 326 were listed as miscellaneous. For Muslims, Christians, and tribals alike, the world consists of this, the middle world, the upper world (the sky), and the world below. Traditionally the world was egg-shaped, seven layers or worlds above and seven below the middle world, the whole being balanced on the head of a buffalo standing on a snake, all surrounded by water. The breathing of the buffalo caused the ebb and flow of the tides. For some people the land of the dead was an underworld; others thought it elsewhere, but did not know where. Its topography was exact, but differed for Muslims, whose view was shared by Christians.

For Muslims, Christians, and tribals alike, the world, the sun, the moon, and the stars were created by Alla-taala, but how is not known. He is remote and little interested in human affairs. All "layers" of the world are inhabited by spirits (*tou*), who, together with humans, animals, and plants, share this middle world. Every being has its own proper place in the world, which is ordered by adat. Overstepping boundaries causes trouble, and most human illness is caused by trespassing on some spirit's living space. Spirits are of many kinds: earth, air, water, forest, etc. Sometimes they are referred to as *ipu'*, who are less malevolent than tou, and may indeed be invited to reside in and protect dwellings. Supernaturals live on the moon and punish disorderly and disrespectful behavior by men, especially mockery of animals. A female guards the entrance to the land of the dead. People are reluctant to call such supernaturals "tou" or "ipu'," but no other term exists for such demigods. Muslims and some pagans call them *melaikat*.

Religious Practitioners. No pagan priests exist. Expert carvers of spirit images, or *bilum*, diagnose what spirit (sometimes also called "bilum" and not "tou") is likely to have caused an illness and, in a short ceremony, forces the spirit into its carved image so that it may be taken to its proper place and forbidden to harm the patient for at least three days. Spirit mediums, with the help of familiar spirits, also cure illness and practice divination. Every village, Muslim and tribal alike, holds an annual cleansing ceremony, *kaul*, to call uninvited spirits that have taken up residence in the village to a feast before they are sent home to their proper places.

Ceremonies. Apart from the annual kaul, private ceremonies of increasing complexity and expense are held for the curing of illness by spirit mediums. Ceremonies for the safety of a child two months before its delivery initiate a series of taboos, culminating in the birth. There are also ceremonies at the wake of a dead person; they may continue for several months, until a secondary burial.

Arts. Among most Melanau groups, tattooing was never widely practiced. Strongly built longhouses, fortresses thirty feet above ground, were traditionally decorated with elaborate wood carving. Bilum carved in sago pith were widely used and are a sophisticated form of sculpture. Ceremonies were accompanied by gong orchestras with distinctive chants and music; bards recited and sang epics, legends, and myths of considerable poetic merit at ceremonies or simply for entertainment.

Medicine. Most illness was attributed to an attack by a spirit, but certain ailments, mostly minor, were attributed to a failure to keep a proper balance between hot and cold conditions in the body. Herbal medicines existed to restore the balance, most of which have been taken over by practitioners of Malay medicine.

Death and Afterlife. An individual's funeral is one of the most important events in the life cycle. At death the soul begins a boat journey, accompanied by attendant spirits—usually called "tou"—to the land of the dead. Chants, ceremonies, and games during the wake ensure the soul a safe journey. Once admitted, the soul is sent to one of seven pagan villages, appropriate to the manner of death, and lives a life similar to that of this middle world. Eventually a second death occurs, and many believe that the soul then becomes dew. Muslims and many Christians also believe that the soul sets out for the land of the dead by boat or, according to some, along a road that comes to a place where the path becomes a sword across a pot of blazing fire. An individual who has led a good life can walk along the flat edge of the sword; the sharp edge of the sword ensures that one who has led a bad life falls into the pot. Beyond the sword is the land of Mohammed, Jesus Christ, and the pagans.

Bibliography

Crocker, W. M. (1876). "A Short Account of the Melanos of Sarawak." *Sarawak Gazette* (Kuching), no. 119.

Morris, H. S. (1953). *A Report on a Melanau Sago Producing Community in Sarawak.* London: H.M.S.O.

Morris, H. S. (1978). "The Coastal Melanau." In *Essays on Borneo Societies*, edited by Victor T. King, 37–58. Oxford: Oxford University Press.

Morris, H. S. (1981). "The Melanau View of Their Environment." *Sarawak Museum Journal* 27 (5).

Roth, Henry Ling (1896). *The Natives of Sarawak and British North Borneo; Based Chiefly on the mss. of the Late H. B. Low, Sarawak Government Service.* London: Truslove & Hanson. Reprint. 1980. Kuala Lumpur: University of Malaya Press.

H. S. MORRIS

Mentaweian

Mentaweians (Mentaweier, Orang Mantawei, Poggy-Islander) inhabit the Mentawei (Mentawai) Islands (Siberut, Sipura, North Pagai, and Utara Selatan) and the islands of Nias and Enggano off the west coast of Sumatra. In 1966, Mentaweians numbered about 20,000. Their language has not been studied extensively, but it is believed to be related to the other languages of western Indonesia.

The traditional social organization recognized patrilineal clans, clan communities, and centralized clan houses (*uma*). With widespread conversion to Christianity, beginning in the 1950s, these traditional cultural features have largely disappeared. In the past women raised taro (the main crop) and tubers and gathered shellfish and small fish. Men fished and hunted. More recently, the government and missionaries have introduced more permanent agriculture, rice being the major crop.

See also Nias

Bibliography

Nooy-Palm, C. H. M. (1968). "The Culture of the Pagai Islands and Sipora, Mentawei." *Tropical Man* 1:152–241.

Wallace, Anthony F. C. (1951). "Mentaweian Social Organization." *American Anthropologist* 53:370–375.

Minahasans

Numbering around 40,000 in 1977, the Minahasans (Minahasa, Minahasser, Minhasa, Tombalu, Tombula, Toumbulu) inhabit the mountainous terrain of the extreme northeastern section of Sulawesi's northern peninsula in Indonesia. Rather than a single group, the Minahasans are a confederation of groups including the Tontemboan, Toulour, Tondano, Tombalu, Tonsea, Tonsawang, Bentenan, Ponosokan, Belang, and Bantik. The purpose of confederation was conflict with the neighboring Bolaang Mongondow. Minahasan is classified in the Northern Sulawesi Group of the Austronesian Language Family. Single-family houses on low piles, each with a hedged yard, are organized into rows. Wet and dry rice are the staples, supplemented by maize, sago, goats, pigs, and chickens. Tobacco, coffee, coconuts, and cloves are grown commercially. Since the late 1600s, the Minahasans have been in regular contact with the Dutch, which over time has led to the Christianization of most of the population (except for the Ponosokan, who are Muslim), the formation of a large Eurasian population, and the virtual disappearance of the traditional culture.

See also Bolaang Mongondow

Bibliography

Kennedy, Raymond (1935). "The Ethnology of the Greater Sunda Islands." Ph.D. dissertation, Yale University.

Minangkabau

ETHNONYM: Menangkabau

Orientation

Identification. The Minangkabau are similar to their neighbors, the Malays, from whom they differ most notably in reckoning descent through females. It is this feature that has attracted the greatest interest of scholars. There are references to the relationships between the two cultures in Minangkabau folklore. For example, the first two Minangkabau persons were Parapatiah (Malay *perpatih*) and Katamangguangan (Malay *temenggong*), corresponding to the terms for systems of customary law governing descent through females (Minangkabau *adaik parapatiah*) and descent through males (Malay *adat temenggong*). The most common folk etymology of "Minangkabau" depends on its resemblance to the words *manang* (victory) and *karbau* (water buffalo). In this explanation, the ethnic name refers to a "buffalo victory" won by clever villagers who selected as their champion an unweaned female calf, armed with a knife on its nose harness, which in its frantic search for nourishment castrated and thereby defeated a champion Javanese bull.

Location. The traditional Minangkabau homeland, West Sumatra Province in Indonesia, is centered on the Padang Highlands (Darek, "land above water"), which are part of a chain of mountains near and parallel to the western coast of Sumatra. Several peaks are more than 3,000 meters in elevation and some are active volcanos. The highlands, in few places more than 60 kilometers from the Indian Ocean, are divided into three territories (*luhat*), each of which is associated with a *rantau* (peripheral area). Additionally the *pasisia* (coastal area) is part of the traditional homeland. Rainfall is adequate for most crops throughout the area. Mountain lakes provide irrigation for wet-rice fields in flat parts of the highlands.

Demography. There are approximately eight million Minangkabau in Indonesia, about half of them in West Sumatra;

300,000 or more live in Malaysia. Minangkabau have been migrating (*marantau*) to other areas in Indonesia and Malaysia for many centuries. Most large cities thus have sizable Minangkabau communities. Populations in rural areas of the traditional homeland tend to be unbalanced in favor of females and the elderly. Those in urban and rantau areas tend to be unbalanced in favor of males and the young.

Linguistic Affiliation. Closely related to Malay, Minangkabau belongs to the Western Group of Austronesian languages.

History and Cultural Relations

According to myth, the first Minangkabau came from the volcanic peak Marapi. In one version, the founders arrived during an immense flood, when the part of the peak above water was no larger than an egg. In another, the founders emerged directly from the crater. Their descendants spread first into the three core areas (*luhak*) in the highlands, and then into the periphery (*rantau*) of the homeland.

This homeland is bordered by the Batak homeland to the north, the Malay homelands of Riau and Jambi to the east, the Kerintji homeland to the south, and the Indian Ocean to the west. From the thirteenth century onward the Acehnese, whose homeland lies north of that of the Batak, were the dominant sea traders along the west coast of Sumatra. They were a major source of Islamic influence on Minangkabau culture. Minangkabau trade also extended eastward to the Malay-dominated Strait of Malacca. A series of fifth-to-sixteenth century Malay and Javanese trading empires (Melayu, Sri vijaya, Majapahit, and Malacca) strongly influenced the development of Minangkabau society and culture. These empires provided the economic context of Minangkabau emigration, and they provided the cultural inspiration for royal institutions at Pagarruyong, the seat of the Minangkabau king.

According to myth, the first king (Maharajo Dirajo) was a son of Iskandar Zulkarnain (Alexander the Great). Traditional history indicates that a Javanese prince or aristocrat named Adityavarman became the first king, but perhaps as late as the fifteenth century.

Tome Pires of Portugal was, in the sixteenth century, among the first western European travelers to mention the Minangkabau. During the seventeenth century the Dutch traded for gold and black pepper in native ports along the Minangkabau coast. The Dutch East India Company contracted with local rulers for a trade monopoly. By 1641, with the capture of Melaka town, the Dutch dominated much of the trade on the eastern coast of Sumatra as well. Nonetheless, the economy and social structure of Minangkabau society did not change significantly until the nineteenth century, after the Dutch colonial government replaced the Dutch East India Company. The Paderi Wars, a factor spurring development of administrative complexity, began early in the nineteenth century as a local expression of the Wahabi fundamentalist movement in Islam. Initially, the conflict was a Minangkabau affair between adat traditionalists and Islamic fundamentalists; but it developed into an anti-Dutch war, which prompted the development of more comprehensive colonial administration.

Colonial government modified native political structure by defining a new, more elaborate hierarchy of administrative districts and leadership positions, and by adhering strictly to inheritance of offices and ignoring traditional ancillary concerns regarding the size and prosperity of rival kin groups. New civil-service positions and schools that provided the necessary Western education for gaining these positions were opened to the Minangkabau. This produced a new type of Minangkabau elite. Broad economic changes also occurred, beginning in 1847 with the forced delivery of crops for export associated with the development of coffee plantations in the highlands, but changing at the beginning of the twentieth century to rapid expansion of commercial agriculture.

Settlements

The basic territorial units are the traditional *nagari* (village states), about 500 of which now constitute the homeland area. Natural and man-made features of the landscape mark the boundaries between them. Each nagari is a self-sufficient community with agricultural lands, gardens, houses, prayer houses, a mosque, and a community meeting hall. Ordinarily there is a central open market and scattered coffee shops, but no business district as such. Some old long wooden houses are propped high on foundations and have roofs that bow down deeply at mid-length and rise steeply to the gabled ends. There are also other styles of house. Houses line both sides of the roads, which link all houses. Fruit trees of many sorts shade the houses, rice fields lie behind the houses, and fields for dry cultivation are beyond the rice fields.

Economy

Subsistence and Commercial Activities. Ecological conditions vary from place to place: well-watered valleys and gentle slopes support wet-rice cultivation; drier hills support commercial crops such as cinnamon, coffee, fruit, and rubber; mountain lakes, rivers, and sea coasts support fishing; forests support collection of wild products; and village compounds support vegetable gardening, crafts, and petty commerce. The economy of each nagari is a particular mixture of these activities. Moreover, the distant rantau communities of emigrants contribute to the economies of their respective home nagari. The coastal towns support businesses of every sort and scale.

Industrial Arts. Blacksmithing, carpentry, wood carving, weaving, tailoring, jewelry, and pottery are the common industrial arts.

Trade. Minangkabau men are among the most widely known and active traders in Southeast Asia. Their heavy involvement in trade outside the Minangkabau homeland area is related to the fact that they cannot inherit Minangkabau rice land.

Division of Labor. Men's work includes the harvesting of rice, commercial agriculture, fishing, metal- and woodworking, and trade. Women's work includes vegetable gardening, transplanting and weeding of rice fields, preparation of food, care of children and the household, and some crafts such as weaving and pottery.

Land Tenure. Individual households ordinarily gain use of traditional wet-rice land and house land through matrilineal inheritance. Newly opened land belongs to those who clear it and plant it. It may be sold or inherited as part of a man's personal property; but it becomes traditional land within a few generations, and then its use is based on matrilineal inheritance.

Kinship

Kin Groups and Descent. Matrilineal descent groups (*suku*) vary in size and segmentary organization, depending on the vicissitudes of reproductive and economic success over many generations. Some scholars cite myths and terms for groups as evidence of moiety and phratry organization, but these features are not actually present in Minangkabau society. The largest social grouping below the nagari level is the matriclan or suku (quarter), of which there are usually four or more. Matriclans are subdivided into subclans that are also referred to as suku except when distinguishing them from other segmentary levels of organization. In that case, the subclan may be called a *payuang,* or "umbrella," in reference to the symbol of office of the elected leader of such a group. Members of the same subclan may not be able to trace genealogical relationships but nonetheless consider themselves close relatives. Each subclan is subdivided into genealogically isolated lineages, for which there is no special term. Lineages are subdivided into lesser units that can be distinguished as *sabuah paruik* or "of one womb." These are the primary corporate landholding units. Finally, the sabuah paruik consists of several small domestic groups called *urang sapariuak* (persons of one cooking pot). Some of these units consist of more than one household. Royal kinship was patrilineal.

Kinship Terminology. Terminology is generational or Hawaiian in type. However, special terms for mother's brother (*mamak*) and for sister's child (*kamanakan*), and other expressions identifying groups of relatives with common interests in property—*dunsanak sa'iniyek* (relatives with the same remote ancestress), *dunsanak sa'uci* (relatives with the same great-grandmother), and *dunsanak sa'anduang* (relatives with the same grandmother)—clearly indicate the importance of matrilineal descent.

Marriage and Family

Marriage. Members of the same matriclan are not supposed to marry. Cross-cousin marriage is preferred, especially between a woman and her father's sister's son. Residence after marriage is uxorilocal. Polygyny is allowed but is not common. Many marriages simply lapse through desertion. Divorce according to Islamic law is possible.

Domestic Unit. The core of the traditional domestic unit consists of a woman, her married and unmarried daughters, and her daughters' children. Her adult sons or grandsons who are not yet married sleep in the local prayer house (*surau*); those who are married sleep as guests in the houses of their wives. Her husband is a guest in her house, as are her daughters' husbands. Each married woman has her own room in which to receive her husband. Members and guests of the household socialize and work in a great common room that runs full length through the middle of the traditional house, with rows of bedrooms on either side. As the original family matures and expands, older women without young children move to small houses built near the great house. Such house compounds are heritable property occupied by succeeding generations of women and their families.

Such traditional houses still exist in most nagari, but now they are often outnumbered by smaller and more modern houses occupied by nuclear or stem families in which men are less clearly guests in the houses of their wives. If a man builds a modern house for his wife using his own resources, the house is his until his wife or daughter inherits it. Households in rantau areas also tend to be nuclear or stem families.

Inheritance. There are two types of property in traditional law (*adaik*): *harato pancarian* (earned property) and *harato pusako* (ancestral property). Earned property generally involves goods produced for exchange: the means of production are individually owned, and can be inherited by children of either sex. Rules of distribution of such inheritance may be Islamic, in which case male heirs receive full shares and female heirs half shares. Or, traditional rules may be followed, in which case the heirs of males are males and the heirs of females females. Examples of harato include craft goods and newly acquired land.

Ancestral property involves goods produced for immediate consumption and the means of production, which are communally owned and can be inherited only by females. The best example of harato pusako is land for wet-rice production. A right to the use of such land passes from mother to daughters and is closely supervised by the matrilineal group that owns it. Usually this is at the sabuah paruik (sublineage) level, but it might be at higher or lower levels depending on the segmentary structure of the actual kinship group and the number of generations since the acquisition of the land. Also, if there are many heirs and the plot of land is not large, the right to use the land may be rotated year-by-year among the different heirs. The male leaders (mamak, or "mother's brother") of the matrilineal group are the arbiters in matters of inheritance.

Minangkabau distinguish between *harato pusako tinggi* or "high ancestral property" and *harato pusako randah* or "low ancestral property." High ancestral property has been inherited over a period of so many generations that the incident of its initial acquisition has been forgotten, whereas low ancestral property has been inherited for only a few generations, and the incident of its initial acquisition through labor or purchase is still remembered. Low ancestral property is available for use only by the heirs of the ancestress who first acquired it. High ancestral property is available for use by a wider range of members of the corporate landholding group.

The relative importance of these two modes of inheritance, one for earned property and the other for ancestral property, varies from place to place in the Minangkabau area. Nagari in the well-watered plains, in which wet-rice production is the main economic concern, are more involved with ancestral property (harato pusako) and matrilineal law (adaik parapatiah). Those located in the dry hills and in urban areas, where the production of commodities is more important than the production of rice, are more involved with earned property (harato pancarian) and patrilineal law (adat temenggong). Also, patrilineal inheritance is more important among royal and aristocratic families and in communities where fundamentalist Islamic precepts are important.

Socialization. Mothers and fathers socialize children. Weaning may be traumatic, but toilet training is not early or harsh. A father helps his children gain an education and he takes a strong interest in helping find appropriate husbands for his daughters. Children also receive the attention of the mother's brother, who as an adult male of the same corporate group has a strong interest in their success. Older siblings are strongly involved in the socialization of their younger siblings.

Sociopolitical Organization

Social Organization.   The various lineage groups constitute the main apparatus of social organization. Social and economic class differences based on differential access to property, leadership positions, and education have always existed.

Political Organization.   Some loose alliances of the past among groups of nagari were organized into permanent districts for modern administrative purposes. Other modern districts are not based on traditional alliances. West Sumatra is now divided into eight districts (*kabupaten*), which are divided into subdistricts (*kecamatan*), and further into nagari. Also, there are six municipalities (*kota madya*) in the province. Each nagari has a mayor (*wali nagari*) elected by the village council but approved by the *bupati*, who is the government-appointed head of the district. At the village-council level and below are the chiefs (*panghulu*) of the various lineage segments who adjudicate property rights and other matters of traditional law and receive labor service (*serayo*) from other lineage members in return.

Social Control and Conflict.   National police and courts as well as traditional (*adaik*) and Islamic courts operate. Conflicts involve disputes over property and leadership positions, and differences between religious beliefs and practices of traditional Shafi'i and modern fundamentalists.

Religion and Expressive Culture

Religious Beliefs.   Minangkabau are Muslims of the Sunni sect and the Shafi'i school of jurisprudence. The requirements of Islamic faith are simple: confession of faith, five daily prayers, fasting during the month of Ramadan, giving alms, and pilgrimage to Mecca (hajj) if possible. Because Minangkabau are born Muslims, many do not follow all of these practices; nor are they aware of the technical aspects of their religious belief and practice, Sunni or Shafi'i. Most simply follow the practices of their parents. A few individuals know a great deal about Islam, having studied in local *madrasah* schools or with religious scholars who have studied in Mecca or Medina.

Religious Practitioners.   Religious officials include the imam (head of the mosque), *khatib* (the preacher), *kadi* (religious judge), and *bilal* (caller to prayer). Additionally, there are *urang siak* and *ulama* (pious persons who know about religion).

Ceremonies.   Important ceremonial occasions include the weekly Friday sermon, beginning and ending the fast each day during the month of Ramadan to honor the Holy Quran, the feast days at the end of Ramadan, the feast days before the month for going on the hajj, the birthday of the Prophet Mohammed, and *khenduri* (ritual feasts) to celebrate any sort of change in social status.

Arts.   Poetry, music, architectural decoration, and portraiture are notable art forms practised by Minangkabau.

Medicine.   Herbal remedies (*jamuan*) and word charms (*jampi*) are used.

Death and Afterlife.   Death is viewed in Islamic terms and burials are carried out according to Islamic law. Deaths of married persons involve changes in relationships between lineage segments of different clans, which are reflected in the series of funeral ceremonies that occurs after a death.

Bibliography

Chadwick, R. J. (1991). "Matrilineal Inheritance and Migration in a Minangkabau Community." *Indonesia* 51:47–81.

Graves, Elizabeth E. (1981). *The Minangkabau Response to Dutch Colonial Rule in the Nineteenth Century*. Monograph Series, Publication no. 60, Cornell Modern Indonesia Project. Ithaca, N.Y.: Cornell University, Southeast Asia Program.

Josselin de Jong, J. P. B. de (1951). *Minangkabau Social Formations: Indonesian Peasants and the World Economy*. Cambridge Studies in Social Anthropology. Cambridge: Cambridge University Press.

Kato, Tsuyoshi (1982). *Matriliny and Migration: Evolving Minangkabau Traditions in Indonesia*. Ithaca, N.Y., and London: Cornell University Press.

Thomas, Lynn L., and Franz von Benda-Beckmann, eds. (1985). *Change and Continuity in Minangkabau: Local, Regional, and Historical Perspectives on West Sumatra*. Monographs in International Studies, Southeast Asia Series, no. 71. Athens: Ohio University Center for International Studies and Center for Southeast Asian Studies.

RONALD PROVENCHER

Mnong

Located in the southern highlands of Vietnam, the Mnong (M.Nông, Mnong Gar, Phii Bree) registered 67,340 in the 1985 census of Vietnam. The scholarly literature is unclear about which groups and subgroups therein should be classified as Mnong. The official classification in Vietnam is apparently a restrictive one, as a population estimate from 1981 lists 180,000 Mnong. The slash-and-burn method of agriculture is used to produce the staple crop, upland rice. Secondary crops are maize, bananas, beans, eggplants, taro, yams, sugar cane, a variety of other vegetables, fruits, and tobacco. Indigo and cotton are grown for weaving, a local art form. Hunting is done by men only, but both men and women fish. Women gather bamboo shoots, saffron, and mint. The Mnong trade pigs and poultry for buffalo, and use cash or produce to obtain salt, jars, and cloth. The Mnong have spirits and rituals for everything in nature, including all animals and inanimate things, for heroes, and for ancestors. Sorcerers are important. Shamans act as medicine men and preside at rituals that often include the sacrifice of buffalo.

Bibliography

Condominas, Georges (1960). "The Mnong Gar of Central Vietnam" (in French). In *Social Structure in Southeast Asia,* edited by George P. Murdock, 15–23. Viking Fund Publications in Anthropology, 29. Chicago: Quadrangle Books; London: Tavistock Publications.

Modang

ETHNONYMS: Dayak, Long Belah (Medéang), Long Glit (Long Gelat), Long Way (Medang), Menggaè (Segai), Wehèa (Wahau)

Orientation

Identification. "Modang" is a generic term covering a complex of culturally related groups living in the Kutai Regency of Kalimantan Timur, Indonesia, along the Mahakam River and its tributaries. Outside Kutai proper (i.e., in Doberai or Bulungan), these people are known by the exonyms "Segai" or "Ga'ai." The term "Modang" also seems to have originated over a very wide area (about 63,000 square kilometers) in the province of East Kalimantan, roughly between 0° and 4° N and 115° and 117° E. They are comprised of five river-based groups loosely identified as Dayak: (1) Long Gelat (middle and upper Mahakam), (2) Long Belah (Belayan), (3) Long Way (Kelinjau), (4) Wehèa (Telen-Wahau), (5) Menggaè (Kelai-Segah, lower Kayan).

Location. Established on the middle and upper reaches of rivers in the lowland areas, the Modang occupy a distinct geomorphic region. It is situated between the rolling hills and mountains bordering the Apo Kayan Plateau and the marshy plains nearer to the river mouths. The Modang subgroups are divided among three drainage basins: Mahakam, Kelai-Segah, and Kayan. They have preferentially settled flat areas along the riverside where good fertile alluvial land is found.

Demography. Judging from field surveys and published census data, the total Modang population does not exceed 5,000 individuals for the five subgroups (1985). Epidemics, intermarriage with other ethnic groups, conversion to Islam, and a low birthrate have all had a negative effect on the population. The Modang Wehèa, the largest group, has a population of 2,100 (1985) concentrated on a relatively narrow stretch of land along the upper Telan and Wahau rivers. It has shown a steady growth (39 percent) in the last fifty years (from 1,266 persons in 1935). Some marriages are taking place between neighboring Modang groups such as the Long Way, Menggaè, and the Wehèa, mostly among aristocratic families. Out-migration to the nearby towns (Tenggarong,

Samarinda, and Balikpapan), of temporary nature, is still unimportant.

Linguistic Affiliation. Modang is part of the Kayanic Family within Western Malayo-Polynesian, but it constitutes a discrete language group. The five Modang isolects are still mutually intelligible. It appears that a process of lexical innovation, combined with rare phonological changes, has been going on for a long time. The subgroups have been separated for more than two centuries. The languages spoken by the Punan Kelay and Punan Mahkam in Doberai are part of this group. These isolects form a dialectal chain with about 6,000 speakers spread from Kutai to Bulungan.

History and Cultural Relations

Oral history and genealogies point to the upper Kayan area, the Apo Kayan Plateau, as the last major settlement area of the Modang before they migrated to the lowlands of Kutai and Doberai or Bulungan in the late eighteenth century. It is known as Kejin/Kejien, according to the various isolects. If one goes further back in time, the Bahau-Punjungan region was occupied by Modang, Kayan, and Bahau subgroups before the Kenyah migrations from Sarawak started in the seventeenth century. During the early nineteenth century (1810–1840), the Modang, as the major Dayak entity in Kutai and Doberai, were challenging the Malay sultanate's power. They were then practicing ritual headhunting on a larger scale than any other Dayak group in eastern Borneo. The Modang show close cultural similarities to the Bahau, the Busang, and Kayan. They are part of a central-northeast Borneo culture area. Social structure, religious beliefs, custom (*adat*), and technology constitute variations on a common background. Within the Kayan-Kenyah-Bahau cultural complex, however, the Modang exhibit a particular differentiation. They distinguish themselves by their village organization: the existence of a men's house (*ewéang* in Wehèa, *petoèh* in Long Way, etc.), and the institution of the chief's "great house" (*msow pwun* in Wehèa). Generally they appear more conservative than the other populations of the region. They have retained cultural elements discarded by others, for instance the great number of taboos (*pli'*) observed during the rice cycle. The description given here applies mainly to the Modang Wehèa.

Settlements

Modang villages (*ekung*) are located on high river banks, usually near the confluence of a major river with a stream. Longhouses (*min*) of three to six apartments or individual houses (*msow*) linked by plankways are built in rows (*telsong min*) parallel to the river course; the ridge beam follows the upstream-downstream orientation. The rows of houses are situated on both sides of a central street (*lan*). They correspond to the two named moieties of the village: *dya' min,* the row of houses closer to the river bank, and *lon min,* the row of houses farther inland. The village as a unit has a territory (*lenih ekung*), where all households are allowed to farm. Villages range from 200 to 600 inhabitants. In the Mahakam area, the politically dominant Long Gelat are sharing multiethnic villages with vassal Busang groups. Within the village territory, settlements used to shift every ten or fifteen years in response to inauspicious omens, deaths, or bad dreams; this is no longer the case. Because population density is very low, the swidden system operates fairly well.

Among central Borneo peoples, the Modang have a distinctive house type (msow). It is built with a strong ironwood structure on two vertical levels: a low platform (*sun tah*) and living quarters (*maè msow*), linked by stairs or a notched log (*hesien*). The same principle is applied to the different buildings: longhouse, individual house, the chief's great house, and even farmhouses. The platform has the same uses as the gallery in Kayan-Kenyah-Bahau longhouses: economic activities and ritual and leisure space. In the past (nineteenth century), houses were very high, 8 or 9 meters above the ground, for defensive reasons. Households of neighboring houses (or longhouse apartments) are related by ties of kinship; according to the Modang's conception, they cannot be separated by nonkin (see "Kin Groups and Descent").

Economy

Primarily subsistence agriculturists, the Modang combine fishing and hunting with gathering of forest products. Fishing is a daily activity whereas hunting, practiced with dogs and spears, is less important. Hill rice (*plaè*), their major crop, is cultivated on swiddens located on flat river banks, usually with long fallow periods (12–20 years). Rattan gardens are also planted. Modang occasionally pan for gold during the dry season. Today men commonly find temporary jobs throughout the year with nearby timber companies.

Kinship, Marriage, and Family

Kin Groups and Descent.   Modang reckon kinship bilaterally, so as to include vertically great-grandparents and colaterally fourth cousins. The personal kindred, however, is not named. It forms a kinship network focused on a young couple or a sibling group, rather than on Ego. No corporate or economic functions are ascribed to this kin grouping aside from the expected solidarity between relatives. Affines are included in the category. Descent is cognatic (ambilateral) and descent lines (*sot*) are linked to apical ancestors of a particular rank. In a village, closely related households constitute clusters of "neighbors/relatives" (*petsah msow/pewellin*), according to the residence pattern. They are established on the principle of *kentèp* (gripped, squeezed), a taboo that forbids nonrelatives (*lun elap*, "other people") to build their houses or to occupy apartments within a longhouse between relatives (affinal or consanguineal kin, especially siblings and cousins). Transgression is punished by supernatural sanction (*ka' kentèp*), which manifests itself as illness, ultimately resulting in death. In practice, these clusters tend to form endogamous units within each row of houses in a community; they show a closer economic and ritual cooperation between their members. Membership in the two named moieties, dya' min, "the lower village," and lon min, "the upper village," is fixed by residence only. In any case the "moieties" are not exogamous; they have a ceremonial function at sowing (*enkuel*). In contrast to the other ranks, the chief's descent line (*waés*), attached to the great house, is characterized by a segmentation process. Minor descent lines (sot) stemming from this main line form aristocratic descent lines of a lesser rank. This happens by means of hypogamous or hypergamous marriages between aristocrats of a higher status (*hepuy pwun*) and other aristocrats (*hepuy so'*), commoners of various statuses, and

even slaves (*megwes, psap*). Very long genealogies (15–20 generations), complete with collateral lines, are memorized by members of the chiefly house or by influential aristocratic women. In relation to rank, matrilateral or patrilateral descent can be stressed by individuals, depending on their ancestors' position, so as to claim preeminence in political or ritual status. For the ruling strata, however, patrilateral line or the "head of the post" (*du' jehoè*) is considered superior to the matrilateral line, the "middle of the post" (*welguak jehoè*).

Marriage.   According to the hierarchy of rank, bride-price is graded for the chiefs (higher aristocrats), the lesser aristocrats, and the commoners. Formerly the traditional wealth objects and heirlooms, like gongs, jars, old beads, swords, etc., were used. Today these have been replaced by cash payments of different sums. But some items (china plates, swords, cloth) are still available. Bride-price is given to the bride's family on two separate occasions. Postmarital residence (*ngeyen*) is uxorilocal, but some couples practice alternating uxorilocal and virilocal residence. Neolocal residence, following the birth of children, is becoming more common. The chiefs usually establish virilocal residence, often after an initial uxorilocal period. There have been reports of polygyny among the chiefs. Marriage prohibitions are restricted to first- and second-cousin marriages and those between relatives in two successive generations, such as uncle and niece.

Domestic Unit.   The household (msow) is the only corporate grouping of Modang society. It is a production and consumption unit; each household owns a separate rice barn (*pèa plaè*). In theory it is an everlasting entity, but after three or four generations some domestic units become extinct (*pe'us*). When longhouses were the dominant housing type, the stem family was the norm; now the nuclear family is a major type (one-third of the sample in Bèn Has, the village studied). On average, family size was found to be five persons. The household is also a ritual unit that can be subject to taboos (pli'), thus closing it to nonmembers. As a rule, birth, marriage, incorporation, and adoption create membership for the household. Partition of the "original household" (msow un) occurs at a slow rate.

Sociopolitical Organization

Social Organization.   Like most of central Bornean peoples, hereditary named ranks characterize Modang social structure. The four main status levels are chief (hepuy pwun), aristocrats (hepuy so'), commoners (pengin) and, formerly, two classes of slaves (megwes, psap). Megwes, slaves captured in war, were possessed only by the chief. The ranks are divided again into intermediate levels. Rank ascription is exclusively based on descent; nonetheless adopted children follow their parents' rank. According to the rule of uxorilocality, children usually have the mother's status, but this is changing slowly. Ideally each rank was endogamous; in fact, anisogamic marriages were common, but only village chiefs would stick to the rule.

Political Organization.   Each village constitutes an independent political unit, although in a river basin the chief of one village may be acknowledged as a paramount chief. The decision-making process is controlled by the chief; a council of elders (bo' be's) and aristocrats takes place in the great house. They discuss community affairs and prepare villagewide ceremonies and rituals. A village crier (*sewün keltèa*) transmits the chief's orders and other information to the villagers. The chief and the important men (*hepuy so'* and *sewún kas*, "influential persons") are entitled to build a men's house (*ewéang*) as a meeting place for their clients (*nèak gua'*). These buildings (there are two or three in a village) function as ritual centers for the men and as bachelors' dormitories. More generally, society is divided into two political groupings: the "people who speak" (*lun kehèa*) and the "populace" (*lun megon*). The former are the aristocrats, sewün kas, and other influential elders.

Religion and Expressive Culture

Religious Beliefs. The Modang cosmology gives an idea of a tripartition of the universe: upper world or sky (*lengèt*), earth (*sun mna'*), and underworld (*dya'mna'*) are differentiated. The skies—divided in seven "layers" (*telsun*)—and the underworld are the dwelling places of the deities (*metà*). At the top of the pantheon one finds a pair of goddesses: Doh Ton Tenyè and Dèa Long Meluen, respectively elder and younger sister. Besides these main figures a complex of deities, malevolent spirits or ghosts (*sekyah*), and supernatural beings is recognized. Among the metà, the thunder-gods (*dlay*) have a predominant position: they punish humans guilty of transgression of taboos and custom or mockery of animals.

Ceremonies. The ritual life is extremely rich. The yearly cycle has two main phases: *Edat na' plaè*, "the Custom of Rice," and *Na'pli'*, "to do the sacred [things]," which are comprised of no fewer than twenty-four rituals of varying scale. Transition rites (birth, naming, marriage, funeral) are carried out by ritual specialists, who are also spirit mediums (*lun enjuk*). Formerly, most of these ceremonies, when done for the chief's family, required human heads, as well as the building of the great house. Headhunting was abolished in the 1920s. Now for the great head-hunting ritual, *Nemlèn*, pieces of old skulls are used.

Death and Afterlife. Conceptions of the soul distinguish between a "soul of the living" (*welgwen lun blom*) and a "soul of the dead" (*welgwen lun lewas*). Eschatological notions refer to a journey of the soul to a village of the dead, Pang Kung Kelung. However, people who have died a "bad death," or *lewas ak* (i.e., by drowning, in childbirth, or violently), go to another place called Pang Kung Néang. In accordance with this belief, there are two graveyards (*keldam*) in the village. The chiefs used to be buried separately from the other villagers, in impressive mausoleums (*belah*) up to 10 meters high. Statues of dead persons (parents, grandparents) of high status are erected in the village toward the end of the Nemlèn ceremony as an expression of prestige. These images (*bo' jöng*), carved on the upper part of posts, display the particular aesthetic values of the Modang.

Arts. The Modang have a rich craft tradition of mat making, basketry, beadwork, iron forging, and wood carving, which has achieved a high degree of skill as evidenced by house posts, boards, doors, and staircases with intricate motifs of spirits, animals, and ornamental designs. Painted murals on the chief's house and mausoleum (especially among Long Gelat and Long Way) show the same symbolic figures. The performing arts are well developed also: collective dances (*enjéak*) and masked dances (*hedo'*)—the masks worn by men only—take place on ritual occasions. Vocal music, expressed in chants (*teluy*) and epics (*tek'na'*), presents more complexity than does instrumental music.

See also Kalimantan Dayaks; Kenyah-Kayan-Kajang; Tidong

Bibliography

Bock, Carl (1882). *The Headhunters of Borneo: A Narrative of Travel up the Mahakkam and down the Barito; also, Journeyings in Sumatra.* London: Sampson, Low, Marston, Searle, & Rivington. Reprint. 1985. Singapore: Oxford University Press.

Dewall, H. von, and A. L. Weddik (1849). "Beknopt Overzigt van het Reijk Koetei op Borneo." *Indisch Archief* 1:78–105, 128–160.

Guerreiro, Antonio J. (1983). "Le nom des ancêtres et la continuité: Remarques à propos d'une généalogie des *hepuy pun* Long Way (Long Bentuk, Kalimantan Timur)." *Asie du Sud-Est et le monde indonésien* 14:51–68.

Guerreiro, Antonio J. (1984). *Min, "maisons" et organisation sociale: Contribution à l'ethnographie des sociétés Modang de Kalimantan-Est, Indonésie.* Paris: École des Hautes Études en Sciences Sociales.

Guerreiro, Antonio J. (1985). "An Ethnological Survey of the Kelai River Area, Kabupaten Berau, East Kalimantan." *Borneo Research Bulletin* 17:106–120.

Guerreiro, Antonio J. (1987). "'Longue maison' et 'grande maison': Considérations sur l'ordre social dans le centre de Bornéo." In *De la hutte au palais: Sociétés "à Maison" en Asie du Sud-Est insulaire*, edited by Charles MacDonald, 45–66. Paris: Éditions du Centre National de Recherche Scientifique.

Guerreiro, Antonio J. (1988). "Le groupe Kayan: Essai d'inventaire ethnolinguistique." In *Le riz en Asie du Sud-Est: Atlas du vocabulaire de la plante*, edited by N. Revel, 174–178. Paris: Éditions de l'École des Hautes Études en Sciences Sociales.

Guerreiro, Antonio J. (1989). "Entités, rhétorique et intention dans le discours rituel Modang Wehèa (Bornéo)." In *Anthropologie de la prière: Rites oraux en Asie du Sud-Est*, edited by S. C. Headley, 89–124. Paris: Études du Centre de l'Asie du Sud-Est.

Nieuwenhuis, A. W. (1904–1907). *Quer durch Borneo: Ergebnisse seiner Reisen in die Jahren 1894, 1896-7 und 1898-1900.* Leiden: E. J. Brill.

ANTONIO J. GUERREIRO

Moluccans—North

ETHNONYM: Orang Maluku (Utara)

The Northern Moluccas constitute the original "Moluccas" sought out for millennia by foreigners for their cloves. Nowadays they form a subdivision of the province of Maluku in the Republic of Indonesia, with approximately half a million inhabitants spread over Halmahera, the Sula and Obi Islands, Bacan, Morotai, and a number of smaller islands. On two of these, Ternate and Tidore, powerful rival Muslim sultanates arose in pre-European times. Their influence reached at times as far as the Philippines, Sulawesi, New Guinea, and the islands in the Timor Sea. After a century-long struggle with the Portuguese and Spaniards in the 1500s, they eventually succumbed to Dutch colonial rule in the seventeenth century. Although strong island identities still exist, the inhabitants are united by their common Islamic faith and a "creole" culture, an amalgamation of many (locally somewhat divergent) indigenous and foreign traits. The Tobelorese on the northern peninsula of Halmahera are Protestant Christians; other pockets of Christianity exist elsewhere. Various "Alifuru" tribal groups in the interior of Halmahera still adhere to animistic religions. Austronesian languages are or were spoken throughout the region except on Ternate, Tidore, and northern Halmahera, where languages are spoken that constitute, together with those in the Bird's Head of West Irian, the West Papuan Phylum. Ternate-Malay is widespread and Bahasa Indonesia, the national language, has become the official means of communication. Besides the cultivation of cloves, the main economic pursuits are horticulture, fishing, and forestry.

See also Tobelorese

Bibliography

Campen, C. F. H. (1890). "Eenige mededeelingen over de Alifuren van Hale-ma-hera." *Bijdragen tot de Taal-, Land- en Volkenkunde* 32:162–197, 511–516.

Ishige, Naomichi, ed. (1980). *The Galela of Halmahera: A Preliminary Survey.* Senri Ethnological Studies, no. 7. Osaka: National Museum of Ethnology.

Riedel, J. G. F. (1886). *De sluik- en kroesharige rassen tusschen Selebes en Papua.* The Hague: Martinus Nijhoff.

DIETER BARTELS

Moluccans—Southeast

ETHNONYM: Orang Maluku (Tenggara)

This far-flung island region between New Guinea and Timor is part of the province of Maluku in the Republic of Indonesia. In this thinly inhabited region, Protestant Christians make up more than half of the population, while the rest is about evenly split between adherents of Roman Catholicism and Islam. Indigenous religious beliefs in nature deities and ancestor spirits still exist. The roughly 250,000 inhabitants are interspersed over three main island groups, Tanimbar, Aru, and Kai, and smaller islands like Babar, Leti, Wetar, Romang, Luang-Sermata, Damar, and Kisar. Beginning in 1978 the populations of Teun, Nila, and Serua have been forcibly removed to Ceram (Central Moluccas), ostensibly to protect them from volcanic activities. Many Austronesian languages are spoken in the area, and often several mutually unintelligible languages are used within one ethnic group, as on Tanimbar. Horticulture and fishing are the main modes of subsistence. Pearls are cultivated at Dobo (Aru islands). Weaving is practiced by women on Tanimbar. The area has remained largely isolated and fairly unimportant economically, and social change has been relatively slow. Ethnographically it is still largely unexplored, although its affinal marriage systems have received much attention. Formerly headhunting was common. There are evident cultural and historical affinities with New Guinea and Timor; the Ambonese of the central Moluccas, who came as administrators, missionaries, and educators, left a strong cultural imprint. The overall cultural picture is quite heterogeneous. The most unique feature is a caste system in the Kai Islands.

Bibliography

Drabbe, M. S. C. (1940). *Het leven van den Tanimbarees.* Leiden: E. J. Brill.

Geurtjens, H. (1921). *Uit een vreemde wereld: Het leven en streven der Inlanders op de Kei-Eilanden.* 's-Hertogenbosch: Teulings.

Nutz, Walter (1959). *Eine Kulturanalyse von Kei.* Düsseldorf: M. Trilitsch.

Wouden, F. A. E. van (1968). *Types of Social Structure in Eastern Indonesia.* The Hague: Martinus Nijhoff.

DIETER BARTELS

Mon

In 1983 the Mon (Mun, Peguan, Talaing, Taleng) numbered about 835,000 in Myanmar (Burma) and between 70,000 and 100,000 in Thailand, with smaller numbers in Cambodia and Vietnam. A more recent estimate places their number at 1.3 million in Myanmar alone. If these figures are accurate, they suggest that the Mon population has nearly doubled since the 1930s. The Mon have evidently been in Burma for at least 1,000 years, with villages in Thailand established within the last 400 years. They live primarily in villages located in monsoon-climatic areas roughly between 13° and 17° N. Mon is classified as an Austroasiatic language in the Mon-Khmer Group. Today, most Mon are bilingual, with Burmese becoming the primary language for many, reflecting a long process of assimilation into the dominant Burmese culture. The Mon were politically independent until 1757, when they were defeated by the Burmese. Today the Mon are involved in the insurgency movement against Myanmar's military government. The economy rests primarily on wet-rice agriculture and fishing, both for consumption and sale. Yams, sweet potatoes, pineapples, and sugar cane are also grown. Mon fishing along the coast has declined in recent years because of competition from Thai commercial vessels, which are allowed there by the Myanmar government. The Mon are Theravada Buddhists, with religious practices similar to those of their Burmese and Thai neighbors.

See also Burmese

Bibliography

"Burma: In Search of Peace." (1989). _Cultural Survival Quarterly_ 13.

Halliday, Robert (1917). _The Talaings_. Rangoon: Superintendent of Government Printing and Stationery.

Monom

The Monom (Bonom) are a group of about 5,000 (1973) located in eastern Gia Lai-Cong Tum Province in Vietnam.

Muna

The Muna (Mina, Moenanezen, To Muna), numbering about 200,000 in 1977, live on Muna Island, adjacent to Buton, south of the southeastern peninsula of Sulawesi, Indonesia. Muna is classified in the West Indonesian Group of the Austronesian Language Family. Plaited-grass houses, raised on piles, formerly were scattered among the swiddens. The only large settlement is the capital, Kota Muna. Maize is the staple crop, supplemented by sweet potato, sugarcane, and vegetables. Muna was ruled by the Butung sultanate from the coming of Islam at the end of the sixteenth century until the early twentieth century.

See also Butonese

Bibliography

LeBar, Frank M. (1972). "Muna." In _Ethnic Groups of Insular Southeast Asia_, edited by Frank M. LeBar. Vol. 1, _Indonesia, Andaman Islands, and Madagascar_, 144–145. New Haven: HRAF Press.

Muong

ETHNONYMS: Mi, Moai, Moal, Moi, Mol, Montagnard

Orientation

Identification. In the last few decades, the word "Muong" has received recognition as the name for this ethnic collectivity, but it is not an autonym. Until the early twentieth century, the Vietnamese used to call all the forest/hill dwellers "Mi" or "Moi" (the savage). The French too used the same derogatory term, "les Mois," and only much later did the French refer to them as "Montagnards" (mountaineers). Now they are designated as ethnic minorities. The Vietnamese term "Muong" initially had no ethnic connotation. It simply referred to any neighboring area inhabited by non-Vietnamese, especially the Muong and the Thai, under the traditional authority of an aristocratic family. The Muong, on the other hand, called themselves "Mol," meaning "man." Through dialectal variations in different regions, "Mol" is also pronounced "Moal" or "Moai."

Location. The Muong inhabit a continuous stretch of about 300 kilometers of land from north to south, from Yen Bai Province to Nghe An Province, without passing through the territory of any other ethnic group. This territorial contiguity has contributed to the extraordinary cohesion and persistence of the Muong culture. In fact, there is very little variation in the material and spiritual life of the Muong in different regions. The Muong regard Hoa Binh Province in the north of Vietnam as the cradle of their culture. The Muong habitat is essentially mountainous, enclosing narrow valleys. The forest cover has been largely decimated. Most of their settlements are located at the foot of the limestone or earthen hillocks in narrow valleys. Usually there are Thai settlements to the west of theirs, and Vietnamese settlements to the east. This midland location has been a source of Muong economic and cultural strength for ages.

Demography. In 1960 the Muong numbered 415,658, and by the mid-1980s they had reached a population of nearly 500,000. They are one of the largest ethnic minorities in the Indochinese region, and the second-largest in Vietnam.

Linguistic Affiliation. Their language belongs to the Mon-Khmer Group of Austroasiatic languages. As yet there is no script, despite concerted efforts in the last few years.

History and Cultural Relations

Little is known about the prehistory of the Muong. Archaeological evidence and local legends suggest that the various ethnic minorities of the region—the Muong, Meo, Zao, Tay, Tho, Nung, Thai, Kmhmu, Coong, Sila, La Hu, and Bo Kho Pa—belonged to a single cultural group (more or less). It was through subsequent geographical dispersion and cultural isolation that diverse ethnic identities emerged and consolidated. Similarly, ethnographic and linguistic research on the Muong and the Vietnamese indicate several crucial similarities between the two societies. Given that the Muong inhabit a region between those of the Vietnamese and the Thai, the presence of cultural and linguistic similarities is not surprising. The Muong nevertheless continue to have their own specific characteristics, often very much distinct from those of their neighbors.

Settlements

The smallest unit of Muong habitation is the *quel* (hamlet), with about fifty households. Their housing design and architecture not only have remained unchanged for generations, but also reflect the structure of the household and the traditional social system in general. The houses are raised on 2-meter wood pilings, creating a rectangular space 6 to 13 meters long and 4 to 6 meters wide. The roof is thatched with elephant grass and the floor is made of both wood and bamboo. The house is then divided into two unequal parts by a shoulder-high bamboo screen. The smaller part is used as a bed-cum-store room and is where the women and unmarried girls spend most of their time. The larger compartment is used as a guest room as well as for cooking and dining. The ancestors' altar occupies the central place. Both the rooms have independent staircases but the front side is reserved for males and the back for females. There is also a conception of upper and lower parts, according to respective positions in the width of the house. The upper part is toward the windows overlooking the valley and the lower part leans towards the hillslope, without any window. The more social status one has, the greater the chance of being seated near the windows. Notables, male elders, and guests are assigned places in the upper side, whereas commoners, females, and children are assigned places in the lower side. Even while eating or gossiping, a similar positioning is still maintained between the males and females and the elders and youngsters in the family.

Economy

Subsistence and Commercial Activities. The Muong economy is based on agriculture, although gathering, hunting, livestock breeding, and handicrafts together constitute an important component. Women gather edible tubers, leaves, vegetables, fruits, berries, mushrooms, bamboo shoots, and, at times, breadfruit, whose flour is used for bread in periods of scarcity. Fuel wood, house-building material, pharmaceutical plants, and other forest products for trade are collected from what remains of the forest. Hunting with traps, crossbows, nets, snares, lime twigs, flintlocks, and rifles remains the prerogative of males. Communal hunting is organized on festive days and a successful expedition is seen as a good omen for the rice harvest. Women are allowed to partici-

pate only as support personnel, but a pregnant woman receives two shares, one for herself and the other for the child she is bearing. According to custom, individual hunters have to give some portions to the headman and elders. Fishing is done by dip, cast, or scoop net, and the Muong are experts in catching fish with bows as well as with knives. During floods, every family catches a large quantity of fish. Animal husbandry is limited to a few pigs, poultry, and a few buffalo for farming. Milking cows is still not popular.

Industrial Arts and Trade. Except for weaving cotton and silk clothes and making baskets for domestic use, handicrafts remain underdeveloped, necessitating dependence on Vietnamese traders and state cooperatives for all pottery, brass, and iron objects as well as other materials.

Division of Labor. The sexual division of labor is rigid and mechanical. Women are involved in transplantation, irrigation, weeding, parts of harvesting, rice husking, weaving, and food gathering. Children are often assigned the task of pasturing the buffalo. The male adults are engaged in plowing, digging, clearing bushes, threshing, hunting, making farm tools, and constructing and repairing the houses.

Land Tenure. Traditionally, the irrigated rice fields were communal and controlled by the hamlet/village headman with the support of a group of nobles belonging to their own clans. The headmen and nobility together occupied about two-thirds of the total irrigated-rice fields and redistributed the rest to the peasants, who were in turn obliged to pay certain dues in kind and to perform corvée in the fields reserved for the headmen and to maintain the local irrigation and drainage network. Whenever a commoner died without a male heir, his family automatically lost the right to land use, and even their cattle, cash, jewelry, and other precious belongings were seized and handed over to the aristocracy. Thus, the aristocracy consistently defended the principle of communal ownership of irrigated lands. The peasants, however, eked out a miserable existence.

In recent years slash-and-burn agriculture has been reduced greatly, but it was always subsidiary to farming maize, cotton, cassava, sweet potatoes, gourds, and pumpkins. Productivity is so low that a hectare of the best shifting land is inadequate to meet the minimum food needs of two adults. The corvées and dues imposed by the seigneurial administration of the past were shared equally by the concerned households. Now the peasants pay between 7 and 10 percent of their produce to the state. There are also bush-rice fields, constituting one-tenth of the total rice fields, which are individually reclaimed and owned by the peasants; but the yield is negligible and they not infrequently remain fallow. The terraced rice fields, sometimes prepared by taking soil from the valley, yield almost twice as much as the shifting lands. Small brooks irrigate these fields on the slopes of the low hillocks before flowing into a stream.

Following the Dien Bien Phu victory in 1954, the last stretch of the Muong territory was liberated. Tribunals against headmen were instituted and the "land-to-the-tiller" campaign followed. Small mutual-aid teams were also established, wherein peasants retaining the individual lands helped one another by sharing the main agricultural tools, animals, and labor. By the mid-1960s, almost every Muong hamlet had formed an agricultural cooperative. This increased productivity through adoption of improved technologies. Soon the cooperatives got involved in animal breeding, tea growing, trading forest produce, rural credit systems, and small-scale industries, and they established schools, dispensaries, etc. Besides shifting lands, about 10 percent of land is left for private gardens where the peasants grow fruits, vegetables, etc., which have great free-market value. Since 1982, there has also been subcontracting of nearly half of agricultural tasks of cooperatives to production teams. According to this system, the households enjoy the right to sell in the free market any produce above the stipulated quota.

Kinship

In traditional Muong society there was a strict hierarchical separation between the nobles and the commoners. Each village or hamlet headman belonged to one of the four dominant clans, namely, Dinh, Quach, Bach, and Hoang. They had the hereditary prerogative of ruling or administering the unit. Clan exogamy is followed strictly. The commoners, on the other hand, mostly carried the patronym "Bui." This is not a clan, but is something like a caste. Intermarriage among the Bui is common, as they are not necessarily relatives; intra-hamlet marriages are frequent. Marriage is strictly forbidden in a patrilineage. Each lineage is divided into two branches, the elder and the younger. Lineage unity is maintained by a lineage head chosen from among those conversant with usage and custom. When any member of a lineage faces any difficulty, others tend to help without being asked. The beneficiary receives the assistance as a matter of right. During marriages, funerals, and other rites, gifts are made willingly to the household and the work is shared. Such reciprocal exchanges are more frequent among the commoners than among the nobility.

Marriage and Family

Marriage. A traditional Muong marriage was normally arranged by the parents, often contrary to the wishes of the partners concerned, and sometimes years before puberty. The groom's family supplied about 100 kilograms of pork, an equal quantity of alcohol, and a few silver coins. The only way to avoid such a system was the simulated elopement, which was, of course, rare and socially despised. It is of little wonder that most of the Muong tragic stories in verse concentrate on the theme of lovers being torn apart by arbitrary acts of the patriarchal and feudal system. Today, although arranged marriages still predominate, the consent of the partners is obtained before finalizing the marriage. Marriage for love is increasing and so also is intermarriage with the Thai, Vietnamese, Tay, and Meo. Bride-price has been reduced considerably. Divorce, though rare, is increasing. Widow remarriage is encouraged. Marriage between cross cousins is allowed while that between parallel cousins is forbidden. The levirate and sororate have fallen into disuse.

Muong are monogamous by tradition. A second marriage is performed only if the first wife has proved sterile. Of course the nobility and the headmen had more wives, as well as concubines, than did commoners.

Domestic Unit. The domestic unit is comprised of one couple and their unmarried offspring. The patriarchal and patrilineal family offered a privileged position to males; the women had to live in absolute submission without any right to family property. It was the prerogative of the eldest son to inherit at least two-thirds of his parents' property. Even the seating arrangements within the Muong house reflect gender, age, and social ranking. Children, irrespective of sex, are always pampered. The status of women has increased both within and outside the family. They neither have to lacquer their teeth nor wear a chignon before reaching the age of puberty; they still wear a rectangular white kerchief on their heads as a cultural sign. The traditionally timid, shy, and reserved Muong woman is now hard to find. In fact during the Vietnam War women effectively handled all agricultural tasks that were once the preserve of males and also participated actively in the guerrilla units. The political transformation, educational expansion, occupational diversification, and changed cultural ethos raised their status, albeit in a relative sense.

Sociopolitical Organization

The basic sociopolitical unit of the Muong was the quel. The long-established hamlets had boundaries defined not on the principle of consanguinity but on neighborhood ties, largely for joint exploitation of an ecological niche. Containing about fifty households, the hamlet had its own communal rice fields, hunting reserves, and shifting lands. For all local matters, the hamlet operated autonomously. Each hamlet was placed under the jurisdiction of a headman (*tao*), who belonged to one of the four dominant clans. He held the hereditary right to redistribute communal rice fields and in turn received tributes and the unpaid labor of the commoners. With the help of the chosen nobility, he arbitrated quarrels that broke out between different family groups. A number of hamlets formed a village, whose headman was called *long cun*. A group of villages constituted a commune and was ruled by a subordinate chief, while a few communes together formed a canton under the control of a chief. Each of these political functionaries had several subordinate guards, servants, and notables. They were the administrators, tax collectors, judges, and military chiefs in their respective domains. A large number of myths indicate that the aristocracy originated from a different source than did the common man, and that every commoner should submit to his lord's authority and defend him in all circumstances in his own interest. This political system was maintained by the French colonial administration. It was only after the revolution of August 1945 that the system began to change. The authority of the headman was abolished and vestiges of the unpaid labor system liquidated.

In the past, greater age, superior clan, greater wealth, and male gender determined power and authority. Today the director of the cooperatives and the administrators of the communes are the key decision makers at the lower level. Muong peasants enjoy the same rights and responsibilities as do their former masters. Until 1975, they had their own administration in the autonomous regions. The administration of the communes is carried out by a committee elected by the people's council, which is elected once every two years, ensuring political equality.

Religion and Expressive Culture

Religious Beliefs. The Muong are mostly animists and believe in the existence of a multitude of spirits and in the transmigration of the soul. Spirits are thought to exert at will a be-nevolent or malevolent influence on human events. The religious universe is a vertical, three-tiered structure. The middle tier is the "flat land," which represents the terrestrial world. The upper tier is the "celestial land," the abode of the all-powerful ruler, the king of heaven. The spirits perform various functions under the king of heaven. The chief spirit maintains a register regarding that king's decisions on the fate of each soul leaving the earth. The influence of Taoism is obvious here. The lower tier is divided into two parts, one under the ground, which is in essence a miniature of the middle tier, and the other under water, the abode of snakes that can change their forms at will.

Ceremonies.   The Muong have several cults, but the cult of ancestors is common. Almost all have a permanent altar dedicated to the souls of the dead members of the family. Food is offered on the death-anniversary days. An Earth Genius, who is supposed to ensure good health for family members and domestic animals, is worshiped. The cults of king, guardian spirit of the hamlet, and the spirit of the ancestor of the hamlet head are also worshiped. The cult of Buddha, a very rudimentary Buddhism, is contradictorily grafted on the archaic linga cult.

Religious Practitioners.   The Muong also practice the occult through the shaman, who channels the reaction of the deceased soul. The sorcerer is still a healer and respected for his occult powers. Before treating the sick, he traces the malevolent spirit and performs a ceremony of exorcism. Muong also have a whole range of superstitions and taboos and a number of agrarian rites. Rice-planting season begins with the Khung Mua rites, entailing the sacrifice of a pig. The new-rice harvest celebration is pompous; offerings of steamed fish are mandatory. The lunar New Year (Tet) is a great occasion for annual celebration, and so on.

With the dissemination of free and compulsory education, the relative improvement of living conditions, and the introduction of modern medicine, many superstitions have declined. The traditional roles of *ong thuos* and *me thuoc* (medicine man and woman) and priest-sorcerer are now insignificant. Sorcery and witchcraft have become things of the past. Accusations of being possessed by the devil are unknown. Feasting and religious rites organized during marriages as well as funeral and housewarming parties have been reduced to the minimum. Nonetheless, invocations to the genie, charms for treating illness, taboos concerning travel, absolute respect for superiors, and expensive marriages still prevail and constitute a serious impediment to sociocultural development.

Arts.   The cultural policy of independent Vietnam has encouraged the aesthetic sense and manual dexterity. The unique house style, decoration and architecture, embroidery patterns, traditional costumes, delicious dishes, musical instruments, spicy popular songs, the famous *sap* dance, and the heritage of trust and cooperation are highly admired, renovated, and popularized across ethnic groups and in schools.

Death and Afterlife.   Death is considered a passage of the soul of the deceased from this body to another. Every living person has ninety souls. Good souls transmigrate into the bodies of happy men, whereas bad souls enter into the bodies of the poor subjects and even those of animals. The Muong soul travels to the celestial land to hear the verdict of the king

of heaven, and visits the ancestors with whom he or she will live and his or her hamlet to bid farewell. The notion of punishment is nowhere explicit, while affections for family and hamlet are reiterated.

In the past, the corpse was often left in the house for several days, up to twelve nights, until the near and distant relatives had arrived. The funeral required the sacrifice of an ox, buffalo, or pig, and feasting for several days by the relatives. The coffin carried the provisions for the dead man's journey into his new existence. The buffalo sacrifice was thought to send the draft animal to join the deceased and continue to plow for him. The funeral song, "The Creation of Earth and Water," recited by the shaman (*po mo*)—a priest specializing in funeral liturgy—refers to the origin and evolution of the universe, to mythical ancestors, and to civilizing heroes. The long series of funeral rites only concludes after a few years. At present the rites are restricted and expenses are greatly curtailed.

See also Kmhmu; Vietnamese

Bibliography

Chi, Nguyen Tu (1972). "A Muong Sketch." *Vietnamese Studies* 32:49–142.

Coedès, Georges (1950). *Ethnography of Indochina.* Washington, D.C.: Joint Publications Research Service.

Cuisinier, Jeanne (1948). *Les Muong: Géographie humaine et sociologie.* Paris: Plon.

LeBar, Frank M., Gerald C. Hickey, and John K. Musgrave, eds. (1964). "Muong." In *Ethnic Groups of Mainland Southeast Asia*, 171–175. New Haven: HRAF Press.

Pathy, Jaganath (1985). "The Muong: A North Vietnamese Tribe in Transmutation." *Eastern Anthropologist* 38: 279–294.

Schrock, J. E., et al. (1966). *Minority Groups in the Republic of Vietnam*, 527–572. Washington, D.C.: Department of Army Headquarters.

JAGANATH PATHY

Murut

ETHNONYMS: Sabah Murut: Idahan, Tagal, Taggal, Tagol, Tagul; Sarawak Murut: Kelabit, Kemaloh Kelabit, Lun Bawang, Lun Daya, Lun Daye, Southern Murut

Orientation

The term "Murut" translates as "hill people," and refers to two culturally distinct peoples living between 5°20′ and 3°20′ N, in central Borneo. Linguistically, there are two main groups. The Sabah (or Idahan) Muruts speak a language that belongs to the North Indonesian Branch of the Austronesian Family, and numbered approximately 35,000 in 1972; the Sarawak (or Kelabitic) Muruts speak a language that belongs to the West Indonesian Branch of the Austronesian Family, and numbered approximately 5,000 in 1987. Though culturally distinct, the two groups share practices pertaining to warfare, burial, and religion.

Settlements

The Idahan traditionally lived in longhouse villages at the confluence of a river and a tributary; they now live in smaller longhouses that are spread out along the tributary, and there are no longer village centers. Kelabits inhabit fairly large longhouses (as long as 75 meters, and housing an average of 100 people), which are built in clusters on alluvial plains.

Economy

Idahan practice swidden agriculture, the most important crop being rice; corn, bananas, sugarcane, tobacco, citrus fruits, etc., are also grown. Wet-rice agriculture is practiced only by three lowland groups. Fishing is important, much of it being done with poison and traps. Idahan raise pigs as a form of wealth; they are used for sacrifices and to pay bride-prices and fines; dogs are raised for hunting. Kelabits, on the other hand, raise rice, primarily through the use of irrigated fields, and also produce large numbers of cattle. The *baya* is their system of labor exchange, in which groups of workers farm each other's land in turn. Surplus rice and cattle, as well as salt, are important items of trade. Kelabit families own parcels of wet-rice land individually.

Kinship

For the Idahan, the nuclear family is of paramount importance; the extended family has an undefined role. The Kelabits reckon descent ambilineally.

Marriage and Family

The Idahan prohibit marriage and sex between members of the nuclear family, with uncles, and with first cousins and their descendants for five generations. Formerly, first cousins who had sexual relations were speared to death, but such relations are now allowed if a payment is made. Polygyny is allowed. A prospective groom's father arranges the details of the betrothal and marriage with the prospective bride's family. His family should pay a betrothal fee, a bride-price, and the expenses of the wedding feast; with the exception of the bride-price (which may be paid much later), these fees are not mandatory. A man without a son may allow a daughter to marry without a bride-price if she and her husband care for him in old age. Residence is patrilocal. Kelabit marriages place a great deal of emphasis on social class; a man need pay a bride-price only when he is of low class and wishes to marry an aristocrat's daughter. There is no firm rule regarding postmarital residence.

Sociopolitical Organization

The Murut have no political unity above the village level. The Idahan once had three classes of slaves. A prisoner of war (the lowest class of slave) could become a member of the tribe as an *ulipon*. Marriage to another ulipon meant that the children would remain ulipon as well, and would also have to live with their owner. A slave's marriage to a free woman meant status as a debt-slave to his father-in-law, with whom he would have to live. Another salient feature of Murut social organization is the class distinction practiced by the Kelabits. There is a large distinction between "good" (Paran or aristocrats) and "bad" (low-class) people; this distinction is based on the amount of inherited wealth (jars, beads, gongs, etc.) a family has. The major difference between the two classes is that until recently the leading aristocrat had legal authority; in still earlier times, headhunting was a pursuit of the aristocrats as well. Presently, the Kelabit longhouse legal authority (Penghulu) is elected by popular vote.

Religion and Expressive Culture

Among the Idahan, women who know how to perform the required rituals may become spirit mediums (*babalian*) and do such things as curing and performing exorcisms of people and houses. Spirit mediums among the Kelabits, however, are old men who contact guardian spirits for advice about things such as rice planting. The Kelabits practice secondary burials. The death feast that accompanies the secondary burial is extremely expensive and takes place only every few years, usually on the occasion of the death of an aristocrat whose family can bear the expense for themselves (and for the poor, who take advantage of the occasion simultaneously to bury their own dead ritually). Kelabits are also known for their megalithic culture.

Bibliography

LeBar, Frank M. (1972). "Kelabitic Murut." In *Ethnic Groups of Insular Southeast Asia*, edited by Frank M. LeBar. Vol. 1, *Indonesia, Andaman Islands, and Madagascar*, 158–163. New Haven: HRAF Press.

LeBar, Frank M. (1972). "Murut." In *Ethnic Groups of Insular Southeast Asia*, edited by Frank M. LeBar. Vol. 1, *Indonesia, Andaman Islands, and Madagascar*, 153–154. New Haven: HRAF Press.

Prentice, D. J. (1972). "Idahan Murut." In *Ethnic Groups of Insular Southeast Asia*, edited by Frank M. LeBar. Vol. 1, *Indonesia, Andaman Islands, and Madagascar*, 154–158. New Haven: HRAF Press.

Saging, Robert Lian R., and Lucy Bulan (1989). "Kelabit Ethnography: A Brief Report." *Sarawak Museum Journal* 40:89–118.

DANIEL STROUTHES

Ndaonese

The Ndaonese, who call themselves "Ndau Ndau" (meaning "men of Ndau") are the inhabitants of the islands of Ndao and Nuse off the west coast of Roti, Indonesia. In 1981, there were an estimated 3,500 Ndaonese living on Ndao, Sumba, Roti, and Nuse. Classified as a Savunese dialect, the language borrows heavily from Western Rotinese. Most Ndaonese men are multilingual. Because of the island's small size, there is limited agriculture and the only domesticated animals are chickens, dogs, and pigs. The men are gold- and silversmiths and trade their jewelry with the peoples of the Timor Archipelago.

See also Rotinese

Bibliography

Fox, James J. (1972). "Ndaonese." In *Ethnic Groups of Insular Southeast Asia*, edited by Frank M. LeBar. Vol. 1, *Indonesia, Andaman Islands, and Madagascar*, 109. New Haven: HRAF Press.

Jonker, J. C. G. (1903). "Iets over de Taal van Dao." In *Album-Kern (Opstellen geschreven ter eere van Dr. H. Kern)*, 85–89. Leiden: E. J. Brill.

Ormeling, F. J. (1956). *The Timor Problem: A Geographical Interpretation of an Underdeveloped Island*. Groningen and Bandung: J. B. Wolters.

Ngeh

The Ngeh (Nghe) are a group of about 4,000 (1981) in the Muong Phine-Bung Sai area of southern Laos. They speak a language of the Mon-Khmer Group. The traditional economy is based on the cultivation of wet rice. Houses are arranged in a circle, and the village is enclosed. Some longhouses are built on pilings.

Bibliography

Hoffet, J. (1933). "Les Moïs de la chaîne annamitique." *Terre, Air, Mer: La Géographie* 59:1–43.

Nias

ETHNONYMS: Niasan (English), Niasser (Dutch and German), Ono Niha, Orang Nias (Indonesian)

Orientation

Identification. Niasans inhabit the traditional homeland of the island of Nias, as well as the Batu Islands (which were settled from South Nias) and Hinako off the west coast of Nias. The name "Nias" is probably a foreign corruption of the indigenous name for the island, "Tanö Niha" (the land of men).

Location. Nias is located between 0°30′ and 1°30′ N and 97°00′ and 98°00′ E, about 120 kilometers west of Sumatra, in Indonesia. It has an area of 5,450 square kilometers. The Batu Islands are a cluster of small islets 80 kilometers southeast, between Nias and Mentawai. The interior of Nias consists of forested hills up to 866 meters high. With 200–250 rainy days annually there are no distinct wet or dry seasons, although rain is heaviest from October to December.

Demography. In 1985 the population was estimated to be over 531,000 (including 22,583 in the Batu Islands) with an average density of 94.5 persons per square kilometer and an annual population growth of 2.6 percent.

Linguistic Affiliation. Nias belongs to the Western Malayo-Polynesian Branch of the Austronesian Language Family. Further research is needed to establish a subgrouping of Nias with other related languages, but attempts have been made to link it with Mentawai and Toba Batak. The language (*li niha*: "the language of men") has five dialects, with a broad division between South Nias and the rest of the island. Batu Islanders speak the southern dialect. The Bible was translated into a northern dialect, and this has become the standard form. Bahasa Indonesia, the language of government bureaucracy and education, is not widely known among ordinary villagers.

History and Cultural Relations

The origin of the Nias people is unknown. There are striking cultural similarities with the Batak, Toraja, Ngaju Dayak, and peoples of eastern Indonesia, all of which belong to the same language family. But similar social systems can be found among peoples of highland Southeast Asia (Kachin, Chin, Naga). A diffusion of so-called megalithic cultures from Assam has been postulated, but more comparative research is needed to substantiate reconstructions. There is a myth of origin from the center of Nias, and clan pedigrees all connect ultimately to a few tribal progenitors. The great cultural variation in Nias cannot easily be explained therefore by a theory of separate waves of migration to the island. The only important external contact recorded before Dutch intervention is with Acehnese slave traders who brought gold, the supreme prestige object, needed for bride-wealth and feasts of merit. The slave trade led to the depopulation of large areas, and was only brought under control in this century. In 1857 the whole island came nominally under Dutch control, but Nias remained marginal to colonial interests until a change in policy toward the Outer Islands, which led to the complete conquest of the island in 1906. Traders from Sumatra, some of whom settled in the port of Gunung Sitoli, brought Islam to many coastal areas. Christianity was introduced by German Protestant missionaries in 1865, its geographical spread coinciding with colonial domination. It made little progress, however, until the traditional social structure and its ideological underpinnings were broken down by missionary and government interference, paving the way for a wholesale rejection of tradition. From around 1915 a series of apocalyptic conversion movements swept across the island. The character of Christianity in Nias today and its relation to traditional culture owe much to this period, which has come to be known as The Great Repentance. Postindependence Nias has seen some economic development and expansion of the administrative capital and an increasing centralization of power away from the villages.

Settlements

Traditional villages (_banua_) are of several types. In the south, which is a distinct region culturally, villages are very large and compact, with several hundred houses. These are ranged close together along the sides of a paved plaza, dominated by the house of the chief, which is built on a much larger scale than are other houses. In the area referred to in the literature as the center (around Gomo, which is actually southeast), many smaller villages of a similar type are found (with a maximum of fifty houses), usually strategically placed on hilltops, as well as small, amorphous clusters of dwellings and dispersed temporary homesteads. In the north, villages may be dispersed or compact but they do not usually have more than between twenty and thirty houses. The present system of administrative villages (Indonesian _desa_) is based on the existing pattern of settlements, sometimes amalgamating several traditional villages or hamlets under a single headman. Most villages were originally founded by a single descent group, later becoming transformed into multiclan settlements. Houses in the center and south are beautiful rectangular structures raised on high pillars, surmounted by roofs of sago thatch up to 20 meters high. In the northern half of the island, houses are oval. Because of dwindling forest reserves and the great expense of feasting that traditional building involves, simple houses of wooden planks or concrete with corrugated roofs are now the usual form of architecture. Stone monuments, which once adorned every village, are no longer erected.

Economy

Subsistence and Commercial Activities. The only major town in Nias is Gunung Sitoli, which has regular maritime commercial links with Sumatra, and is the principal market for cash crops and the source of imported goods. There is a small tourist industry in the south. Coastal dwellers (mainly Muslim) practice fishing from outrigger canoes. The vast majority of the population is engaged in agriculture and pig farming. Sweet potatoes, cassava, and rice are the staple crops, cultivated in swiddens and gardens mostly by traditional methods (no plows, draft animals, or fertilizer are used). Wet-rice farming is restricted by hilly terrain and low technology. Little primary forest remains, and short swidden cycles (owing to pressure on land) have led to lower yields. Cash crops include coffee, raw rubber, cloves, patchouli oil, and copra. While all commodities are integrated in the market, traditional rates of exchange between pigs, gold, and rice are adhered to in some areas for customary transactions. In the center, where feasts of merit are still held and bridewealth is extremely high, a traditional economy based on relations of prestige and reciprocity persists, despite modern influences. Hunting for wild pigs is practiced in many areas. Compared with Sumatra and most of Indonesia, Nias is very poor.

Industrial Arts. Niasans are highly skilled builders, producing some of the finest domestic architecture in Southeast Asia. Imported clothing long ago replaced locally produced bark cloth. Mats and baskets are still made in the villages.

Trade. Small weekly markets usually serving several villages are held all over Nias, providing an outlet for surplus crops and a living for small local traders, who obtain goods from town.

Division of Labor. Women perform domestic chores, tend gardens, weed fields, and prepare pig food. Men clear forest for swiddens, hunt, fish, and spend much time in customary transactions. Planting in many areas is done by teams, who receive payment in rice and pork.

Land Tenure. Great variation occurs, but there is usually a distinction between original tenants and recent settlers. The latter may not sell or transfer the land they work or plant coconut trees, which are signs of permanent ownership. In the south, communal village ownership of land with allocation of it by the chief has been reported. In the north and center, land belongs to the person who first cleared it, and to his descendants or lineage. Segments of the lineage or nuclear families work individual plots of lineage land. Forest land or land that has remained fallow for more than twenty years may be claimed by anyone.

Kinship

Kin Groups and Descent. Descent is patrilineal. Clans (_mado_) are dispersed. In the center, the local lineage is the largest corporate descent group. It has a depth of about six generations and its members, who call themselves _sambua motua_ (those of one ancestor), generally share land, cooperate in festive and economic ventures, venerate the same set of ancestor figures, and live in the same or adjoining houses. Variant marriage forms have no effect on patrilineal recruitment. Fostering of agnates or a sister's child is common but adoption of nonkin is rare and was formerly associated with servitude. In the south patrilineal descent groups of varying compass are called _mo'ama_. Precise details on descent organization in the north and south are lacking. There is great variation in adherence to the ideal of clan exogamy, both within a region and between regions.

Kinship Terminology. Great regional variety and a complexity of contextual options prevent a simple classification. In all areas matrilateral cross cousins are distinguished from other cousins and siblings. Distinctions of relative age in sibling sets are carried through all levels down to grandchild. There are separate terms for wife givers and wife takers but no prescriptive equations.

Marriage and Family

Marriage. Bride-wealth (*böli niha, bövö*) consists of up to thirty named prestations, mainly of gold and pigs, raised by loans from agnates and neighbors. Recipients include the members of the bride's lineage and the agnates of her mother, mother's mother, mother's mother's mother, etc. These groups of agnates form a series of affines who are collectively viewed as wife givers (direct or indirect) to the groom. As such they (and the man's own mother's agnates) are ritually superior and are owed lifelong allegiance and tribute on festive occasions. A prohibition on the reciprocal exchange of women gives an asymmetric slant to the pattern of affinal relations. In the south the ideal marriage is with a matrilateral cross cousin, but there is no terminological prescription. Postmarital residence is typically patrilocal. Variant forms of marriage include uxorilocality, polygyny, bride-service, and widow-inheritance. Divorce is rare.

Domestic Unit. There is a range of household types from nuclear family, which forms a unit of production and consumption, up to joint family of brothers with their sons and grandchildren and incoming wives. In central Nias a whole local lineage may reside in one large building with separate family quarters and a common social area.

Inheritance. Sons receive almost everything, with rules varying on how seniority and personal qualities affect entitlement. In some areas uxorilocal sons-in-law and sisters' sons can be endowed if they have been loyal and generous allies to the deceased.

Socialization. Infants are raised by all members of the household, including older siblings. Division of chores by gender begins in early childhood. Full moral responsibility and social adulthood are only attained on marriage and parenthood. The moral qualities valued in a man are filial piety, cleverness and skill in speech, firmness, and initiative; in women, chastity and diligence.

Sociopolitical Organization

Social Organization. In South Nias there are two hereditary classes: nobles (*si'ulu*) and commoners (*sato*). Slaves (*savuyu*) were bonded laborers, captives, or ransomed criminals. Children of a nobleman and a commoner woman (in a secondary marriage) are *ono ba zato* (child by a commoner), an intermediate rank that is not heritable. A council of elders (*si'ila*) is appointed from the commoner class. In the north and center there is an analogous hierarchy of ranks rather than classes, with greater social mobility and emphasis on achieved status. Hamlet or village chiefs are called *salawa; satua mbanua*, village elders, are men who have demonstrated superior qualities and mastery of custom by staging feasts of merit (*ovasa*). Ordinary villagers are called *ono mbanua*. There are further informal gradations of status subject to continual revision. Status is validated and raised in feasts of merit. Influence is won by gaining credit in the system of festive payments. This system is insulated from other forms of exchange (e.g., mutual aid, bride-wealth) by elaborate rules and different systems of measurement. In parts of North Nias, however, the size of bride-wealth was formerly integrated with social rank in a single scheme of "steps" (*bosi*).

Political Organization. Nias is a *kabupaten* (regency) of the North Sumatran province of Indonesia. Its thirteen subdistricts (*kecamatan*) contain an average of fifty villages each. Many areas had traditional federations of villages (*öri*), which legislated on rates of exchange and interest on loans, and within which headhunting and war were prohibited. The *öri* were renamed *negeri* after independence and dissolved in 1967. Prior to the Dutch "revival" of the öri system, there was no political unit above village-level in the center; nor was there a paramount chief until the Dutch imposed one. Leadership in the village was informal and unstable as the prominent men of each lineage vied for supremacy. In the south the traditional ruler is the senior nobleman, the *balö zi'ulu*, who rules in concert with his councillors or elders. The status and functions of traditional chief and government headman overlap to some extent.

Social Control. Serious crimes are now dealt with by government authorities. In disputes over matters of custom (e.g., bride-wealth, adultery, land borders), long debates, led by elders and chiefs, have the aim of restoring social harmony and reaching a settlement, rather than simply imposing a penalty. Fines, in pigs and gold, include a meal for participants. Offenses against church rules (e.g., polygyny, funeral feasts) are punished by expulsion from the church and denial of the sacraments.

Conflict. Prior to colonial government, warfare and headhunting between villages (or between öri) were endemic. Heads or human sacrifices were required for funerals and certain feasts of merit. The slave trade with Aceh led to increased insecurity.

Religion and Expressive Culture

Religious Beliefs. In 1985 80 percent of the population was Protestant, 15 percent was Catholic, and 5 percent was Muslim. Affiliation to an official religion is compulsory under national law.

Aspects of the traditional religion survive in the vernacular Christianity (e.g., in concepts of sin and misfortune). The ethos of social life derives from a non-Christian value system. Some spirit beliefs persist. Feasts of merit are intended partly as a means of winning the blessing and fertility dispensed by wife givers, who are thus in a position analogous to the gods (cf. "Batak"). In the old cosmology a creator god, Lowalangi, and his younger brother Lature Danö (center: Nazuva Danö) control the upper and lower world respectively. There was a priestly cult of the goddess Silewe. Man's daily welfare depended on the placation of patrilineal ancestral spirits and on the blessing of wife givers. His ultimate destiny lay with Lowalangi, who keeps men as his pigs. Sacrifices to forest spirits ensured success in the hunt. There were no clan totems.

Religious Practitioners. Traditional ritual experts (male or female) called *ere* performed life-cycle rituals, divination, and healing, interceding with ancestral spirits (represented in carved wooden figures), and with God in various manifestations. Some were experts in reciting oral traditions. The charismatic leaders of the conversion and revivalist movements have often been ere, and evangelists often claim the ere's oracular skills, albeit in Christian guise.

Ceremonies. Most stages of the life cycle are marked by ceremonies and, usually, by feasting. The complex systems of exchange and measurement were regulated by ritual. Epidemics, thought to be caused by profiteering, were remedied by expiatory sacrifices and a lowering of interest rates. In the center, annual clan ceremonies (_famongi_) involving abstention from work took place after the harvest. For any venture, the household ancestor figures were adorned and given offerings. Large-scale feasts of merit today retain an important place only in central Nias.

Arts. Fine wooden ancestor figures were once carved, as well as larger statues that were venerated before raids. Ornamented stone columns are found in South Nias; limestone seats with animal heads as well as a variety of columns are found in the center. Traditional arts are no longer practiced except in making souvenirs for tourists. Many fine statues and carvings are now in museums and collections abroad.

Medicine. The remedy for illness is indicated by the diagnosis of the cause by a diviner, healer, or Christian priest: counter-magic for sorcery, herbal palliatives for poisoning, placation of the ancestors by sacrifice to remove a curse, tribute to disgruntled wife givers, repentance to the Christian God (who, it is believed, punishes sin with disease and death).

Death and Afterlife. Only men who had performed feasts of merit, whose festive debts had been paid off, and who had been buried with full honors (including human sacrifice) could enter the Golden Paradise, _tete holi ana'a_, which seems to have been a replica of the earthly village. Ordinary men were left to rot and "became food for the worms."

See also Batak; Mentaweian

Bibliography

Beatty, Andrew (1992). _Society and Exchange in Nias_. Oxford: Clarendon Press.

Marschall, Wolfgang (1976). _Der Berg des Herrn der Erde: Alte Ordnung und Kulturkonflikt in einem indonesischen Dorf_. Munich: Deutscher Taschenbuch Verlag.

Schröder, Engelbertus Eliza Willem Gerards. (1917). _Nias: Ethnographische, geographische en historische aanteekeningen en studiën_. Leiden: N. V. Boekhandel en Drukkerij Voorheen E. J. Brill.

Suzuki, Peter (1959). _The Religious System and Culture of Nias, Indonesia_. The Hague: Excelsior.

ANDREW W. BEATTY

Ogan-Besemah

ETHNONYMS: Dempo, Pasemah

Orientation

Identification. The name "Ogan-Besemah" refers to an ethnolinguistic grouping of peoples living primarily in the province of South Sumatra, Indonesia. Members of the several peoples comprising this grouping consider themselves more akin to each other than to their neighbors—the Komering to the south, Malay speakers to the east, and Rejang to the north. Residents of the area sometimes refer to the entire grouping as "Ogan" or "Dempo" people, but more often distinguish between two subfamilies (hence the hyphenated name used here): the Besemah subgroup to the west (often written "Pasemah") and the Ogan subgroup to the east.

Location. The Ogan-Besemah area covers most of South Sumatra Province, from the outskirts of Palembang city on the east to the mountainous border with Bengkulu on the west. The area rises from the eastern peneplains to a high coffee-growing region in the west.

Demography. The province of South Sumatra (103,688 square kilometers) had about 6 million inhabitants in 1989; probably about half that number are of the Ogan-Besemah grouping (censuses do not ascertain language or ethnic affiliation). During the past quarter-century Besemah peoples have expanded southward into Lampung Province.

Linguistic Affiliation. The Ogan-Besemah dialects are in the Western Indonesian Branch of the Austronesian Family and are closely related to Malay. They form a continuum or chain of intelligibility across the area. Speakers distinguish among dialects on the basis of degree of difficulty. Within the Besemah category speakers group the Lematang, Kikim, Lintang, and Besemah dialects as highly mutually intelligible, and the Semende (or Semendo) dialect as somewhat more distant. Among Ogan dialects are Enim, Musi, Rawas, and Ogan proper, all highly mutually intelligible. These languages were once written in a local Sanskrit-derived script (generally called Ka-Ga-Nga), which is rarely used today; only Latin and Arabic scripts are taught in the schools. Nearly all Ogan-Besemah speakers are also fluent in the Palembang dialect of Malay, and many also command the national language, Bahasa Indonesia, which is derived from Malay.

History and Cultural Relations

The Ogan-Besemah region was relatively independent of coastal Malay rulers. Dutch rule began in 1816, but was largely limited to the area around Palembang city. Local rulers carried out active resistance to Dutch conquest, and only in 1866 was the entire area officially under colonial control. The dialectal differences within the area are not the basis for clear-cut contrastive social identities. Since independence in 1945, Ogan-Besemah people have occupied important posts in local and national government. Within the province they have alternated with Komering people for control of the governor's office and the patronage positions that follow, accentuating the local sense of a division between the two groups. Besemah people have played the most important political role within the Ogan-Besemah grouping.

Settlements

People in the area live largely in villages (*dusun*) ranging from several hundred to several thousand persons in size. In the western half of the area villagers may spend much of the year living in small dwellings (*talang*) near their garden sites a considerable distance from the village. In the 1980s, most houses were single-family wooden structures with iron roofs, divided into a front reception area, a back kitchen, and one or more sleeping rooms.

Economy

Subsistence and Commercial Activities. Agriculture is the principal economic activity for most people in the area and is based on the three crops of rice, rubber, and coffee. Rice is grown primarily for producer consumption and rarely yields over two tons per acre (low by current Indonesian standards). Much of the rice land is either in swampland or in highland areas, where it competes with coffee for farmers' time and capital, and can be marketed only with difficulty. Farmers work wet-rice (usually irrigated) plots by hoeing or plowing with oxen or water buffalo. Planting is done by small groups working for wages or by a rotating work group. Harvesting is done by work groups, the farming family, or, increasingly, by a small number of day-wage laborers. Rubber became an important cash crop early in this century, but poor quality and a declining international market led to price declines in the 1970s and 1980s. Rubber tapping in the late 1980s was a low-status and stopgap occupation. Coffee seedlings, long planted as part of a swidden-rice cycle, became the object of full-time activity by some farmers after price rises in the 1970s.

Industrial Arts. People construct fishnets, traps, and weirs, and women in the eastern part of the area may weave ceremonial cloths and embroider them with gold thread. Certain villages specialize in crafts such as woodworking and goldworking.

Trade. Farmers sell coffee and rubber in village markets to local agents. Trade flows through Palembang. Sundries are purchased in shops located in larger villages and towns, owned by local people or by Chinese.

Division of Labor. Most agricultural tasks are performed by people from within a village or, in the case of harvest groups, from a neighboring village. Work groups for planting or harvesting may be mixed-sex or all-male. Plowing and preparing fields for planting are done by men, as are the pruning and harvesting of coffee trees. Trade is a specialized occupation.

Land Tenure. Land is controlled by individuals but is considered to be within the territory of a particular village. It may be sold to other villagers; land sale outside the village is permitted but not frequent. Sharecropping, renting, and mortgaging land are common. Land that has not previously been cropped may be cleared and planted by a village member; he or she then assumes ownership.

Kinship

Kin Groups and Descent. There is considerable variation across the area in descent categories and groups. In much of the area a village may be divided into two or more descent-based categories (*jurai* or *rogok*) within which ties are reckoned through men or women. In the central Ogan area both kinds of tie are found in the jurai; in the west one finds systems strongly favoring patrifiliation (e.g., Besemah) and systems strongly favoring matrifiliation (e.g., Semende).

Kinship Terminology. In general one finds modified Iroquois-type terms, with variation a function of the local marriage options and rules; namely, where there is a differentiation among cousins with respect to marriageability, a cross/parallel distinction is found for that generation; otherwise not.

Marriage and Family

Marriage. Marriage rules are the main feature distinguishing among societies within the Ogan-Besemah area. Two types of marriage exist in all these societies. In the type generally called *belaki*, payment of bride-wealth before marriage establishes the couple's residence in the groom's household, and all children from that marriage remain affiliated with that household. In the type generally called *ambig anag*, the groom moves into the bride's household, making no major payments, and children are classified as part of the bride's descent line. These alternatives are weighted differently across the area. In Besemah society the norm is the virilocal marriage; in nearby Semende the norm is the uxorilocal variant. In these last two cases this rule applies most strongly to the eldest child, who then inherits the bulk of the property. Most societies in the area permit first-cousin marriage, and in some a preference for the matrilateral cross cousin is stated. Divorce is subject to permission of the office of religious affairs.

Domestic Unit. Households vary in composition from one person to three generations. A married son or daughter rarely resides with the parents for longer than one or two years after marriage.

Inheritance. Inheritance is largely a function of the marriage form found in the particular society. Inheritance is usually to one or two children who remained in the village. Common throughout the area is the institution of the *tunggu tubang*, in which one or sometimes two children, with their spouses, receive house space and land from the parents and continue the descent line. In most societies only these children inherit the family estate. Two consequences follow: land is relatively unfragmented, and noninheriting children seek their livelihood elsewhere. Devolution of property onto just one child is the most common pattern in Besemah and Semende societies, and these are the peoples who have been most active in clearing new agricultural land in the region and in migrating to Palembang and to other Sumatran provinces.

Socialization. Both parents are care givers. Children who remain in the household after marriage share in care giving and support of younger siblings. Circumcision is a major stage in the life cycle for boys, as is learning the Quran for boys and girls. Primary education, largely in state schools, is nearly universal. Physical punishment is rare; feelings of shame and embarrassment are major incentives for obedience.

Sociopolitical Organization

Social Organization.   From the precolonial and through the colonial periods, and until recently, the _marga,_ a supra-village territorial unit, was the primary sociopolitical unit in most of the Ogan-Besemah area. The marga had residual rights over land, and the marga head, the _pasirah,_ held high status. More recently the village has assumed many of these rights (including land rights), and the pasirah office has gradually faded away. Within each descent-based unit in a village (the jurai or rogok), men who can trace their descent from an apical ancestor through firstborns (in some villages, through firstborn males) have high status.

Political Organization.   In precolonial and early colonial times an independent ruler (_pangeran_) ruled in some parts of the area. Today the village head (_tuo dusun_) is the primary leader in the village, and often is of high status owing to his descent line. He has gradually assumed much of the former role of the pasirah, and by the 1980s reported directly to the government-appointed subdistrict head (_camat_) and not, as before, to the pasirah. In the Indonesia of the 1970s and 1980s the state party, Golkar, also had considerable local power.

Social Control and Conflict.   The village head calls meetings of male villagers to resolve most local conflicts, but the Indonesian representatives of the army and police may also intervene. Open physical confrontations are rare here, as elsewhere in Sumatra. Little conflict with other groups is apparent.

Religion and Expressive Culture

Religious Beliefs.   Virtually all Ogan-Besemah people are Muslims. Islam spread into the eastern part of the area in the sixteenth century, but the Besemah districts in the west were converted only in the latter part of the nineteenth century. Megalithic shrines on the Besemah plateau continue to be objects of vows and dedications. Much of the later work of conversion was carried out by the Nagshbandiyya Sufi order. In the 1950s leaders of this order formed a political party in the province; this party continues today as a nonpolitical religious association.

Religious Practitioners.   Although in theory any adult male may serve as worship leader (_imam_), in practice several men of learning or high status function as unofficial leaders of worship. They may also be the village-level heads of the Sufi order. These heads lead chanting sessions in which a chain of authority (_silsilah_) is recited that links the head to the founder of the order, and in turn to the archangel Gabriel. Participants recite names of God and other Arabic phrases as a means to gnosis and as a way of expiating sins. Several major religious schools (_pesantren_), located in the eastern part of the area, are centers of religious learning from which many villagers return to take up local positions of religious leadership.

Ceremonies.   Most men (not women) attend Friday congregational worship at least some of the time. The event also serves as the occasion for the village head to disseminate information. Ritual meals (_sedekah_) are held to celebrate a birth, ward off danger, give thanks for a crop, or bless the deceased. Chants generate merit that God then converts to blessings on villagers' activities or relatives. Muslim calendrical feast days are also celebrated.

Arts.   Art is largely verbal and ranges from the telling of myths, to the exchanging of short couplets, to the singing of songs with stringed accompaniment.

Medicine.   Older practices involving leaves and spells continue in use alongside the clinics, traveling doctors, and readily available powerful antibiotics and vitamins.

Death and Afterlife.   Funerals are followed by ritual meals, at which men chant Arabic phrases that generate blessings for the dead. Following general Muslim ideas, people believe in resurrection and a final day of judgement.

Bibliography

Bowen, John R. (1981). _The Ethnography of a South Sumatran Village._ Cambridge: Harvard Institute for International Development.

Collins, William (1979). "Besemah Concepts: A Study of the Culture of a People of South Sumatra." Ph.D. Dissertation, University of California, Berkeley.

Lekkerkerker, C. (1916). _Land en Volk van Sumatra._ Leiden: E. J. Brill.

Marsden, William (1783). _The History of Sumatra._ London: Privately printed. Reprint. 1986. Singapore and New York: Oxford University Press.

JOHN R. BOWEN

Okinawans

The Okinawans (Amamijin, Loochoo Islanders, Okinawajin, Ryuku Islanders, Ryūkyūjin, Sakishimajin) are Japanese people who inhabit the Ryukyu Islands, a group of small islands 640 kilometers south of Japan. Most Okinawans live on Okinawa, the largest of the Ryukyu Islands. Okinawans speak a dialect of Japanese, and in some ways they differ culturally from the Japanese. Okinawan people were independent for most of their history, until they were conquered by the Meiji regime in 1872. The Okinawan king was removed, and the Japanese have followed a forceful policy of assimilation since that period. The Okinawans lost 150,000 people in the Allied invasion of World War II, many killed by Japanese soldiers who doubted their allegiance.

Okinawa remained under the control of the United States until 1972, with the agreement of Japan but without consultation with the Okinawans themselves. During the late 1940s the United States built military bases, intended to be permanent, that take up 20 percent of the land on the island of Okinawa. During the 1950s and 1960s, the Okinawan economy grew quickly as it adapted to servicing the needs of the U.S. bases and military personnel.

The Okinawan people supported the return of Japanese control in 1972, but many now regret the transfer because they have less autonomy than they did under U.S. control. A special problem has been the opening of Okinawa to Japanese economic competition, which has resulted in high unemployment. There is now a movement toward independence, led by a number of groups including Shima-okoshi (Island Revival Society). Agriculture is now almost nonexistent and the new growth industry is tourism.

A small percentage of the people living in Okinawa face an unusual and distinctive problem. These are the children of American fathers and Okinawan mothers. They are frequently the object of abuse by Okinawans, and, owing to the vagaries of Japanese and U.S. laws, they have no legal citizenship whatsoever.

See also Japanese

Bibliography

De Vos, George A., William O. Wetherall, and Kaye Stearman (1983). *Japan's Minorities: Burakumin, Koreans, Ainu, and Okinawans*. London: Minority Rights Group.

Kanaseki, Takeo (1978). *Ryūkyū minzokushi* (Ryuku folklore). Tokyo: Hōsei Daigaku Shuppankyoku.

Oy

The Oy (also spelled Huei or Oi) are a group of about 10,000 (1981) located on the slopes of the Boloven plateau in Attopeu Province in southern Laos. A subgroup, the The, are considered by some to be a distinct group, although they may now be totally assimilated. The influence of both Buddhism and Roman Catholicism has altered their traditional way of life.

Bibliography

Hickey, Gerald C. (1964). "Oy." In *Ethnic Groups of Mainland Southeast Asia*, edited by Frank M. LeBar, Gerald C. Hickey, and John K. Musgrave, 145. New Haven: HRAF Press.

Pacoh

The Pacoh (Khas Pakho) are a group of about 15,000 (1973) located in the highlands of Thien province in Vietnam and bordering Laos.

Bibliography

Burr, Angel (1977). "Group Ideology, Consciousness, and Social Problems: A Study of Buddhist and Muslim Conception of Sin in Two Southern Coastal Villages." *Anthropos* 72:433–446.

Pak Thai

Also known as the "Pak Tai" and "Southern Thai," the approximately 4,500,000 (1981) speakers of Tai who reside in about fourteen different provinces in southern Thailand are called "Pak Thai" by the Thai. They are primarily wet-rice agriculturalists and cattle breeders. Although most Pak Thai are Buddhists, more than a million of them are Muslims. They speak a variety of dialects of Tai, often referred to as *dambrö*.

See also Central Thai

Palaung

ETHNONYMS: Dang, Humai, Kunloi, La-eng, Palong, Ra-ang, Rumai, Ta-ang

Orientation

Identification. While the name "Palaung" is Burmese in origin, the Palaungs call themselves "Ta-ang," along with several dialectal variants of that name. They are known as "Palong" as well as "Kunloi" (mountaineer) by the Shans. The name "Rumai" or "Humai" is occasionally applied to all Palaungs but actually refers specifically to one of their subgroups.

Location. The Palaungs are found in the Shan States of east central Myanmar (Burma) with the majority found in Taungpeng State (approximately 23° N and 97° E). They are also in the adjacent states of Hsipaw, North and South Hsenwi, Möngmit, and as far south as the Shan State of Kengtung. Palaungs are also reported in the southern part of Kachin State and in southwestern Yunnan, China. They occupy a region of ridges up to 2,000 meters, separated by narrow valleys. In addition to cultivated lands, there is some open grassland, but the upper elevations are mostly temperate forest. The climate is typical continental Southeast Asian monsoon, with rainy summers and dry winters.

Demography. While there is no available population estimate for Palaungs in Myanmar today, in 1931 the total Palaung population was estimated at 140,000.

Linguistic Affiliation. The precise linguistic classification of Palaung has not yet been determined; it is however agreed that the various dialects of the Palaung language belong to the Mon-Khmer Group in the Austroasiatic Family. In the literature the Palaung are often associated with the Wa, another northern upland Mon-Khmer group, and they may appear cited as a single group, the Palaung-Wa. There appears to be no close affiliation between them, however, and it is reported that the two groups do not recognize any affiliation.

History and Cultural Relations

The Palaungs probably preceded Shan and Kachin settlement of the east central and northeast region of Myanmar. During the nineteenth century Taungpeng, the political focus of the Palaungs, was marginal to the neighboring Shan principalities and its relationship to the Burmese state was even more marginal. Although there were tributary relations and trade with the Burmese, the greatest cultural influence on the Palaungs appears to have been that of the Shans. Although there are Burmese loanwords in Palaung, the Shan language is both the written language of the Palaung and the lingua franca not only between Palaungs and Shans, Kachins, and other neighbors, but also between Palaung dialect groups. The few existing legendary chronicles of the Palaung are written in Shan and most Palaung adult males speak some Shan. Because the most recent ethnographic descriptions based on field research among the Palaungs are now more than sixty years old, it is possible that there is currently an even greater degree of acculturation between the Palaungs and their more dominant neighbors. Given the lack of recent data, descriptions of their cultural patterns in this article should be regarded as referring to their traditional way of life; it would be conjecture to attempt to describe how their culture may have changed in the context of the modern Burmese state. However, since many small tribal groups in the world are conservative and make an overt effort to maintain their cultural distinctiveness, it may be that the Palaungs have changed relatively little in the past sixty years.

Settlements

The Palaungs live in compact villages located on hilltops or ridges between hills. The villages range in size from two to fifty houses, with an average of about ten. Houses cluster along both sides of a main road; in larger villages, there are additional houses flanking these down the slopes. The center of the village contains a market area, a rest house for visitors, a monastery, and a structure to house images of the Buddha. Additional structures include granaries and spirit shrines. Villages were formerly surrounded by protective stockades whose gates were closed at night, and some still have gates on which incantations or Buddhist scriptures are written for the purpose of warding off disease. There are also auxiliary houses in the tea gardens; they are used at plucking time, when most villagers work for extended periods picking and processing tea leaves. Houses are raised on wooden posts that vary from 3 to 12 feet in height, depending on the slope of the ground. The frames, floors, external walls, and internal partitions are usually of bamboo, although those who can afford it may have wooden-plank walls. The roofs, which extend to within a few feet of the ground, are of grass thatch. Beneath the house is a fenced area for keeping livestock and doing household tasks such as rice pounding. Houses vary in length from 9 to 24 meters, depending on the number of families in a dwelling. In Palaung villages just south of the Chinese border, as many as three to six families may occupy a single dwelling. In the central Palaung area in Taungpeng, one or at the most two families per house is normal. In single-family houses, verandas at each end are used for entrances and for kitchen tasks. In two-family houses in the central Palaung area, each veranda opens into a separate entrance room for each family. Additional smaller rooms are used for sleeping and storage. Entrance and sleeping rooms have fireplaces but are otherwise largely bare of furnishings.

Economy

Subsistence and Commercial Activities. The Palaungs are agriculturalists whose hunting and gathering activities are minimal or reported only for some northern groups. Since they are predominantly vegetarians, virtually no hunting activities have been reported, although some freshwater fish and eels are caught for food. Likewise, no livestock is kept for food. Agricultural activities center on garden produce for food and trade, tea production for cash, and livestock raising for trade. Most areas practice swidden agriculture with rice as the main crop, although wet rice is also grown in areas where suitable lowland is available. Swidden and kitchen gardens also produce tobacco, hemp, beans, peas, sesame, maize, chilies, tomatoes, eggplants, onions, mustard, and sugarcane. Many wild fruits are used, but domestication is limited to bananas, jackfruit, and mangoes. Whereas both opium and betel nut are grown in the Shan States, the Palaungs do not raise either, even though both men and women use betel extensively. Tea production, which appears to have begun around 1910, is the chief economic pursuit of the central Palaungs, particularly those in Taungpeng state. All aspects of growing, processing, and transportation of tea for export are handled directly by the Palaungs, who have some large-scale enterprises with paid labor. Tea is exported in two forms: fermented or pickled (the latter eaten in Myanmar) and as dried leaves.

Since the Palaungs are predominantly vegetarians, few animals are raised for food. Pig raising is reported for some marginal areas and only the Rumai subgroup, north of the central area, is reported to slaughter animals. Since women neither eat nor cook meat, men prepare it when it is used. This may include either beef or pork obtained from Chinese butchers or neighboring Lisu and Kachins, or animals killed by predators. Palaungs also obtain salted, smoked, and fermented fish from the Burmese. Cocks are raised for crowing and fighting, but poultry are not eaten and eggs are rarely consumed. Cattle and buffalo, along with horses, which are sold in lowland Myanmar, are raised as beasts of burden; though cattle are raised, milk is not used.

Industrial Arts. The production of material goods by the Palaungs is fairly limited. It can be assumed that tea production takes up much of their productive labor time, and they buy or trade extensively for material goods. They make baskets but also buy them. Cloth to make bags for plucking tea is acquired from the Shans, as well as the white homespun cotton upon which the Palaung women weave distinctive patterns, although some women were reported to be still weaving cloth. Men's clothing is also made from cloth imported into the area. While some villages have silversmiths, most jewelry is acquired from Shans. Likewise there are Palaung blacksmiths, but cast-metal tools such as plowshares are acquired from the Chinese. Much carpentry, masonry, and decorative work, such as in monastery and pagoda construction, is done by lowland Burmese. Virtually no Palaung crafts are produced for trade.

Trade. Palaung trade is based on tea, both dry and pickled, and livestock, especially horses. The Palaungs carry on trade directly or through intermediary itinerant Chinese, Burmese, Indians, or Shans. Trade is conducted in Palaung villages as well as in towns such as Möngmit, Hsenwi, Hsipaw, and Namkham, and even as far away as Yangon (Rangoon) and Mandalay. Import trade from outside the area is shared with other cultural groups, although there is some area specialization such as that among the Shans and Kachin, who supply the Palaungs with salt and preserved fish. At the time of the most detailed ethnographic accounts of the Palaungs, most of the tea trade was in the pickled form, which moved south to the Burmese and north and east to the Shans of Burma and China.

Division of Labor. Men plow, tend livestock, build and repair houses, transplant tea, pack and load tealeaf, cook meat dishes, and prepare the slash-and-burn garden plots. Women fetch water, clean the houses, cook, spin, weave, make clothing, prepare the nurseries for the tea plants, and plant the gardens. Both men and women cut and gather firewood, cut and carry timber for houses, and gather grass for horses.

Kinship

Kin Groups and Descent. Published accounts mention "clans" for the Palaung, but it is unclear exactly what this term means. They are apparently named groups comprised of most of the population of a contiguous area, although it is reported both that villages of different clans occur side by side and that members of clans may be widely distributed among villages. The clans are said to differ in respect to dialect and a variety of practices such as marriage rules, courtship, wedding procedures, naming, and women's clothing. Information on descent rules is not available.

Kinship Terminology. There is no complete description or analysis of Palaung kin terms; however, Milne provides some terminology in her 1931 dictionary.

Marriage and Family

Marriage. Villages are normally endogamous units in which polygyny is permitted, though rare. A man may not marry his father's sister's daughter nor the daughter of his own sister or brother. There is some indication that the preferred marriage is with a mother's brother's daughter. Courtship takes place at the woman's house, late at night, after her parents have gone to sleep. In the central Palaung area this takes place in the entrance room where one or more men may visit a woman to engage in conversation, which follows a stylized convention. In other areas the men must stand under the house and converse with the woman through cracks in the floor of her sleeping room. Sex relations are apparently uncommon. A man who fathers a child and refuses to marry the mother must pay a fine. If she refuses to reveal his identity, her father must pay a fine to the elders to appease the local tiger spirit. Parents usually learn the identity of a woman's suitors and may praise or criticize them, but more direct interference is not the norm. Engagements are entered into without explicitly informing parents or obtaining their permission. In the central Palaung area marriage is traditionally by elopement, whereas elsewhere elopement may occur only because of parental disapproval. The eloping couple may go to the house of an older male relative of the man's father while several days of marriage negotiations are carried out by two part-time specialists skilled in traditional rhetoric. The woman's family expects a sum of money from the man's family, but this is regarded as help toward the wedding meal provided by the bride's family rather than as bride-price. The wedding is formalized by a blessing of the elders, after which the woman is surrendered and her parents send with her a dowry of household goods. Residence is initially patrilocal and a widow may either remain in her husband's home or return to her father's.

Domestic Unit. Information is not precise, but the domestic unit is probably the nuclear family along with some semi-detached individuals such as an unmarried brother or widowed parent.

Socialization. Spirit worship and Buddhism are strong forces for socialization. Young children are cared for almost exclusively by their mothers. Older children enjoy considerable freedom while learning work tasks and are taught to regard work as a source of enjoyment. Specially chosen young adults teach children poetry and customs of courtship, and prepare them for the *prüh* ceremony, a preadult initiation occurring around 10 years of age. Childhood training emphasizes courteousness, Buddhist merit, knowledge of spirit forces, and the learning of a vast corpus of poetry, songs, and metaphorical phrases necessary for social interaction. Almost every Palaung village has a monastery compound that serves as the traditional school in which boys receive their few years of formal education.

Sociopolitical Organization

Social Organization. Little information is available on social organization among the Palaung. Status differentiation according to wealth is reported for the central tea-growing area. Those who are well off may have Palaung servants whose status is regarded as inferior. Witches are reported, whose power is believed to be hereditary and who live apart and marry among themselves.

Political Organization. The Palaungs of Taungpeng have a state system with a prince (*saohpa*) and a petty court patterned after that of the Shans. Most other Palaungs live in traditional Shan chieftaincy domains. In both cases, at least in the early part of this century, the village community appears to have been the primary unit of political organization. In Taungpeng local administration was carried out by village officials who functioned somewhat independently of the capital at Namhsan. In the state of Möngmit, the clans had chiefs who were chosen by the elders, but who were usually the oldest surviving male relatives. The choice had to be reported to the saohpa of Möngmit. Chiefs were in charge of heads of village groups, who were in turn responsible for the village headmen in their respective areas. Except where personal influence had made them hereditary, other positions were filled by men chosen by villagers and confirmed by the clan chief.

Social Control. In more recent times, judicial cases were tried by headmen of villages or, if serious, by the chief and the elders. Traditionally, however, the guilt or innocence of a person was determined by a variety of trials by ordeal. The strongest forces for social control are the requirements of proper behavior to gain Buddhist merit or to avoid reprisals by spirits.

Conflict. Nondivisiveness is taught as a moral precept. There are reports of in-fighting over succession to the office of clan chief. Otherwise, being under pressure from the more dominant Shans and Kachins, the Palaungs are described as a peaceful, timid people.

Religion and Expressive Culture

Religious Beliefs. The basis of Palaung religion is belief in spirits, and their aid is constantly invoked. Buddhism has been incorporated into spirit worship with the Buddha regarded as a beneficent spirit. Orthodox Buddhism, with the training and functioning of monks and nuns, parallels but seldom overlaps the functions of spirit worship. Two forms of Theravada Buddhism are followed: the Burmese school, practiced by the northern Palaungs, and the Yuan or Shan school, practiced by all others. The latter is differentiated from the Burmese school by the existence of a series of grades among monks, each marked by ceremonies of increasing cost, which are born by the monk's relatives and godparents. There are two classes of spirit: the *kar-bu*, in people and animals, which survive death for about a week; and *kar-nam*, in plants and inanimate objects. The kar-bu of persons who have suffered violent deaths or who do not proceed along the road of death become malevolent kar-nam spirits. Some kar-bu become the *pe-aet*, which are reminiscent of European ghosts. Other supernaturals include two guardian spirits for each human; guardian spirits of the house, village, roads, gardens, etc.; and numerous ogres and others of Burmese derivation.

Religious Practitioners. Although Buddhism guides Palaung religious belief, monks have no dealings with the host of supernaturals or supernatural practices that pervade Palaung belief. Offerings to supernaturals are usually made by ordinary people, even in cases of illness. Identification of the spirit causing an illness or misfortune is made by a specialist, the *hsa-ra*, a combination of diviner and medical practitioner. The diviner's advice is also sought in matters such as naming a child or choosing a house site, and for his knowledge of amulets and incantations, which he sells to those seeking success in love or against enemies. He is likely also to be the local tattooer. The *bre*, a witch or wizard, is said to be able to possess the body of another or to assume the shape of a tiger. Attached to the court of Taungpeng is also an older man, known as the *ta pleng* (old man of the sky) who acts as intermediary in dealing with spirits.

Ceremonies. Major ceremonies are calendrical ones associated with Buddhism. In the central area there is a state spirit festival conducted every September by the ta-pleng. The people assemble and, following a meal for the elders and monks and scripture reading by the monks, the ta-pleng and his assistants summon all spirits, great and small, to receive offerings.

Arts. Poetry, both recited and used as song texts, is the most important Palaung art. Nearly any context is suitable for the use of poetry or poetic phrases, but courting poetry, love songs, wedding songs, tea-picking songs, and dirges are especially important. All songs are sung, apparently unaccompanied, to a single tune. Ensembles of drums, gongs, and cymbals perform at all ceremonial occasions. Circle dancing is also prominent. Decorative art includes embroidery, tattooing of the entire body except the head, decorative roof gables, and carved and decorated entrance-door frames.

Medicine. While most people know and use many simple remedies, illness is believed to be caused by spirits whose influence, in Buddhist belief, cannot be warded off without the accumulation of merit. Some illnesses, such as insanity, are regarded as spirit possession by another person. The affected person makes offerings to the responsible spirit and, if necessary, seeks the help of a hsa-ra, who delivers incantations and remedies of plant and animal derivation. There are also women who employ massage and charms as cures. In childbirth, the woman is attended by one or more married friends who have had normal deliveries. For about thirty days after birth, the mother and child remain in the sleeping room by the fire, which is tended by her husband. She observes dietary rules and is periodically caused to sweat, after which she is massaged by her friends.

Death and Afterlife. The soul has two parts: the kar-bu, or general animal spirit, composed of parts, some of which may leave the body during sleep, and the *vin-yin*, the intellect, which is the immortal part of a person. At death the kar-bu is thought to wander for about seven days seeking a new mother through whom it may be reincarnated. The idea of the kar-bu's wandering causes Palaungs to fear death. In cases of abnormal death, such as by violence, by lightning-strike, or in childbirth, burial takes place as soon as possible, without a coffin, in an isolated place. Occasionally monks, nuns, clan chiefs, headmen and their wives, or other notables who died normal deaths are cremated. Ordinary people are washed, dressed, and buried in a coffin in an unmarked grave no later than a day after death. Buddhist scriptures are read in the entrance room of the house for a week, food offerings are made to the Buddhist images of the monastery, and monks are presented uncooked rice. On the seventh day, a larger than usual amount of food is taken to the images and the spirit of the dead person is called upon to depart for the road of the dead and the afterlife.

Bibliography

Cameron, A. A. (1912). "A Note on the Palaungs of the Kodaung Hill Tracts of Momeik State." *Appendix A* in *Census of India*, 1911, 9, Pt. 1: i–xiii. Rangoon: Superintendent of Government Printing and Stationery.

Maring, Joel M., and Ester G. Maring (1973). *Historical and Cultural Dictionary of Burma*. Metuchen, N.J.: Scarecrow Press.

Milne, Mary Lewis (Harper) (1924). *The Home of the Eastern Clan: A Study of the Palaungs of the Shan States*. Oxford: Clarendon Press.

Milne, Mary Lewis (Harper) (1931). *A Dictionary of English-Palaung and Palaung-English*. 1st and 2nd pagination. Rangoon: Superintendent of Government Printing.

Musgrave, John K. (1964). "Palaungs." In *Ethnic Groups of Mainland Southeast Asia*, edited by Frank M. LeBar, Gerald C. Hickey, and John K. Musgrave, 121–126. New Haven: HRAF Press.

JOEL M. MARING

Palawan

The Palawan (Ira-an, Palawano, Palawanon, Paluanes, Palawanin) are located mainly in the interior of the island of Palawan in the southern Philippines. Palawan is the fifth-largest Philippine island and also the least-heavily populated of the larger islands. It stretches from 8°20′ N to 11°30′ N, running northeastward, and is nowhere more than 40 kilometers wide. The number of Palawan people is estimated at about 70,000. About 10 percent are Muslims (mainly those living along the coast) and the rest of the people practice their traditional religion. The Palawan cultivate upland rice. They build their homes in the fields and make sure that they are out of sight of their neighbors.

Bibliography

Warren, Charles P. (1964). *The Batak of Palawan: A Culture in Transition*. Philippine Studies Program, Research Series, no. 3. Chicago: University of Chicago.

Palu'e

ETHNOMYMS: Ata Nuha, Ata Nusa, Ata Pulo, Hata Lu'a, Hata Rua, Orang Palu'e

Orientation

Identification.   Throughout the Lesser Sunda Islands the people of Palu'e (Palu) Island are usually referred to by the Indonesian term "Orang Palu'e." When referring to themselves as one people they call themselves "Hata Lu'a" (people of Lu'a). Various ethnic groups of the neighboring Flores Island employ the general vernacular term for "islander." Thus, in coastal Ngada they are called "Ata Nusa," in Sika, "Hata Pulo," and in Tana 'Ai, "Ata Nuha." The people of coastal Lio call them "Ata Rua." On sixteenth- and seventeenth-century Portuguese maps, the island is listed variously as Ilha de Nuca Raja, Lusa Raja, Rusa Raja, Lucaraje, and Illusartaia. Dutch designations include a number of variations of the name "Palu'e" (Paloeweh, Pulowe, Palu, Palue), a name possibly traceable to *palu-palu*, the Bugis term meaning "a conically shaped headdress." The official Indonesian designation is "Pulau Palue."

Location.   Palu'e is located some 15 kilometers off the north coast of Flores at 8°19′ S and 121°44′ E. The conically shaped and nearly circular island extends over 72 square kilometers. It rises gradually from the north shore and drops sharply to the sea in the south, forming the mountain Manu Nai (875 meters) and the adjoining volcano of Rokatenda. The people of Palu'e refer to the mountain as "Ili" and to the volcano as "Mutu." Periodic volcanic activity has marked mainly the southern part of the island. Throughout the island, along the lines of volcanic fissures, there are fumaroles and solfataras. Deep erosive ravines run down all sides of the mountain to the sea, creating steeply inclined ridges. Remains of primary forest are found at higher locations and in several isolated patches. Most of the secondary tree coverage has been removed for agricultural purposes. Apart from two minor springs on the western mountain slopes, there is no surface water on Palu'e. The island is part of the arid tropics. There are clearly demarcated dry and rainy seasons. The latter lasts from the month of December through March. There is an average annual rainfall of 180 centimeters.

Demography.   The total population is about 14,000, some 2,500 of whom have recently been transmigrated to coastal locations on central Flores. Small groups have also established coastal settlements on several of the Lesser Sunda Islands. The population density is approximately 180 persons per square kilometer. Because of volcanic activity, about one-third of the island's surface is not suitable for settlement or agriculture.

Linguistic Affiliation.   The people of Palu'e speak their own distinct language, called Sara Lu'a. It is classified as a member of the Bima-Sumba Group, which belongs to the Central Malayo-Polynesian Branch of the Austronesian Language Family. Its use is confined to the island. In every one of the twelve traditional domains of Palu'e a mutually intelligible but different dialectical variation of Sara Lu'a is spoken.

History and Cultural Relations

In 1511-1512, after the seizure of Malacca, Afonso de Albuquerque sent out a fleet to discover the Moluccas. On their way along the Flores north coast the Portuguese ships passed Palu'e. A panoramic drawing was made by the pilot Francisco Rodrigues, picturing the island against the background of Flores. In their mythology, all groups of the island ultimately trace their origins to a place located far away in the west. The final stages of these myths are concerned with the crossing from the Lio region on the Flores north coast. To this day, these groups honor long-standing alliances in warfare with a number of ethnic groups of central and east Flores. In some cases they retain rights to land use and ritual sites on Flores. In a document dated 1699, the raja of Gowa in South Sulawesi claimed supremacy over the island and stated his intention to reinforce this claim by means of warfare. It is doubtful whether this claim was ever upheld. The lack of drinking water on Palu'e was first noted by the Scotsman Cameron, who visited the island briefly in 1860. Cameron also mentioned the islanders' reputation among the neighboring islands as boatbuilders (Palu'e boats were commonly exchanged for guns and ivory tusks). Nineteenth-century sources mention the island in the context of piracy and slave trade. Palu'e boats were said to be raiding the Flores Sea and well-armed Bugis vessels. Ancestral treasures on Palu'e are often associated with these past activities and ties with Bugis groups of the kingdom of Bone on Sulawesi are still recognized. Toward the end of the century the Dutch military staged several unsuccessful punitive expeditions against coastal villages. In 1906 the island was pacified with the help of an indigenous coastal group and forced to accept the supremacy of the raja of Sika, the Dutch-appointed indigenous ruler of Maumere Regency on Flores. A succession of Sikanese relatives of the raja became his representatives on the island. They held the title of _kapitan_ and were charged with collecting a head tax and enforcing communal labor. Later holders of this office were recruited from the abovementioned coastal group and educated by the Catholic mission (Society of the Divine Word, or SVD) on Flores. Only in some cases were members of descent groups holding traditional political offices appointed as village headmen. In 1928 the volcano Rokatenda erupted, killing several hundred people and devastating large parts of the island. In the eyes of the people this eruption had been caused by Dutch attempts to dig for water on the island. Missionary activity by the Floresbased SVD mission began in the first quarter of the century and was mainly aimed at collectively baptizing the population and educating future native administrators and religious instructors. In 1938 the mission established a permanent presence on the island, which was only interrupted during the period of Japanese occupation (1942–1945). During nearly forty years, schooling and medical care were provided by the SVD. At present, approximately 90 percent of the population is nominally Catholic. Schooling and medical care are now provided by Indonesian government agencies, and the two Palu'e parishes are run by priests of the Indonesian Catholic church. In 1966 Palu'e adopted the _desa_ system, whereby groups of traditional villages were united into administrative units (desa). With few exceptions these followed the boundaries of traditional domains, but in some cases the traditional system of political alliance was crosscut by grouping together

long-standing enemies. Administratively, Palu'e is now classified as a subdistrict (_perwakilan_) and incorporated into the district (_kecamatan_) of Maumere on Flores. Its remoteness from the administrative center, periodic volcanic eruptions of various intensities, and the notorious lack of water have, for the last thirty years, made the people of Palu'e a target for transmigration to Flores. Since 1982 these efforts by the provincial government have been partially successful, and transmigration settlements have been established on the Flores north coast. To date only one desa has been moved to its new location.

Settlements

There are approximately 40 villages (_nata_) on Palu'e, varying in size from 30 to 500 people. Villages are connected to the administrative center by a network of footpaths. Because of interdomain warfare, slave raids, and piracy, villages were traditionally fortified and positioned on easily defensible ridges at higher locations. In successive stages of settlement, they have generally been moved from higher to lower locations. Coastal villages have been built only by more recently settled population groups. There are two types of village: main villages, where houses are typically oriented around a central ritual courtyard, and subsidiary villages, where mainly topographic and demographic factors dictate the settlement pattern. Traditional houses consist of rectangular wooden structures elevated on pillars. The interior sleeping and cooking chamber and the surrounding bamboo sitting platforms are covered by a high conical elephant-grass thatched roof reaching to the ground. The high roof also serves as storage space for harvest goods. Modern houses, termed _rumah sehat_ (healthy houses) are rectangular bamboo structures built on the bare ground and covered by a pitched coconut-palmfrond thatched roof. Increasingly, cemented stone and brick houses with corrugated iron roofs are being built.

Economy

Subsistence and Commercial Activities. The people of Palu'e are traditionally shifting horticulturalists growing various types of tuber, mung beans, and maize as well as a number of minor crops. Land shortages induced by population pressures have caused rotation cycles to be reduced from five years to one year. In many cases they have given way to permanent cultivation. An ancestral proscription against the growing of rice is strictly enforced throughout the island. The sale of surplus harvest goods—coconut, tamarind, candlenut, betel pepper, areca nut, fruits (mango, banana), bamboo, and palm-leaf products—in local markets and in markets on Flores is subject to ceremonial restrictions. Domestic animals include goats, sheep, dogs, and poultry. Pigs are kept for purposes of ceremonial exchange and sacrifice. Offshore fishing is conducted by means of traps, poison, lines, spears, and bows and arrows. Bomb fishing by coastal groups has in recent times greatly reduced the fish population. Because of the lack of surface water, banana trunks, bamboo, and a number of trees are tapped for water. In some locations volcanic steam is trapped in earth catchments and condensed in bamboo poles. Rainwater tanks are beginning to replace the traditional ways of water collection during the rainy season. Volcanic spots with high ground temperature are used as earth ovens for the preparation of various types of bean and tuber. Throughout the island the lontar palm (*Borassus flabellifer* or *B. sundaica*) is tapped twice daily and is the most important source of fluid. An islandwide ancestral prohibition on the distillation of palm juice is observed.

Most men on Palu'e are seasonal migrants. At the beginning of the dry season they take their boats to various locations along the Flores north coast and establish temporary settlements from which they return home periodically. The rainy season is spent back on Palu'e. Their occupations are occasional and include agricultural labor, construction of houses, logging, fishing, and trading.

Industrial Arts. The construction of boats used to be an important source of wealth. Boats are built on the mountain and ceremonially dragged down to the shore. The scarcity of trees now limits boat construction. Tie-dyed textiles and baskets woven from lontar-palm leaves are sold at markets on Flores.

Trade. Goods include livestock, fish, rice, textiles, and various commodities. Trade routes follow the major weekly markets on Flores.

Division of Labor. Major agricultural work, such as the initial clearing of fields and the threshing of mung beans, is shared by men and women. Planting, harvesting, and tending of the fields are done by women. Allocation of harvest goods is the domain of women. Livestock are raised and fed by women; the disposition of animals, however, is the domain of men. Traditionally women never left the island but increasing numbers of women now go to Flores to attend secondary schools. Construction of boats, dwellings, and fishtraps, palm-juice tapping, and harvesting of coconuts are exclusively male pursuits.

Land Tenure. Titles to arable land are patrilineally inherited and are held by the male members of a minimal descent group. Allocation of rights to land use by the father favors the firstborn male sibling. Female members are allocated land but relinquish their rights after marriage. Dowry can be converted into land and titles may be transferred to wife-taking groups. Land can be bought and sold as well as pawned in lieu of legal fines. Boundary disputes between domains are an important cause of warfare. Increasingly, titles are registered with the district administration. Titles to communal land and village grounds are nominally held by the priest-leader. As first-settling groups, descent groups of priest-leaders usually claim the largest number of titles to land within a given domain. Other descent groups were initially assigned land by them and hold roughly the same number of titles. Individual strategies of acquisition can alter this situation significantly. The size of holdings varies greatly according to domain affiliation.

Kinship

Kin Groups and Descent. Society on Palu'e is house-based in that individual houses, *nua*, constitute the localized minimal descent groups. A nua is mostly coincident with the physical structure of a house. Membership in a house is acquired by way of patrilineal descent or adoption. Members share a set of ancestral names, privileges and obligations, ritual offices, and access to land and resources, as well as ritual prohibitions. The core of larger groups, *kunu* (coconut husk), is constituted by houses tracing descent to common ancestors. The kunu can, however, also incorporate houses of different ancestral origin. Genealogical knowledge generally does not extend over more than two to three generations.

Kinship Terminology. The relationship terminology is neither clearly lineal nor cognatic, but shows mixed characteristics.

Marriage and Family

Marriage. Marriage is effected by the exchange of goods following extensive formal negotiations. The wife-taking group (*hata wedda*, "sister people") exchanges conceptually male goods (pigs, ivory tusks, golden ear pendants, money) with the wife-giving group (*hata naja*, "brother people") for conceptually female goods (harvest goods, household goods, textiles, ivory arm rings, ancestral beads, or land). Payments by wife takers are effected in three major stages. The schedule of payment varies according to domain. Obligations for support in everyday life and ceremonial exchange between wife-giving and wife-taking groups remain binding over a minimal period of two generations. The groups involved are primarily of the spouse's natal house and to the houses of its kunu. Additionally, there are throughout the island individual houses of quasi-consanguineal kin status (*huju-bako*, "bundle and heap") who traditionally assist in payment of goods. If a given house lacks marriageable women, the daughters of huju-bako houses can act as classificatory substitutes. For the purposes of a specific marriage, another kunu of the same domain may also contribute to the payments. This form of assistance is always reciprocated and can lead to lasting ties. Kunu fission can occur when individual houses repeatedly do not contribute to a given marriage. Such houses may fuse with a different kunu on the basis of repeated contributions to its marriages. Matrilateral cross-cousin marriage, termed "marriage of the afterbirth" (*wai kuni-laja*), is traditionally prescribed. Under Catholic and local government pressure the prescribed categories have become partially classified together with a proscribed category, which includes siblings and parallel cousins. Matrilateral cross-cousin marriage can now only be contracted after a lapse of a minimum of two generations. Marriage is kunu-exogamous and mostly domain-endogamous. A given kunu usually has a number of wife-giving kunu. Every three to four generations, the direction of alliance is reversed. Polygyny is permitted but infrequent. Divorce is mostly initiated by the husband and effected by returning the wife to her parents. In some cases part of the bride-price is then returned to the wife-taking group. The frequency of divorce is low. Postmarital residence is patrilocal. As long as no goods have been exchanged, the groom resides with the parents of the bride. In such cases children are affiliated with their mother's natal house.

Domestic Unit. A given house (nua) may shelter parents, several married male siblings and their spouses and children as well as any unmarried siblings. A nua averages five to six persons. A married male sibling, his spouse, and their unmarried children constitute a separate "hearth" (*labo*). Food and most resources are shared by the members of one labo. In cases where a labo has been established for several generations, ritual activities of the house may be carried out separately by each labo. Scarceness of living space can lead to the construction of a separate though ritually dependent dwelling.

Inheritance. Inheritance is predominantly patrilineal. In the transference of tangible and intangible property from father to sons, the firstborn son is generally favored. Objects associated with one gender can be passed on to others of the same gender. Objects related to agricultural magic are handed down matrilineally upon completion of bride-wealth payments.

Socialization. On the third day after childbirth the mother ceremonially presents the infant to the village community. The child is given an ancestral name and is ritually incorporated into the house by cutting the forelock and reciting prohibitions and qualities specific to the house and to the child's gender. During the ceremony a child of the opposite sex and, depending on its gender, a member of a traditional wife-giving or wife-taking group, is symbolically married to it. Subsequent stages of socialization are not ceremonially marked but occur gradually and informally. For young men an important threshold toward adulthood is crossed at the age of 12 to 15 years by participating for the first time in seasonal migration. A similar threshold for women is represented by the informal allocation of a garden at the age of 5 to 7 years. In the past these thresholds were crossed at a more advanced age and were marked by the wearing of a first loincloth.

Sociopolitical Organization

Social Organization. Society on Palu'e is stratified in that there exist three categories of houses (nua): houses from which priest-leaders are recruited, houses of commoners, and houses of slave descent. Members of the first category are referred to as "father-people," as opposed to members of the latter two categories, who are referred to as "child-people." "Father-people" claim to represent the first settlers who cleared the land. They hold most of the major ritual offices. Within the group (kunu) of houses of this category, one house assumes a traditional position of seniority (*hata ka'é*, elder sibling). It is from this house that the priest-leader, *lakimosa*, is recruited. Strictly speaking, all male members of the "father-people" can be called "lakimosa" (strong man); in practice only the most senior member is addressed by this title. The kunu referred to as "child-people" represent subsequently settled groups. Among these there is no clear-cut order based on precedence in settlement; rather, individual actions and events determine differences in their status. One house within each group assumes the senior position. It is this house that is prominent in ritual and is the guardian of kunu-specific ancestral treasures. Houses of slave descent have in recent times become absorbed into the category of commoners. Within each domain there are two separate kunu of the "father-people" category, one of which is of lesser status. In some domains this lesser kunu has regressed to a position of such inferiority that it no longer lays claim to "father-people" status. In most domains one commoner house has managed by way of marriage strategies to achieve an elevated position of influence. It is then referred to as "mother-people." In some cases this position is maintained by the normally prohibited practice of sister exchange with a house of "father-people" status.

Political Organization. The twelve traditional domains (*tana*) on Palu'e constitute ceremonial, political, and territorial entities. They can be divided into two categories according to the practice of different ceremonial systems. The seven tana practicing the offering of water-buffalo are referred to as *tana laja karapau*, "domains of water-buffalo blood." The five domains lacking the water-buffalo sacrifice are called *tana laja wawi*, "domains of pig blood," in reference to their main sacrificial animals. All domains on Palu'e are linked by a system of political cum ritual alliance and enmity that crosscuts the adherence to one or the other form of sacrifice. Alliances between domains are often reinforced by huju-bako relationships between the houses of the respective priest-leaders. Each domain classifies its traditional allies in warfare according to their size and strength as either conceptually male or female, thereby implying a position of relative superiority or inferiority. The population of a domain varies from 300 to 1,500 people; its size ranges from 2 square kilometers to 16 square kilometers. Only in recent times have efforts been made to stabilize boundaries by means of cement markers. Traditionally the territory of a domain is defined by a set of place-names, but boundaries are periodically renegotiated through warfare. The firstborn son of the senior house of the leading kunu of "father people" in a domain is usually appointed to the position of lakimosa. He is the traditional ritual, political, and juridical head of the domain. As such he receives, as a form of tax, part of the harvest of commoner houses as well as specific cuts of animals sacrificed in the domain. In most domains the former obligation no longer applies. The appointment to lakimosa status is made by the preceding lakimosa at the moment of his death and is subject to confirmation by the traditional allies of the domain. In those cases where a second kunu of "father-people" successfully upholds claims to full lakimosa status, separate spheres of influence and separate ritual centers are maintained. Ceremonial cycles are synchronized and in decisions affecting the whole of the domain the leading lakimosa takes precedence. In most cases traditional political authority is entirely delegated to him.

Social Control. At the most general level the concept of *hada* encompasses the totality of ancestral knowledge. It stands for the correct way of doing things. The content of hada is transmitted orally from parents to children and from grandparents to grandchildren. Much of hada is encoded in a poetic form of ritual speech. Knowledge of the parts of hada related to domain-specific ritual and to warfare is restricted to the lakimosa. He is the guardian of hada for all of the domain, as firstborn sons are the guardians of hada for their respective houses. Breaches of hada are considered offensive to the ancestors and to the Supreme Being and members of an offender's house will eventually incur misfortune or even death. In many cases fear of these supernatural sanctions will drive offenders to admit breaches to the lakimosa and plead for his mediation with the Supreme Being by way of ritual and sacrifice. In precolonial days all breaches of customary law were adjudicated by the lakimosa. Traditional sanctions are codified and range from fines in goods to corporal punishment, including the death penalty. Since the establishment of regency courts on Flores only minor offenses such as theft, extramarital affairs, land disputes, and slander of reputation are adjudicated by the lakimosa. Sentences are established in consultation with local government representatives and in accordance with the norms of customary law. Sentences can be appealed in government courts at district and regency level.

Conflict. Boundary disputes are the most important source of conflict in that they present a major potential for escalation. Within a domain disputes over boundaries between fields are ultimately dealt with by various forms of divine ordeal under the auspices of the lakimosa. Disputes over boundaries between domains generally lead to warfare. Leadership in warfare rests with the lakimosa but may be delegated to skilled warriors. In most domains it is a stipulation of hada to go to war with the traditional enemy at intervals of five years. An auspicious moment for warfare is after the completion of the ceremonial cycle, when offerings to the Supreme Being have been laid out along the domain's boundaries. War is fought by men who use flintlock guns, bows and arrows, spears, and bush knives. Women participate by throwing stones and insulting the enemy. A truce between the priest-leaders involved is usually arrived at after both sides have suffered some minor casualties. Recent battles have often been aborted prematurely by the arrival of military forces from Flores. Boundary disputes are then temporarily settled in district courts.

Religion and Expressive Culture

Religious Beliefs. The mythology of most water-buffalo-sacrificing groups contains an account of the voyage of an ancestral pair coming from the far west and arriving at the present location of the island. Their boat carried the "stone and earth," a metaphor for the island, which grew to become Palu'e. These first ancestors brought along all knowledge of hada. In another myth of origin, seven boats traveled together. During the voyage the boats containing rice and water went astray and this accounts for their lack on Palu'e. The universe is layered, with seven levels constituting the terrestrial realm and eight levels making up the firmament. One myth recounts how the ties between the skies and the island became severed. In ritual terms, Palu'e is imagined as a living body with streams of blood circulating beneath the surface, the seaboard representing its "feet" and the mountain its "head." One abode of the ancestors is inside the volcano, where the island, with all of its domains, is replicated. Earthquakes and volcanic eruptions are met with the exclamation "We are here!" in order to remind the mythical animals on whose back the island rests of the existence of human beings. Lunar eclipses are caused by the morning star spearing the moon. In analogy to the growing "stone-and-earth" motif, every domain has as its ritual centers two monolithic structures (*tupu*) that are increased in size with every ceremonial cycle. The tupu is the place where the priest-leader can, by way of ritual and offering, establish contact with the first ancestors and with the Supreme Being. The Supreme Being stands at the origin of everything and is referred to as "Sun-Moon/Stone-Earth" (*era-wula/watu-tana*). There are several categories of supernatural being: nonpersonified spirits associated with specific places such as trees or rocks (*nitu*), and named personified spirits associated with natural phenomena such as rain and drought. By far the widest range of spirits dwells outside the island and incorporates both indigenous concepts and those from outside groups. The human soul has essentially two aspects, one that remains with the body until death and another, referred to as the "shadow-soul," which can leave the body during its lifetime and take on a number of human and animal disguises. It is this soul that the witch employs for his flight. Dogs bark at disguised witches, thereby providing the means for differentiation between these and other types of supernatural beings. Ancestral spirits that have not been able to leave the island are of a similar type.

Religious Practitioners. The efficacy of a practitioner ultimately depends on his relationship with the Supreme Being. As priest-leader, the lakimosa can establish the closest relationship to era-wula/watu-tana within his domain. Because of his close affinity with the sun and the moon, the life of a lakimosa is endangered during a total eclipse. The ritual activities performed by him and, by way of delegation, by members of his descent group, ensure the well-being of all of the domain. He is the guardian of the entrance to the ritual center and, as such, he controls access to the Supreme Being. The healer-sorcerer (*hata pisa*) can act only with his consent. With the help of his ancestral auxiliary spirits, the hata pisa can contact the realm of spirits and ancestors and locate and manipulate the cause of illness and misfortune befalling individuals or houses. These faculties also allow the hata pisa to assist the lakimosa in domain-specific ceremonies. The acquisition of the powers of a healer-sorcerer involves a period of illness or mental disturbance in the hata pisa's youth. This is rarely followed by a formal apprenticeship. In most cases the healer-sorcerer is male. Payment of his fees (livestock, ivory, golden ear pendants, money, land) is ensured by his capacity to cause harm. Most hata pisa are also considered to be witches (*hata nutu*), male or female individuals whose "shadow-soul" has the capacity to fly by night and enter people's dreams in order to cause harm. Witches can be expelled from a domain or taken to court for such activities. Minor practitioners include members of houses who hold special skills ascribed to named ancestors (e.g., influencing rain and wind, healing specific afflictions, and finding lost or stolen objects) and those who possess magical qualities related to agriculture, fishing, boat building, dyeing, food preparation, warfare, and navigation.

Ceremonies. The theme of ritual heat and coolness pervades Palu'e ritual and ceremonial life. All new things are hot, breaches and mistakes of hada create heat, and the general accumulation of negative influences generates heat. Such heat is noxious to human beings and needs to be cooled down regularly by way of ritual. The cooling agent is mostly coconut milk. All ritual cooling is accompanied by an offering of food and/or blood. Blood offerings are ranked according to ritual potency in the following order: water buffalo, pig, chicken, dog. Most ceremonial events involve the exchange of goods. Not all domains practice the sacrifice of water buffalo. A domain can also lose its capacity to do so if attempts to raise sacrificial animals have repeatedly been unsuccessful. The ritual cycle extends over a period of five years, beginning with the ceremonial purchase of yearlings from allies on Flores and ending with the sacrifice at the ritual centers of the domain. Several years of prohibition on the construction of boats and houses and on the export of harvest goods follow the sacrifice. The number of animals sacrificed varies between domains. The water-buffalo sacrifice is essentially the prerogative of the kunu of priest-leaders. It ensures the welfare of the domain and establishes its prestige by acting as host to other domains of the island, and specifically to its allies. The water-buffalo sacrifice and the ceremonial inauguration of boats make up a category termed *kua ca*, "large ceremonial events."

Both employ similar texts recounting the myth of origin and involve the presence of other domains. All other ceremonies are termed *kua lo'o,* "small ceremonial events." This category includes the inauguration of houses, life-cycle rituals, healing rituals, rituals connected with fishing, and the rituals of the agricultural cycle. Every major stage of the agricultural cycle is initiated by the lakimosa on a ceremonial field and is followed by a ritually marked period of restriction on agricultural activities. In all domains the kua lo'o are essentially the same. In recent times the "domains of pig blood" have increased the scale of a ritual aimed at controlling the population of rats in an attempt to match the prestige of the "large ceremonial events" of the "domains of water-buffalo blood."

Arts. Graphic and plastic arts are restricted to tie-dyed textiles, decorated objects for everyday use, and carved and decorated implements for ceremonial use. The creation of chants during ceremonial dances is a major means of artistic expression. Chants are accompanied by three gongs and two drums. Musical instruments include the bamboo zither, Jew's harp, flute, tambourine, and ukulele.

Medicine. Relief from minor afflictions is sought by applying the common but limited knowledge of medicinal properties of herbs. Afflictions such as skin disease, intestinal worms, or toothache can be successfully dealt with by minor practitioners. Illness is generally caused by breaches of hada or witchcraft. In cases of severe illness the priest-leader mediates between the individual and his ancestors by way of ritual and the sacrifice of a pig. The sacrificial animal takes on the illness and is consumed by all members of the domain. In the last instance the help of the healer-sorcerer is enlisted. Knowledge of the ways of the healer-sorcerer is secret.

Death and Afterlife. Death occurs when the soul leaves the body through the fontanel. The body is wrapped in textiles provided by wife givers, and wife takers place golden ear pendants in its mouth. The deceased is buried in the vicinity of the house on the same day. The body is interred in a pit in reclining position with the feet pointing toward the rising sun. This orientation is reversed if death has been caused by an accident. A banana trunk can be substituted for a missing body. Personal belongings of the deceased are destroyed and disposed of in the direction of the setting sun. A general prohibition on agricultural labor is imposed throughout the domain for three days. A period of mourning of one year applies to members of the house of the deceased, entailing prohibitions pertaining to food, dress, agricultural labor, and general behavior. A widow of advanced age may be subject to prohibitions for the rest of her life. Prohibitions are announced on the third day after death, when the soul of the deceased has returned to the house. It is then sent off to commence its journey to the ancestral place of origin in the west. Elaborate secondary mortuary rituals entailing the setting of monoliths as points of communication with the deceased take place collectively for all of the deceased of a domain before the beginning of the final stages of the water-buffalo-sacrificing cycle. In some domains this is carried out separately by individual houses at any given time depending on the availability of harvest goods and livestock for ceremonial exchange. There are three conceptually interconnected abodes of the ancestors: the place of origin in the west; the inside of the volcano; and a banyan tree (*Ficus benjamina*) on the moon, from which the ancestors can observe the doings of their descendants.

Bibliography

Cameron, J. (1865). "On the Islands of Kalatoa and Puloweh." *Proceedings of the Royal Geographical Society,* 1st ser. 9:30–31.

Neumann van Padang, M. (1930). "Het vulkaaneiland Paloeweh en de uitbarsting van den Rokatinda in 1928." *Vulkanologische en Seismologische Mededeelingen,* no. 11. Bandung: Dienst van den Mijnbouw in Nederlandsch-Indië.

Wichmann, Arthur. (1891). "Bericht ueber eine im Jahre 1888–89 im Auftrage der Niederlaendischen Geographischen Gesellschaft ausgefuehrte Reise nach dem Indischen Archipel." *Tijdschrift Nederlandsch Aardrijkskundig Genootschap* 8:187–293.

MICHAEL P. VISCHER

Pear

Also known as the "Bahr" or "Pohr," the Pear number about 1,000 (1981) and live in southwest Cambodia. They are now largely assimilated into Khmer society. The Pear are closely related to the Chong and the Saoch.

See also Khmer

Bibliography

Hickey, Gerald C. (1964). "Pear." In *Ethnic Groups of Mainland Southeast Asia,* edited by Frank M. LeBar, Gerald C. Hickey, and John K. Musgrave, 159–160. New Haven: HRAF Press.

Penan

ETHNONYMS: Pennan, Poenan, Poonan, Pounan, Punan

Orientation

The Penan consist of one large ethnic group of nomadic forest people living in Borneo's interior; they may be distinguished from other "Punan" (a general term for Bornean forest dwellers) by language and other cultural features. Most live in Sarawak, though some live in Kalimantan and Brunei. Their range is approximately 2°45′ to 4°15′ N and 113°25′ to 115°50′ E. The Penan recognize two main groups among them, and these may be called the East Penan and the West Penan; the groups are culturally distinct and are geographically separated by the Baram River. The Penan hold no exclusive territory, but rather live alongside other groups. There are approximately seventy small Penan groups, and total population likely falls under 3,000 people. Overall migratory inclination has been in the direction of the China Sea. The Penan habitat consists of climax forest with streams and rivers. The Penan language belongs to the Kenyah Group, and includes two dialects (Eastern and Western, spoken by the two main groups respectively), dialects that are sometimes mutually intelligible. Much linguistic borrowing has taken place from settled populations nearby.

History and Cultural Relations

The Penan know little about their history, but probably they arrived in their present location by traveling through the Lio Matu area from Pejungan. The trend toward settlement and agriculture has a long history, and this trend has been encouraged by colonial governments. The Penan have occupied settlements on the Niah, Suai, and Buk rivers since the early nineteenth century. Western Penan can trace their genealogies that far back as well. Assimilation is occurring at an increasing rate. Both Eastern and Western Penan have borrowed cultural features from the settled longhouse dwellers. They secure their manufactured trade goods from settled patrons, who profit greatly from the Penan's gathered goods.

Settlements

Eastern Penan build a semipermanent base camp inside a new territory; from there they move around the forest using a series of temporary camps. The base camp serves also as a storage facility. Western Penan, in contrast, live in a settlement for as long as two years; groups of one or two families each spread out from the camp to gather forest products, leaving the sick and elderly behind. Penan houses are made of saplings, and roofed with palm leaves; Eastern Penan build their houses on pilings, and Western Penan on the ground.

Economy

The Penan staff of life is the wild sago, which grows in lower elevations and sporadically in the mountains. Animals are hunted as well, using spears and blowguns with poisoned darts, though firearms are becoming common. The game is primarily gibbons and macaques, though the wild pig is most desired. Fish are caught with hook and line, as well as poisoned with derris root. Food is shared. The Western Penan also make iron tools. The Penan trade with Kenyah people at the latter's longhouses three times annually, giving such things as hornbill feathers, wild latex, damar, and anteater scales. In return, they receive, at a disadvantageous rate, spearheads, knives, cookware, jewelry, matches, etc. Goods that they receive in trade are not shared. Land is not owned, but goods that the Penan trade with others are the property of the collectors. The Penan do not prevent other people from using the land that they themselves use.

Kinship

The Penan have no descent groups. Kinship is reckoned bilaterally, but patrilineal links are more important than matrilineal ones; offspring take their father's name.

Marriage and Family

The Penan allow marriage outside the nuclear family; also, Eastern Penan may marry their first cousins, but Western Penan may not. Polygyny is accepted, but rare. Marriage to another member of the same group is desirable. Marriage does not entail ceremony or official approval. Ideally, the groom should pay a bride-price of swords, blowguns, etc., but this is rarely done. Postmarital residence is with the wife's group for a year if different from the husband's group. The domestic unit is the nuclear family. Divorce takes place at the choice of either party. With little to inherit, there are no formal rules of inheritance; siblings and offspring decide among themselves who is to have what goods.

Sociopolitical Organization

The Penan group has an official headman, but he is without much power. His office is frequently passed from father to son. There is no political organization above the level of the group. The Penan have no formal means of ensuring social control.

Religion and Expressive Culture

The Penan creator divinity is Peselong. The Western Penan believe that their society originated in the upper Lua river region. The Penan cure illness through a shaman (*dayung*), who removes illness-producing spirits from the sick. Christianity has spread to some Penan groups since World War II.

See also Kenyah-Kayan-Kajang

Bibliography

Hoffman, Carl (1986). *The Punun: Hunters and Gatherers of Borneo.* Ann Arbor, Mich.: UMI Research Press.

Needham, Rodney (1972). "Penan." In *Ethnic Groups of Insular Southeast Asia,* edited by Frank M. LeBar. Vol. 1, *Indonesia, Andaman Islands and Madagascar,* 176–180. New Haven: HRAF Press.

DANIEL STROUTHES

Philippine Negritos

ETHNONYMS: Aeta, Atta, Baluga, Batak, Dumagat, Mamanwa, Pugut

The Negritos of the Philippines are comprised of approximately twenty-five widely scattered ethnolinguistic groups totaling an estimated 15,000 people. They are located on several major islands in the country: Luzon, Palawan, Panay, Negros, Cebu, and Mindanao. They are assumed to be the aboriginal inhabitants of the archipelago. The religion of most groups remains animistic, often with a thin overlay of Roman Catholic influence. All the Negrito languages are Austronesian, as are all the native languages of the Philippines. The Negrito languages do not form a subfamily among the Philippine Austronesian languages. Rather, they tend to be most closely related to, but usually mutually unintelligible with, the languages of the non-Negrito peoples in their particular geographical areas. All Negrito adults in every area are bilingual, able to converse in and understand the major languages of their non-Negrito neighbors with only minor difficulty. The population of the Negritos has declined greatly since the early Hispanic period (1600) and continues to decline today because of high death rates resulting from encroachment by outsiders, deforestation, depletion of their traditional game resources, and general poverty and disease. These Negroid peoples are phenotypically quite different in appearance from the Mongoloid peoples of the Philippines, who today outnumber the Negritos by 4,000 to 1. In spite of their Negroid appearance, all scholars reject the theory that their ancestors came from Africa. Rather, the accepted theory today is that Philippine Negritos are descendants of groups of *Homo sapiens* who migrated into the Philippines during the Upper Pleistocene from mainland Southeast Asia, and subsequently developed their phenotypic traits in situ, through processes of microevolution, some 25,000 years ago. All of the Negrito groups are or were hunter-gatherers. Today they are found in various stages of deculturation. Most practice some marginal cultivation themselves, and all groups carry on intense symbiotic relationships with neighboring non-Negrito peoples, trading forest products for cash or starch food (rice or corn), serving as forest guides, and especially working as casual laborers on nearby farms.

See also Agta; Tasaday

Bibliography

Eder, James F. (1987). *On the Road to Tribal Extinction: Depopulation, Deculturation, and Adaptive Well-Being among the Batak of the Philippines.* Berkeley and Los Angeles: University of California Press.

Fox, Robert B. (1953). *The Pinatubo Negritos: Their Useful Plants and Material Culture.* Manila: Bureau of Printing.

Garvan, John M. (1964). *The Negritos of the Philippines,* edited by Hermann Hochegger. Vienna: Verlag Ferdinand Berger Horn.

Omoto, Keiichi (1985). "The Negritos: Genetic Origins and Microevolution." In *Out of Asia: Peopling the Americas and the Pacific,* edited by Robert Kirk and Emoke Szathmary, 123–131. Canberra: Journal of Pacific History.

THOMAS N. HEADLAND

P'u Noi

The P'u Noi (Kha P'ai Pu Noi, Phunoi) are a group numbering about 32,000 (1981) who reside in the uplands of northern Laos. The linguistic affiliation of the P'u Noi language is unclear. They are primarily swidden rice horticulturalists; maize is an important secondary crop. Each village has a headman and several other important figures, with several villages under the control of a chief and five of these groupings forming a *tasseng.* The P'u Noi are Buddhists.

Bibliography

Hickey, Gerald C. (1964). "P'u Noi." In *Ethnic Groups of Mainland Southeast Asia,* edited by Frank M. LeBar, Gerald C. Hickey, and John K. Musgrave, 126–128. New Haven: HRAF Press.

Izikowitz, Karl Gustav (1951). *Lamet: Hill Peasants in French Indochina.* Ethnologiska Studier, no. 17. Göteborg: Etnografiska Museet.

Rengao

The Rengao (Reungao, Rongao, Ro-ngao) are a group of about 15,000 (1973) in the Gia Lai-Cong Tum province in the central Vietnam highlands. They are considered by some scholars to be a subgroup of the Bahnar or the Sedang.

Bibliography

Hickey, Gerald C. (1964). "Rengao." In *Ethnic Groups of Mainland Southeast Asia,* edited by Frank M. LeBar, Gerald C. Hickey, and John K. Musgrave, 145–146. New Haven: HRAF Press.

Rhadé

The Rhadé (E-De, E Dê, Raday) are a group in the southern highlands of Vietnam and neighboring Cambodia. The 1985 Vietnam census places the population at 194,710, an increase from the roughly 120,000 reported in the 1960s. In Vietnam, Rhadé is spelled "E Dê." Rhadé subgroups include the Rhadé Kpa, Rhadé M'dur, Rhadé A'dham, K'tul, Epan, Blo, K'ah, K'drao, and Hwing. Their language is Austronesian.

Rhadé villages consist primarily of longhouses arranged along paths, with kitchen gardens behind. Within the longhouses, each nuclear family has its own compartment with additional compartments for old people and for female members and their guests. Each village has a stand of bamboo that is considered sacred. Rice is the primary subsistence crop and is grown in upland swiddens, or, whenever possible, in paddy fields, with two annual harvests. Maize is the most important secondary crop grown along with vegetables in the longhouse gardens.

Prior to French rule, villages were autonomous and were the basic political units. They were generally self-governing until the French instituted a system based on districts and provinces. Villages were ruled by an alliance of families, formed in part through marriage. Descent is matrilineal, with matrisibs and two phratries. The head of each longhouse is a male, while women control the family property. Rhadé religion centers on a pantheon of deities and numerous rituals honoring the deities and spirits. The most important deities and rituals center on agriculture, especially the growing of rice.

Bibliography

Hickey, Gerald C. (1964). "Rhadé." In *Ethnic Groups of Mainland Southeast Asia,* edited by Frank M. LeBar, Gerald C. Hickey, and John K. Musgrave, 251–255. New Haven: HRAF Press.

Rotinese

ETHNONYMS: Atahori Rote, Hataholi Lote

Orientation

Identification.   The Rotinese have long taken their name from some version of their Indonesian island's name and combined this with a dialect word for "man" (Atahori Rote, Hataholi Lote). The principal name for Roti in ritual language is "Lote do Kale," and the expression for "man" is *Hataholi do Dae Hena.* The Rotinese insist that Rote or Roti is a Portuguese imposition. One seventeenth-century Dutch map shows the island as Nusa Da Hena, which would translate as the "Island of Man." By ancient tradition, the population is divided into two territorial divisions, Lamak-anan for the eastern half of the island, which is also known simply as "Sunrise," and Henak-anan for the western half, also known as "Sunset." Whether these names formerly had political or other significance is difficult to ascertain. This dual classification now serves to characterize differences in custom, dialect, and topography between the east and the west. Within these divisions, the island is subdivided into eighteen autonomous states, each ruled by its own "lord." These domains are the maximal native political units. Each domain cultivates its own distinctive variation of dress, speech, and customary law. The Rotinese tend to be of short stature, of light build, and of Malay appearance. They are characteristically identified by their broad, sombrerolike leaf hats.

Location.   Roti, off the southwestern tip of Timor, is the southernmost island of the Indonesian archipelago. The Rotinese have migrated in large numbers to the northeastern plains of Timor, to Kupang, and to the island of Semau. There they work as rice growers, lontar tappers, retailers, and, in Kupang, as civil servants. Rotinese also live on Sumba and Flores. Because of a long tradition of education, many educated Rotinese are to be found in the large cities of Indonesia. Roti consists of level areas of cultivation, bare rolling hills, palm or acacia savannas, and occasional patches of secondary forest. The east monsoon (April to October) brings a dry season of gusty, hot winds. The west monsoon, which brings a sporadic rain, is irregular; it begins sometime between November and January and continues until April.

Demography.   Census figures for 1980 record a population of just over 83,000. There are probably another 50,000 Rotinese on Timor and Semau. Chinese merchants and Indonesian government officials live in the town of Baä. Roti has traditionally assimilated the excess population from the tiny island of Ndao.

Linguistic Affiliation.   Rotinese, according to Jonker, shows closest affinities with the Belu (Tetum) languages, Timorese (Uab Meto), Galoli, and Kupangese, and more distant affinities with the languages of Kisar, Leti, Moa, and Roma. Each of Roti's eighteen domains cultivates its own manner of speech, and Jonker distinguishes nine mutually intelligible dialects. One dialect, that of the central domain of Termanu, has gained some prominence as a lingua franca. The Rotinese, in addition, possess a form of ritual, poetic, or high language that crosscuts dialect boundaries. Included within the political boundaries of Roti is the small island of Ndao, whose population of approximately 3,500 persons speaks a distinct language closely related to that of the island of Savu.

History and Cultural Relations

The Rotinese claim to have migrated from the north in separate groups by way of Timor. They also possess a tradition of accepting client-strangers from other islands. Each domain has its own traditional narratives associated with its ruling dynasty. Portuguese Dominicans established a mission on the island (then known as Savu Pequeño) in the late sixteenth century, but by 1662 the Dutch East India Company had signed treaties of contract with twelve of the domains of present-day Roti. The domains (*nusak*) were recognized as autonomous states until the twentieth century. Until 1969, the Republic of Indonesia recognized the eighteen domains plus Ndao within an administrative structure of four districts (*kecamatan*). This has since been altered to a system of six districts, each of which combines two or more former domains. The existence of an extensive school system in the nineteenth century gave the population an educational advantage in eastern Indonesia; it also stimulated emigration. Rotinese now participate at all levels of Indonesian national life.

Settlements

Traditions assert that before the formation of domains, each clan or origin group identified with a particular named ancestor held its own territory in the vicinity of some defensible walled redoubt. After the formation of the domains, these clans were assigned positions in the defense of the walled fortifications of their lords. With the establishment of peace under the Dutch, settlements became scattered. For administrative purposes, the Dutch attempted to recognize villages or village areas (now identified by a church or local school), but houses are still dispersed individually and in small clusters wherever there is sufficient fresh water for drinking and gardening. The traditional house, the center of Rotinese life, is a rectangular structure with gabled ends and a thatched roof that extends nearly to the ground. The house proper, divided into male and female halves, is raised on posts beneath the roof. The roof also envelops a ground-floor area with resting platforms where guests are received. Cooking is most often done in an adjacent thatched structure. Since 1970, traditional houses have been replaced by rectangular structures built on the ground. Because of a lack of wood, both cement and stone are now used in building houses.

Economy

Subsistence and Commercial Activities. A large proportion of Rotinese subsistence is derived from tapping and reducing to syrup the juice of the lontar palm (*Borassus flabellifer*). This syrup, mixed with water, provides the normal daily sustenance of most Rotinese. Solid foodstuffs, especially rice and millet, are eaten sparingly and usually saved for feasting, when they are consumed in great quantities with boiled meat. Some syrup is processed into thin square cakes of crystallized sugar. Syrup is also fermented to make a dark beer, which may be distilled to a fine sweet gin. Rice is the prestige food, but maize, millet, sorghum, a variety of tubers, various kinds of bean, green grams (or mung beans), peanuts, squash, sesame, onions, garlic, and several kinds of cucumber are grown in dry fields and also in household gardens fertilized with animal manure. The principal fruit trees are the banana, papaya, breadfruit, nangka, djeruk, mango, and coconut. The Rotinese also grow tobacco, cotton, betel (the nuts rather than the leaves of the plant are preferred for chewing), and areca. Located in a dry region with an irregular monsoon, the Rotinese are remarkably capable wet-rice cultivators who divert rivers and streams and use natural springs to water their fields. Although rice plots are individually owned, planted, and harvested, wet-rice fields are organized into corporate complexes whose members maintain a common fence and who appoint individuals to apportion water. Dry fields are usually cleared by burning in November. Over the past hundred years, wet rice and maize have predominated but have not entirely replaced dry rice, millet, and sorghum. Wet-rice fields are worked by driving herds of water buffalo through them after rain has softened the earth; other fields are worked with steel digging sticks and hoes.

Fishing is a common daily occupation in the dry season. Offshore stone weirs trap fish as the tide recedes, and rivers yield a variety of small shrimp and eel. Women fish with scoop nets; men use spears or cast nets. Basket traps, poison, and hook and line are used to a lesser extent. Hunting is confined to small birds, a few remaining deer, and an occasional domestic pig gone feral. Honey, mushrooms, seaweed, and agar-agar are gathered to supplement the diet. The Rotinese have herds of horses, water buffalo, sheep, and goats and most households have dogs, cats, pigs, and chickens.

Industrial Arts. Weaving of tie-and-dye cloths and basketry are the major domestic arts. Pottery, made in only a few areas with suitable clay, is traded throughout the island. Wandering Ndaonese goldsmiths attach themselves briefly to wealthy households, for whom they work gold and silver jewelry.

Trade. There is extensive trade between Roti and the town of Kupang on the island of Timor. On Roti, trade is mainly with Chinese and Muslim residents. Animals and foodstuffs are traded for broadcloth, cotton thread, kerosene, tobacco, and areca nuts. Apart from native pots, occasional flintlocks, and betel, the Rotinese trade little among themselves. The interisland trade with Kupang is becoming increasingly important. Clans possess rights to water and thus the right to appoint a ritual head over the corporation of individuals who hold plots of land irrigated by that water. Land, trees, and animals are the property of individual households. Native cloths, gold and silver jewelry, ancient *mutisalah* beads, and old weapons are the chief forms of movable wealth.

Kinship

Kin Groups and Descent. Each domain is comprised of a number of named origin groups or clans (*leo*), which constitute its political units. Clans are divided into named lineages (*teik*) and these, in turn, into smaller "birth groups" (*bobongik*), and finally individual households (*uma*). Neither clans nor lineages are localized, though "birth groups" tend to cluster in the same general village area. In conventional terms, "descent" may be described as ideally "patrilineal." In fact, the continuity of origin groups is based on genitor lines that trace relations through a system of inherited, altering names. Since these "hard names," no matter from whom they are inherited, are associated with the masculine aspect of the person, origin groups are conceived of as symbolically "male." If bride-wealth has been paid, the child of the marriage belongs to his father's group and takes a part of his "hard name" from that of his father. This is the statistically overwhelming form of lineage ascription and name inheritance on Roti. The child of a woman for whom no bride-wealth has been paid belongs necessarily to his or her mother's group and acquires a part of the mother's "hard name." Although not exclusively lineal, there is no personally "optative" element in Rotinese lineage ascription.

Kinship Terminology. The Rotinese kin terminology has several levels of articulation. Father and father's brother are distinguished from mother's brother; mother and mother's sister are distinguished from father's sister. Same-sex siblings and parallel cousins are classified according to relative age; opposite-sex cross cousins are distinguished from parallel cousins. There is a special progenitor relationship, marked in the terminology, between mother's brother and sister's child.

Marriage and Family

Marriage. The Rotinese recognize three levels of marriage, depending on (1) the amount of bride-wealth given for the woman, (2) the reciprocal prestations on the part of the woman's family, (3) the amount of ceremony and feasting accompanying the marriage, and formerly (4) the length of bride-service performed by the groom. Bride-wealth may be paid in gold, in old silver rupiah, in water buffalo, or in sheep and goats; there exists a fixed conversion rate among these different forms of wealth. Polygyny is permitted and is the ideal of the rich and the noble. Rotinese clans are not exogamous, although lineages are. Marriage is prohibited between siblings and close parallel cousins; more distant parallel cousins are, however, potential marriage partners. Marriage is preferred but in no way prescribed between cross cousins, the stated preference being for marriage with the mother's brother's daughter. In Thie and Loleh, there exists a moiety system that partially regulates marriage. Divorce is relatively easy, but permission must be obtained from the lord's court. Levirate, sororate, and adoption are extremely rare.

Domestic Unit.   Elder sons and all daughters leave at marriage, but the youngest son resides with his parents after marriage. The youngest son inherits the paternal house and brings his wife to live there. All elder sons must establish a new residence before or shortly after marriage, usually in the same village area but never too close to the paternal house. The domestic unit is based on the nuclear family and generally consists of husband, wife, and unmarried children, except for the youngest son and his wife. Widows can maintain their own households and raise their children on their own.

Inheritance.   The eldest son inherits the right to represent his father in affinal ceremonies and inherits all affinal prestations; the youngest son inherits the house. Other wealth is divided equally among all sons. A daughter (or daughters) may inherit only when the household lacks a male heir.

Sociopolitical Organization

Political Organization.   Traditionally each domain was ruled by a "male" lord (*manek*), a complementary and executant "female" lord (*fettor*), and a number of court lords chosen, ideally, from each of the clans of the domain. In every domain, one court lord was Head of the Earth (*dae langak*). He was the acknowledged upholder of customary law and had the right, in certain instances, to abrogate the lord's decision. His clan claims settlement priority and ritual rights over the land. Nobility is associated with the clans of the "male" and "female" lords; all others in a domain are commoners. The wealthy are frequently described as forming a separate class, but it is theoretically and, in fact, practically impossible for a wealthy commoner to become a noble. A former slave class has been absorbed within the other social categories. When the domain system was abolished in the 1970s, many of the functions of the domain, particularly rights to settle local disputes, devolved on the village headman. Much of Roti's traditional clan structure has been preserved under modern guises.

Social Control and Conflict.   Means of settling disputes existed within the lineage and the clan and at the lord's court. There existed no traditional means of settling disputes between domains, and in the past such disputes led to warfare. Since approximately 1850, domain warfare has given way to a pattern of lesser feuding and some raiding across borders that persists to this day. Headhunting may have been ritually associated with agricultural fertility but, as an institution, it appears to have been eliminated or transformed, perhaps as early as the eighteenth century.

Religion and Expressive Culture

Religious Beliefs.   Christianity has been preached on Roti since 1600 and has long been associated with some knowledge of Malay. Early in the twentieth century less than one-fifth of the population were baptized Christians, but wholesale conversion followed a national literacy campaign and government certification of its success. Traditional religious practice centers on ancestral spirits and their opposites, malevolent spirits associated with the bush. Lontar-leaf representations of the ancestors were hung within the house, which itself can be regarded as a shrine to the ancestors.

Religious Practitioners.   There was no class of priests, although there exist men who are regarded as chanters and who recite long ritual poems at major feasts. Any man may make offerings to the spirits. A mother's brother must perform all life-cycle rituals for his sister's children.

Ceremonies.   Major ceremonies are concerned with marriage, house building, and death. Minor ceremonies occur in the seventh month of the first pregnancy, at hair-cutting, baptism, naming, whenever human blood has been shed, at specific times during the agricultural and palm-tapping year, and at times of illness and upon recovery from illness. An annual clan-focused "feast of origin," *hus*, marking the transition from one year to another, has been abandoned in all domains except Dengka. In the hus cycle each clan that possessed ceremonial rights performed its own rituals according to a prescribed sequence of celebration. The cycle ran for several weeks in August, September, or October, depending on the domain and the number of its participating clans. Each hus involved ancestral invocations and requests for animal and plant fertility. Rituals also included horse racing, dancing, mock battles, and animal sacrifices. In the cycle there was usually one clan that performed rain rituals on a hilltop.

Arts.   The Rotinese have maintained a vast oral literature and weave magnificent tie-and-dye textiles. This literature and textile tradition were once an integral part of Rotinese ritual life.

Medicine.   Native curers, who use a variety of (secret) native medicines, have diminished in number. Formerly, for serious illness, a small feast was held to make offerings to the spirits. Now Christians gather at these feasts to pray for the sick.

Death and Afterlife.   The souls of those who have died a violent death are separated from other ancestral souls and become malevolent spirits who wander the earth. Funeral practices are the most elaborate of the Rotinese rituals. The deceased's mother's brother and mother's mother's brother, or their direct descendants, prepare the coffin and dig the grave. Dog sacrifice may accompany the making of the coffin, called the ship of the dead. There exist numerous formal ritual chants in praise of the dead. Burial is usually on the third day after death; feasts are given on this day and on the seventh, ninth, and fortieth day, and further commemorative feasts may be given a year or even three years later. There are no secondary burial rites involving the exhumation of the corpse. The mother's brother "cools" or purifies the close mourners on the day following burial and releases them from their expected fast.

See also Ndaonese

Bibliography

Fox, James J. (1971). "A Rotinese Dynastic Genealogy: Structure and Event." In *The Translation of Culture*, edited by T. O. Beidelman, 37-77. London: Tavistock.

Fox, James J. (1971) "Semantic Parallelism in Rotinese Ritual Language." *Bijdragen tot de Taal-, Land- en Volkenkunde* 127:215-255.

Fox, James J. (1971). "Sister's Child as Plant: Metaphors in an Idiom of Consanguinity." In *Rethinking Kinship and Marriage*, edited by Rodney Needham, 219-252. London: Tavistock.

Fox, James J. (1974). "'Our Ancestors Spoke in Pairs': Rotinese Views of Language, Dialect, and Code." In *Explorations in the Ethnography of Speaking*, edited by R. Bauman and J. Sherzer, 65-85. Cambridge: Cambridge University Press.

Fox, James J. (1975). "On Binary Categories and Primary Symbols: Some Rotinese Perspectives." In *The Interpretation of Symbolism*, edited by Roy Willis, 99-132. London: Malaby Press.

Fox, James J. (1977). *Harvest of the Palm: Ecological Change in Eastern Indonesia*. Cambridge: Harvard University Press.

Fox, James J. (1980). "Obligation and Alliance: State Structure and Moiety Organization in Thie, Roti." In *The Flow of Life: Essays on Eastern Indonesia*, edited by James J. Fox, 98-133. Cambridge: Harvard University Press.

Fox, James J. (1988). "'Chicken Bones and Buffalo Sinews': Verbal Frames and the Organization of Rotinese Mortuary Performances." In *Time Past, Time Present, Time Future: Essays in Honour of P. E. de Josselin de Jong*, edited by D. S. Moyer and H. J. M. Claessen, 178-194. Verhandelingen van het Koninklijk Instituut voor Taal-, Land- en Volkenkunde, 131. Dordrecht: Foris Publications.

Jonker, J. C. G. (1905). "Rottineesche verhalen." *Bijdragen tot de Taal-, Land- en Volkenkunde* 58:369-464.

Jonker, J. C. G. (1908). *Rottineesch-Hollandsch woordenboek*. Leiden: E. J. Brill.

Jonker, J. C. G. (1913). "Bijdrage tot de kennis der Rottineesche tongvallen." *Bijdragen tot de Taal-, Land- en Volkenkunde* 68:521-622.

Jonker, J. C. G. (1915). *Rottineesche spraakkunst*. Leiden: E. J. Brill.

Ormeling, F. J. (1956). *The Timor Problem: A Geographical Interpretation of an Underdeveloped Island*. Groningen and Bandung: J. B. Wolters.

JAMES J. FOX

Sagada Igorot

ETHNONYMS: Igorot, Kankanay, Katangnang, Lepanto Igorot, Northern Kankanai, Western Bontok

Orientation

Identification and Location. The Sagada people are the northernmost extension of the Northern Kankanai Igorots, who occupied the former province of Lepanto to the west and south of Bontok. An individual's ethnic identification is most commonly associated with his or her village or local settlement area. Sagada is centrally located in Mountain Province on the eastern shoulder of the Cordillera Central in western Bontok Province, the Philippines, at about 1,500 meters above sea level. This area is formed from partly eroded limestone basins drained by tributaries of the upper Abra and Chico river systems. Largely deforested, this region has a nine-month rainy season and temperatures ranging from 40° to 90° F (4° to 32° C).

Demography. In 1981 the Lepanto Igorot numbered approximately 60,000, of whom some 20,000 resided in Sagada municipality.

Linguistic Affiliation. Lepanto is classified in the Hesperonesian Group of the Austronesian Language Family. There is a shared basic language as between Northern Kankanay and Bontok.

History and Cultural Relations

The Sagadans probably established their culture about two centuries ago in the process of interaction with the Bontok villages to the north and east; they borrowed and adapted much of the central Bontok culture. Sagada then came under the control of the Spanish military government, which resulted in the long history of acculturation through churches and mission schools established since the Spanish-American War. Sagadans have been able to maintain much of their indigenous culture, including most of their ceremonial activity.

Settlements

Sagada proper is composed of two named territorial divisions, which are subdivided into a series of wards (*dapay*) and correspond to the Bontok *ato* (compact villages divided into wards). Houses are two or three stories high, constructed of wood, each with a high thatched roof and an enclosed area underneath. The low boxlike room at ground level is used for sleeping, cooking, and eating, whereas the upper level or "granary" is used primarily for the storage of food, wood, jars of rice wine, and other possessions. Surrounding each building is a rectangular field where sweet potatoes are grown, and also nearby are pens in which villagers keep pigs. The compact villages of from 300 to 2,000 persons are located near streams and are surrounded by terraced rice fields.

Economy

Subsistence and Commercial Activities. The Sagada people subsist on irrigated rice grown in stone-walled terraces, in addition to sweet potatoes and other root crops that are grown in village gardens and on hillside farms. They raise livestock such as pigs, chickens, dogs, and *carabao* (buffalo), some of which they sacrifice on ceremonial occasions.

Division of Labor. Among the Sagada, the men do the heavy work such as breaking the soil and preparing the rice terraces, dams, and ditches. In addition, they secure pine timber for houses and coffins; they do metalwork, weave baskets, and hunt and fish for sport. The men stand guard as the women go to the spring or river for water or to the clay pits for potters' materials. Men assist with the children and even with the cooking without encountering ridicule. The women tend the crops in the fields and are responsible for keeping the terraces in repair. They take care of the children and all aspects of household work.

Kinship

Kin Groups and Descent. In Sagada, there are six major bilateral descent groups or "families," which are composed of all the descendants of certain prominent ancestors, founding fathers, and important living individuals, regardless of the line of descent. These groups are further subdivided into lesser groups that trace their ancestry back eight or ten generations to a male founding ancestor. These groups do not regulate marriage directly, but they do conduct certain ceremonial activities and hold corporate rights over various hillsides and trees, exercised through appointed "wardens." Corporate ownership does not extend to rights in rice land, possibly because the groups stem from an earlier period of shifting agriculture. The personal kindred is formally recognized; it includes the descendants of the eight pairs of great-grandparents and thus extends laterally to include all third cousins. These are the relatives responsible for revenge and wergild, and they also constitute the proper exogamous range.

Kinship Terminology. The Sagada terminological system is bilateral, is organized on the basis of generation, and has a wide but indefinite range.

Marriage and Family

Marriage. Marriage is the most important social event in Sagada and is the focus of a variety of ceremonies designed to unite individuals and invite prosperity. Most marriages are contracted through the *olag* (girls' dormitory), generally after a period of experimental mating; wealthy families, however, may betroth their children at birth to ensure the continuance of their wealth. Unions such as these are often within the family, although not with first cousins. These marriages link the two kindreds through a series of reciprocal associations, privileges, and responsibilities. Families of the newlyweds give land and other wealth; however, if they separate or divorce

without having children, the gifts revert to their former owners. Children are essential to making the union of marriage permanent. If no children are born, a series of rituals is performed, and if these fail the marriage usually breaks up. If there are children, however, divorce or separation is difficult and rare. For Sagadans monogamy is the rule and adultery is a crime with serious repercussions involving the possible death of children, community and kin ostracism, and rituals of repentance.

Domestic Unit. The Sagada household is the smallest social unit that has a territorial base. Each residence is occupied by both parents and their offspring, together with perhaps a widowed parent or other relatives. The latter and the children over 6 years of age take meals with the family but normally spend their evenings in the dapay or *ebgan*. The average size of the household group in Sagada in 1952 was 4.4 persons.

Inheritance. Children usually receive their portions of inherited property when they marry. The parents then retain only a small amount of land to provide for themselves. Children have an obligation to care for their parents and to provide animals for sacrifice if they fall ill, and they have other obligations to fulfill when the parents die.

Socialization. Parents are primarily responsible for training their children in economic tasks. Girls receive much of their training from their mothers and other female relatives in the home and fields, as well as through participation in the ebgan activities. Young boys help their fathers in gathering wood, preparing fields, and caring for the carabao. Children are also usually responsible for gathering food for the pigs and chickens, which are kept in pens or cages near the house. A boy receives much of his education from the old men in the dapay. There he learns the traditional history of the village and the ward, the ceremonies and the prayers, and the songs and legends that are part of the annual round of work and ceremony. Moreover, boys are disciplined by their peers under the watchful eyes of the old men and develop patterns of loyalty to the village and ward, as well as to their kin. Parents seldom punish their children by whipping, and after the age of 6 they usually discipline them only by scolding.

Sociopolitical Organization

Sagada is divided into two geographical divisions, Dagdag and Demang, which are separated by irrigation systems. These territorial groups are rivals in ceremonies and in games, alternating in the performance of certain rituals for village welfare. They are opponents in the annual "rock fight" of the village boys. Moreover, evidence suggests that they may have formerly buried each other's dead. In addition, each group has its own sacred grove, guardian spirits, and sacred springs. These two divisions are divided further into a series of wards (dapay): Sagada has twelve wards, five in Dagdag and seven in Demang. Each ward has a ceremonial platform that is attached to both the men's and girls' sleeping houses.

Houses within a ward form a social unit (*obon*) that is not kinship-based. There are no fixed rules for residence in Sagada. Following marriage, parents usually give their house to the new couple and move to a vacant one. There is no evidence to suggest ward patrilocality. The ward is governed by a council of elders who make up an informal council (*amam-a*). These elders settle disputes within their jurisdiction and organize and carry out rituals and ceremonies essential for ward and village welfare.

The range of differences in wealth in the Sagada region is not great. There are basically two categories, the "rich" (*kadangyan*) and the "poor" (*kodo*). The kadangyan are expected to validate their position by elaborate and expensive marriage celebrations. Also of significance is the fact that some kadangyan customs, particular burial practices, and special ceremonial obligations are associated with membership in certain descent groups, regardless of whether the individual is rich or poor. Those with fewer assets often impoverish themselves, going into debt to the wealthy to obtain the necessary animals for sacrifice and feast giving.

Religion and Expressive Culture

For Sagadans, the spirits of their deceased ancestors (*anitos*) make up the most important category of supernatural. Great emphasis is put on death ceremonies to ensure the future welfare of the soul in the "house of anitos." Full ceremonial rites, which include the initial placement of a corpse in a death chair and coffin burial in ancestral caves or stone-lined mausoleums underground, are performed for deceased married persons only. There is a lengthy mourning period, which is slowly terminated by a series of animal sacrifices. Sagadans bury infants and young children in clay jars beside the house, without prayer or special ceremony.

People consider the old to be the keepers of customs and performers of rituals essential to the continuance of Sagadan society. Consequently elders assume a greater status when they die, that of anito ancestors, in which they continue to look after the welfare of their descendants and to protest against neglect by sending illness and other disasters.

See also Bontok

Bibliography

Cooper-Cole, Fay (1909). "Distribution of the Non-Christian Tribes of Northwestern Luzon." *American Anthropologist* 11:329–347.

Cooper-Cole, Fay (1945). *The Peoples of Malaysia.* New York: D. Van Nostrand.

Eggan, Fred (1960). "The Sagada Igorots of Northern Luzon." In *Social Structure in Southeast Asia,* edited by George P. Murdock, 24–50. Viking Fund Publications in Anthropology, no. 29. Chicago: Quadrangle Books; London: Tavistock Publications.

Keesing, Felix M., and Marie Keesing (1934). *Taming Philippine Headhunters: A Study of Government and of Cultural Change in Northern Luzon.* New York: AMS Press; London: George Allen & Unwin.

LeBar, Frank M. (1975). "Lepanto (Sagada)." In *Ethnic Groups of Insular Southeast Asia,* edited by Frank M. LeBar. Vol. 2, *Philippines and Formosa,* 86–87. New Haven: HRAF Press.

MAYRA DIAZ

Saluan

The Saluan (Loinan, Loinanezen, Loindang, Madi, To Loinang), who numbered about 74,000 in 1979, inhabit east-central Sulawesi Island, Indonesia. Saluan is classified in the Hesperonesian Group of the Austronesian Language Family. Villages range in size up to no more than about 700 inhabitants. Individual nuclear or extended families live in rectangular, raised houses made of wood and bamboo. Subsistence is based on rice, maize, sago, and millet, supplemented by chickens, dogs, and goats. Descent is bilateral. The aboriginal religion of the Saluan is based on ancestor worship, though both Islam and Christianity have gained a hold since the early 1900s.

Bibliography

LeBar, Frank M. (1972). "Loinang." In *Ethnic Groups of Insular Southeast Asia,* edited by Frank M. LeBar. Vol. 1, *Indonesia, Andaman Islands, and Madagascar,* 136–138. New Haven: HRAF Press.

Samal

ETHNONYMS: Badjaw, Bajao, Bajau, Sama, Samah, Sinama

Orientation

Identification. The term "Samal," or more generally "Sama," covers a diverse congeries of Sama-Bajau–speaking peoples whose scattered settlements are found throughout a vast maritime zone stretching from the central Philippines to the eastern coast of Borneo and from Sulawesi to Roti in eastern Indonesia. In the Philippines most Sama speakers, with the exception of Yakan, Abak, and Jama Mapun, are referred to as "Samal," a Tausug term used also by Christian Filipinos. Elsewhere, in Indonesia and Malaysia, related Sama-speaking groups are known as "Bajau" (variously spelled Bajao, Badjaw, etc.), a term of apparent Malay origin, while in the Philippines the term "Bajau" is reserved more narrowly for boat-nomadic or formerly nomadic groups referred to elsewhere as "Bajau Laut" or "Orang Laut." The most common term of self-designation is "Sama," or "a'a Sama" (*a'a,* people). In addition, most groups identify themselves by toponymic modifiers (referring typically to a particular island or island cluster) to indicate their geographical and/or dialect affiliation. As a whole, the Sama are a highly fragmented people, without overall political integration. In the past, these smaller populations were divided between the principal trading states of the region, in each polity occupying a subordinate status relative to the dominant ethnic groups, notably the Tausug and Maguindanao in the southern Philippines, the Brunei in western Sabah, and the Ternatans, Bugis, and Makassarese in eastern Indonesia. Among the principal subgroups of Sama, the most divergent, culturally and linguistically, are the Abak of Capul Island, northwest of Samar in the central Philippines. The Abak are believed to derive from an early northward migration of Sama speakers and are today the only Christianized Sama subgroup. The Yakan of Basilan Island and coastal Zamboanga are thought to be descendants of another early offshoot community. While acknowledging the symbolic suzerainty of the Tausug and Maguindanao sultanates, the Yakan-speaking groups, unlike the majority groups, are today an inland agricultural people with no close ties to the sea.

Location.   Sama-Bajau speakers are probably the most widely dispersed ethnolinguistic group indigenous to Southeast Asia. Their widely scattered settlements are found from the central Philippines, with small enclaves in Zambales and northern Mindanao, through the Sulu Archipelago of the Philippines to the eastern coast of Borneo and from Palawan and western Sabah (Malaysia) to coastal Sulawesi, southward through the Moluccas to Aru, Roti, and western Timor.

Demography.   In all of Southeast Asia Sama-Bajau speakers number some 650,000 to 730,000. Those in the Philippines referred to as "Samal" form the largest single group, estimated at 243,000 in 1975. The Yakan numbered over 115,000 and the Jama Mapun about 25,000, including an estimated 5,000 in Sabah. The total Bajau population of Sabah was nearly 73,000 in 1970, exclusive of recent Philippine immigrants. The latter comprise a further 30,000 to 40,000 (a conservative estimate). No reliable population figures exist for eastern Indonesia, but recent estimates place their numbers there at between 150,000 and 200,000.

Linguistic Affiliation.   Until recently the Sama Language Family was thought to be affiliated with the Central Philippine Language Group; today, however, it is generally assigned a separate status within the Hesperonesian Branch of Austronesian, probably coordinate with that of the Philippine languages as a whole. Sama-Bajau has been proposed as a general name to cover all of its various dialects and languages. Included are an estimated ten languages, most of them strongly dialectalized. The most divergent are Abaknon (spoken by the Abak), Yakan, and Sibuguey. The Sibuguey are comprised of a number of small, relatively isolated Sama groups living mainly around Sibuguey Bay in western Mindanao. Another relatively divergent language, Western Sama, is spoken in North Ubian and the Pangutaran island group west of the main Sulu chain. Small numbers of Ubian speakers are also found in northern and western Sabah. More closely related are Northern Sama, spoken chiefly in the islands of Basilan Strait, including Balanguingui in the Samales island group, and central and southern Sama, spoken in the Tapul, Tawitawi, and Sibutu island groups and throughout the adjacent eastern coastal districts of Sabah, from Kudat to Tawau. In Sabah, these latter varieties of the Sama subgroup live mainly on Cagayan Sulu and neighboring islands (Balabac, Bakungan, etc.) near the eastern coast of Sabah, with additional small enclaves in southern Palawan. In Sabah, dialects of a separate Sama language, West Coast Bajau, are spoken in the western and northern coastal districts of the state, from Kuala Penyu to Terusan. Another distinct group of dialects, known generally as Indonesian Bajau,

is spoken by a variety of closely related peoples from Sulawesi and eastern Kalimantan to Timor.

History and Cultural Relations

Linguistic evidence suggests that Sama speakers began to disperse, sometime in the first millennium A.D., from an original homeland located in the islands and coastal littoral separating southwestern Mindanao from the northeastern islands of Sulu. While some groups moved northward, settling on Sibuguey Bay and along the Zamboanga coast of Mindanao, most moved south and westward, establishing themselves along the main Sulu Archipelago, southward to Cagayan Sulu and the eastern Borneo coast. A major impetus behind this movement appears to have been a rapid growth of Chinese trade, beginning in early Sung times, and the attraction of the area's rich marine resources. When these migrations began, the Sama appear to have incorporated a wide range of ecological variation, from land-based to strongly sea-oriented groups. However, with the rise of Tausug hegemony in Sulu, beginning in the thirteenth century, ecological specialization seems to have intensified, with the dominant Tausug assimilating the more land-based groups, particularly in Siasi and eastern Jolo, leaving the Sama numerically dominant only in the smaller, mainly coralline islands near the northern and southern ends of the archipelago. The subsequent founding of the Sulu sultanate in the fifteenth century, and the related expansion of maritime trade, appear to have accelerated this southward spread of Sama speakers. While some groups settled the western coast of Sabah, where they came under the loose jurisdiction of the Brunei sultanate, others moved eastward through the Straits of Makassar to southern Sulawesi. From here, their subsequent scattering over much of eastern Indonesia appears to have occurred within the last 300 years and was closely bound up with the development of a trepang (bêche-de-mer) trade and the expanding economic and political influence of Bugis and Makassarese traders. Later, with the rise of the Tausug port of Jolo as a major entrepôt for slaves, Samal living in the islands of the Balanguingui group and along the southern shores of Mindanao emerged as a major piratical force. From bases, particularly on Balanguingui Island, Samal slavers carried out annual raids on coastal settlements from Luzon to the central Moluccas. In 1848 Spanish forces destroyed the main Samal bases on Balanguingui Island, and, by the end of the century, European intervention broke the power of the Sulu sultanate, ending its role as an independent polity. Following the imposition of American colonial rule in 1899, the sultanates of Sulu and Mindanao were shorn of secular power and their domains were brought under the direct administrative control of Manila. However, resistance to central rule has continued. Since the early 1970s the Sulu Archipelago has become the site of intense secessionist conflict. The ensuing civil war, which reached its peak in the mid-1970s, has resulted in a massive dislocation of peoples. Tens of thousands of Sama have migrated or fled to Zamboanga, Tawitawi, and the Sibutu island group or crossed the Malaysian border into eastern Sabah. At the same time, large numbers of Tausug have moved from Jolo and Siasi, centers of Islamic-secessionist fighting, into the formerly Sama islands of Tawitawi and Sibutu, forcing large numbers of Sama further westward into Sabah. Here their presence, as refugees, threatens an already precarious balance of ethnically defined political alignments.

Settlements

Settlements, particularly those oriented around predominantly maritime economies, take the form of densely clustered houses situated along a well-protected stretch of shoreline. In central and southern Sulu, villages are characteristically built directly over the sea, in channels or tidal shallows, often within or behind a line of fringing reef. Elsewhere they are more often located along or immediately behind the beachfront. Houses, which are raised on piles 1 to 3 meters above the ground or high-water mark, usually consist of a single rectangular room with an attached kitchen. Size and construction materials vary with the wealth of the owner. The dwellings of the relatively poor are typically constructed of thatched roofing and split-bamboo walls and floor; those of wealthier families are more likely to be made of commercially milled lumber and corrugated roofing and may include several additional sleeping rooms, a porch, and a separate kitchen. Houses built over the water are typically connected by catwalks and planks. Households are grouped into larger units called *tumpuk*, or "clusters." These consist of households that are both physically adjacent and genealogically related by close cognatic ties. Core members are most often siblings or spouses of siblings. Within the community one household head, having the support of the majority of the others, is acknowledged as the cluster spokesman. Clusters coincide in some instances with parishes, local groups whose members are affiliated with a single mosque. More often parishes consist of a number of clusters, all of whose members recognize a common leader in political and legal matters. This leader is usually the owner or sponsor of the mosque. Larger villages occasionally contain more than one parish, with one parish leader generally acknowledged as the village head.

Economy

Subsistence and Commercial Activities. Sama adaptation is varied, typically combining, with differing local emphasis, fishing, farming, seafaring, and trade. For island and strand communities, fishing is generally a major economic activity. Virtually all locally available fish are exploited, using a wide range of equipment—hand lines, longlines, lures, jigs, fish traps, spears, spear guns, drift nets, and explosives. In addition, shellfish, crustaceans, turtle eggs, sea urchins, and edible algae are collected. The crews formed for drift netting and handline trolling are generally recruited from among the net or boat owner's cluster members. Today nearly all fishing is market-oriented, with catches sold through local vendors, or through wholesalers, most of them Sama, or to carriers for transport to local retail markets. Some fish is sold (either dried or salted) to larger-scale dealers for export to areas outside Sulu and eastern Sabah. Cassava, dry rice, maize, and bananas are the principal food crops, with yams, beans, tomatoes, onions, ginger, sugarcane, and fruit being the main secondary crops. Throughout much of Sulu and eastern Sabah copra constitutes the major cash crop, providing both markets and capital for a variety of other commercial activities such as storekeeping and interisland transport. Copra holdings are small, however, and few families own enough palms to support themselves entirely from copra sales.

Industrial Arts. Historically, different Sama groups have specialized in different lines of trade and craft production. The Laminusa Samal are well known, for example, for their especially fine pandanus mats, while the Sibutu Samal enjoy a reputation as expert boat builders. Other groups specialize in pottery making, which, in Sulu, is entirely a Samal craft. Historically, in most regions, specialization was linked to patterns of intercommunity trade. For example, in the Semporna District of Sabah, the Sama Banaran community traditionally produced *kajang* matting and gathered boat-caulking resin for local trade with other groups, while Sama Kubang villages specialized in boat building, ironworking, and the manufacture of tortoiseshell combs and ornaments and carved wooden grave markers.

Trade. Trade has long occupied a central place in Sama life. European accounts as early as the seventeenth and eighteenth centuries describe Sama communities as being dependent on trade for even basic foodstuffs. Throughout Sulu and eastern Indonesia, sea-oriented groups historically were valued for their navigational skills and as seafarers and suppliers of trepang, dried fish, pearls, pearl shell, and other marine commodities of trade. In addition, specialized Sama groups historically engaged in intercommunity barter, exchanging, for example, fish for kajang matting, cassava, and seasonal fruit. Such trade involved, in some regions, both Sama and non-Sama groups. Today trade in fish, farm produce, fruit, and craft goods is channeled almost entirely through regularly constituted local markets, while copra and, to some degree, dried and salted fish are handled by larger-scale wholesalers. Along the Zamboanga coast, Samal traders historically dominated the external coastwise trade of the Subanun, while in Palawan the Jama Mapun maintained similar relations with swidden cultivating groups inhabiting the interior of the island.

Division of Labor. Both sexes share in agricultural labor; fishing, boat building, and ironworking are primarily male occupations. Both men and women engage in trade, while women weave pandanus mats and make and market pottery.

Land Tenure. Farm and residential land is subject to individual use and/or tenancy rights. Fish-trap and lift-net sites and coral fish corrals may be owned individually; otherwise fishing grounds are available for common exploitation.

Kinship

Kin Groups and Descent. Kinship is strictly bilateral and genealogical knowledge is generally shallow. There are no permanent kin groups with corporate functions. A bilateral kindred (*kampong*) is recognized, consisting of all persons with whom some kin relationship exists, whether traceable or not. Obligations owed to close kindred include attendance at funerals, children's weddings, and thanksgiving rites; lending and borrowing of property, food, and money; and exchange of visits and hospitality. Among the Jama Mapun, a localized kin group (*lungan*) is recognized, its members descended bilaterally, over three to eight generations, from a common ancestor. Such groups constitute the primary basis of support of local and regional leaders.

Kinship Terminology. Kin terminology displays some variation, although all systems emphasize lineality, relative age, and generation. Among the Jama Mapun, nobles reportedly have a Hawaiian system of terminology distinct from the more general Eskimo system of commoners and other Sama groups.

Marriage and Family

Marriage. Marriage between kindred is preferred, provided partners are close to the same age. Marriage may be parentally arranged, often with the help of a go-between, or be initiated by elopement or, less often, abduction. In the case of elopement, either a couple may place themselves under the protection of a village headman or other local leader, or the woman may act on her own, going to the house of a village headman or other local leader and there declaring her intention to marry a particular suitor. In all cases bride-wealth is paid. In the case of abduction, the groom may be required to pay an additional fine. Weddings typically occasion the largest gathering of kindred and neighbors of any life-cycle rite. An imam or a group of *paki* (religious officials) officiate, witnessing the ceremony and confirming the transfer of bride-wealth, designated by the bride's father. The couple live for at least the first three or four days with the bride's family. After that they are expected to visit the groom's parents; they may either remain there or return to the woman's family. Most couples are expected to set up their own household by the second or third year of marriage. There is some preference that new households be located near the wife's relatives, with the result that clusters are commonly formed around a core of closely related women. Polygyny is allowed but is most infrequent. The frequency of divorce varies; for some Sama groups it is described as common, while for others it is relatively infrequent. There is some evidence that its frequency is highest for polygynous unions, somewhat high for arranged marriages, and lowest for elopement. Little stigma attaches to divorce, and remarriage is relatively easy for both partners.

Domestic Unit. The primary domestic unit consists of those who eat together and share a common hearth, a group normally coterminous with the household. Most domestic groups consist of a stem or nuclear family often augmented by several additional kin, and occasionally comprised of more than one married couple (normally, married siblings with their spouses and children). Houses are individually owned and the house's owner is usually acknowledged as the household head.

Inheritance. Inheritance is bilateral, with each child, regardless of sex, entitled to a share of its parents' property. The Sama distinguish between property acquired in the course of a marriage and that inherited independently, to which the owner's husband or wife has no claim.

Socialization. Children tend to be highly valued and for the first six or seven years are made to assume few responsibilities. Preadolescent children undergo a ritual haircutting (*maggunting*) and weighing ceremony. Boys are circumcised at puberty, whereas girls undergo a form of partial clitoridectomy between the ages of 2 and 6. At adolescence some children are taught to recite from the Quran, either under the guidance of a personal tutor or through attendance at special Quranic schools. Those who complete instruction demonstrate their proficiency in a public reading (*magtammat*), at which both they and their instructor are honored. Following puberty, girls are usually kept close to home, where they are expected to help with housework and child care; boys are allowed greater freedom of movement, accompanying their fathers when they go fishing and marketing. Today most children attend public school, although few complete more than primary education.

Sociopolitical Organization

Social Organization. Historically some Sama groups, such as the Jama Mapun, Balanguingui, and Pangutaran Samal, enjoyed considerable trading and political independence within the Sulu sultanate. Like the dominant Tausug, these Sama groups were divided into ranked strata: nobles, commoners, and slaves. Other groups were more egalitarian. Among the more stratified Sama, the nobility, consisting of both *datu* and *salip,* tended to enjoy privileged access to wealth and power through their involvement in trade and raiding and from their control of slaves and the labor services of commoners. Today these hereditary privileges are no longer acknowledged. Inherited titles, however, continue to carry prestige, and class distinctions are based chiefly on wealth and political influence.

Political Organization. Political relations are organized primarily in terms of leader-centered networks, or coalitions. Locally these coalesce around cluster, parish, and village leaders. Above the village level, factional rivalry tends to be endemic. Today, as under the former sultanates, central authorities seek to integrate local Sama communities into the larger polity by placing them under the jurisdiction of regional authorities representing the state. In Sulu the sultan formerly appointed *panglima* or maharajas as community headmen and regional chiefs. Today regional leaders operate largely in the context of electoral politics, linking local community leaders to the wider administrative structure through a hierarchy of municipal, district, and state officials.

Social Control. Responsibility for settling disputes falls chiefly on parish and village leaders. As a result, disputes that cross village and/or parish boundaries are often difficult to resolve and sometimes escalate, without outside intervention, into open violence. In rendering judgments, local leaders appeal to custom (*adat*) and Islamic law (*sara'*).

Conflict. In contrast to the situation among the neighboring Tausug, endemic armed conflict is generally not found among the Samal. However, piracy and occasional vendettas occur. In the past regional leaders were in frequent contention and many erected stone or coral forts (*kuta'*) where their followers might take refuge in times of raiding or during interregional feuds between rival leaders.

Religion and Expressive Culture

Religious Beliefs. Except for the Abak, all Sama-Bajau speakers are Sunni Muslims of the Shafi school. The Five Pillars of Islam are acknowledged: confession of faith in Allah and Mohammed, his prophet; the five daily prayers; the fast during Ramadan; the pilgrimage to Mecca; and the payment of religious tax. Few, however, can afford to make the pilgrimage to Mecca and only the most pious regularly observe all five daily prayers. Every Samal parish contains a mosque (*masjid*), serving as a center of public worship and a weekly gathering place. Parish families contribute to its maintenance and to the support of the imam, *hatib*, and other mosque officials, chiefly through a tithe (*zakat*) collected annually at Hari Raya Puasa. Traditionally, the appointment of mosque officials was a privilege of authority, descending from the sultan to parish elders. God (Tuhan) is believed to be the creator of heaven and earth, of the first man and woman, and of both the archangels and Iblis (Satan), who leads people to evil. Also in this world is a multitude of local spirits (some free-moving, others identified with features of the natural landscape), ghosts, and other potential agents of misfortune.

Religious Practitioners. Those who are well versed in religious matters, including the imam and other mosque officials, are called paki, or *pakil*. As a group, the paki preside over all life-crisis rites, act as religious counselors, and conduct minor rites of thanksgiving (*dua'a salamat*). The latter are held in fulfillment of a pledge (*janji*) offered in return for a special favor, such as recovery from illness or a safe return from a difficult journey. A number of traditional religious practitioners are also consulted, including midwives, herbalist-curers, diviners, and spirit mediums.

Ceremonies. Friday prayers performed in the parish mosque climax a weekly cycle of daily prayers. In addition an annual religious calendar is observed that includes a month of fasting (Ramadan); a feast day (Hari Raya Puasa) to mark the end of Ramadan; a feast of sacrifice (Hari Raya Hadji) during the month of Jul-Hadj; the birthday of the Prophet (Maulud); and a day of ritual bathing (Tuak Bala'), performed usually in the sea, to remove evil during the month of Sappal.

Arts. The Samal are well known among Muslims of the Philippines for their developed dance and song traditions, percussion and xylophone music, dyed pandanus mats and food covers, and decorative wood carving (*ukil*).

Death and Afterlife. As soon after death as possible, the body is bathed and shrouded. It is then buried in a grave niche with the head facing Mecca; the grave is covered, usually with sand or crushed coral, and marked with a wooden marker. Burial is followed by a period of vigil, lasting up to seven nights for an adult. Each evening male relatives and neighbors gather in the house of the bereaved family for readings, prayers, and a meal or light refreshments. If the family is particularly wealthy, it may hold additional memorial rites on the twentieth, fortieth, and hundredth day after death and on the first anniversary. Following a period of atonement a person's soul is believed to ascend to heaven, while the body descends to hell where it suffers punishment proportional to the person's misdeeds and accumulated merit. Spirits of the dead are thought to remain in the vicinity of their graves. Here they require remembrance and expressions of continued concern from the living; some graves become sources of miracle-working power. During the month of Shaaban God permits the souls of the dead (*roh*) to return to this world. To honor their return, the living offer special prayers to the dead and clear their graves.

See also Bajau; Samal Moro; Sea Nomads of the Andaman; Selung/Moken; Yakan

Bibliography

Casiño, Eric (1976). *The Jama Mapun: A Changing Samal Society in the Southern Philippines*. Quezon City: Ateneo de Manila Press.

Geoghegan, William (1975). "Balangingi." In *Ethnic Groups of Insular Southeast Asia*, edited by Frank M. LeBar. Vol. 2, *Philippines and Formosa*, 6–9. New Haven: HRAF Press.

Geoghegan, William (1984). "Sama." In *Muslim Peoples: A World Ethnographic Survey*, edited by Richard V. Weekes, 654–659. London: Aldwych.

Pallesen, A. Kemp (1985). *Culture Contact and Language Convergence*. Manila: Linguistic Society of the Philippines.

Pelras, Christian (1972). "Notes sur quelques populations aquatiques de l'Archipel Nusantarian." *Archipel* 3:133–168.

Sather, Clifford (1984). "Sea and Shore People: Ethnicity and Ethnic Interaction in Southeastern Sabah." *Contributions to Southeast Asian Ethnography* 3:3–27.

Szanton, David (1973). "Art in Sulu: A Survey." *Sulu Studies* 2:3–69.

Warren, James F. (1978). "Who Were the Balangingi Samal? Slave Raiding and Ethnogenesis in 19th Century Sulu." *Journal of Asian Studies* 37:477–490.

CLIFFORD SATHER

Samal Moro

ETHNONYMS: Muslim Samalan, Sama, Samal

Orientation

Identification. "Samal" is a covering term for Muslim Samalan speakers. One of the many ethnic-minority groups in the Philippines, they are one of ten Islamic groups presently living in the southern Philippines. They speak a Malayo-Polynesian language, Siamal or Samalan, perhaps the oldest in the Sulu Archipelago. In the Philippines, ethnic identity is usually determined by language. For the Samal Moro, their minority status is a double bind: they are at once speakers of a less-known language and Muslims in a Christian country. Christians call them "Moros" (as in "Moors"), a reference the Samal consider insulting. Referring to themselves as "Sama" or "Samal," they clearly distinguish themselves from the Sama-laut, known in the literature as "Bajaus" or "Sea Gypsies." Typically, Samal identify themselves more with a particular island or island group.

Location. The Philippines lies in the severest cyclone belt of Asia. It is extremely volcanic, and its climate is tropical with marked rainy and dry seasons except in Sulu. Of 7,100 islands and islets, only 700 are inhabited, and most of them have a simple north-to-south structural alignment. The southernmost group of islands form the Sulu Archipelago where the Samal live. South of Jolo and Siasi, the Samal are found mainly in the TawiTawi area and outlying islands beyond.

Demography.   The 1992 national population estimate for the Philippines was 62,380,000, of which 5 to 10 percent are Muslims, the largest minority group. National population density averages 208.2 persons per square kilometer. There are concentrations of forty-five other major ethnic groups in the islands of Luzon, Mindanao, and the Visayas. The annual population growth estimate is 2.49 percent and average life expectancy is 62 years for males and 64 for females. In 1985 the national population was estimated at 56,808,000, of whom an estimated 126,100 were Samal Moro. In Sulu, the Samal are the second-largest indigenous ethnic group (after the Tausug).

Linguistic Affiliation.   Around eighty-seven languages and dialects are spoken in the Philippines; with the exception English, Spanish, and Chinese, they all belong to the Austronesian Family. Eight Philippine languages are spoken by 86 percent of the population, with Cebuano (24 percent) and Tagalog (21 percent) being the most widely used. Tagalog has formed the basis for the national language, Pilipino, as it is the major language of Manila. The official languages of the country, Pilipino and English, are used in government, mass communication, and commerce, and beyond grammar school.

History and Cultural Relations

Prior to European colonization, the Philippines had been an outpost of Southeast Asian kingdoms in various periods, the most notable of which was the Majapahit. In the fourteenth century, Islam, by way of Malaysia and Indonesia, had gained a foothold in many coastal regions of the Philippines, leading to a replay of Christian-Muslim conflicts when the Spaniards arrived in 1521. Spanish Christianity was successfully superimposed on the majority of the native cultures, except among interior tribal groups and the southern people of the Philippines. The end of the Spanish-American War brought the Philippines under United States control between 1899 and 1946. Throughout the American occupation, the southern part of the country remained Islamic, separatist in ideology, and hostile. Pacification tactics and containment differed little from those used previously by the Spaniards or those adopted later by the Marcos regime. The short Japanese occupation of the Philippines (1941–1945) left no significant imprint. During the Marcos regime considerable effort was exerted to align the Philippines with its Southeast Asian neighbors, but its cultural links to the West are profound. It is a Roman Catholic country, historically related to Latin America, that champions an American-style government and a public-school system directed toward mass education and modernization; the American experiment on Philippine soil was successful, if only briefly. Until the twentieth century the Chinese presence in the Philippines had been intermittent and confined to trading activities. Today Chinese constitute 2 percent of the population.

Settlements

Philippine settlements are classifiable as cities, towns, and villages. While the national capital, Manila, stands alone, chartered cities form the second-highest level of urban organization. Small cities and large towns are often interchangeable. Both are based on the number of villages included under their jurisdiction. In Christian areas a Catholic church identifies the town. In Sulu a mosque marks a specific ethnic neighborhood or a village. Typically, Samal villages are of the strip kind, with houses built on stilts along the coastal lines. Denser villages are built out further into the sea and are accessible by platforms serving as passageways. Samal mosques, schoolhouses, and health dispensaries are built inland, as are the homes of more affluent and acculturated families. A typical house has two sections: one part roofed, the other not. Most household chores are done in the latter, while formal activities and sleeping take place in the former. The traditional thatched roofs and walls have given way to more durable materials such as galvanized iron, lumber, and concrete.

Economy

Subsistence and Commercial Activities.   As a maritime people, Samal Muslims have pursued varied patterns of livelihood: cassava and coconut horticulture (*huma*), household and commercial fishing, contraband trade, and, mostly among the Sibutu Samal, boat (*kumpit*) building. Early acceptance of public schooling has given the Samal an advantage over the Tausug in the training of local civil servants, whose salaries augment household income and sometimes cause relative wealth differentiation between households. Coastal households often fish and also raise a few chickens and ducks, mainly for eggs. Inland households may also raise a goat or a cow for slaughter during ceremonials, especially weddings. Otherwise, the Samals' dietary needs are met via food purchased from the trading centers of Tawitawi and Sitangkai: rice (an expensive supplement to cassava), canned goods, and vegetables.

Industrial Arts.   Part-time motorcycle mechanics, sewing-machine operators, blacksmiths, carvers, and bricklayers are usually found in the Samal villages. Mat weaving is a specialized activity for some women and often a source of additional income.

Trade.   Commercial activities in Sulu exist on two levels: legitimate and illegitimate. Legitimate trade involves the sale of dried fish, copra, or a newly built boat to Chinese merchants throughout the markets of Sulu, Zamboanga, and North Borneo. Cash from these transactions is used to smuggle goods from North Borneo into the islands. Smuggling trips involve the cooperative activities of young men in the villages and call for a facility for eluding the naval patrols. A typical village has one or two *sari-sari* stores, where daily needs such as oil, soap, condiments, spices, and pain remedies are easily bought.

Division of Labor.   Except in farm work, division of labor by gender is fairly clear-cut. Men exclusively fish, build boats, and trade. Women do such domestic chores as housecleaning, food preparation, and child care. Men assist in child rearing after infancy.

Land Tenure. Homesteading by people from the northern islands created permanent settlements on many Samal islands and changed their form of adaptation away from sea roving. By 1910 the larger islands like Subutu, Simunul, Bongao, and Pangutaran had settled populations. As late as the 1960s, homesteading was still attracting migrants to Cagayan de Sulu. Residential and farming plots and cemetery grounds are family- or kin-owned. Village founders are well remembered by the first mosques they built or the first trees they planted to mark off their communities.

Kinship

Kin Groups and Descent. Kin-based groups are readily identifiable as households (*magtoteyanak, dambua'luna, dapaningan*) ranging in composition from nuclear to four-generational extended families. The nuclear family, *mataan*, is distinguished clearly from the household unit. A group of kin-related households, located in the common residential land, form neighborhoods or work teams. Two or more of these localized kindred groups constitute the village (*kaum*), the unit of worship. Descent is bilateral, tempered by status.

Kinship Terminology. The traditional distinction between nobility (*datus*) and commoners is reflected in the separate sets of address terminology employed within each group. Both use Eskimo cousin terms, but whereas commoners use lineal terms for the first ascendant generation, the nobility employs generational terms. As a result, mixed marriages produce semblances of bifurcate merging and bifurcate collaterality depending on the respective status of the spouses. Kin terms also reflect the significance attributed to relative age.

Marriage and Family

Marriage. Monogamy is the norm but polygyny is tolerated, although second and third wives have less status than the first wife. Patrilateral and matrilateral cross cousins are considered equally suitable spouses. Unions between patrilateral parallel cousins, sororate marriages when the second wife is senior to the first wife, and intergenerational marriage between Ego and a parent's first cousin are less preferred. These marriages are considered "hot," or *panas*, and thus require extra ritual treatment. Matrilocal residence is a more prevalent practice. High frequency of marriage between kin mutes the distinction between consanguineal and affinal relatives. Divorce, though sanctioned by Islamic law, rarely occurs.

Domestic Unit. Mainly a residential and often an economic unit, the household group ranges from single families of six members to extended units that include grandparents, grandchildren, aunts, uncles, and children of spouses. In multifamily households, the family as the consumption unit stands distinct from the residential group. The latter may have two or three hearths from which individual families prepare their separate meals. House repairs require collective labor or financing by the members.

Inheritance. Equal division of property among children is subscribed to and technically prescribed by law. Because land is held in common by kin groups and houses do not last, inheritable property consists of jewelry, cash, or other salable articles. In this connection, the child, ideally a daughter who cares for and lives with the aging parents, may get the better share.

Socialization. Children are raised by both parents at different stages. Infants are tended almost exclusively by the mother. After children are weaned, they are cared for by their father and older siblings. While physical punishment is rare, teasing is used in sanctioning. Parents are extremely affectionate toward their children, in whom they instill the importance of social relationships and loyalty to the community over self-centeredness.

Sociopolitical Organization

The modern Philippines is a constitutional democracy with a president, vice-president, and congressional and local officials, all popularly elected.

Social Organization. Principles of hierarchy that apply throughout Philippine society are based on age, occupation, wealth, residence, ethnicity, and, in Sulu, on inherited status. Class mobility has obscured status at both regional and local levels: poor datu families and rich commoner families have emerged. The priestly class (*pakil*) stands above the status conflict. Patron-client relationships are also hierarchical and often involve petty bureaucrats and their relatives in the chain.

Political Organization. The province, each with its capital, is the major political and administrative division in the country. Provinces are organized into districts; each district, into municipalities; and each municipality, into *barrios* and/or *baranggays*. The barrio often corresponds to a village or a group of hamlets. The province is run by an elected governor and council, and it sets policies for its constituent municipalities. Municipalities, in turn, elect their mayors and councils, and their barranggay constituency elects the baranggay captain and council. The seat of the municipality is the *poblacion*, where some measure of urbanism is recognizable. Chartered cities are specialized municipalities governed in parallel to the provinces. Districts elect representatives to the national congress but senators, like the president and vice-president, are elected at large. The national government, through its appropriate bureaus, provides for its citizenry free elementary and selected secondary schools, competitive national universities, public health dispensaries and selected hospitals, public records, tax collection, courts, police, national highways, and water systems. As a rule, the political regions closer to Manila have better access to these facilities. In Sulu many of these services are nonexistent.

Social Control. In Samal villages gossip provides an effective but informal source of social control. Fear of strangers and evil spirits is also invoked in socialization techniques. Both the barranggay captain and the pakil in their advisory capacity can influence or arbitrate on matters that concern the village, via the village council. Beyond the village, the religious court, *agama*, is the ultimate source of social control.

Conflict. Status distinction between the nobility and commoners often translates into political campaigns for public office, competition for government appointments in a patronage system, and marriage alliance and preference.

Religion and Expressive Culture

Religious Beliefs.   Islam, the religion of submission to God, is the main unifying factor for many groups in the southern Philippines. Of the four schools of the Sunni branch of Islam, the Muslims of Southeast Asia belong to the Shafi school, in which equal weight is given to the authority of the Quran and of the Hadith.

Religious Practitioners.   The pakil (priestly) class is composed of imams, *hatibs*, and *bilars*, who are ranked according to knowledge of the Quran, experience, and seniority. Traditionally appointed by the agama, these officials are now appointed by the mayor. Their ranking is usually evident during major religious ceremonies; otherwise each may substitute for the others in delivering sermons, leading chants, and performing critical rituals. Attendance at Friday worship (Jumaat) in the mosque is virtually all male. If women do go, they sit in the back, behind the men. Other practitioners include curers and diviners. Sorcerers are widely believed to exist. The Muslim jinn are locally known as *saitans* (evil spirits), to which the typical Samal makes daily reference in connection with illness, misfortune, failure, and unhappiness. Invocation of Tuhan (God) is comparatively rare and is made in the more abstract assessment of the human condition. Sometimes bogey men with supernatural qualities are imagined.

Ceremonies.   The Muslim calendar has twelve months of thirty days each. Important feasts and festivals include the New Year (Muharram) celebration; Maulud en-nabi, the Prophet Mohammed's birthday; Ramadan; Hari Raya Puasa, at the close of the fasting month; the Feast of Sacrifice surrounding the hajj (pilgrimage to Mecca), locally known as "Hari Raya Hadji"; and the Festival of Mohammed's Night Journey.

Arts.   Carved designs are found in the more traditional homes and on burial markers, boats, and machete handles. Brass gongs, drums, and xylophones are typical instruments used in festivities, as well as battery-run radios and phonographs. Dance troupes visit villages, although at long intervals. Competitive sports among school districts (usually interisland) provide great entertainment, as do traveling movies.

Medicine.   Spirit possession, spirit loss, and sorcery (*kulam*) are often blamed for lingering illness. Curers usually diagnose and prescribe relief alongside a Western medical agent. Sickly children are attended by the pakil, who performs renaming and weighing (*pagtimbang*) rituals as remedies.

Death and Afterlife.   Funeral rites are held immediately after a death, and before sundown the body is buried. The soul (*aluwa*) of a good person is believed to go to heaven, via Mecca; a bad soul goes to hell. The bad soul is feared as a potential ghost and requires the ritual of forgiveness (*kipalat*) conducted on its behalf by the living relatives.

Bibliography

Casino, Eric S. (1976). *The Jama Mapun: A Changing Samal Society in the Southern Philippines*. Manila: Ateneo de Manila University Press.

Ducommun, Dolores (1962). "Sisangat: A Sulu Fishing Community." *Philippine Sociological Review* 10:91–107.

Flores-Meiser, Enya P. (1969). "Division and Integration in a Sibutu Barrio (Sulu, Philippines)." In *Anthropology: Range and Relevance*, 511–526. Quezon City: Kayumanggi Press.

Orosa, Sixto Y. (1923). *The Sulu Archipelago and Its People*. Yonkers, N.Y.: World Book Co.

Spoehr, Alexander (1973). *Zamboanga and Sulu: An Archeological Approach to Ethnic Diversity*. Pittsburgh: University of Pittsburgh Press.

ENYA P. FLORES-MEISER

Sangir

The Sangir (Sangirezen, Talaoerezen) are the indigenous inhabitants of the Sangihe (Sangir) and Taluad island chains located between southern Mindanao and northern Celebes. They speak Sangir, sometimes referred to as Sangil, Sangihé, or Sangirese, an Austronesian language. In 1987 the entire population, including those along the southern coast of Mindanao in the Philippines, numbered about 205,000. Those living in Indonesia have been subject to both Muslim and Christian influences for centuries; they are now mostly Christian and are being assimilated into the national economic and political system.

The Sangir are sometimes confused with the Sangil, a group of about 4,000 who live on islands off the southern coast of Mindanao. The Sangil are a contemporary population of Philippine Muslims descended from Sangir who migrated to Mindanao in the seventeenth century or perhaps earlier. They are seen as a group now distinct from the Sangir and as Filipinos rather than Indonesians.

Bibliography

Gowing, Peter G. (1975). "The Growing List of Filipino Muslim Groups." *Dansalan Research Center Reports* 2:5–6.

Saoch

A group of about 500 (1981) in southwest Cambodia, the Saoch are closely related to the Pear and Chong. The Saoch, who were once hunter-gatherers, are largely assimilated into Khmer society today.

Bibliography

Taillard, Paul (1943). "Les Saoch." _Bulletins et Travaux pour 1942, Institut Indochinois pour l'Étude de l'Homme_ 5:15–45.

Sasak

ETHNONYMS: Sassak, Waktu Lima, Wetu Telu

Orientation

Identification. The Sasak are speakers of the Sasak language and are the dominant population on the island of Lombok, Indonesia. Traditionally they have classified their population, villages, and culture into two native categories: the Wetu Telu, or traditional Sasak, and the Waktu Lima, the more strongly Islamized and market-oriented Sasak. This classification has changed recently. Whereas prior to 1965 whole villages were considered to be Wetu Telu, since that time few Sasak have openly declared themselves to be such.

Location. The island of Lombok, located in the Indonesian archipelago to the east of Bali, is 112 kilometers long by 80 kilometers at its widest point, or about 4,680 square kilometers. The Sasak population is concentrated in the fertile central plains area of the island, but it is also spread over the island in the mountain ranges of the north and southeast as well as in the more arid areas of the south and east. The dry season occurs between May and August, the rainy season between November and March. The greatest precipitation occurs in the west. A central plain running west to east divides this mountainous island, with the highest ranges located in the north, culminating in the volcanic peak of Gunung Rindjani. Some thirty rivers, most originating in the north, make up the island's drainage system, so important to its agrarian economy.

Demography. In 1980 the population was estimated to be near 2.3 million, with a population density of approximately 152 people per square kilometer; however, the population density of the fertile plains is closer to 700 people per square kilometer. The population is growing at an average rate of about 2.37 percent. Well over 90 percent of the population of the island is Sasak; Lombok Balinese predominate in the remainder of the population and are concentrated in the western part of the island, followed by Sumbawanese in the east.

Linguistic Affiliation. The Sasak language, closely related to Balinese and Javanese, is a branch of the Malayo-Polynesian Language Family.

History and Cultural Relations

Prior to the Balinese conquest of Lombok, the island was divided into a number of frequently warring Sasak princedoms. These Hinduized Sasak states converted to Islam in the sixteenth century, but they retained a syncretized religion that had some indigenous ancestor worship, Hindu elements, and newer Muslim beliefs and practices. Conflict between and within these princedoms was common at the time. Such divisiveness enabled the Balinese to conquer Lombok and to become the ruling caste, reducing the Sasak to vassaldom. The Balinese rulers instituted a number of techniques to reinforce their position, including language etiquette relating to caste, in which they spoke down to the Sasak, who were required to use the superior language level in speaking back to them; marriage levels, in which the Balinese could marry Sasak women, but Sasak men could not marry Balinese women; and corvée, in which Balinese could command Sasak labor. The Balinese collected tribute in rice and confiscated Sasak land. Several unsuccessful Sasak revolts against the Balinese were attempted. The Dutch, interested in greater economic control, landed in Lombok in 1894, proclaiming themselves liberators of the Sasak from their Balinese oppressors. The Balinese and their Sasak supporters' engagement in another conflict aided the Dutch conquest in 1895, leading to the _puputan_, or ritual suicide, of the Balinese ruling dynasty after their defeat. The Dutch colonial government dissolved the ties of allegiance to earlier rulers by setting up a new administrative system under the rule of a resident in Bali, and the Dutch obtained major revenues from the agrarian sector.

During this period the division of the Sasak population into traditional Wetu Telu and the more orthodox Muslim Waktu Lima was pronounced. Dutch-appointed Sasak administrators were usually Waktu Lima, and this provoked Wetu Telu discontent, sometimes taking the form of messianic and revivalistic movements during the early twentieth century. The Waktu Lima Sasak villages were most numerous along the main roads and in market centers, while Wetu Telu villages tended to be more self-sufficient and isolated. Political and economic centers were Waktu Lima, with Waktu Lima officials whose beliefs and practices conflicted with Wetu Telu customs. There was increasing Muslim proselytizing by Waktu Lima missionaries. In the increasing conflict between the two Sasak groups many villages that had been previously considered Waktu Lima became designated as Wetu Telu, particularly in eastern Lombok. Although not predominant in the population, the syncretistic Wetu Telu, united by personal and kinship ties and economic redistribution, were found in the more isolated Sasak villages. In the early 1970s the Wetu Telu disappeared as a culturally distinct category. In 1942 the Japanese invaded Indonesia, ousting the Dutch. The Sasak remember this as a time of forced labor, poverty, and oppression. After Indonesian independence, missionary Muslim leaders called "Tuan Guru" gained great political and economic power on Lombok, ensuring Waktu Lima dominance. The president stressed economic self-sufficiency and mutual aid. Economic conditions were deteriorating. The Land Reform Program of 1960 proved problematic, and attempts to implement it ended by 1965. In 1965 an attempted coup, crushed by the military and blamed on the Communists, led to a bloodbath of alleged Communist sympathizers and a concomitant swelling of the ranks of the followers of the Tuan Guru as the Sasak attempted to avoid persecution. In the late 1970s BIMAS, or the "Green Revolution," had a major economic impact on Lombok. The most recent changes have been an upsurge of economic development projects and tourism.

Settlements

Villages range in population from several hundred to about 15,000 people. They tend to be clusters of houses around a road or path, surrounded by fields that separate one village settlement from another. The village mosque, administrative office, and marketplace are located along the main road, usually in the middle of the village. House construction varies by village type and by affluence of owners, with houses made of native materials predominating in the more isolated and traditional villages as well as among the less affluent in the more populous villages. Typically, these houses are one- or two-roomed, thatched-roofed, windowless structures built on platforms of packed earth, with bamboo frames and walls of bamboo, earth, and woven grass or palm fronds. Rice barns, containing raised platforms used for entertaining or working, are associated with houses of this type. The more modern housing style often contains several rooms. These are also single-storied structures but are made of concrete or wood with a few windows and roofs of corrugated iron.

Economy

Subsistence and Commercial Activities. The Sasak economy is primarily agrarian and dominated by the production of wet rice as the dietary staple and for sale. Most of the population is engaged in farming and lives in rural peasant villages. The economy is labor-intensive. Plows drawn by water buffalo or oxen, hand harvesting, and transportation by horse still predominate despite development efforts. Very important to the production of wet rice is the extensive irrigation system of canals and dikes managed by the *subak,* irrigation societies that oversee the equitable distribution of water. Other crops such as cassava, soybeans, maize, sweet potatoes, and coconuts are grown for subsistence; rice, coffee, tobacco, peanuts, and onions are among the crops grown for sale as well as for local consumption. In addition to irrigated rice, the Sasak cultivate rainfall-dependent rice in the less-fertile areas, and they practice some swidden cultivation or *ladang.*

Industrial Arts. Some villages have part-time and seasonal specialists who make earthenware pottery for sale, weave baskets, or are blacksmiths or charcoal makers.

Trade. There is a proliferation of petty traders among the landless Sasak. Small shops, itinerant peddlers, and sellers in the markets are common in all but the most isolated villages. Most petty trade is done by women, while men tend to control larger-scale and off-island trade.

Division of Labor. While both sexes engage in cultivation and work as farm wage laborers, some of the tasks differ along gender lines. Men clear land, build and repair fields and irrigation works, guard crops, plow, build houses, and work as blacksmiths. Women pound rice, clean house, fetch water, weave, and cook (though men cook for feasts). Both sexes plant, weed, harvest, collect, fish, weave baskets, and tend babies.

Land Tenure. Population growth and increasing commercialization have led many smallholders to sell their land, creating an increasingly large landless population. Many have become seasonal laborers or traders. While farming one's own land is the ideal, few landless Sasak can hope ever to save enough money over subsistence needs to purchase land. Many syncretists remain reluctant to sell land or rice, but rapid change is occurring in this regard.

Kinship

Kin Groups and Descent. The Sasak social system is composed of three hierarchically ranked title levels (sometimes referred to as castes), with two levels for the aristocracy and one for commoners. Nobles and commoners often live in segregated neighborhoods. Caste regulates marriage and affects descent. Descent is bilateral with an emphasis on the patrilineal kin. Kin share labor, jointly contribute to rituals, and provide other help.

Kinship Terminology. Kinship terms of reference are Eskimo, but terms of address are Hawaiian. Relative age is important.

Marriage and Family

Marriage. Most marriages are monogamous, although polygynous marriages are allowed. The ranking system is important in determining marriage. Men may marry women of lower rank, but women marry below their rank only at the risk of being disowned by their families. First-cousin marriages are often arranged among nobility. Many marriages take place through elopement, which the Sasak call "bride capture." Cousin marriage is preferred and is common. Within the limitations imposed by caste there is considerable freedom of choice of spouses. Residence is neolocal. Divorce is common and is generally the male's option, following Muslim custom.

Domestic Unit. Households consist of people who live together, share meals, and cooperate economically. They are usually composed of nuclear-family members, perhaps including a grandparent or, in grandparental households, a grandchild.

Inheritance. The most important form of heritable property is land, especially irrigated fields or orchards. Inheritance rules vary by village. In many villages daughters receive one share to every three shares inherited by sons. In some villages women do not inherit land and older sons may inherit more than younger sons. Daughters may share equally in inheritance of houses, furnishings, cattle, and money, and they are provided for from the land inherited by their male kin.

Socialization. Child care is provided by both parents, other available adults, or older siblings (especially sisters). Infants and very young children are always carried; physical punishment is avoided.

Sociopolitical Organization

The Indonesian government is headed by a president with other elected officials. Political parties operate through popular vote.

Social Organization. Sasak society has a ranked system of titled levels (arguably called "castes") with two levels for the aristocracy and one for commoners. Additionally, the society is hierarchically organized by relative age, wealth, religious attainment, occupation, and residence.

Political Organization. The island of Lombok is part of the province of Nusa Tenggara Barat, composed of Lombok and Sumbawa. There is a provincial governor. Lombok has three districts, *kabupatan*, each of which has a district headman, *bupati*. These districts are Western Lombok, Central Lombok, and Eastern Lombok. Each district is subdivided into subdistricts, *kecamatan*, which vary greatly in population and have subdistrict headmen called *camat*. There are several hundred Sasak villages, or *desa*, with village headmen, *kepala desa*. Most desa are subdivided into hamlets, *gubug*, with neighborhood headmen, or *keliang*. The village council of elders, *kerama desa*, is an important decision-making body in many villages and works by discussion and consensus.

Social Control. Direct conflict is avoided. Gossip and ostracism are key mechanisms of control. District courts handle problem cases beyond the village level. In the more isolated areas local problems are adjudicated by the kerama desa.

Conflict. Conflicts over succession and control led to warfare in the past. Present disputes over water rights or inheritance are often resolved through adjudication.

Religion and Expressive Culture

All Sasak claim to be Muslim, whether of the more pervasive Waktu Lima orthodox type or of the syncretistic religion embraced by a small percentage of the population. Villages have mosques, and many also have *pesantren*, informal religious schools, and *madrasah*, schools offering more formalized religious education. These institutions are often operated by Tuan Guru, influential religious leaders who have exercised considerable political power among the Sasak.

Religious Beliefs. While the distinctions between Wetu Telu and orthodox Muslims have almost disappeared, a small number of Sasak in more isolated villages still embrace the traditional ancestor cult, with life-crisis ceremonies, agricultural feasts, and beliefs in local holy places, local spirits, and ritual inheritance. Generally Sasak today maintain that they are orthodox Muslims obeying the Five Pillars of Islam: the confession of faith in Allah and Mohammed as his prophet; the five daily prayers, *salat*; the fast during the month of Ramadan, *puasa*; the pilgrimage to Mecca, *hajj*; and the payment of religious tax for charity and mosque upkeep, *zakat*. Traditional belief in ancestral spirits, the rice mother, and spirits that possess people and cause misfortunes are less prevalent than they were formerly. Waktu Lima Sasak believe in Allah, the supreme being; Mohammed, the major prophet; Iblis, the satanic being; evil spirits, witches, and spirit doubles or jinn.

Religious Practitioners. The religious officials present in all Sasak villages are the *kiyai*, of whom the *penghulu* is the official religious leader. However, a few isolated traditional villages still have *pemangku*, officials of sacred places.

Ceremonies. Once prevalent *adat* ceremonies (rituals relating to traditional law), which varied by village, have declined. Replacing them are Islamic ceremonies, which tend to be more individualistic than were the ritual feasts held for life-cycle and agricultural events, and which entail a network of kinship and villagewide obligations.

Arts. Traditional arts include making musical instruments such as gongs, drums, and wooden xylophones (often in carved and painted wooden stands), dance dramas, shadow puppet plays, and Islamic songs and dances. Traditionally large wooden horses for carrying celebrants were made.

Medicine. Illness may be attributed to spirit possession, sorcery, supernatural retribution, reactions to adversity, and disease. The services of *belian*, native healers, are often used.

Death and Afterlife. Islamic officials preside at funerals, and, in traditional communities, at mourning ceremonies held at specified times afterward. The body is washed by kiyai and kin of the same sex, orifices are plugged, and it is shrouded. Burial takes place soon after death. The corpse is laid on its side facing Mecca, with the head pointed south. Traditionalists believe that deceased kin continue to influence future generations. Orthodox Muslims believe in an afterlife earned by the individual through personal actions.

See also Balinese

Bibliography

Cederroth, Sven (1981). *The Spell of the Ancestors and the Power of Mekkah: A Sasak Community on Lombok*. Göteborg: Acta Universitatis Gothoburgensis.

Ecklund, Judith (1977). "Marriage, Seaworms, and Song: Ritualized Responses to Cultural Change in Sasak Life." Ph.D. dissertation, Cornell University.

Krulfeld, Ruth (1974). "The Village Economies of the Sasak of Lombok: A Comparison of Three Indonesian Peasant Communities." Ph.D. dissertation, Yale University.

Krulfeld, Ruth (1986). "Sasak Attitudes towards Polygyny and the Changing Position of Women in Sasak Peasant Villages." In *Visibility and Power: Essays on Women in Society and Development*, edited by Leela Dube and Eleanor Leacock, 194–208. Delhi: Oxford University Press.

RUTH M. KRULFELD

Sea Nomads of the Andaman

ETHNONYMS: Chaolay, Moken, Sea Gypsies

Bands of hunter-gatherers of the sea once ranged freely through the many tiny isles and reefy shoals strewn across the eastern Andaman Sea. These Sea Nomads now inhabit an oceanic fringe extending from the seas off southern Myanmar (Burma) southward along the Malay Peninsula past Thailand to Malaysia. After World War II, many of the islands among which they roamed were settled by mainland peoples moving out to escape a spate of onshore epidemics. From that contact the Sea Nomads began to change, although not extensively at first. It was in the 1980s that their transformation drastically accelerated as mainland entrepreneurs built and staffed tourist industries linking many of the pristine islands off Thailand and Malaysia.

From north to south, from the multitudes of tiny islands along Myanmar's coast down past Thailand to Malaysia, there is today a spectrum of adaptation. Off Myanmar the Sea Nomads are fully animistic and nomadic. To the south there are varying degrees of seminomadism and Islamic influence. The most nomadic of the shore-settling groups build rude temporary shelters close to the tide line on one island after another, inhabiting each for several weeks or months before moving on. The least nomadic have permanent home communities stretching into their islands, from which they go out to sea. Between these poles are those who have central sites they prefer and consider their "home," but who spend much time in temporary shelters on different isles. On a few large islands near the mainland, some groups live and work among mainland people and have abodes in separate zones within alien communities.

The most widespread term applied to these "people of the sea," both by themselves and by others, is "Chaolay." In English they are usually referred to as "Sea Nomads" or "Sea Gypsies." They retain this designation as long as they live within their own groups. Individuals who integrate with mainland-style communities, sometimes by marriage, are no longer called "Chaolay," and are no longer thought of as "people of the sea." The Sea Nomads of the Andaman are related to similar Sea Nomads in the Sulu and South China seas.

Athough it is possible to discern subgroupings within the Sea Nomads of the Andaman, they are essentially a single people. Despite their dispersal and differentiations among them, they have overlapping legends and matching practices. They all speak mutually intelligible dialects of Malay, to which they have added terms from languages they have encountered. They raise their children in similar ways. They seek their livelihood in much the same ways, by freely taking from the abundant mélange of seafood offered by the various shoals and reefs among which they circulate.

The northernmost, those off Myanmar, still live, love, marry, and raise children roaming on handmade outrigger boats. They have no dwellings ashore. They are fully nomadic hunter-gatherers, and call themselves "Moken." Whatever they might gain by luck or labor is shared spontaneously with everyone at hand, including nearby strangers, a practice that slowly fades when they settle down. No mental ledger sheets are kept. They have a sensual sense of unity extending to the sea, to the life in it, and to nature's forces. The sea produces all the things they like, in diverse profusion. Those in the north say: "We have a good life." Those further south say: "We had a good life with few worries in the past."

Traditional Sea Nomads eschew personal ownership. They do not store largesse, nor do they hoard: accumulated goods impede a nomadic way of life. Among the Sea Nomads keeping goods for oneself undermines the subtle social impulse that infuses them with joy, an experience they value deeply. The sociality that is the basis of their way of living engenders a rapport that is not easy to reconcile with the practice of private ownership. To have more of anything than does another, or to domineer by wealth (or in any other way) is a crassness, an atavism, a behavior incompatible with and destructive of their cultivated system and of their collective sense. Where anger, selfishness, deceit, or fraud enter Nomad life, as they do when entrepreneurs come to settle, traditional

Sea Nomad bands must depart or suffer a traumatic collapse of their basic way of being.

The boats they live on, together with their simple seafood-gathering tools, are held in common by those who live and work together. As subsistence hunter-gatherers, not commercial fishers, they take from the sea just what they need for their daily livelihood. They do not catch to sell, have no use for nets, and take no joy in a large catch.

Underlying their adaptive and consensual way of life is their deep social impulse. This basic feature of their culture emerges from a neonatal milieu of profuse and communicative tactile stimulation, which forestalls many of the usual kinds of child frustration. Trust and fondness follow from it as the youngsters grow.

Growing up in such a milieu, children seize on patterns of behavior that increase collective joy. To do this effectively they must first assimilate the desires and states of mind of those around them. The rapport thus cultivated deepens and solidifies during adolescence. The sharpened state of feeling that suffuses Nomad teenage groups creates a deep but subtle intuitive rapport that fosters behavioral and economic consonance.

This social impulse is also a measure of their kinship. Because the impulse was expansive, traditional kinship was accretive, or extendable to outsiders. Spontaneous appreciation of a member of a group by an outsider, followed by continuing joint endeavors, was enough for the outsider to become an accepted member of that group. Such incomers, even temporary ones, were welcomed, thought to be desirable, and usually looked upon with favor.

This type of system is stable in isolation. Faced with predatory commerce and formal law, or even just bad manners, it withers and ultimately collapses. Traditional Sea Nomad bands typically recoil when touched by unkind social forces. When challenged steadily, their deep sociality gives way, collapses irrevocably, sometimes abruptly. Western manners had a ravaging impact, including transient cognitive paralysis and a blanking of intuitive response.

As befits a segmenting, roving people, Sea Nomad legends recount many origins. Because they did not marry within their economic group, Nomad youths made boats to sail beyond, often with an age-mate friend, or several—in part to experience more of the world, in part to find a woman to marry.

When money first came in, the Sea Nomads avoided it. To their way of thinking it could not bring a life half as good as what they had. To avoid it, they formed client-patron relationships with friendly merchants and interposed these patrons between themselves and encroaching commerce. They gave prized seafoods and rare seashells to their merchant patrons. The merchants gave friendship and protection, rice and other foods, alcohol, motors, and fuel. The Nomads rarely counted what they gave and got. They preferred "trust barter" with a friend. The merchants also liked the system, since the commercial value of what they took substantially outweighed what they gave back. In the early phase of adaptation, some Sea Nomads became plunderers of the sea, not for their own commercial gain but for that of patrons. After cultural collapse, they started to exchange larger catches for larger dispensations of alcohol, and, later, money.

When domineering peoples first settled in their regions, the Nomads fled. When there was no longer any place to hide, most turned to Islam for protection. Egalitarian in philosophy, it struck a chord. More important, it offered political protection. Conversion was simple and nominal. Islamic practices were introduced gradually by Muslim teachers who later established mosques.

Nomad legends also speak of animistic groups fleeing Islam to sustain traditional animistic lives in remote regions to the north. Their descendants still follow their traditional life-style off the coast of Myanmar, thanks in part to the isolationistic policies of that country, but also to the pirates ranging there. Pirates long discouraged commerce in the eastern Andaman Sea by their continual predations, but they ignored the Nomads because they had no wealth. Piracy bestowed on the Sea Nomads an additional century of isolated freedom.

Further south, government and commerce began pressing in after World War II. Thailand and Malaysia slowly squelched the pirates off their coasts (though not effectively near Burma). Mainland administrators began insisting that the Nomads join some nation or another, cease their random roaming in seas and isles of other lands, obey national laws, settle down, and be "civilized." By the law mainlanders brought and enforced, the once free islands of the Nomad range became the property of various claimants, people who knew the laws on claiming. Nomads were allowed to live on sites the new owners had no use for—until those sites were also wanted. Eventually they became an underclass on unwanted fringes of their previous domain. Some built shelters on the tide line, the open side facing toward the sea, a land-bound replica of how they had once lived on boats.

In these situations their collective sociality sometimes collapsed. It could not meld with the social forces pushing out among them with deceit and selfishness, anger and contempt. Where such pressure increased, the traditional Nomad mentality gave way, sometimes suddenly, in a catastrophic spate of intense epidemic mental anguish, after which it did not reappear.

Following such collapse, the Nomads turned to massive alcoholic intake (in some places a bit of opium, more recently marijuana); the birth rate increased. Temperaments akin to those of pirates began emerging. Where Islam had been adopted, Muslim social concepts filled some of the existential void. More recently government schools, especially in Thailand, brought a different kind of structure, one still more attuned to twentieth-century commerce.

As fringe destitutes on the disappearing edges of a once prolific range, many Sea Nomads took up low-wage day labor to obtain alcohol. Diseases rarely seen started breaking out—epidemic dysentery, urinary failure, rampant funguses and parasites, and viral epidemics. Half of those Sea Nomads who had been caught by invasive social change were soon dying before the age of 2. Elders all agree that there was very little of such sicknesses in the old days.

Seemingly impelled by imprints from the past, young teenage boys, spurred in part by the venturesomeness of youth, began going off in boats, sometimes for weeks. They would say "We're going off to snare a catch," but it was just an excuse to get away, to be nomads for a while, to live solely from the sea in close-knit harmony. The catches they brought back were usually very small, often none at all. As old ways kept fading and money started catching on, they began increasing the size of their catches. Many of today's modern Sea Nomads are commercial fishermen.

Economic style and the deep sociality changed together. As traditional hunting-gathering gave way to the "new-world" economic order, the deep social impulse was replaced by other behavioral patterns.

As communities became more clearly Islamized, females were increasingly protected by Islamic mores and isolated from maturing boys. Pubescent boys could no longer sleep within their family houses. They went off with older boys to whom they were attracted, joined their ad hoc gangs of friends, and often moved through several such groups. They found and ate their food in these teenage clusters; they slept together on boats, in "boy houses" on the shore, on the pier or in vacant buildings, and sometimes under houses. Such teenage groups became part of the structure of the Sea Nomad communities in this phase of change.

A parallel rapport united teenage girls within extended family households. Such households turned into wealth-accumulating economic units to which boys began contributing after marriage. The bonds forged in the teenage peer groups were transformed into business and political associations after marriage. The male associations linked extended family groups, provided for a new type of cooperation based on in-group self-interest. Catching fish to sell became an accepted practice. Some families started getting wealthy.

In the last stage of conversion, schools and media came in, and then tourists. Mores, traditional and Islamic, started fading. When television comes to an island, the fading drastically accelerates.

"Modern" youths then emulate boy/girl social styles and dress seen on television, adopt brusque offhand manners, deliberately misunderstand, and espouse callousness. Traditional Muslims begin marrying 14-year-old girls to be certain of their purity. These modernizing youths become exploitative entrepreneurs, make sharp deals, and explore techniques of cheating in league with their gang, often with great verve. They take what they can squeeze from strangers, with a sense of triumph and without pity.

See also Bajau; Samal; Selung/Moken; Tausug

Bibliography

Sorenson, E. R. (1991). _Psychosexual Transformation in the Eastern Andaman_, manuscript.

Sorenson, E. R. (1979). "Early Tactile Communication and the Patterning of Human Organization: A New Guinea Case Study." In _Before Speech: The Beginning of Interpersonal Communication_, edited by Margaret Bullowa, 289–305. Cambridge: Cambridge University Press.

E. RICHARD SORENSON

Sedang

The Sedang (Ha[rh] ndea[ng], Xó dâng) are a group located in the highlands of Gia Lai-Cong Tum Province in Vietnam, centered approximately at 17° N by 107° E. The 1985 census of Vietnam counted 96,766 Sedang. "Sedang" is the French name for the group. They call themselves "Ha(rh) ndea(ng)" and are called "Xó dâng" by the Vietnamese. The actual composition of the group is unclear, with some authorities considering the Danja, Rengao, Ca-Rong, Hre, and Halang as subgroups. The Sedang have had much contact with the Bahnar and other local groups, but they strongly resisted French colonization. Traditional villages consisted of longhouses around a central men's house. The economy is based on a combination of swidden and wet-rice cultivation, with millet being an important secondary crop. The village is the most important social unit, with important intervillage alliances and a fairly rigid social structure of a chief, village headman, household chiefs, shamans, smiths, slaves, animals, and spirits and ghosts. Extended households are still the norm, though they have decreased in size over the course of the twentieth century. The traditional religion focuses on the powerful creators and ghosts, particularly of ancestors.

Bibliography

Devereux, George (1937). "Functioning Units in Ha(rh)ndea(ng) Society." *Primitive Man* 10:1–8.

Sek

The Sek (Saek) are a group of about 20,000 (1981) located on both sides of the Mekong River in northeastern Thailand and central Laos. Through extensive contact, the Sek have been largely assimilated into Lao society.

Bibliography

Hickey, Gerald C. (1964). "Sek." In *Ethnic Groups of Mainland Southeast Asia*, edited by Frank M. LeBar, Gerald C. Hickey, and John K. Musgrave, 149–150. New Haven: HRAF Press.

Selung/Moken

ETHNONYMS: The names used by and for nomadic boat people typically refer to the people's connections with the sea. "Moken" (Mawken, Maw khen) is the name people living around the Mergui Archipelago of Myanmar (Burma) use to identify themselves. Originating from a Moken story, the name means "drowned people" or "people of the drowning,"

maw or *l'maw* (drowning, to dip), *o'en-ken* abbreviated to *oke'n* ("salt water"), according to Bernatzik and to White. Anderson mentions people calling themselves Manoot (*menut* or *manut,* people) Ta'au (*teau* or *t'ow,* sea) or "people of the sea." Similar terms for "people" are found in Thailand (*chao*) and Malaysia (*orang*) with words for "sea" (Thai *le;* Malay *laut*) or "water" (Thai *nam*); hence Thais call Moken "Chao Nam" or "Chao Le" and Malays use "Orang Laut." The meaning and etymology of the Burmese name Salon, Selon, Selong, Selung, or Silung is not clear; it may derive from the Thai-Malay placename Salang (Thalang) Phuket, where Moken may have lived. Other names for Moken are associated with sociopolitical status, geography, and environment; these include "Orang Rayat" (Malay, "subject") or "Rayat Laut" ("the sea subjects"), "Orang Pesukuan" ("people divided into clans"), and "Bajau" (Bugis, "subject"), a term denoting sea people of north Borneo and the Sulu Archipelago (often equated with pirates). Local groups may take the name of geographic places where they live (e.g., Orang Barok, for Baruk Bay, on the island on Singkep).

Orientation

Identification. This grouping encompasses diverse, semi-nomadic boat dwellers scattered along the coasts and offshore islands throughout Southeast Asia from Tenasserim in southwest Myanmar down the coasts of Thailand and Malaysia, Singapore, southeast Sumatra, Borneo, and into the Sulu Sea region. "Sea nomads," as they are labeled in the literature, are a maritime-dwelling boat people oriented to the strand, including sand beaches, coral reefs, rocky shores, mangroves, and the sea. The most commonly used name for sea nomads, "Orang Laut," results in confusion, since this name refers not only to boat-dwelling sea peoples but also to strand-living people (in contrast to inland-residing communities known as "Orang Darat").

Location. Within similar nomadic boat adaptations, additional group distinctions can be made based on location, origin, dialect, and recent history. Along the Tenasserim coast and the Mergui Archipelago, the major islands on which Moken wander include Tavoy (Mali), King (Kadan), Elphinstone (Thayawthadangyi, Dung), Grant, and Ross (Daung) in the north; Domel (Letsok-Aw), Kisseraing (Kanmaw), Sullivan (Lanbi), Owen, Malcolm, and Bentinck islands to the south; and the southernmost point of Myanmar at Victoria Point (Kawthaung), including Saint Matthew's (Zadetkyi), Saint Luke's (Zadetkale), and the Loughborough Islands. Moken reside along the Thai coast down to Ko Phra Thong, Tongka, at the foot of Phuket. The Burmese/Thai communities include four distinct dialect groups: Dung (Doang) residing in the northern end of the archipelago around the islands of Elphinstone, Grant, and Ross; the Ja-it dialect group living around Lampi Island and Bokpyn; Lbi speakers living around Victoria Point; and the Lawta dialect group of Lawta and Tongka, Thailand. Farther south along the Thai coast at Ko Lanta Yai and Ko Lanta, in the Trang area, are Orang Laut Kappir (from the Arabic *kafir,* "unbeliever"). Down the Malay Peninsula along the Pontian coast live Desin Dolaq (Orang Kuala, Duano) and Orang Seletar (Selitar, Sletar), Orang Laut communities that the Malaysian government considers part of the Orang Asli community. On Pulau Brani in Singapore Harbor live the Selat. Documented

Johor-Singapore communities that are either extinct or unknown today include Orang Akik, Sabimba, and Orang Biduanda Kallang; with the establishment of Port Swettenham, the British removed the Sabimba and Biduanda Kallang inland to sites in Johor. Orang Laut groups from around the Riau-Lingga archipelago include Orang Tambusa, Galang, and Mantang originally from the Pulau Mantang group of islands south of Pulau Bintan; Orang Moro from Pulau Sugi Bawah in the Riau Archipelago; and Orang Pusek (Persik), Orang Barok, and Orang Sekanak from Singkep in the Lingga Archipelago. The sea nomads of Billiton and Bangka Islands include the Orang Sekah (Sekak, Sekat, Sika). Communities related to the Johor-Singapore and Riau-Lingga groups can also be found along the southeast coast of Sumatra (e.g., Desin Dolaq migrated from Pulau Bengkalis and until World War II visited their kin at the mouth of the Siak River).

Demography. Population statistics are based solely on estimates. Bernatzik estimated the Moken population of Burma to be around 5,000 in 1939. This figure included settled boat nomads. The population for all sea nomads decreased over the past century because of disease and because of attrition as more boat dwellers settled as a result of government intervention (e.g., Skeat and Ridley reported that there were only 8 Orang Biduanda Kallang families left out of the 100 families removed from Singapore to Johor in 1847). 1983 population figures for Orang Laut in Malaysia include 1,924 Desin Dolaq and 542 Orang Selitar. Figures for Riau-Lingga, Bangka, and Billiton Orang Laut in the nineteenth century are unknown, but it is clear that the pattern of decreasing population fits them as well.

Linguistic Affiliation. All sea nomads traditionally spoke non-Malay Austronesian dialects and languages. Today the few remaining Orang Laut communities that maintain their cultural identity speak Malay, with a distinctive pronunciation. When Baptist missionaries established a school among the Moken in 1946, they wrote a Moken script "primer."

History and Cultural Relations

Moken oral history and reconstruction of historical materials postulate origins in the southern end of the Strait of Malacca, suggesting a cultural and historical connection between Moken and peninsular Malaysia's Jakun. Orang Laut history is full of stories of Malay slave raiding and exploitation that forced the sea nomads' settled ancestors to flee in boats and adopt a nomadic maritime life-style. A characteristic consistently recorded about Moken is their timidity and the likelihood of their fleeing outsiders. The transition of sea people into settled coastal fishing peoples, integrating cultural features of the locally dominant culture of the region and accelerating during this past century, was occurring long ago. The sea nomads' maritime mobility and their intermittent and scattered sedentization had a profound effect by carrying and spreading "Malay" cultural traits.

Settlements

Nuclear families form the primary residential boat unit. Five to ten boats form a community and travel together. Communities come together annually, forming flotillas of up to thirty or forty boats. During the southwest monsoon, boat flotillas form in protected bays to wait out the bad weather. Most Moken communities rarely wander more than about 50 kilometers in any direction from their home-base island. For most of the year, maritime Moken reside on 6- to 8-meter-long dugouts constructed with a deck and sailing mast made from palm sheets. The sides of the boat are built up with stems of a palm placed one on top of the other, caulked with tree resin, and lashed together. Amidship, Moken build a hearth with earth on the deck to avoid fire. A sheltered living area, built on deck toward the boat's stern, is constructed of split bamboo arch supports covered with a removable palm-leaf roof, which can be rolled up and stowed away or used as a shelter on shore. When Moken anchor near shore they either build small temporary beach huts or, more typically, continue to reside on boats. Sedentarized Moken construct single-room houses on stilts on the strand or out in the water.

Economy

Subsistence and Commercial Activities. Maritime and sedentarized Moken depend on the sea, fishing and collecting strand life. Moken, who seem never to have been totally self-sufficient, depend on trade for food and other material needs. Most boat dwellers do not grow food, but White mentions sporadic planting of fruit trees. Sedentarized sea nomads (e.g., Orang Laut Kappir and Moken on King Island) do cultivate fruit trees and subsistence crops.

Although an otherwise advanced marine-oriented people, Orang Laut traditionally have used only simple technology. The practice of fishing with nets, lines, and traps, found among many non–Orang Laut strand communities and sedentarized Orang Laut communities, is absent among the sea-dwelling Moken. Spearing and harpooning of fish, turtles, dugong, trepang, and crustaceans at low tide are the most common techniques. Sedentarized and acculturated boat people (e.g., Desin Dolaq) use more elaborate fishing technologies learned from neighboring peoples.

Low-tide strand collecting is the most important activity. Shellfish, including oysters, clams, snails, and crabs, as well as other mollusks and crustaceans, turtle eggs, and sea slugs are collected along the beaches for subsistence and barter. Shallow-water diving for such bartering items as sea slugs, pearl oysters, rays, and sea snails is also important. Forest products collected include wild fruits, roots, honey, and wax. Moken hunt pig and deer with dogs and spears. Domestic animals typically include dogs used in hunting, and chickens; a few households also keep cats.

Traditionally Moken worked for traders, washing tin ore or gathering mangrove wood for charcoal. The Orang Sekana and Galang were both involved in piratical activities with support and promotion by Malay chiefs who had nominal political control over them. Pirate activities had economic, social, and demographic consequences not only for pirating groups but also for the Orang Laut communities being preyed upon. Pacification of many groups is complete, but some piratical activities still continue.

Trading. Much of the collecting Moken do is for barter. The sea products they exchange include trepang, tortoise-shell, mother of pearl, agar, pearls, sea slugs, and shark fins. They barter forest products including birds' nests, woven pandanus mats, and tree resins with Malay and Chinese dealers for rice, sago, cloth, tobacco, alcohol, opium, and iron tools. Bernatzik reported traders marrying Moken women so the women's kin would become their exclusive trading partners. Traders established an exploitative monopoly by putting Moken into debt and dependence through opium addiction. Traders also acted as intermediaries for Moken with the outside world.

Division of Labor. Women were as efficient boat handlers as men. Women gathered strand fauna and wove pandanus mats for sleeping and barter. Men hunted, built boats, and dived for marine life, which women processed by cooking or drying.

Industrial Arts. Wood, grass, liana, bamboo, and pandanus are basic raw materials. Men's boat-building skills are highly praised, as are women's skills in making pandanus mats. Women's potting and men's blacksmithing all but disappeared with the introduction of cheap trade articles.

Kinship

Kin Groups. There are no permanent corporate kin groups. Boat groups are composed of bilateral kin who could provide aid. The large flotillas that come together are probably larger bilateral kin groups.

Kinship Terminology. In White's account gender is distinguished only for parents, parents' siblings, Ego's younger siblings, and people in the second ascending generation. However, Ambler and Anderson include general terms for sister (*lua*) and daughter (*me'*). Kin terms not distinguished by sex may be marked with the designation *kanai* (man) or *binai* (woman) (e.g., *aka binai*, for "elder sister"). Cousins are called "friend" (*ja*), suggesting they are outside the family's "inner circle."

Marriage and Family

Marriage. Moken recognize couples as married when they begin having sexual relations. Couples arrange their own marriages with the consent of the bride's parents, whom the groom asks through an intermediary. The groom may provide a small bride-price to the bride's parents. Marriage ceremonies are only found among Islamized communities. Among some communities (e.g., Sekah and Kallang), a man must have his own boat before he can marry. Few restrictions are placed on the selection of a spouse; partners may be from within or outside a boat community. Marriage between Moken women and non-Moken men is not uncommon. While there is no proscription against polygyny, it is uncommon. There are no reported cases of marriage after widowhood, but according to White there is a stepparent kin term suggesting the possibility. Patrilocality predominates; with the birth of a child, a couple takes up residence on its own boat. The exceptions to this include Orang Sekah and Orang Sama, who reside matrilocally, and Moken, who do not reside with the husband's boat group until after the birth of the couple's first child. White suggests that the Moken see divorce as "sinful."

Domestic Unit. Nuclear families predominate; cases of extended households include young newlyweds and elderly parents. Average household size ranges from four to ten people.

Sociopolitical Organization

Boat communities are autonomous. Mergui boat communities are under the nominal direction of a headman who provides some amount of leadership to boat groups' movements and activities. Among some Riau-Lingga and Billiton groups, headmen had more than nominal authority. Adjacent dominant cultures sometimes imposed community leaders, so office titles vary depending on the dominant culture. Malay lords of Johor and later Binton and Lingga forced Riau-Lingga sea nomads to become their feudal vassals, calling them Orang Rayat ("sea subjects") and persuading the sea people to perform services, including pirating coastal villages and boats.

Religion

Religious Beliefs. Traditional animistic beliefs are allied to Malaysian Orang Asli ideology. Islamic, Christian, and Buddhist beliefs have filtered into the belief systems of local groups to varying degrees. Moken of Mergui are the only group Islam has not penetrated. Orang Laut range from nominal Muslims who continue to eat pork and do not fast during Ramadan to more conservative Muslims.

Nineteenth-century missionaries and government officers recorded Mergui Moken belief in a spirit called Thooda (Thida), which Carrapiett argues derives from the Thai Theoda. A more widespread belief is in good and malicious spirits. Spirits are thought to cause illness and death, storms, thunder and lightning, or provide food and protection from other spirits. Moken believe that spirits require propitiation with food and drink left at temples and carved spirit posts.

Religious Practitioners. Shamans lead ceremonies; they communicate with and make offerings to spirits and exorcise illness from the sick. Shamanic ability is not inherited. Women may become shamans. Sorcerers are believed to be capable of causing sickness and death.

Ceremonies. Reminiscent of B'sisi' and Jah Hut on the Malay Peninsula, Orang Laut shamans pull pain spirits from the sick and lure them into carved figures that are disposed of later. Moken have an annual ceremony for which a number of neighboring boat groups come together to "feed the spirits" and ask for good health and a good year's sea harvest.

Medicine. Nineteenth-century reports of Moken all mention the decimating effects of cholera and smallpox on Moken populations. Illness and death are believed to be caused by evil spirits who enter a body through a wound. The shaman holds healing ceremonies in which he or she enters a trance and calls for spiritual help in bringing about a cure. Sick people propitiate spirits and ask for good health at the annual festival. Midwives assist in the birthing process. There is no ceremony following birth. Mothers name their newborn without ceremony.

Death and Afterlife. Souls go to the east but evil spirits remain near the grave. Moken fear evil spirits so cemeteries are located on an out-of-the-way island. The traditional method of disposal was to place the corpse on a four-post platform wrapped with bamboo sticks; boat owners were buried in their boats, which were cut in half. The boat then became part of the grave goods, which also included the individual's personal possessions. By 1850 platform burials were abandoned for burial on the beach.

See also Bajau; Samal; Sea Nomads of the Andaman

Bibliography

Ambler, G. M. (1938). "A Vocabulary of the Mawken, Salon, or Sea Gypsy Language of the Mergui Archipelago." _Journal of the Royal Asiatic Society of Bengal, Letters_ 4:195–216.

Anderson, John (1890). _The Selungs of the Mergui Archipelago._ London: Trübner & Co.

Bernatzik, Hugo Adolf (1951). _The Spirits of the Yellow Leaves._ London: Robert Hale.

Carrapiett, W. J. S. (1909). _The Salons._ Ethnographical Survey of India, Burma no. 2. Rangoon: Office of the Superintendent, Government Printing.

Lewis, M. Blanche (1960). "Moken Texts and Word-List: A Provisional Interpretation." _Federation Museums Journal_ (Kuala Lumpur) 4:1–102.

Skeat, W. W., and C. O. Blagden (1906). _Pagan Races of the Malay Peninsula._ 2 vols. London: Macmillan.

Skeat, W. W., and H. N. Ridley (1900). "The Orang Laut of Singapore." _Journal of the Straits Branch of the Royal Asiatic Society_ 33:247–250.

Sopher, David E. (1977). _The Sea Nomads: A Study of the Maritime Boat People of Southeast Asia._ Singapore: National Museum of Singapore.

White, Walter Grainge (1922). _The Sea Gypsies of Malaya: An Account of the Mawken People of the Mergui Archipelago with a Description of Their Ways of Living, Customs, Habits, Boats, Occupations._ London: Seeley, Service & Co.

BARBARA S. NOWAK

Semang

ETHNONYMS: Negritos, Pangan; subgroups: Batèk De', Batèk Nòng, Kensiu, Kintak, Jahai, Lanòh, Mendriq, Mintil

Orientation

Identification. The term "Semang" (probably from Central Aslian _sema'_, "human being") was used by nineteenth-century writers for the small, dark-skinned, curly-haired people living in the forests of the Malay Peninsula. Occasionally those on the eastern side of the peninsula were distinguished as "Pangan." Although the ideas that the Semang are a separate race and that race and culture are coterminous have now generally been abandoned, there are enough cultural similarities among the groups called "Semang" to warrant considering them as a single category. Malays usually call Semang and other aboriginal peoples "Sakai" ("savages," "subjects") or "Orang Asli" ("original people"); Thais call Semang "Ngò' Pa" ("frizzy [-haired] people"). Terms used for themselves are variations of "Meni'," among northwestern groups, and "Batèk," among southeastern groups, meaning "human beings of our type." At least nine distinct cultural-linguistic subgroups still exist: Kensiu of eastern Kedah (near Baling) and southern Thailand (Yala Province); Kintak of northwestern Perak (near Gerik); Jahai of northeastern Perak and northwestern Kelantan; Lanòh of northwestern Perak (near Gerik); Mendriq of central Kelantan; Batèk Dè' of southeastern Kelantan and northern Pahang; Batèk Nòng of central Pahang (near Jerantut); Mintil of north-central Pahang (near Cegar Perah), and Mos (or Chong) of the Pattalung-Trang area in southern peninsular Thailand. There may be a few other small groups in southern Thailand.

Location. Semang generally live in the lowlands and foothills in primary and secondary tropical rain forest of southern Thailand and northern peninsular Malaysia between 3°55' and 7°30' N and between 99°50' and 102°45' E. Only the Jahai inhabit higher elevations.

Demography. The population of Semang has remained at about 2,000 since the beginning of the twentieth century, but individual groups have increased or decreased as conditions changed. The 1986 Department of Aboriginal Affairs census reports: Kintak 107, Kensiu 135, Jahai 873, Mendriq 144, Batèk (including Batèk Dè', Batèk Tè', Batèk Nòng, and Mintil) 822, and Lanòh 229.

Linguistic Affiliation. All Semang languages—except that of the Lanòh, who speak a Central Aslian language—are in the Northern Aslian Family of the Aslian Stock of Mon-Khmer languages. Most Semang also speak Malay, and many Malay loanwords have been absorbed into all Semang languages.

History and Cultural Relations

The Semang are probably descendants of the Hoabinhian rain-forest foragers who inhabited the Malay Peninsula from 10,000 to 3,000 years ago. After the arrival of agriculture in the peninsula about 4,000 years ago, some Hoabinhians probably became farmers while others—ancestors of the Semang—continued foraging, possibly supplementing their stores by trading with the agriculturalists. Semang probably traded with early Malay-speaking settlers as well, but relations gradually soured with the growth of the Malay population and its political power, culminating in extensive Malay slave raiding of Semang and other aboriginal peoples (i.e., Orang Asli) in the nineteenth century. The British colonial government banned slavery in the late nineteenth century and instituted policies to protect Orang Asli. The Department of Aboriginal Affairs, established in 1954 to win Orang Asli away from Communist insurgents, is now charged with providing education, health care, and economic development to Orang Asli. Relations with Malays tend to be strained because of the condescending attitude of the Malays and government pressures on Semang to become Muslims. Relations with non-Malays (Chinese, Indians, and other Orang Asli) are generally more amiable.

Settlements

Until recently most Semang were nomadic, living in temporary camps lasting from one night to six weeks, and some still are. The camps consist of a cluster of lean-to shelters, each housing a conjugal family, a widow or widower, or a group of unmarried adolescent boys and/or girls. Camps range from two to twenty shelters—about six to sixty people. Camp composition varies as families move in or leave to join other camps. Since the 1960s the Department of Aboriginal Affairs has attempted to settle many Semang in "regroupment projects" with Malay-style wooden houses. Typically these are used only as base camps by groups that also live in forest camps. The agricultural Semang groups—Lanòh, Mendriq, and Batèk Nòng—live in small semipermanent villages.

Nomadic groups make small lean-tos of palm thatch. Western Semang groups sometimes arrange their lean-tos in two rows facing each other to form a communal tunnel-hut with openings at each end. More permanently settled Semang live in small Malay-style bamboo and thatch houses or, in the regroupments, in plank houses built by the Department of Aboriginal Affairs.

Economy

Subsistence and Commercial Activities. Until recently most Semang lived by hunting and gathering wild foods and trading forest products for cultivated foods and manufactured goods. Some groups, such as the Batek Dè', still live this way. Yet even the most nomadic groups plant a few crops from time to time, and most work temporarily for outsiders (e.g., helping Malay farmers harvest rice in return for a share of the crop). This economy is characterized by frequent switching of activities as opportunities change. Collecting forest products for trade is usually the most favored activity, followed by wage labor, subsistence foraging, and horticulture. The Lanòh, Mendriq, and Batèk Nòng have been semi-settled swidden horticulturalists since early in this century. The Department of Aboriginal Affairs has attempted to persuade all Semang to live in government settlements, where occupants are trained in commercial crop production. Many Semang who move to these settlements—after being displaced by dams, logging, or development projects—resist full-time farming, opting instead to collect forest products for trade. The staple carbohydrate of the foraging economy is wild yams (*Dioscorea*) of at least twelve species, which are found in relative abundance year-round. Other wild foods include bamboo shoots, nuts, seasonal fruits, and honey. Hunting with blowpipes and poison darts provides most of the meat, mainly from arboreal animals such as monkeys, gibbons, and birds. Digging bamboo rats out of their burrows and fishing with hook and line, nets, poison, and spears also provide animal protein. Some Semang formerly used bows and arrows to kill larger game, but this practice disappeared, for no obvious reason, early in this century. Semang seldom set traps. Slash-and-burn horticultural crops include dry rice, cassava, maize, and sweet potatoes. Foragers share foods throughout the camp; among horticulturalists food sharing is concentrated within extended families.

Some nomadic Semang keep dogs, valued as watchdogs but useless in blowpipe hunting. Young monkeys, birds, etc. may become pets. Settled groups sometimes keep dogs and cats as pets and raise chickens for food or trade.

Industrial Arts. Semang utilize forest materials, such as bamboo (for blowpipes, dart quivers, cooking vessels, water containers, combs, sleeping platforms, rafts), wood (for knife handles, sheaths, meat-drying racks), pandanus (for mats and baskets), bark (for baskets and, formerly, bark cloth), and rattan (for bindings, baskets, ladders, belts). They use metal knives and axes obtained through trade and rework metal scraps into harpoon points, spear tips, and digging-stick blades.

Trade. The Semang have traded forest products for cultivated foods and manufactured goods at least since the early nineteenth century and probably since the advent of agriculture in the peninsula. Their survival does not depend on trade, however, although life would be much more difficult without iron tools, for example. Many items obtained through trade are luxury goods, such as tobacco, or substitutes for natural foods and materials, such as rice and flour for wild tubers, sugar for honey, cloth for bark cloth. Semang have lived without trade during periods of hostilities: during intense slave raiding, the Japanese occupation, and the 1948–1960 Communist insurrection (known as "the Emergency"). Forest products collected by Semang for trade—resins, wax, thatch, plant medicines, honey, rattan, and resinous woods—vary according to demand. Trade partners include both Malay and Chinese wholesalers and shopkeepers. In the last century some Malays established patron-client relationships with groups of Semang.

Division of Labor. A division of labor by gender exists, but it is a statistical tendency apparently resulting from practical considerations rather than norms or ideology that define certain tasks as appropriate only to one sex. Most activities are done by both sexes, often working together in mixed groups or husband-wife teams. For example, both men and women dig tubers and care for small children, but women spend more time on these tasks. Most blowpipe hunting and making and repair of hunting equipment is done by men, but women may hunt and own blowpipes. Men generally do tasks that take great strength (e.g., felling or climbing large trees) or mobility (blowpipe hunting) or that are incompatible with child care, and women do tasks that take less strength and mobility (because they have to carry babies), such as digging up tubers and bamboo rats, fishing, and weaving pandanus. Individual specialization is almost entirely absent except in the religious sphere.

Land Tenure. Each group regards a certain area as its home (the *saka'*), although claims of exclusive rights to an area vis-à-vis other groups (Semang or others) are seldom made and, in any case, are unenforceable. People have access to all wild resources found in their group's area and have the right to clear any land for planting that is not already in use. Crops, but not the land, are the property of the conjugal family that planted them, although food-sharing rules apply after harvest. Western Semang allow individuals to own poison trees and perennial fruit trees they plant or discover (a concept similar to that of the adjacent Temiar Senoi), but Batèk Dè' regard such trees as free to all. The Malaysian government does not recognize any traditional Semang rights over land or resources.

Kinship

Kin Groups and Descent. The only corporate group among the Semang is the conjugal family. Many camps contain one or more extended families, but these are transitory entities, forming and breaking up as the component conjugal families move. There are no "bands" of fixed membership that always camp together. There are no descent groups or descent ideology.

Kinship Terminology. Semang relationship terminologies are bilaterally symmetrical. They merge sibling and cousin terms but distinguish collateral relatives at the +1 and −1 generation levels. Cousin-sibling terms contain relative age distinctions. Some groups classify cousins as "older" and "younger" according to their ages relative to Ego and some according to the relative ages of the linking parents.

Marriage and Family

Marriage. Semang generally choose their own spouses; parents have little influence. Most Semang prohibit marriage between traceably related consanguines or affines. In theory the prospective husband should ask the girl's parents for permission, but this does not always happen. The marriage "ceremony" may consist only of the couple setting up a household together. Often the couple holds a small feast. Some groups expect the groom to give gifts, usually trade goods, to the wife's parents, and the wife to give handmade items to the groom's parents. Horticultural groups expect a new husband to perform bride-service for a year or two, helping in the wife's parents' garden. Polygyny and polyandry are permitted but rare. There is no fixed postmarital residence rule. If the bride is young, the couple may stay near her parents until she feels secure. Later they may alternate between the camps of the parents or camp apart from them. Horticultural groups expect the couple to settle with the bride's parents during the bride-service year(s). But most groups prohibit physical contact between opposite-sex affines and postpubescent consanguines.

The acceptability of divorce varies (Batèk Nòng prohibit it), but it occurs in most groups, especially among young couples without children. Either spouse can initiate divorce, which is accomplished by moving out of the joint shelter. Some divorces are acrimonious, but it is not unusual for former spouses, both remarried, to live amiably in the same camp. Prohibitions between in-laws continue even after a couple divorces. Young children of divorced couples usually stay with the mother; older children make their own choices and often alternate between parents. Stepparents usually treat the spouse's children like their own.

Domestic Unit. The family shelter houses parents and their preadolescent children. Adolescent daughters sleep in an extension or share a separate shelter with other girls. Adolescent boys usually share separate lean-tos. Western Semang tunnel-houses provide contiguous housing for conjugal family units. Occasionally more than one family in a settled group will share a Malay-style house, but each family has its own section and cooking fire.

Inheritance. Principles of inheritance of personal possessions vary. Among the Batèk Dè', personal possessions go to the surviving spouse, if there is one, who may distribute some of them to the children. Some personal items are left on or in the grave. Among the Western Semang, ownership of poison and fruit trees passes to the deceased's children of both sexes.

Socialization. Both parents look after their offspring from earliest childhood, although mothers spend more time with them, especially when they are still nursing. Children learn most skills and social norms casually, by observation and practice, often in play groups of mixed ages and sexes. Children have great freedom; corporal punishment is rare. Parents teach adolescents complicated skills such as pandanus weaving or blowpipe hunting.

Sociopolitical Organization

Social Organization. Conjugal families are the basic units of society. They are linked flexibly by bonds of kinship and friendship. There are no social classes.

Political Organization. No adult Semang has authority over any other adult or the means of coercing others. Individual autonomy is highly respected. Competent or persuasive individuals, male and female, may emerge as natural leaders, but people need not follow their advice. Some men are designated as "headmen" by the Department of Aboriginal Affairs, but they are only mediators between the group and outsiders and have no authority within the group.

Social Control. There are no coercive control mechanisms. Antisocial behavior is discouraged by informal social pressure and through concepts of disease that blame anyone who mistreats or frustrates another as the cause of illness in the victim. Some norms, such as the prohibition on incest, are believed to be enforced by the thunder god, who kills the offender with a violent thunderstorm or disease.

Conflict. Semang abhor violence. Disputes between Semang are infrequent and are usually settled by a public airing of grievances resulting in a consensus solution. Individuals who do not get along tend not to camp together. They usually respond to conflict with outsiders by moving where they cannot be found.

Religion and Expressive Culture

Religious Beliefs. As the Semang have no religious authorities or written scriptures, beliefs vary from group to group and even person to person, but many elements of the belief systems are shared among Semang and between Semang and other Orang Asli. The earth is generally pictured as a disk of land resting on a huge snake (_naga'_) or turtle that floats in an underground sea. Above the atmosphere is the firmament, a cool, sandy land with flowers and fruits. The earth is connected to the firmament by one or more stone pillars, an image probably drawn from the limestone hills of the peninsula. The firmament, underworld, and stone pillars are populated by immortal superhuman beings who created the rain forest to supply human needs on earth.

All groups believe that numerous immortal superhuman beings live on the firmament and stone pillars and under the earth. Some superhumans once lived on earth as humans and return occasionally to visit or listen to the singing of the Semang; they may be met in dreams. Most superhumans are anonymous and grouped in broad categories, often associated with natural phenomena such as wind and fruit (e.g., the Cenoi of the western groups). Some have individual names and identities and may be termed "deities." The most prominent is the thunder god (Karey; Batèk Dè'; Gobar) who sends thunderstorms to topple trees on Semang who break prohibitions (*telañ* or *lawac*), for example, against mocking certain animals or mixing incompatible foods. In punishing humans, the thunder god may collaborate with a female deity of the underworld—called the "Grandmother" (Ya') and sometimes confounded with the earth-supporting snake (naga')—who produces a flood beneath the offender. The thunder god also punishes offenders with disease or a tiger attack. To avert his wrath the offender makes a blood offering by scraping a small amount of blood from the shin with a knife, mixing it with water, and throwing it to the thunder god and Grandmother. Most groups personify one or more other celestial beings (e.g., Kensiu; Tapn). After death Semang become immortal superhumans and can visit earth.

Religious Practitioners. Ritual specialists (*hala'*) are thought to communicate with the superhumans through dreams or trance, or even to be superhumans themselves. The latter, called "big hala'" among the western groups, can take on the body of a tiger and protect the Semang by driving off ordinary tigers. "Small hala'" are ordinary mortals who know some curing techniques. The potential to be a big hala' is hereditary, descending bilaterally to both sexes, but a big hala' must learn songs, spells, medicines, and techniques. Big and small hala' receive such knowlege from superhumans through dreams or from other hala'. The best method is to wait at the grave of a "dead" shaman until he appears in tiger form, then return him to human form by blowing incense over him; the shaman will then teach the novice.

Ceremonies. The major rituals, including the blood offering, center on communication with the superhumans. Some western groups believe the Cenoi can possess shamans in trance, speak to the people through them, and convey songs or instructions for curing. The Batèk Dè' hold singing sessions to ask superhumans for fruit and, after the fruit season, to thank them. In cases of serious illness, singers may go in trance to meet the superhumans, who may teach them cures. Rites of passage are little developed except in connection with death.

Arts. Blowpipes, quivers, and bamboo combs are decorated with geometric and floral patterns. Both sexes wear flowers, leaves, and pigments, especially at singing sessions.

Medicine. Semang attribute most diseases to breaking prohibitions or to the intrusion of noxious substances from the environment, especially in food. Herbal medicines are drunk in infusions or massaged into the skin. Curing songs and spells are acquired from superhumans. Shamans may convey the healing power of the superhumans to the patient through magical quartz crystals (*cebu*), in the west, or cooling dew (*mun*), among the Batèk Dè'.

Death and Afterlife. Most groups believe that after death the shadow-soul goes to an island afterworld at the western horizon, but it may first linger at the grave as a dangerous ghost. Tigers are thought to come to devour the corpse. Thus death rituals combine protective measures, such as fleeing the site of the death and erecting symbolic barriers around the grave, with measures to hurry the shadow-soul on its way, such as burning incense. Most groups bury the corpse in a shallow grave. Some personal possessions are placed with the body or in a leaf shelter on top of the grave, and food and water are provided for the deceased. The Batèk Dè', who believe that the afterworld is above the firmament, place the corpse on a platform in a tree to assist the shadow-soul in reaching the sky and to protect the body from tigers. Most groups reserve tree burial, or burial with the head above ground, for great shamans.

Bibliography

Endicott, Kirk (1979). *Batek Negrito Religion*. Oxford: Clarendon Press.

Evans, I. H. N. (1937). *The Negritos of Malaya*. Cambridge: Cambridge University Press.

Schebesta, Paul (1928). *Among the Forest Dwarfs of Malaya*. Translated by Arthur Chambers. London: Hutchinson.

Schebesta, Paul (1954). *Die Negrito Asiens: Wirtschaft und Soziologie*. Vienna and Mödling: St. Gabriel-Verlag.

Schebesta, Paul (1957). *Die Negrito Asiens: Religion und Mythologie*. Vienna and Mödling: St. Gabriel-Verlag.

KIRK ENDICOTT

Senoi

ETHNONYMS: Sakai (Malay for "infidel slave"); Senoi or Mai in the Central Aslian language; Smaq or Mah in South Aslian; Orang in Malay with words added from Malay or other languages for "hill" (Bukit), "upriver country" (Darat, Seraq, Seroq, Ulu) or "forest" (Bri, Hutan, Rih). Local groups take the name of the watersheds where they live.

Orientation

Identification. The criteria used to classify people as "Senoi" are inconsistent. "Senoi" generally refers to peoples who speak Central Aslian languages and subsist by means of swidden agriculture. These include the Semai (central Sakai), Temiar (north Sakai, Temer, Ple), and Jah Hut (south Sakai). Also included are the Che Wong (Beri Chuba); the Semelai, former South Aslian speakers who now speak an Austronesian language; the Semoq Beri; and the Btsisí (Mah Meri, Besisi, Betisek). The language criterion is used inconsistently with these groups. Excluded are the Lanòh, Semnam, and Sabum classified as Semang, although they speak Central Aslian. In this summary, "Senoi" is used in the cultural sense to include the Che Wong and Semelai and exclude the Btsisí peoples whom the Malaysian government has only recently pressured into agriculture.

Location.   Most Senoi live in rain-forested mountains and foothills of the Main mountain range, which bisects Malaya from north-northwest to south-southeast. Temiar inhabit south Kelantan and northeast Perak; Semai inhabit northeast Pahang and southeast Perak. The other four groups are in south-central Pahang. Government programs are encouraging the rapid clearing of the forests covering the steep slopes.

Demography.   Official 1983 figures listed 18,500 Semai, 1,300 Temiar, 2,500 Jah Hut, 200 Che Wong, 1,800 Semoq Beri, and 3,000 Semelai. The Senoi consititute less than 0.5 percent of the Malaysian population. Rapid Senoi population growth and the loss of traditional lands have led to overcrowding in several west Semai settlements. Men outnumber women in all age groups, perhaps because of the number of deaths in childbirth.

Linguistic Affiliation.   Senoi languages are classified in the Aslian Branch of the Austroasiatic Family: Che Wong is North Aslian; Temiar, Semai, and Jah Hut are Central Aslian; and Semelai and Semoq are South Aslian.

History and Cultural Relations

The Senoi arrived on the peninsula around 8000–6000 B.C., perhaps mixing with Semang peoples already there. Malays arrived millennia later, at first trading peacefully and even mixing with the Senoi. The rise of Malay statelets turned the Senoi first into dependents and then, following Malay conversion to Islam, into despised pagans who served as raw material for Indonesian slavers who murdered adults and kidnapped children under the age of 9. The word *sakai* recalls this history, which Senoi over 50 years of age experienced personally and relate to their children. Although mistrust of the Malays remains strong, government policy is designed to convert the Senoi to Islam and bring them into the mainstream as landed or unlanded peasants.

Settlements.   Traditionally, the Senoi live in settlements of 30–200 people who rarely leave their home watershed (*sakaq*, traditional territory). Few people in their lives travel more than 20 kilometers from their birthplace. Settlements are usually strung along high ground near the junction of a stream and river. Dwellings are occupied by nuclear or small extended families, with most settlements having a large house or longhouse for community meetings and ceremonies. Some hill Temiar bands live in 30-meter-long longhouses that hold up to sixty people in nuclear-family compartments. In low-population-density areas (east Semai, Temiar), bands settle for three to eight years, moving on when the land is exhausted. Where population density is increasing, because of population growth and encroachment by non-Senoi (west Semai), people live in compact settlements except just before and during harvest, when each family moves to a simple house in its own swidden. Finally, the wet-rice agriculturalists such as the Jah Hut live in more permanent settlements. Houses of bamboo, bark, and woven palm-frond (*plook*) shingles are built on stilts 1 to 3.5 meters high, or up to 9 meters high where tigers and elephants are common. Even where people can afford Malay-style planks, kitchen floors are slatted for easy waste disposal.

Economy

Subsistence and Commercial Activities.   Subsistence rests mainly on growing rice and manioc, supplemented by hunting, fishing, and the sale of forest products like rattan, resin, and wild banana leaves. The ancient starch staples were Job's tears and foxtail millet; they have been replaced in the last 200 years by maize and manioc, which were introduced by Portuguese traders. Rice seems to have spread widely only about seventy years ago. Fruit-tree groves are especially important in settled communities since inherited trees bind people more closely to their *sakaq*. In the last twenty-five years, some Senoi have begun growing rubber as part of a government campaign to settle them in Malay-style villages. Traditional agriculture is slash-and-burn, using only dibbles and machetes. Cereals are planted in midsummer, with the option of a smaller planting in spring. The goal is to plant cultivars of all crops so that some will survive no matter what happens. Swiddens are plagued by *lalang* grass, pests such as rats and rice-eating birds, deer, and elephants. Harvesting is done year-round as the need dictates; only rice harvests are marked by ritual. Basket traps are the main fishing tool. Poisons, weirs, corrals, baskets, spears, and hooks are also used. Men hunt with blowguns and poisoned darts and the Semai and Temiar use spears. Most wild meat is taken via snares, deadfalls, spear traps, and birdlines. The whole community shares any large animal such as a deer, pig, python, or binturong (an arboreal civet cat). Dogs, chickens, goats, ducks, and cats are bred, the chickens for food and the goats and ducks for sale to the Malays.

Industrial Arts.   Bamboo, rattan, and pandanus are the basic raw materials. Bark cloth from four species of tree is now worn only ritually. Basketry is sophisticated, especially among settled groups. Aboriginal pottery making and metallurgy apparently disappeared as a consequence of the need to flee from slavers. Bamboo rafts and, rarely, dugouts are used for water transport.

Trade.   Traditional Senoi share on the basis of need rather than trade with one another. Silent trade with the Semang is no longer important. Rattan, resin, lumber, fruits, and butterflies are traded with Malay or Chinese dealers for metal tools, salt, cloth, tobacco, and sugar or sold for money. The Jah Hut, with government encouragement, sell sculpture to tourists. Traditional Temiar trade was handled by two *mikong*, men descended from Thais married to Temiar women. These trusted intermediaries distributed machetes and other trade goods among their clients.

Division of Labor.   Although there are no formal sanctions and many exceptions occur, there is a statistical division of labor by sex with men hunting, making blowpipes and traps, and felling large trees and women gathering plant products and making and fishing with baskets. Male and female activities are often complementary, as in planting and house building.

Land Tenure.   A family has exclusive rights to the land it clears until it stops producing food. Ties between bands and their *sakaq* are sentimental, not jural. Land cannot be sold. Neither British nor Malay law recognizes Senoi land rights.

Kinship

Kin Groups and Descent. Nuclear families, which own the fields, are unstable but basic. Extended families and households, mutually hard to distinguish, are less important. The local group, usually a village but sometimes several villages, has corporate ties to a sakaq. As people move to a new sakaq freely, local groups often split or coalesce. Owners retain rights to trees after moving. Larger kin groups including kindreds (west Semai, *jek*) and ramages (west Semai, *guw*) spread through several sakaq and do not include affines. Ramages occur within major watersheds because of the easy travel on the river, with the groups taking their names from the rivers. Members sometimes cooperate in fish drives. Although ramages are seen as territorial, the west Semai talk of affiliation on the basis of descent from a common ancestor. Informal age grading is reflected in the kinship terminology, which has a special designation for an adolescent who has not yet settled down.

Kinship Terminology. There are differences among the six Senoi groups in the emphasis placed on lineality and generation in kinship terminology: Central Aslian distinguishes elder and younger siblings but not brother and sister; South Aslian distinguishes elder brothers from elder sisters; Semelai distinguishes nonlineal from lineal kin in the parents' generation. With some exceptions, Semai and Temiar use one term per generation for the six generations above and one below oneself. Kin terms also reflect informal age grades of neonate, child, adolescent boy/girl, old woman/man. Teknonymy is widely used and people are expected to use respectful teknonyms for mature and old people, at least so long as their children are young enough to need such protection.

Marriage and Family

Marriage. Casual east Semai and Temiar liasons shade into marriage with little ritual, although local elders may intervene in inappropriate teenage love affairs. Other Senoi have modified Malay weddings. West Semai have a form of bride-price. Less than 5 percent of marriages are polygynous, sometimes sororal. These marriages are often unstable, as first wives feel neglected and leave. West Semai polygynists usually have wives in separate settlements, spending some time with each. Only the Temiar have polyandry, often fraternal. East Semai brothers have limited access to each other's wives, if the wives consent. Since most sakaq residents are kin, marriage tends to be exogamous. Postmarital residence is ambilocal, with the couple living first in the wife's sakaq, then the husband's, then the wife's again and so on until they settle. Divorce is common, often following long periods of living apart. Children and the parents decide on where the children will then live.

Domestic Unit. Nuclear families predominate in most Senoi groups, with extended families found in all groups, ranging from the hill Temiar longhouses to the more amorphous arrangements resulting from overcrowding among the east Semai.

Inheritance. Land goes to the surviving spouse, with siblings or children receiving movable goods, depending on the need. West Semai divide land or trees acquired after marriage equally between widow(er)s and close blood relatives of the deceased.

Sociopolitical Organization

After the traditional social structure was destroyed by slave raiding, Senoi government was consensual. Persuasive people, usually men, were "elders." Taboos against interfering in individual autonomy, expressed as taboos against violence, left no sanctions available to elders who were not persuasive enough to keep people from ignoring them or from moving away. Thus verbal facility, not wealth or generosity, was the prime prerequisite for leadership. Spiritual wisdom generated through contact with familiar spirits and manifested in dreams was also important, so that rivals might criticize a man for representing his wife's dreams as his own. The end of slaving in the 1930s increased contact with outsiders who wanted to deal with "spokesmen," thus creating Senoi "headmen," who almost always were men modeled on the outsider's own pattern. A Communist insurrection in the 1950s speeded the infiltration of state sovereignty into the interior, as the British made headmanship official by giving a letter of investiture as headman to one man in each band, following the model established by the Malay sultans for the dependent Senoi. The emphasis on individual autonomy still limits a headman's authority, and other elders (west Semai "field heads," for example) retain some power. Ultimate authority rests with the Malay-run Jabatan Orang Asli (Indigenes' Department).

Religion and Expressive Culture

Religious Beliefs. Fear of violence and respect for individual autonomy pervade Senoi life. Children, who are especially vulnerable, need protection by taboos, but parents will infringe a taboo to see if it applies to their particular child. Parents may threaten boisterous children to make them stop behavior that is believed to unleash thunder squalls; but because they regard children as controlling their own lives they will ask children barely old enough to talk if they want a penicillin shot. Everyone fears thunder squalls, but individuals, not communities, make the "blood sacrifice" that appeases storms. For the Senoi, human beings are free, alone, and in constant danger. Individual autonomy applies to religious belief, creating a formless animism. The cosmic order is seen as so fragile that people must always be careful not to destroy it and unleash obscene, ravening horrors into the world, a belief that may be related to the slaving experience. People, most animals, and other entities have several detachable "souls" each. Pain spirits abound. Jah Hut carvings give outsiders some insight into the Senoi spirit world. Christian missionaries were active in the 1930s, producing the first written text. Government proselytizing for Islam is unpopular.

Religious Practitioners. People become "adept" by having familiars. A familiar appears in dreams, attracted by a dreamer's body. A dreamer who chooses to adopt the familiar becomes adept, able with the familiar's help to diagnose and cure diseases caused by pain spirits. Women may reject the offer, since trance is exhausting, but some become "adept" anyway, as midwives. Midwives and adepts tend to marry one another.

Ceremonies. Spirits are so timid that most ceremonies are conducted in darkness at night. Because spirits love fragrance and beauty, dark ceremonial areas are decked with flowers and fragrant leaves. Adepts sing to attract their familiars.

Spirit possession and trance occur everywhere but take local forms. Ceremonies, usually lasting two or six nights, are held only for diseases involving pain spirits or loss of spiritual health by individuals (midwives, pregnant women) or communities. The only annual ceremony is after the rice harvest, now synchronized with the Chinese New Year. Teknonymy for both parents begins with pregnancy. Both the pre- and postnatal periods contain ritual restrictions, most of which apply to the mother.

Death and Afterlife.   Everyone has several souls, but it is the shadows that become ghosts. Corpses are buried across the stream from the settlement, as ghosts cannot cross running water. Great adepts may be afforded a tree burial. The former practice of abandoning a settlement after someone dies is no longer followed. Mourning lasts a week to a month, during which there are taboos on making music, dancing, and getting dressed up. Six days after the burial a feast "closes the grave." Despite the use of grave goods and vague ideas about a flower-fragrant afterlife, the Senoi are dubious about life after death.

See also Semang; Temiar

Bibliography

Benjamin, Geoffrey (1976). "Austroasiatic Subgroupings and Prehistory." In *Austroasiatic Studies*. Part 1, edited by Philip N. Jenner, Laurance C. Thompson, and Stanley Starosta, 37–128. Honolulu: University Press of Hawaii.

Couillard, Marie-Andrée (1980). *Tradition in Tension: Carving in a Jah Hut Community*. Penang: Penerbit Universiti Sains Malaysia.

Dentan, Robert Knox (1979). *The Semai: A Nonviolent People of Malaya*. Fieldwork edition. New York: Holt, Rinehart & Winston.

Fix, Alan (1977). *The Demography of the Semai Senoi*. Anthropological Papers, no. 62. Ann Arbor: University of Michigan, Museum of Anthropology.

Gianno, Rosemary (1989). *Semelai Culture and Resin Technology*. Memoir of the Connecticut Academy of Arts and Sciences, no. 22. New Haven.

Hood, H. M. S. (1979). "The Cultural Context of Semelai Trance." *Federation Museums Journal* (Kuala Lumpur) 24:107–124.

Howell, Signe (1983). *Our People: Chewong Society and Cosmos*. Oxford: Oxford University Press.

Robarchek, Clayton A. (1979). "Conflict, Emotion, and Abreaction: Resolution of Conflict among the Senoi Semai." *Ethos* 7:104–123.

ROBERT KNOX DENTAN

Shan

ETHNONYMS: Burmese Shan, Chinese Shan, Dai, Hkamti Shan, Ngiaw, Ngio, Pai-I, Tai Khe, Tai Khun, Tai Long, Tai Lu, Tai Mao, Tai Nu, Thai Yai

Orientation

Identification.   The people refer to themselves as "Tai," often with a second term identifying their particular Tai group. "Shan" is a Burmese term that Europeans use. The word "Shan," used by colonial writers, refers to any non-Siamese Tai group. Burmese refer to these people as "Shan" and many of these people also use "Shan" as a broad label to refer to themselves and other lowland Tai peoples in Myanmar (Burma), southern China, and northern Thailand. Siamese refer to Shan living in Thailand and in the northern area of the Shan State as "Thai Yai" (big Thai); the people in this area refer to themselves as "Tai Long" (great Tai). Northern Thai refer to Shan as "Ngio" or "Ngiaw," a term Shan find pejorative. Chinese refer to Shan living in southern China as "Dai" or "Pai-I." There are a number of different Tai groups living in this area, including the Tai Lu, similar to the Northern Thai; Tai Mao, similar to the Tai Long, who refer to them as "Tai Nu" (northern Tai) or "Tai Khe" (Chinese Tai). Those in Kengtung, Myanmar, refer to themselves as "Tai Khun."

Location.   Shan are widespread in mountain valleys in southern China, eastern Myanmar (the Shan State), and northern Thailand. As in the rest of monsoon Asia, there is a hot dry season from February until June, when the rains begin. These last until October or November, followed by a colder season until February. In the higher elevations of Myanmar and southern China there are frosts.

Demography.   Population estimates are practically meaningless. Reports from Myanmar systematically underreport minority populations; a 1931 British census reported 1.3 million Shan in Burma. Thai census figures do not include a separate Shan figure since most are Thai citizens. The third Chinese national census, in 1982, lists the number of Dai as 839,000.

Linguistic Affiliation.   Shan speak Thai, linguistically related to Siamese and Lao. Tai Long, Tai Mao, Tai Khun, and Tai Lu all have separate scripts: Tai Long resembles Burmese; Tai Mao, an angular Tai Long; and Tai Khun and Tai Lu, Northern Thai. The scripts were primarily used for religious texts and court chronicles. Most men learned to read and write when they were ordained as novices or monks; some women also learned to read and write.

History and Cultural Relations

Shan migrated from southern China around A.D. 1000, eventually establishing numerous small states in the mountainous region of northern Burma. Shan princes have been involved in the politics of the region, paying tribute to Burma, China, and Chiang Mai at various times. After the British conquest of Burma, most Shan states paid tribute to Burma, although the more easterly states were establishing relationships with Chiang Mai and Central Thailand. At this time there were eighteen major states ruled by princes and twenty-five states ruled by lesser officials. During the British period the Shan states were administered indirectly, through their ruling princes. During this period, borders were drawn administratively separating the Shan in Thailand from those in Burma. At Burmese independence the Shan states were consolidated into the Shan State. Since the 1950s Shan in Burma (now Myanmar) have been engaged in a military struggle to regain control of their area. Their goals range from forming an independent state to being federally associated with a changed Burmese state. Shan in Thai areas are not engaged in this struggle.

Settlements

Shan villages are nucleated settlements ranging from 10 to 500 or more households.

Economy

Subsistence and Commercial Activities. The majority of Shan are farmers growing rice to eat and a variety of crops to sell. Ideally Shan grow rice in irrigated fields; however, in areas where there is limited irrigable land, they also slash-and-burn fields to grow hill rice. In Thailand farming is becoming mechanized as people buy small tractors to replace water buffalo and as they use threshing machines for both rice and soybeans. Farming in Myanmar is not mechanized. What cash crops people grow depend on local ecology and the village's location; near towns and larger villages people grow vegetables to sell in the market. Elsewhere, they grow soybeans, peanuts, garlic, onions, sunflowers, pumpkins, sesame, chili peppers, pineapples, bananas, coconuts, and betel nuts.

Industrial Arts. People use bamboo to make a variety of baskets, mats, and handles for knives and other implements. Metal parts such as knife blades are purchased. In Myanmar, Shan make traditional carrying bags, clothes, carvings, and paintings.

Trade. In the past, Shan men participated in the oxen caravan trade moving industrial goods from India and Burma into northern Thailand. With the development of roads, this caravan trade has disappeared. Now industrial goods move through Thailand into Myanmar in exchange for gems, cattle, and traditional Shan goods. Shan act as wholesalers, moving these goods through northwestern Thailand and eastern Myanmar. In the past, Shan women engaged in more local trade in food and domestic goods. With better transportation, most of this trade has been replaced by markets where women are the retailers.

Division of Labor. Men plow and harrow the irrigated fields and women transplant irrigated rice, although occasionally men may help transplant. Men hunt. Women do most of the domestic work such as laundry, cooking, and carrying water. These tasks are often delegated to a competent girl or occasionally to a boy.

Land Tenure. Hill fields are held in usufruct and not sold. Traditionally irrigated fields were held in usufruct but could be used as security for loans or mortgaged. In Thailand people are now acquiring legal title to their irrigated fields, gardens, and house sites.

Kinship

Kin Groups and Descent. Descent is bilateral. Kinship is not an organizing principle in Shan society; people recognize a wide range of others who are their kin and those who behave toward them as if they were kin.

Kinship Terminology. Kin terms distinguish relative age and sex with different terms for older/younger siblings and older/younger siblings of one's mother or father. Kin terms are used primarily as terms of address because Shan do not refer to people by their name without an address term or title. Even when using titles such as "teacher" or "ex-monk," a kin term precedes it.

Marriage and Family

Marriage. There are no preferred marriage partners. With the restriction that children of siblings are considered too closely related to marry, choice of marriage partner is left to the individual. Once a marriage partner is chosen and meets with parental approval, the parents negotiate the gifts from the groom's side to the bride and the contributions from the bride's side. If the match does not meet with parental approval the couple may elope, although this usually entails smaller exchanges. Postmarital residence is usually initially with the wife's household, although this arrangement is negotiable; after a period of time, the couple establishes an independent household. Divorce is easy; the couple separates and divides any common property. If there are children, older relatives may encourage the couple to settle their disputes. Children may choose to live with either parent or some other relative.

Domestic Unit. A household consists of the people who live, work, and eat together, minimally a couple and their children. Occasionally one person or a divorced or widowed spouse and his or her children will maintain an independent household. Households may also contain grandparents, married children, and distant relatives. Unlike among Northern Thai, there is no restriction on more than one married couple living in the same household.

Inheritance. Inheritance is bilateral; half siblings have shares in their parent's property and in property their parent helped develop.

Socialization. Children are taken care of by their parents and other relatives. Small children are indulged and humored but are taught early to share with younger children. Once they reach age 6 or 7 they are expected to understand and do what they are told. Children are allowed to play together without adult supervision, although if there is fighting adults quickly break it up. Both boys and girls take early responsibility for washing their own clothes, but girls are likely to have more domestic chores.

Sociopolitical Organization

Social Organization. Shan social organization is inherently hierarchical, based on age, gender, and wealth.

Political Organization. Traditionally Shan were members of numerous small states ruled by princes having relationships with China, Burma, and northern Thailand. Other lower-ranking officials dealt with clusters of villages and individual villages. Government officials were viewed as one of the five natural disasters. Shan villages in Thailand are administered as is the rest of Thailand, with elected village headmen and village-cluster headmen responsible to an appointed district officer. Shan in China are administered as a minority group in an autonomous region.

Social Control. Within communities, gossip and the desire to maintain a good reputation are important means of maintaining order. If there are fights or thefts people may appeal to the police.

Conflict. In the precolonial period Shan fought with Burmese, other Shan, Chinese, Northern Thai, and other neighboring groups in succession disputes and assorted alliances. Now Shan in Myanmar are actively in conflict with the Burmese, the national Communist party, and, occasionally, other Shan groups.

Religion and Expressive Culture

Religious Beliefs. In some characterizations of Theravada Buddhism, Shan beliefs and practices may be considered unorthodox. Nevertheless, Shan identify themselves as Theravada Buddhists. By so doing, they classify themselves with other lowland groups and distinguish themselves from upland "tribal" peoples. Although they are Buddhist, the worldview of the Shan centers on the idea of "power protection" and its unequal distribution. Power protects people from the consequences of their actions, allowing them to behave as they choose. Because more powerful beings exist and may behave capriciously, people need to enter into a relationship with more powerful others for their own protection. One gains power protection through the practice of restraint or relying on the protection of more powerful others. Buddhas and Buddhist monks are the most powerful beings. Powerful beings associated with Buddhism are more reliably benevolent while others, such as government officials or spirits, are less likely to be benevolent. The world is populated with beings ranked on a continuum of power, with human beings falling somewhere near the middle. Beings with more power than humans include Buddhas, cadastral spirits of the village, and spirits associated with fields, households, and the forest. Beings less powerful than humans, although still dangerous, include spirits that arose from violent deaths or from women dying in childbirth and disease spirits. People, rice, and water buffalo have spirits whose loss causes illness or death.

Religious Practitioners. There are Buddhist monks, novices, and nuns; temple lay readers; traditional curers; and caretakers of the cadastral-spirit altar. All except the caretaker of the cadastral-spirit altar draw on the power associated with Buddhism. The traditional curer's ability to cure comes from his keeping of precepts, his practice of restraint, and his reliance on his teachers and on the Buddhas.

Ceremonies. The Buddhist lunar calendar structures the ceremonial cycle with four holy days each month falling on the days of full, dark, and half-moons. There are temple festivals celebrating events in the Buddha's life, such as the anniversaries of his birth, his enlightenment, his first sermon, and his death; other festivals entail the construction of sand pagodas, and the firing of rockets before or after the rainy season and to honor the end of the retreat during the three months of rain. Wealthy villages and temples celebrate more of these events than do poorer ones. However, all villages at least hold a festival after the end of the rains' retreat. Once a year villages as a whole invite monks to chant to remove misfortune and to renew the village and its constituent households' barriers against misfortune. The village cadastral spirit is also feasted at least once a year. Households may sponsor a range of ceremonies including Buddhist ordinations, funerals, merit making for the dead, marriages, first bathing ceremonies for infants, and invitations for monks to chant in the house.

Arts. Mostly these are impermanent decorations such as carved and decorated fruit offered to the Buddha image or monks and elaborately decorated coffin carriers, money trees, and pagodas celebrating the end of the rains' retreat. In Myanmar, Shan still weave traditional shoulder bags and carve small objects such as Buddha images from marble and jade. Shan in Chiang Mai were known for their silverwork.

Medicine. Shan accept and use Western medicine where available and when the ailment responds to such treatment. They also use the four elements—earth, water, wind, and fire—together with hot and cold to diagnose and treat illness. Buddhist verses are important in curing, either being blown over the patient or recited over water for the patient to drink.

Death and Afterlife. Funerals occur three to seven days after death. In Thailand everyone is cremated, although in the recent past people dying "bad deaths" were buried. Shan in Myanmar and China still bury people who die a "bad death." Buddhist monks officiate at funerals; Shan believe that only monks can transfer merit from the living to the dead. After a short period, during which the spirit may remain waiting for people to make merit for it, it is reborn.

Bibliography

Durrenberger, E. Paul (1981). "The Southeast Asian Context of Theravada Buddhism." *Anthropology* 5:45–62.

Durrenberger, E. Paul, and Nicola Tannenbaum (1989). *Analytical Perspectives on Shan Agriculture and Village Economics.* Yale University Southeast Asian Studies Monograph Series, no. 37. New Haven.

Mangrai, Sao Saimong (1965). *The Shan States and the British Annexation.* Cornell University Southeast Asia Program, Data Paper no. 57. Ithaca, N.Y.

Tannenbaum, Nicola (1989). "Power and Its Shan Transformation." In *Ritual, Power, and Economy: Upland-Lowland Contrasts in Mainland Southeast Asia,* edited by Susan D. Russell, 67–88. Occasional Paper no. 14. DeKalb: Northern Illinois University, Center for Southeast Asian Studies.

Tannenbaum, Nicola (1987). "Tattoos: Invulnerability and Power in Shan Cosmology." *American Ethnologist* 14:693–711.

Yangwhe, Chao Tzang [Eugene Thaike] (1987). *The Shan of Burma: Memoirs of a Shan Exile, Local History and Memoirs.* Singapore: Institute of Southeast Asian Studies.

NICOLA TANNENBAUM

Singaporean

The Singaporeans are not an ethnic group, but simply citizens of the Republic of Singapore, which was established in 1959. Before that time Singapore was a part of Malaysia, one island at the southern tip of the peninsula. The term "Singaporean" was little-used in the literature before independence.

The name "Singapore" was adopted on 23 February 1819 by Sir Stamford Raffles to designate the town he had founded. It was, however, a name of considerable antiquity, for in the form of "Simhapura," Sanskrit for "lion-city," it had been applied to a trading town of some importance in this locality since about the fourteenth century, when it had been established by Malay or Javanese settlers. (Other etymologies have been proposed.) Although Singapore was originally a name for both the island and Raffles's town on its southern coast, spreading urbanization in the twentieth century has now covered almost the entire island with the city, a total area of 544 square kilometers.

The climate, like that of Malaysia, is one that formerly supported a tropical rain forest. Ethnically, the population of 3,062,000 (1992) is about 76 percent immigrant Chinese, and it is these people who, settling there for trade purposes over the past 150 years, now dominate the population. Malays, who were the original inhabitants of the area, are today only a small minority in Singapore, and Islam is consequently a minority religion (16 percent of the population). Nearly a fifth of all Singaporeans (18.7 percent) are Christian, while the great bulk are—like Chinese elsewhere—followers of a mélange of Mahayana Buddhism, Taoism, and Confucian philosophy. In addition to these faiths, 4.9 percent of Singaporeans are Hindus of Indian origin, and there are also small communities of Sikhs and Parsis.

The small country has four "official" languages, Chinese, Malay, English, and Tamil, and owing to excellent schools and universities it can boast one of the highest literacy rates in Asia. This achievement reflects the fact that good schooling is available in all four of the official languages. The standard of living is also one of the highest in Asia.

Although there is considerable unemployment, nearly all those who do work are employed in service industries, commerce, education, and administration, and very few in agriculture. Singapore is in fact one of the world's great commercial centers; the impending reversion of Hong Kong to China in 1997 has had the effect of moving many industrialists with their families and capital from there to a new home in Singapore. The republic's government has naturally been very supportive of all movement for further economic growth.

See also Chinese in Southeast Asia

Bibliography

Blaut, James M. (1953). "The Economic Geography of a One-Acre Farm on Singapore Island: A Study in Applied Micro-Geography." *Journal of Tropical Geography* 1:37–48.

Chan, Hong Chee (1971). *Singapore: The Politics of Survival, 1965–1967.* Singapore: Oxford University Press.

Maday, Bela C., et al. (1965). *Area Handbook of Malaysia and Singapore.* Washington, D.C.: American University, Foreign Studies Division.

Milne, R. S., and Diane K. Mauzy (1990). *Singapore: The Legacy of Lee Kuan Yew.* Boulder, Colo.: Westview Press.

Moore, Joanna (1960). *Singapore: City of the Lion.* Singapore: D. Moore, for Heinemann.

PAUL HOCKINGS

So

A group of about 130,000 (1981), the So are located on both sides of the Mekong River in Thailand and central Laos. Through extensive contact with the Sek and the Lao they have largely been assimilated into Laotian society. Included under the So are a number of subgroups including the So Trong, So Slouy, So Phong, So Tri, and So Makon.

Bibliography

Hickey, Gerald C. (1964). "So." In *Ethnic Groups of Mainland Southeast Asia*, edited by Frank M. LeBar, Gerald C. Hickey, and John K. Musgrave, 150. New Haven: HRAF Press.

Sork

The Sork or Sok are a group of about 1,600 (1981) in Attopeu Province in southern Laos.

Sou

The Sou (Souk) are a group of about 1,000 (1962) in Attopeu Province in southern Laos, who by now may be totally assimilated into Laotian society.

Bibliography

Hoffet, J. (1933). "Les Moïs de la chaîne annamitique." _Terre, Air, Mer: La Géographie_ 59:1–43.

South Asians in Southeast Asia

There is a fairly large Indian and Pakistani population in Southeast Asia, primarily in Myanmar (Burma), Malaysia, and Singapore. The great majority of these people were, and still are, plantation laborers, though a sizable minority are traders, and today many may be found in the urban professions of law, medicine, education, and administration. In 1947, in undivided Malaya (which then included Singapore), there were a total of 545,385 people of South Indian origin and a further total of 54,231 of North Indian or Pakistani origin. Today there are an estimated 1,466,000 people of Indian origin in Malaysia (excluding those of Pakistani or Bangladeshi origin). Although these immigrants came from many parts of South Asia, and included Hindus, Sikhs, Muslims, Zoroastrians, and Christians, they were seen by most Malays as falling into two categories, "Bengalis" or North Indians, and "Klings" (possibly meaning Kalingas) or South Indians. In Myanmar the demographic picture is less clear. By about 1956 there were some 800,000 Indians and Pakistanis there, of whom about 100,000 were Pakistanis from what later became Bangladesh; the latter were concentrated in the area of Arakan. (Recent figures on the Indians in Myanmar are unobtainable.)

The main group of Indian immigrants in Malaysia and Singapore is the Tamils, of whom there were, in 1947, a total of 460,095 in undivided Malaya. Today there are approximately 1,260,000 Tamils in Malaysia, and many thousands more in Singapore. Most came from South India, some from Sri Lanka, during the past century, primarily to work as plantation laborers. There are, however, a number of Tamils in modern, urban professions. There were formerly many Tamils in Myanmar, especially members of the Nadukottai Chetti money-lending caste, who used to be major landowners in the Irrawaddy Delta.

Also scattered throughout Malaysia and Singapore, though fewer in number than the Tamils, are the Telugus, Pathans, Malayalis, Punjabis, and Sikhs. These groups together currently number about 145,000 in Malaysia alone. A few (perhaps 20,000) Bengalis also live in Myanmar, Malaysia, and Singapore.

Other countries of Southeast Asia that include populations of Indian or Pakistani origin are Thailand (about 50,000), Cambodia (about 200), Vietnam (about 6,000), Indonesia (about 40,000), and the Philippines (about 1,300). These figures relate to an estimate made in 1956, when Malaysia included about 696,000 and Singapore a further 91,000 Indians or Pakistanis.

Stieng

The Stieng (Budip, X. Tiêng) are a group of about 70,000 (1981) located in Song De Province in Vietnam and bordering areas of Cambodia. The population in Vietnam was enumerated at 50,194 in 1985. Swidden rice cultivation is the primary economic activity, supplemented by hunting and fishing. The Stieng lack any sort of tribal-level political organization, with each family constituting the basic social and political units. Similarly, religious beliefs focusing on spirits are centered in the family, where all rituals are performed.

Bibliography

Gerber, T. (1951). "Coutumier Stieng." _Bulletin de l'École Française d'Extrême-Orient_ 45:228–269.

Subanun

ETHNONYMS: Subanen (Eastern Subanun), Subano (early Spanish documents), Subanon (Western Subanun)

Orientation

Identification. The Subanun are pagan shifting cultivators of rice who inhabit the mountainous, forested interior of the Zamboanga Peninsula, a southwestern extension of the island of Mindanao in the southern Philippines. Subanun groups share a similar culture that sets them off from Christian and Muslim lowlanders. This article refers specifically to the Eastern Subanun living in the north-central part of the peninsula.

Location. The Zamboanga Peninsula extends a length of some 300 kilometers from 6°53′ to 8°38′ N and from 121°54′ to 123°53′ E. Were the peninsula a separate island, it would be, with an area of 17,673 square kilometers, the third-largest island in the Philippines, after Luzon and Mindanao. It is divided into four political units, from northeast to southwest: Misamis Occidental, Zamboanga del Norte, Zamboanga del Sur, and Zamboanga City.

Linguistic Affiliation. The Subanun language is comprised of a set of closely related dialects, divided into two groups, Eastern and Western Subanun. The language belongs to the huge, Pacific-wide Austronesian Language Family. Among Austronesian languages it is affiliated most closely with the Central Group of Philippine languages.

Demography. The Subanun probably number about 75,000. Population density is highly variable by region and distance from the coast. A careful census has never been conducted. During the 1970s and 1980s many Subanun groups have suffered depopulation from devastating raids by warring Christian and Muslim bands.

History and Cultural Relations

The Subanun first enter recorded history in the accounts of seventeenth-century Spanish Jesuits, who described them as living in scattered settlements with "scant social life." Jesuit attempts to bring the Subanun together into nucleated villages were unsuccessful. Until the time of the American conquest and occupation of the southern Philippines in the years prior to World War I, the major outside relations of the Subanun were with Muslim traders and raiders who came both overland from the east and by sea along the coasts. Muslims settled along the coasts and set up trading centers to collect Subanun forest and agricultural products, as well as slaves, in exchange for Chinese porcelains, gongs, beads, and iron. This trade was highly exploitative and it set the pattern for outsider relations to this day. The Subanun never developed any effective political organization to counter outside exploitation, nor have they attempted to resist it militarily. During the American period, warfare and raiding in the southern Philippines was fairly well suppressed, but since World War II, and especially during the Marcos regime, Christian-Muslim hostilities became increasingly violent. In several areas of the Zamboanga Peninsula, the Subanun have been caught in the cross fire and have been victimized by the marauding bands that flourish under such conditions.

Settlements

The Subanun live in dispersed settlements of single-family households. The focus of nucleation is the cluster of agricultural fields cut and burned each year in the forest. Houses, which are rectangular, raised on piles, and thatch-roofed, are relocated and rebuilt every three or four years. They are typically perched on ridges and hillsides overlooking the family's fields. In grassland areas of dry-field plow agriculture, settlements tend to be more nucleated.

Economy

Subsistence and Commercial Activities. The Subanun practice swidden agriculture. Rice is the major crop but they grow a large variety of other grain, root, and tree crops for food, materials, and medicines. Each family cuts and burns a new rice swidden annually. No plow or hoe is used. The crop is harvested and processed by hand. The swiddens of previous years are given over to secondary crops and then, as these are harvested, to secondary growth fallow. After a period of up to

fifteen years, when a good mature secondary forest has reestablished itself, the area can be recut. A group of kin and neighbors generally tries to cluster its swiddens each year to share some of the labor of watching and tending fields. This ideal cycle assumes relatively abundant forested land. In recent decades increasing pressure on the forest from commercial lumbering, cattle raising, lowlanders' encroachments, and population growth has led to shortening of the cycle or its abandonment altogether for dry-field plow agriculture in grassland. The Subanun raise pigs, chickens, and sometimes cattle or water buffalo. They hunt wild pigs and deer and fish mountain streams for small fish and crustaceans. They also gather a variety of forest products. They largely depend on their own agriculture, hunting, and gathering for subsistence and for technological materials. They also sell rice and forest products, especially rattan, in lowland markets. Cash is needed for purchasing market goods, especially clothing, utensils, and tools, and for a variety of internal transactions.

Industrial Arts. The Subanun practice weaving on backstrap looms, basketry, forging of iron knives and axes, and house and granary construction. The extent to which they engage in these crafts varies greatly from place to place and is decreasing everywhere. One very important Subanun product is rice wine, fermented in treasured old Chinese jars and brought out for any interfamily social occasion.

Trade. The Subanun have long been dependent on external markets for many of their tools, utensils, musical instruments, and precious objects. These markets are controlled entirely by outsiders: Christian lowlanders, Muslim traders, and Chinese merchants. In former times, when Muslims controlled external trade, access to trade goods was typically channeled through titled Subanun leaders, subordinates to Muslim authorities. Internally among the Subanun there is informal trade of agricultural produce, heirloom objects, and labor, transactions motivated by the perpetual need for cash to purchase goods, pay fines, provision rituals, and finance weddings.

Division of Labor. The formal division of labor by any criterion, even sex, is quite minimal for a human society. Men and women participate in agricultural and domestic activities. Men fell trees, burn swiddens, and dibble planting holes for grain. Women plant grain seed. Otherwise each does any chore: slashing undergrowth, weeding, and harvesting. Women are usually responsible for cooking and child care, but men freely take over when needed. Men, women, and children share in the daily task of pounding rice or grinding maize. Men tend to assume roles of legal and religious leadership, but both sexes participate fully in ritual and ceremonial life. There is little significant specialization by occupation or stratification by wealth and power. Everyone is a farmer. Everyone is poor and everyone is powerless.

Land Tenure. Traditionally land per se has been a free good. Crops are individually owned by the person who planted them and this right gives the planter (or in the case of tree crops, his or her descendants) control over the land on which the crop is growing. New swidden land is allocated among neighbors each year by negotiation and ritual divination. Claims of previous use are relevant to these negotiations but not as claims to "ownership" of the land per se. The traditional system of land allocation has, of course, no legal status in Philippine law. Subanun land frequently has been appropriated by outsiders with better access to the legal system. Some Subanun have succeeded in officially declaring a plot of land, but cultivating a single plot requires changing the method of agriculture and, thereby, one's way of life.

Kinship

Kin Groups and Descent. Beyond the nuclear family there are no discrete, bounded, or corporate kin groups. Each family is embedded in a network of its members' cognatic and affinal kin. This network, combined with propinquity and shared history, provides the basis for the formation of settlement groups that jointly cultivate adjacent swiddens, for the staffing of ritual and ceremonial occasions, and for support in life-crisis situations. There are no unilineal descent groups of any kind; descent is bilateral or cognatic.

Kinship Terminology. The basic distinctions in kinship terminology are those of generation, consanguinity, and collaterality. Parents are distinguished from their siblings. There is a cover term for all siblings and cousins, as in the Hawaiian system, but there are also separate cousin terms. The gender of relatives is distinguished only in the parental generation. In affinal terminology, there are terms used exclusively between males. Relative age in one's own generation can be distinguished in address terminology. Kinship terms and special relational nicknames are widely used to classify, name, and address a wide circle of associates regardless of actual genealogical connection.

Marriage and Family

Marriage. Although polygyny, including sororal polygyny, sometimes occurs, the overwhelming majority of marriages are monogamous. Marriages are generally arranged by families among neighbors and kin. Cousins may marry but are expected to pay a ritual fine that increases with the degree of closeness. A bride-price is paid by the groom's kin, to be distributed among the bride's kin. A period of bride-service in lieu of full bride-price is common. Because of bride-service obligations, a new couple generally lives near the bride's parents. Independent residence in one's own household is the goal of all nuclear families. Informal separation and formally negotiated divorce are common. Bride-price and bride-service obligations, as well as fines for misconduct, can make divorce negotiations difficult, especially between the recently married. Remarriage of the divorced and widowed is the norm. Once married, it is difficult to rejoin one's natal family unit as a dependent member.

Inheritance. Property is divided equally among surviving children. The most valuable property consists of heirlooms in the form of Chinese jars and brass gongs.

Socialization. Child care is relaxed and nonpunitive. It can, however, be a burden on young couples because of the relative isolation of homesteads and the need for both spouses to participate in agricultural work. The biggest problem in child rearing is not discipline but disease.

Sociopolitical Organization

The Subanun are subjects of the Philippine Republic. They occupy a marginal, almost outcast position in the national society and economy. Their contacts with the arms and agencies of the national government have rarely been happy ones. They have no formal political organization at all. Apart from local appointees of outside powers, either the national government or Muslim traders, leadership among the Subanun is self-achieved by participation in the social arenas that require skills of decision making and persuasion. These are largely contexts of legal debate about local infractions, sexual offenses, and marital and property disputes. The use of formal titles to name leadership positions is common among the Western Subanun and was probably more often the practice everywhere in the Muslim-influenced past.

Social Control. Legal authorities are those with the social influence and persuasive power to impose fines. Force or violence is never used or threatened in local litigation. In the background, however, there is always the fear of a case coming to the attention of government authorities. Although verbal dispute is common enough, physical violence is extremely rare. Even though they are quite dispersed and lack anything in the way of formal political organization, the Subanun greatly enjoy social gatherings. Their legal cases, rituals, and feasts are marked by rice wine drinking, dancing, singing, gong playing, storytelling, joking, and lively conversation by both sexes and all ages.

Religion

Religious Beliefs. At the core of a culture that enables the Subanun to maintain a meaningful identity distinct from both Catholic Filipino lowlanders and coastal Muslims is a shared system of belief and ritual that is uniquely Subanun. (A number of Subanun speakers have become Catholics and have merged into the lowland population. Others in the Western Subanun area have become Muslim and thereby have been given a new identity by outsiders as "Kalibugan" or "half-breed." American Protestant missionaries have been active in some areas. Their converts have yet another identity.) Sharing the Subanun universe with human mortals are named gods, spirits, demons, and ghosts. These supernatural beings can all help or harm humans—just as humans can, through agricultural activities, for example, cause the beings damage. The agricultural cycle is punctuated with requisite offerings to the supernaturals. Speaking through mediums during séance rituals, the gods and ancestors may demand offerings for the cure of illness. Human enemies can be attacked by luring their mortal souls to a nocturnal offering and then ambushing them at the doorway. This type of indirect assault on the invisible spirit of a distant antagonist is one kind of violence the Subanun do practice. The constituents of offerings vary with the demands of particular supernaturals, but they always include rice, meat, wine, and a betel chew—the essential ingredients of a festive meal. Unlike the agricultural cycle, the stages of the human life cycle, other than birth and death, are not strongly demarcated by rituals. There is no social observance of puberty for either sex.

Religious Practitioners. Ritual specialists and mediums learn their craft either through apprenticeship or directly through divine revelation. Their status is one of the few specifically named and relatively clearly defined nonrelational social positions in Subanun society. Most specialists are older men, but women are not excluded from the role.

Medicine. The Subanun distinguish religious practice centered on offerings from the use of substances and spells for the treatment and prevention of disease and other misfortune. Hundreds of wild and cultivated medicinal plants are distinguished and routinely used. Medicinal treatment of this type is generally tried before one resorts to the more expensive route of religious offerings.

Death and Afterlife. The dead are buried, but grave sites are not conspicuously nor permanently marked. A death initiates a major ceremonial occasion, during which there are rituals, exhortations, and offerings to ensure that the ghost of the diseased departs this world of mortals and demons, journeying to the other world to become a spirit among the gods. Ancestral spirits play an important role in séances by acting as intermediaries between the supernaturals and their mortal descendants. There is, however, no attempt to remember long lines of ancestors from the distant past.

See also Kalibugan

Bibliography

Christie, E. B. (1909). *The Subanuns of Sindangan Bay*. Division of Ethnology Publications, no. 6. Manila: Bureau of Science.

Combés, Francisco (1667). *Historia del las Islas de Mindanao, Iolo, y sus Adyacentes*. Madrid. Reprint. 1897. Madrid: W. E. Retana.

Frake, Charles O. (1980). *Language and Cultural Description*. Edited by Anwar S. Dil. Stanford, Calif.: Stanford University Press.

Hall, William C. (1987). *Aspects of Western Subanon Formal Speech*. Dallas, Tex.: Summer Institute of Linguistics.

CHARLES O. FRAKE

Sulod

The Sulod (Buki, Bukidnon, Mondo, Mundo, Putian) are a mountain people numbering about 14,000 in 1980, who live along the banks of the Panay River on central Panay Island in the Bisayan Islands in the central Philippines. Sulod is classified in the Hesperonesian Group of the Austronesian Language Family. Small, autonomous settlements consist of from five to seven four-walled, one-room houses, raised on bamboo or wooden posts. Subsistence is based on cultivation of rice, maize, and sweet potato, supplemented by hunting and fishing. Descent is bilateral. Leadership is in the hands of the oldest man of each settlement. The Sulod believe in several spirits and deities and hold at least sixteen annual ceremonies, most of which are conducted by the religious specialists (*baylan*).

Bibliography

Jonaco, F. Landa (1968). *Sulod Society: A Study of the Kinship System and Social Organization of a Mountain People of Central Panay*. Institute of Asian Studies, Monograph Series, no. 2. Quezon City: University of the Philippines Press.

Sundanese

ETHNONYMS: Orang Sunda, Urang Prijangan, Urang Sunda

Orientation

The Sundanese are a group of nearly 25 million whose territory (Sunda) is western Java (Jawa Barat) as far east as the Cipamali river (though many Sundanese live elsewhere in Java). The Sundanese language is Austronesian; an interesting aspect of the language is that it is obligatory for speakers to distinguish in their speech the status of the addressee and the degree of intimacy between them. With the exception of the Badui subgroup, Sundanese are Muslim. Although culturally similar to the Javanese, the Sundanese see themselves as far less formal in their social relationships.

History and Cultural Relations

Because the Sundanese (especially those who lived in the hills) were long culturally isolated from the outside world, their culture is still very traditional. In Sundanese history there has been only one state, the kingdom of Pajajaran (1333–1579), which came into existence as a result of the defeat of the Sumatran kingdom by the Javanese kingdom of Singhawari. Indian traders introduced Islam in the fifteenth century; Sundanese Islam then spread outward from the ports where the Indians traded. The nobles of Sunda were converted in 1579 at the order of the sultan of Banten, who first killed the royal family. Shortly thereafter, the Islamic Javanese kingdom of Mataram gained control of Sunda, and not long after this, European power became dominant. The Dutch introduced plantation farming of coffee. On two separate occasions, in 1880 and following World War II, the Sundanese began holy wars against the Dutch with the goal of independence; both wars failed to achieve their aim. At present, the Sundanese are under Indonesian control.

Settlements

Sundanese villages are larger than those of Java, and usually have between 1,000 and 7,000 or more residents. The usual settlement pattern is one of clusters of houses separated by agricultural fields. One's fields are typically small and dispersed. Although traditional housing no longer exists, Sundanese housing may be distinguished from Javanese in that it is built on pilings.

Economy

The mainstay of Sundanese subsistence is wet-rice agriculture, though some groups in the southwest portion of Sunda still practice swidden agriculture. Up to three rice crops are grown annually, and between these crops farmers raise peanuts, yams, chilies, vegetables, and soybeans. Cash crops include corn, root crops, chili peppers, and tobacco. In coastal areas, many people also fish or practice fish farming. Bulls and water buffalo are raised to provide transportation and for plowing; otherwise, animal husbandry is insignificant. Because landholdings are typically too small to support their owners, many peasants trade, make handicrafts, or work as laborers on the farms of others.

Although there is much private land, there is also communal land set aside in most villages. There is also land that is for the exclusive use of original members of the village and for those who have benefited the community. Additionally, land is reserved for the usufruct of village administrators, who receive no salary.

Kinship

The Sundanese reckon kinship bilaterally, and the kinship terminological system is geared more toward the distinctions between generations and age than between lines of collaterality or gender. Peasants rarely acknowledge kinship ties more distant than two ascending generations and one degree of collaterality; nobles, on the other hand, have an interest in their genealogies for the purpose of establishing their kinship to ancient Sundanese kings. The nuclear family (_kulawarga_) is the basic unit of society; it is to the kulawarga that the individual has the greatest obligations. There is also the _golongan_, or kindred, who function occasionally in the performance of life-cycle ceremonies. Finally, there is the _bondorojot_, an ambilineal kin group that exists among some members of the higher social classes and functions in the context of ancestor-worship ceremonies.

Marriage and Family

Subject to parental acceptance, Sundanese choose their own spouses, though in the past marriages were arranged by the parents. Polygyny is accepted but rare; men claim cost and wives' opposition as barriers to multiple wives. The marriage itself involves much ritual revolving around the rice goddess, Dewi Sri, and also includes the following stages: the groom's family formally presents a gift to the bride's parents; the marriage contract is concluded by a district Muslim religious official (_naib_); and there is a formal meeting of the bride and groom. Residence is ideally neolocal, but in practice most young couples cannot afford to live alone, so for a period of years they will live with either set of parents.

Sundanese socialization is the responsibility of the mother alone; the father is seen as the one responsible for the physical existence of the child. Perhaps for this reason, children are considered to have a spiritual connection with their mothers rather than their fathers.

An individual's property is divided equally among the surviving spouse and offspring; when no spouse survives, all property is divided equally among the offspring, without regard to sex. This customary rule (_adat_) violates Islamic law, which stipulates that males receive twice what females receive; to avoid this, the male is given two-thirds of the estate, and he in turn gives one-third of what he has received to his sister. The house and surrounding gardens, however, go to the offspring (usually the youngest daughter) who has lived with the parents to care for them.

Sociopolitical Organization

Dutch colonization resulted in a new class of administrative elite. Administrative personnel (_pamong pradja_) enjoy the highest status in Sundanese society, and Western education and the ability to speak Dutch became the best means for raising one's status. The Sundanese are presently under Indonesian rule.

Religion and Expressive Culture

Sundanese religion is syncretic, mixing pre-Islamic and pre-Indian beliefs and practices with Islamic ones. Although the Sundanese have been Muslim for a long time, it is only since World War II that Islam has been taught. The _lebbe_, who teaches Islam, also records births and deaths in the official records. As a result of this instruction, many practices and beliefs that predated the introduction of Islam are being altered. Non-Islamic spirits are being given Islamic identities and meanings; for example, ceremonial visits to the graves of ancestors (a central, but non-Islamic, feature of Sundanese religion) and the ritual cleaning of weapons are being incorporated into Islamic celebrations such as Maulud.

See also Javanese

Bibliography

Hirokoshi, Hiroko (1978). "Islam and Social Change among the Moslem Sundanese in West Java." _Kabar Sekarang_ 4:41–47.

Palmer, Andrea Wilcox (1967). "Situradja: A Village in Highland Priangan." In _Villages in Indonesia_, edited by R. M. Koentjaraningrat, 299–325. Ithaca, N.Y.: Cornell University Press.

Thomas, Murray, et al. (1975). _Social Strata in Indonesia: A Study of West Javanese Villagers._ Jakarta: Antarkarya.

Wessing, Robert (1978). _Cosmology and Social Behavior in a West Javanese Settlement._ Southeast Asia Series, no. 53. Athens: Ohio University Center for International Studies.

DANIEL STROUTHES

Tagalog

ETHNONYM: Pilipino (also Wikang Pambansa—"national language")

Orientation

Identification. The Tagalog language is the basis of Pilipino, the national language of the Republic of the Philippines since 1937, and has been taught from the first grade throughout the archipelago since the early 1950s. Thus most Filipinos (60–70 million) under the age of 50 speak, read, and write Tagalog as at least a second language, while some 10 to 15 percent (perhaps 10 million) have learned it as their first language. This article deals only with the latter group. The usual derivation of the name "Tagalog" is from *taga ilog*, meaning "inhabitants of the river."

Location. The Tagalog-speaking area is oriented toward Manila Bay and is concentrated mostly within 80 to 320 kilometers of the megalopolis of Manila on the island of Luzon. It lies within the Tropic of Cancer from 10° to 16° N and from 119° to 123° E. It consists of the provinces of Bataan, Bulacan, Rizal, Cavite, Batangas, Laguna, Quezon, parts of Nueva Ecija and Camarines Norte, Marinduque, Polillio, parts of Mindoro and Palawan, and many smaller islands. The topography includes mountains up to 2,000 meters and uplands with tropical rain forest cover as well as a wide range of lowland coastal and inland environments. Monsoon seasons vary from location to location, and there are dramatic differences in annual rainfall (152 to 457 centimeters) and length of wet and dry periods. Typhoons, earthquakes, volcanic eruptions, droughts, floods, and malarial vectors form ever-present threats for the people of the area.

Demography. As of 1991 the population in this "heartland" of the Tagalog area (Katagalugan) was over 10.9 million in approximately 23,920 square kilometers (325 persons per square kilometer). Probably another 100,000 people whose first language is Tagalog live elsewhere in the Philippines and abroad.

Linguistic Affiliation. Tagalog belongs to the Malayan Branch of the Austronesian Phylum. The dialect of Tagalog spoken in Manila is often called "Taglish" because of the high percentage of American English words.

History and Cultural Relations

Tagalog civilization has been a distinctive configuration for at least one thousand years, subject to the various cultural influences operative in mainland and insular Southeast Asia since the Neolithic period. Long before the Spanish began colonization in the last half of the sixteenth century, Tagalog society on Luzon was organized in loose "confederations" of local groupings sometimes called "kingdoms." In general, Tagalogs had a system of writing (a syllabary derived from Sanskrit), an advanced technology including metallurgy, a complicated social system with hierarchical classes (including a category of individuals termed "slaves" by early Spanish sources), and religious patterns that varied regionally. The Indonesian empires of Sri Vijaya and Majapahit left their imprint on language, religion, and technology—through both trade and settlement. The Chinese for centuries used ports along the western coast of Luzon as stopping points in their trade with the Spice Islands to the south and local trading centers. Islamic sultanates had been established around Manila Bay not long before the Spanish began almost 350 years of occupation in the middle of the sixteenth century. During the seventeenth and eighteenth centuries Manila was one of the major seaports of the world as the transshipment point in the famous Manila galleon trade that exchanged silver from Mexico for silks and other luxury wares of China. By the middle of the nineteenth century, strong resistance to Spanish rule had developed in the Philippines, especially in the Tagalog area, which produced the national heroes José Rizal, Andres Bonifacio, and Emiliano Aguinaldo. Before Americans came to the Philippines during the Spanish-American War in 1898 there was a full-scale insurrection in process, which continued against the American occupation until 1902. The first Republic of the Philippines was established during this time at the Barasoin Church in Malolos, Bulacan, 48 kilometers northwest of Manila, in the midst of what is considered the land of the deepest (*malalim*) and purest dialect of Tagalog. American colonial control officially lasted almost fifty years. During World War II, the battles of Bataan and Corregidor, as well as the Death March, occurred in the Tagalog area. Independence was granted in 1946 after a three-year occupation by the Japanese. Until 1952 the insurgent Hukbalahap army waged some of its most intensive battles against the new Republic of the Philippines in the Tagalog provinces. Recently the American presence and influence have lessened, with Japan, Australia, New Zealand, and European countries becoming important economically and technologically. In the early Spanish period most of the people of the Philippines were called "Moros" and later "Indios." The term "Filipino" then referred to persons of Spanish descent born there.

Settlements

In lowlands where irrigated rice was the basis of subsistence, settlements were distributed along waterways before the introduction of highways and railroads during the Spanish period. As this network of roads and railroads expanded, housing was extended along them even in upland areas where houses were usually dispersed in clusters oriented to landholdings and water supply. In both areas larger settlements served as markets and religious centers. Coastal settlements were clusters near sources of fresh water. Nonunilineal kinship ties were, and still are, foci for neighborhood and community. With the introduction of Roman Catholicism under the Spanish, the settlements became centralized around a church, chapel, or shrine (possibly continuing pre-Spanish patterns). By the beginning of the nineteenth century the larger settlements had complex central plazas with concentrations of population. Manila and several of the provincial capitals developed into urban centers. The houses have been of two major types: movable and nonmovable. Movable houses were built on stilts of bamboo and wood with thatch or metal roofs. Until recently, masonry houses were built mostly in the towns and cities. Manila and the other urban centers of the Tagalog area are rapidly becoming truly metropolitan districts. Manila, though an integral part of Tagalog society, is also a nexus for integration of almost all segments of the nation.

Economy

Subsistence and Commercial Activities. There have been extensive changes in rural areas since independence, brought on by improved communication, roads, and expansion of electrical power resources. There are several distinct types of land use. North of Manila, the Tagalog provinces form the southern edge of the "rice bowl" of the Philippines. South and west of Manila the provinces of Cavite and Batangas form a predominantly upland dry-farming and fruit-producing region. The latter is noted for its peddlers, who have traditionally roved the length and breadth of Luzon. To the south and east is a mixed region of sugarcane, coconuts, and terraced rice. In many areas mechanization is replacing water buffalo, horses, and oxen. Fishing, both deep-water and riverine, is important wherever possible. There is an almost unending inventory of local enterprises, including production of salt, vinegar, hard-boiled and fertilized duck eggs (_balut,_ a national delicacy), alcoholic beverages, clothing and mosquito netting, implements, and containers. Commercial activities on a large scale take place mostly in Manila, but there are regional centers for the commercial processing of copra, sugarcane, and other products. Rice is a basic commodity around which life is oriented. Many Tagalog families living in Manila or other nonagricultural areas usually have ties to one or more rural communities within commuting distance and receive a share of crops raised by their relatives or tenants.

Industrial Arts. For centuries even remote communities have been part of networks of trade because people depended on the markets for things they could not make for themselves. There have been, however, certain regional specialties, for example the famous _balisong,_ a collapsible pocket knife made in the province of Batangas, and the wood carving of the towns of Laguna Province, just south of Manila.

Trade. The ancient, highly developed, and fascinating market system connects local networks to Manila and its international port. A crucial commercial relationship is the institution of the _suki,_ a self-reciprocal term referring to the tie between a seller and a regular customer. Overseas Chinese have been important in trade and financial institutions over the centuries.

Division of Labor. Division of labor (_hanapbuhay,_ occupation) by gender is highly variable. Both men and women hold professional positions in medicine, law, education, and politics. Traditionally, men in lowland rice areas were responsible for the care of irrigation systems, preparation of fields, and heavier work (although women could participate). Teenaged women under the supervision of an older woman planted, and everyone harvested. In some upland areas, however, planting and harvesting were not divided so specifically. New methods of rice production are bringing about changes in all of this. Sugarcane production is usually a commercial enterprise requiring seasonally determined wage labor. Copra production, intensive fishing, and fish-pond management are predominantly male occupations. In general, division of labor within the family is highly contingent; either gender can be called upon for both household duties and economic activities. Women often control family finances and enterprises.

Land Tenure. Patterns of ownership and rights to the use of land are also variable. In pre-Spanish times usufruct operated in both lowland and upland areas because both paddies and swiddens were prepared on new land. During the Spanish period, with its imposed regulations and land grants, large areas of land came under the ownership of a relatively few Tagalog and non-Tagalog families and the various religious orders. Thus most Tagalogs came to live on land that belonged to someone else and worked the land either as tenants or as paid laborers. Frequently, the tenancy rights were inherited according to local custom within interrelated extended families. Cadastral surveys over the years have established legal boundaries, often with permanent markers. Since the early twentieth century, legislation has slowly caused division of some large holdings. Further, in some regions tenants have been able to buy the land, often renting it as a tenancy to others.

Kinship

Kin Groups and Descent. The basic unit is the sibling group, _kamagkapatid_ (_kapatid_ = sibling). Usually there are terms for firstborn and lastborn: _panganay_ and _bunso._ In some communities and families, terms borrowed from Chinese are used for numerical order of birth. Each marriage produces a nuclear family, _kamaganakan_ (_anak_ = child), which is part of a bilaterally extended family with genealogical ties traced from specific ancestors (or sibling groups). Extended families are further affiliated in complex webs of obligation and rights (reckoned polylineally) through ties of marriage into a grouping sometimes called the _angkan_ or _pamilia_ and identified by patrilineal inheritance of surnames, which can be retained by women after marriage. The angkan may be a fairly definite unit, but more often it is similar to the U.S. pattern called the "family of the Smiths, Jones, etc." Kinship is extended as far as can be determined, so that strangers often begin interaction by comparing names of relatives to see if there are any ties. Affinity and ritual kinship are strongly embedded in the formation and recognition of wider relationships between individuals and families. Relationships, though dependent on genealogical and ritual ties, are continually instigated, maintained, and strengthened by proper behavior on the part of individuals showing acceptance of obligation and responsibility. This reciprocity is most often expressed by the term _utang na loob,_ or debt (_utang_) of volition-free will (_na loob_). Some analysts have emphasized the other meaning of _loob,_ "inside" (as opposed to _labas,_ "outside"), which signifies a recognition that two individuals fall within the same network of inherited obligation. Utang na loob is initially produced by an unsolicited "gift," which creates or increases obligation within the receiver. The greatest obligation is to God and parents, who give life to the individual. Kinship relations are extended to nonrelatives or intensified between relatives through ritual sponsorship of individuals at baptism (_binyag_), confirmation (_kumpil_), and marriage (_kasal_).

Kinship Terminology. Referential and vocative terminologies including alternatives are mixtures of Tagalog, Spanish, and Chinese and vary from area to area. Referential terminology is very close to "Yankee" or Eskimo, while vocatively it can be more Hawaiian. There is no unilateral emphasis. Great-grandparents, grandparents, and parents' siblings are differentiated by gender. Cousins are not distinguished vocatively from siblings, and parents' siblings can be equated with parents. However, cousins are differentiated referentially from siblings to the third degree by numerically distinctive terms; beyond that, they are considered *malayo* (distant). There is a basic term for sibling (kapatid) and another for cousin (pinsan), either of which can be modified by adding a term indicating gender. Own children, grandchildren, and great-grandchildren are differentiated from the descendants of siblings and cousins by separate basic terms with gender and generation modifiers. The prefix *mag-* attached to a term indicates a dyadic relationship: *magama*, father and child; *magina*, mother and child; *magkapatid*, two siblings; etc. Some affinal terms are not gender-specific: *asawa* (spouse); *biyenan* (parent-in-law); *manugang* (child-in-law). Some affinal terms *are* gender-specific: spouse's own siblings are *hipag* (female) and *bayaw* (male); but their spouse's siblings of either gender are *bilas*. Ritual terms are: *kumari/kumpari* (cogodmother/godfather) used between sponsors and parents of sponsored individuals; *inaanak* (godchild); and the usual kinship terms are extended to all sides of the ritual connection. Vocative terminology is primarily age- or status-based. Most frequently the personal name of the younger or junior person is used while the older or senior is addressed by a derivation of the referential term: *ina* is derived from *nanay* (mother); *ka* is from kapatid; etc. Relative status as to age or prestige of relatives and nonrelatives is often indicated by the use of *po*, *ho*, or *oh* in a descending order during conversation.

Marriage and Family

Marriage. Marriage (kasal) generally follows the proscriptions of the Roman Catholic church, but cousin marriages of all degrees occur. The degree permitted or encouraged varies from area to area and from family to family; however, there is frequently pressure to marry within the third degree and if possible within the local group. Divorce (diborsiyo) has not been legal for centuries, but separation (hiwalay) occurs.

Domestic Unit. In rural areas, where dwelling space is less limited, the preferred pattern is for each nuclear family to have a separate dwelling as soon as possible. Normally one child and spouse remain in the parental home, but as population pressure increases multiple households are increasingly becoming the rule. Parents share household chores and care of children. As children are able, they take over many household duties including care of their younger siblings and cooking. Frequently, the wife begins to engage in more intense economic activities. There are usually three or more generations present in the household, but in most cases only one or two nuclear families with young children.

Inheritance. The root term for inheritance is *mana*. Personal property is inherited equally by siblings. Houses usually become the property of the child who has remained to care for the parents. Rights to tenancies or ownership of land can either descend in a strictly bilateral fashion leading to segmentation of holdings of sibling groups over the generations, or be maintained by naming one sibling steward, with all having a share in the land's output dependent upon input.

Socialization. Young children are cared for by members of the household, extended family, and neighbors in general (*mga kapitbahay* or *paligid*). Probably one of the more crucial experiences a Tagalog undergoes comes upon assuming responsibility for a younger sibling, cousin, or other relative. The residential and extended family group is the nurturing environment, and provides opportunities for the building of much utang na loob.

Sociopolitical Organization

The head of state in the Republic of the Philippines is a president (*pangulo*). There are two legislative houses (one elected by district and the other at large) and a series of appointed courts and judges with a supreme court at the summit.

Social Organization. Tagalog society seems to have a strongly kinship-based set of parameters, although nonkin are generally incorporated in networks of reciprocal obligation and interaction. There are horizontal class distinctions based on wealth and closeness to economic resources and political power, which are crosscut vertically by genealogical and ritual ties of kinship so that the lower and upper classes are linked at various levels into a series of pyramidal (but ill-defined) networks. Their boundaries and internal relationships are constantly being rearranged.

Political Organization. The Tagalog-speaking area (Katagalugan), as part of the Philippines (Bayan ng Pilipinas), is divided into provinces (singular, *lalawigan*), each with an elected governor and legislative body. Provinces are divided into municipalities (singular, *bayan* or *munisipyo*). One of the municipalities is designated provincial capital. Each municipality has an elected mayor and council. There is usually a central area (also called the bayan or munisipyo) where municipal business is carried on, with an administration building, frequently a market, and religious center. The municipality is divided into segments called *baryo*, *nayon*, or *baranggay*. These basic units have had an elected head since the middle 1950s called *tiniente del baryo*, who was promoted to *kapitan del baryo* a few years later. There is also an elected baryo council representing subdivisions called *sitio* or *pook*. At each level police, education, public works, etc. are managed by presidential appointees.

Social Control. Aside from the legal system and police functions, most Tagalog communities outside the urban centers operate according to local custom similar to the *adat* found elsewhere in insular Southeast Asia. Local officials exert power insofar as they are personally respected and have influence with people involved in disputes. Ostracism and ridicule are often used as means for social control.

Religion and Expressive Culture

Religious Beliefs. Tagalogs are predominantly Roman Catholic, but there are several other formal religious groups with significant membership. Most Protestant sects are represented in the area to a minor degree. However, both the Iglesia ni Cristo (Church of Christ), a Protestant group established locally in the Philippines, and the Aglipayan Church, a group founded by a priest (Gregorio Aglipay) who broke away from Catholicism, have significant memberships. There are also many local sects and cults.

There are generally two levels to religious belief. One is the expressed set of tenets of Roman Catholicism or other formal religion. The other is interpretation and modification of these as individual and local belief systems. Education and exposure to general scientific knowledge long ago penetrated to most parts of the Tagalog area, but mysticism is still strong and individuals seek personal experience with the unknown and unseen through acts of penitence and contrition. The continuing vagaries of life in an environment prone to catastrophic storms, earthquakes, volcanic eruptions, and social upheaval reinforce the traditional fatalism expressed in the phrase *bahala na,* or "it's all up to God."

Religious Practitioners. The religious hierarchies are centered mostly in Manila and are staffed predominantly by Tagalog priests and ministers. Most municipalities have resident Roman Catholic clergy in a church (*simbahan*) who service chapels (*bisitas* or *ermitas*) in outlying barrios. There are still individuals who have special powers for curing and making contact with spirits of the deceased. The terminology for these and their specialties is highly variable from region to region. Most communities have annual fiestas celebrating a patron saint, the Virgin Mary, or a local manifestation of Christ. These are usually sponsored and managed by a highly organized group of volunteers who are in charge of one year's activities.

Ceremonies. The annual cycle universally includes Christmas and Easter and their phases. Among others, the day of Saint John the Baptist is widely celebrated, especially in relation to waterways. Good Friday each year produces activity from penitents of various sorts, including whipping and actual crucifixion at spots considered especially sanctified. Baptism, confirmation, marriage, and funerals are regular parts of all lives.

Arts. Tagalogs have long been noted for excellence in all the arts. Since the introduction of printing in 1593 at Binondo, Manila, there has developed an extensive literature published in Tagalog (and other Philippine languages), Spanish, and English, including poetry, drama, novels, short stories, essays, and criticism. As early as 1606, poems were being printed in Tagalog by Fernando Bagonbanta. Among many famous writers since then have been Francisco Baltazar (Balagtas, "Prince of Tagalog Poets"), whose *Florante at Laura* is a classic and whose pseudonym is associated with the traditional *balagtasan* or contest in verse. The works of José Rizal, especially his romantic novels *Noli me tángere* and *El filibusterismo,* which eventually brought on his execution by the Spanish in 1896 and made him into a national martyr, have been published in many languages. There is a flourishing Tagalog movie and television industry and all the media use Tagalog extensively. A traditional art form that survives is the *kundiman* or love song.

Medicine. Modern medical treatment is available in all parts of the Tagalog area through medical schools, hospitals, clinics, and a national health service. Traditional knowledge of herbs is still important and used. Dietary regimes and bodily care reflect long-held concepts of the relationship between good health and adaptation to the environment.

Death and Afterlife. Although the usual Christian beliefs regarding death and afterlife are followed, there are at least two widespread conceptual frameworks present. One holds that the body returns to the four elements: earth, water, fire, and air. The other maintains that the spirit (*kaluluwa*) of the deceased spends a certain amount of time in the immediate neighborhood before departing to an afterworld. Secondary burial has frequently been practiced (i.e., placement of the body in a grave or niche, followed after a period by transfer of the bones to an ossuary). All Souls' Day (Araw ng mga Kaluluwa) is the occasion for visiting the cemetery (*libingan*).
    See also Filipino

Bibliography
Blair, Emma Helen, and James Robertson (1903–1909). *The Philippine Islands, 1493–1898. . . .* 55 Vols. Cleveland, Ohio: A. H. Clark Co.

Eggan, Fred (1955). *The Philippines.* 4 Vols. New Haven: Human Relations Area Files.

Hollnsteiner, Mary R. (1955). *The Dynamics of Power in a Philippine Municipality.* Quezon City: University of the Philippines, Community Development Research Council.

Kaut, Charles (1961). "*Utang na Loob*: A System of Contractual Obligation among Tagalogs." *Southwestern Journal of Anthropology* 17:256–272.

Kaut, Charles (1965). "The Principle of Contingency in Tagalog Society." *Asian Studies* 3:1–15.

Lynch, Frank, and Ronald S. Hymes (1984). "Cognitive Mapping in the Tagalog Area." In *Philippine Society and the Individual: Selected Essays of Frank Lynch, 1949–1976,* edited by Aram A. Yengoyan and Perla Q. Makil, 127–164. Ann Arbor: University of Michigan, Center for South and Southeast Asian Studies.

CHARLES KAUT

Tagbanuwa

The Tagbanuwa (Tagbanoua, Tagbanua) are one of the indigenous peoples of Palawan Island in the Philippines and, aside from the Batak, the only group on the island to have been studied extensively by anthropologists. At the time of first Spanish contact the population of Palawan and nearby islands was comprised of Batak, Tagbanuwa, Palawan, Kenoy, Moro, Kalamian, Agutayano, Kuyono, and Kagayano peoples. In the early 1980s, the total number of Tagbanuwa speakers in the Philippines was estimated at about 14,000. The central regions of Palawan island are the homeland of the Tagbanuwa, with groups now also living in the northern portions of the island and in Quezon Province. Tagbanuwa is an Austronesian language, with a distinction sometimes being made between Central Tagbanuwa and Northern Tagbanuwa.

The traditional economy involved the growing of rice supplemented by maize, millet, taro, cassava, and sweet potatoes. Fishing and hunting provided supplemental foods. The Tagbanuwa are the only people in central Palawan who collect Manila copal, a gum found in the bark of a tree

(*Dammara orientalis*) of the pine family. A large portion of trade income comes from the sale of gum, rice, split rattan, wax, and honey. The traditional religion centered on a world of deities, evil spirits, spirit relatives (*tiladmanin*), and the cult of the dead. This is not ancestor worship, and usually includes only veneration of the mother, father, brothers, and sisters.

See also Palawan

Bibliography

Fox, Robert B. (1954). "Religion and Society among the Tagbanuwa of Palawan Island, Philippines." Ph.D. dissertation, University of Chicago.

Warren, Charles P. (1975). "Tagbanuwa." In *Ethnic Groups of Insular Southeast Asia*, edited by Frank M. LeBar. Vol. 2, *Philippines and Formosa*, 64–67. New Haven: HRAF Press.

Tai Lue

ETHNONYMS: Bai-yi, Dai, Lawa, Lü, Lua', Lue, Pai-I, Pai-yi, Shui Bai-yi, Shui Dai, Tai

Orientation

Identification. The Tai Lue are the Tai-speaking inhabitants of Sipsongpanna. (This name is written "Xishuangbanna" in Pinyin; when the status of the prefecture as part of the People's Republic of China is being referred to here it will be written in its Pinyin form, and when the Tai sociopolitical unit is the important issue it will be written in romanized Tai. It should also be mentioned that "Dai" is the Pinyin form of "Tai," which is the conventional spelling in English. There is no difference in pronunciation.) Sipsongpanna means "the twelve thousand fields" or "the twelve principalities." The extent of the kingdom varied over time, but in the precolonial period it included Muang Sing, now in Laos, and parts of the Tai-speaking areas of Myanmar (Burma). Today, however, there are Lue communities throughout northern Thailand, and it is not easy to make distinctions between the Lue and the Yorng and Khoen of Myanmar. There is now also a sizable Lue population in Taiwan. The term "Tai" is used for all Tai-speaking peoples. In the southwestern part of Yunnan these are mainly the Lue and the people known variously as Tai Nuea (Northern Tai), Chinese Shans, Tai Khorn, and Tai Mao. There is considerable difference between the Tai Lue and Tai Nuea languages and they should be considered mutually unintelligible.

Location. Xishuangbanna Dai Autonomous Prefecture lies in the southernmost part of Yunnan Province of the People's Republic of China (PRC), roughly between 21°10′ and 23°40′ N and 99°55′ and 101°59′ E. The capital of the prefecture is the city of Jing Hong (Ceng Hung, "the city of the dawn"). Jing Hong is situated on the Lancang Jiang, the Mekong River. The Tai Lue mostly live in the river valleys. As in upper Myanmar and north Thailand, the year is divided into three seasons with the rains falling from about June to October.

Demography. In 1923 the population of Tai Lue in Xishuangbanna was estimated at just under 100,000. Recent estimates indicate a figure of 240,000. There have also been major changes in relative populations. In 1923 it was estimated that the Tai Lue constituted slightly over 70 percent of the population of Xishuangbanna. In 1945 this had probably fallen to about 50 percent. During the Korean War, when there was an embargo on the sale of rubber to China, Xishuangbanna proved to be one of the more suitable areas for its growth and there was a massive movement of Han into the prefecture, which reduced the percentage of Tai Lue to about 35 percent. The Lue population of Thailand was estimated at about 50,000 in the 1960s.

Linguistic Affiliation. Tai Lue belongs to the Southwestern Group of Tai languages and is very similar to the languages known as Yorng, Khoen, and Kam Muang (the language of northern Thailand). The writing systems, which are also similar, are derived from the Mon and look like the Burmese script. In the 1950s the PRC reformed Tai scripts in Yunnan, and for Lue additional tone markers were added and all characters were written on the line. These reforms have created some problems. There are complaints that there is not sufficient material to read in the new script and that those educated in the new script cannot read the old Tai Lue documents. One of the major differences between the phonology of Tai Lue and Kam Muang of northern Thailand is that Lue appears not to use diphthongs. In vocabulary, the massive borrowing of Central Thai into Kam Muang has not taken place in Lue; instead, there has been extensive recent borrowing from Chinese.

History and Cultural Relations

There is dispute as to the movements of the Tai-speaking peoples to the area they now occupy. According to tradition, the Tai Lue entered this area and displaced earlier inhabitants, who included the modern-day Akha, in about the eighth and ninth centuries. No evidence is available to verify these claims. Tai came into contact with the Han in the fourteenth century. Nineteenth-century European scholars suggested that the kingdom of Nan Chao (seventh to thirteenth century) was Tai. This view is now generally rejected. Tai speakers probably formed only a small, nondominant section of the population. Under the Mongol Yuan dynasty, Yunnan was incorporated into China, but control was little more than nominal until 1325 when a Lue chieftain was appointed Chinese commander-in-chief based in Jing Hong. Suzerainty over Sipsongpanna fluctuated among the Ming emperors (fourteenth to seventeenth centuries), local rule, and the Toungoo dynasty of Burma. Ming control of Sipsongpanna was greater than that of the Mongols. They interfered with the hereditary succession of Lue chiefs and demanded silver tribute. Ming control was extended to the Mekong River and was mainly peaceful to the middle of the seventeenth century. The conquest and pacification of the southeastern region proceeded with much turbulence during the eighteenth and nineteenth centuries. The prizes sought were the region's tea and cotton. During the middle years of the nineteenth century much of

Sipsongpanna was in revolt against Chinese attempts to impose land taxes and remove the powers of the Lue chieftains. In many parts of the country the outcome was joint authority vested in Chinese magistrates and Tai chiefs. The chief of Jing Hong was recognized as suzerain over the chiefdoms, which constituted the twelve _panna_. He had the title of _cawphaendin,_ which is translated as "king." During World War II Yunnan suffered badly in the conflict between the Allies and the Japanese. Siam was then occupied and an ally of the Japanese, and Sipsongpanna was subject to rather indiscriminate bombing because of the alleged presence of Chinese troops. Many Lue fled to Burma and northern Thailand at this time. With the victory of the Communists and the establishment of a Communist administration in Sipsongpanna, the kingdom ceased to exist: the last king is now an academic in Kunming. There was much movement out of Sipsongpanna. Among the nobility and elite many Tai had thrown in their lot with the Kuomintang and so most fled to Taiwan. There were divisions within the court on purely factional lines and this determined, to some extent, who stayed and who fled. Many, including both nobility and common people, also fled to Burma and Thailand. During the hundreds of years that Chinese rule was being extended into Sipsongpanna, the region and the Lue also had cultural links, political alliances, and conflicts with Tai speakers in Burma, Thailand, and Laos. Sharing very similar languages with these peoples, the Lue developed similar forms of Theravada Buddhism, a common literary tradition, and much familial contact. The twentieth century has seen these lessen, although contacts improved during the 1980s. There has been much recent movement of population between China, Myanmar, and Thailand. At the elite level this movement has been by air between Bangkok and Kunming, but there is also a probably more important movement of ordinary people, by foot, motorcycle, boat, and pack animal. The reasons for this movement include trade, family visits, religious purposes, and professional pursuits.

Settlements

Settlements tend to be nucleated, either on raised ground surrounded by rice fields or on high ground on either side of a road or pathway. No detailed information on village size is available for Sipsongpanna as a whole, but figures are available for four villages (Chang Chai, Thung, Dorn Taen, and Thin) within easy reach of Jing Hong, from 1940 and from 1987. In 1940 the populations ranged from 106 to 195; in 1987, from 416 to 600. Houses are built on stilts, and are of bamboo or timber, often with tiled or shingled roofs. Houses are usually occupied simultaneously by three generations. Traditionally, ordinary farmers' houses were said to be built of bamboo and thatch, while those of village officials were of timber. Not all villages have temples (_wat_) today, because many were destroyed during the Cultural Revolution. Traditionally, each village had a piece of forest land (_dong sya_), which was sacred to the tutelary deity; hunting was prohibited there. Population pressure and acquisition of land for rubber plantations have now deprived many villages of such land.

Economy

Subsistence and Commercial Activities. Traditionally the Tai Lue have been wet-rice agriculturalists using the stan-

dard technology of Southeast Asian rice cultivation. Plowing, raking, and leveling are done with wooden equipment with steel blades and rakes, which are buffalo-drawn. Mostly glutinous rice is grown for consumption and sale, the dark purple variety being particularly favored. Tractors are now used, but they seem to be valued more as an efficient and cheap means of transport than as an agricultural tool. Some smallholding rubber is cultivated, though most Xishuangbanna rubber is grown on state plantations with Han labor. A wide variety of other crops—cotton, sugar, and tobacco being among the most important—are also grown, as are maize, beans, and a variety of vegetables. Many villages have communal fish ponds, and under the new system villages are allotted shares in the catch. They also keep a range of domestic animals, buffalo, cattle, pigs, and chickens.

Industrial Arts. Weaving and the manufacture of elaborate textiles were important aspects of rural life, but although Lue textiles are still well known, they seem to be becoming rarer around Jing Hong. In recent years individual villagers have set themselves up with equipment for such tasks as rice milling and noodle making. Some of these enterprises compete with state factories. The refugee population of northern Thailand, particularly in the town of Mae Sai, warrants special mention. Because of Thai government restrictions on their movement they depend heavily on such things as the making of reed brooms and employment in factories as cutters and polishers of precious stones.

Trade. There are markets everywhere and many local areas seem to rotate markets on a five-day cycle. Markets are not ethnically exclusive: there are Tai, Han, and other minorities selling a range of goods—cloth, shoes, and manufactured articles that have come up from Thailand through Myanmar; vegetables, meat, fish (often still alive), chickens, eggs, cooked food, and all kinds of forest produce. Whereas most Han traders are men, most Tai traders are women, though men may sell freshly butchered pork or beef. Not much is known of how the cross-boundary trade is organized, but it is clear that Tai Lue control a large part of it. It is also clear that there is some smuggling of jade and precious stones.

Division of Labor. In agriculture the major division of labor is that the heaviest tasks, such as plowing, are confined to men, and it seems that the cultivation of vegetables and small cash crops is done by women, but not exclusively. In the domestic sphere, cooking is done mainly, but not exclusively, by women. Village officials, both traditionally and under Communist rule, have almost always been men.

Land Tenure. Traditional land tenure in Sipsongpanna is thought to have been based on village communities under the control of chiefs. Certain lands were reserved for the chief and his senior officials and these plots would be worked either with the nobles' own retainers or with corvée. Other village officials, including ritual officials, had special allocations of land that included the right to free labor. The commoners had access to what land was left, but even here there were said to be divisions. There were first the "native" Lue who occupied the best villages, had major duties, and did not marry with other types of villager. The second major group was comprised of the "dependents of the lord's house," who were migrants from other Tai _muang_ (chiefdoms) or prisoners of war. They cultivated state land, but could cultivate a small portion for themselves. They performed domestic duties and other labor for which they were paid wages. The third group consisted of the remote kin of the nobility, who were granted land as free peasants. It appears their land was not liable to reallocation. Much effort by Chinese officials throughout the centuries appears to have been directed at making cultivators directly liable to pay taxes to the emperor for the land they cultivated, thus breaking the power of the traditional rulers. Although this appears to have succeeded in the north, it was only imperfectly achieved in the southeast and west. During Communist rule, though Sipsongpanna was never completely communized, there was a period during which individual control of production and access to produce was very limited. Today the village decides how much land is available and how it should be divided each year—it seems mostly to be done on a per capita basis. Under the system that began in Xishuangbanna about 1985, each household is allotted land for five years and contracts to pay specified amounts to the government during that period. As an example, a household that has been given rice land at the rate of 1.3 *mou* per person (1 mou equals about 0.06 hectare) would be expected to pay 26 kilograms of paddy per person per year. The government acquires another 80 kilograms at about half the market price. The farmer may sell additional paddy to the government at slightly below the market price, but may prefer to take his chances elsewhere.

Kinship

Kin Groups and Descent.   No detailed studies of Tai Lue kinship are available. There is reason to believe that the multigenerational household and compound has been the major unit of social organization. It also appears that even villages close to the capital of Jing Hong have a strong tendency toward endogamy, suggesting that kin ties within villages are pervasive and that it is probable that villages act very much as kinship units. The literature suggests that succession in princely families was patrilineal and followed rules of primogeniture. However, experience with other Tai groups and the region in general suggests that though this may have been an expectation, dynastic disputes may have brought quite different outcomes. The question of matrilineal descent is also a problem. Many groups with close cultural connections to the Lue have a system of matrilineal descent particularly concerned with a cult of domestic spirits. There is no clear evidence about this for the Lue, but Kon Muang from Chiang Mai, who have family connections with the Lue, claim that a similar system was traditionally present.

Kinship Terminology.   The Lue system is very like that of northern Thailand—generational, but distinguishing "elder" from "younger" in one's own and senior generations. The skewing of nephew/niece and grandchild terms is also present. In address the terms *ai* and *ii*, ambivalent in northern Thailand, are used as normal terms of address for adults as well as children.

Marriage and Family

Marriage.   Traditionally, ordinary Tai Lue marriage appears to have been characteristically informal and largely monogamous. Sources suggest that evening weaving on public platforms (compared to open verandas in northern Thailand)

was an institutionalized occasion for courting—as were the festivals associated mainly with religious occasions. If villages were largely endogamous, this pattern of working while courting is consistent with the informality of courting and marriage. Premarital sexual relations seem not to have been disapproved, but a permanent relation required agreement on such matters as how long the bridegroom would reside with his new wife's family. Many modern Tai Lue homes do not contain the Tai matrilineal ancestral shrines characteristic of northern Thailand that are involved in marriage and the control of sexual behavior. Contemporary information also suggests that postmarital residence is decided pragmatically according to which household requires the residence and services of the couple. This decision is known as *aw koei/aw njing*, "taking a son-in-law/daughter-in-law." Traditionally divorce by mutual consent was easy.

Domestic Unit.   Many Tai houses around Jing Hong are large and may contain more than one elementary family. They appear to operate as a single economic and ritual unit. Today allocation of agricultural land is calculated per capita but assigned by household units.

Inheritance.   Very little is known about the intricacies of traditional inheritance. If land was administered as indicated earlier, it seems that the major inheritance pattern was bilateral right to communal land. Today the youngest daughter, if there is one, remains with her parents and expects to inherit the family home.

Socialization.   Fathers and mothers are the prime care givers for children, though the household members and neighbors appear to take over duties when required. Both boys and girls attended traditional school in the wat, though only boys went on to be ordained as novices. Today children attend state primary schools where, depending on the population of the area, they may be taught Tai as well as Chinese. In secondary schools, however, Tai is no longer taught. Traditionally the Lue ordained their boys as novices, and not many adults were ordained as monks. Today their numbers are slowly increasing after the destruction of temples during the Chinese Cultural Revolution.

Sociopolitical Organization

Xishuangbanna is a Dai Autonomous Prefecture of the province of Yunnan in the People's Republic of China and is therefore today part of that political system.

Social Organization.   The fundamental class division of the traditional social structure was between the nobility, with the king and royal family at its peak, and the common people. Both groups, however, were themselves arranged hierarchically. The king—"the lord of the land" (cawphaendin)—was in theory the owner of all land in the kingdom. His hereditary chiefdom was based in Jing Hong, where he held court. The rest of the kingdom was divided into *meng* or muang, which may be translated as "chiefdoms." Other members of the nobility held various titles and performed duties toward the king or chief, in return for which they held land and rights over serfs. The commoners were referred to as *khaphai* by the nobility. This term in fact brought together two different statuses: *kha*, which meant "slave" and was also generally used of non-Tai, Mon–Khmer-speaking peoples; and *phai*, which may be variously interpreted as "serf" or "freeman." The senior commoner officials had special status and rights to land, as did certain ritual experts. This division among commoners was expressed in the contrast _kanmeng/kanban_, "the work of the chiefdom (or state)/the work of the village." Officials had a duty to the state itself, while other commoners had a duty to the village community. Today in Sipsongpanna the old class division expresses itself somewhat in the pattern of sinicization. Many Tai have now taken Chinese names, the old nobility having the surname "Dao." Members of the former ruling families hold positions of influence and authority in the provincial administration. This phenomenon is not confined to Tai. The present governor of Yunnan is from the Naxi minority. Around Jing Hong traditionally owned land has been converted into businesses of various kinds, particularly those related to the tourist trade, such as restaurants and guest houses. Within the village there is now general social equality and equal access to land resources. There are, however, clear signs that village officials and party cadres have special privileges. One phenomenon is the different style of house—brick and mortar—favored by some village officials.

Political Organization. Traditional political organization has been reported as being very formalized, and we should keep in mind the possibility that the actual working of the system was much less formal and also that the history of warfare and conflicting claims to suzerainty would have greatly modified it. The king was also part of the Chinese administration and was known by a title translated as the "Cheli Pacification Commissioner" ("Cheli" being a Chinese name for Jing Hong). Below the king was the _upalat_ (a comparable rank in Siam was translated by nineteenth-century Europeans as "second king"). Government was conducted by two councils—the Royal (or outer) Council and the Private (or inner) Council. The Royal Council was presided over by a representative of the territorial princes (the rulers of the meng). The membership consisted of senior-ranking princes, the younger brothers of the king, four senior ministers (the prime minister, in charge of general administration, finance, and revenue; the minister of justice and recorder of population; the minister in charge of government rations; and the president), an official in charge of sacrificial rites at markets, and all the rulers of meng or their representatives. This council discussed all matters to go before the king, as well as proposals by the king. Ultimate authority, however, appeared to remain with the monarch. The Private Council was made up of members of the royal family, of four grades. The council was presided over by the chief official of the palace. When the king did not attend a meeting of the outer council, a member of the inner council took his place. The Private Council appears to have been an advisory body of close kin, who kept watch over the activities of the Royal Council. The councils of the meng chiefs were patterned on the central bodies. Below the chief were the president of the council, a senior _phya_ (lord) who acted as "prime minister," and two or three other lords. There were also representatives of local organizations such as the _ho sib_, literally the "head of ten." At the village level the officials were phya, ca, and _saen_, which may be glossed as "lord," "lieutenant," and "noble" (the latter also means "one hundred thousand"). Sources also say that large villages would have an official responsible for ceremonies and rites, one responsible for irrigation, one responsible for the

registration and reception of strangers, and one who managed lost and found property. There was also a leader for each youth group, male and female. In the modern administration, village officials have Chinese titles that translate as "headman," "treasurer," "chief of women," and "constable."

Social Control. In traditional times, in communities with recurrent warfare, where political authorities had constant recourse to armed might, control was tight in settled areas. But as the history of flight and migration shows, there was always a means of escape. There are Lue law codes, but like the codes of the Mangrai in northern Thailand, it is not known to what extent and how these were enforced. There are no detailed studies of village life, so comments on social control at that level must be speculative. There is evidence that patterns of witchcraft accusation, as reported particularly from northern Thailand, are also found among the Lue. These are extreme mechanisms, perhaps better interpreted as mechanisms of oppression rather than social control. But they do suggest that public opinion, gossip, and similar mechanisms are manipulated in Tai Lue villages as elsewhere in the Tai-speaking world.

Conflict. The history of Sipsongpanna is a history of conflict—between heirs to high office, between meng, with conquerors coming out of Burma, Thailand, and Laos—as well as against the continuing push of the Chinese for suzerainty. The Communist conquest has brought an end to warfare, and since the early 1950s there appears to have been no significant movement to change the political status of the Tai Lue. Little, if anything, is known about the resolution of conflict within the general population.

Religion and Expressive Culture

Religious Beliefs. The Tai Lue are Theravada Buddhists, with historical links to the Yuan tradition of the Tai speakers of upper Myanmar and northern Thailand. The term "Hinayana" is generally used in Chinese sources to refer to the religion of the Tai Lue, and it also has some indigenous currency. Spirit beliefs are widespread and, particularly among the elite and upper classes, there is evidence of beliefs from Chinese religion. More recently, a small but significant strain of skepticism has appeared. The Tai Lue, like Tai groups in Thailand and Myanmar, believe in spirits known as _phi_ as well as in the hierarchy of the Hindu-Buddhist pantheon. Of major importance are the territorial deities. The deity Phya Alawu (sometimes called Arawi) parallels legendary figures in northern Thailand and Luang Prabang, and appears to have the status of protective spirit for the entire kingdom. Information on domestic spirits is limited.

Religious Practitioners. Because of the Cultural Revolution the number of monks and novices now in Sipsongpanna is small. The Tai Lue traditionally preferred to be ordained as novices, leaving the monkhood as a specialized category. Many monasteries are still struggling to build up their numbers. During the Cultural Revolution monks were forced to leave the order, and stories are told of many fleeing to monasteries across the border in Burma; a few defied the worst excesses of the time, maintaining their vows under threat of death. Villages have lay elders who are necessary in the performance of Buddhist ritual and there are officials who perform the territorial spirit-cult activities. Presumably many of these are also healers and diviners.

Ceremonies.   The Tai Lue celebrate the full cycle of Buddhist festivities. In recent years, as part of the Chinese government's promotion of tourism, the Buddhist New Year in April has become an international event, known as the "Dai water-splashing festival." To the Lue, ceremonies of major importance are the beginning and end of the Buddhist "Lent," the period of the rains when Buddhist monks are constrained to sleep in the precincts of their monasteries, and Vesak, the day associated with the major life events of the Buddha. The celebration known in the literature as *pai* has become synonymous with the Tai Lue. Some scholars theorize that the term "Pai-yi" (or "Bai-yi") derives from this ceremony; the more popular interpretation is that it means "white barbarian." The Chinese representation of "Pai" (in Pinyin "Bai") does not seem to be an accurate representation of the pronunciation of this word. The major purpose of this ceremony is the installation of a Buddha statue in a wat. Sponsors gained status through this activity. Ceremonies are held to propitiate tutelary deities, *sya ban*, at village shrines called *cai ban* ("the heart of the village").

Arts.   Traditionally the Lue practiced a range of arts and crafts, such as the production of textiles, basket weaving, temple murals, music, and theatricals. Two items are worthy of brief mention here. One is the distinctive decorated and covered well, characteristic of Sipsongpanna and Dehong (Tai, but not Tai Lue) farther north. The other is the musical form *kap*, which is akin to the *sor* of northern Thailand. This is now encouraged by the government and there are regular performances on Jing Hong radio. The most popular is the *kap langka*, the Lue version of the Ramayana.

Medicine.   Tai Lue practice both supernatural and herbal treatment of the sick. Chinese sources say their procedures for diagnosing illness are similar to those of the Han: observation, listening and questioning, and taking the pulse. There are numerous Lue medical texts and pharmacopoeia, some of which have been published in Lue and Chinese.

Death and Afterlife.   Traditionally the Lue cremated only monks and very old people, burying others, except those having "unfortunate" deaths. This is the opposite of Central Thai (Siamese) practice, but it is similar to the traditional practice of the Kon Muang of northern Thailand. It is not known why these differences occur. It is reported that Lue villagers long settled in northern Thailand have practices like those of the Siamese. The Lue subscribe to Buddhist beliefs about the nature of heavens and hells, rebirth, and final enlightenment.

Bibliography

Chen Han-Seng (1949). *Frontier Land Systems in Southernmost China.* New York: Institute of Pacific Relations.

Lemoine, Jacques (1987). "The Tai Lue Historical Relation with China and the Shaping of the Sipsong Panna Political System." *Proceedings of the International Conference on Thai Studies* 3, pt. 1:121–134. Compiled by Ann Buller. Canberra: Australian National University, Department of Anthropology.

Moerman, Michael (1965). "Ethnic Identity in a Complex Civilization: Who Are the Lue?" *American Anthropologist* 67:1215–1230.

Moerman, Michael (1968). *Agricultural Change and Peasant Choice in a Thai Village.* Berkeley and Los Angeles: University of California Press.

Thai-Yunnan Project Newsletter (1988). Canberra: Australian National University, Department of Anthropology (numerous items).

GEHAN WIJEYEWARDENE

Taiwan Aboriginal Peoples

Orientation

The indigenous people of the island of Taiwan (Formosa) are now only a small minority of the Taiwan population, which is mainly Han Chinese. Many of the aboriginal groups are now assimilated almost completely into the mainstream culture. Anthropologists conventionally have divided the seven major remaining groups into three categories based on location, as follows. (1) Eastern Lowland Groups: Ami (Amia, Mo-amiami, Mo-quami, Pangtash); Puyuma (Panapanayan, Pelam, Pilam, Piuma, Pyuma). (2) Western Lowland Group: Saisiat (Saiset, Saisirat, Saisiyat). (3) Central Mountain Groups: Atayal (Atazan, Etall, Taiyal, Tayal); Bunun (Bunum, Vonum, Vunun); Paiwan-Rukai (Tsarisen); Tsou (Alishan, Arisan, Northern Tsou, Tsu'u, Tsuou, Tzo).

The aboriginal peoples of Taiwan speak or used to speak Austronesian languages of two or possibly three branches: Atayalic (Atayal and Sedeq), Tsouic (Tsou, Kanakanabou, and Sa'aroa), and possibly Paiwanic (all others). The speakers of Atayalic and Tsouic languages inhabit or inhabited the central mountain area, whereas Paiwanic speakers inhabit primarily the coastal plains.

Although Chinese pirates had been settling Taiwan from the sixteenth century, it was not until the seventeenth century that Chinese began to have much of an impact on aboriginal societies and cultures. From that time on, however, the relationship between Han and non-Han peoples has been one of profound acculturation and assimilation for the latter. By the early nineteenth century, there were 2 million Han in Taiwan, and most of the aboriginal peoples living on the plains had been assimilated or driven into the mountains. By the mid-1960s, one-third of Taiwan's 13 million aboriginal people lived in large cities. Today many of the aboriginal people of Taiwan cannot be considered to exist as identifiable groups, and so they are not included in this article. The following are the groups that still exist.

Eastern Lowland Groups

Ami. The 90,000 (in 1975) Ami were indigenous to the east coast between Hualien and Taitung. They have been growing rapidly in number (their 1939 population was 52,000). The influences of the Japanese after 1900 and the local Han peasantry have led to a great deal of acculturation, although the Ami are one of the few aboriginal peoples on Taiwan who still speak their own language.

The Ami were originally swidden agriculturalists who adopted wet-rice agriculture and the water buffalo (used for plowing) from the Han in approximately 1900. They raised dogs for hunting and pigs and chickens for ritual sacrifice. They made their clothing from bark cloth. Prior to Japanese occupation, the members of villages owned land corporately; it was parceled into units worked by younger men's age-grade groups. Since then, private ownership has become common. Hunting and fishing territories are administered by age-grade groups.

The Ami are matrilineal (with 50 clans) and generally matrilocal. The _ambil-anak_ form of marriage, however, allowed those without daughters to pay a bride-price to gain patrilocal residence for the couple. Owing to Chinese influence, at least in part, this pattern is being used more and more by those with daughters.

Political structure is dualistic. Secular authority resides in the men's age-grade groups. Ritual authority is provided by the matrilineal _kakitaan_, or hereditary priestly families, though it is the men and not the women of these families who function as priests.

Social control of murder depended less on law than on blood vengeance by the deceased's kindred. Warfare against the Atayal, Bunun, and Puyuma peoples involved headhunting; pacification circa 1930 ended this. Traditionally the taking of heads was integral to the _irisin_ renewal and fertility ceremony, celebrated following the millet harvest. Ami villages were once protected against their enemies by sharp bamboo stakes and trenches.

Puyuma. The approximately 6,000 (in 1975) Puyuma are now essentially assimilated among Han peasants. Traditionally they were agriculturalists who also hunted and fished. Land was owned by heads of aristocratic families, who rented it to commoners for part of the agricultural and faunal goods they produced.

The Puyuma lived in permanent villages of approximately 600 people. Each village was politically independent and almost entirely endogamous. Leadership was inherited among chiefly families. The Puyuma are matrilineal and matrilocal.

Of special importance was the moiety and age-grade system. The age-grade groups functioned as military training schools, among other things, and the moieties would practice attacking each other. From the ages of 18 to 22, a young man lived segregated from females in a men's house and learned to fight. At 22 he was allowed to marry, and he left the men's house to live with his wife's family.

The Puyuma believe that each person has three souls, one of which resides in the head, and one of which resides on each shoulder. Illness is caused by the departure of a shoulder soul, and death by that of the head soul. Female shamans treat illness by returning a shoulder soul.

Western Lowland Group

Saisiat. The 2,800 (in 1966) Saisiat live in the coastal cities of Miaoli and Hsinchu in northwestern Taiwan. Their culture has been greatly affected by their contact with the Atayal and the Han.

The patrilineal Saisiat are organized into seventeen exogamous sibs, which now bear Chinese names. Governmental pressure and the introduction of wet rice have weakened the sib ownership of land in favor of private ownership.

Sister exchange was the preferred marriage pattern, although in some cases bride-service was practiced.

Villages were composed of localized sib segments. Although villages were autonomous, they did cooperate for defense.

Central Mountain Groups

Features common to all mountain groups include their great reliance on millet and their extensive acculturation.

Paiwan-Rukai. The 51,000 (in 1966) Paiwan and Rukai live in the southern reaches of Taiwan's central mountain area. They are known for their monumental wood and stone artwork and their bronze dagger handles.

The Paiwan-Rukai traditionally lived in close-settled villages of from 100 to 1,000 people on hillsides. Because relations with other groups were hostile and alliances rare, the villages were protected by bamboo and stone walls and by guard patrols. Villages were autonomous and independent. Houses were semisubterranean.

These peoples were swidden horticulturalists and hunters and fishers. All land belonged to chiefly lineages, although commoners had rights of usufruct.

Descent was ambilineal and residence ambilocal. Divorce, usually attributable to adultery, was common. Inheritance was by primogeniture without regard to sex.

Social control was primarily legal; chiefs adjudicated disputes and levied fines. The amount of fines varied inversely with social class, and aristocrats were immune to prosecution for many offenses, including theft. Tattoos indicated noble status, with the exception that young men gained the right to have tattoos through successful head-hunting. They also blackened their teeth as youngsters and pierced their earlobes.

The deceased were buried under their houses; all members of one family were buried in a single grave.

Bunun. A full article on the Bunun is included in this volume.

Tsou. The 3,100 (in 1966) Tsou traditionally lived in the western central mountains near Mount Ami. In the 1930s, the government relocated them to lower elevations and encouraged the farming of wet rice. The Tsou traditionally lived in hamlets of three to ten households, although at one time there were core villages with men's houses at the center of several hamlets. Tsou houses were unique in Taiwan, being oval in shape and having thatched roofs that reached nearly to the ground. Nuclear-family houses were considered complete only if they had a shelf for the bones of animals killed in hunting, a millet field, and a storage basket for sacred millet. The wall-less men's houses once had shelves for heads taken in battle.

The Tsou are known for their strict enforcement of gender roles. Men hunt, burn fields, and make baskets, nets, and weapons. Women make cloth, pottery, and embroidery, take care of pigs, and weed the fields. According to traditional belief, to touch the tools used by, or the goods made by, members of the other sex was to risk supernatural sanction (such as scarcity of game) for oneself and for the group.

The Tsou are patrilineal, and lineages own hunting territories; people who are not members of the lineage may use these lands by paying a tribute.

The functions of political leader, ritual leader, and war leader were usually performed by one man.

Atayal.   The Atayal occupy nearly a third of Taiwan's mountainous area, in north-central Taiwan. They speak two languages, Atayal proper (with dialects Seqoleq and Tse'ole') and Sedeq.

The Atayal traditionally lived in hamlets or isolated huts above 1,500 meters in elevation. They lived in almost entirely subterranean houses that one entered by climbing down a ladder from the door. There was a shelf for the heads of enemies, and the bones that were trophies of hunting hung from rafters. Pigs lived in their own huts in fenced yards. Japanese and Han Taiwanese forced the Atayal to move to lower elevations in this century, and now they live in typical Chinese-style houses.

The Atayal subsisted mainly by horticulture, but they also hunted (often in groups) for boars, deer, goats, bears, bats, squirrels, and monkeys. Fishing was done with poison.

The preparation for marriage could be a lengthy affair. First, the prospective groom would have a male relative propose and negotiate on his behalf. Then came the haggling over the bride-price, which could take as many as four years. The bride-price was paid in the form of shell money, pigs, and embroidered clothing. Some practice sister exchange, but since this practice violates taboo there must be an accompanying pig sacrifice and ritual feast. The incest prohibition extends to fourth patrilateral and third matrilateral cousins, though one may marry a third patrilateral cousin upon payment of a fine. There are no lineage groups. Inheritance is patrilineal and by primogeniture.

Traditional political organization lay in hamlet groups that were patrilineally related and that observed the same rituals and taboos. Social control was by law and by taboo. In some types of case, headmen imposed fines. In others, violations of taboo required confession and a pig sacrifice, in which the injured parties would eat the meat of the pig.

Although all Taiwanese aboriginal peoples practiced head-hunting, the Atayal were the most feared. The group's reason for warfare was usually to gain or defend territory, but the individual's reason to fight was for honor and prestige. The use of an enemy head was crucial to ancestor worship, and the skull, teeth, and hair were used for personal protection from spirits.

See also Bunun; Taiwanese

Bibliography

Beauclair, Inez de (1956). "Present-Day Conditions of the Aborigines of Formosa (Atayal and Bunun)." *Sociologus* 6:153–169.

Chang, Kwang-chih (1969). *Fengpitou, Tapenking, and the Prehistory of Taiwan.* Yale University Publications in Anthropology, no. 73. New Haven: Yale University, Department of Anthropology.

Chen, Chi-lu (1965). "Age Organization and Men's Houses of the Formosan Aborigines." *Bulletin of the Department of Archaeology and Anthropology* 25–26:93–111. Taipei: National Taiwan University.

Chen, Chi-lu, and Michael D. Coe (1954). "An Investigation of Ami Religion." *Quarterly Journal of the Taiwan Museum* 7:249–262.

Dyen, Isidore (1971). "The Austronesian Languages of Formosa." In *Current Trends in Linguistics,* edited by Thomas Sebeok. Vol. 8, *Linguistics in Oceania,* edited by J. Donald Bowen, Isidore Dyen, George W. Grace, and Stefan A. Wurm, 169–199. The Hague and Paris: Mouton.

Ferrell, Raleigh (1969). *Taiwan Aboriginal Groups: Problems in Cultural and Linguistic Classification.* Monographs of the Institute of Ethnology, no. 17. Taipei: Academia Sinica.

Ferrell, Raleigh (1971). "Aboriginal Peoples of the Southwestern Taiwan Plain." *Bulletin of the Institute of Ethnology* 32:217–235. Taipei: Academia Sinica.

LeBar, Frank M., ed. (1975). "Part IV. Formosa." *Ethnic Groups of Insular Southeast Asia.* Vol. 2, *Philippines and Formosa,* 115–148. New Haven: HRAF Press.

Mabuchi, Toichi (1960). "The Aboriginal Peoples of Formosa." In *Social Structure in Southeast Asia,* edited by George P. Murdock, 127–140. Chicago: Quadrangle Books.

Tang, Mei-chun (1970). "Han and Non-Han in Taiwan: A Case of Acculturation." *Bulletin of the Institute of Ethnology* 30:99–110. Taipei: Academia Sinica.

DANIEL STROUTHES

Taiwanese

ETHNONYMS: Formosan, Republican Chinese

The Chinese who live on the island of Taiwan are of fairly recent mainland origin. The indigenous people of the island are represented by seven tribes who speak Malayo-Polynesian languages and who numbered 338,151 in 1991. The Chinese, in contrast, speak either Hakka or Hokkien, although many soldiers and bureaucrats prefer Mandarin, the official language. The island was once claimed by the Dutch, who founded the town of T'ai-pei in 1624; China annexed the island in 1683. There was a brief British presence toward the end of the nineteenth century, and then Taiwan was under Japanese colonial administration from 1895 to 1945. In 1949 Taiwan was cut off from the mainland by civil war and became a separate republic. The official point of view in Beijing, however, is that it is a breakaway province of the People's Republic of China.

Taiwan is located in the South China Sea, just to the north of the Philippines and east of Fukien Province. It is one of the most densely inhabited parts of the world, with 20.4 million people (1991), nearly all Chinese, living on 36,179 square kilometers of land, three-quarters of which is unarable. Rice is the major crop, but the relative success of the Taiwanese economy in recent years has been dependent on heavy and effective industrialization initiated by the Japanese. Over the past forty years Taiwan has had an annual real economic growth rate that averaged 8 percent, one of the highest in the world.

See also Bunun; Taiwan Aboriginal Peoples; in volume 6, Hakka; Han

Bibliography

Wolf, Margery (1968). *The House of Lim: A Study of a Chinese Farm Family*. New York: Appleton-Century-Crofts.

PAUL HOCKINGS

Tasaday

ETHNONYMS: none

Orientation

In 1971 the news story broke of the discovery of a band of cave-dwelling people called "Tasaday," who were said to be living in a secluded area of rain forest in the Philippines. The discovery team was led by Manuel Elizalde Jr., the Filipino politician who headed PANAMIN (Presidential Assistant on National Minorities), the government agency then in charge of all Philippine tribal peoples. These twenty-six Tasaday individuals were reported to be following a Stone-Age life-style, surviving solely on wild foods, and wearing leaves for clothing. They reportedly knew nothing of the outside world, nor of the large village of agriculturalists located just a three-hour walk from their cave home. They knew neither how to hunt nor how to grow food, and ate only what they could forage: roots, wild bananas, grubs, berries, and crabs and frogs fished by hand from small streams. News reports said that they had no pottery, cloth, metal, art, houses, weapons, dogs, or domestic plants. The cave site where they are said to have lived is located in dense rain forest in South Cotabato Province in southern Mindanao, at 6°18′ N and 124°33′ E, at an elevation of 1,200 meters.

The story gained worldwide attention mainly through the National Geographic Society, both from the publication of their famous cover story on the Tasaday (in *National Geographic* in 1972), and from their Tasaday film shown repeatedly on television stations worldwide in 1972–73. The fame of the Tasaday spread farther with the publication in 1975 of

the book *The Gentle Tasaday* by American reporter John Nance. Politicians, movie stars, journalists, and film makers were flown in by PANAMIN helicopters to visit the Tasaday for short periods in 1972 and 1973. About a dozen scientists were invited by PANAMIN to visit the site, though only one, ethnobotanist Douglas Yen, was able to stay for more than a few days. (Yen was there for 41 days.) Most of these scientists published short articles in local Philippines publications. Then, in 1974, all contact with the Tasaday was stopped by the PANAMIN authorities. A blanket of silence fell over the Tasaday for thirteen years, until the termination of the Marcos government.

Then, just a month after the fall of Philippines President Ferdinand Marcos in February 1986, sensational reports on the Tasaday again hit the international press, this time saying the whole story was a hoax. Although rumors had quietly circulated in the Philippines academic community for years that the Tasaday were not all they had been made out to be, independent researchers and reporters alike had always been forbidden by Elizalde, PANAMIN, and the Marcos government from investigating these stories or visiting the Tasaday. In the chaotic month following Marcos's downfall, foreign journalists were able to slip into the area. The first was Swiss journalist Oswald Iten. In March of 1986 he found the Tasaday living in houses and wearing regular clothes. But a week later the German magazine *Stern* sent in their reporters. They photographed the same Tasaday man that Iten had photographed, this time wearing leaves, but with a pair of cloth underpants showing underneath the leaves. In the following months, most of the hundreds of news articles in the worldwide press argued that the Tasaday story was a complete fabrication.

For the public, the issue by the end of the 1980s had been simplistically reduced to two polar alternatives: were the Tasaday (in 1971) a group of primitive isolated foragers living off wild foods alone and unaware of the outside world, or were they rain-forest phonies? As *Asiaweek* stated in November 1988, the Tasaday discovery is either "one of the major anthropological events of the century," or "the hoax of the decade."

Actually, neither of these extreme views is correct. As anthropologists have analyzed the issues, a consensus perhaps halfway between these viewpoints has developed. The no-hoax theorists had by 1991 moved away from the viewpoint that the Tasaday had lived completely isolated in a cave for hundreds of years, that they had a stone-tool technology, that they are windows into the Pleistocene epoch. Some of those anthropologists at the other extreme—those who claimed a hoax—have also retreated from their position that these people were "paid performers" brought in from outside to fake a primitive life-style before scientists and media cameras.

While the thirty or so scholars involved in the controversy in the late 1980s still disagree sharply on many of the details, almost all of them agree that the Tasaday were not following a Paleolithic foraging subsistence. They still disagree as to whether or not the Tasaday were living without iron tools, independently of cultivated foods, and with no interaction with farming peoples. But no scholar argues that they were a Stone Age people. On the other side, no anthropologist today claims that the Tasaday never existed. All seem to agree that they are a genuine minority tribal people who have always lived in South Cotabato in the general vicinity in which they were found in the early 1970s. Disagreement continues, among anthropologists especially, as to whether these twenty-six people (increased to about seventy in 1986) were a separate ethnic population, or merely a group from a nearby Manobo farming village who were asked by PANAMIN officials to live at the cave site whenever visitors were flown in.

A Hypothesis of Tasaday History before 1971

As of 1991, there are still few facts known about how the Tasaday lived in the recent past. Based on the data available, however, most anthropologists are led to accept the following tentative interpretation: it may be inferred that during the first half of the twentieth century the Tasaday were a group of foragers who lived not very differently from other hunter-gatherer groups in Southeast Asia (such as the Agta, Batak, Philippine Negritos, and Semang, who are described elsewhere in this encyclopedia). Linguistic analysis of the Tasaday language in 1989 provided strong evidence that sometime in the nineteenth century they separated from a Cotabato Manobo agricultural group and moved deeper into the rain forest of South Cotabato, near where they live today. Their economy then shifted from farming to a seminomadic foraging subsistence. They probably lived in simple huts and slept in rock shelters only during occasional overnight foraging trips. They ate wild foods, but also domestic foods, some of which they may have planted themselves in tiny gardens but most of which they secured by trading minor forest products with Manobo farmers living up to 40 kilometers away. In this hypothetical scenario, they had at least periodic interaction based on trade with other Manobo groups living in South Cotabato, especially with the people of Blit, the name of the agricultural village located in the late 1960s just 4 kilometers southwest of the Tasaday cave.

Some Little-Known Facts

While the above is a plausible but still hypothetical description of Tasaday history, there are some facts that have recently emerged concerning the pre-1970 Tasaday that indicate that the journalists, if not the early scientists, exaggerated the "primitiveness" of the Tasaday and led the public to assume that they were more isolated than they actually were. These eight facts, which no anthropologist disputes, are listed below. Explanation and documentation for these may be found in the 1991 volume by Headland that is listed in the bibliography at the end of this article.

(1) *The Tasaday were not wearing leaves* when discovered in 1971, as the public was led to believe. They were wearing commercial cloth. They were asked at that time by Elizalde to discard their cloth and to "wear their traditional" coverings. Thereafter, published films and photographs always showed them either naked or wearing orchid leaves.

(2) *The Tasaday had trade goods* before they were discovered in 1971; they were not isolated, out of contact with the modern world, or Paleolithic. Besides cloth, they had, for example, brass, metal-tipped arrows, bows made from cultivated (not wild) bamboo, iron bush knives, imported baskets, glass beads, and tin cans.

(3) *Farming peoples in nearby towns were eating meat from wild game that had been killed and smoke-dried by Tasaday* before 1971. This was probably an important trade item the

Tasaday exchanged for the goods above. Wild meat is a main trade product exchanged for cultivated foods by tropical forest hunter-gatherers all over the world.

(4) *The South Cotabato rain forest lacks sufficient wild plant foods to sustain a pure foraging group.* The evidence is strong for this. Although the Tasaday ate wild fruits, roots, palm pith, etc., these are so widely scattered and difficult to harvest that foragers could not depend on such resources to provide adequate carbohydrate needs unless they also had access to some cultivated starch foods.

(5) *No one ever observed the Tasaday subsisting on wild foods.* It was assumed a priori that their diet was based solely on nondomestic foods, and the original dozen scientists never learned otherwise during their fieldwork periods there in the 1970s. But from June 1971 they ate rice, often two and sometimes three times per day, during the periods when the scientists were there. What is significant is that the rice was often given to them secretly by the PANAMIN staff. The scientists, not knowing this, thought the Tasaday were fulfilling their nutritional needs from wild foods. It was not until later that a few of them discovered that rice was being smuggled to the Tasaday.

(6) *The Tasaday stone tools displayed in Manila and shown in photographs were not genuine tools.* The Tasaday were said to have had three simple stone tools in 1971, but these were reportedly taken to Manila by Elizalde, where they strangely disappeared. They were never photographed, and no one has seen them since. The stone tools subsequently published in photographs and displayed in the PANAMIN Museum in Manila were made by Manobo Tasaday at the request of PANAMIN personnel for the benefit of newspaper correspondents. The Tasaday may have used some stone in their technology, but they did not use stone tools in the sophisticated way that humans did during the Upper Paleolithic period.

(7) *The Tasaday do not speak a separate language or an unintelligible dialect.* They speak a dialect of the nearby Cotabato Manobo language. About 85 percent of Tasaday words are identical to Manobo. The percentage of shared cognates would, of course, be much higher. In 1989, Tasaday conversations tape-recorded in 1972 were played by linguist Clay Johnston in several Manobo villages. The Manobo had no trouble understanding them, although they did notice that the "tune" (i.e., the accent) was different. It is important to note, however, that all the linguists who reviewed the Tasaday language data agree that the Tasaday speak a separate dialect of Manobo. Their speech is not identical with Manobo speech. This suggests that the Tasaday have lived geographically separate from Manobo people for at least 100 to 150 years. The Tasaday speak a dialect of Cotabato Manobo, one of more than twenty languages making up the Manobo Subgroup of the Southern Philippine Austronesian Language Family.

(8) *The bamboo in which the Tasaday cooked their food was cultivated* bamboo (*Dinochloa* spp.), not wild bamboo. This bamboo could not have come from the rain forest. They either planted it themselves or got it from Manobo farmers. Since the Tasaday were using a cultivar for their cooking vessels, they could not have been as ignorant of agriculture as was originally claimed.

The above eight points do not prove that the Tasaday were "a hoax"; in fact, the linguistic data (point 7) support the no-hoax theory. These points do indicate that they were not as isolated and "primitive" as first reported. The media circus surrounding the story was more the fault of the news reporters and PANAMIN officials than that of the original dozen scientists, who were much more conservative in their analyses. Discoveries of lost Stone-Age cavemen make for great press coverage, but poor science.

Critical Research Needed

The original claims in 1972 were that the Tasaday had been living for hundreds of years in a cave (actually, three adjacent caves, but they dwelled mainly in "Cave III," the largest). Although many outsiders visited the Tasaday at this cave site in 1972–73, PANAMIN never allowed any archaeological investigation to be done at the site. The research most needed at present, then, is in archaeology. As archaeologist William Longacre stated in 1989, it would only take a "blue-ribbon" team of archaeologists three or four days of digging at the cave site to collect the data needed to find out when and for how long humans lived in the cave, if ever, and what their subsistence was like. A simple dig into the cave midden (if there is one) would furnish valuable data, and would probably settle the hoax controversy once and for all.

Bibliography

Bower, Bruce (1989). "The Strange Case of the Tasaday: Were They Primitive Hunter-Gatherers or Rain-Forest Phonies?" _Science News_ 135:280–281, 283. Reprinted in _Anthropology Newsletter_ 30(7): 25–26 (October 1989).

Elizalde, Manuel, Jr., and Robert B. Fox (1971). "The Tasaday Forest People: A Data Paper on a Newly Discovered Food Gathering and Stone Tool Using Manubo Group in the Mountains of South Cotabato, Mindanao, Philippines." [Typescript, viii + 20 pp., + 5 unnumbered pages of 10 photographs. Dated July 1971.] Washington, D.C.: Smithsonian Institution, Center for Short-Lived Phenomena.

Fernandez, Carlos A., and Frank Lynch (1972). "The Tasaday: Cave-Dwelling Food Gatherers of South Cotabato, Mindanao." _Philippine Sociological Review_ 20:275–330.

Headland, Thomas N., ed. (1991). _The Tasaday Hoax Controversy: An Assessment of the Evidence._ Washington, D.C.: American Anthropological Association.

MacLeish, Kenneth (1972). "Stone Age Cavemen of Mindanao." _National Geographic_ 142(2): 219–249.

Nance, John (1975). _The Gentle Tasaday: A Stone Age People in the Philippine Rain Forest._ New York: Harcourt Brace Jovanovich. Reprint, with a new afterword by the author, pp. 453-471. 1988. Boston: David R. Godine.

Yen, D. E., and John Nance, eds. (1976). _Further Studies on the Tasaday._ Panamin Foundation Research Series, no. 2. Makati, Rizal: PANAMIN.

THOMAS N. HEADLAND

Tau-Oi

The Tau-Oi (Ta Hoi, Tà ôi) are a group of swidden rice farmers and fishers located in Saravane Province in Laos and in neighboring areas of Vietnam. In Vietnam, they numbered 26,004 in 1985; their entire population was estimated at 30,000 in 1981.

Bibliography

Hickey, Gerald C. (1964). "Tau-Oi." In _Ethnic Groups of Mainland Southeast Asia,_ edited by Frank M. LeBar, Gerald C. Hickey, and John K. Musgrave, 151. New Haven: HRAF Press.

Tausug

ETHNONYMS: Joloanos, Jolo Moros, Suluk, Sulu Moros, Sulus, Taw Sug

Orientation

Identification. The Tausug ("people of the current"—_tau_, "people"; _sug_, "sea current") are the numerically dominant group in the Sulu Archipelago of the southern Philippines. Jolo Island, strategically located near the heart of the archipelago, constitutes the cultural and political center of Tausug society. Major concentrations of Tausug are also present on Pata, Tapul, Lugus, and Siasi islands, on the north and eastern coasts of Basilan, and in the Mindanao provinces of Zamboanga del Sur and Cotabato. Additional populations are found in eastern Sabah (Malaysia), from Labuk-Sugut southward to Tawau. In Sulu the Tausug typically occupy the larger high islands, suitable for intensive agriculture, leaving the low coraline islands to the more maritime Samal. The Tausug are a culturally unified group, and regional differentiation is minimal. On Jolo Island, coastal-dwelling Tausug refer to themselves as "Tau Higad" (_higad_, "seacoast") and to inland dwellers as "Tau Gimba" (_gimba_, "hinterland"), whereas both groups refer to Tausug living on islands other than Jolo as "Tau Pu" (_pu_, "island"). In Sabah the Tausug are known officially and in the ethnographic literature as "Suluk."

Location. The 400 or so islands of the Sulu Archipelago, bounded on the west by the Sulu Sea and on the east and south by the Celebes Sea, lie between 4°30′ and 6°50′ N and 119°10′ and 122°25′ E. Jolo, the largest of the group, is a rugged, high island, 59 kilometers long by 16 kilometers wide. Fertile volcanic soils make possible intensive dry-field cultivation over approximately one-half of its area; the rest is either unarable mountain land, remnant forest, or former farmland turned to _imperata_ grass. Rainfall is abundant, 178 to 254 centimeters annually, but erratic, particularly during the northeast monsoon (November–March). Jolo Island is surrounded by coral reefs and fringed with sand beaches and mangrove swamps.

Demography. The Tausug population of the Philippines was estimated at 325,000 in 1970, of which 190,000 lived on Jolo Island. Following the destruction of Jolo town in 1974 in fighting between Muslim separatists and Christian soldiers, this latter figure has probably declined, as considerable numbers of Tausug were evacuated or fled, many to Basilan, Zamboanga, and Sabah. In Sabah locally born Tausug numbered 10,900 in 1970. Current estimates of their number, together with recent refugees, run from 20,000 to as high as 100,000.

Linguistic Affiliation. The Tausug language belongs to the East Mindanao Subgroup of Central Philippine languages. Its closest affiliation is with Butuanun, spoken at the mouth of the Agusan River (northeast Mindanao), from which it is believed to have separated some 900 years ago. It also exhibits extensive linguistic convergence with Sama-Bajau, indicating a long and close association. Tausug shows little dialectal variation and served historically as the lingua franca of the Sulu sultanate. A Malay-Arabic script is used for religious and other writings.

History and Cultural Relations

The Tausug appear to have come to Sulu from northeastern Mindanao as a result of contact with Sama-Bajau traders. This movement probably began in early Sung times and was related to the growth of Chinese trade during the Sung (A.D. 960–1279) and Yuan (A.D. 1280–1368) periods. Linguistic evidence suggests that a Tausug-speaking community may have originated from a bilingual population established in Jolo by Sama traders and their Tausug-speaking wives and children between the tenth and eleventh centuries. By the end of the thirteenth century the Tausug emerged in the islands as a regionally powerful commercial elite. The date of earliest Islamic penetration is uncertain, but initial contact possibly began in late Sung times, when Arab merchants opened direct trading links with southern China by way of the Sulu Archipelago. There also seems to have been some early proselytizing by Chinese Muslims. Islam was later reinvigorated in Sulu by Sufi missionaries, who came from Arabia or Iraq via Malaya and Sumatra. The Sulu sultanate was established in the mid-fifteenth century, putatively by the legendary Salip (Sharif) Abu Bakkar or Sultan Shariful Hashim. Its establishment consolidated the ascendancy of the Tausug and appears to have furthered their social and economic differentiation from the Sama-Bajau-speaking Samal. The sultanate reached the height of its power in the eighteenth and early nineteenth centuries, when its influence extended from Sulu through the coastal foreshores of Mindanao and northern Borneo. Jolo emerged as a major center of trade and piracy and as an entrepôt for slaves, most of them taken in the Christian Philippines. Slavery made possible an intensification of trade-related production and, in addition to being practiced by Tausug slavers, was carried out by Ilanon and Balangingi Samal under the commission of Tausug aristocrats. Following Spain's colonization of the Philippines in the sixteenth century, warfare with the Spanish was almost continuous for the next 300 years. The first Spanish attack on

Jolo town occurred in 1578. The town was occupied briefly in the seventeenth century and a permanent garrison was established for the first time in 1876. After Spain's defeat in the Spanish-American War, American troops occupied Jolo town in 1899, but stiff resistance prevented them from gaining control over the interior of the island until 1913. The Pax Americana that followed saw the abolition of slavery, confiscation of firearms, and temporary curtailment of piracy and feuding. In 1915, under the terms of the Carpenter Agreement, Sultan Jamal ul-Kiram II relinquished all claims to secular power, while retaining his religious role as an Islamic sovereign. Since World War II indigenous forms of armed conflict have revived. Sulu today is a major center of Islamic separatism, the birthplace of many of the founding leaders of the present Moro National Liberation Front, and the site of some of the most destructive fighting of the recent past.

Settlements

Except for towns and coastal fishing villages, Tausug communities are typically dispersed, with individual houses located close to family fields. The household, or cluster of two or three adjacent households, comprises the smallest territorial grouping. The next larger unit is the hamlet (*lungan*). Still larger is the community (*kauman*), having a common name and headman. The unity of a kauman depends on intermarriage, the existence of a core kin group among its members, their attendance at a common mosque, recent history of conflict, and the political skills of the community's headman. Boundaries between kauman tend to be ill-defined, varying according to the dynamics of alliance and feuding and the relative power of successive headmen. The Tausug house typically consists of a single rectangular room, bamboo- or timber-walled, with a thatched roof, raised on posts about 2 to 3 meters above the ground. The structure is generally surrounded by a series of elevated porches leading to a separate kitchen at the rear and is often enclosed within a protective stockade encircling the house compound.

Economy

Subsistence and Commercial Activities. Subsistence is based primarily on agriculture, fishing, and trade, with some livestock raising (cattle, chickens, ducks). The Tausug practice plow agriculture, growing dry rice on permanently diked, nonirrigated fields, using cattle or water buffalo as draft animals. Rice is intercropped with corn, cassava, and a small amount of millet, sorghum, and sesame. There are three annual harvests: first, corn and other cereals; second, rice; and third, cassava. The harvesting of cassava continues until the following dry season. Farms are typically fallowed every third year. Other crops, generally planted in separate gardens, include peanuts, yams, eggplants, beans, tomatoes, and onions. The principal cash crops are coconuts (for copra), coffee, abaca, and fruit. Fruit, some of it wild, is an important source of seasonal cash income and includes mangoes, mangosteens, bananas, jackfruits, durians, *lanzones*, and oranges. Today many coastal Tausug are landless and make their living from fishing or petty trade. Fishing, as either a full- or a part-time occupation, is carried out in coastal waters, mainly using nets, hook-and-line, or traps.

Industrial Arts.   Most farm and household items are made of bamboo. Iron implements are forged locally and the manufacture of bladed weapons has historically been an important local craft. Women produce pandanus mats and woven headcloths for both home use and sale.

Trade.   From the founding of the Sulu sultanate until the mid-nineteenth century, the Tausug conducted an extensive trade with China in pearls, birds' nests, trepang, camphor, and sandalwood. Historically, considerable interisland trade has also existed within the archipelago. Today copra and abaca are sold primarily through Chinese wholesalers, while most locally consumed products are handled by Tausug or Samal traders. Smuggling between Sulu and nearby Malaysian ports is an important economic activity to many with capital and commercial connections and is a major source of local differences in wealth and power.

Division of Labor.   Both sexes share in farm work, men doing much of the heavier work such as clearing, plowing, and fencing fields; planting, weeding, and harvesting are done jointly. Women tend the smaller vegetable gardens and gather fruit. Both sexes engage in trade. Fishing, metalwork, interisland trade, and smuggling are largely male occupations, although, in the latter case, women often manage the financial side.

Land Tenure.   Landholdings typically are dispersed, with a man having rights of usufruct or tenancy in farms in several different locations. These rights are individually held. In contrast water holes, pasturelands, and beaches are by tradition unowned and available for common use. In the past, titular rights were held by the sultan over all land within the state and secondarily by local or regional leaders acting as his representatives.

Kinship

Kin Groups and Descent.   The bilateral kindred (*usbawaris*) extending to second cousins is the major kinship category. Lineal descent has no special functional or ideological significance, and a hallmark of Tausug society is the absence of enduring corporate groups of any kind. According to the Tausug interpretation of the Shafi marriage law, children are filiated with the father and his kindred (*usbaq*), but in other contexts, aside from marriage and divorce, ties are acknowledged bilaterally without distinction. Relations with kin are markedly dyadic; relatives act as a group only during life crises, in times of sickness or special need, or when family honor is at stake. Sibling solidarity is especially intense. Bonds between brothers and first cousins are particularly important in forging political allegiances and in garnering support in times of armed conflict. In addition to kinship, a variety of ritual-friendship relations is recognized. These include sworn alliances between allies and ritual friendships between rivals, or potential rivals, entered into—often at the instigation of regional leaders—to forestall open enmity or bring it to an end. Having many friends is essential for success in armed feuds and litigation and for safety in traveling outside one's home region.

Kinship Terminology.   Terminology emphasizes generation, relative age, and lineality; cousin terms are of the Eskimo type.

Marriage and Family

Marriage.   Marriage is ideally arranged by parents. Contacts between the sexes are restricted and marriageable women are kept in relative seclusion to protect their value to their family as political and economic assets. First and second cousins are favored spouses (with the exception of the children of brothers). A series of negotiations precedes marriage, concluding with an agreement on the amount of bride-wealth and other expenses to be paid by the boy's family. In addition to arranged marriages, wives may be obtained by elopement or abduction, both common alternatives. Weddings are held in the groom's parents' house immediately upon payment of bride-wealth and are officiated by an imam. Newly married couples generally reside uxorilocally for the first year, or until the birth of a child, after which they are free to join the husband's family, remain with the wife's family, or, preferably, build a new house of their own, typically close to the husband's natal community. Independent residence is the eventual ideal. Relations between husband and wife are characteristically close and enduring. Divorce is permitted but is infrequent, occurring in less than 10 percent of all marriages and, although polygyny is allowed, few men take more than one wife.

Domestic Unit.   The Tausug household consists of either a nuclear family or a stem family, the latter being comprised of parents, unmarried children, plus a married child, spouse, and grandchildren. Fully extended families are rare.

Inheritance.   Land is usually divided between sons, with some preference given to the eldest. Other property is generally inherited bilaterally.

Socialization.   Children are looked after by both parents and older siblings. A newborn infant's hold on life is thought to be precarious; therefore, children are commonly protected with amulets (*hampan*) and temporarily secluded immediately after birth. At around 1 or 2 years of age, both boys and girls undergo a ritual haircutting and immediately afterward are named. Most preadolescent children attend Quranic school or study the Quran with a private tutor, and when proficient they demonstrate their skills at recitation in a public ceremony called *pagtammat*. This is typically a festive occasion, its scale reflecting the family's status and economic means. Boys are circumcised (*pagislam*) in their early teens; girls undergo a similar rite (*pagsunnat*), but without ceremony and attended only by females, when they reach the age of 5 or 6. Socialization emphasizes sensitivity to shame, respect for authority, and family honor. Today children attend public schools, but few attain more than a primary education. Only one in five who begin school complete grade six.

Sociopolitical Organization

The major cultural focus of Tausug society is on conflict, politics, law, and litigation.

Social Organization.   Tausug society is hierarchically stratified and has been since at least the founding of the Sulu sultanate. Three major rank categories were formerly recognized: nobles, commoners, and slaves. The nobility consisted of *datu*, men holding patrilineally inherited titles who exercised regional power, and *salip*, religiously revered men and women who claimed descent from the Prophet. As in other Malay polities, those of datu status were internally differentiated into what have been called "royal datus" and "ordinary datus" (i.e., those directly related to the line of the ruling sultan and others related only distantly or not at all). Commoners, who comprised some 80 percent of the population, lacked ascribed titles and ranking. The position of each category was defined by law. Commoners and slaves were required to pay allegiance to a particular datu, although they exercised some choice in the matter, as individual datus were not assigned unambiguously bounded territories. To a considerable degree wealth and power were achieved independently of inherited titles, so that men of humble origin often gained great influence and, in acknowledgment, received bestowed titles and recognized positions of prominence in the alliance hierarchy. This status system has thus been characterized as one of "status-conscious egalitarianism."

Political Organization. Although centralized as a polity, political power within the traditional sultanate operated primarily through networks of interlocking leader-centered alliances. Person-to-person bonds of friendship and patronage linked smaller alliances to larger ones in a ramifying network that extended from community headmen and local factional leaders to the sultan and his kindred at the apex of the system. Within the archipelago, the sultan's authority was strongest at the geographical center of the state, on Jolo and neighboring high islands, shading to symbolic hegemony at its outer peripheries. Recognition of a leader's authority and his position in the alliance hierarchy were expressed through ranked titles (*panglima*, maharaja, *orangkaya*, *parukka*, etc.); part of the sultan's authority derived from his powers of investiture and control over the title system. At each level of the alliance network, leaders acted as representatives of the law, performing legal functions, mediating feuds, and imposing fines. They also offered their followers physical protection and, from the sultan downward, were responsible for administering religious law and for appointing local and regional religious officials. At the capital the sultan was advised by a state council (*ruma bichara*) made up of religious advisers and leading datus, which, in addition to its advisory role, reserved the right to determine succession. Today traditional political values remain largely intact. Minimal and medial alliances still operate, whereas maximal alliances are now led by acculturated Tausug operating within the setting of Philippine electoral politics. Sulu is divided into two provinces, Sulu (Jolo) and Tawitawi. Jolo in turn is divided into eight municipalities, each with elected officials: mayors, vice-mayors, and municipal councillors. Provincial officials include a governor, a provincial board, and a national congressperson. Their powers derive mainly from their ability to obtain government largesse and to guarantee their followers legal immunity. Although the secular power of the sultan is greatly diminished, he continues to preserve, mainly through the *agama* (religious court), much of his traditional religious function. Since the death of Sultan Jamal ul-Karim II, the office has been represented by two lines of claimants.

Social Control. The Tausug recognize three categories of law: pure Quranic law; interpreted religious law (*sara*), codified by the sultan and other Tausug officials; and customary law (*adat*), including offenses of honor.

Conflict. Armed feuds are endemic. The pattern is chiefly one of individual revenge. A widely ramifying feud may result in battles involving more than 100 persons on each side. In the past, external warfare took the form of piracy and coastal raiding, organized at the levels of medial and maximal alliance, chiefly for slaves and booty. In the nineteenth century, following the establishment of a precarious Spanish military hegemony over Sulu, a pattern of ritual suicide (*sabbil*) developed as a form of personal jihad, or religious martyrdom.

Religion and Expressive Culture

Religious Beliefs. The Tausug are Sunni Muslims, followers of the Shafi school. The Five Pillars are observed, although only the elderly practice daily prayers regularly. All illness, accidents, and other misfortunes are ultimately God's will. However, the Tausug retain elements of pre-Islamic belief and, additionally, see the world as inhabited by local spirits capable of causing good or ill fortune. Folk curers (*mangungubat*) may be sought in time of illness. Traditional medical specialists, who obtain their powers through dreams or by the instruction of older curers, heal mainly by herbal remedies and prayers.

Religious Practitioners. The imam is an important community figure. He officiates at life-crisis rites, offers religious counsel, and leads the faithful in prayer. Religion is central to Tausug identity and traditionally played a major role in maintaining the hierarchical structure of the state. The sultan, as head of an Islamic polity, was invested with religious authority. Official genealogies traced his descent to the Prophet and in his person he was expected to exemplify ideal qualities of virtue and religious devotion. Paralleling the political pyramid was a religious one, united at its apex in the sultan's person, and consisting, from state to community level, of *kadi*, *ulama*, imam, *hatib*, and *bilal*, juridical and religious advisors, and mosque officials.

Ceremonies. Major events in the religious calendar include fasting during Ramadan; Hari Raya Puasa, a day of feasting immediately following Ramadan; Hari Raya Hadji, the feast of sacrifice on the tenth day of the month of Jul-Hadj; Maulideen Nabi, the birthday of the Prophet, on the twelfth day of Maulud; and Panulak Balah (lit., "to send away evil"), a day of ritual bathing on the last Wednesday of Sappal.

Arts. Dancing, instrumental music, and song are popular forms of entertainment, but the decorative arts are unelaborated.

Death and Afterlife. Four acts must be performed at death: bathing the corpse, enshrouding it, reciting the prayer for the dead, and burial. Burial is followed by a seven-day vigil. Depending on a family's economic circumstances, commemorative feasts may be held on the 7th, 20th, 40th, and 100th day, and on the first, second, and third anniversaries of death. Each person is believed to have four souls that leave the body at death. The body goes to hell, where the length of punishment it suffers is determined by the misdeeds and accumulated religious merit of the deceased. On the fifteenth day of the month of Shaaban, one of the souls (*ro*) of the dead is sent back to earth: here the deceased is honored with prayers and on the following day graves are cleared.

See also Samal

Bibliography

Bruno, Juanito (1973). *The Social World of the Tausug: A Study in Philippine Culture and Education*. Manila: Central Escolar University Research Center.

Hart, Donn V. (1984). "Tausug." In *Muslim Peoples: A World Ethnographic Survey*, edited by Richard V. Weekes, 764–770. Westport, Conn.: Greenwood Press.

Kiefer, Thomas (1972). "The Tausug Polity and Sultanate of Sulu: A Segmentary State in the Southern Philippines." *Sulu Studies* 1:19–64.

Kiefer, Thomas (1972). *The Tausug: Violence and Law in a Philippine Moslem Society*. New York: Holt, Rinehart & Winston.

Kiefer, Thomas (1975). "Tausug." In *Ethnic Groups of Insular Southeast Asia*, edited by Frank M. LeBar. Vol. 2, *Philippines and Formosa*, 2–5. New Haven: HRAF Press.

Majul, Cesar Adib (1973). *Muslims in the Philippines*. Quezon City: University of the Philippines Press.

Warren, James F. (1981). *The Sulu Zone, 1768–1898: The Dynamics of External Trade, Slavery, and Ethnicity in the Transformation of a Southeast Asian Maritime State*. Singapore: Singapore University Press.

CLIFFORD SATHER

Tay

"Tay" (Tày, Tho, Thu) is a general term used in reference to the large, rural, Thai-speaking population in Vietnam, primarily in northern Vietnam. In 1985, the total number of people classified as "Tay" was 1,190,342, making them the largest ethnic population in Vietnam other than the Vietnamese themselves. Tay are an official national minority in Vietnam. It is not clear, however, what specific groups fall within the official definition of "Tay." The Tay were previously often referred to as "Tho," meaning "soil," but the term is now considered derogatory and "Tay" is preferred. The Tay have traditionally been agriculturalists, growing rice in paddies and by swiddening and also raising maize, buckwheat, watercress, sugar cane, manioc, and various other vegetables for home use. Tay villages were centers of regional economic activities, with local markets rotating among a series of villages. Markets often involved trade between the Tay and Vietnamese and Chinese merchants. Today, the Tay are highly assimilated into Vietnamese society.

Bibliography

Hickey, Gerald C. (1958). "Social Systems of Northern Viet Nam: A Study of Systems in Contact." Ph.D. Dissertation, University of Chicago.

Hickey, Gerald C. (1964). "Tho." In *Ethnic Groups of Mainland Southeast Asia*, edited by Frank M. LeBar, Gerald C. Hickey, and John K. Musgrave, 232–235. New Haven: HRAF Press.

Temiar

[*Editor's Note*: This entry is longer than most others in the volume, to provide information about the current state of indigenous peoples in Southeast Asia, especially in regard to their relationships with other dominant groups and national governments.]

ETHNONYMS: northern Sakai, Ple, Ple-Temiar, Tembé, Temer, Tmèèr, Tmiir, Tummior

Orientation

Identification. The Temiar are one of the larger component groups of the Orang Asli (Malay, "original people," i.e., Aborigines), the name currently applied to the non-Muslim tribal (or recently tribal) populations of peninsular Malaysia. The name "Temiar" (Tembé, Temer, Tummior) has been common in the ethnological literature since the mid-1930s. Earlier the Temiar were usually referred to as "Northern Sakai" (primarily to distinguish them from the "Central Sakai," now known as the "Semais"). The ethnonym "Ple" has also been applied, usually in the compound form "Ple-Temiar," which refers nevertheless to a single population.

"Temiar" is an anglicized form of the Semai name (Tmiir) for the language spoken by the Semais' northerly neighbors. This word has no apparent meaning in any Aslian language, but it probably derives from the Austronesian etymon **tembir* (edge) and implies that some earlier peninsular population saw the Temiar as geographically peripheral to themselves.

The Temiar have usually referred to themselves as "Sèn'òòy Sròk" (the people of the hilly interior) or "Sèn'òòy Bèèk" (the people of the forest); they call their language "Kuy Sròk" (hilly interior speech). Since the mid-1960s, they have also begun to refer to themselves by the name others call them, in the form "Tmèèr."

Location. Temiar occupy a continuous area amounting to some 5,500 square kilometers, situated between 4°30′ and 5°25′ N and between 101°08′ and 101°52′ E at its extreme points. This places them mostly in the interior parts of Perak and Kelantan states, with two or three villages in the northwestern part of Pahang State. The region is mountainous, and Temiar can be found living at elevations ranging from 100 meters to around 1,400 meters. Except where commercial loggers have recently denuded the forest, Temiar country is cloaked in large-tree primary tropical rain forest, changing to small-tree/dwarf montane forest at higher elevations beyond the inhabited areas. This rich growth sits on rather infertile lateritic soil, maintained by nutrients derived from the ground-level litter of fallen leaves. Although relatively uniform, the environment is extremely rich in plant and animal species, a high proportion of which have been utilized by the Temiar for food, medicine, construction, and trade. The many rivers provide a degree of localized diversity and are utilized as communication routes and sources of water and fish.

The area is under a tropical monsoonal regime that brings winds and rain from the northeast at the turn of the year and from the southwest in the middle of the year. Seasonality is so slight at these latitudes, however, that rain (amounting to around 200 centimeters annually) can fall or cease at almost any time. Dry periods are carefully monitored, as they are necessary to the swidden-farming cycle. The seasonal appearance of certain forest and cultivated fruits is also monitored, for these play an important part in Temiar religion and social organization.

At lower elevations, communication with the people of neighboring valleys is easy, and the downstream Temiar make considerable use of Malay-type dugout canoes for the purpose. At high elevations too, communication on foot with neighboring valleys is relatively easy. Throughout the greater part of the valleys, however, the steep terrain makes it rather difficult to get out of one valley and into the next. This topographical constraint has given rise to a degree of cultural conservatism. As a result, most of the population of each valley (i.e., those who inhabit the middle stretches) come to see themselves as differentiated from people in other valleys by certain diagnostic cultural features that they think of as attached directly to the land rather than to people. To some extent these valley populations take on the character of "demes"—large-scale units tending statistically to endogamy, each consisting of many distinct, usually exogamous, local groups.

Demography. The Temiar numbered 11,593 in the census of 1980. They thus maintain an overall population density of about 2 persons per square kilometer, though local densities are higher. Until the recent residential shifts brought about by the government's relocation program, Temiar lived in small or very small villages, lying some few kilometers from each other. The modal village population was about 30, but ranged from 12 to about 150. In such circumstances, with kinship and relative age as the main principles of social categorization, relationships were necessarily of the "face-to-face" type: at the village level Temiar society has usually been highly solidarist in character.

Linguistic Affiliation. Temiar belongs to the Aslian Subfamily of Mon-Khmer, and hence to the Austroasiatic Stock; along with its closest relatives (Lanoh, Semai, and Jah Hut), it belongs to the Central (or "Senoic") Division of Aslian. Its wider affiliations therefore lie with the several hundred Mon-Khmer languages of mainland Southeast Asia. Temiar has also incorporated lexical and grammatical elements from a variety of Austronesian languages, including some that are no longer spoken in the peninsula.

There are two mutually intelligible major dialects—Northern and Southern—with a few smaller variants on the western and southern parts of their area of distribution. Temiar is also spoken as a localized lingua franca by members of neighboring Orang Asli groups and by some Malays. It remains unwritten, apart from the private notations of Temiar-language radio broadcasters and some printed pamphlets circulated by Baha'i religionists.

All adult males can speak Malay, and most of the women have at least a passive knowledge of that language. Since the 1960s increasing numbers of Temiar children have attended government primary schools, and so a high proportion of younger Temiar is now literate in Malay. A smaller number have also learned some English at secondary-school level.

Linguistic and archaeological data suggest that the Aslian-speaking peoples may have formed a separate linguistic division within Mon-Khmer for perhaps 4,000 years. Nevertheless, the Temiar are typical in many ways of the Mon-Khmer-speaking hill peoples of mainland Southeast Asia. They have followed their own religion in an area where the religion of civilization was formerly Mahayana Buddhism and is now Islam. They have lived, probably for millennia, by swidden (slash-and-burn) farming supplemented by hunting and fishing, while the plains dwellers have lived variously by wet-rice cultivation, collecting for trade, and coastal fishing. In addition, they have no recorded history or writing in a country where indigenous literary records extend back to the fourteenth century.

History and Cultural Relations

Interference by outsiders may well have been an ancient feature of Temiar life, but the evidence allows us to date it with assurance only to the second third of the nineteenth century. At that time some upland Malay leaders claimed authority over all the Temiar living upstream, presumably for reasons of their own aggrandizement. These Mikong (a word of obscure, possibly Thai, origin) intermarried with Temiar women and remained in place as a loosely knit alliance of hereditary chiefs until World War II. Their home settlements were at the river-mouth villages of Kuala Betis in Kelantan and Temengor and Lasah in Perak, locations that allowed them to control most of the Temiars' external trade. The mediative activities of these Mikong probably had much to do with generating the sharp social distinction between Temiars and Malays. There is evidence, however, that relationships between the two peoples were closer in earlier times and that Malays sometimes ventured more readily into the interior than most commentators have assumed.

The picture was not untroubled, however, for downriver Malays (aided on occasion by Temiars from other valleys) are known to have raided Temiar communities for slaves. The victims were taken against their will to serve as domestic servants in settlements outside Temiar country. The raids continued until the 1930s in some areas, and the folk memory of them persists today. Indeed, it is likely that the fear of enslavement helped to generate the relative shyness toward strangers and the intense local communalism that Temiar life still exhibits.

Since the 1950s, the role of the Mikong has effectively been taken over by other agencies, most notably by the federal Department of Aboriginal Affairs (Jabatan Hal Ehwal Orang Asli, or JOA). The Temiar went along with these various arrangements, not out of any feeling of obeisance to authority, but simply to put their external relations on a stable basis. In 1948 the British established the Federation of Malaya; this was immediately followed by a Communist insurrection known as the "Emergency," which lasted until 1960. It was led mainly by Chinese guerrillas who were fearful they would be squeezed out of an independent Malay state. During the Emergency some Temiar village leaders gave the appearance of having become followers of the Communist insurgents, who sometimes accorded them letters of authority. As "tribespeople," it made sense for Temiar to play all sides in the game of maintaining their distance from all powerful outsiders with whom they nevertheless had to deal. The game has changed since then, of course. Individual Temiars, no longer "tribal" in outlook, are as likely as any other Orang Aslis to seek a place in Malaysian society through more symmetrical arrangements, the most important of which is the recently formed Orang Asli Association of Malaysia. The older institutions of headman and village leader are still utilized widely at the local level by officers of the JOA, however.

A major influence on Temiar relations with the wider world is the Malaysian Aboriginal Peoples Act of 1954, revised in 1974. This piece of legislation, among its other features, empowers the JOA or the local police to control who may enter an Orang Asli village, and it empowers state governments to decide on the allocation of land rights to Orang Asli. The original purpose of the legislation was to accord governmental protection to the Orang Asli during the period of the Communist insurgency, when protection was sorely needed. The legislation remains in effect, however, leading to a reduction in the intensity of contact that the more remote Orang Asli (such as the Temiar) have with the rest of Malaysian society. This has somewhat delayed their attainment of civic maturity, while doing little to guarantee their rights of ownership or usufruct over the land that they occupy.

Increasing economic peasantization, literacy, and improved health have brought the Temiar face to face with the evaluations that others hold of them. These opinions are potent elements in the formulation of the various policies and plans that now affect Temiars' lives. Upper-level officers of the JOA tend to see the Temiar as an economically backward community needing "development." Military officers have seen them as an interference in what they think should be a free-fire zone. The police (whose Field Force has had very close relations with the Temiar and to which several Temiars belong) have regarded them ambivalently as both "eyes and ears of the nation" and possible subversives.

Other government officers have focused on ethnological issues. In accordance with the official inclusion of the Orang Asli within the "Malay" census category, they have often seen the Temiar as incomplete Malays who should become more fully so (through conversion to Islam) as soon as possible. Officers of the Forest Department and lumbermen working for the many logging companies now operating in Temiar country have seen the Temiar simply as people who waste forest resources—a particularly unjust evaluation.

Since the mid-1970s many Temiar have been living in "relocation settlements," furnished with permanent Malay-style housing. These settlements were built by the JOA in response to the Malaysian security authorities' desire to leave the forested areas open for anti-insurgency operations.

The Temiar share a common genetic heritage with other Orang Asli populations, as well as with the now-dominant Malay population of the peninsula and the population of Southeast Asia at large. According to this view, the Temiar are the descendants of the people who produced the archaeological remains uncovered at several Hoabinhian and Neolithic sites within their territory. Temiar "origins" are in principle no more mysterious than those of the other indigenous populations of the Malay Peninsula, whether "aboriginal" or Malay. The Temiar form part of an ethnic and cultural array generated within the Malay Peninsula by sociopolitical processes relating to such issues as ecological differentiation and state formation.

Despite this, much popular and scholarly writing still treats the Temiar (along with other so-called "Senoi" populations) as having origins distinct from those of both the Malays and the Negritos, who are both commonly thought of as the residues of distinct migratory waves coming from southwest China in earlier times. Few archaeologists or biological anthropologists now accept this "wave" view, however.

Settlements

Currently many Temiar live in large relocation communities built on the modern rural Malay pattern, with raised zinc-roofed plank houses arranged in streets. Others still live in, or are moving back into, houses and villages of a more traditional kind situated in forest clearings along the major rivers. Houses here—which follow no special pattern of orientation—are raised off the ground on unshaped wooden pillars, to heights varying between 1 and 4 meters. The under-house space is used for work activities and as a shelter for domestic animals. The flooring is made of split-bamboo laths and the walls are of plaited bamboo strips or sheets of tree bark. This open construction allows air to circulate freely, unlike in the houses in the relocation communities. The overhanging roofs are of leaf thatch, which keeps out most of the rain and solar heat. The structure is held together with tightly knotted rattan strips, requiring a minimum of carpentry or tools. Temiar houses are generally rectangular (although circular houses are found in one valley). Internally, there is a common central floor space employed for cooking, dancing, threshing, and receiving visitors. The separate household compartments are situated on all sides of this central space, often separated by only knee-high partitions.

Economy

Subsistence and Commercial Activities. The swidden cultivation of cassava, rice, and other crops provides the main source of food and is the primary factor in shaping the preferred pattern of settlement and consociation. Where the rivers have not been disturbed by commercial logging, fishing (with drop net, barricade, or hook-and-line) also provides a regular food source. These foods are not usually shared beyond the household or household cluster. Trapping and hunting (with blowguns and shotguns) provide extra protein several times a week; larger catches are obligatorily shared throughout the village community and sometimes beyond. Apart from their chickens, Temiar normally cannot bear to eat livestock that has been raised in their own village, for they regard these animals as pets. They will sometimes sell them to others for meat, however.

There are four main sources of cash: "internal" bartering and trading of special locally produced items; the selling of forest produce to outsiders; paid employment (as laborers at inland administrative posts and tea estates, or as porters for forest travelers), either full-time or casual; and prestation from wage-earning friends and relatives. This last source (backed by special sanctions) ensures that money, clothing, and other items are widely shared within and beyond the village.

Industrial Arts. Temiar are locally renowned for the decorated mats, tobacco pouches, and grain storage bags that they plait from strips of pandanus leaf. Although these items are produced for domestic use, they are also sometimes traded in exchange for other items (such as homegrown tobacco). Occasionally a few pieces find their way into the tourist curio market, though not in any organized way. Basket weaving provides such items as storage containers or fish traps made of bamboo and rattan strips. A special long-internode wild bamboo is the source of the very fine double-tubed blowguns that Temiar men use for hunting arboreal game. Finished blowguns and unworked bamboo tubes are traded over long distances, among the Temiar and between them and other Orang Asli groups. Where the local conditions are appropriate, Temiar make dugout canoes and massive bamboo rafts. The latter—which cannot be poled against the flow—are often sold to Malays at the end of a journey downstream for the valuable large bamboo pieces they contain.

Trade. The main item of trade has long been rattan cane, in a variety of species, gathered from the wild during the agricultural off-season. The canes are coiled up and rafted downstream in large quantities, for sale to wholesalers—usually Chinese Malaysians—connected with the rattan furniture industry. Also traded is the coagulated latex of a forest tree known as *jelutong*, which is used commercially as a cheap ingredient in chewing-gum manufacture. Until 1948, external trade was mostly mediated by local upstream Malays under the leadership of the Mikong. The JOA now plays a similar role. Some Temiar, however, have made tentative moves to place the manufacture of commercial cane furniture more directly in their own hands. A similar development has been the emergence of small-scale "adventure" tourism through Temiar country, in cooperation with a nationwide Orang Asli trading cooperative.

Locally and seasonally, Temiar sell fruit, wild game, and hill rice to non-Temiars. Fishing for trade has become available to Temiar living on the shores of the large lake formed by the damming of the Temengor River in Perak during the 1970s. Rubber is tapped and processed in a few areas; these plantations were established by the JOA, but the trees are owned by Temiars themselves. This has been a major influence in the development of permanent villages; however, the generally low market price of rubber in recent years has restricted the growth of this enterprise.

Nowadays Temiar seek to purchase much the same consumer goods as other Malaysian rural dwellers: canned food, tea, sugar, dry batteries, cooking vessels, radio sets, clothing, kerosene. This demand for goods has been a major force pushing them further into the cash economy. Formerly they relied on trade to supply them with such essentials as iron bush knives and ax heads, without which their farming activities would be impossible.

Division of Labor. The Temiar have not usually imposed a rigorous system of occupational specialization, although they do sometimes express generalized ideas about the different roles of men and women. Most activities, including farming, fishing, cooking, and child minding, are carried out indiscriminately by men, women, or children. Tree felling, shooting animals, and raising roof beams seem, however, to be exclusively adult male activities, while pandanus plaiting is thought of as typically female. Women and children do catch animals by other means, however, and men make baskets. Children are not normally prevented from undertaking adult activities if they wish to do so, even when the activities are dangerous.

Status bears no obvious relation to specialization in work activities, except when a headman takes a coordinating role in decisions about communal work. Otherwise, headmen work just as hard as anyone else and for no obviously greater gain. This arrangement has been modified, however, where commercialized production is being followed, such as the processing of rubber and rattan for the wider market. The leaders of such enterprises need to be especially charismatic or thick-skinned to overcome a still widely felt egalitarianism.

Land Tenure. Under swidden farming, the cultivable soil around the village is depleted after two years. The community must then move, usually to a previously inhabited area of secondary forest that has been left untouched for fifteen or more years. Most such sites are barely distinguishable from the surrounding forest, although Temiar will recognize them by their untidy orchards of seasonal fruit trees.

Each of these fruit trees is, in principle, owned. The owner is either a particular individual or, if some time has passed since the tree was first claimed, a corporate group formed from among his or her descendants. The Temiar until recently had no concept of the ownership of land. Apart from movable goods, all that might be owned as heritable property were the products of the land (i.e., crops and individually claimed wild plants) or structures built upon it, such as houses or weirs. Of these, only long-lived trees would survive to bear witness to the linkage that once existed between the people of an earlier generation and "their" land.

It is only through this continued acknowledgment of proprietary rights to fruit trees that Temiar are able to talk in any determinate way about the relationship through time of social groups to specific localities. The similarity of the distribution of village sites to bounded plots of land or spheres of influence has led many observers to claim that these areas (*sakaa'*, from Malay *pusaka*, "inherited property") are the units of landownership in Temiar culture. But this belief results from a misunderstanding, at least as regards premodern arrangements. Nevertheless, ever since this misunderstanding became the basis of modern administrative practice, the Temiar have begun to accept the sakaa' concept, especially where relations with non-Temiars are involved. The notion of the ownability of land has consequently been spreading among them since the 1950s, but the idea is still communally rather than individually based, and no land registration has taken place. Under modern Malaysian law this means in effect that individual Temiar have as yet no recognized right to the land they and their ancestors have occupied for millennia. This is bound to become a problematic issue in the years ahead as roads are built, timber extracted, and valleys flooded without Temiar permission or with very small—or no—compensation payments.

Kinship

Kin Groups and Descent. The tree-owning village core group previously described constitutes the operational aspect of a corporate cognatic descent group, or ramage. Any one individual may thus claim potential membership in several such ramages, through his or her mother, father, or other consanguines. The ramage associated with a person's natal village is usually thought of as his or her primary ramage, even if that person has lived elsewhere, such as in the spouse's village. In most situations, however, decisions about membership in local groups do not involve active acknowledgment of descent as such. It is one's continuing relations with the living, not the dead, that provide the basis for such decisions. Thus, while it is siblingship (and cousinship) that is concerned in the day-to-day operation of village membership, descent is brought into play only when the group's continuity through time or individual cases of village membership are in doubt. Ramages as such do not enter into alliances, either marital or political. They do, however, provide a basis for the allocation of political authority: the most able member of the senior core-sibling group in each community becomes in effect the village leader.

Kinship Terminology. The referential kinship terminology is thoroughly classificatory and bilateral; it is also basically generational in structure. Since cousins and siblings are referred to and addressed in the same way, the terminology is of the Hawaiian type. This overriding of collaterality applies to some other generations too, so that aunts might optionally be called "mother," uncles "father," and nieces or nephews "child"; however, distinctive terms do exist for these relatives, and they are frequently employed.

All Temiar—and indeed all members of the neighboring Orang Asli groups—are regarded as potential kin. Two strangers will search their genealogical knowledge until they find one or more relatives in common, whereupon they will enter into an appropriate kinship relationship. In practice, for all except close kin, categorization reduces to just a few basic decisions: whether the other person is of the same or of an adjacent generational level, and whether he or she is related by marriage or by birth. Finer distinctions may then be made on the basis of the two kinspersons' relative ages ("older" or "younger") and, if they choose to be affines, relative sex ("cross" or "parallel"). With this simple calculus in mind individual Temiar can travel for 160 kilometers or so, even into Semang or Semai (and sometimes Malay) territory, building up a chain of kinship-based rights and obligations as they go.

Temiar thus have the means to extend their kinship links at will to considerable distances. They are able to do this because of the primary structural importance they ascribe to the sibling linkage, which underlies both the sociology of group formation (where a principle of sibling solidarity applies) and the cultural logic of kinship reckoning (where a principle of sibling equivalence applies). Analysis of the kinship terminology and of the personal naming system shows that both of these cultural paradigms embody the same model of social structure: the progressive generation of a group of siblings out of a set of affinal and filiative links that simultaneously undergo progressive degeneration.

Marriage and Family

Marriage. Temiar marriage is characterized by the establishing of wider and highly marked affinal relations, and not just by the cohabitation of the two partners. There is little restriction on sexual relations as such, either before marriage or out of marriage, and a couple may live and sleep together without being regarded as "married." Indeed, there is no special word for "marry" in Temiar: the idea is expressed through a transitive or reciprocal usage of the verb "sleep." Despite this relative openness, senior members of the woman's community (such as her father, brother, or village leader) will usually seek to regularize the union by exacting public avowals from the couple that they will keep together. Some marriage gifts may be given, although there are no formal bride-wealth or dowry requirements.

The first months or years of marriage are usually spent in the wife's community. Thereafter the couple may move to the husband's community, or to any other community that is prepared to let them settle. Roughly half of Temiar couples stay permanently in one community, while the remainder move frequently between different communities. They usually try to occupy their own compartment in a communal house: compartments might contain more than one conjugal family, but only as a temporary expedient.

Relations between husband and wife are expected to be warm, amicable, egalitarian, and based on free will. This is usually the case in practice, for there are few constraints to prevent an aggrieved or dissatisfied partner from simply leaving and ending the marriage. Many Temiar have been married more than once, engaging in what were effectively trial marriages. Spouses work together or in complementary ways in such activities as farming, gathering forest materials, and domestic work.

No rule of marriageability, positive or negative, attaches to the Temiar ramage as a unit. But Temiar frequently say that marriage is forbidden between people born in the same village, even though such marriages are not particularly rare in practice.

Thus several principles act together in guiding the individual Temiar as to whom he or she may marry: (1) degree of residential propinquity; (2) quality and degree of consanguineal relationship; and (3) prior affinal relationship.

Temiar marriage generates a new pattern of relations, not just between husband and wife but also between their relatives. Former "extended" consanguines become close affines—a change that adds a degree of complicatedness to their interaction, for formalized avoidance, joking, or respect relations now apply. Affines of opposite sex are especially constrained by these rules, which also apply (with some dilution) to the siblings and cousins of the affected parties.

Between "spouse's parent" and "child's spouse" of opposite sex, complete avoidance is expected. In contrast, a sexually charged joking relationship holds between opposite-sex siblings-in-law (_mneey_). There is an institutionalized understanding that mneey may have sexual relations with each other if they wish, whether or not they are already married. The few polygamous marriages that occur are almost always between siblings-in-law, usually a man and two sisters.

Domestic Unit. It is usually possible to discern three levels of residential organization within each local community. First is the household, usually a single conjugal family. Second is the household cluster, a grouping of two or more closely related conjugal families who live in adjoining sections of the house, often sharing the same hearth, and usually stay together if they migrate to another village. And third is the village (Temiar, *déék*, which also means "house"), the total local community, which is usually thought of as a familial grouping too.

Inheritance. Traditionally, the Temiar were so little concerned with inheritance that they buried most of a deceased person's property, including money, along with the corpse. Nowadays, when personal property has come to include such items as electronic goods and permanent housing, this might be expected to change; but no reliable data are available as yet on recent changes. As previously described, the major corporate property consists of seasonal fruit trees. These are inherited by cognatic transmission between whole sibling sets. When a tree is claimed for the first time, it may be individually owned; after the owner's death, it simply becomes one of the corporately owned trees. Inheritance of status is not usually an issue: the senior surviving sibling of the senior generation of siblings is normally recognized as village leader. Where outsiders have intervened by instituting a more formal headmanship, this has tended toward the more patrilineal mode of succession favored by Malay political structures.

Socialization. Child rearing is shared so easily between the parents and other kin that it often seems as if all the villagers were jointly responsible for the care of all the children. Fathers undertake the same care-giving activities as mothers. Mother, father, and child are all bound by the same set of food taboos until the child is safely out of infancy. Children are allowed a great deal of freedom, and discipline is limited to verbal advice or warnings of possible intervention by the thunder deity. Physical punishment or constraint is strongly avoided, even when the child throws a tantrum. This nonviolent approach is absorbed into the child's emerging personality: children may threaten each other in play, but the blows freeze in midair. When they play soccer or other ball games, no teams are formed—they all cooperate in helping one of the players land a goal.

There is little educational or initiatory formality. Childbirth and first-menstruation rituals are private, and weaning is so gradual that even 6-year-olds will be breast-fed if they ask. There are no rites of adulthood. Children are allowed to learn by experimentation, whether it concerns using knives, building rafts, smoking, or having sex. Other matters are explained, as the need arises, by citing the appropriate portion of Temiar mythology.

Nowadays most Temiar children attend government primary schools set up within their own territory. These have achieved basic national-language (Malay) literacy, but little more as yet.

Sociopolitical Organization

Social Organization. Viewed in its own terms, Temiar social organization is segmentary and nonhierarchical; each village community runs its own affairs. There are no formal rules of organization apart from the kinship and descent structures already described. More important than formal rules, however, are two dialectically conjoined values that pervade Temiar social life: noninterference in other individuals' wishes and a profound concern for communality. This dialectic is not always easy to maintain, but a variety of cultural mechanisms, rooted in language, religion, and kinship, serve to keep it embedded in daily life.

Political Organization. Two kinds of political role may be distinguished: leadership, which operates at the household cluster and village levels, and which relates primarily to autonomous day-to-day affairs; and headmanship at the village level, which operates in the context of external relations with politically dominant outsiders. A specialized form of headmanship, which we may call chieftaincy, operates at the supravillage level and depends on formal appointment through a letter of authority, issued ostensibly by a sultan.

As already noted, the Temiar village leader's main function is to act as the symbolic guardian of the descent group's estate. Any practical authority to run village affairs that he may possess depends entirely on his strength of character, not on his social position. His most important practical role lies in mediating discussion about such joint productive activities as farming, the collecting and trading of forest products, or the selling of village livestock to outsiders.

The headman (*twaa', tunggò'*), by contrast, has virtually no role to play in village affairs. Even a Temiar "senior chief," regarded by some outsiders as the ruler of a thousand or more people living in some dozen villages, dresses exactly like the other men of the village and is accorded no special deference by his fellows. The ranking that this appears to generate, and that some writers have claimed was an indigenous feature of Temiar social organization, is a chimera. The roles of headman and chief were created more to bolster the importance of those outsiders who were forced to have dealings with the Temiar (such as the local Malay chiefs or the British military authorities) than in response to needs arising within the Temiar community.

Despite the headman's relative insignificance in day-to-day affairs, the institution of headmanship has allowed certain structural notions (such as hierarchy by rank and patrilineal succession to office) to enter Temiar culture. These have served as alternative models of social organization, available for use if the political situation seems to demand it. Under the social and ecological changes that the Temiar are currently experiencing, these ideas could become more significant. It is more likely, however, that the relinquishment of a "tribal" outlook will make this a less attractive option than the espousal of an altogether more individualistic mode of operation.

Conflict and Social Control. The main sources of conflict are: (1) sexual jealousy, occasioned by the permissiveness of Temiar "in-law" joking relations; (2) differences of wealth within the community, generated by differential involvement in the cash economy; and (3) pulling out of the village to live elsewhere, instead of giving long-term help and commitment to village activities. Because of a general reluctance to enforce one's wishes on others, there is little that can be done about these circumstances. Gossip and complaining behind people's backs are quite common, but direct confrontation is rare. Things may sometimes get so bad, however, that a communitywide meeting is called by the village leader. Even here, moralizing rather than direct accusation fills the speeches. If discussion does not solve the problem, one of the disputing parties will usually move away to live elsewhere.

Temiar social interaction is underpinned by a general

anxiety that one's actions might cause someone else to suffer unsatisfied desires, for this is thought to leave that person open to accident, disease, or misfortune. An assortment of diffuse sanctions is aimed at reducing the likelihood of such an occurrence. One should always share food; one should accede to a direct request for a service or object; and one should avoid setting up a definite future meeting for fear that the promise cannot be kept. These ideas are linked closely to Temiar religious attitudes.

Religion and Expressive Culture

Religious Beliefs and Practitioners. The Temiar have become famous among psychotherapists and dream researchers as the supposed inventors of the "Senoi dream therapy" currently practiced by several groups in the United States. The relation between these American therapeutic systems and the practices of the Malaysian Aborigines is now known to be tenuous, even spurious, but this revelation has left undisclosed the reasons for the high regard the Senoi peoples have for dreams and trance states. To the extent that the Temiars' propensity for dream-based activities has anything to do with their mental health, their mental well-being results not from any psychotherapeutic counseling techniques that they are reputed to have developed but from the way in which their trancing and (lucid) dreaming puts them in direct touch with what their cosmological notions lead them to think of as the fundamental basis of existence.

Like everyone else, the Temiar are forced to map less graspable notions onto a more familiar surrogate. The Temiar mode of surrogation represents the cosmos, and the religious and social relations that occur within it, not in terms of things or words but in terms of the direct experience that individual human beings have of their own subjectivity. This psychocentrism is founded, moreover, on a thoroughly dialectical orientation of attention as between self and other. Unlike more familiar modes of orientation, in which either self or other is suppressed as the explicit focus of attention, the dialectical mode takes as its starting point the very mutuality of self and other. In Temiar culture, this dialectic serves as the tacit, prereflective notion out of which coherence is constructed: the Temiar self can be perceived and discussed not as an autonomous entity but only in ways that also implicate the other (and vice versa).

This construction derives its plausibility from individual Temiars' experience of their own subjectivity as being simultaneously a controlling actor and an undergoing patient. The closest they come to articulating this central unspoken mystery verbally is when talking of the various "souls" (i.e., subjectivities capable of communication) that are thought of as animating the people, animals, plants, and other salient things that inhabit their world.

In human beings these souls are the *hup* (heart) and the *rwaay* (head-soul), the corporeal seats of doing (or willing) and of experiencing (or undergoing), respectively. The same animistic imagery extends throughout the rest of the cosmos: any entity that appears capable of attracting to itself the attention of a human being is thought of as being able to do so by virtue of the simultaneously hup- and rwaay-like subjectivity that constitutes its essential core. The same holds, in reverse, for the supposed ability of nonhuman entities to become aware of and to act on the subjectivity of individual human beings.

This dialectical mutuality of actor and patient, subject and object, colors all domains of the Temiar worldview. Ordinary social relations (as already mentioned) exhibit a complicated balance between extreme communalism and extreme individual autonomy, which would be very difficult to maintain under any nondialectical mode of orientation. The cosmos itself is thought of as a subjectivity, linked somehow with thunder. It is simultaneously both the creator and the world it creates, constantly employing the "bootstrap" cosmogonic power of its own thought and imagination to maintain the differentiated character of the physical world as the Temiar know it. If human beings (or any other agency) should by their actions distract the cosmos's subjectivity away from this task, then it is thought likely that the world will dedifferentiate, through the agency of thunder (the cosmos's voice) and flood, into a muddy undifferentiated chaos. If that should happen, all things would lose their identity and disappear, through the cosmic merging of subjectivity and objectivity.

Plants and animals are thought to partake in this interplay just as fully as human beings. It is the temporarily disembodied upper- and lower-body souls of various mountains, animals, and plants (seasonal fruit trees, especially) that become the personal spirit guides to which Temiar direct their religious action. These souls are called by various special names, but they are uniformly reported to take the same shape when they appear in dreams or trances: upper-body souls become young men or women; lower-body souls become tigers.

Individuals enter into initial communication with their spirit guides through dreams. If they feel so inclined, they may then make their spirit guide's power-for-good available to the rest of the community by serving as a *halaa'* (an adept spirit medium). Mediumship centers on nighttime trance-dancing ceremonies involving one or more halaa', performing to the accompaniment of contrapuntally sung music. Each song is supposedly passed on by its composer (i.e., the spirit guide) to its initial performer (the halaa') in revelations that occurred while the latter was in a waking dream, most typically around dawn. The halaa' will often be called on to perform healing rituals on the sick during the ceremonies and also in nonceremonial circumstances during the daytime.

Trancing and (lucid) dreaming are altered states of consciousness in which one becomes simultaneously one's own subject and object, since one is then undergoing whatever one is doing. In Temiar terms, these are activities in which one's rwaay is experiencing what one's hup is simultaneously willing into existence. Trance, for example, is talked of as "forgetting one's hup"; but the trancer still retains his or her own rwaay, or there would be no means of experiencing the trance. Lucid dreaming, on the other hand, requires one to retain one's hup, as the locus of one's active participation in whatever is going on in the dream (which is thought of in turn as being located in one's rwaay's experience). Thus the rwaay/hup dialectic is founded on the trance and lucid-dream experience of simultaneously undergoing and controlling the products of one's own imagination, as if those products were autonomous "real-world" entities. By giving themselves over to trance and lucid dreaming, Temiar are thus able to experience directly the selfsame subjective processes that the cosmos itself is thought to employ in keeping itself going. But that experience is ineffable in character, formed of notions, not concepts. It involves the dreamer or trancer in a symbolic condensation that fuses mind, body, social relations, and the world into a dialectically self-transforming, indescribable (and hence unspoken) unity. Relatively few Temiar become specialists in these activities, but virtually all seek to enter into trance and lucid dreaming on occasion, if only once in their lives. They thus disguise the surrogational character of their psychocentrically constructed cosmos by fusing it with what for them is the "really real": the direct experience of controlling and being controlled by the creatures of their own imagination. They thereby provide themselves with an authentically unmediated experience of the very state of mind that supposedly holds everything together on both the cosmic and mundane levels.

Such a complicated way of approaching the world poses a problem, however. Unlike the easily expressible ideas of the various monotheistic religions, the traditional Temiar conception is far too complex to be put into words and talked about explicitly. It is therefore hard to share with others and far from easy to maintain in one's own mind. Many younger Temiar have responded to this situation in recent years by embracing more easily catechized and apparently "rational" religions. The highly monotheistic Baha'i faith found many adherents during the 1970s, especially among Temiar looking for a religion comparable to those that the Malaysian authorities had been urging people to follow. This suited these younger Temiars' desire for an easily explained religion and for one that better fitted their emerging sense of individualistic modernity.

Paradoxically, although Baha'i sees itself as an autonomous religion, some Malaysian authorities regarded it as an Islamic heresy, not appropriate for adoption by a population seen as Malay-like. Some Temiar, on the other hand, complained that Islam was being offered to them by individuals who made a poor job of explaining it and that, while Baha'i employed the national language (Malay), Islam employed a language (Arabic) that neither they nor their would-be teachers could understand. There are reports, nevertheless, that many Temiar have lately become Muslims—how spontaneously is not clear.

Ceremonies.   The ceremonial centerpiece of Temiar life consists of public performances by spirit mediums, at night within the house, involving choral singing, dance, and trance. (These have continued even in communities that have adopted the Baha'i religion. Trance is not always present, however.) Performances are put on when there is a demand for shamanic healing rituals or when someone's spirit guide has indicated in a dream that it wishes to be entertained. The sessions are known as gnabag (singsongs). Most of the community is involved, with the women and children singing responses in overlapping canon to the lead verses sung by one or more mediums. The song lyrics are considered to be the spirit guide's own, sung through—not by—the medium.

A much rarer kind of performance involves tiger shamanism, performed by a medium squatting within a special palm-leaf hut set up inside the house. This is performed only by a "big" halaa', without dancing, with the fires extinguished, and with distinctively minor-key melodies.

Other rituals are performed more casually and on a small scale. These include the pouring of warmed (i.e., encultur-ated) water over a newly delivered woman or into the post holes of a new house, or the special treatment accorded to some specially selected rice grains at the beginning of the planting season.

There are also what might be called antirituals. These are an open-ended collection of rather oddly chosen acts that must be avoided if the thunder deity is not to strike. One should not laugh at butterflies, display colored mats outdoors, dress animals in human clothing, laugh too loudly, and so on. Such acts are classed as misik (probably from the Malay bising, "disturbing noise"), and seem to have in common only the property of attracting undue attention. As already explained, one should avoid disturbing the cosmos's subjectivity for fear of causing disastrous floods and storms. If such disasters do nevertheless occur, then individuals who feel themselves guilty of having committed misik might slash their shins with a bamboo sliver, gather up some blood, mix it with water, and throw it up as an appeasement offering to the thunder deity. This blood sacrifice is also found among other Orang Asli groups (especially the Semang), but it is very rare among the Temiar. Another such rite involves slashing at the ground with a knife, sometimes while hammering a lock cut from one's own (or one's child's) hair into the soil; this is still sometimes done by Temiar during violent thunderstorms.

Arts.   The designs woven into or inscribed on mats, pouches, the walls of houses, and bamboo dart quivers are abstract and geometrical. The greatest degree of indigenous aesthetic attention is directed to the tightly woven rattan caps that cover the geometrically decorated bamboo quivers in which Temiar men carry their blowgun darts. Unlike some other Orang Asli groups, the Temiar do not produce representational images of any kind. Music, dance and storytelling, however, are cultivated with enthusiasm, and certain individuals gain considerable local fame for their abilities in these domains. The women's singing, in particular, is among the finest indigenous choral music to be heard in Southeast Asia. Appreciation for this art form is now so keenly developed among the Temiar that they make and circulate among themselves homemade tape recordings of their own musical performances. This activity was stimulated initially by the example of Malaysian Radio, which has been airing field recordings of Temiar music since around 1960 as the major component of its Temiar-language broadcasts.

Medicine.   Indigenous Temiar ideas about disease relate mainly to fears of improper interpenetration between domains or agencies that should remain separate. This can occur between spatial domains, or through soul loss and spirit invasion. The attendant symptoms do not always fit tidily into a biomedical framework of analysis, though they certainly are often real enough. Thus goutlike or arthritic symptoms are often explained as the result of letting one's leg get trapped in mud: human beings belong in the domain of off-the-ground, not in-the-ground. Depressive or neurotic symptoms may be regarded as resulting from rwaay loss; more severe psychosislike behavior may be thought to have been brought about through an invasion by the disembodied soul of an animal. Contravention of food taboos (most of which are either completely personal or affect young children together with their parents) is often blamed for convulsions and other symptoms.

Treatment includes herbal and mineral remedies ingested or rubbed on the body, enforced shady segregation within the house, casual "blowings" performed through cupped hands by anyone with halaa' powers, or full ceremonial shamanism performed in trance by several halaa' acting together. Some of the herbal remedies undoubtedly have pharmacological effect, but they have not been investigated systematically. Jennings's work on dance and Roseman's on music has gone a long way to explaining the efficacy of Temiar mediumship as therapy.

Modern treatment is also available to the Temiar, through the medical section of the JOA. This started in the late 1950s and two special hospitals for Orang Asli have been in operation for several decades. Tuberculosis and fungal skin diseases, once the scourges of Temiar communities, have become rare as a result of these services; malaria and childbirth are considerably less dangerous than they were formerly; and, most important, the medical service has provided regular paid employment (and even a career) for young Temiars.

Death and Afterlife.   Burial takes place on the day of the death, usually at a site across the river from the village. The body is wrapped in matting and placed in an alcove within the grave, on a split-bamboo platform. More split bamboo is placed on top, to ensure that the body does not come into direct contact with the soil when the grave is filled in. The grave is usually oriented in line with the sun's track, in accordance with the belief that the deceased will be transported to an afterlife in a special "flower garden" situated at the sunset.

Most of the deceased's possessions are buried with the body, and mourners also leave some of their own prized possessions (such as money or watches) in or on the grave—thus effectively blocking property inheritance. For the first few days after the burial, lights or fires will be placed on the grave. Eventually, however, the grave is left untended so that the forest may reclaim the site; Temiar thereby avoid the development of any memorial cult—an idea they regard with unease. They also firmly avoid uttering the name of a deceased person, referring instead to "Old Man X" or "Old Woman X," where X is the place-name of the burial site. In this way, detailed genealogical accounting of earlier generations is lost, for distinct individuals come to share the same burial name after they die. Genealogies thus become recitations of formerly inhabited village sites, enabling the cognatic descent-group structure (described previously) to function in a less ambiguous manner than it otherwise would.

In another expression of the wish to put death behind them, Temiar villagers used to burn the deceased's house to ashes the same day and move immediately to a new site a short distance away. This custom has now become rare, as the ownership of material goods has put a premium on staying in place.

Alternative patterns of disposal exist. "Big" halaa' are ideally left on a platform in a tree when they die; dead babies may be left suspended in a bag from a tree. These practices probably represent the remnants of the formerly more widespread Southeast Asian custom of tree burial, for the pattern of burial now usually followed by the Temiar seems to have been learned from the Islamic practices of the Malays.

See also Semang; Senoi

Bibliography

Benjamin, Geoffrey (1968). "Temiar Personal Names." _Bijdragen tot de Taal-, Land- en Volkenkunde_ 124:99–134.

Benjamin, Geoffrey (1970). "Headmanship and Leadership in Temiar Society." _Federation Museums Journal_ (Kuala Lumpur), n.s. 13:1–43.

Benjamin, Geoffrey (1985). "In the Long Term: Three Themes in Malayan Cultural Ecology." In _Cultural Values and Human Ecology in Southeast Asia_, edited by Karl Hutterer, A. Terry Rambo, and George Lovelace, 219–278. Ann Arbor: University of Michigan Center for South and Southeast Asian Studies.

Jennings, Sue (1986). "Temiar Dance and the Maintenance of Order." In _Society and the Dance_, edited by Paul Spencer, 47–63. Cambridge: Cambridge University Press.

Noone, H. D. (1936) "Report on the Settlements and Welfare of the Ple-Temiar Senoi of the Perak-Kelantan Watershed." _Journal of the Federated Malay States Museums_ 19:1–85.

Roseman, Marina (1991). _Healing Sounds: Music and Medicine in Temiar Life._ Comparative Studies of Health Systems and Medical Care. Berkeley and Los Angeles: University of California Press.

GEOFFREY BENJAMIN

Ternatan/Tidorese

ETHNONYMS: Orang Ternate, Orang Tidore, Suku Ternate, Suku Tidore

Orientation

Identification.   Ternatan and Tidorese are the inhabitants of the islands Ternate and Tidore in the northern Moluccas of eastern Indonesia; they have partly settled also along the coast of adjacent islands, Halmahera among others. They distinguish themselves from other Moluccans by the use of the language of Ternate or Tidore. The people of Ternate and Tidore call themselves in the Malay or Indonesian language "Orang Ternate" or "Orang Tidore" (_orang_, "people"). Ternatan and Tidorese are closely related to each other linguistically, historically, sociologically, and culturally, but in relation to each other they tend to set a high value on maintaining their own identity. No Ternatan likes to be classified as a Tidorese, nor does a Tidorese like to be seen as a Ternatan. For ages Ternatan have been more closely in touch with people from the more western parts of the Indonesian archipelago than with the Tidorese; as a result Tidorese are generally less educated and less cultivated than Ternatan. The Tidorese are viewed as the more industrious but also the more boorish people in relation to the Ternatan.

Location. The small islands of Ternate and Tidore are two volcanoes, very close to each other and very close to the equator, off the west coast of the large island Halmahera in the northern part of the Moluccas (Maluku) Province, Indonesia, 1° N and 127° E. The peaks of these islands are over 1,700 meters high. Both Ternate and Tidore are more than 40 kilometers in circumference. The volcano of Ternate is active; that of Tidore has not shown any signs of activity for ages. The islands have a healthy climate.

Linguistic Affiliation. Ternate and Tidore can be classified as two dialects of one language, Ternate-Tidore, which is one of the four related languages spoken on the northern half of the island of Halmahera and on the offshore islands to the north and the west. These form a non-Austronesian enclave in Austronesian language territory. These non-Austronesian languages have linguistic ties with the languages of the Bird's Head Peninsula, Irian Jaya. The superordinate group to which all these languages belong is the West Papua Phylum. The teaching medium in schools is the Indonesian national language, Bahasa Indonesia; the languages of Ternate and Tidore are reduced to a position of minor social importance, used in daily conversation but no longer in writing. Until World War II the local language was the official language of the courts of Ternate and Tidore and also was used in writing (in Arabic script).

Demography. The number of Ternatan is about 35,000 and approximately half of them live on Ternate Island; the number of Tidorese is about 70,000 and approximately half of them live on Tidore Island.

History and Cultural Relations

The area of Halmahera and adjacent islands is the homeland of cloves, and until the sixteenth century the cultivation of cloves remained confined to this area. At the time the Portuguese arrived in the Moluccas, in 1512, this area numbered four sultanates: Ternate, Tidore, Bacan, and Jailolo. Together these four sultanates, of which the competing realms of Ternate and Tidore were the most important, controlled the total world production of cloves. The power and prestige of the sultanates were based on the control of the sale of cloves to foreign traders and, later on, to Europeans. In the fifteenth and sixteenth centuries, Ternate and Tidore succeeded in extending their military power and political and cultural influence over the surrounding islands. Ternate directed its expansion mainly to northern Halmahera, to the islands south of Ternate, and to the east coast of Sulawesi. Tidore directed its expansion mainly to southern Halmahera, the Raja Ampat Islands, and the adjacent coast of Irian Jaya and to eastern Ceram. In the sixteenth century the Portuguese, who had settled themselves on Ternate Island, attempted without success to establish a monopoly on the purchase of cloves, but later on in the seventeenth century the Dutch, who took over the position of the Portuguese, succeeded in this objective. The Dutch restricted the cultivation of cloves to Ambon (central Moluccas) and a few adjacent islands, producing just enough to supply the world market. For any other islands in the Moluccas, including Ternate and Tidore, the cultivation

of cloves became strictly forbidden. This interdiction was maintained into the nineteenth century. In compensation for the loss of revenues from clove production and allied trade, the sultans of Ternate and Tidore and their principal officials were provided an annual allowance by the Dutch. Nevertheless, the interdiction of clove production and allied trade resulted in a drastic economic decline for the sultanates and, at the same time, an absolute dependence on the Dutch, cultural isolation, and internal social and political ossification. The abolition of the interdiction on clove production in the nineteenth century brought no change whatsoever because the price of cloves had fallen to a level that made the cultivation of cloves unattractive, and the system of allowances was maintained. Under Dutch protection Ternate and Tidore remained semiautonomous states until Indonesia's independence in 1949. The Indonesian government has pursued a policy of total integration of the sultanates into the modern state. The autonomous sultanates have been abolished by gradually integrating the internal administration with the provincial organization of the Moluccas. The sultanates have virtually ceased to exist now and institutions of the former sultanates survive only in folklore, not as politically significant elements.

Throughout the ages Ternate and Tidore have been influenced culturally by the Islamic northeast coast of Java, by the Portuguese, and by the Dutch. Nevertheless there has always been a strong cultural radiation from the political centers of Ternate and Tidore to the surrounding islands.

Settlements

Ternate and Tidore each has its own capital, namely, Ternate City and Soa Siu. Both these towns developed from neighborhoods that came into being near and in connection with the residence of the sultan. However, the greater part of the Ternatan and Tidorese live in villages that lie scattered along the coast of the islands. These villages number from about 200 to 5,000 people. Most villages on Ternate and Tidore lie along the road that runs along the coast, but there are also some villages situated off the road on the lower slopes of the volcano; the latter can only be reached by footpaths. A village usually consists of a number of houses of farmers and fishermen, without any special layout, and with a mosque more or less in the center of the village.

Economy

Subsistence and Commercial Activities. Ternatan and Tidorese, when not in a town, live mainly on subsistence agriculture supplemented with some fishing. Only a few people are professional fishermen. Formerly the principal food was sago, which grows on Ternate and Tidore only in negligible quantities and had to be supplied mainly from Halmahera, Morotai, Bacan, and Sula. There was and there is yet some dry-rice cultivation on Ternate and Tidore, but not so much that rice could at any time serve as the principal food of the population. Sago has now been replaced as the principal food by cassava and maize, which are cultivated on Ternate and Tidore. The cassava is prepared and eaten in the same manner as sago (i.e., as *popéda*: by pouring boiling water on the flour one gets a kind of paste that is eaten by preference with a fish sauce). Bananas, taro (*Colocasia antiquorum*), and batatas (*Ipomaea batatas*) are also an important part of the daily diet. If possible the meal is completed with a bit of dried and salted, smoke-dried, or fresh fish. Vegetables are seldom eaten and meat even less. Besides their work in the gardens and their fishery, the villagers also keep a few hens, ducks, goats, and so on. In the town the people live mainly as employees of the government and of Chinese employers, or as retailers at the marketplace.

Industrial Arts. Almost no artisans are to be found in the villages of Ternate. On Tidore there is a traditional division of labor between the villages: for example, the village of Gurabati is known for its makers of _atap_ (traditional roofing) and the village of Toloa for its blacksmiths and boat builders, whereas artisans on the little island of Mare near Tidore specialize in commercial pottery.

Trade. The stores of Ternate City and Soa Siu, like businesses in general, are almost without exception in the hands of Chinese and a few Arabs. Ternatan and Tidorese play only a small role in the trade in fruits, vegetables, and fish in and around the market: the surplus of agricultural products and fish are supplied from the villages to the town market directly or by wholesalers.

Division of Labor. The men do the incidental hard labor in the gardens, such as felling trees. They do some fishing and they see to building and maintaining the house. The women do the daily work in the gardens and the cooking, take care of the children, and try to make some money for the daily budget by selling garden produce and fish.

Land Tenure. In the villages there is still enough land available for nearly every family. People who no longer have enough land to make the necessary gardens can move to Halmahera, to make clearings there in sparsely populated areas.

Kinship

Kin Groups and Descent. Because descent is cognatic, there are no clear-cut kin groups. On closer inspection, however, various lineages or descent groups are to be distinguished, without having a name; they go back to some ancestor who held an office important enough to still be remembered. Lineages or descent groups derive their status and identity from offices held by their members in state organizations or in the organizations of the religious community. The descent groups are neither exogamous nor endogamous. Succession and inheritance of rights are by preference but not necessarily in the male line. The position of an individual is not exclusively conditioned by descent in the patriline. To be sure, one belongs in the first place to one's father's house, but one also has relations with and rights in one's mother's house.

Kinship Terminology. The kinship terminology is of the Hawaiian type.

Marriage and Family

Marriage. Marriage usually is at an early age. Only by marriage can one become a full member of the society and community. In upper-class families, marriages are frequently arranged by parents to protect and enhance the status and honor of the family involved and to avoid misalliances. It often happens that young people are forced into a marriage.

On the whole, however, there are now fewer prearranged marriages. As tolerated by Islamic law, marriage may be among relatives, for example, between parallel or cross cousins, and these kinds of marriages do occur. Marriages frequently end in divorce. Polygyny also occurs. Newlywed couples often go to live for some time with the parents, sometimes with the boy's parents but usually with the girl's. The house that is eventually built by the young couple is in most cases situated close to the house of the parents of the girl or the boy.

Domestic Unit. The domestic unit usually consists of a married couple, their children, and, frequently, their coresident parents.

Inheritance. Property is usually divided more or less equally among the children. The outcome of the division, however, is to a great extent the result of a (subtle or crude) play of forces, because inheritance is informally arranged entirely within the family, without the interference of persons not directly involved.

Socialization. Socialization of the children is by the parents, grandparents, and siblings, although frequently uncles and aunts are involved to a certain extent. There is only a vague borderline between play and learning the really important things of life. When the boys are at an age when they might be expected to marry, they are not expected to do heavy physical labor. They are the pride of the families and, in contrast to the girls, they are not expected to demonstrate their fitness for marriage by a show of diligence and industry. Only after marriage does the seriousness of life begin for boys.

Sociopolitical Organization

Ternate and Tidore now are part of the national state of Indonesia. Their sultanates have ceased to exist.

Social Organization. Ternatan and Tidorese identify themselves by means of descent from one of the traditional units of sociopolitical organization, _soa_, each soa having its own name. The meaning of "soa" is literally "ward," "quarter," or "hamlet," but the soa were by no means pure territorial units. One did not belong to a soa on account of residence but rather on account of descent. Membership in a soa was transmitted in the patriline. The soa was not a clan or lineage, however, because the members of the soa did not claim a common descent from one ancestor and because the kinship organization is not unilinear but cognatic. The soa was headed by a chief who was appointed by the sultan. With the abolition of the sultanates, the soa as units of sociopolitical organization have become obsolete; they are no longer accepted by the government as units of administration, and they do not have a function in the field of kinship organization. The soa chiefs have been replaced by democratically chosen village chiefs.

Political Organization. Since Ternate and Tidore are part of the Indonesian state, the political organization is the same as everywhere else in Indonesia. All government employees are members of Golkar, a semipolitical grouping that is closely related to the government. In the elections one can vote for Golkar or for one of the two other political groupings in parliament. When there are no elections for parliament coming up, political parties are almost completely inactive.

Social Control.   Social control is exercised by neighbors, fellow villagers, and members of the family. Generally violators of commonly accepted norms are not dealt with too harshly, provided that the transgression of the norm is done in an inconspicuous way. If people feel forced by a public scandal to maintain the norms, measures tend to be taken without delay. For example, young people who have been caught in the act of extramarital intercourse are immediately forced to marry, more often than not after a severe beating.

Conflict.   Ternatan and Tidorese are not aggressive people. If they do not like other people, they tend to avoid them rather than fight with them. People of foreign origin are easily integrated into the society, provided they profess Islam.

Religion and Expressive Culture

Religious Beliefs and Practices.   Ternatan and Tidorese are convinced Muslims, as is expressed by the rituals at circumcision, marriage, and death; in the strict maintenance of the fast during Ramadan; in the celebration of the holy days; and in the high value placed on the pilgrimage to Mecca. At the same time they retain a great number of traditional local customs that are incompatible with orthodox Islam, such as the belief in shrines that are visited to pray for recovery from illness and for other pragmatic purposes. There also exists a widespread belief in guardian spirits, who are venerated and beseeched for help by means of shamanistic rituals.

Religious Practitioners.   Formerly Arabs especially acted as religious teachers. The leaders of religious ritual, imams and *khatibs*, were appointed by the sultan, who acted as head not only of the polity but also of the religious community (*ummat*). That situation changed after World War II. Indonesia has created a nationwide educational system for the training of religious teachers. The bureaus of the Department of Religion are filled with graduates from the schools for religious training. This department has its branches on Ternate and Tidore, where it appoints imams and khatibs and takes care of religious jurisdiction, as it does elsewhere in Indonesia. The traditional position of Arabs as teachers of religion has been strongly undermined by this new educational system for religious teaching. The modern teachers of religion are more orthodox than the traditional Arab teachers and are inclined to cleanse Islam of traditional customs incompatible with orthodoxy. Leaders of shamanistic rituals, however, are still tolerated for traditional reasons.

Arts.   There are no conspicuous art performances on Ternate or Tidore.

Medicine.   People value modern medicines highly, but besides these most people also believe strongly in traditional forms of surgery and in traditional ceremonies to prevent illness and all kinds of mischief.

Death and Afterlife.   Ideas about death and afterlife are borrowed wholly from Islam.

   See also Moluccans—North; Tobelorese

Bibliography

De Clercq, F. S. A. (1890). *Bijdragen tot de Kennis van de Residentie Ternate*. Leiden: E. J. Brill.

Polman, K. (1981). *The North Moluccas: An Annotated Bibliography*. Bibliographical Series, Koninklijk Instituut voor Taal-, Land- en Volkenkunde, no. 11. The Hague: Martinus Nijhoff.

van Fraasen, Ch. F. (1987). "Ternate, de Molukken en de Indonesische Archipel: Van soa-organisatie en Vierdeling: Een studie van traditionele samenleving en cultuur in Indonesie." Ph.D. dissertation, University of Leiden.

   CH. F. van FRAASEN

Tetum

The label "Tetum" (Belu, Teto, Tetun) refers to the more than 300,000 speakers of the Tetum language on the island of Timor in Indonesia. The people call themselves "Tetum" or "Tetun," and are referred to as "Belu" by the neighboring Atoni. The traditional Tetum territory is located in south-central Timor. While the Tetum are often described as a single culture, there are numerous subgroups that differ in some ways from each other. One classification scheme differentiated among the Eastern, Southern, and Northern Tetum, with the last two sometimes lumped as the Western Tetum. Tetum is an Austronesian language and either the primary language or the second "official" language in south-central Timor.

   The Tetum are swidden farmers; the main crop varies according to location. The people of the hills cultivate rice and breed buffalo, the latter being consumed only during major rituals. The people of the coastal plains cultivate maize and breed pigs that are eaten regularly. Each household maintains its own garden and raises chickens to supplement the diet. There is little hunting and fishing. A weekly market provides a social meeting place and allows the people to trade produce and wares. The Tetum traditionally make iron tools, textiles, rope, baskets, containers, and mats. They express themselves artistically through carving, weaving, engraving, and dyeing cloth.

   Groups in the east generally have patrilineal descent, whereas matrilineal descent is the norm among those in the west. Although lineages are localized, the members of a given phratry or clan are dispersed among a number of villages. Tetum have a variety of marital arrangements, including bride-price, bride-service, marriage to form alliances, and concubinage. Traditionally there were four social classes: royalty, aristocrats, commoners, and slaves. Political organization centered on princedoms, which formed kingdoms. Catholicism has become the primary religion, although traditional beliefs and ceremonies survive.

   See also Atoni

Bibliography

Hicks, David (1972). "Eastern Tetum." In _Ethnic Groups of Insular Southeast Asia_, edited by Frank M. LeBar. Vol. 1, _Indonesia, Andaman Islands, and Madagascar_, 98–103. New Haven: HRAF Press.

Tidong

"Tidong" (Bolongan, Camucones, Nonukan, Tarakan, Tedong, Tidoeng, Tidung, Tiran, Tirones, Tiroon, Zedong) is the name used for an Islamized population found in northeastern Kalimantan and Sabah. In Malaysia, the population is estimated at about 10,000. People labeled Tidong were probably early inhabitants of the region or people who migrated there from the interior. Contact with the Tausug and Bugis led to large-scale cultural change and conversion to Islam. Even so, Tidong have remained distinct from other groups in the region.

Bibliography

Sather, Clifford (1972). "Tidong." In _Ethnic Groups of Insular Southeast Asia_, edited by Frank M. LeBar. Vol. 1, _Indonesia, Andaman Islands, and Madagascar_, 167–168. New Haven: HRAF Press.

T'in

ETHNONYMS: Chao Dol, Htin, Katin, Kha Ché, Kha Pai, Kha T'in, Lawa, Luaʔ, Lwaʔ, Maí, Pai, P'ai, Pral, P'u Pai, Thin, Tiê, Tin

Orientation

Identification. The T'in are hill horticulturalists of northern Laos and northern Thailand. Some, especially in Pua District, call themselves "Mai," as in _phuam maí_ (Mai people) or _ngang maí_ (Mai language), meaning "life force" or "life essence." Those to the north and east of the Mai call themselves "Prai" (in Thailand) or "P'ai" (in Laos), a Yuan (Northern Thai) or Lao word meaning "commoner, lawless, or vulgar person." The Yuan terms "Ka," "Kha," "Lawa," "Luaʔ," "Lwaʔ," "P'u," and various other combinations and transliterations are derogatory terms used indiscriminately for Mon-Khmer and Palaung-Wa groups. The Thai refer to them as "Htin," "Tin," "T'in," or "Thin" (all transliterations signifying an aspirated _t_), related to the Thai word for "place" or "locality," hence "the locals," "the native inhabitants of a place." Only those heavily influenced by the Thai, as in relocation centers, use this term as a self-designation. The T'in appear physically similar to Kmhmu, Lamet, and other Mon-Khmer hill peoples in Thailand and Laos: short and stocky with black hair and a darker complexion than their valley neighbors. Physical anthropologists classify them as Paleo-Mongoloids.

Location. The T'in live in Nan Province, Thailand, and Xagnabouri (Sayaboury) Province, Laos, to the southwest of Luang Prabang. Except where they have been resettled by lowland authorities, they prefer the mountain ranges between the Mekong and the Mae Nam Nan rivers.

Demography. William Dessaint estimated 14,548 T'in in Thailand in 1964 and George Tubbs estimated 5,000–6,000 in Laos in 1960. Assuming an annual population growth rate of 2 percent, the total number of T'in in Thailand and Laos in 1989 would be about 34,100.

Linguistic Affiliation. T'in is in the Mon-Khmer Family, closely related to Kmhmu. There has been extensive borrowing of vocabulary from Yuan (Northern Thai) and Lao. Filbeck differentiates two major branches in Thailand: Mal (three dialects spoken, mainly in Pua District) and Prai (at least five dialects). Most T'in (men more than women) are fluent in the Nan dialect of Yuan or in Lao. In some acculturated villages, Yuan has become the primary language. A small number of T'in, those who purchase opium or hire themselves out as laborers, speak Hmong. There is no written language.

History and Cultural Relations

The T'in have probably lived in the same general area for centuries. Large numbers probably moved from Laos to Thailand in the late nineteenth and early twentieth centuries as a result of internecine warfare between highlanders and lowlanders in Laos, as in Muang Ngol in 1876. Other migrations occurred before and since, both from Laos to Thailand and from Thailand to Laos, spurred by political conditions and availability of good land. There is regular trading between T'in and lowlanders. In Thailand, they have been exposed to strong acculturative pressures by the presence of Thai Border Patrol Police and Thai and Lao military forces. Several thousands were moved into resettlement centers beginning in 1967. A small number of T'in have become nominal Buddhists. American Protestant missionaries have had little success among them.

Settlements

Most T'in live at mid-level elevations near the headwaters of the Mae Nam Nan, between Tai groups (Yuan, Lue, Lao) in the river valleys, and between Hmong and Mien in the higher mountains. T'in villages are located between 300 and 1,300 meters, close to a reliable source of drinking water. Villages vary in size from 4 or 5 households to over 100, and they often include scattered hamlets or individual houses with varying degrees of autonomy. T'in villages are sometimes interspersed with those of their Tai, Hmong, or Mien neighbors. The largest and most stable villages are those with a sound economic basis: salt wells, _miang_ (fermented tea leaves chewed as a mild stimulant), or access to favorable agricultural land at lower elevations. Village gates with carved wooden spirit posts may still be found, though more and more they fall into disrepair through neglect. Several households, who may or may not be related, cooperate in house building. A house should face west, with an entrance porch reached by a wooden ladder or notched log. Houses are built on wooden piles, usually windowless, with walls and floors of bamboo or wood and thatched roofs. The roof may overhang to cover the family's rice pounder. Flimsy bamboo walls partition off bedrooms in the corners. Rattan mats are used for sitting and sleeping. Rice is stored in a granary set on piles or in large rattan containers inside the house. Villagers move whenever they believe the soil to be exhausted, or when sickness, accidents, or bad omens occur too frequently. Village stability among T'in is greater than among highlanders such as Lisu or Hmong.

Economy

Subsistence and Commercial Activities. Glutinous rice is the main crop. Maize, millet, and vegetables and condiments (including gourds, squash, capsicum, cucumbers, eggplants, Chinese mustard, and chili peppers) are also grown. Swiddens are cleared in January and February using axes and machetelike knives. Old swiddens that have lain fallow several years require less work to clear and are therefore favored. In April or May, the cut brush is burned. T'in plant crops in May or June before the monsoon, using digging sticks; they weed with hand hoes. The fields must be guarded against birds and other predators. The rice harvest begins in August, though most rice is harvested in October and November, using sickles. It is threshed by beating it against a bamboo frame or trampling it underfoot, and it is transported to the village in baskets using head tumplines. Rice swiddens are used for one or two years: a few are irrigated, though none is terraced. Households cooperate in agricultural labor: usually a couple, their married daughters, and their sons-in-law will exchange labor. In larger villages, miang is a major commercial product. T'in cultivate only small amounts of betel and tobacco for their own use. Opium has been grown by a few households (usually on fields abandoned by Hmong), but most of it is bought from highlanders. Domesticated pigs and chickens usually fend for themselves, though they may also be given rice bran, banana stems, vegetable leftovers, and maize. Only a few households own cattle (water buffalo and zebu). Pigs and cattle may be sold to outsiders or for village sacrifices. Chickens, pigs, dogs, and occasionally cattle are used as sacrifices to the spirits, though the meat is eaten later. Men and boys hunt with crossbows or rifles for wild fowl, rabbits, wild pigs, barking deer, bears, tigers, and rhinoceroses (the last two are now almost extinct). Fishing is less important; both nets and poison are used. Collecting of wild fruit, honey, medicinal herbs, benzoin, stick-lac, and firewood is done mostly by women and children. Until recent disturbances in the area, salt was collected from salt wells in two communes near the headwaters of the Mae Nam Nan, Bo Klüa Nüa, and Bo Klüa Tai rivers. (The water was boiled in large kettles until only the salt remained.) As a last resort, the T'in occasionally hire themselves out as agricultural laborers to the Hmong or Mien.

Industrial Arts. Most containers, rattan mats, rattan baskets, utensils, and everyday articles are made by hand in each household.

Trade. Miang is peddled door-to-door in Yuan or Lao communities. Yuan or Lao caravanners buy salt. Pigs, cattle,

and hides (deer, bear, and tiger) are also sold to lowlanders. T'in buy rice, medicine, blankets, clothes, towels, pots, pans, axes, sickles, flashlights, matches, beads, earrings, and other manufactured goods.

Division of Labor. Both men and women perform agricultural chores, but men do the heavier clearing. Men hunt, trade, deal with lowlanders, hold the offices of headman and village priest, brew liquor, and are responsible for religious observances. Women are primarily responsible for child rearing, food preparation, hulling rice, fetching water and firewood, and cleaning clothes. Children fetch firewood and water, tend younger siblings, and collect wild foods. Elders take care of grandchildren, prepare food, weave baskets, make fishnets, and tend livestock.

Land Tenure. Whoever clears a piece of land enjoys its usufruct until it is abandoned. No claim on a piece of land can be maintained by someone who does not work it. These usufruct rights are sometimes rented or sold for a small sum. While the rice crop belongs to the sower, anything else— vegetables, condiments, trees, animals—found in a swidden can be taken by anyone. Villages do not have an exclusive territory: people from different villages (and ethnic groups) may be working adjacent fields. The headman may confirm field boundaries and inform villagers of areas that the government does not wish disturbed.

Kinship

Kin Groups and Descent. The descent system is bilateral. There are no lineages, clans, or other social institutions based on kinship apart from the family and household. The spirits of the last two generations are honored.

Kinship Terminology. Kinship terms stress relative age, reflecting its importance in determining status relations. Differences between patrilateral and matrilateral, lineal and collateral, and consanguineous and affinal relatives are expressed. Distant relatives of a person's own generation are often called elder or younger brother or sister; thus one's kinship group may include most members of a village community. The T'in have adopted Thai personal names and surnames; often a whole village shares the same surname.

Marriage and Family

Marriage. Premarital sex is a serious insult to the village guardian spirit and calls for an expensive sacrifice, usually a calf. It is rare. Courtship is carried out in groups, and the boy indicates his interest in a girl to his parents, who in turn contact the girl's parents. Women marry in their mid-teens, men in their late teens. The ideal is village endogamy (resulting in first-cousin marriages) and monogamy, and these are usually practiced. The marriage ceremony, which may take place after a man and a woman have begun living together, involves a feast for the groom with the men of the village at which the *khawcam* (village priest) invokes the blessing of the village spirit and notifies the groom's ancestor spirits that the groom will be leaving his house. Another feast is held at the bride's house to introduce the groom to the bride's ancestor spirits. Divorce is common, especially during the period of brideservice, which in some communities is a trial marriage. Requests are made to the headman who with the elder men of the village, attempts a reconciliation. If this is not possible, they discuss with the families of husband and wife the division of property and children.

Domestic Unit. The basic social unit is the matrifocal nuclear or extended family. After marriage, there is matrilocal residence with bride-service (which averages one or two years). An older married daughter and her husband and children will move out and build a house nearby. The youngest daughter will remain in her parents' house, take care of her old parents, and eventually inherit the house. Patrilocal residence occurs only when a family has no daughters.

Socialization. Parents, siblings, grandparents, and other relatives share child-care duties. As soon as they are able, boys take part in male activities and girls begin helping their female relatives. Many villages in Thailand now have government schools.

Sociopolitical Organization

Social Organization. There is no tribal consciousness. The village is the largest sociopolitical entity. There are no clan ties, and few marriage ties crosscut village boundaries; there are no leaders with power in more than one village. Even religious beliefs and rituals differ somewhat from village to village. There is strong pressure for harmonious social relations within a village. Only minor differences in status, wealth, or personal influence exist, based largely on age and secondarily on sex.

Political Organization. Anyone in the village may attend meetings of the informal village council and participate in discussions, but in practice it is the male household heads who have a real say. Men enjoy prestige according to their age, experience, and reputation for sound reasoning. The khawcam also has influence. The office of headman seems a more recent innovation in response to pressures from lowland authorities. The headman is often recommended by an outgoing headman, selected by the village council, and appointed by the Thai or Lao district officer. He forms the link between lowland administration and villagers, carries out government directives, assigns numbers to each house, keeps count of the members of each household, assesses taxes, coordinates unpaid village labor, and reports crimes to lowland police. He receives a small monthly stipend, and he may appoint assistant headmen.

Conflict. The _riit_ is an unwritten code of T'in tradition. Any infraction of riit, such as quarrels or fights, is offensive to the village spirit, who may turn his anger on anyone in the village or the village as a whole, causing illness, epidemics, crop failure, or other calamities. Disputes between houses are mediated by elder men. Serious infractions of riit are dealt with by the khawcam who, in consultation with village elders, may impose fines, require the sacrifice of a chicken or pig to the village spirit, or expel the wrongdoer from the village. Witchcraft accusations occur between people of different villages.

Religious and Expressive Culture

Religious Beliefs. Following religious tradition is essential to good health and agricultural success. The T'in strive to attain and maintain harmony between themselves, the natural world, and the supernatural world through ceremonies and taboos. There are many types of spirit: ancestor spirits, village guardian spirits, field spirits, jungle spirits, and spirits associated with mountains, water, or other natural features or phenomena. Spirits may become harmful if offended, whether the offense is intended or not, resulting in disharmony that must be corrected through offerings and sacrifices. One propitiates spirits before undertaking any major activity, including any major phase of the agricultural cycle. Offerings and sacrifices, preventive or curative, are made by the khawcam or by any household head. All spirits can be appeased, though none can be controlled.

Religious Practitioners. There are no full-time specialists. A khawcam is selected by divination by his predecessor or influential elders. He acts as the villagers' representative to the village spirits, sees to it that villagers observe ceremonies and respect taboos, settles disputes, judges infractions of religious customs, makes offerings and performs sacrifices on behalf of the village, and presides at weddings, funerals, house blessings, and annual rituals. Other adult males have specialized knowledge to carry out specific rituals; they may know formulas with curative powers or incantations against witchcraft, or they may have power to deal with certain spirits. Each of these specialists may work for other villagers with little or no remuneration.

Ceremonies. The T'in observe a ten-day week, of which one day (differing from village to village) is a holy day; no physical labor may be done in the rice fields on that day. The new year usually falls in mid-April and lasts three days, during which spirits of the old year are driven out and spirits of the new year are welcomed. Villagers drink specially prepared rice liquor through long reeds, and the khawcam is possessed by the village spirit, who makes his wishes known. The religious calendar is intertwined with the agricultural cycle: the major ceremonies are related to rice, the staff of life. Before villagers plant rice, the khawcam sacrifices a pig (paid for by all households), and before the rice shows its head, he sacrifices a chicken to preserve the crop from insects. The head of each household should also sacrifice a dog to the spirit of the household's field. After the rice begins to grow, a major festival lasting several days is held to reintegrate the _mai_ (life force or life essence) of rice. Rice is the only item for which there is such a ceremony. At harvest, _taieo_ (a Yuan loanword for star-shaped markers made of bamboo strips) are placed around the village as protection against evil spirits intent on destroying the crop. When a field is abandoned, a simple ceremony with food offerings is made to return the land to the spirits.

Medicine. Human beings are believed to have more or less mai. Like the Thai or Laotians, some T'in say they have thirty-two mai. Loss of mai is caused by an offended or angry spirit and results in sickness. Loss of all mai results in death. If only part of it is lost, that part can be regained through a ceremony involving the recital of incantations and the sacrifice of a chicken or pig, for blood is believed to be indispensable to appease an offended spirit and to retrieve lost mai.

Death and Afterlife. At death, the men of the village hold a loud wake, singing and drinking to keep the dying company. After death, the body is wrapped in a blanket and bamboo mat, and men bury it in the jungle. If the deceased was a woman, betel, tobacco, and rice are buried with her. The grave diggers and the house of the dead must be cleansed ritually to get rid of evil spirits; the family of the dead performs a ceremony to increase their mai. On the tenth day after death, ashes are placed in a winnowing tray and the deceased is asked to walk across: the type of imprint made will show whether the deceased has become a pig, a dog, a chicken, or—if no imprint is visible—an ancestral spirit. Those who die in violent or unusual circumstances become ghosts or evil spirits that are much feared.

Bibliography

Dessaint, William Y. (1973). "The Mai of Thailand and Laos." *Bulletin of the International Committee on Urgent Anthropological and Ethnological Research* 15:9–25.

Filbeck, David (1971). "T'in: A Historical Study." Ph.D. dissertation, Indiana University.

Filbeck, David (1971). "The T'in of Northern Thailand: An Ethnolinguistic Survey." *Behavior Science Notes* 6:19–31.

ALAIN Y. DESSAINT

Toala

The Toala (East Toraja, Luwu, Sada, Telu Limpoe, To Ale) numbered around 30,000 in 1983. They live in the mountains of southwest Sulawesi Island, Indonesia. Toala is classified in the West Indonesian Group of the Austronesian Language Family. Formerly hunter-gatherers, the Toala now work copra plantations and grow rice, maize, and vegetables in their gardens. The people are largely pagan, although Islam has made some converts among them. The Toala were traditionally divided into three subtribes ruled by a hereditary chief; they have since changed to an elected chieftainship.

Bibliography

Kennedy, Raymond (1935). *The Ethnology of the Greater Sunda Islands.* Ann Arbor, Mich.: University Microfilms.

Tobelorese

The Tobelorese (Orang Tobelo, Suku Tobelo) live on the northern peninsula of Halmahera Island, Indonesia, and number about 20,000. Tobelorese is classified in the North Halmahera Group of the Papuan Language Family. Subsistence is based on rice, maize, cassava, bananas, and vegetables, supplemented by fish. Nearly all Tobelorese are Protestant Christians. In the past the Tobelorese were organized into four tribal villages headed by a single leader (*kimelaha*).
See also Moluccans—North

Bibliography

LeBar, Frank M. (1972). "Tobelorese." In *Ethnic Groups of Insular Southeast Asia*, edited by Frank M. LeBar. Vol. 1, *Indonesia, Andaman Islands, and Madagascar*, 121–122. New Haven: HRAF Press.

Tomini

Numbering around 74,000 in 1980, the Tomini (Tiadje, Tialo, Toli-toli, Tominers) occupy the northern Sulawesi Island peninsula in Indonesia. Tomini is classified in the West Indonesian Group of the Austronesian Language Family. Villages, small and comprised of houses on stilts, are located on the coast. Maize and sago are the staples, wet rice having been introduced in the early 1900s. Copra is raised commercially. Tomini are Sunni Muslims, although there are still small animist enclaves in the mountains. The animist population is referred to as *suku terasing*, meaning "foreign tribes," and they have been the object of Indonesian government acculturation programs including relocation. The Tomini are presently very much involved in commercial clove production and are active participants in the Indonesian state.

Bibliography

Nourse, Jennifer W. (1984). "Tomini." In *Muslim Peoples: A World Ethnographic Survey*, edited by Richard V. Weekes, 789–793. Westport, Conn: Greenwood Press.

Toradja

The name "Toradja" refers to the indigenous people of the central highlands of Sulawesi (Celebes) in Indonesia. It means "men of the mountains," in contrast to the peoples of the lowlands. There are numerous named groups within the region, all of whom are culturally similar and usually lumped under the general designation of Toradja. Anthropologists have conventionally classified these groups as Western Toradja, Eastern Toradja, and Southern Toradja. This system reflects both geography and degree of cultural contact with Hindu-Javanese groups in southern Sulawesi. These three groupings never existed as distinct political units and traditional organization was localized at the village and multivillage level. The Toradja were of considerable interest in the early twentieth century because of unique and highly developed cultural traits such as head-hunting, elaborate funerals, cave burials, and carved stone statues. Named groups of peoples classified as Western Toradja include the Mountain Toradja, Pipikoro Toradja, Palu, and Parigi; the Eastern Toradja include the Poso-Todjo groups, Poso Lake groups, Palende, Lampu, Wana, and Ampana. The total number of Toradja exceeds 500,000.

See also Toraja

Toraja

ETHNONYMS: Sa'dan Toraja, South Toraja, Tae' Toraja, Toraa, Toraya

Orientation

Identification. The Sa'dan Toraja reside in the highlands of the province of South Sulawesi in Indonesia, speak the Sa'dan Toraja (Tae' Toraja) dialect, and are predominantly Christians. As these Sulawesi highlanders have never developed their own writing system, most early references to the Toraja derive from the written records (_lontara_) of neighboring lowland Buginese (Bugis) and Makassarese kingdoms. There is general agreement among scholars that the name "Toraja" derives from Buginese, probably from "To-ri-aja," _to_ meaning "people" and _ri-aja_ meaning "upstream" or "above" (Sa'dan is the name of the region's major river). The Toraja began to adopt this externally imposed name only in the twentieth century.

Location. Most of the Sa'dan Toraja reside in the Indonesian regency of Tana Toraja. This district on the island of Sulawesi is 3,657 square kilometers in area and lies between 2°40′ and 3°25′ S and 119°30′ and 120°25′ E. Tana Toraja Regency ranges from 300 to 2,884 meters above sea level. The climate is tropical, with a rainy season lasting from November until April.

Demography. In 1987 the population of Tana Toraja Regency was estimated as 346,113. Population density averages 84 per square kilometer. Figures are not available for the number of Sa'dan Torajans who have left their homeland to reside in the larger cities of Indonesia (the one exception is a 1973 estimate of 30,000 Toraja in Ujung Pandang).

Linguistic Affiliation. The Sa'dan Toraja speak Tae', an Austronesian language that is thought to be related to the neighboring languages of Duri and Buginese. Tae' has two levels of speech—a daily language and a high language of the priesthoods. Today, as citizens of Indonesia, most Toraja also speak Bahasa Indonesia.

History and Cultural Relations

It is speculated that the Toraja migrated to Sulawesi from Indochina some 4,000 years ago. There is evidence of relations with the coastal Buginese and Luwunese as early as the sixteenth century. By the late nineteenth century, trade between Toraja highlanders and Muslim lowlanders intensified: coffee and slaves were exported in return for guns, salt, and textiles. Toraja traditionally resided in autonomous and at times mutually hostile mountain villages. It was not until the arrival of the Dutch colonial forces in 1906 that the Toraja were united under a single political authority. By 1913 missionaries from the Calvinist Reformed Church had arrived, precipitating dramatic sociocultural changes. Scholars suggest that the activities of these Protestant missionaries stimulated a unifying sense of Toraja identity. The region was occupied by the Japanese during World War II. Following that war, in 1949, the region was declared a part of the new nation of Indonesia. Today, Tana Toraja Regency has become a major tourist destination (in 1988 179,948 tourists visited the area).

Settlements

Toraja traditionally resided in isolated mountaintop settlements; however, the Dutch relocated many of these villages into the major valleys for administrative convenience. Today the population of villages averages 4,170, although there is variety in size and constellation. Traditionally villages consist of clusters of elevated plaited bamboo houses, rice barns, and kindred houses (_tongkonan_). The tongkonan is a most significant aspect of Toraja culture. The tongkonan is more than a physical structure—it is a visual symbol of descent (see under "Kinship"). According to ritual prescriptions, the tongkonan must face north. Tongkonan are constructed of wood, without nails, and are raised on stilts; they also have arched bamboo roofs, although today these are being replaced by corrugated iron. In precolonial times, elaborately carved tongkonan were associated with the nobility. Commoners were restricted to carving only specified sections of their tongkonans and slaves were strictly forbidden to carve their tongkonans. In front of the tongkonans one finds a plaza that is used for ritual occasions. Across this ritual plaza is a row of rice barns. They vary in construction, but all rice barns have a lower deck area that is used for receiving guests and socializing. Rice barns may be constructed of wood with elaborate stylized motifs or they may be of simple plaited bamboo. Surrounding the village are gardens and rice fields. Today villages also have Buginese-style houses elevated on stilts, and modern cement homes. Most villages also have a church and a school nearby.

Economy

Subsistence and Commercial Activities. Most residents of Tana Toraja Regency (90 percent) are subsistence agriculturalists. Rice, grown in terraced paddies, is planted and harvested by hand. Single metal-blade plows drawn by water buffalo or men are still in use. Toraja farmers also grow maize, cassava, chilies, beans, yams, and potatoes. Cash crops include coffee and cloves. The Toraja also gather snails, eels, and small fish from unplanted wet-rice fields. Domestic animals include pigs, chickens, and water buffalo, which are sacrificed on ritual occasions.

Industrial Arts. A number of Toraja supplement their income by carving (for traditional or touristic purposes). Certain villages are known to specialize in particular crafts: knife forging, pottery making, mat making, and hat plaiting.

Trade. Most villages have a couple of tiny stores that may sell only two or three items (cigarettes, sweets, instant noodles, soap, etc.). Markets rotate on a six-day cycle. Women bring fruit and vegetables to sell at the market. Men bring livestock, palm wine, hand-forged knives, or carvings. Full-time market vendors tend to be Buginese or from Duri, rather than Toraja.

Division of Labor. Both men and women fish and tend the fields. Men and children care for water buffalo, while women generally feed the pigs. Women are occupied with the traditional home tasks, although men often cook meat and tend babies.

Land Tenure. Although remote mountain slopes are still being converted into new terraced wet-rice fields, changes in agricultural technology have been minimal. Steady population growth has resulted in land shortage. Rice fields are highly prized and the majority of court cases in Tana Toraja involve land-tenure disputes. By the 1960s land shortage and limited local economic opportunities began to drive many Toraja to seek wage labor away from the homeland. Today many Toraja work in a variety of professional and blue-collar jobs in Indonesian cities. Still others work for lumber and oil companies as far away as Irian Jaya, Kalimantan, or Malaysia.

Kinship

Kin Groups and Descent. As noted earlier, Toraja kinship is organized around the tongkonan (kindred house). Each tongkonan has its own unique name and history. A given tongkonan belongs to all male and female descendants of its two founding ancestors (husband and wife). As Toraja descent is bilateral, an individual may claim links to a number of tongkonan on both the mother's and father's side. A group of kin who trace their descent to a common pair of tongkonan-founding ancestors is called a *pa'rapuan*. In some areas, smaller, splinter branches of pa'rapuan are called *rapu*. Pa'rapuan members come together for ritual occasions and share in the expenses of rebuilding the tongkonan.

Kinship Terminology. There is some confusion as to whether Toraja kinship terminology should be classified as Hawaiian or Eskimo. Although terms for different degrees of cousins (first, second, third, etc.) exist, in everyday practice these are avoided and sibling terms are substituted. The system is generational in nature and kin terms tend to convey the relative age (and sometimes gender) of individuals.

Marriage and Family

Marriage. Today Toraja marriages are monogamous, although in the past polygyny was sometimes practiced by the aristocracy. Some marriages continue to be arranged by the parents; however, most contemporary Toraja select their own mates. Marriage with first and second cousins is prohibited (although in previous times one could circumvent this taboo through ritual offerings). In certain regions the nobility were the exception to this rule, often marrying first cousins to keep wealth within the immediate family. Residence is ideally neolocal, but many couples reside initially with either the husband's or the wife's family. Divorce is frequent, and divorce compensations are determined prior to marriage (to be paid by the divorcing party). There are no prohibitions on remarriage.

Domestic Unit. The people who cook and share meals around a hearth are considered the most basic family unit. The average size of this household group is five persons, although grandchildren, cousins, aunts, etc. are frequent overnight visitors. As a household member, one is expected to share in the tasks of everyday living—cooking, cleaning, farming, or contributing part of one's wages to the family.

Inheritance. One's surviving children and grandchildren have the right to inherit property. To claim such rights one must sacrifice water buffalo at the funeral of the deceased.

Socialization. Children are reared both by parents and by siblings. Adoption is common: family ties are extended and strengthened by adopting infants out to relatives and friends. Often children will move back and forth between the households of their adoptive and biological parents. Emphasis is placed on respect for one's elders, diligence, and the importance of the family over one's individual needs.

Sociopolitical Organization

Social Organization. Toraja society is hierarchically organized on the basis of age, descent, wealth, and occupation. In traditional times there were three basic ranks: the aristocracy (*puang, to parengnge'*), commoners (*to makaka, to buda*), and serfs/slaves (*kaunan*). Women were prohibited from marrying down, and the eating utensils of slaves were considered polluting and were carefully segregated from those of the nobility. Today slavery is illegal and the topic of rank is particularly sensitive. Wealth is much respected in Tana Toraja, particularly as it allows one greater visibility in ritual contexts. Tongkonan leaders also have a great deal of prestige and are chosen on the basis of their intelligence, charisma, bravery, descent, and wealth. Government officials and the clergy are also afforded high status.

Political Organization. The head of Tana Toraja Regency is called a *bupati* and is appointed by the Indonesian government. A council of local representatives (DPRD) assists the bupati in decision making. The regency is divided into nine smaller administrative districts called *kecamatan*, each overseen by a *camat*. Each kecamatan consists of several villages (*desa*), each with a village head (*lurah*). The Indonesian government provides the basic range of services including schools, police, health posts, tax collection, and road maintenance.

Social Control. Gossip and shaming are important means of social control. Personal disputes are often mediated by tongkonan leaders. When traditional leaders are unable to resolve such disputes, the state apparatus (police, military, etc.) is called upon.

Conflict. Prior to the twentieth century lowland Buginese periodically raided the Toraja highlands for coffee and slaves. Relations between Toraja settlements were often tense as well. Headhunting raids to avenge the death of a kinsman were common until the beginning of this century.

Religion and Expressive Culture

Religious Beliefs. Christianity is central to contemporary Toraja identity, and most of the population has converted to Christianity (81 percent in 1983). Only about 11 percent continue to practice the traditional religion of Aluk to Dolo (Ways of the Ancestors). These adherents are primarily elderly and there is speculation that the "Ways of the Ancestors" will be lost within a few generations. There are also some Muslims (8 percent), primarily in the southern areas of Tana Toraja. The cult of the ancestors plays an important role in the autochthonous religion of Aluk to Dolo. Ritual sacrifices are made to the ancestors who, in turn, will protect the living from illness and misfortune. According to Aluk to Dolo the cosmos is divided into three spheres: the underworld, the earth, and the upperworld. Each of these worlds is presided over by its own gods. These realms are each associated with a cardinal direction, and particular types of rite are geared toward particular directions. For example, the southwest represents the underworld and the dead, while the northeast represents the upperworld of the deified ancestors. The dead are believed to voyage to a land called "Puya," somewhere to the southwest of the Toraja highlands. Provided one manages to find the way to Puya and one's living relatives have carried out the necessary (and costly) rituals, one's soul may enter the upperworld and become a deified ancestor. The majority of the dead, however, remain in Puya living a life similar to their previous life and making use of the goods offered at their funeral. Those souls unfortunate enough not to find their way to Puya or those without funeral rites become *bombo*, spirits who threaten the living. Funeral ceremonies thus play a critical role in maintaining the harmony of the three worlds. Christian Toraja also sponsor modified funeral rituals. In addition to the bombo (those who died without funerals), there are spirits who reside in particular trees, stones, mountains, or springs. *Batitong* are terrifying spirits who feast on the stomachs of sleeping people. There are also spirits that fly at night (*po'pok*) and werewolves (*paragusi*). Most Christian Toraja say that Christianity has driven out such supernaturals.

Religious Practitioners. Traditional ceremonial priests (*to minaa*) officiate at most Aluk to Dolo functions. Rice priests (*indo' padang*) must avoid death-cycle rituals. In prior times there were transvestite priests (*burake tambolang*). There are also healers and shamans.

Ceremonies. Ceremonies are divided into two spheres: smoke-rising rites (*rambu tuka*) and smoke-descending rites (*rambu solo'*). Smoke-rising rites address the life force (offerings to the gods, harvest thanksgivings, etc.), whereas smoke-descending rites are concerned with death.

Arts. In addition to elaborately carved tongkonan houses and rice barns, life-sized effigies of the dead are carved for certain wealthy aristocrats. In the past these effigies (*tautau*) were very stylized, but recently they have become very realistic. Textiles, bamboo containers, and flutes may also be adorned with geometric motifs similar to those found on the tongkonan houses. Traditional musical instruments include the drum, Jew's harp, two-stringed lute, and gong. Dances are generally found in ceremonial contexts, although tourism has also prompted traditional dance performances.

Medicine. As in other parts of Indonesia, illness is often attributed to winds in the body or the curses of one's enemies. In addition to traditional healers, Western-style doctors are consulted.

Death and Afterlife. The funeral is the most critical life-cycle event, as it allows the deceased to leave the world of the living and proceed to Puya. Funeral ceremonies vary in length and complexity, depending on one's wealth and status. Each funeral is carried out in two parts: the first ceremony (*dipalambi'i*) occurs just after death in the tongkonan house. The second and larger ceremony may occur months or even years after the death, depending on how much time the family needs to amass its resources to cover the expenses of the ritual. If the deceased was of high status, the second ritual may last more than seven days, draw thousands of guests, and entail the slaughter of dozens of water buffalo and pigs, buffalo fights, kick fights, chanting, and dancing.

See also Toradja

Bibliography

Koubi, Jeannine (1982). *Rambu solo', "La fumée descend": Le culte des morts chez les Toradja du sud.* Paris: CNRS.

Nooy-Palm, C. H. M. (1979). *The Sa'dan Toraja: A Study of Their Social Life and Religion.* Vol. 1. The Hague: Martinus Nijhoff.

Nooy-Palm, C. H. M. (1986). *The Sa'dan Toraja: A Study of Their Social Life and Religion.* Vol. 2, *Rituals of the East and West.* Dordrecht and Cinnaminson: Foris Publications.

Volkman, Toby (1985). *Feasts of Honor: Ritual and Change in the Toraja Highlands.* Urbana and Chicago: University of Illinois Press.

KATHLEEN M. ADAMS

Vietnamese

ETHNONYMS: Annamese, Cochinchinese, Kinh, Tonkinese

Orientation

Identification. The Vietnamese speak the Vietnamese language and live in the Socialist Republic of Vietnam. Significant numbers of Vietnamese, especially since 1975, are now found in most Western countries, including the United States, France, Australia, and Canada. Remnants of earlier Vietnamese migrations still exist in northeastern Thailand and New Caledonia. Many Vietnamese have also lived in Cambodia and Laos for many decades. Under French colonial rule Vietnam was divided into three separate political entities: Tonkin (north Vietnam), Annam (central Vietnam), and Cochinchina (south Vietnam). Foreigners have sometimes used these terms as designators of ethnicity (e.g., the "Tonkinese"), sometimes employing the term "Annamese" to include all Vietnamese. This usage is offensive to Vietnamese, who all refer to themselves as "Vietnamese," sometimes using "northern," "central," or "southern" as adjectives to designate region of origin. Ethnic Vietnamese also refer to themselves as *kinh*, meaning "lowlanders," as opposed to highland "tribespeople."

Location. Vietnam is located between 8°30′ and 23° N and between 102° and 109° E. Very narrow and elongated in the center, it is wider in the south and in the north. The country lies to the south of China and east of Laos and Cambodia, with a long coastline on the South China Sea. Although some three-quarters of Vietnamese national territory is hilly or mountainous, ethnic Vietnamese have lived mainly in the lowland plains.

Demography. The population of Vietnam is about 68.5 million, over 20 percent of whom live in urban areas. Population density is over 207 per square kilometer. About 85 percent of the total population is ethnic Vietnamese. There are many highland ethnic minorities, including numerous Tai-speaking groups as well as Hmong (Meo), Nung, and Muong in the northern highlands and Austronesian-speaking groups (e.g., Rhadé and Jarai) and Mon-Khmer (Austroasiatic)-speaking groups (e.g., Bahnar, Sedang, Stieng, Mnong, and Katu) in the southern highlands. A sizable and long-established ethnic Chinese population lives mostly in urban areas of the south, although many left the country between 1975 and 1980. Many ethnic Khmer live in parts of the Mekong Delta. The Red River and Mekong deltas, containing less than a quarter of the total land area, hold almost 60 percent of the population and over 70 percent of all ethnic Vietnamese. Population density in these core areas is often very high (over 2,000 persons per square mile), but in highland areas it is often under 25 per square mile and rarely exceeds 150 per square mile. Both the southern and the northern regimes during the division of Vietnam (1955–1975), as well as more recently the Socialist Republic of Vietnam, had programs to resettle Vietnamese into the highlands, but they encountered numerous difficulties and achieved only limited results.

Linguistic Affiliation. Vietnamese is a monosyllabic and tonal language of composite origin, basically Mon-Khmer (Austroasiatic), but with elements derived from Tai and Sinitic languages.

History and Cultural Relations

The early inhabitants of the area apparently were Negritos. Some 4,000 years ago Austronesian (Indonesian) migrants from the north were moving into the area that is now north Vietnam. Later, Austroasiatic (Mon-Khmer and Malayo-Polynesian) peoples arrived. Then, about 2,500 years ago Viet (Yueh) and Tai peoples moved down from southern China. Out of this mixture of genes, languages, and cultures arose Van Lang, considered to have been the first Vietnamese kingdom. In mid–third century B.C. Van Lang was overrun by and incorporated into another state to the north, forming the kingdom of Au Lac. Then Au Lac was incorporated into an even larger and more powerful state: Nam Viet (Nan Yueh in Chinese), centered on Canton. Local leadership and culture were little disrupted in the Red River Delta, although new cultural elements entered from the north. In 111 B.C. the region was incorporated into the expanding Han Empire in China and the Red River Delta was part of the Chinese empire for a thousand years. Local hereditary leadership was used by both Nam Viet and early Han rulers, but as infrastructure and more intensive production techniques developed, pressure increased for more complete Sinicization of local culture and administration. In A.D. 39 the Trung sisters led the traditional local elite in a popularly supported revolt that flourished briefly but was suppressed in A.D. 43, ending hereditary leadership. The new hybrid elite of the Red River Delta kept and developed a sense of regional identity; the local language and many non-Chinese customs were retained. Revolts came periodically until A.D. 939 when independence from Chinese rule was achieved, although China would remain a military threat and a continuing source of cultural influence. What is now central Vietnam was then the kingdom of Champa. The Cham spoke an Austronesian language, had a powerful Indian influence on their culture and political organization, and also had a strong maritime orientation. Over the next six centuries Vietnam displaced or assimilated the Cham and extended Vietnamese territory down the coast to the plains and foothills east of Saigon, which they took and occupied during the seventeenth century. The Vietnamese then expanded at the expense of Cambodia, settling the western Mekong Delta in the eighteenth century and the eastern portion in the nineteenth. But between 1859 and 1883 all of Vietnam fell under French colonial control. South Vietnam (called Cochinchina) was a French colony; central Vietnam (called Annam) and northern Vietnam (called Tonkin) became protectorates. Together with Cambodia and Laos, they constituted French Indochina. A public school system established by the French in 1908 disseminated elements of Western culture in Vietnam, influencing but not destroying Vietnamese culture. In 1945 a popular revolution erupted against French rule. As this movement came under increasingly strong Communist control, however, some Vietnamese became disaffected. In 1955 Vietnam gained independence from France but was divided into the Socialist Republic of Vietnam in the northern half and the anti-Communist Republic of Vietnam in the southern half. About

900,000 Vietnamese relocated from the north to the south, while 90,000 or so others moved from south to north. A Communist-led revolution in the south evoked heavy American support for the Republic of Vietnam, adding American influence to the already heterodox southern region, and led to the invasion of the south by northern troops. After a devastating war, Communist forces in 1975 took over all of Vietnam, the foreign troops departed, and the Socialist Republic of Vietnam was established in 1976.

Settlements

The traditional Vietnamese village, typical of lowland northern and central Vietnam, was a highly nucleated settlement surrounded by a bamboo hedge or sometimes by an earthen wall. Each village had a communal hall (*dinh*) that served as a sanctuary for the cult of the village guardian spirit and as a public meeting hall. Mahayana Buddhist temples were also common. These villages tended to be tightly bounded and relatively closed communities (both physically and socially) with an elaborate community structure, located along roads or waterways or on knolls or hillsides. Houses were built with mud or brick walls, thatched or tile roofs, and earthen or concrete floors. In the more recently settled southern region, especially in the western Mekong Delta, settlements have been more scattered and less tightly bounded, with a less well-defined community structure. Some southern villages had no dinh. Most are strung out along roads or waterways and some households are scattered over the countryside. Houses have walls of woven bamboo, brick, or wood, earthen or concrete floors, and roofs of palm leaves, thatch, or, in recent decades, corrugated iron or metal sheets made from recycled aluminum cans.

Economy

Subsistence and Commercial Activities. Vietnam is a poor country, with an annual per capita income of less than U.S. $200. Agriculture, the dominant sector of the economy, emphasizes the cultivation of wet rice, but the production of secondary food crops (maize, yams, manioc, beans) and industrial crops (rubber, tea, coffee, pineapple, citrus fruits, sugar, tobacco, jute) has increased in recent decades. Despite efforts to mechanize agriculture, water buffalo and human beings still do most of the farm work. Pigs, chickens, ducks, cattle, and fish ponds are common. Many coastal villages specialize in fishing. Home gardens play an important role in the household economy.

Industrial Arts. Small-scale food processing, charcoal making, and handicrafts (furniture, lacquerware, pottery, silk, baskets) play an important economic role. Sewing machines are widespread. Mining and metalworking are important in the north. Some industries (cement, textiles, chemicals, steel) are well established, but efforts to build heavy industry have been impeded by war and a weak economic base.

Trade. While small shops, stalls, street peddlers, and market squares are common, and Vietnamese women are especially active in petty retail and trade, until recently ethnic Chinese dominated many wholesale activities. Government efforts to socialize the economy in 1978 closed tens of thousands of small private businesses that were replaced by a state

trading network, but some private enterprise has now returned.

Division of Labor. Traditionally women have had charge of domestic affairs, including finances. Men dominated public affairs, the professions, and agricultural activity. Extended warfare and government regulations have given women greater opportunities in all areas, but much de facto division of labor by gender persists.

Land Tenure. The ratio of people to arable land is one of the most unfavorable in the world for an agricultural country. Most landholdings have been collectivized under Communist rule. Each household in a collective is permitted to have some land for its own use; private plots (about 5 percent of the land area) typically produce from 10 to 20 percent or more of the total yield.

Kinship

Kin Groups and Descent. The structure of Vietnamese kinship involves logical opposition and functional complementarity between two models. Especially in northern and central Vietnam, patrilineage has been the dominant form, with emphasis on hierarchy and solidarity. But bilateral tendencies, with greater egalitarian emphasis, have always been present, most strongly in the south. In recent years Socialist policies have reinforced bilateral tendencies, weakened patrilineage, and strengthened the nuclear family. Descent is patrilineal, but with increasingly strong bilateral tendencies.

Kinship Terminology. Vietnamese kinship terminology is of the Sudanese type, highly descriptive. There are different terms for father's siblings and mother's siblings, and father's older brother is terminologically distinguished from his younger brother.

Marriage and Family

Marriage. Although free choice in marriage is now the law and is quite common, arranged marriages and the use of matchmakers persist, and parents and important elders wield much influence. In the northern and central regions, village endogamy and patrilocal residence have been the norm and are still common. Polygynous marriage, once common, is now illegal; but it has not disappeared.

Domestic Unit. Households average from five to seven persons, but they vary greatly in size. Most consist of a nuclear family, often supplemented with one or more other close relatives, and function as a single economic unit, sharing the work and resources.

Inheritance. In general, all children inherit equally, although sons, especially eldest sons, are sometimes favored. The oldest, or sometimes the youngest, son (or even the youngest daughter) may stay at home to care for aging parents and inherit the house.

Socialization. The attitude toward young children is very permissive, but older children are much more strictly controlled and disciplined. Boys have somewhat more freedom than girls and, although the tendency is weakening, are likely to get more education. Family solidarity is emphasized over independence, and nurturance/dependency relationships over self-reliance.

Sociopolitical Organization

Social Organization. Vietnamese social organization entails complex interaction between two contradictory sets of ideas. Traditionally, individual Vietnamese have been firmly embedded in powerful corporate groups, first and foremost in a family. A family was part of a lineage and of a village. Villages were aggregated into the state through a national civil service. Within families, lineages, and villages a strict, male-dominant hierarchy was common. These biases persist in Vietnamese society. Relative age, rank, titles, degrees, and other status markers remain significant determinants of attitudes and behavior in social interaction. Yet at each level a distinct set of more open and egalitarian institutions has always been present: bilateral family ties, mutual aid groups, shamanistic cults, and Buddhist practices. Situational shifting between these two logically contradictory but on the whole functionally complementary domains at every level has been and to a large extent remains the essence of Vietnamese social organization. In recent decades state ideology and legal codes have weakened the strength of traditional social groupings and hierarchies; but the new Socialist men and women and the new Socialist society envisioned by state planners since 1955 in the north and 1975 in the south remain more of an ideal than an actuality as older patterns reemerge in new forms. Vietnamese social organization is changing, but the extent and precise nature of change is still unclear and unevenly distributed from region to region.

Political Organization. The Socialist Republic of Vietnam is a Communist state divided into thirty-nine provinces and three autonomous municipalities. Provinces are divided into districts, districts into villages and townships. Each such unit has its own People's Council, the main public organ of state authority, and a People's Committee, the executive agent of the People's Council and the major administrative body. The Communist party of Vietnam plays a major role in all spheres at all levels, however, imposing parameters of discourse and action and setting social and economic goals. The Communist party is designated by the constitution to be the "sole force leading the state and society," and the executive branch of government is virtually an extension of the Central Committee of the party.

Social Control. Traditionally families, lineages, and villages could be held corporately responsible for the actions of their members. Concern for the welfare and reputation of one's family has served to constrain misbehavior. Gossip and ridicule have been important weapons for social control because of a concern for "face." Now neighborhood committees and Communist party cells and organizations monitor behavior and rebuke deviance. Self-criticism and public-criticism sessions are used to check antisocial tendencies.

Conflict. Local disputes have often involved competition for scarce water or land; historically much conflict has arisen from Vietnam's southern expansion and from resistance to encroachment upon Vietnam's territorial integrity and independence from the north. Ideological disputes have torn the country and region apart for the past fifty years, while regional rivalry has reemerged with national independence. Within groups, conflict often involves perceived slights in regard to respect behavior and relative status. Underlying such sensitivities there are both high psychological stakes and competition over the control of resources. Vietnam, with the twelfth-largest population in the world, has maintained the fourth-largest army and a large public-security apparatus, despite a weak economy.

Religion and Expressive Culture

The official ideology of the Socialist Republic of Vietnam is basically atheistic, and the state is committed by its constitution to combat "backward life styles and superstitions." While official policy guarantees freedom of religion, secular activities of religious groups are severely circumscribed, and activist religious leaders have been jailed.

Religious Beliefs. Popular Vietnamese religion is a mixture of ritual and belief derived from animist, Confucian, Taoist, and Buddhist sources. Veneration of ancestors is a very important part of this syncretic system, as are many elements of Mahayana Buddhist practice and belief. But only a minority of Vietnamese could properly be called Confucianists or Buddhists. Beliefs in astrology, geomancy, and the intervention of spirits in human life are all widespread. Traditional villages had cults to a village guardian spirit. There are perhaps over 5 million Roman Catholics in Vietnam. Many Vietnamese are nominally Buddhists, but active members of organized Buddhist churches probably number only 3 or 4 million, mostly in and around Ho Chi Minh City and Hue. The Cao Dai, numbering between 1 and 2 million and limited to the south and south-central regions, combine folk religion and Christian beliefs. The Hoa Hao, limited to one portion of the western Mekong Delta, with about 2 million adherents, are a puritanical, poor, peasant-based sect committed to a simplified and austere Buddhist doctrine. There are also a small number of Protestant Christians and other small sects built around prophets or charismatic leaders. For some Vietnamese, Marxism seems to function as a secular religion and appears to have acquired some sacred aspects. Ho Chi Minh, "the father of independence," is to some a cult figure similar to traditional heroes worshiped as powerful spirits after their death.

Village guardian spirits were once important cult figures, but now less so. Some spirits are believed to provide assistance if venerated, or illness and misfortune if ignored. People who die violent deaths are thought to linger as angry spirits and bring misfortune if not propitiated. There are many categories of malevolent or potentially malevolent spirits, among them ghosts (*ma*), and demons (*guy*). There are numerous minor deities who may intervene in human life for good or ill, and a generally benevolent category of supernatural, *tien*, a "fairy" or "genie."

Religious Practitioners. Buddhist monks are to be found in many villages. They do not automatically enjoy high respect or exert influence in village affairs, although some may achieve these things. Catholic priests and many Cao Dai and Hoa Hao leaders are respected leaders in their communities. Shamans, fortune-tellers, and a variety of other specialists in dealing with the supernatural may build up a group of clients or followers.

Ceremonies. The most widespread and important ceremonies involve the ancestors. Death-anniversary celebrations, New Year's festivities, and other events bring the ancestors back to visit the family, where they must be ritually greeted. The Midyear (Wandering Souls) festival is widely observed. Christians celebrate Christmas and Easter. Many households have, in addition to altars for the ancestors, small shrines to various spirits (the earth god, Shakyamuni, the goddess of mercy, the god of wealth, etc.) and present ritual offerings once or twice a month.

Arts. Literary arts, especially poetry, are highly prized. A wide variety of musical forms and instruments is popular. Many southerners enjoy reformed opera, musical dramas with humorous elements. Some people like Western music, everything from classical to rock and roll. While guitars and pianos are popular, some people still play traditional stringed instruments with great skill. Fine arts and architecture reveal both Western and Chinese influence. Skits and impromptu musical performances or recitations of verse are popular at many kinds of gatherings.

Medicine. Illness is attributed to many causes: it may be organic or owing to germs, but it also may be caused by fright or hardship, heartbreak, an imbalance of elements, a curse, or spirit possession. Picking the right kind of treatment is essential. There are many specialists in the supernatural who diagnose and treat illness in a variety of ways, often sharing clients with modern medical centers and with Vietnamese or Chinese herbalists. Vitamin injections, tonics and elixirs of many kinds, and special dietary regimens are also used. Sometimes women feel called to worship a particular spirit or deity, and illness is the penalty for failure to make offerings. Protective talismans and amulets and ritual support for protector spirits are used to ward off illness.

Death and Afterlife. Funerals (and sometimes reburials) were elaborate and costly affairs, especially for the well-to-do, but they are now less so. Ritual support for the deceased is most crucial. Those not honored by a cult become errant spirits, unhappy and harmful. A series of rituals elevates the deceased into the ranks of the ancestors. Ancestors return to visit the family on death-anniversary celebrations and special family occasions. Major life events are reported to the ancestors.

Bibliography

Gourou, Pierre (1936). _Les paysans du delta tonkinois._ Paris: École Française d'Extrême-Orient. Translated as _Peasants of the Tonkin Delta._ 1955. New Haven: Human Relations Area Files.

Hickey, Gerald C. (1964). _Village in Vietnam._ Chicago: Aldine.

Hy Van Luong (1989). "Vietnamese Kinship: Structural Principles and the Socialist Transformation in Northern Vietnam." _Journal of Asian Studies_ 48:741–756.

Le Thi Que (1986). "The Vietnamese Family Yesterday and Today." _Interculture_ 92:1–38.

Rambo, Arthur Terry (1973). _A Comparison of Peasant Social Systems of Northern and Southern Viet-nam: A Study of Ecological Adaptation, Social Succession, and Cultural Evolution._ Monograph Series, no. 3. Carbondale: Southern Illinois University Center for Vietnamese Studies.

Rambo, Arthur Terry (1982). "Vietnam: Searching for Integration." In _Religion and Societies: Asia and the Middle East,_ edited by Carlo Caldarola, 407–444. Berlin: Mouton.

NEIL JAMIESON

Visayan

Visayan (Bisaya, Bisayan, Pintado) is a general term for a large segment—about a quarter—of the Philippine population. In 1962–1963 they numbered about 10,836,000, and the total may be closer to 15 million today. The term "Visayan" refers to people who inhabit the islands surrounding the Visayan Sea, mainly the Samarans (1,488,600 in 1962–1963), Panayans (2,817,300), and Cebuans (the largest Christian group, 6,529,800). Their territory lies between 9° and 13° N, and between 122° and 126° E, in the central Philippines. These people generally inhabit the islands of Bohol, Cebu, Leyte, Masbate, Negros, Panay, Samar, and Siquijor, although many have migrated elsewhere, especially to Mindanao and Manila.

Most Visayans are Roman Catholics, and they make up a large part of the Christian population that is loosely labeled Filipino. On first being discovered by the Spaniards they were named "Pintados" because they used to paint their bodies. They are not the only inhabitants of their islands, for they share them with such shifting-cultivation groups as the Agta, Bukidnon, and Sulod (all covered earlier in this volume). The popular image of Visayans is of a passionate, fun-loving, brave, and musical people. Many are professional fighters. Their major economic activity is the cultivation of maize and irrigated rice. Those who have settled in Mindanao in recent decades have often become involved in fighting local Muslims ("Moros") for land.

Visayans speak either Cebuano, Panayan or Samaran, three languages of the Malayo-Polynesian Family (to which all Philippine languages belong). English and Pilipino are widely used as second languages today, and there is also a pidgin language called "Chabakano," which is based on Spanish, Cebuano, and Subanun.

See also Filipino

Bibliography

Dumont, Jean-Paul (1991). _Visayan Vignettes: Ethnographic Traces of a Philippine Island._ Chicago and London: University of Chicago Press.

Hart, Donn V. (1954). _Barrio Caticugan: A Visayan Filipino Community._ Ph.D. dissertation, Syracuse University.

Hart, Donn V. (1959). _The Cebuan Filipino Dwelling in Caticugan: Its Construction and Cultural Aspects._ New Haven: Yale University, Southeast Asia Studies.

Hart, Donn V. (1969). *Bisayan Filipino and Malayan Humoral Pathologies: Folk Medicine and Ethnohistory in Southeast Asia*. Southeast Asia Studies, Data Paper no. 76. Ithaca, N.Y.: Cornell University.

Lieban, Richard W. (1967). *Cebuano Sorcery: Malign Magic in the Philippines*. Berkeley and Los Angeles: University of California Press.

Nurge, Ethel (1965). *Life in a Leyte Village*. Seattle: University of Washington Press.

PAUL HOCKINGS

Yakan

ETHNONYMS: none

Orientation

Identification. The Yakan are one of the Muslim peoples of the southern Philippines. They live on the island of Basilan, just off the southwestern point of Mindanao.

Location. Basilan is located at 6°40′ N and 122°00′ E, with a total area of 1,283 square kilometers. The climate is tropical with a rainy season from April to October and a dry season from November to April. The interior is mostly mountainous. The Yakan live predominantly in the interior, mostly in the eastern, central, and southwestern part, whereas Samal and Tausug, who are also Muslim, live along the coasts. Nowadays there is also a large Christian population, which emigrated from other parts of the Philippines, mostly from the Visayan Islands. A few Yakan live on Sacol Island.

Demography. The number of Yakan is usually estimated at between 90,000 and 100,000, though variations between 60,000 and 196,000 may be found. The Yakan constitute a little less than half the population of Basilan.

Linguistic Affiliation. The Yakan language is Malayo-Polynesian. It is closely related to the Sama and Bajau languages, and is considered by some to be a Sama dialect.

History and Cultural Relations

The Yakan are probably the original inhabitants of Basilan, and may once have inhabited the whole island. Later the coastal areas were occupied by Sama and Tausug from the Sulu Islands and, more recently, some Christian Filipinos settled not far from the coast, where they established rubber and coconut plantations. The sultan of Sulu once claimed Basilan as part of his possessions. Christian occupation started when the Spanish colonial government established a fort at Isabela on Basilan's northwest coast in 1842. In the 1870s the Yakan were conquered by a Christian Tagalog, who had escaped from a penal colony in nearby Mindanao. After some resistance the Yakans recognized him as their leader, with the title of *datu*. He adopted Islam, but he also restricted the hostilities between Yakan and Christians. He was succeeded first by a nephew, later by that man's son, who in 1969 was proclaimed sultan of Basilan. The unrest in the southern Philippines in the 1970s hit the Yakan very badly. In the early seventies a considerable part of Basilan was controlled by the rebels, and many Yakans were evacuated for some years. The Yakan are in many respects culturally related to other Muslim groups (Moros), not merely in religion. There has been contact with the Tausug and Sama, and especially with the Sama there is much cultural similarity. However, the Yakan have their own identifiable culture.

Settlements

The Yakan have no compact villages; the houses are scattered among the fields, and there are vegetables and fruit trees around the house. Usually it is difficult to see where one settlement ends and the next begins. The center of the community is the mosque (*langgal*), which is a simple building. The houses are rectangular pile dwellings housing nuclear families. The traditional house has a steep thatched roof, although today corrugated iron is also used. The walls are made of either plaited reed or bamboo, or of wooden boards; the floor may be of bamboo, but is more often of timber. Usually the house has only one big room with no special quarters for the women. To the house is joined a kitchen. The house is entered through a porch, which is an important part of the house. The inhabitants of a settlement may be related, but it is not the rule. Some changes have recently taken place. Though houses may still be scattered, this is no longer the case everywhere. Some people now build closer to one another, which was formerly done rarely and only when the occupants of the houses were closely related. Also, some who can afford to do so now build better, more modern houses.

Economy

Subsistence and Commercial Activities. The Yakan are agriculturalists who practice dry farming with water buffalo-drawn plows. The main crop is upland rice, harvested once a year, but camote and cassava are also important. Other crops are grown, including maize, eggplants, yams, beans, coffee, and sugarcane, as well as many fruits including papaya, banana, mango, pineapple, jackfruit, and durian. Stimulants, betelpepper, areca nuts, and tobacco are also cultivated. For the growing of the main crops, rotation of fields is practiced. Usually only one crop of rice is grown in a field, and after it is harvested camote or cassava is planted in that field. When this second crop has been harvested, the field is usually left fallow for a couple of years, and then rice is planted again. Few people have enough rice to last them from one harvest to the next. On the whole, the crops mentioned are grown primarily for private use.

The same was formerly the case with coconuts. In more recent years, however, coconuts have become increasingly important as the production of copra has become an essential source of income. Coconuts now supplant other crops, even rice. The Yakan have few domestic animals. Formerly they had great herds of cattle, but this ended during World War II; now a household may have only a few cows and water buffalo. They also keep a few goats and chickens. Pigs, of course, are not kept, since the Yakan are Muslims. Hunting was formerly important but this is no longer the case, and although fish play an important part in the diet, the Yakan seldom fish; they mostly buy fish from the Samal.

Industrial Arts. A few Yakan are smiths. In some places there are skillful boat builders, though the Yakan themselves are not a seafaring people. The boats are sold to the coastal peoples. The only important craft is weaving: Yakan women weave beautiful cloths of various kinds on backstrap looms. Formerly these were for personal use only, but they now make textiles for sale. Some of these are of the same kind they use for their own clothing, others are tourist wares made in the old weaving style.

Trade. Barter was practiced in the past, but now money is in universal use. The Yakan bring their products (aside from copra, some vegetables, and weavings) to the markets. In most settlements there is a small Yakan-owned store where the most important goods can be purchased.

Division of Labor. There is no marked division of labor in agriculture. It is most common for men to plow and harrow, but women also perform these tasks, and other forms of agricultural work are done by both men and women. The increasing importance of coconut growing is changing this because the men do most of the work in connection with the production of coconut and making the copra. Household chores are mostly done by women, but men may help. The crafts are gender-specific: smithing is done by men, weaving by women.

Land Tenure. Land is individually owned, but until recently ownership was only by tradition, without legal titles. This has caused problems as non-Yakans have tried to acquire Yakan land in some areas. Now more and more Yakans have acquired land titles legally.

Kinship

Kin Groups and Descent. Descent is bilateral: father's and mother's kin are of more or less the same importance. There is a great feeling of solidarity among relatives. At any great event, such as a wedding or a funeral, as many relatives as possible will come together. A settlement may consist of related persons, but that is not the rule.

Kinship Terminology. There are special terms for father and mother. There is no distinction in terms between father's and mother's relatives. The terms for aunt and uncle respectively are the same whether they are father's or mother's sibling. The same is the case in connection with cousins. As to the older generation, there is no distinction between grandparents and their siblings, and grandparents use the same term for their own grandchildren as they do for their siblings' grandchildren. Sibling terms distinguish between elder and younger siblings.

Marriage and Family

Marriage. As Muslims, Yakan men are allowed to have four wives, but polygyny is becoming increasingly rare. Most Yakans have only one wife, although some have two and a very few have three or more. Formerly marriages were arranged by the parents, but now the parents will often consider their children's wishes. The bridegroom and his family must pay a bride-price to the bride, which however is hers only until she has children; then it will be transferred back to them. A greater bride-price is paid to the parents of the bride. All expenses in connection with the wedding are met by the bridegroom's side. It was formerly preferred that the young couple be related, but this is now considered of less importance. Usually the newly married couple will live for some time with the parents of either the bride or the groom; later they will establish their own household on land belonging to either of them. Husbands and wives have separately owned property; what they acquire in common will be their common property. Divorce is not uncommon, and may be initiated by either spouse. If the wife wants a divorce the bride-price must be returned, whereas this is not the case if it is the husband who wants a divorce.

Domestic Unit. The nuclear family, consisting of man and wife with unmarried children, is the most common domestic unit. Often newly married children stay with the parents. A parent or sibling of either the husband or the wife may join the household, usually if the person in question is single.

Inheritance. Property is divided equally between the children in spite of the precepts of the Quran that a daughter's inheritance shall be only half as big as a son's.

Socialization. The children are brought up in the family; they begin at an early age to help with family work. Older siblings often take care of smaller brothers or sisters. Formerly the only education the children had was to learn to read the Quran, although there were a few schools before World War II. Today there are several private and public schools. At first many parents did not want their children to go to these schools, but now an increasing number go, although many also attend the Quranic school.

Sociopolitical Organization

The sultan of Sulu once claimed Basilan as his property, and it must be because of this claim that there were a small number of datus among the Yakan. They were all Tausug and apparently representatives of the sultan. Neither sultanate nor datuship is part of Yakan traditional culture. On the whole the sultan's influence seems to have been rather limited. Now, of course, the Yakan are under the Philippine government.

Social Organization. The settlements are small political units based on mosque affiliation. At the head of the community are the imam and a council. Wealth or leading position is respected, and so is age. But on the whole there is no pronounced social stratification. It should be mentioned that although the Yakan are Muslims, there is no segregation of women. Formerly young women were said to have had more limited freedom of movement, but that is no longer the case. Veiling has never been practiced.

Political Organization.   There are two sorts of political organization: the traditional, with parishes centered around the langgal and a council taking a role in local matters, and the modern organization of the government of the Republic of the Philippines. Basilan is a province with a city and municipalities headed by mayors, and, more important to the Yakan, *barrios* (which are composed of several smaller communities called *sitios*) headed by barrio captains.

Social Control and Conflict.   Formerly fighting among Yakans was not uncommon. Conflicts may still occur. As far as possible they are handled by the council and the imam, though it seems that nowadays it is most often the imam and the barrio captain who handle the cases. This goes also for marriage quarrels, though more serious affairs may be brought before the sultan. Serious matters, such as killings, are settled at the official courts.

Religion and Expressive Culture

Religious Beliefs.   The Yakan are Muslims, but many beliefs and practices deriving from an older religion are still retained and are, to a great extent, incorporated into their Muslim rituals and life; the Yakan consider them to be part of Islam. One important example is connected with rice growing. Rice is, to some extent, personified; planting and harvesting are initiated with religious ceremonies, and other religious precautions are taken to secure a good rice harvest. The Muslim center of religious practice, where the official prayers are conducted, is the langgal. There is a belief in various spirits, some of whom may sometimes attack people. Some places are believed to house spirits (e.g., a special kind of tree); one spirit may be encountered near the grave of a newly buried person. There is also a belief in a special devil who may attack and torture people during the second month of the year; people born in that month are especially in danger. To avoid the danger, a bathing ritual is performed on three successive Wednesdays of that month.

Religious Practitioners.   The head of the langgal is the imam, who has two helpers, the *habib* and the *bilal,* both in accordance with Islam. The imam conducts the service in the langgal, and officiates at the life-cycle rituals and at the rice ceremonies. An important part of his position is to lead household prayer (e.g., to ask for recovery in case of sickness, or to bless a new house). There are other religious practitioners, however, who probably derive from an older, pre-Islamic religion. The most important is the *bahasa,* a kind of shaman, who will summon spirits to help him cure sickness or to tell fortunes. Whereas the bahasa will never work with the imam, another practitioner, the *tabib,* may sometimes assist the imam in performing certain semi-Muslim ceremonies outside the langgal. He may also perform the rice ceremonies and cure sickness. These practitioners are all male; the person teaching Quran-reading, the *guru,* is most often a woman.

Ceremonies.   The Yakan follow the Muslim calendar and celebrate both the orthodox and the less common annual Muslim festivals. The most important are the fasting in the ninth month, concluded with a big celebration, and the celebration in the twelfth month during the pilgrimage. Among the Yakan the most important feast, however, is the birthday of the Prophet Mohammed in the third month. Very important also are the three bathing rituals in the second month.

The Yakan have annual Islamic celebrations during seven months of the year. Ceremonies are also performed in connection with the life cycle: after birth, at the end of the Quranic studies, at weddings, and a series of ceremonies after death. The wedding usually consists of two ceremonies, an Islamic and an older, pre-Islamic ritual. This is typical of the religious syncretism of the Yakan. Rice ceremonies have already been mentioned.

Art.   The Yakan have various musical instruments, most of them percussive, but also flutes and Jew's harps. Percussion instruments are mostly played on certain important life-cycle occasions such as weddings. One special instrument is played while the rice is growing to make it happy so that it will give a good harvest. Dancing is restricted to a war dance performed at weddings. Visual arts are nonexistent.

Medicine.   To cure sickness the imam will pray. Sometimes he may also apply roots and herbs, although that method is more typical of the tabib. The bahasa will summon spirits to help him.

Death and Afterlife.   The funeral must take place within twenty-four hours after death. The body is placed in the grave on its right side, facing Mecca. After the grave has been filled the imam reads a prayer that teaches the deceased to utter the right words on its way to the Judgment. The spirit is supposed to stay in the home of the deceased person for seven days, during which a prayer is said in the house each evening. After the seven days the spirit begins the journey to the next world, which takes 100 days. On the way the spirit passes certain places, and each time the spirit reaches one of these places a prayer is said in the house. Part of the way to the next world crosses a sea. To help the spirit get across, a goat is sacrificed. The last and biggest ceremony is performed on the hundredth day, when the spirit reaches its destination. The grave is finally arranged, and a grave marker is placed on top of it. This grave marker symbolizes a boat that is intended not for the passage across the sea but for the spirit's use in the next world. In very recent times these cycle-of-death ceremonies have been shortened. In some places there are no longer any rituals after the burial. Recently Muslim missionaries have worked among the Yakan, teaching a more orthodox Islam and trying to do away with the many non-Islamic elements of Yakan religion. In some areas they have been successful, but older people especially prefer the old ways.

Bibliography

Frake, Charles O. (1969). "Struck by Speech: The Yakan Concept of Litigation." In *Law in Culture and Society,* edited by Laura Nader, 147–167. Chicago: Aldine.

Wulff, Inger (1974). "Features of Yakan Culture." In *The Muslim Filipinos,* edited by Peter G. Gowing and Robert D. McAmis. Manila: Solidaridad Publishing House.

Wulff, Inger (1978). "Continuity and Change in a Yakan Village." In *Social Change in Modern Philippines,* edited by Mario D. Zamora, Donald J. Baxter, and Robert Lawless. Vol. 2, 25–38. Papers in Anthropology, 19 (2), University of Oklahoma.

Wulff, Inger (1979-1980). "Economic Activities of the

Yakan—With Special Reference to the Part Taken by the Women." *Folk* 20–22:35–43.

INGER WULFF

Yao of Thailand

ETHNONYMS: Iu Mian, Man, Mian

Orientation

Identification. The people officially known as the "Yao" in Thailand call themselves "Mian" or "Iu Mian." Historically, the Chinese called them "Yao," which means "dog" or "savage." In Yao, the word *mian* means "people." In Laos and Vietnam the word *man* also means "people."

Location. At present, Yao villages can be found in the provinces of Chiang Rai, Chiang Mai, Phayao, Lampang, Nan, Kamphaeng Phet, and Sukhothai in Thailand. Recently one village was also located in Tak Province. There has been a large-scale migration of the Yao from Chiang Rai Province to the south to find fertile land for farming; when the soil was exhausted they moved back and settled in Lampang. A number of the Yao who cultivated the land in the reserved forest were forced to settle in Kamphaeng Phet.

Demography. In 1986-1988 the Yao population in Thailand was officially placed at 36,140 persons, living in 4,814 households in 205 villages in 8 provinces: Chiang Mai, Chiang Rai, Phayao, Nan, Lampang, Kamphaeng Phet, Sukhothai, and Tak. The most populous provinces are Chiang Rai and Phayao. The Yao population is rapidly increasing owing to a high birth rate and immigration. In 1972 there were only 19,990 Yao people living in 111 villages.

Linguistic Affiliation. The Yao language is closely related to that of the Miao, both belonging to the Miao-Yao Pateng Branch of the Sino-Tibetan Language Family. Many Yao also speak Yunnanese or the closely related Mandarin Chinese; literacy in Chinese has long been found among them. In Thailand, the dialect spoken by the Yao of different regions is essentially the same, with the addition of some new words from Yunnanese and Thai. More men than women speak the Thai language, especially the northern Thai dialect.

History and Cultural Relations

About three-quarters of the Yao live in China, mostly in the southern provinces of Guangdong, Guangxi, and Yunnan. The remainder are scattered through northern Vietnam, Laos, and Thailand. Books written thirty years ago mentioned some 130 Yao living in Kiang Tung of Shan State in Burma. It is reported that they have lived in the mountainous areas of China's Hunan province for at least 2,000 years and that they gradually moved southward, probably to Vietnam, as early as the eleventh century to escape from the imperial Chinese administration and to find new hill farmlands. From Laos, some Yao of the Nam Tha areas entered Nan and Chiang Rai provinces of Thailand in the late nineteenth century, and a greater number arrived after World War II.

Young described the Yao as industrious and friendly but shrewd businesspeople eager to trade and to improve their lot. They have considerable contact with their neighbors. Their villages are located among those of different peoples. In the past marriage with the Yunnanese was common; today marriage with other groups still occurs, particularly with Thai men. Since the Yao live at lower elevations than do the Miao and Lisu, their villages are more easily reached by plains-dwelling traders and missionaries. The Yao have frequent contact with the lowland markets, where they buy clothing. Only a few Yao have converted to Christianity. Close contact with Thai society has changed the Yao way of life.

Settlements

Villages range in size from about 80 to 300 persons. Compared to the households of the other groups Yao households are the largest, averaging 7.3 persons. Yao households in Tak, Phayao, and Lampang provinces are even larger, with an average of 10.4, 8.3, and 8.0 persons respectively. In the past, Yao lived in large villages supported by abundant primary forest land. Later, when the land was exhausted, they split the villages and formed smaller ones. The average village has twenty-one houses, fewer than among the Karen, Akha, Lahu, Lisu, and Miao. The traditional Yao house is of the rectangular type and uses the ground as the floor. The house is made of bamboo (only some parts, such as the poles, are made of solid wood) and has *cylindrica*-thatch roofing. Houses are arranged in a line facing the lower part of the mountain. Water is brought from the mountain slopes to the village via bamboo tubes. Since Yao are Thai citizens and it is now difficult to move as freely as they did in the past, they tend to settle permanently and construct their houses off the ground, with planked floors and tile or galvanized iron roofs.

Economy

Subsistence and Commercial Activities. Dry-rice agriculture dominates the economy: 86.2 percent of Yao grow rice for domestic consumption. In the past maize was grown for family and animal consumption, and the opium poppy was the only cash crop. At present, with opium cultivation considered illegal and the traffic in opium effectively suppressed, most Yao have turned to maize as the cash crop. They also grow chilies, eggplants, and lettuce. Domestic animals include pigs, chickens, horses, and dogs.

Industrial Arts. Most villages have at least one blacksmith who can make farm tools such as knives, axes, and hoes. These tools are also traded between villages. The traditional costume of Yao women is very elaborate and usually embellished with colorful embroidery. Some kind of coat over loose trousers is most common and many hours are devoted to stitching intricate multicolored patterns over the coarse blue or black cotton of these garments. There is some degree of specialization by silversmiths.

Trade. Small stores are found in most villages. Some Yao families also have shops in towns. For commercial crops, lowland merchants come to Yao villages to purchase maize, cotton, and chilies.

Division of Labor.   There is some division of labor by gender. Men clear the fields, hunt, butcher, build houses, and make traps. Women weed the fields, gather firewood and wild greens, and care for the animals (mainly hogs). Both sexes participate in planting and harvesting rice. Only men engage in ritual and political activities.

Land Tenure.   Everyone living in a Yao village believes in the concept of communal ownership. The land around the village belongs to the village and is under the authorized management of the village headman. The persons who cleared the land have the right to cultivate it, and it will be theirs for as long as they stay in that village. If a man leaves the village, his kin in the village have a prior right to cultivate the land, subject to the headman's decision. If nobody in the village uses the land, outsiders may be asked to cultivate it. Since the Yao have come to live in permanent villages, about 97.2 percent of families own the land they work and very few rent land in the reserved forest.

Kinship

Kin Groups and Descent.   The extended family of three generations is the typical Yao family. Marriage is strictly exogamous with different clans. Traditionally the Yao group is patrilocal and patrilineal with a slight matrilineal tendency. The bride-price plays an important role in determining the residence of the couple after marriage. When the bride-price is paid in part, the residence may be virilocal and the balance is paid annually in labor. The husband may live with his parents-in-law during the agreed number of years corresponding to the number of silver ingots he has yet to pay. One year of service working with his parents-in-law is equivalent to one silver ingot. He can take his wife and his children to his parent's house when the payment is completed. When the man lives with his wife's parents, the affiliation of children born during that residence is matrilineal. The residence may be permanently matrilocal if the man is poor or if his wife is the only daughter; the latter situation can be modified by the adoption of another boy who will be the clan descendant. Adoption is in fact widely practiced. Although marriage is traditionally endogamous, intergroup marriage also exists. Polygamy is also acceptable, especially among rich families. A man will take a second wife if the first wife has no children and gives her consent.

Kinship Terminology.   Yao kin terms distinguish among elder and younger relatives, and kin behavior is marked by respect for age. Yao bear a clan name for life but, although well disposed toward fellow members of the clan, they are not bound by the same obligations and restrictions that apply to members of their lineage, a much narrower grouping of those able to trace a genealogical connection in the patriline.

Marriage and Family

Marriage.   Premarital sexual experimentation is permitted and young people are expected to choose their own marriage partners, with advice from their elders. Fathers retain an intermediary to make arrangements; the couple's horoscopes are examined and, if these are compatible, the girl's parents are approached and the bride-price is discussed. Yao marriage ceremonies are formal, elaborate, and very expensive affairs. Their principal purpose is to transfer the girl, and her fertility, from her father's lineage to that of her husband.

Domestic Unit.   The basic unit of Yao social organization is the extended family, a group of people living under the same roof. Most Yao households are made up of a couple, their unmarried children, and one or more married sons with their families. People who cook and eat meals and farm together are considered a family. The Yao prefer to live in an extended family, and under the same roof there may be many related families who help each other in agriculture. The families of the elder sons will eventually depart to build their own houses, leaving the younger son's family with the parents.

Inheritance.   Property is divided equally among the surviving sons, but the youngest son will receive the family homestead. Unmarried daughters also inherit a share.

Socialization.   The Yao prefer boys over girls, but they love them equally. Infants and children are raised by both parents and by siblings. Physical punishment in child rearing is very rare.

Sociopolitical Organization

Social Organization.   There is no single leader for all Yao groups in northern Thailand. Traditionally the village's headman or chief is the same person who established the village, and the members of his clan are numerous. In some areas, the headman of one village takes the leadership role for several villages as well as over the other groups. The position of the village headman is passed from father to son or to someone selected by the retired headman. Old people are highly respected, and they may form an elder council giving advice to the headman on domestic problems.

Political Organization.   Under the Thai official administration, every Yao village is registered as an official hamlet (*muban*) or classified as part of an official hamlet. The village headman may be elected, if qualified, to the position of Phy Chuai Phuyai Ban under the lowland Thai Phy Yai Ban. Or he may be elected to be Phuyai Ban if his village is officially registered as a hamlet. He administers the affairs of the community under the supervision of the commune (*tambon*) and district office (*amphur*).

Social Control.   A number of taboos are strictly observed by both men and women. Behavioral rules are also respected by younger people when dealing with older people. Traditionally the Yao avoid conflict among themselves. Conflicts are resolved by the headman, assisted ritually by the religious practitioner. Fines are also used in recompense.

Religion and Expressive Culture

Religious Beliefs.   Evidence for the centuries of Yao association with Chinese civilization is most clearly seen in their religious beliefs and practices. There is a cult of the ancestors. They celebrate the lunar New Year. They also have a pantheon of spirits believed to have an influence on human beings. The Yao recognize eighteen principal deities whose finely painted portraits they preserve on scrolls. These are usually kept rolled up on the spirit altars in their houses and are displayed on important ritual occasions. Most of these are believed to derive from Chinese deities, the Jade Emperor, the Three Celestial Ones, the earth god, Tichu, and even the deified Lao Tzu. In Thailand, some Yao have converted to Christianity. Like the Chinese, Yao propitiate a host of minor supernaturals, gods, deceased heroes, and even spirits of natural phenomena. Considerable attention is paid to evil spirits in exorcistic and propitiatory rites, which are carried out on such occasions as harvest or when there is illness.

Religious Practitioners.   The position of priest-exorcist is important in Yao society. Although these practitioners are skilled at divining with chicken bones and bamboo sticks, their real power lies in their knowledge of incantations taken from books written in Chinese characters. During their teens boys are given special instruction in this art and they may become shamans when they grow up. Yao shamans are called in on occasions of illness and also officiate in various village ceremonies. These shamans are of crucial importance to the maintenance of harmony between the world of the living and the supernatural world beyond.

Ceremonies.   Boys between 12 and 20 years of age go through a coming-of-age ceremony lasting several days. There are communal rites as well as an individual rite. The ceremonies performed in honor of the village guardian spirit and the mountain guardian spirit are activities shared by the whole village. The individual ceremonies include the Souls calling ceremony, the initiation ceremonies, and all kinds of merit-making ceremonies. The older generation invests in merit-making ceremonies and marriage on behalf of the younger, expecting recompense before or after death. Prosperity and health attend the living who make offerings to and merit for their forebears, while illness and misfortune are often attributed to dissatisfied ancestors.

Arts.   Singing is very popular among the Yao, but dancing is never seen. Songs have been recorded in books. Traditional musical instruments such as the gong, clappers, drums, and cymbals are used only for ritual purposes.

Medicine.   The properties of herbs are widely understood by the Yao; plants are used to cure sickness and especially to restore a woman to health after she gives birth. Because Yao believe that most illnesses are caused by evil or malevolent ghosts and spirits, however, most curing rites are exorcistic in nature. Illness is thought to be the result of soul loss; the function of the shaman is to placate the ghost responsible for this condition, thus restoring the patient to health. The rituals performed usually involve blood sacrifice and the burning of strips of paper on which the names of offending spirits are written. Ceremonial instruments are sacred knives, bells, and sticks.

Death and Afterlife.   Death is always announced by gunshot. The indigenous method of disposing of the corpse is cremation. The body is washed, dressed, and placed in a wooden coffin in front of the altar, with the funeral usually lasting for two to three days after death. The Yao in Thailand usually cremate their dead. The burial place for the ashes is selected by the shaman after consulting the sacred book on burials. Some old people may select their own burial place before death. Periodic ceremonies are held for the souls of deceased ancestors one year after death; their purpose is to purify the souls, enabling them to ascend into the spirit world.

Bibliography

Chob Kacha-ananda (1977). "Étude ethnographique du groupe ethnique Yao en Thailand du Nord." Doctoral dissertation, Université de Paris.

Kandre, Peter (1965). _Autonomy and Integration of Social Systems: The Iu Mien ("Yao" or "Man") Mountain Population and Their Neighbours._ Göteborg: n.p.

LeBar, Frank M., Gerald C. Hickey, and John K. Musgrave, eds. (1964). "Thailand Yao." In _Ethnic Groups of Mainland Southeast Asia,_ 91–93. New Haven: HRAF Press.

Lemoine, Jacques (1982). _Yao Ceremonial Paintings._ Bangkok: White Lotus.

Shiratori, Yoshiro (1978). _Tōnan Ajia sanchi minzokushi: Yao to sono rinsetsu shoshuzoku: Jōchi Daigaku Sheihoku Tai Rekishi Bunka Chōsadan hōkoku (Ethnography of the Hill-Tribes of Southeast Asia . . .)._ Tokyo: Kōdansha.

Takemura, Takuji (1975). _Clan Organization and Merit-Making Systems of the Yao, Northern Thailand._ Report submitted to Thailand NRC, Bangkok.

Takemura, Takuji (1978). _An Ethnography of the Yao Religious Life in Northern Thailand._ Osaka.

Young, Gordon Oliver (1961). _The Hilltribes of Thailand: A Socio-Ethnological Report._ Bangkok: Government of Thailand.

CHOB KACHA-ANANDA

Yuan

The Yuan (Lanatai, Lao, Youanne, Youon, Yun) are Tai speakers who inhabit primarily the Chiang Mai region of northern Thailand. They numbered 6,000,000 in Thailand in 1983, and there were 3,000 to 5,000 in Laos in 1962. They share with the Lao, Khün, Lü, and Nüa a complex of cultural traits associated with northern Pali-language Buddhism (script, polite terms, temple architecture). Although assimilating to the national culture, the Yuan may be distinguished from other Thais by their long cultural and historical ties to the Mekong region. The Yuan may also be distinguished from the Lao of northeastern Thailand in that the former once tattooed their bellies, and by dialectal differences.

In the middle and late nineteenth century, although ostensibly under the rule of the king of Siam, the Yuan of Chiang Mai were actually under the absolute control of the Chiang Mai prince. The landed nobility came to his court once a year to offer their allegiance. Well into the twentieth century, the nobility imposed limitations on the property and personal rights of farmers and artisans, including corvée and military conscription. Also, farm products and manufactured items were taxed and requisitioned. (In one ironworking village, for example, the tax was to be paid in the form of elephant chains and cooking pots). Slavery was still extant in the nineteenth century. Warfare and resettlement caused massive social dislocations. There was, as well, great exposure to external influences in the form of trade. Annual Chinese trade caravans ran from Yunnan to Chiang Mai, Moulmein, and back. The Yuan operated trade caravans, which included cattle, to Burma. In addition, the river was an important trade link with Bangkok and other downriver settlements.

Bibliography

Freeman, John H. (1910). *An Oriental Land of the Free*. Philadelphia: Westminster Press.

McGilvary, Daniel (1912). *A Half Century among the Siamese and the Lao*. New York and London: Fleming Revell.

Seidenfaden, Erik (1958). *The Thai Peoples*. Bangkok: Siam Society.

Sharp, Lauriston, Hazel M. Hauck, Kamol Janlekha, and Robert B. Textor (1953). *Siamese Rice Village: A Preliminary Study of Bang Chan, 1948–1949*. Bangkok: Cornell Research Center.

Yumbri

"Yumbri" is the name used for themselves by small bands of hunter-gatherers in northern Thailand and neighboring Laos. Their population was estimated at about 150 in 1938. Their traditional hunter-gatherer subsistence economy may now have largely disappeared. Yumbri are known to the Lao and Thai as "Phi Tong Luang" and are called "Ma Ku" by the Meo.

Bibliography

Boeles, J. J. (1963). "Second Expedition to the Mrabri ('Khon Pa') of North Thailand." *Journal of the Siam Society* 51:133–160.

Pookajorn, Surin (1985). "Ethnoarchaeology with the Phi Tong Luang (Mlabrai): Forest Hunters of Northern Thailand." *World Archaeology* 17:206–221.

Weaver, Robert W. (1956). "Through Unknown Thailand." *Natural History* 65:289–295, 336.

Glossary

adat/adet The customary law of the indigenous peoples of Indonesia. Also used in a more general sense to mean the overarching rules governing social behavior.

affine A relative by marriage.

agglutinative language A language in which morphemes are combined into words without their form being substantially modified or their meaning lost.

agnatic descent. *See* patrilineal descent

agnatic kin Kin related to one another through the male line.

ambilineal kin. *See* cognatic kin

ancestor spirits Ghosts of deceased relatives who are venerated because they are believed to have supernatural powers that can influence the living.

animal husbandry. *See* pastoralism

animism The worship of spiritual beings.

archipelago A sea or broad expanse of water interspersed with islands or groups of islands; often the term is used for island groups themselves, such as Indonesia.

asymmetric alliance A form of social organization in which several groups are linked by affinal ties, with each group receiving their wives from one group but giving wives to another one; such a system has also been called a circulating connubium.

avunculocal residence The practice of a newly married couple residing with the husband's mother's brother.

Bahasa Indonesia The modern national language of Indonesia, largely based on Javanese and English.

bilateral descent The practice of tracing kinship affiliation more or less evenly through both the female and male lines.

bride-price/bride-wealth The practice of a groom or his kin giving substantial property or wealth to the bride's kin before, at the time of, or after marriage.

Buddhism A world religion, founded by Siddhartha Gautama or Sakyamuni, "the enlightened one," in the sixth century B.C. The two major branches of Buddhism are Mahayana Buddhism and Hinayana (Theravada) Buddhism; the former is a relatively liberal missionary religion while the latter stresses more the original traditions of Buddhism. Mahayana Buddhism, with its strong missionary tradition, is more widespread throughout Asia, including China, Japan, Korea, and Vietnam; but Theravada Buddhism is predominant on the Southeast Asian mainland. (*See the article* "Buddhist")

cassava A starchy root crop (*Manihot esculenta*), also called manioc, yuca, or tapioca, that was introduced to Asia from the New World following the arrival of Europeans.

clan/sib A group of unilineally affiliated kin who usually reside in the same community, recognize a common ancestor, and share common property.

classificatory kin terms Kinship terms, such as aunt, that designate several categories of distinct relatives, such as mother's sister and father's sister.

cognates Words that belong to different languages but have similar sounds and meanings.

cognatic kin/ambilineal kin Kin related to one another through the male line, the female line, or both (ambilineal).

collaterals A person's relatives not related to him or her as ascendants or descendants; one's uncle, aunt, cousin, brother, sister, niece, nephew.

Confucianism A moral and philosophical religious tradition based on the teaching of Confucius (Kongzo), who lived in northern China from about 551 to 479 B.C.

consanguine A relative by blood (birth).

corvée A labor system under which members of a cultural or other group are required to work on public projects for a set period of time each year.

cousin, cross Children of one's parent's siblings of the opposite sex—one's father's sisters' and mother's brothers' children.

cousin, parallel Children of one's parent's siblings of the same sex—one's father's brothers' and mother's sisters' children.

datu In the southern Philippines, a chief; in Sumatra, a shaman.

descriptive kin terms Kinship terms that are used to distinguish different categories of relative such as mother or father.

dowry The practice of a bride's kin giving substantial property or wealth to the groom or his kin before or at the time of marriage.

dry rice Varieties of the rice plant (*Oryza sativa*) grown in rain-fed fields without irrigation.

Ego In kinship studies Ego is a man or a woman whom the anthropologist arbitrarily designates as the reference point for a particular kinship diagram or a discussion of kinship terminology.

endogamy Marriage within a specific group or social category of which the person is a member, such as one's caste or community.

exogamy Marriage outside a specific group or social category of which the person is a member, such as one's clan or village.

horticulture Plant cultivation carried out on a small scale by relatively simple means, usually without permanent fields, artificial fertilizers, or plowing.

Indochina That area of mainland Southeast Asia occupied by the nations of Vietnam, Laos, Cambodia, and Thailand. The region is so named to reflect the strong cultural influences from both India and China.

kindred The bilateral kin group of near kin who may be expected to be present and participant on important ceremonial occasions, usually in the absence of a unilineal descent system.

kinship Family relationship, whether traced through marital ties or through blood and descent.

kin terms, Crow A system of kinship terminology in which matrilateral cross cousins are distinguished from each other and from parallel cousins and siblings but patrilateral cross cousins are referred to by the same terms used for father or father's sister.

kin terms, Dravidian. *See* kin terms, Iroquois

kin terms, Eskimo A system of kinship terminology in which cousins are distinguished from brothers and sisters but no distinction is made between cross and parallel cousins. Sometimes also called European kin terms.

kin terms, generational A system of kinship terminology in which all kin of the same sex in the parental generation are referred to by the same term.

kin terms, Hawaiian A system of kinship terminology in which all male cousins are referred to by the same term used for brother and all female cousins are referred to by the same term used for sister.

kin terms, Iroquois A system of kinship terminology in which parallel cousins are referred to by the same terms used for brothers and sisters but cross cousins are identified by different terms.

kin terms, lineal A system of kinship terminology in which direct descendants or ascendants are distinguished from collateral kin.

kin terms, Omaha A system of kinship terminology in which female matrilateral cross cousins are referred to by the same term used for one's mother and female patrilateral cross cousins are referred to by the same term used for one's sister's daughter.

kin terms, Sudanese A system of kinship terminology in which there are distinct terms for each category of cousin and sibling and for aunts, uncles, nieces, and nephews.

levirate The practice of requiring a man to marry his brother's widow.

lineage A unilineal (whether patrilineal or matrilineal) kin group that traces kinship affiliation from a common, known ancestor and extends through a number of generations.

magic Beliefs and ritual practices designed to harness supernatural forces to achieve the particular goals of the magician.

matrilineal descent/uterine descent The practice of tracing kinship affiliation only through the female line.

matrilocal residence/uxorilocal residence The practice of a newly married couple residing in the community of the wife's kin. Uxorilocal is sometimes used in a more restrictive sense to indicate residence in the household of the wife's family.

moiety A form of social organization in which an entire cultural group is made up of two social groups. Each moiety is often composed of a number of interrelated clans, sibs, or phratries.

monogamy Marriage between one man and one woman at a time.

neolocal residence The practice of a newly married couple living apart from the immediate kin of either party.

Pagans A name used for those indigenous peoples of the Philippines who did not convert to Christianity following the arrival of the Spanish in the sixteenth century.

pastoralism A type of subsistence economy based on the herding of domesticated grazing animals such as sheep or cattle.

patrilineal descent/agnatic descent The practice of tracing kinship affiliation only through the male line.

patrilocal residence/virilocal residence The practice of a newly married couple residing in the community of the husband's kin. Virilocal is sometimes used in a more restrictive sense to indicate residence in the household of the husband's family.

peasant/peasantry Small-scale agriculturalists producing only subsistence crops, perhaps in combination with some fishing, animal husbandry, or hunting. They live in villages in a larger state but participate little in the state's commerce or cultural activities. Today many peasants rely on mechanized farming, produce a food surplus, and are involved in the national economy, so they may be called "postpeasants" by anthropologists.

phratry A social group consisting of two or more clans joined by some common bond and standing in opposition to other phratries in the society.

polyandry The marriage of one woman to more than one man at a time.

polygyny The marriage of one man to more than one woman at a time.

prestation A form of reciprocal gift giving, often associated with marriage negotiations and ceremonial exchange.

ramage An ancestor-focused bilateral descent group consisting of an entire community whose members trace their descent from a common ancestor, with graded ranks based on closeness to the senior line of descent.

refugee An individual who has left his or her homeland as a result of political or military events in that nation or for other ideological reasons.

seer One who foresees the future; a diviner.

sib. *See* clan

sister exchange A form of arranged marriage in which two men marry each other's sisters.

slash-and-burn cultivation. *See* swidden cultivation

social-class stratification A form of social organization in which the society ranks individuals or groups in a hierarchical system based on both ascribed and achieved status.

sorcery The attempt to use supernatural forces to further the interests of the sorcerer, primarily through verbal formulas and the ritual manipulation of material objects.

sororal polygyny The marriage of one man to two or more sisters at the same time.

sororate The practice of a woman being required to marry her deceased sister's husband.

stem family A residential group composed of a nuclear family and one or more additional members who do not comprise a second nuclear family.

sultan A Muslim prince or ruler (in postclassic Arabic).

sultanate The rule of a dynasty of sultans.

swidden cultivation A form of horticulture in which plots of land (swiddens) are cleared and planted for a few years and then left fallow for a number of years while other plots are used. Also called shifting or slash-and-burn cultivation.

Taoism (Daoism) An ancient Chinese philosophy that seeks to recognize and control the essential forces (ch'i) in nature and all living things.

taro A starchy root crop cultivated throughout Oceania. When "true taro" is intended, the term applies to *Colocasia esculenta*, but recent usages extend it to other aroids such as *Alocasia macrorrhiza*, *Cyrtosperma chamissonis*, and *Xanthosoma* spp.

teknonymy The practice of addressing a person after the name of a close relative rather than by the individual's name. For example, "Bill" is called "Father of John."

topolect The speech of a particular place.

transhumance Seasonal movements of a society or community. It may involve seasonal shifts in food production between hunting and gathering and horticulture or the movement of herds to more favorable grazing locations.

tribe Although there is some variation in use, the term usually applies to a distinct people who view themselves and are recognized by outsiders as having a distinct culture. The tribal society typically has its own name, territory, customs, dress, and subsistence activities, and often its own language.

unilineal descent The practice of tracing kinship affiliation through only one line, either the matriline or the patriline.

unilocal residence The general term for matrilocal, patrilocal, or avunculocal postmarital residence.

urbanization   A sociodemographic process through which an increasingly large percentage of a nation's population resides in cities or urban areas.

usufruct   The right to use land or property without actually owning it.

uterine descent. *See* matrilineal descent

uxorilocal residence. *See* matrilocal residence

virilocal residence. *See* patrilocal residence

wet rice   Varieties of the rice plant (*Oryza sativa*) grown in irrigated fields.

witchcraft   The attempt to use supernatural forces to control or harm another person. Unlike sorcery, witchcraft does not require the use of special rituals, formulas, or ritual objects.

Filmography

The following list of films is not exhaustive, but it does reflect what is currently (1992) available for rental in North America. The subjects are indicated in parentheses. Included are a few feature films that have significant anthropological or historical interest. In many cases, only a selection of distributors has been indicated—usually one on the West Coast, one in the Midwest, and one in the East. In most cases, too, there are also prints of these films available for sale, though not necessarily through the distributors listed here. To find the appropriate sales organization, one should either check with a rental distributor or a film librarian, or check for further details in the references listed at the end of the index to this filmography.

1. *The Age of the Shoguns.* (Tokugawa Japan) 1989. Color, 51 minutes, VHS, U-mat. (FFHS)
2. *Aging in Japan: When Traditional Mechanisms Vanish.* (Elderly, Japan) 1989. Color, 45 minutes, VHS, U-mat. (FFHS)
3. *Angkor: The Lost City.* (Medieval Cambodia) 1965. B&W, 12 minutes, 16mm. (IU, PSt, WaPS)
4. *Art of the Southern Barbarian—The Discovery of Japan.* (Europeans in Japan) 1990. Color, 30 minutes, VHS, U-mat. (FFHS)
5. *Asian Heart.* (Filipino mail-order brides) 1987. Color, 38 minutes, VHS. (FL)
6. *The Asianization of America.* (Asians in the United States) 1988. Color, 26 minutes, VHS, U-mat. (FFHS)
7. *The Bajau: Seagoing Nomads.* (Bajau) 1983. Wayne Mitchell. Color, 18 minutes, 16mm, VHS. (BFA, IU, MnU)
8. *Bali beyond the Postcard.* (Balinese arts) 1991. Nancy Dine and Peggy Stern. Color, 60 minutes, VHS. (FL)
9. *Bali Today.* (Balinese) 1969. Color, 18 minutes, 16mm. (CU, IU, NSyU)
10. *Balinese Family.* (Balinese) 1951. Produced by Gregory Bateson and Margaret Mead. B&W, 17 minutes, 16mm. (CU, NYU, PSt)
11. *A Balinese Trance Seance.* (Balinese, mental health) 1980. Timothy Asch, Linda Connor, Patsy Asch. Color, 28 minutes, 16mm. (DER, MiEM, PSt, WaU)
12. *Bathing Babies in Three Cultures.* (Bali, New Guinea, United States) 1952. Gregory Bateson and Margaret Mead. B&W, 11 minutes, 16mm. (CU, IU, PSt)
13. *Big Problems for Little People.* (Philippine rural economy) 1975. George and Helen Guthrie. Color, 23 minutes, 16mm. (IU, PSt)
14. *Borobudur: The Cosmic Mountain.* (Javanese monument) 1973. Color, 40 minutes, 16mm. (CU, MiU)
15. *Buddha in the Land of the Kami (7th–12th Centuries).* (Japanese Buddhism) 1990. Color, 30 minutes, VHS, U-mat. (FFHS)
16. *But I'll always Continue to Write* (Poverty in Jakarta) 1987. Color, 30 minutes, VHS. (FI)
17. *Ca Dao: The Folk Poetry of Vietnam.* (Vietnamese music) 1984. Produced by David Grubin. Color, 9 minutes, VHS, U-mat. (PSt)
18. *Cambodia: Year Ten.* (Cambodia, civil war) 1990. Color, 58 minutes, VHS, U-mat. (FFHS)
19. *The Cave People of the Philippines.* (Tasaday) 1972. Produced by Gerald Green for NBC. Color, 39 minutes, 16mm, VHS, U-mat. (IU, PSt, WaU)
19a. *Celso and Cora.* (Urban Philippines) 1983. Gary Kildea. Color, 109 minutes, 16mm, VHS. (FRIF)
20. *Centuries of Prints—Woodblock Prints, Their Traditional Technique and History.* (Japanese art) 1974. Color, 27 minutes, 16mm. (CU, PSt)
21. *Ceramic Art: Potters of Japan.* (Japanese crafts) 1968. Color, 37 minutes in two parts, 16mm. (IU, PSt, UU)
22. *China and Japan: 1279–1600.* (China, Medieval Japan) 1985. Color, 26 minutes, 16mm, VHS. (CU, NSyU, OKentU)
23. *The Coming of the Barbarians (1540–1650).* (Portuguese in Japan) 1990. Color, 52 minutes, VHS, U-mat. (FFHS)
24. *Community Medicine: A Training Center in the Rural Philippines.* (Philippines, public health) 1980. Produced by George and Helen Guthrie. Color, 22 minutes, 16mm. (PSt, WaPS)
25. *Coup d'État: The Philippines Revolt.* (Philippine guerrillas) 1986. Color, 60 minutes, VHS. (CU, MnU)
26. *Crafts of Edo.* (Japanese crafts) 1980. Color, 29 minutes, 16mm. (CU, IU)
27. *Curios and Customs—The World of Japanese Antiquities.* (Japanese arts) 1976. Color, 29 minutes, 16mm. (CU, IU)
28. *Day for All People—Politics in Japan.* (Japan) 1975. Produced by the U.S.-Japan Trade Council. Color, 16 minutes, 16mm. (CU, TxU)
29. *Discovering the Art of Korea.* (Korean arts) 1979. Color, 58 minutes, 16mm. (FFHS, IU)

30. *Electronics in Japan Today.* (Japan) 1982. Color, 30 minutes, 16mm. (CU, IU, PSt)
31. *The Eleven Powers (Bali).* (Balinese festival) 1980. Larry Gartenstein and Orson Welles. Color, 48 minutes, 16mm, VHS. (FL)
32. *The Essence of Being Japanese.* (Japanese) 1990. Color, 48 minutes, VHS, U-mat. (FFHS)
33. *Farewell to Freedom.* (Hmong refugees) 1981. Color, 55 minutes, VHS, U-mat. (InU, WaU)
34. *The Feast in Dream Village.* (Sumba festival, Indonesia) 1989. Laura S. Whitney and Janet Hoskins. Color, 27 minutes, 16mm, VHS. (CU)
35. *Fighting Festival.* (Japanese festival) 1985. Keiko Ikeda. Color, 30 minutes, VHS. (CU)
36. *Floating in the Air, Followed by the Wind.* (Malaysia, Hindu trance) 1973. Gunther Pfaff and Ronald Simons. Color, 34 minutes, 16mm. (CU, InU, PSt)
37. *Footnotes to a War.* (Vietnam War) 1980. UN Production. Color, 15 minutes, 16mm. (CU, IU)
38. *A Forest Village in Thailand.* (Thai teak industry) 1976. Color, 26 minutes, 16mm, VHS. (IU)
39. *Formosa: Blueprint of a Free China.* (Taiwan government) 1953. B&W, 27 minutes, 16mm. (IU)
40. *Four Families: Part 2.* (Japanese) 1960. Gregory Bateson and Margaret Mead. B&W, 30 minutes, 16mm, VHS, U-mat. (CU, IU, PSt)
41. *Future Wave: Japan Design.* (modern Japanese society) 1988. David Rabinovitch. Color, 27 minutes, VHS. (CU)
42. *The Gods of Japan.* (Shintō) 1973. Produced by ABC. Color, 30 minutes, 16mm. (FTS, OrPS, PSt)
43. *The Graying of Japan: Rural and Urban.* (Japanese) 1980. Color, 29 minutes, 16mm. (CU, PSt)
44. *Growing Up Japanese.* (Japanese) 1975. Produced by the U.S.-Japan Trade Council. Color, 25 minutes, 16mm. (CU, FTaSU, MiU)
45. *Gyoshu Hayami: Pioneer of Modern Japanese Painting.* (Japanese art). Color, 20 minutes, 16mm. (CoU, IU, PSt)
46. *The Hanawa Family.* (Japanese) 1981. Color, 29 minutes, 16mm. (CU, IU, PSt)
47. *Hanunoo.* (Hanunóo) 1958. Harold C. Conklin. Color, 17 minutes, 16mm. (PSt, WaPS)
48. *Head of the Class: Motivation in Japanese Schooling.* (Japan) 1988. Color, 14 minutes, VHS, U-mat. (FFHS, MnU, PSt)
49. *Hirohito: Japan in the 20th Century.* (Japan) 1989. Color, 58 minutes, VHS, U-mat. (FFHS)
50. *Hiroshima and Nagasaki: The Harvest of Nuclear War.* (Japan) 1969. B&W, 16 minutes, 16mm, VHS. (CU, IU, PSt)
51. *Hiroshima: The Legacy.* (Japan) 1987. Color, 30 minutes, VHS, U-mat. (FFHS, MoU, NmPE)
51a. *Horses of Life and Death.* (Sumba festival, Indonesia) 1991. Laura S. Whitney. Color, 25 minutes, 16mm, VHS. (CU)
52. *Horyuji Temple.* (Japanese Buddhism) 1958. Color, 23 minutes, 16mm. (InTI, PSt)
53. *House of the Spirit: Perspectives on Cambodian Health Care.* (Khmer, public health) 1984. Ellen Bruon and Ellen Kuras. Color, 42 minutes, VHS. (AFSC, NIC)
53a. *How to Behave (Chuyen tu te).* (Vietnamese society) 1987. Tran Van Thuy. Color, 43 minutes, 16mm, VHS. (FRIF)
54. *Indonesia: When Invaders become Colonists.* (Dutch in Indonesia) 1991. Color, 50 minutes, VHS, U-mat. (FFHS)
55. *Invitation to Kabuki.* (Japanese theater) 1970. Color, 33 minutes, 16mm. (InTI, PSt)
56. *Invitation to Traditional Japanese Music.* (Japanese music) 1970. Color, 25 minutes, 16mm. (CoU, IaAS, PSt)
57. *Iyomande: The Ainu Bear Festival.* (Ainu) 1935, released 1970. Neil Gordon Munro. Color/B&W, 26 minutes, 16mm. (CU, IU, PSt)
58. *Japan.* (Japan) 1974. Color, 80 minutes, 16mm. (CU, IU, PSt)
59. *Japan: A Nation Transformed (1945–1965).* (Japan) 1972. B&W, 22 minutes, 16mm. (FI, OKentU, PSt)
60. *Japan: An Interdependent Nation.* (Japan) 1980. Color, 24 minutes, 16mm. (CoU, InU, PSt)
61. *Japan: Emerging Superstate.* (Japan) 1973. Color, 22 minutes, 16mm. (CU, OkS)
62. *Japan, Inc.: Lessons for North America.* (Japan) 1981. Produced by the National Film Board of Canada. Color, 28 minutes, 16mm, VHS. (CU, IU, NSyU)
63. *Japan: Land of the Kami.* (Japan) 1965. Color, 29 minutes, 16mm. (InU, OrPS, PSt)
64. *Japan: The Collective Giant.* (Japan) 1973. Color, 20 minutes, 16mm. (FI, IU, PSt, WU)
65. *Japan: The Frozen Moment.* (Japanese arts) 1965. B&W, 60 minutes, 16mm. (PSt)
66. *Japan Today and Yesterday: Food and Tastes.* (Japan) 1977. Color, 20 minutes, 16mm. (CU)
67. *The Japanese.* (Japanese family) 1968. Edwin O. Reischauer. Color/B&W, 52 minutes, 16mm. (CU, IU, PSt)
68. *Japanese Armor.* (Japan) 1974. Color, 30 minutes, 16mm. (PSt)
69. *The Japanese Economic Miracle.* (Japan) 1987. B&W, 20 minutes, VHS, U-mat. (FFHS)
70. *Japanese Farmers.* (Japan) 1969. Color, 17 minutes, 16mm. (FI, IU, PSt, UPB)
71. *Japanese Nonverbal Communication.* (Japanese) 1978. Color, 20 minutes, 16mm. (InU, MtU, PSt)
72. *The Japanese, Part I: Full Moon Lunch.* (Japanese family) 1976. John Nathan. Color, 58 minutes, 16mm. (PSt, IU, TxU)
73. *The Japanese Sword as the Soul of the Samurai.* (Japan) 1969. Color, 24 minutes, 16mm. (PSt)
74. *The Japanese Tea Ceremony.* (Japan) 1989. Color, 30 minutes, VHS, U-mat. (FFHS)
75. *The Japanese Version.* (Japan, Westernization) 1991. Louis Alverez and Andrew Kolker. Color, 55 minutes (high school version, 40 minutes), VHS. (CNAM)
76. *Japanese Village.* (Japan) 1966. Color, 17 minutes, 16mm. (PSt)
77. *Japan's Mass Media.* (Japan) 1980. Color, 25 minutes, 16mm. (CU, PSt)
78. *Jero on Jero: A Balinese Trance Seance Observed.* (Balinese, mental health) 1981. Timothy Asch, Linda Conner, and Patsy Asch. Color, 17 minutes, 16mm, VHS. (DER)
79. *Jero Tapakan: Stories in the Life of a Balinese Healer.*

(Balinese, mental health) 1983. Timothy Asch, Linda Conner, and Patsy Asch. Color, 25 minutes, 16mm, VHS. (DER)

80. *Kabuki.* (Japan, Kabuki theater) 1987. Color, 56 minutes, VHS, U-mat. (FFHS)

80a. *Kampuchea after Pol Pot.* (Cambodia) 1982. Mark Stiles. Color, 49 minutes, 16mm, VHS. (FRIF)

81. *Karba's First Years.* (Balinese) 1950. Gregory Bateson and Margaret Mead. B&W, 19 minutes, 16mm. (CU, NIC, WU)

82. *Katsura Imperial Villa.* (Japan) 1972. Color, 21 minutes, 16mm. (CU, IU, PSt)

82a. *Kembali—To Return.* (Bali, gamelan music) 1991. Color, 46 minutes, VHS. (FL)

82b. *Kim Phuc.* (Vietnamese girl) 1984. Manus van de Kamp. Color, 25 minutes, 16mm, VHS. (FRIF)

83. *Kites of Japan.* (Japanese toys) 1976. Color, 28 minutes, 16mm. (CU, IU, PSt)

84. *Korea.* (Korean children) 1977. Color, 25 minutes, 16mm. (IU, OKentU, MoU)

85. *Korea: Ancient Treasure, Modern Wonder.* (Korea, modernization) 1990. Color, 25 minutes, VHS, U-mat. (FFHS)

86. *Korea: Overview—The Face of Korea.* (Korea, geography) 1980. Color, 23 minutes, 16mm, VHS. (InU, MnU, WU)

87. *Korea: Reflections on the Morning Calm* (Korean arts) 1982. Color, 29 minutes, 16mm. (IU)

88. *Korea: The Circle of Life—Traditional Customs and Rituals.* (Korean customs) 1980. Color, 35 minutes, 16mm. (InU, IU, OrPS)

89. *Korea: The Family.* (Korea, family) 1980. Color, 18 minutes, 16mm. (InU, OrPS)

90. *Korean Backgrounds.* (Korea) 1951. B&W, 17 minutes, 16mm. (InU)

91. *Korean People.* (Korea) 1961. Color, 11 minutes, 16mm. (WaPS)

92. *The Korean War: The Untold Story.* (Korean War) 1988. Color, 24 minutes, VHS. (OKentU, PSt)

93. *Land Dayaks of Borneo.* (Dayaks) 1965. William R. Geddes. Color, 38 minutes, 16mm. (CU, NYU, PSt, WU)

94. *Last Reflections on a War.* (Vietnam War) 1968. B&W, 44 minutes, 16mm. (CtU, CU, IU)

95. *The Last Tribes of Mindanao.* (Tasaday) 1972. National Geographic Society. Color, 50 minutes, 16mm. (IU, PSt, WaU)

96. *Latah: A Culture-Specific Elaboration of the Startle Reflex.* (Malaysia) 1982. Gunter Pfaff and Ronald C. Simons. Color, 38 minutes, 16mm. (PSt)

97. *Late Spring.* (Japanese family) 1949. Yasujiro Ozu. B&W, subtitled, 107 minutes, 16mm, VHS. (Facets, NYF)

98. *Learning to Dance in Bali.* (Balinese dance) 1978. Gregory Bateson and Margaret Mead. B&W, 13 minutes, 16mm. (CU, NYU)

99. *Life in the Jomon Period.* (Japan, prehistory) 1976. Color, 47 minutes, 16mm. (CU, IU, JF, PSt)

100. *The Life of Women in Japan.* (Japanese women) 1977. Color, 20 minutes, 16mm. (CU, PSt)

100a. *Lines of Fire.* (Myanmar, politics) 1990. Brian Beker. Color, 62 minutes, 16mm, VHS. (FRIF)

101. *The Living Treasures of Japan.* (Japanese artists) 1980. National Geographic Society. Color, 58 minutes, 16mm. (PSt, WU)

102. *The Long Search: 8—Religion in Indonesia: The Way of the Ancestors.* (Toraja, tribal religion) 1977. Color, 52 minutes, 16mm. (PSt)

103. *The Long Search: 9—Buddhism: The Land of the Disappearing Buddha—Japan.* (Zen Buddhism) 1977. Color, 53 minutes, 16mm, VHS. (IU, PSt)

104. *Lord Jim.* (Indonesia; Conrad's novel) 1965. Richard Brooks. Color, 154 minutes, 16mm. (FI, IU, NSyU)

105. *"Love" to the Rising Sun: The Dutch Arrival in Japan.* (Dutch in Japan) 1991. Color, 50 minutes, VHS, U-mat. (FFHS)

106. *Ma'Bugi': Trance of the Toraja.* (Toraja, trance) 1974. Eric Crystal and Lee Rhoades. Color, 19 minutes, 16mm, VHS. (CU, PSt)

107. *Made in Japan.* (Japan) 1981. Color, 38 minutes in 2 parts, 16mm, VHS. (CU, IU)

108. *Malnutrition in a Third World Community.* (Philippine economy) 1979. George and Helen Guthrie. Color, 26 minutes, 16mm, U-mat. (IU, PSt, WaPS)

109. *Manga: The Cartoon in Contemporary Japanese Life.* (Japan) 1982. Susumu Hani. Color, 28 minutes, 16mm. (CU, PSt)

110. *Mashiko Village Pottery, Japan 1937.* (Japanese crafts) 1937, restored 1984. B&W, silent, 22 minutes, 16mm, VHS, U-mat. (CU [1984], PSt [1937])

111. *The Medium Is the Masseuse: A Balinese Massage.* (Balinese, mental health) 1983. Timothy Asch, Linda Conner, and Patsy Asch. Color, 30 minutes, 16mm, VHS. (DER)

112. *The Meiji Period (1868–1912).* (Japan, modernization) 1990. Color, 52 minutes, VHS, U-mat. (FFHS)

113. *The Meo.* (Meo, Vietnam War) 1972. Jacques Lemoine. Color, 53 minutes, VHS. (FI, PSt)

114. *Metos Jah Hut (Jah Hut Myth).* (Senoi myth) 1987. Duncan Holaday, Betin Long bin Hok, and Shantyhi Ramanujan. Color, 10 minutes, VHS. (DH)

115. *Miao Year.* (Miao) 1971. William R. Geddes. Color, 62 minutes, 16mm. (CU, InU, PSt)

116. *Mind and Body: Judo Worldwide* (Japanese wrestling) 1978. Color, 20 minutes, 16mm. (CU, IU, PSt)

117. *The Miracle at Tsubosaka Temple* (Japanese puppets) 1974. Color, 28 minutes, 16mm. (CU, IU, PSt)

118. *Narcotics File: The Connections.* (Golden Triangle, drugs) 1974. Color, 28 minutes, 16mm. (IU, NSyU, WU)

119. *Narcotics File: The Source.* (Golden Triangle, drugs) 1974. Color, 28 minutes, 16mm. (IU, NSyU, WU)

119a. *No More Hiroshima!* (Japan, nuclear war survivors) 1984. Martin Duckworth. Color, 26 minutes, 16mm, VHS. (FRIF)

120. *Nomads of the Jungle: Malaya.* (Sakai) 1948. C. F. Kahn. B&W, 20 minutes, 16mm. (CU, InU, PSt)

121. *On a Wind from the South: The First European Impact on Japanese Culture.* (Europeans in Japan) 1982. Color, 30 minutes, 16mm. (CU, PSt)

122. *The Path* (Japanese tea ceremony) 1972. Don Rundstrom and Ron Rundstrom. Color, 33 minutes, 16mm. (CU, IU, PSt)

123. *Peasant Ecology in the Rural Philippines.* (Philippine

economy) 1971. George M. Guthrie. Color, 26 minutes, 16mm, U-mat. (PSt)

124. *People and Productivity: We Learn from the Japanese.* (Japan) 1982. Color, 28 minutes, 16mm, VHS. (CU, IU, NSyU)

125. *People Are Many, Fields Are Small.* (Taiwanese agriculture) 1974. Color, 32 minutes, 16mm. (MtU, InU, CU)

126. *Philippines: The Price of Power.* (Igorot resistance movement) 1986. Jeffrey Chester and Charles Drucker. Color, 28 minutes, 16mm, VHS. (FRIF)

127. *Postwar Japan: 40 Years of Change.* (Japan) 1990. Color, 56 minutes, VHS, U-mat. (FFHS)

128. *Preventing Malnutrition by Reinforcing Improved Diets.* (Philippine public health) 1980. George and Helen Guthrie. Color, 26 minutes, 16mm, U-mat. (PSt)

129. *The Principles and Practice of Zen.* (Japanese Buddhism) 1987. Color, 100 minutes, VHS, U-mat. (FFHS)

130. *Rice Farmers in Thailand.* (Thailand, modernization) 1969. Color, 19 minutes, 16mm. (OKentU, PSt)

131. *Rural Cooperatives.* (Taiwanese agriculture) 1974. Color, 16 minutes, 16mm. (MtU, InU, CU)

132. *Sacred Trances of Java and Bali.* (Javanese, Balinese, Islam, trance) 1976. Color, 29 minutes, 16mm. (NIC, PSt)

133. *The Sakuddei of Indonesia.* (Indonesia, egalitarian society) 1987. Granada Television. Color, 52 minutes, VHS. (FL)

134. *The "Salary Man": Japan's White-Collar Worker.* (Japanese) 1975. Color, 26 minutes, 16mm. (CU, PSt)

135. *Sanctuary of the Earth Goddess.* (Minangkabau, Sumatra) 1986. Katherine S. Frey. Color, 42 minutes, 16mm, VHS, U-mat. (NIC)

135a. *Senso Daughters.* (Japanese army prostitution) 1989. Noriko Sekiguchi. Color, 54 minutes, 16mm, VHS. (FRIF)

136. *Shinto: Nature, Gods, and Man in Japan.* (Shintō) 1977. Japan Society, Inc. Color, 48 minutes, 16mm, VHS. (IU, PSt, WaPS)

137. *Showa.* (modern Japan) 1987. B&W, 200 minutes, VHS, U-mat. (FFHS)

138. *Silk Makers of Japan.* (Japanese crafts) 1961. Robert Lang and Sterling S. Beath. Color, 16 minutes, 16mm. (IU, PSt, WaU)

139. *Song of Yellow Skin.* (Americans in Vietnam) 1970. Michael Rubbo for the National Film Board of Canada. Color, 58 minutes, 16mm. (CU, OKentU, PSt)

140. *The Sounds of Bamboo.* (Japanese music) 1976. Color, 42 minutes, 16mm. (CU, IU, PSt)

141. *Strength, Bulk, and Balance: The World of Sumo.* (Japanese wrestling) 1977. Color, 28 minutes, 16mm. (CU, IU, PSt)

142. *Sulawesi: Island of Discovery.* (Sulawesi) 1985. Color, 27 minutes, 16mm. (PSt)

143. *Taiwan: China's Western Dragon.* (Taiwanese) 1971. Color, 54 minutes, 16mm. (WaPS)

144. *Taiwan: Silk and Strings.* (Taiwanese arts) 1973. Color, 18 minutes, 16mm. (OKentU, OrPS)

145. *Taiwan: The Face of Free China.* (Taiwanese) 1960. Color, 26 minutes, 16mm. (InU, WU)

145a. *Taksu: Music in the Life of Bali.* (Balinese music) 1991. Jann Pasler. Color, 24 minutes, VHS. (CU)

146. *Temple of Twenty Pagodas.* (Mahayana Buddhism, Thailand) 1971. Color, 21 minutes, 16mm. (PSt)

147. *They Call Him Ahkung.* (Taiwanese agriculture) 1974. Color, 24 minutes, 16mm. (MtU, InU, CU)

148. *This Bloody, Blundering Business.* (Philippines) 1978. 30 minutes, 16mm, VHS. (CU, MiU, NIC)

148a. *Tobelo Marriage* (Tobelorese) 1990. Dirk Nijland. Color, 106 minutes, VHS. (CU)

149. *Tokyo Story.* (Japanese family) 1953. Yasujiro Ozu. B&W, subtitled, 139 minutes, 16mm. (BUD, Facets [VHS], NYF)

150. *The Tokyo Trial.* (modern Japan) 1987. B&W, 279 minutes, VHS, U-mat. (FFHS)

151. *Tokyo: World's Safest City.* (Tokyo Police) 1973. Color, 26 minutes, 16mm. (CU, FTaSU, MiU)

152. *Tomorrow's World.* (Thailand) 1984. Produced by the United Nations. Color, 24 minutes, 16mm. (CU, IU)

153. *Too Far, Too Fast.* (Japanese) 1982. Color, 20 minutes, 16 mm. (CU)

154. *Traditional Bunraku Theater.* (Japanese puppets) 1976. Color, 29 minutes, 16mm. (PSt)

154a. *Traditional Dances of Indonesia.* (Dances of Java, Bali, and West Sumatra) 1990. William Heick. Color; series of 12 films, each 12–32 minutes; 16mm, VHS. (CU)

155. *Traditional Japanese Architecture.* (Japanese architecture) 1989. Color, 30 minutes, VHS, U-mat. (FFHS)

156. *Trance and Dance in Bali.* (Balinese) 1951. Gregory Bateson and Margaret Mead. B&W, 20 minutes, 16mm. (CU, IU, NYU)

157. *Trinkets and Trust: Japanese Open-Air Markets.* (Japanese markets) 1978. Color, 29 minutes, 16mm. (CoU, IU, PSt)

158. *Ukiyo-e Printing: Art for the People.* (Japanese art) 1969. Color, 23 minutes, 16mm. (CU, PSt)

158a. *Uminchu: The Old Man and the East China Sea.* (Japanese fishing) 1991. Color, 101 minutes, 16mm, VHS. (FRIF)

159. *The Very Remarkable Yamato Family.* (Japanese family) 1975. Color; 118 minutes in two parts, 59 minutes each; 16mm. (CU, InU, PSt)

160. *The Village Potters of Onda.* (Japanese crafts) 1966. B&W, 25 minutes, 16mm. (MtU, PSt, WaU)

161. *Voices of Young Japan.* (Japanese education) 1979. Color, 30 minutes, 16mm. (CU, IU, PSt)

162. *The Water of Words: A Cultural Ecology of a Small Island in Eastern Indonesia.* (Lesser Sundas) 1983. Timothy Asch and James J. Fox. Color, 30 minutes, 16mm. (DER)

163. *The Wave: A Japanese Folktale.* (Japanese folklore) 1968. Color, 9 minutes, 16mm, VHS. (CU, NSyU, OKentU)

164. *Wet Culture Rice.* (Taiwanese agriculture) 1974. Color, 17 minutes, 16mm. (MtU, InU, CU)

165. *The Whale Hunters of Lamalera.* (Lamaholot) 1988. Robert Barnes. Color, 52 minutes, VHS. (FI, PSt)

166. *Women of Giriloyu.* (Indonesian women) 1985. Produced by the United Nations. Color, 20 minutes, 16mm. (CU, IU)

167. _World at War, 22: Japan: 1941–1945._ (Japan) 1975. Color, 51 minutes, 16mm, VHS. (CU, IU, PSt)

168. _World of the Heike Monogatari._ (Japan) 1969. Color, 24 minutes, 16mm. (CoU, IaAS, PSt)

169. _The World's Safest City: Public Security in Tokyo._ (Japan) 1976. Color, 29 minutes, 16mm. (CoU, PSt)

170. _Yoshi No Yama._ (Kabuki dance) 1951. Color, 20 minutes, 16mm. (PSt)

171. _Young Jiro: A Day at a Japanese School._ (Japanese education) 1976. Color, 29 minutes, 16mm. (CoU, IU, PSt)

172. _Zen Culture, Zen Spirit._ (Zen Buddhism) 1979. Color, 29 minutes, 16mm. (CU, IU, PSt)

Index to Filmography

Bibliography

Grilli, Peter, ed. (1984). *Japan in Film: A Comprehensive Annotated Catalogue of Documentary and Theatrical Films on Japan Available in the United States.* New York: Japan Society.

Heider, Karl (1983). *Films for Anthropological Teaching.* 7th ed. Special Publication no. 16. Washington, D.C.: American Anthropological Association.

InterOptica Publishing (1991). *The Orient–InterOptica's Multimedia Travel Encyclopedia.* Hong Kong: InterOptica Publishing. (This is one CD-ROM disc available for a variety of computers, available from the publisher at 1213–1218, Shui On Centre, 6–8 Harbour, Hong Kong; FAX no. 852-824-2508. It gives basic multimedia information on sixteen countries and forty-two cities of East and Southeast Asia.)

Jeung, Michael (1992). *Crosscurrent Media: Asian American Audiovisual Catalog.* San Francisco: CrossCurrent Media.

Volkman, Toby Alice (1985). *Film on Indonesia.* New Haven: Yale University, Southeast Asian Studies.

Directory of Distributors

AFSC	American Friends Service Committee, 15 Rutherford Place, New York, NY 10003
BFA	BFA Educational Media, 468 Park Ave. S., New York, NY 10016
BUD	Budget Films, 4590 Santa Monica Blvd., Los Angeles, CA 90029
CNAM	CNAM Film Library, 22-D Hollywood Ave., Hohokus, NJ 07423
CoU	Academic Media Service, University of Colorado, Stadium Bldg., Box 379, Boulder, CO 80309-0379
CtU	Center for Instructional Media and Technology, University of Connecticut, 249 Glenbrook Rd., Storrs, CT 06269-2001
CU	Center for Media and Independent Learning, 2176 Shattuck Ave., University of California, Berkeley, CA 94720
DER	Documentary Educational Resources, 101 Morse St., Watertown, MA 02172
DH	Duncan Holaday, Annenberg School of Communications, University of Pennsylvania, Philadelphia, PA 19174
Facets	Facets Multimedia, 1517 W. Fullerton St., Chicago, IL 60614
FFHS	Films for the Humanities and Sciences, P.O. Box 2053, Princeton, NJ 08543-2053
FI	Films Inc., 5547 N. Ravenswood Ave., Chicago IL 60640
FL	Filmmakers Library, Suite 901, 124 E. 40th St., New York, NY 10016-1199
FRIF	First Run/Icarus Films, 153 Waverly Place, New York, NY 10014
FTaSU	Instructional Support Center, Florida State University, Tallahassee, FL 32306-1019
FTS	Film and Video Library, University of South Florida, 4202 Fowler Ave., Tampa, FL 33620
IaAs	Media Resources Center, 121 Pearson Hall, Iowa State University, Ames, IA 50011
InTI	Audio Visual Center, Stalker Hall, Indiana State University, Terre Haute, IN 47807
InU	Center for Media and Teaching Resources, Indiana University, Bloomington, IN 47405-5901
IU	Film and Video Center, University of Illinois, 1325 S. Oak St., Champaign, IL 61820
JF	Journal Films, 930 Pitner Ave., Evanston, IL 60202
MiEM	Instructional Media Center, Michigan State University, East Lansing, MI 48826-0710
MiU	Film and Video Library, 207 ULG, University of Michigan, 919 S. University Ave., Ann Arbor, MI 48109-1185
MnU	Film and Video Center, Suite 108, 1313 Fifth St. SE, University of Minnesota, Minneapolis, MN 55414
MoU	Film and Video Rental Library, University of Missouri, 505 E. Steward Rd., Columbia, MO 65211
MtU	Instructional Media Services, Montana State University, Missoula, MT 59812
NIC	Audio-Visual Resource Center, Cornell University, 8 Research Park, Ithaca, NY 14850
NmPE	Film Library, Eastern New Mexico University, Portales, NM 88130
NSyU	Film Rental Center, Syracuse University, 1455 E. Colvin St., Syracuse, NY 13210
NYF	New Yorker Films, 16 W. 61st St., New York, NY 10023
NYU	Film Library, New York University, 26 Washington Place, New York, NY 10003
OKentU	Audio Visual Services, Kent State University, Kent, OH 44242
OkS	Audio Visual Center, Oklahoma State University, Stillwater, OK 74078
OrPS	Continuing Education Film and Video Library, Portland State University, 1633 SW Park St., P.O. Box 1383, Portland, OR 97207
PSt	Audio Visual Services, Special Services Building, Pennsylvania State University, University Park, PA 16802-1824
TLF	Time-Life Film and Video, 100 Eisenhower Dr., Paramus, NJ 07652
TxU	Film Library, University of Texas, Box W, Austin, TX 78713-7448
UPB	Audio Visual Services, 101 Harvey Fletcher Bldg., Brigham Young University, Provo, UT 84602
UU	Instructional Services, 207 Milton Bennison Hall, University of Utah, Salt Lake City, UT 84112
WaPS	Film/Video Center, Instructional Media Services, Washington State University, Pullman, WA 99164-5602
WaU	Educational Media Collection, 35 Kane Hall, DG-10, University of Washington, Seattle, WA 98195
WU	BAVI, University of Wisconsin Extension, P.O. Box 2093, Madison, WI 53701-2093

Ethnonym Index

This index provides some of the alternative names and the names of major subgroups for cultures covered in this volume. The culture names that are entry titles are in boldface.

Acehnese
Achehnese—**Acehnese**
Achinese—**Acehnese**
Aeta-**Philippine Negritos**
Agta
Aini—**Akha**
Aino—**Ainu**
Ainu
Aka—**Akha**
Ak'a—**Akha**
Akha
Aki—**Banggai**
Akka—**Akha**
Alak
Alakong—**Bahnar**
Alifura—**Ambonese**
A-Liko—**Melanau**
Alishan—**Taiwan Aboriginal Peoples**
Aloreezen—**Alorese**
Alorese
Alta—**Agta**
Amamijin—**Okinawans**
Ambonese
Ami—**Taiwan Aboriginal Peoples**
Amia—**Taiwan Aboriginal Peoples**
Angkola-Sipirok—**Batak**
Annamese—**Vietnamese**
Anung—**Lisu**
Apayao—**Isneg**
Arisan—**Taiwan Aboriginal Peoples**
Arta—**Agta**
Arut—**Kalimantan Dayaks**
Ata Bi'ang—**Ata Sikka**
Ata 'Iwang—**Ata Tana 'Ai**
Ata Kangae—**Ata Tana 'Ai**
Ata Kiwan—**Lamaholot**
Ata Krowé—**Ata Sikka; Ata Tana 'Ai**
Ata Manggarai—**Manggarai**
Ata Nuha—**Palu'e**
Ata Nusa—**Palu'e**
Ata Pulo—**Palu'e**
Ata Sikka
Ata Tana 'Ai
'Ata Ende—**Endenese**
'Ata Jaö—**Endenese**
Atahori Rote—**Rotinese**

Atayal—**Taiwan Aboriginal Peoples**
Atazan—**Taiwan Aboriginal Peoples**
Atchinese—**Acehnese**
Atjehnese—**Acehnese**
Atoin Meto—**Atoni**
Atoin Pah Meto—**Atoni**
Atoni
Atta—**Philippine Negritos**

Badjaw—**Bajau; Samal**
Bagobo
Bahau—**Kenyah-Kayan-Kajang**
Bahnar
Bahr—**Pear**
Bai-yi—**Tai Lue**
Bajao—**Samal**
Bajau
Bajau—**Samal; Selung/Moken**
Bajau Laut—**Bajau**
Bajo—**Bajau**
Balantak
Balinese
Balud—**Bilaan**
Baluga—**Agta; Philippine Negritos**
Banggai
Baraan—**Bilaan**
Baru—**Bru**
Batak
Batak—**Philippine Negritos**
Batèk De'—**Semang**
Batèk Nòng—**Semang**
Baweanese
Bawean Islanders—**Baweanese**
Belu—**Tetum**
Benguetano—**Ibaloi**
Benguet Igorot—**Ibaloi**
Beri Chuba—**Senoi**
Biadju—**Kalimantan Dayaks**
Bidayuh—**Kalimantan Dayaks**
Bilaan
Bilanes—**Bilaan**
Binokid—**Bukidnon**
Binukid—**Bukidnon**
Biraan—**Bilaan**
Bisaya
Bisaya—**Visayan**

Bisayan—**Visayan**
Blann—**Bilaan**
Boeginneezen—**Bugis**
Bolaang Mongondow
Bolongan—**Tidong**
Boloven—**Loven**
Bonerate
Bonom—**Bahnar; Monom**
Bontoc—**Bontok**
Bontoc Igorot—**Bontok**
Bontok
Boolaang-Mongondonese—**Bolaang Mongondow**
Boyanese—**Baweanese**
Brao
Bru
B'ru—**Bru**
Buddhist
Budip—**Stieng**
Buginese—**Bugis**
Bugis
Buki—**Sulod**
Bukidnon
Bukidnon—**Sulod**
Bulalakao—**Hanunóo**
Buluan—**Bilaan**
Bunun
Burakumin
Burmans—**Burmese**
Burmese
Burmese Shan—**Shan**
Butonese

Calagan—**Kalagan**
Calinga—**Kalingas**
Cambodian—**Khmer**
Camucones—**Tidong**
Cau Ma—**Ma**
Central Kankanaey—**Kankanai**
Central Moluccans—**Ambonese**
Central Thai
Cham
Chaobon
Chao Dol—**T'in**
Chaolay—**Sea Nomads of the Andaman**
Che-nung—**Lisu**

Che Wong—**Senoi**
Chinese in Southeast Asia
Chinese Shan—**Shan**
Chong
Chosŏn—**Korean**
Chrau
Cochinese—**Vietnamese**
Corinchee—**Kerintji**
Co Sung—**Lahu**
Cotabato Manobo
Cò Tu—**Katu**
Co Xung—**Lahu**
Cua

Dai—**Shan; Tai Lue**
Dairi-Pakpak—**Batak**
Dajak—**Kalimantan Dayaks**
Damugat—**Agta**
Dang—**Palaung**
Dashan—**Kachin**
Da Vach—**Hre**
Davak—**Hre**
Daya—**Kalimantan Dayaks**
Dayak—**Iban**
Delang—**Kalimantan Dayaks**
Dempo—Ogan—Besemah
Duane
Dulangan—**Cotobato Manobo**
Dumagat—**Philippine Negritos**
Dusun
Dyak—**Iban**

East Toraja—**Toala**
Édang—**Kédang**
Edaw—**Akha**
E-De—**Rhadé**
E Dê—**Rhadé**
Emischi—**Ainu**
Endenese
Eta—**Burakumin**
Etall—**Taiwan Aboriginal Peoples**
Ezo—**Ainu**

Filipino
Formosans—**Taiwan Aboriginal Peoples**

Gadan—**Gaddang**
Ga'dang—**Gaddang**
Gaddanes—**Gaddang**
Gaddang
Gajo—**Gayo**
Gayo
Gorontalese
Gorontalo—**Gorontalese**
Guianes—**Bontok**
Guozhou—**Lahu**

Halang Doan
Hampangan—**Hanunóo**
Han'guk—**Korean**
Hani—**Akha**
Hanono-o—**Hanunóo**
Hanunóo
Ha[rh] ndea[ng]—**Sedang**
Hataholi Lote—**Rotinese**
Hata Lu'a—**Palu'e**
Hata Rua—**Palu'e**
Higaonan—**Bukidnon**

Higaunen—**Bukidnon**
Hinin—**Burakumin**
Hkamti Shan—**Shan**
Hmong
Ho Drong—**Bahnar**
Hokkaidō Ainu—**Ainu**
Holo—**Lamaholot**
Holontalo—**Gorontalese**
Houni—**Akha**
Hre
H.Rê—**Hre**
Htin—**T'in**
Huaqiao—**Chinese in Southeast Asia**
Huaren—**Chinese in Southeast Asia**
Huei—**Oy**
Hulontalo—**Gorontalese**
Humai—**Palaung**
Hwach'ŏk —**Kolisuch'ŏk**

Ibaloi
Ibaloy—**Ibaloi**
Iban
Ibilao—**Ilongot**
Ibilaw—**Ilongot**
Idäan—**Dusun**
Idahan Murut—**Murut**
Ifugao
Ifugaw—**Ifugao**
Igodor—**Ibaloi**
Igorot—**Bontok; Kankanai; Sagada Igorot**
Ikaw—**Akha**
Ikho—**Akha**
Ilanon
Ilanum—**Ilanon**
Ilanun—**Ilanon**
Illanun—**Ilanon**
Ilongot
Ilungut—**Ilongot**
Ilyongut—**Ilongot**
Indonesian
Inibaloi—**Ibaloi**
Inibaloy—**Ibaloi**
Inibioi—**Inbaloi**
Ipugao—**Ifugao**
Ira-an—**Palawan**
Iranon—**Ilanon**
Iraya—**Gaddang Irianese**
Isnag—**Isneg**
Isned—**Isneg**
Isneg
Itneg
Iu Mian—**Yao of Thailand**

Jahai—**Semang**
Jah Hut—**Senoi**
Japanese
Javanese
Jinghpaw—**Kachin**
Joloanos—**Tausug**
Jolo Moros—**Tausug**
Jo Long—**Bahnar**

Kachin
Kadazan—**Dusun**
Kagan—**Kalagan**
Kalagan
Kalamantan—**Dusun**

Kalibugan
Kalimantan Dayaks
Kalina'—**Isneg**
Kalingas
Kalingga—**Kalingas**
Kammu—**Kmhmu**
Kampuchean—**Khmer**
Kaniang—**Karen**
Kankanaey—**Kankanai**
Kankanai
Kankanay—**Kankanai; Sagada Igorot**
Karagan—**Kalagan**
Kareang—**Karen**
Karen
Kariang—**Karen**
Karo—**Batak**
Kaseng—**Kasseng**
Kasseng
Katang—**Kattang**
Katangnang—**Sagada Igorot**
Katin—**T'in**
Kato—**Katu**
Kattang
Katu
Ka-Tu—**Katu**
Kaw—**Akha**
Kayin—**Karen**
Kebahan—**Kalimantan Dayaks**
Kédang
Kelabit—**Murut**
Kelemantan—**Melanau**
Kemaloh Kelabit—**Murut**
Kensiu—**Semang**
Kenyah-Kayan-Kajang
Kerinchi—**Kerintji**
Kerintji
Kha Ché—**T'in**
Khae Lisaw—**Lisu**
Khae Liso—**Lisu**
Kha Kho—**Akha**
Kha Ko—**Akha**
Kha Lamet—**Lamet**
Khamu—**Kmhmu**
Khang—**Kachin**
Kha Pai—**T'in**
Kha P'ai—**P'u Noi**
Kha Quy—**Lahu**
Khas Pakho—**Pacoh**
Kha T'in—**T'in**
Khmae—**Khmer**
Khmer
Khmu—**Kmhmu**
Kho Ko—**Akha**
Kho' Mu—**Kmhmu**
Khon Thai—**Central Thai**
Khua
Khua—**Cua**
Khu Xung—**Lahu**
Kiam—**Cham**
Kiaus—**Dusun**
Kinalinga—**Kalingas**
Kinh—**Vietnamese**
Kintak—**Semang**
Kmhmu
Kmhmu'—**Kmhmu**
Koeboe—**Kubu**
Kolibugan—**Kalibugan**
Kolisuch'ŏk

The Editors

Editor in Chief
David Levinson (Ph.D., State University of New York at Buffalo) is vice-president of the Human Relations Area Files in New Haven, Connecticut. He is a cultural anthropologist whose primary research interests are in social issues, worldwide comparative research, and social theory. He has conducted research on homelessness, alcohol abuse, aggression, family relations, and ethnicity. Among his dozens of publications are the award-winning text, *Toward Explaining Human Culture* (with Martin J. Malone), *The Tribal Living Book* (with David Sherwood), and *Family Violence in Cross-Cultural Perspective*. Dr. Levinson also teaches anthropology at Albertus Magnus College in New Haven, Connecticut.

Volume Editor
Paul Hockings (M.A., University of Toronto; Ph.D., University of California, Berkeley) is also editor of the journal *Visual Anthropology*. He is a professor of anthropology at the University of Illinois, Chicago, and a research associate at the Field Museum of Natural History, Chicago. Although primarily a cultural anthropologist and linguist, he has done archaeological and bibliographic work, and he has also made anthropological films. Among those films is *The Village*, made in Ireland with Mark McCarty. He has written or edited ten books and dozens of articles, most of them dealing with the Badagas and related South Indian peoples. His most recent books are *Blue Mountains: The Ethnography and Biogeography of a South Indian Region* (written with several collaborators), and *A Badaga-English Dictionary* (with Christiane Pilot-Raichoor). Paul Hockings is a Fellow of the Royal Anthropological Institute of Great Britain and a life member of the American Anthropological Association.